THE LOST HISTORY OF SEXTUS AURELIUS VICTOR

Edinburgh Studies in Later Latin Literature

Series Editors
Gavin Kelly and Aaron Pelttari, University of Edinburgh

Ground-breaking scholarship on Latin literature from the later Roman and post-Roman world

Edinburgh Studies in Later Latin Literature offers a forum for new scholarship on important and sometimes neglected works. The later Roman and post-Roman world, between the second and seventh century, saw the creation of major texts and critical developments in writing. Texts of all kinds are treated here with careful attention to their various historical contexts.

Volumes include scholarly monographs and editions with commentaries. Modern critical and theoretical methods together provide new interpretations of the surviving Latin literature; these approaches include textual history, transmission, philology in the broad sense, and reception studies. This series provides access to our best understanding of what survives in the written record and makes modern interpretations of later Latin literature more widely available.

Editorial Advisory Board
Therese Fuhrer, University of Munich
Lucy Grig, University of Edinburgh
Isabella Gualandri, University of Milan
Philip Hardie, University of Cambridge
Calum Maciver, University of Edinburgh
Justin Stover, University of Edinburgh

Books available
Judith Hindermann, *Sidonius Apollinaris' Letters, Book 2: Text, Translation and Commentary*
Giulia Marolla, *Sidonius: Letters Book 5, Part 1. Text, Translation and Commentary*

https://edinburghuniversitypress.com/series-edinburgh-studies-in-later-latin-literature

THE LOST HISTORY OF SEXTUS AURELIUS VICTOR

Justin A. Stover and George Woudhuysen

EDINBURGH
University Press

Edinburgh University Press is one of the leading university presses in the UK. We publish academic books and journals in our selected subject areas across the humanities and social sciences, combining cutting-edge scholarship with high editorial and production values to produce academic works of lasting importance. For more information visit our website: edinburghuniversitypress.com

Edinburgh University Press Ltd
The Tun – Holyrood Road
12(2f) Jackson's Entry
Edinburgh EH8 8PJ

Typeset in Bembo
by R. J. Footring Ltd, Derby, UK, and
printed and bound in Great Britain

A CIP record for this book is available from the British Library

ISBN 978 1 4744 9287 4 (hardback)
ISBN 978 1 4744 9289 8 (webready PDF)
ISBN 978 1 4744 9290 4 (epub)

CONTENTS

CONTENTS

Contents

Illustrations

Figure

Maps of Victor's world

Tables

PREFACE

This is a book about a man and his work, a historian and his world, an empire and its past. It is a study of Sextus Aurelius Victor (*ca.* 320-390), the best attested but least understood of the historians of the later Roman Empire. For a man honoured by two emperors, Julian and Theodosius, praised by Ammianus Marcellinus, and read by St Jerome, Victor has managed to lead an afterlife of remarkably quiet obscurity. He is, at best, an eccentric curiosity in the life and letters of the fourth century – little known and even less studied.

At the heart of this book is a deceptively simple question: what exactly did Victor write? Since the end of the nineteenth century, the answer has seemed obvious, self-evident even: Victor wrote the *De Caesaribus*, presented to the world in AD 360. This scrappy and incoherent narrative of the emperors, bombastic in style and moralising in tone, has long lurked in the footnotes of the history of the ancient world, occasionally promoted to the main text when its difficult evidence has been thought to cast light on a more interesting and important topic. As the weight of the volume in your hands might suggest, things are not so simple as they first appear.

Victor's work has never received the kind of sustained and systematic attention that it deserves, has never had fundamental questions about its scope and nature adequately asked or answered. The current understanding of him – and with it far more than has generally been realised – rests on the slenderest of foundations. To rectify these omissions is the task of the first part of this book, which offers the first proper analysis of Victor and his work. Its argument may – for all the proof it requires – be stated simply: Victor wrote a monumental *Historia* in Latin, of which today we have only fragments. To study him is fundamentally to reconstruct his work. That realisation requires – demands – a revolution in our understanding of the historians of the fourth-century Roman Empire. The second part of this book suggests how we might begin.

A chance conversation over lunch in the Buttery on a grey spring day in 2015 first brought us to Victor. The key ideas contained in this book then emerged remarkably quickly, as though an image suddenly coming into focus for the first time. Working them out, and writing this study, has been a rather longer and more arduous task, one in which we have incurred profound debts. Our first is to the Warden and Fellows of All Souls College, whose support made much of the work contained herein possible – the number of institutions that sustain genuinely adventurous research in the humanities is few, and no others would have done so so generously and for so long. Thanks are due also to Colin Burrow, the former Fellow Librarian, and the staff of the Codrington (Norma Aubertin-Potter, Gaye Morgan, and Gabrielle Matthews in particular), who offered crucial support for a project that draws on a baffling array of books and articles – it is no small thing to have at one's disposal the resources of such a fine library. Philipp Nothaft helped us to resolve some difficult matters of chronology and Chris Wickham gave guidance on matters early medieval and Italian. Elsewhere in Oxford, we are grateful to Neil McLynn and Bryan Ward-Perkins, who offered us the first opportunity to air the ideas in this book to an audience at the Late Roman Seminar. Joshua Bennett read Chapter VI in draft and helped to steer our course through German intellectual culture at the end of the nineteenth century. Much of the research for the book was conducted in the Bodleian Library, to whose staff we are indebted – in particular, Oliver House and Matthew Holford responded with speed and precision to vague queries about the Bodley Refs. On Victor, as on so many other subjects, Mark Whittow helped to tire the sun with talking – we like to think that the book would have appealed to his infectious enthusiasm and to his sense of mischief. Another departed friend, Richard Sharpe – who attended our first paper in Oxford and, in conversation after, endorsed the then-tentative suggestion that Paul the Deacon was responsible for the *Epitome* – might have been pleased to peruse Chapter II, a tribute of a sort to his *Titulus*.

Deep gratitude is also owed to colleagues in Edinburgh and Nottingham. Without the encouragement, criticism, and acute eye for English and Latin style of Gavin Kelly, this book would be very different and much inferior – there is no page herein that does not reflect his advice. We would also know considerably less about the usage of the word *umbilicus* without his kind assistance in Munich. His fellow series editor, Aaron Pelttari, also offered unstinting aid, reading the entire manuscript with a careful eye for clarity and good sense and giving us the benefit of his enormous expertise in the far reaches of later Latin literature (even the prelapsarian). Carol MacDonald at Edinburgh University Press welcomed a book project that must have seemed odd even in its first iteration and which has undergone several revolutions and dilations since then – we are grateful for her combination of patience and enthusiasm. Rachel Bridgewater calmly guided the manuscript through the thickets of review and submission – we are in her debt. We can but admire the diligence and accuracy of Ralph Footring, who undertook the difficult task of copy-editing and setting this book, with speed and good humour. Doug Lee read a version of the project when it was still an overgrown essay and gave judicious feedback and careful encouragement. Simon Malloch has heard much of the argument in convivial conversation over the years and offered wise advice on the Latin historians. David Laven was characteristically generous with his time and company, as well as guidance on matters Italian. Heroically, Oliver Thomas checked the accents on our Greek and saved many a slip. The staff of the Hallward Library, in particular the Interlibrary Loans team, went to remarkable lengths to obtain obscure items, for which we are very grateful. We owe thanks also to the School of Humanities at Nottingham for funds to obtain a reproduction of the Brussels manuscript of the *Corpus Tripertitum* and to Lorna Collison in the SMRO for arranging the purchase.

Friends and colleagues further afield have also given generously of their time and expertise. Simon Corcoran read an early draft, provided stimulating correction, and has continued to offer advice on Roman law and Roman lawyers – there can be few who rival his knowledge of the subject and none who offers it so open-handedly to others. David Potter's enthusiasm for the ideas in this book gave our work important early impetus. Alan Ross's kindness in tracking down and sharing items of scholarly literature sustained the project in the season of bibliographical famine during the pandemic. Michael Kulikowski – the prince of reviewers – read the entire manuscript with remarkable speed and generosity. Graham Barrett offered expert advice on matters Iberian. Paweł Janiszewski and Aleksander Paradziński generously invited us to Warsaw to discuss the project at Ewa Wipszycka's Late Antique Seminar, an exhilarating intellectual experience; they also read the entire manuscript in draft, with criticism that was both penetrating and collegial. Silvio Roggo and Brigid Ehrmantraut invited one of us to Cambridge to deliver a paper to the CLANS seminar and bore the fact that the event attracted some protests with remarkable fortitude. Dirk Elbert of the Stadtbibliothek in Soest provided us with images of fragments of a manuscript with speed and graciousness. John Monfasani guided us on the annotating hands in manuscripts of the *Corpus Tripertitum*, Maya Maskarinec helped us to chase down an important manuscript of Paul the Deacon's *Historia Romana*, while Pierfrancesco Porena and Leonhard Schumacher generously shared articles they had written with us. Michael Crawford kindly allowed us to examine a study of the *Scholia Vallicelliana* in draft. The team at the Tesserae Project at the University of Buffalo uploaded texts of Victor's work to allow us to hunt for more obscure allusions.

The bulk of the book was written in the somewhat peculiar circumstances of 2020 and 2021. As a result, even more than usual, we both owe weighty domestic debts – George would like to thank his wife Katie, his son Isaac, and his parents, Deborah and Henry (particularly the latter for advice on matters bibliographical). Justin would like to thank, as ever, Nikki for her patience, and Lizzy, Max, Christian, Hugo, Ferdinand, Viviane, Anton, and Geoffrey, for listening to too many anecdotes about Roman emperors with good humour. Our families have tolerated a project that has at times been all consuming (and for four of them has lasted their entire lives).

Any joint project inevitably invites questions about who really did what, from people (often academic bureaucrats) who believe that in any co-authored work each individual contributed one-third and the rest somehow emerged from the ether. We can but say that this book is an entirely joint production and that we are both equally responsible for all of it. If it was possible at one stage to recall that one of us had drafted this section or first framed that idea, then years of revision and expansion have obliterated the memory. On this score, it seems fitting to quote from the preface of W.E. Plater and H.J. White's *The Grammar of the Vulgate*:

> As to the share which each of us has had in the work … [s]hould reviewers award the book any praise, each will gladly appropriate it; should there be blame, each will gladly pass it on to his colleague. Of one thing we feel quite sure – that neither of us could have written the book without the help given by the other.[1]

In fine, we would like to mention Fergus Millar. Fergus heard the very first iteration of the argument when it was aired at Oxford. Ever generous, his encouragement at the time meant a great deal to us, as we advanced what seemed then (and still seem now) some rather radical notions. We would like to think that this book reflects some small quantum of the approach to ancient history that he embodied: a respect for the evidence, a ruthless clarity of ideas and interpretation, and a sense that there is work to be done and one uses what one has. It is to his memory that this book is dedicated.

Veluniate et Snotingeham
pridie Kal. Aug.
in festo S. Germani
MMXXII

1. Plater and White 1926: vi.

CONVENTIONS AND ABBREVIATIONS

Conventions in the citation of ancient works

We cite standard editions of ancient texts, but the punctuation and orthography are occasionally our own.

We follow the *Oxford Classical Dictionary* and the *Thesaurus Linguae Latinae* in our abbreviations of the titles of most ancient works.

All translations are our own, unless otherwise indicated (referenced by surname of translators).

For manuscripts, we generally offer an abbreviated shelf-mark – full shelf-marks can be found in the Index of Manuscripts Cited. Manuscript sigla are given in **bold**.

We refer to Latin inscriptions using the abbreviations of the *Epigraphik-Datenbank Clauss/Slaby* (https://db.edcs.eu/epigr/epi.php), with some trivial variations.

We refer to Greek inscriptions using the abbreviations of the Packard Humanities Institute database (https://epigraphy.packhum.org), with some trivial variations.

We refer to papyri using the standard abbreviations (https://papyri.info).

We use the following conventions when citing ancient works. Our customary abbreviations are in bold:

Ammianus Marcellinus – we use the abbreviation **AM** for the *Res gestae* of Ammianus.

Aurelius Victor – in referring to the Victorine texts we use the abbreviation *HAb* for the *Historiae abbreviatae* (*vulgo Liber de Caesaribus*) and *LB* for the *Libellus breviatus* (*vulgo Epitome de Caesaribus*). In Chapters I and II, we give a dual format for citations of these works: *Caes.* [*HAb*] and *Epit.* [*LB*].

Cassius Dio – we cite Dio's *Roman History* in the reformed numbering of books introduced by the edition of UP Boissevain (1895–1901): *Cassii Dionis Cocceiani historiarum Romanarum quae supersunt*, 3 vols, Berlin. That edition was also used by Cary in his Loeb translation, probably the most accessible text – E. Cary (1914–1927): *Dio Cassius. Roman History*, 9 vols, London and Cambridge, Mass. A convenient introduction to the numbering of Dio's books can be found in P.M. Swan (2004): *The Augustan Succession: An Historical Commentary on Cassius Dio's Roman History, Books 55–56 (9 B.C.–A.D. 14)*, Oxford, 383–385.

Chronography of 354 – we cite the *Chronography of 354* (by the abbreviation *Chron. 354*) with the page (and, when relevant, line number) in the edition of Th. Mommsen (1892): *Chronica Minora saec. IV, V, VI, VII volumen I*, Berlin.

Codex Justinianus – we use the abbreviation *CJ* for the *Codex Justinianus*.

Codex Theodosianus – we use the abbreviation *CTh* for the *Codex Theodosianus*.

Constantinian *Excerpta* – we cite these from the edition of T. Büttner-Wobst, C. de Boor, and UP Boissevain (1903–1910): *Excerpta historica iussu imp. Constantini Porphyrogeniti confecta*, 4 vols in 6 parts, Berlin. We use the following abbreviations for the different collections: *EI* = *Excerpta de insidiis*, *ELG* = *Excerpta de legationibus gentium*, and *ES* = *Excerpta de sententiis*.

Corpus Tripertitum – we use the abbreviation *CT* for the *Corpus Tripertitum*, the compilation consisting of the *Origo gentis Romanae*, *De viris illustribus*, and *Historiae abbreviatae*.

De viris illustribus urbis Romae – we use the abbreviation *DVI* for the *De viris illustribus urbis Romae*.

Ecclesiastical Histories – we use the abbreviation *HE* for the ecclesiastical histories of Eusebius, Rufinus, *etc.*

Eunapius – we use the abbreviation *VS* for the *Vitae sophistarum* of Eunapius. We cite his history in a dual format, with the number of the fragment given from the Constantinian *Excerpta* (see above) or the *Suda* (see below) and from R.C. Blockley (1981–1983): *The Fragmentary Classicising Historians of the Later Roman Empire: Eunapius, Olympiodorus, Priscus and Malchus*, 2 vols, Leeds.

Fragmentary historians:

We cite fragments of the Latin historians from before the fourth century AD from T.J. Cornell (ed.) (2013): *Fragments of the Roman Historians*, 3 vols, Oxford. We use the abbreviation *FRH* and the number assigned to each historian, with the author(s) of the entry given in parentheses.

We cite fragments of the Greek historians from *Brill's New Jacoby*. We use the abbreviation *BNJ* and the number assigned to each historian, with the author(s) of the entry in parentheses.

Grammatici Latini – we cite the Latin grammarians from H. Keil (ed.) (1857–1880): *Grammatici Latini*, 8 vols, Leipzig. We use the abbreviation *GLK* and give the volume and page number where necessary.

Historia Augusta – we use the abbreviation *HA* for the *Vitae diversorum principum et tyrannorum a Divo Hadriano usque ad Numerianum a diversis conpositae (vulgo Historia Augusta)*. Individual lives are cited by their standard abbreviations. We list these below, with the manuscript title of each life and (in parentheses) the number in the edition of E. Hohl (1927): *Scriptores Historiae Augustae*, 2 vols, Leipzig:

Ael. = *Aelius* (II)

Alex. = *Alexander Severus* (XVIII)

Antonin. = *Antoninus Pius* (III)

Aurel. = *Divus Aurelianus* (XXVI)

Avid. Cass. = *Vita Avidii Cassii* (VI)

Car. = *Carus et Carinus et Numeriani* (XXX)

Carac. = *Antoninus Caracallus* (XIII)

Claud. = *Divus Claudius* (XXV)

Clod. Alb. = *Vita Clodii Albini* (XII)

Comm. = *Commodus Antoninus* (VII)

Diad. = *Diadumenus* (XVI)

Did. = *Didius Iulianus* (IX)

Gall. = *Gallieni duo* (XXIII)

Geta = *Antoninus Geta* (XIV)

Gord. = *Liber de rebus gestis Gordianorum* (XX)

Hadr. = *De vita Hadriani* (I)

Heliog. = *Antoninus Varius Heliogabalus* (XVII)

Macr. = *Opilius Macrinus* (XV)

Marc. = *Vita Marci Antonini philosophi* (IV)

Max. Balb. = *Maximus et Balbinus* (XXI)

Maximin. = *Maximini duo* (XIX)

Pert. = *Helvius Pertinax* (VIII)

Pesc. = *Pescennius Niger* (XI)

Prob. = *Vita Probi* (XXVIII)

Quadr. = *Firmus Saturninus Proculus et Bonosus* (*Quadriga Tyrannorum*) (XXIX)

Sev. = *Severus* (X)

Tac. = *Tacitus* (XXVII)

Tyr. = *Tyranni Triginta* (XXIV)

Val. = *Valerianus pater et filius* (XXII)

Verus = *Verus* (V)

Jerome – we cite Jerome's *Chronicon* (by the abbreviation *Chron.*) from the edition of R. Helm (1956): *Die Chronik des Hieronymus*[2], Berlin, using his pagination and alphabetisation of entries.

John of Antioch – we cite the fragments in the numeration by U. Roberto (2005): *Ioannis Antiocheni Fragmenta ex Historia chronica*, Berlin and New York.

Julian (the emperor) – we cite Julian's letters (by the abbreviation *ELF*) in the numeration of J. Bidez and F. Cumont 1922: *Imp. Caesaris Flavii Claudii Iuliani epistulae leges poematia fragmenta varia*, Paris.

Justinian – we refer to the *Institutes* of Justinian as the *Institutiones*.

Kaisergeschichte – we use the abbreviation *KG* for the hypothesised *Kaisergeschichte*.

Lactantius – we use the following abbreviations for the works of Lactantius: *DI* for the *Divinae institutiones*, *Epit.* for the *Epitome divinarum institutionum*, and *DMP* for the *De mortibus persecutorum*.

Landolfus Sagax – we use the abbreviation *HM* for the *Historia Miscella* of Landolfus Sagax.

Nonius Marcellus – we give the Mercier page number (**M**) in references to the *De compendiosa doctrina* of Nonius Marcellus.

Origo Constantini Imperatoris – we use the abbreviation *OCI* for the *Origo Constantini Imperatoris*.

Origo gentis Romanae – we use the abbreviation *OGR* for the *Origo gentis Romanae*.

Paeanius – we cite Paeanius' Greek translation of Eutropius' *Historia Romana* in the edition of H. Droysen (1879): *Eutropi Breviarium ab urbe condita cum versionibus Graecis et Pauli Landolfique additamentis*, Berlin.

Panegyrici Latini – we use the abbreviation **Pan. Lat.** for the *Panegyrici Latini*, which we cite in the numeration of R.A.B. Mynors (1964): *XII Panegyrici Latini*, Oxford.

Patrologia – we use the abbreviation *PL* for the *Patrologia Latina* and *PG* for the *Patrologia Graeca*, which we cite by column and section number (where necessary).

Paul the Deacon – we use the abbreviations *HL* for the *Historia Langobardorum* and *HR* for the *Historia Romana*.

Photius – when referring to the *Bibliotheca*, we use the edition of R. Henry (1959–1991): *Photius. Bibliothèque*, 9 vols, Paris. We list the Bekker page number in parentheses for specific points in each entry.

Polemius Silvius – we cite Polemius Silvius' list of emperors and usurpers in the numeration of D. Paniagua (2018): *Polemii Silvii Laterculus*, Rome.

Sallust, *Historiae* – we cite the *Histories* of Sallust in a dual format, with the number of the fragment given from both J.T. Ramsey (2015): *Sallust: Fragments of the Histories, Letters to Caesar*, Cambridge, Mass. (**R**); and B. Maurenbrecher (1891–1893): *C. Sallusti Crispi Historiarum reliquiae*, 2 fascicles, Leipzig (**M**). Fragments not assigned to books are prefaced by 'fr.'

Suda – we cite this by the Greek letter and number in the edition of A. Adler (1928–1938): *Suidae Lexicon*, 5 vols, Leipzig.

Conventions and abbreviations for modern works

We use the following abbreviations and conventions in the citation of modern works.

Bischoff, *Katalog* – B. Bischoff (with B. Ebersperger) *Katalog der festländischen Handschriften des neunten Jahrhunderts (mit Ausnahme der wisigotischen)*, 4 vols, Wiesbaden, 1998–2017. Cited by the number Bischoff assigned to each manuscript.

BNP – *Brill's New Pauly*, cited by headword, with the author(s) of the entry in parentheses.

Briquet – C.-M. Briquet, *Les filigranes, dictionnaire historique des marques de papier dès leur apparition vers 1282 jusqu'en 1600* ^{2}, 1907, 4 vols, Paris and Geneva.

CDS – Brepols' *Cross Database Searchtool* (http://clt.brepolis.net/cds).

CLRE – R.S. Bagnall, A. Cameron, S.R. Schwartz, and K.A. Worp (1987): *Consuls of the Later Roman Empire*, Atlanta, GA, cited by page number.

CTC – *Catalogus Translationum et Commentariorum*, cited by volume and page, with the author(s) of the entry in parentheses.

HLL – *Handbuch der Lateinischen Literatur der Antike. HLL 4* – K. Sallmann (ed.) (1997): *Die Literatur des Umbruchs. Von der römischen zur christlichen Literatur, 117 bis 284 n. Chr.*, Munich. *HLL 5* – R. Herzog (ed.) (1989): *Restauration und Erneurung: Die lateinische Literatur von 284 bis 374 n. Chr.*, Munich. Cited by volume and section number, with the author of the entry in parentheses.

Lewis and Short – C.T. Lewis and C. Short (1879): *A Latin Dictionary Founded on Andrew's Edition of Freund's Latin Dictionary*.

LSJ – H.G. Liddell and R. Scott, rev. H.S. Jones, *A Greek English Lexicon*[9].

OCD – *Oxford Classical Dictionary Online* (https://oxfordre.com/classics), cited by headword, with the author(s) of the entry in parentheses.

ODLA – O. Nicholson (ed.) (2018): *The Oxford Dictionary of Late Antiquity*, 2 vols, Oxford. Cited by headword, with the author of the entry in parentheses.

PHI 'Classical Latin Texts' – the Packard Humanities Institute Database of Latin Texts (https://latin.packhum.org).

PIR[2] – *Prosopographia Imperii Romani, editio altera*, 8 vols in 14 parts, 1933–2015, Berlin and Leipzig.

PLRE – A.H.M. Jones, J.R. Martindale, and J. Morris (eds) (1971): *The Prosopography of the Later Roman Empire, Volume I: A.D. 260–395*, Cambridge.

PLRE II – J.R. Martindale (ed.) 1980: *The Prosopography of the Later Roman Empire, Volume II: A.D. 395–527*, Cambridge.

RE – *Realencyclopädie der classischen Altertumswissenschaft*, Stuttgart and Munich, cited by volume, fascicle, and (where necessary) column, with the title of the entry in quotation marks and the author in parentheses.

RIC – *The Roman Imperial Coinage*, 10 vols, London, cited by volume, fascicle, and page number.

RPC – *Roman Provincial Coinage Online* (https://rpc.ashmus.ox.ac.uk), cited by volume, fascicle, and the number assigned to each coin type.

TLG – *Thesaurus Linguae Graecae* (http://stephanus.tlg.uci.edu/index.php).

TLL – *Thesaurus Linguae Latinae*, cited by volume, fascicle, column, and line, with the author of the entry in parentheses.

T&T – L.D. Reynolds (ed.) (1983): *Texts and Transmission: A Survey of the Latin Classics*, Oxford. Cited by the name of the ancient author or work in quotation marks, with the author(s) of the entry in parentheses.

USTC – *Universal Short Title Catalogue* (https://www.ustc.ac.uk).

General conventions and abbreviations

All URLs mentioned were active at the date of the preface.

All dates are AD (*anno domini*) unless otherwise specified:

AM   *anno mundi*

AUC   *ab anno urbe condita*

BC   Before Christ

Other abbreviations

ad loc. *ad locum*, used in references to commentaries and *apparatus* to indicate that they touch on a particular part of the text of an ancient author

ca. *circa*

cos. consul

d. died

fr. fragment

ps. pseudo-, *e.g.* ps.-Dionysius

r. reigned

s. *saeculum, i.e.* century (s. II = second century, *e.g.,*)

In memory of Sir Fergus Millar
(1935–2019)
Scriptor historicus, vir sobrietatis gratia aemulandus.

Part One
The Lost *Historia*

Ces vers tendus, sombres, sentant le fauve, pleins de termes de langage usuel, de mots aux sens primitifs détournés, le requéraient, l'intéressaient même davantage que le style pourtant blet et déjà verdi des historiens Ammien Marcellin et Aurelius Victor, de l'épistolier Symmaque et du compilateur et grammairien Macrobe; il les préférait même à ces véritables vers scandés, à cette langue tachetée et superbe que parlèrent Claudien, Rutilius et Ausone. Ceux-là étaient alors les maîtres de l'art; ils emplissaient l'Empire mourant, de leurs cris; le chrétien Ausone, avec son *Centon Nuptial* et son poème abondant et paré de *la Moselle*; Rutilius, avec ses hymnes à la gloire de Rome, ses anathèmes contre les juifs et contre les moines, son itinéraire d'Italie en Gaule, où il arrive à rendre certaines impressions de la vue, le vague des paysages reflétés dans l'eau, le mirage des vapeurs, l'envolée des brumes entourant les monts.

Joris-Karl Huysmans
À rebours (1884)

In the first part of this study, we present an extended case that the *Historia* of Sextus Aurelius Victor (*ca.* 320–*ca.* 390) does not survive, and that the two works attributed to him in the manuscripts, the so-called *De Caesaribus* and *Epitome de Caesaribus*, are in fact two independent abbreviations of his larger original work. What we present is a cumulative argument, building on general knowledge and previous scholarship, while forging a new synthesis, and (in Chapter V) bringing forward new evidence to support this theory. At the same time, this part of the book functions as a traditional monographic treatment of an ancient author, with the five chapters devoted to (I) the author's life, (II) his works and their manuscript transmission, (III) their genre, (IV) their individual character and relationships to other texts, and (V) their reception.

1

CHAPTER I

THE HISTORIAN VICTOR

Ammianus Marcellinus had a harsh and unforgiving opinion of the condition into which the art of writing history had fallen in his own day. Few of his contemporaries had turned their hands to that noble but demanding endeavour and of their efforts the less said, the better.[1] More than grumbling generalities, his *Res gestae* offers specific (though implicit) criticisms of the brief epitomes that passed for history at the time. Ammianus knew and alluded to two recent summaries of Roman history, the *breviarium* of Eutropius and the still shorter work of Festus, the allusions designed to subtly insinuate how different his own work was from their meagre epitomes.[2] Both of the breviarists had pursued a career in government and risen to positions of rank and power: Ammianus had occasion to mention them in narrating events of the 370s.[3] Yet in spite of their fleeting appearance in his pages, in spite of the rather deeper impress left by their works on his own, Ammianus veiled their writings in a decent obscurity, making no explicit mention of the literary efforts of either Eutropius or Festus. 'Brevity ought only to be praised when it takes away nothing from our understanding of events', he declared elsewhere, and left his readers to draw their own conclusions.[4] Nor was the dire state of history-writing likely to improve. The close of the *Res gestae*, with its defiant declaration that those who would write about the *reliqua* must 'forge their tongues to grander styles', is less a conclusion than a gauntlet, hurled with some force and more feeling.[5] It dares aspirant historians to write of recent events without the crutches of silence or mendacity, confident that, caught between the demands of history and the requirements of politics, they will fall short.[6] His own achievement, Ammianus implies, is unrepeatable, or at least unlikely to be repeated. In that sense, at least, he appears to have been a truly lonely historian.[7]

A single contemporary was an exception to this uniform and dismal picture. In narrating the long year AD 361, when the threat of civil war between Julian and Constantius II loomed over the Roman

---

1 On the problems faced by the historian, see *e.g.* AM 26.1.1.

2 For Festus, see Mommsen 1881: esp. 605–609. For Eutropius, see Kelly 2008: 240–253, esp. 252–253 on the purpose of such allusion.

3 *PLRE* 'Eutropius 2', 'Festus 3', collect the details (in particular, AM 29.2.22 for Festus and 29.1.36 for Eutropius). Burgess 2001 (*n.b.* esp. 77, n. 2) is sceptical about most modern attempts to reconstruct Eutropius' career, but his case has not found wider favour and rests primarily on dismissing the evidence of the *tituli* in the Bamberg manuscript, Msc. Class. 31 (E.III.22). Reeve 1997 makes a convincing case that this manuscript in fact goes back to an ancient edition of Eutropius and Festus combined, which would seem to lend its testimony significant weight (*cf.* Chapter III). Reeve's restoration of the correct

reading of the first sentence of Festus also makes it very likely that he did refer to Eutropius' work there, which would solve the chronological problem of two *magistri memoriae* apparently writing history at the same time raised by Burgess. Burgess (*ODLA*, 'Festus') is similarly sceptical about identifying Festus the historian with the bureaucrat Festus of Tridentum, but see Woudhuysen 2021a: 232.

4 AM 15.1.1: *laudanda est brevitas, cum . . . nihil subtrahit cognitioni gestorum.*

5 AM 31.16.9: *procedere linguas ad maiores . . . stilos.* This is an obvious engagement with the not dissimilar conclusion of Eutropius (10.18.3) (*cf.* Chapter VI).

6 On the *sphragis* of the *Res gestae*, see Kelly 2007; 2008: 319–320.

7 *cf.* Momigliano 1974 and below, Chapter IX.

world, Ammianus describes how, after his sudden descent on the Balkans, the rebel Caesar and aspirant Augustus settled at Naissus.[8] For the moment, it looked as though Julian's challenge to Constantius had met with almost complete success: without a battle, Illyricum had fallen into his lap and his cousin was tied down on the eastern frontier, where the Persian war was once again threatening to turn hot.[9] Increasingly assertive, Julian made clear that there could be no peaceful settlement to the political crisis, attacking the character and deeds of Constantius and Constantine in a sharp address to the Roman Senate.[10] Of his other actions at this time, Ammianus details only one:

> Victor, the historian (*scriptorem historicum*), whom he had seen at Sirmium and ordered to come from there, Julian appointed *consularis* of Pannonia Secunda and honoured with a statue made of bronze. He was a man worth imitating on account of his seriousness and much later was prefect of the city [*sc.* of Rome].[11]

Ammianus evidently thought highly of Victor, but his praise goes beyond a conventional admiration for his upright character. In the pages of the *Res gestae*, *scriptor* was a term rich in praise and only selectively deployed. Sophocles was a *tragoediarum scriptor*, Herodotus was a *scriptor*, and more generally the *scriptores* – *veteres*, *historici*, *antiqui* – were those wise ancients on whose learning Ammianus leant and in whose tradition he wrote.[12] Ammianus' contemporary St Jerome employed the same expression to describe no less a figure than Sallust himself.[13] To pick out a contemporary as a *scriptor historicus* was, then, a rare compliment indeed – it placed him in a different, a more elevated class, suggested that his work had achieved canonical status almost instantly. Victor, Ammianus implied, was a historian of real substance, a man whose work towered over the feeble efforts of his peers. Julian evidently agreed.

Only one individual combines the name, the literary inclinations, and the career which Ammianus attests: Sextus Aurelius Victor.[14] We happen to know a good deal about Victor, at least in outline, much of it derived from his own testimony.[15] Precisely when Victor was born is uncertain, but he could remember the reign of Constantine and he was still alive – and holding office – in 389, so a date a little after 320 is likely to be right.[16] Like his compatriot St Augustine a few decades later, he came from the countryside of Roman North Africa, son to a father who was 'poor and uneducated' (he said).[17] While Victor professed that his origins were humble, his *praenomen*, Sextus, perhaps hints at his family's desire to mark themselves off from ordinary folk. By the fourth century, *praenomina* – the original individuating names of the

---

8 AM 21.10.5.
9 AM 21.9, 13.1–5.
10 AM 21.10.7–8
11 AM 21.10.6: *Victorem apud Sirmium visum, scriptorem historicum, exindeque venire praeceptum Pannoniae secundae consularem praefecit et honoravit aenea statua, virum sobrietatis gratia aemulandum, multo post urbi praefectum.*
12 AM 22.15.28 (Herodotus); 25.4.2 (Sophocles); 15.9.2, 23.4.10, 23.6.30.
13 Jerome, *Chron.* 235ᵃ.
14 *PLRE* 'Victor 13'.
15 Bird 1984: 5–15 offers a detailed overview, though inclined to push the evidence further than it should go. Some of the inferences he makes from emphases

or silences in Victor's work should be discounted. The sketch in Dufraigne 1975: ix–xv is also useful.
16 *Caes.* [*HAb*] 40.14. A significantly earlier date would make him a very ancient urban prefect and a much later one is hard to square with his statement about Constantine.
17 *Caes.* [*HAb*] 20.5: *rure ortus tenui atque indocto patre.* We ought of course to be cautious about taking such statements too literally. Augustine describes his father (*Confessions* 2.3) as *municipis Thagastensis admodum tenuis*. On Augustine's background, see the evocative first chapter of Brown 2000. The parallel in Augustine (whose father as a decurion was *honestior*) should force us to entertain the possibility that Victor is not using *tenuis* here as a synonym for *humilior* (see below).

Romans – were vanishingly rare, archaic even.[18] The common people of the later Empire – the poor, the peasantry, the ordinary – were mostly Aurelii. They traced their citizenship (and hence their name) back to the universal grant of AD 212 by the Emperor Marcus Aurelius Antoninus, better known as Caracalla.[19] There is something defiant about 'Sextus', some pride in it: 'we are Aurelii, but not like *them*'.[20] We might wonder if (like Augustine) Victor's family were poor only by the standards of country squires. There were plenty of gentlemen in the provinces who must have looked very rustic and uneducated, seen from the lofty circles in which Victor spent his later life.[21]

Whatever his precise background, Victor received a good education, of which he was later rather proud: it had been his escape from the rural poverty of his upbringing and had raised his station in life.[22] Good schooling was by no means confined to a narrow elite: the example of Augustine, whose education was partly bankrolled by a wealthy neighbour, is again instructive.[23] However it was funded, Victor's schooling certainly gave him an exceptionally thorough grounding in both Latin and Greek language and literature, while his interest in legal matters perhaps indicates some training in the law as well.[24] In a passage that has some difficulties, Victor proffers the Emperor Septimius Severus as the outstanding example of *gens nostra*: 'my people', the North Africans.[25] He goes on to say of Severus that 'though of humble origin, he was first immersed in literature, and then in the law courts'.[26] Is there perhaps an element of autobiography in this description? An affectionate reference to Carthage as 'the earth's ornament' may suggest that he had spent time in the city; Augustine went there for higher education and perhaps Victor had done so too.[27] He may well also have resided in Rome at some stage: he had a detailed knowledge both of the city's history in his own day and of its various monuments that suggests personal acquaintance.[28] His curious emphasis on the failure to celebrate the Secular Games at Rome in 348 might even hint that he was in the city at the time.[29] His outrage at that omission certainly reveals his sympathies with the traditional, the ancestral, and the Roman, as he identified them. That attitude

18 Salomies 1987: 390–413, esp. 410–413. As Salomies's list makes clear, *praenomina* seem to have clung on longest in North Africa, but even there they were hardly common. Long before the fourth century, the *praenomen* had generally become fossilised: fixed as a single name that was paired with a *gentilicium* and that indicated descent (Salomies 1987: 378–388; Salway 1994: 130–131). In a vanishingly small number of cases, aristocratic *gentes* continued to vary *praenomina* within the family into the fourth century (Cameron 1999: 484–486).

19 On the Aurelii in Africa and elsewhere, see Stover and Woudhuysen 2022a. Sex. Aurelii are not common and there seem to be no distinguished ones (from whom the family might have taken their name on receiving citizenship). It seems almost too good to be true that the epitaph of one S. Aurelius . . . was inscribed on the same stone later used for the famous Maktar Harvester inscription (*ILS* 7457, but see Shaw 2013, Appendix 2), that other great document of rural social mobility in the later Empire. Shaw 2013: 56–64 dates the harvester's long poetic epitaph to the middle of the fourth century, or perhaps even later – could the same stone have earlier been used to commemorate a relative of Victor?

20 Compare the way that the Symmachi, also Aurelii, stubbornly maintained individual *praenomina* long after they were otherwise defunct: Cameron 1999: 484–488. Cameron does not consider the possibility that they were motivated by the ubiquity of the *nomen* Aurelius, but it may well have been a factor.

21 Compare the neighbours of Augustine's childhood, who were not much taxed with their sons' education (*Confessions* 2.3) or his *consobrini* Lartidianus and Rusticus, who had not even been trained by a *grammaticus* (*De beata vita* 1.6).

22 *Caes.* [*HAb*] 20.5.

23 Augustine's patron was Romanianus: *Contra Academicos* 2.2.3.

24 Chapter IV.

25 *Caes.* [*HAb*] 20.6.

26 *Caes.* [*HAb*] 20.28.

27 *Caes.* [*HAb*] 40.19; Augustine, *Confessions* 3.3–4.

28 *Caes.* [*HAb*] 42.6–8, the revolt of Nepotian in 350; 40.26–27, Maxentius' building activity, *e.g.* It is generally accepted that Victor had spent some time in Rome for education or early in his career, *e.g.* Bird 1984: 6–7.

29 *Caes.* [*HAb*] 28.2.

extended to religion. Though he came from North Africa, the Bible Belt of Latin Christianity, and lived in a rapidly Christianising empire, Victor was no Christian. What he says about the world in which he lived barely hints at the epochal religious transformation that was underway. Unlike his contemporaries Eutropius and Ammianus, Victor never refers to Christianity explicitly.[30] A lawyerly description of how under Diocletian – most famous of the persecutors – 'the most ancient cults were most piously cared for' shows where his religious sympathies lay.[31]

It is possible that after his education Victor became a part of the sophisticated bureaucratic machine that ran the Roman Empire – he certainly had a precise understanding of administrative arrangements and strong feelings about them. What he says occasionally has the flavour of life in the *officia* – the pride in his specific task that a minor civil servant felt and the rivalry with those just over the partition wall who were always getting in the way.[32] In reflecting on his education, Victor says that his *studia* had offered him a *vita honestior*, 'a more honourable mode of life'.[33] Later-Roman law acknowledged a distinction between the *honestiores* and *humiliores*, the honourable and the lowly.[34] *Honestiores* enjoyed certain legal privileges, among which some immunity from the routine brutality of the criminal law seems to have loomed largest to contemporaries.[35] It is plausible that Victor meant to say precisely that his legal status had been elevated as a result, in some way, of his education.[36] Various groups are mentioned in our juridical sources as *honestior* – senators, equites, decurions (or town councillors), soldiers, and veterans – but it is hard to shake the feeling that we do not have a comprehensive list.[37] It is most unlikely that Victor became a senator, a soldier, or the syndic of some town fresh from higher education, but by the fourth century even quite junior positions in the bureaucracy attracted equestrian rank.[38] There is one item of contemporary evidence that is tantalising in this connection. Towards 360, Constantius II sent an order to an official at Rome.[39] In it, the emperor first sternly warned that those serving in various administrative offices at Rome had to be of distinguished education and literary talent.[40] Waxing lyrical on 'literary learning,

---

30 Eutropius 10.16.3. Ammianus refers to Christians fairly frequently and discusses Church affairs at moderate length from time to time (*e.g.* 15.7.7–10). On Ammianus and Christianity, see Barnes 1998, esp. ch. VIII, and Matthews 1989: 435–451.

31 *Caes.* [*HAb*] 39.45.

32 *e.g. Caes.* [*HAb*] 33.13 on the *actuarii*.

33 *Caes.* [*HAb*] 20.5.

34 On this distinction, which can evade precise definition, but was no less real for that, see Cardascia 1950; Garnsey 1970: 221–276. The vocabulary for each group varied considerably (Garnsey 1970: 220–233).

35 This is dramatically illustrated in the proceedings recorded in Optatus, *Appendix* 2, where, having prepared to question one Ingentius under torture, the proconsul Aelianus asks him what his *condicio* is and, on hearing that he is a decurion (and thus *honestior*), has him unbound.

36 Though it is not certain: his description of Septimius Severus as *ortus medie humili* (20.28) guarantees that he did not invariably use the words in a technical sense. If Victor *is* using *honestior* in a technical sense (*cf. CTh* 2.17.1), then that probably means his father was not a decurion.

37 Garnsey 1970: 234–259, with reference mostly to the jurists. There is some need for a focused study of *honestiores* as a category in the fourth century.

38 Particularly the elevated grade of *perfectissimus*, which gradually swallowed other equestrian status in the general inflation of titles: see Davenport 2019: 553–606 on these developments.

39 *CTh* 14.1.1. Seeck 1919: 47 emended the transmitted date (Constantius *cos.* IX and Julian *cos.* II = 357) to 360 (Constantius *cos.* X, Julian *cos.* III), on the grounds that the place of issue was Constantinople and Constantius was not there in the prior year. That date, however, is when the law was received at Rome, not necessarily when it was issued, and receipt in May of 357 (as transmitted) would make a good deal of sense, since that was during Constantius' famous visit. Perhaps the place of issue is wrong? The recipient was called Julianus and the suggestion (Seeck 1919: 207) that he was *vicarius* of the city (*cf.* AM 22.11.1 for a Julian, *ex-vicario*) is attractive.

40 The law relates to the *decuriae* at Rome, guilds of officials who seem to have served the prefect of the city. On these, see Sinnigen 1957: 78–79.

the greatest of all the virtues', he then held out the prospect of 'more honourable' (*honestior*) status to those 'who seem worthy of prime position by their education (*studia*) and eloquence (*eloquio*)'.[41] It is very tempting to imagine Victor as a (perhaps slightly earlier) beneficiary of Constantius' enthusiasm for learning, to see him happily ensconced in a comfortable berth in the bureaucracy.

Some official position is certainly compatible with what we otherwise know or can deduce about Victor's career. In the later 350s, he seems to have fallen into the orbit of Anatolius, the praetorian prefect of Illyricum – the most significant relationship of his career so far.[42] Anatolius, a mover and shaker in both the politics and culture of the mid-century Empire, was a powerful patron.[43] He came from Berytus, the great law school of the east Roman world, and had the extensive training in government and Latin that it could provide.[44] He was also closely connected to sophistic and sophisticated circles in the Greek east. His tastes and culture are amply documented by the famous sophist Libanius' tangled, riddling, and allusive letters to him and the historian Eunapius' rather irritated account of a visit he made to Athens (on which 'he descended like the hosts of Persia'), where he first offered sacrifices in the temples and then held a rhetorical competition in which he set out to bamboozle the professors.[45] In the aftermath of the devastating civil war of 350–353, Anatolius had had his pick of the high offices of the Empire. In 355, he was offered the prefecture of the city of Rome – no small mark of favour to an easterner – but turned it down.[46] His name had then been canvassed as a potential praetorian prefect of the East, but he had ultimately (in late 356) been appointed to the same office in Illyricum.[47] Conventionally, the prefecture of Oriens would have been a greater honour than that in the Balkans, but at the time Constantius II was resident largely in Milan, and from 357 to 359 he was normally at Sirmium, or campaigning on the Danube.[48] Anatolius was thus frequently in the imperial presence, with all the opportunities for peculation and influence-peddling that that offered – Libanius took full advantage of the 'imperial feed-trough', as

41 *CTh* 14.1.1: *qui studiis et eloquio dignus primo loco videbitur, honestiorem faciet nostra provisio.*

42 *Caes.* [*HAb*] 13.6: praise of his administration in the account of Trajan. That this occurs so far from its natural chronological position is a strong indication of the connection between them.

43 Basic details, *PLRE* 'Anatolius 3'; see also Petit 1994: 33–37 and the insightful Bradbury 2000.

44 On Berytus, see in general Hall 2004, esp. 192–217 for the law school.

45 Letters: Petit 1994: 33–35. Eunapius, *VS* 10.6. The question of whether Libanius and Eunapius are describing the same Anatolius is controversial, for the former's letters were sent in the 350s whereas the latter seems to be relating events that took place in the 340s. In a lucid overview, Bradbury 2000: 183–186 comes down against, while admitting that Libanius' and Eunapius' 'portraits converge perfectly and convey the overwhelming impression that we are dealing with one and the same man' (184). Goulet, the recent Budé editor of the *VS*, maintains their identity (2014: 496–497). We favour a single Anatolius for the following two reasons. (i) Eunapius' two indications of the date of the story in question are both vague (*VS* 10.6.1 – Κατὰ δὲ τούτους

τοὺς χρόνους; 10.7.1 – οὐ πρὸ πολλοῦ χρόνου). Crucially, while his arrangement implies the event occurred under Constans, he avoids saying that explicitly – it seems most likely he did not actually know. (ii) Mere coincidence of name and office would not suggest identifying the Anatolii – it is the extraordinary similarity of *character* between them in Libanius and Eunapius that really demands they must be the same person. Hence, we are not proposing a *solution* to the prosopographical conundrum, but instead stipulating that, however it is worked out, it is virtually impossible that the character described by Eunapius should be attributed to someone other than the Anatolius of Libanius. This is further confirmed by Himerius' oration to the prefect Anatolius (*Or.* 32), which depicts the honorand in exactly the same terms as those used by Libanius and Eunapius: there has been debate about whether his Anatolius is that of Eunapius or Libanius (*cf.* Penella 2007: 215). The fact that his description is perfectly congruent with both of them should lead one to suspect Eunapius' chronology.

46 Libanius, *Ep.* 391.

47 Libanius, *Ep.* 509, 512 (the East); 549 (Illyricum).

48 Barnes 1993: 222–223.

he vividly described it.[49] That did not stop (characteristically) him from also praising Anatolius' probity.[50] 'Sublimity, magnificence of judgement, independence of tongue, hands that cannot be bribed, a yearning for friendship, love of the truth, a steadfast mind' – all of these characterised Anatolius, 'the great prefect' according to the sophist Himerius.[51] Ammianus and Victor shared this favourable view of the prefect and noted in particular his management of the *cursus publicus*, the imperial postal service.[52] Anatolius' ability to keep messengers, supplies, and information flowing may well have recommended him to an emperor soon to embark on war in the Balkans.

Anatolius summoned to his service in Illyricum men educated in law and letters.[53] One of those recommended for his staff by Libanius was described by him as 'a craftsman of eloquence' (*Ep.* 27.3: λόγων δημιουργός), and Eunapius tells us that an unnamed member of his household was an intimate of the foremost Athenian sophist of the middle of century, Prohaeresius.[54] Because the bulk of our evidence for Anatolius is found in the missives of the Latinless Libanius and the work of the reactionary Hellene Eunapius, it is easy to think of his intellectual interests as a phenomenon of the Greek world – that is how they have been generally understood.[55] This picture is only partial: Latin was the language of law and of government, and Anatolius was expert in both. Only someone with a fluency that extended beyond the linguistic to the cultural could have been seriously canvassed as prefect of the city of Rome, with its snobbish and self-satisfied aristocracy. Anatolius was probably bicultural by inclination, something also suggested by a report Libanius had received from Italy of his ridiculing 'some counterfeit sophist'.[56] His jurisdiction included the university (so to speak) of the Greek world at Athens, but it also encompassed the Latin provinces – Pannonia, Moesia, Noricum – that were the ancestral stamping ground of the ruling dynasty. As long as the emperor was campaigning on the Danube, the region was the beating heart of the Roman state, with a ceaseless flow in and out of soldiers, officeholders, petitioners, and messengers, from the west as much as the east. In this context, it is easy to see why the prefect of Illyricum might have wanted a bright young man with serious Latin culture, like Victor, on his staff. If we now see this cultivated prefect largely through the lens of Greek and sophistry, then he was in reality more Janus-faced, looking also to Rome, the imperial court, and Latin culture. Victor was both a product and a beneficiary of this double world.

Anatolius died unexpectedly in 360, precisely when is not clear.[57] His office had been drawing to a close the year before and it is worth noting that the emperor, finished with his Danubian campaigns, was heading east to face the Persians.[58] Perhaps Anatolius was to have followed him to Antioch? It is possible that there was a vacancy in Oriens at the time.[59] His death left Victor stranded in Illyricum, where the new

---

49 Libanius, *Ep.* 333.5: βασιλική φάτνη. The unimprovable translation is Bradbury's.
50 Libanius, *Ep.* 552.6 *e.g.*
51 Himerius, *Or.* 32.14 (trans. Penella 2007: 240): ὕψος ψυχῆς, μεγαλοπρέπεια γνώμης, ἐλευθέρα φωνή, χεῖρες ἄδωροι, φιλίας πόθος, ἀληθείας ἔρως, ἄτρεπτον φρόνημα. The sobriquet 'great prefect' (ὁ μέγας ὕπαρχος) comes from the same oration.
52 AM 19.11.2–3; *Caes.* [*HAb*] 13.6.
53 *e.g.* Libanius, *Ep.* 582 on his attempt to secure the service of Domitius and Aristaenetus.

54 *VS* 10.6.10: ὁ δὲ θεραπεύσας τινὰ τῶν οἰκείων αὐτοῦ.
55 Bradbury 2000 *e.g.* Eunapius' aversion to Latin culture may have been overstated: Chapter X.
56 Libanius, *Ep.* 552.1.
57 AM 21.6.5.
58 Libanius, *Ep.* 81.3; Barnes 1993: 223.
59 AM 21.6.9 implies that Hermogenes, praetorian prefect in Oriens from 358 onwards (*PLRE* 'Hermogenes 3'), died in office in late 360/early 361, but Libanius, *Ep.* 138.1, perhaps suggests he had resigned (or given up) a little before then. His successor, Helpidius, may have

prefect, Florentius, was an old comrade of Constantius and a man who had never been accused of harbouring intellectual interests – not a promising patron.[60] Paradoxically, however, Victor's unlucky turn ended up the making of him. It meant that when Julian and his army arrived in Illyricum, he was conveniently close at hand (Florentius had made himself scarce in the interval).[61] Hence that significant second meeting at Naissus in which he obtained both a bronze statue and position as consular governor of Pannonia Secunda.[62] To accept these honours was not without risk at the time, for Constantius II was still on the throne. Soon he would be on his way west with an army hardened by years of service in civil and foreign strife.[63] As a governor in Illyricum, Victor would be in the thick of the action. How kindly might the vengeful emperor view a cultured bureaucrat who had been so accommodating to his rival? The gamble, however, paid off. Constantius died suddenly, leaving the Empire to Julian: Victor's rank and reputation were now secure, perhaps even enhanced by their daring date. Not bad for a farm boy from North Africa.

We hear nothing of Victor during his governorship – the eye of the Julianic storm swiftly moved on to Constantinople, Antioch, and Persia, and our evidence for the Balkans declines in bulk and quality. It is just possible that a milestone near Mursa (in Pannonia Secunda) that honours Julian with the unusual formulation *ob deleta vitia / temporum preteri/torum* ('on account of the defects of former times now destroyed') was his work.[64] Beyond that, we have at most plausible supposition. Victor was probably normally resident at Sirmium, a major city, very well connected, and frequently the residence of emperors.[65] We can surmise that he might have found his superior congenial, for Claudius Mamertinus, the new praetorian prefect, was the author of an elegant Latin panegyric to the Emperor Julian.[66] Ammianus tells us that in 363 Lucillianus, the father-in-law of the new emperor, Jovian, was residing at Sirmium when messengers arrived to suddenly make him commander-in-chief, but makes no mention of Victor.[67] The brothers Valentinian and Valens, who next inherited the wreckage of Empire left by Julian, had been born at Cibalae, which lay within Victor's province.[68] They entered Sirmium together in the summer of 364 to divide the Empire, but again, Victor does not appear in the sources.[69] By May 365, another man was in office.[70] That is about as much as we can say. Throughout his years as governor, Victor was tantalisingly on the edge of the action, close to multiple important events, but for his role in them we have no evidence.

In the years after his governorship, Victor remains elusive. It has been suggested that he held a string of undocumented offices after he left Pannonia, pursuing the *cursus honorum* of the later Roman Empire:

been in post by early 360 (*CTh* 11.24.1 of 4 February), though the law does not specify his office at the time.

60 *PLRE* 'Florentius 11'.

61 AM 21.9.4.

62 The question of where that statue was to be located is an interesting one, to which there is no obvious answer. Ammianus' description might be read to imply that the statue was in Naissus itself. On the other hand, the statues of Prohaeresius, Marius Victorinus, and Claudian were all at Rome (see Chapter V), and it is not unimaginable that Julian would in 361 have wished to present himself as a patron of culture in the city.

63 AM 21.13.16.

64 *CIL* 3.10648b = *ILS* 8946 = Conti 2004, no. 73 (who suggests the Victor connection). See also Greenwood

2014: 113–114. The only parallel for the phrase is Servius, *Ad Georg.* 1.512, who talks of the *tanta . . . vitia temporum praeteritorum*, though they have not been destroyed (quite the opposite in fact). The usage in the *Brevis expositio Vergilii Georgicorum* 1.512 is derived from Servius. On Servius and Victor, see below, Chapter IX.

65 See AM 15.3.7 for an unfortunate governor there in the 350s.

66 *PLRE* 'Mamertinus 2'.

67 AM 25.8.9.

68 AM 30.7.5 (Eutropius 10.5 specifies that the town was in Pannonia Secunda).

69 AM 26.5.4.

70 *CTh* 8.5.27 is addressed to this successor, one Fortunatus.

a proconsulship of Africa has been canvassed as a possibility.[71] For somewhat technical reasons to do with appellate jurisdiction in the later Roman Empire, this is most unlikely.[72] Moreover, the period from the 360s to the 390s is one of the most densely documented in later Roman history: that Victor appears by name neither in the law codes nor in the letters of Symmachus (or Libanius), nor in Ambrose of Milan, that most politic of bishops, ought to give us pause. We might also expect Ammianus to have noted some senior position, if such there was – that he says Victor was prefect only *multo post* perhaps also hints at a hiatus between offices.[73] If he did continue to serve the imperial government, it is hard to believe that it was one the great offices of state, or some evidence would have turned up somewhere to hint at it.[74]

There is an alternative. The governorship had given Victor senatorial status – it would also have offered him an opportunity to gentle his condition.[75] After it ended, he may simply have decamped to Rome or its environs, places he probably knew well, and enjoyed a life of cultured leisure, punctuated by Senate meetings. His reputation as a historian grew impressively in this period. In the years before 380, we find Jerome writing to a correspondent, keen to borrow from him the *Historia* of one Aurelius Victor, no small compliment.[76] Probably a little before that, an enthusiastic, though not particularly skilful excerptor had used Victor's history in compiling a summary version of Rome's past: in his preface, he put Victor in the same category as Livy.[77] Ammianus was clearly far from lonely in his judgement.

However he may have spent the years after his governorship, Victor reappears in office in 389, when he was made prefect of the city of Rome.[78] While this was by no means the most powerful position

---

71 Bird 1984: 12–13, *cf.* Penella 1980b: 123 (unspecified but further offices); Dufraigne 1975: xiii was more sceptical.

72 In the inscription on the base of the statue that he erected to Theodosius (below), Victor is listed as *urbi praef(ectus)*, *iudex sacrarum cognitionum*. The latter phrase was used to designate those officials who had appellate jurisdiction (delegated by the emperor). Jones 1964: 481–482 is a very clear discussion of this complex topic; see also Peachin 1996: 188–199, a path-breaking analysis of the creation of the system under Constantine. In addition to being the judge of first instance in Rome itself and the region within 100 miles of it (*Digest* 1.12.1.4), the urban prefect had appellate jurisdiction over parts of Italy (the precise regions changed over time; in 357, Constantius II seems to have removed much of Italy from it: *CTh* 11.30.27). The phrase *vice sacra iudicans* was also used to describe appellate jurisdiction and there seems to have been no difference between the two terms: Ceionius Rufius Albinus, Victor's contemporary, is described as both *iterum vice sacra iudicans* (*CIL* 6.3179a–b, 36959) and *iudex iterum sacrarum cognitionum* (*ILS* 8950, fragmentary, but the key words are secure) on inscriptions from Rome during his stint as urban prefect. Besides the praetorian and urban prefects, proconsuls also had such jurisdiction (*CTh* 11.30.3 of 315 for the proconsul of Africa *e.g.*) and recorded it on inscriptions (*ILS* 1220 for Anicius Paulinus in 334; *IRT* 526 for Decimus Hilarianus Hesperius in the 370s); so too did *vicarii* (the deputies of praetorian prefects; see *CTh* 11.30.16 of 331; *ILS* 4152 of Sextilius Agesilaus Aedesius, erected in 376; *CJ* 1.15.7 of 377) and Constantine's *comites*, probably the *comites*

provinciarum (*CTh* 11.34.1 of 334). Crucially, individuals tended to tot up the number of times they had held such appellate jurisdiction (*e.g.* Memmius Vitrasius Orfitus did so in 359: *CIL* 6.1739, 1740, 1742). In other words, if Victor had held an office with appellate jurisdiction before being prefect at Rome, he would have recorded it in 389 by saying *iterum iudex sacrarum cognitionum*.

73 Ammianus does note the proconsulship of the urban prefect Ampelius *e.g.* (28.4.3), saying that he held the latter office *multo postea*. There is no evidence that the well-documented Ampelius had any official position in between.

74 If Victor did serve in administration between the 360s and 389, then the most plausible offices are palatine ones: he would have made an excellent *quaestor*.

75 Jones 1964: 106–107.

76 See Chapter V.

77 See Chapters II and V.

78 The date of the prefecture is not certain. It must be before Ammianus was writing in the early 390s, since he mentions it, and after 379 when Theodosius became emperor. It ought really to fall after August 388 (the death of Magnus Maximus), because it would be odd for an urban prefect to so extravagantly honour Theodosius (seemingly alone) when he was not emperor in the west (in any case Rusticus Julianus, the nominee of Maximus, seems to have died in office late in the usurper's reign – AM 27.6.2). Since Ceionius Rufius Albinus and Faltonius Probus Alypius (*PLRE* 'Albinus 15', 'Alypius 13') are well attested as urban prefects from mid-389 to 391, late 388 to early 389 appears to be the only period for Victor's tenure of the office.

ve̅ ʃERVM · PRINCIPVM · CLEMENTIAM
sa̅ NCTITVDINEM · MVNIFICENTIAM
SVPERGRESSO
D · N · FL · THEODOSIO · PIO · VICTORI
5   SEMPER·AVGVSTO

SEX · AVR·VICTOR·V·C·VRBI·PRAEF
IVDEX · SACRARVM · COGNITIONVM
D · N · M · Q · E

FIGURE 1.1 – CIL 6.1186: THE BASE OF THE STATUE THAT VICTOR ERECTED IN HONOUR OF THEODOSIUS

in the Empire, it was one of the most prestigious: the peak of a senatorial career.[79] The prefect, splendidly clad, transported in a special carriage, president of the Senate in session, was the intermediary between the aristocracy of Rome and the emperor.[80] Many sons of noble houses, with pedigrees stretching back into Rome's past (and even further, if some were to be believed), never attained the position. Few born in rural poverty ever did.[81] Victor's office is attested by a now lost statue-base that was discovered in 1563 during building work in a private house near the church of S. Maria di Loreto (then still under construction), which stands opposite Trajan's column. The base was broken already when it was found, but still measured an impressive five and a half feet in height. Its inscription (**FIGURE 1.1**) reads:

> To the one who has surpassed the gentleness, holiness, and liberality of ancient emperors, our lord Theodosius, pious, victor, emperor forever, Sextus Aurelius Victor, of senatorial rank, prefect of the city, judge in the emperor's place, consecrated this to his divine majesty.[82]

This elegant, historical compliment to the reigning emperor by his urban minister is the last we hear of Sextus Aurelius Victor during his lifetime.

Victor, who walked with princes yet retained the admiration of Ammianus, who had served Julian but still appealed to Jerome, who combined high office with higher culture, is a tantalising prospect as a writer of history. He was by education and situation ideally equipped for the task at hand. Yet, every historian of the later Roman Empire knows that Victor wrote an incoherent epitome of events from Augustus down to AD 360, the year in which it was finished, a work that is paradoxically both rambling

79 On the urban prefecture, see (still) Chastagnol 1960; our richest evidence survives in the *Relationes* of Symmachus.

80 Chastagnol 1960: 66–68 (intermediary), 68–69 (president of the Senate), 196–203 (dress and insignia), 203–205 (carriage, the *carpentum*).

81 Chastagnol 1962 remains the most accessible compilation of material on individual urban prefects. Those from non-senatorial backgrounds were not unknown (compare Victor's predecessor Sextus Rusticus Julianus:

Symmachus, *Or.* 7.4), but they were not common either.

82 *CIL* 6.1186: *<ve>terum · principum · clementiam / <sa>nctitudinem · munificentiam / supergresso / d(omino) n(ostro) Fl(avio) Theodosio pio victori / semper Augusto / Sex(tus) Aur(elius) Victor v(ir) c(larissimus) urbi praef(ectus) / iudex sacrarum cognitionum / d(evotus) n(umini) m(aiestati) q(ue) e(ius).* The formula at the start of the inscription is rare, but cf. *AE* 1978, 716 (to Valentinian): *virtute pariter ac pro/visione veterum princi/pum transgresso.*

and scrappy.[83] The *De Caesaribus*, as it is generally known, is certainly a history and one which tells us a good deal about Victor, but it seems incompatible with what Ammianus suggests about its author, let alone with what Jerome and the anonymous compiler say. It is a rather perplexing text: written in the grand style, with attempts at literary allusion and plenty of historiographical and moral reflection, yet undoubtedly an epitome, it seems almost self-contradictory. This may be a work with rather greater self-regard than the other *breviaria*, but it is hardly a greater achievement – 'not exactly . . . an artistic or historical high water mark in Roman literature' as Den Boer put it, attempting to defend it.[84] To say that its author, unlike Eutropius or Festus, was a *scriptor* is palpably absurd – he was instead (like them) 'typical of the careerist type of historian' in the fourth century.[85] Indeed, what most modern scholars think – that 'Victor was an imperial bureaucrat who wrote . . . one short work in his spare time' (Bird) – is a complete reversal of what Ammianus tells us about him, that he was a writer of history who happened to hold a couple of offices over the course of his lifetime.[86] Equally troubling, there is in Ammianus no apparent trace of Victor's work: no allusion yet identified, no intellectual debt, no hint of any acquaintance.[87] At first sight, it appears that Ammianus, that most careful and deliberate author, deigned (unusually) to mention a work that he had never read and from which he would have recoiled, had he bothered to flick through its (few) pages. The Emperor Julian appears to have been duped as well, elevating Victor to the rank of governor (a *consularis* to boot) as a reward for a rather inferior work of only 11,000 words. Julian's Latin was not good, but surely it was not *that* bad.[88] Muddying the murky waters still further, there is another short work of Roman history (similar in scope, but not in style), the *Epitome de Caesaribus*, which is attributed to Victor in the manuscripts that transmit it.[89]

Victor is, then, something of a conundrum and he remains an awkward figure in modern scholarship. In spite of the high regard in which both he and his work were held in the fourth century, he has never attracted the attention that Ammianus clearly thought he deserved, for a host of overlapping reasons. His work is just long enough to deter glancing interest, but just short enough to make him unpromising territory for sustained study. He is an author almost too full of character, too willing to beat the reader round the head with his opinions, not an easy guide to the plain facts of Roman imperial history.

---

83 The date of the work can be deduced from *Caes.* [*HAb*] 42.20: *At Iulius Constantius, annos tres atque viginti Augustum imperium regens, cum externis motibus modo civilibus exercetur, aegre ab armis abest.* This is a statement about circumstances as Victor writes (note the tense of the verb and *cf. dedit* in 42.21, describing events of 358). Constantius II became Augustus on 9 September 337 (*Consularia Constantinopolitana* p. 237 Burgess 1993b), so twenty-three years yields a date in 360. The testimony of Ammianus (21.10.6), which suggests that Victor's historical work was known when Julian arrived in the Balkans, points in the same direction. Nixon 1991: 120–121 concluded that the work was still being written in 361. He argued from *Caes.* [*HAb*] 42.17, which refers to multiple famous kings captured by Julian, that the text cannot have been finished until after Vadomarius had been arrested in early 361, since up to that point Julian had captured only one famous king (Chnodomarius), according to Ammianus. This seems a

little literal-minded, but in any case Ammianus' narrative is not as comprehensive as Nixon imagines. Julian had captured royal barbarians unmentioned by him before 360: Eunapius, *ELG* 1 = Blockley fr. 18.6.

84 Den Boer 1972: 19. *cf., e.g.,* Syme 1971a: 228 on Victor's 'stylistic pretensions'; calling him a 'thinker' is also not a compliment.

85 Kaldellis 2017: 44. Matthews 1989: 457–458 suggests that Ammianus' 'real interest' in Victor was the latter's ability to fill him in on Balkan events in 361. That would certainly justify a kind word about a helpful witness, but it is no real explanation for sharply distinguishing Victor from Festus and Eutropius. On the idea of Victor as Ammianus' informant, see Chapter IX.

86 Bird 1981: 463.

87 Kelly 2008: 241.

88 AM 16.5.7

89 On these works, see Chapter II.

At the same time, his Latin is unusually difficult and obscure – the reward for untangling its complexities has generally seemed disappointing. He falls just a little before that great efflorescence of Latin letters that marked the later fourth century, confined instead to the barren wasteland of secular literature that is the age of Constantine's sons. In the company of the *Itinerarium Alexandri*, Firmicus Maternus, Marius Victorinus, and some doubtful grammarians, it is difficult to contextualise him. Above all, perhaps, Victor has been annexed by the *Kaisergeschichte* (*KG*), the common source supposedly used by most of the later Latin historians, first hypothesised by Alexander Enmann in 1884, on which the *De Caesaribus* was (he argued) largely based.[90] Enmann's thesis turned Victor from an author and historian in his own right into one witness among many to a lost and more important text. The *Kaisergeschichte*'s rapid acceptance and more leisurely transformation into part of the scholarly furniture had an obviously deleterious effect on opinions of Victor's originality, his achievement, and of how much attention he merited – issues on which scholars before 1884 had taken varying, but generally favourable, stances. The effect can be seen in the scathing judgements of Victor's work that proliferated in the generations after Enmann. The character-istically sharp statement of Otto Seeck can stand for others: 'for the most part it was nothing more than a poor excerpt from the work of earlier writers'.[91] As later scholars moved the date of the *Kaisergeschichte* closer and closer to the point at which Victor was writing, so his originality dropped in proportion, until he was little more than the opinionated stenographer of an author writing only a year or two before him.

This is not to say that Victor has been entirely neglected, but a brief résumé of literature specifically devoted to him – at the risk of compiling a *Schimpfkatalog* – shows quite how marginal he remains and how low judgements of his historical ability reach. The first modern critical edition of Victor did not appear until the twentieth century, a 1911 Teubner edition edited by Franz Pichlmayr. Four decades later, the British philologist P. B. Corbett assumed that this would also be the last: 'I imagine it is unlikely that future editors of the De Caesaribus will be forthcoming for so ungrateful a task. Pichlmayr will reign in solitary splendour'.[92] After all, Victor's work 'has little historical and almost no literary value'.[93] In the 1950s, he attracted attention both as a supposed spokesman for the Senate and a 'historian of empire'.[94] This did not, however, involve a reassessment of his value. 'Aurelius Victor's work is little known', wrote a reviewer in *Classical Outlook* in 1963; 'it is certainly of no value as a source of accurate information about the facts it purports to relate'.[95] In his classic *The World of Late Antiquity* (1971), Peter Brown quoted Victor's description of his background (discussed above) as an illustration of how the classical culture of the fourth century was a 'success culture': 'its most egregious product was a mere thirty-page "briefing" – a *breviarium* – of Roman history for the new rulers of the empire'.[96] The 1970s saw a brief flowering of scepticism about the *Kaisergeschichte*, with Den Boer calling the *KG* 'manufactured in 1874 (*sic*)' and Dufraigne warning against the study of 'auteurs fantômes'.[97] It is perhaps not a coincidence that both scholars also took Victor rather more seriously, as an interesting and intelligent historian in his own right, than had generally been common thereto. The challenge to the *KG* failed, but interest in Victor

---

90 See, *in extenso*, Chapter VI below.
91 Seeck 1911: 193.
92 Corbett 1949: 256.
93 Corbett 1949: 254.

94 Alföldi 1952: 112 *ff.*; Starr 1956.
95 Gries 1963: 55.
96 Brown 1971: 30.
97 Den Boer 1972: 21; Dufraigne 1975: xxvii. See also Chastagnol 1974: 55–56.

continued to bubble gently away. In 1984, H.W. Bird produced a monographic survey, though he opened with the rather deflating judgement that 'Aurelius Victor was not a major fourth-century figure either historically or historiographically'.[98] As a result, his work did little to shift the needle: 'Œuvre mineure certes que celle de Victor qui ne permet pas de voir en lui un historien', wrote one reviewer.[99] Another reviewer, C.E.V. Nixon, summed up the consensus on the *Caesares*: 'its author's stylistic pretensions outrun his literary ability; much (though not all) of the period is better known from other accounts; and the work is punctuated by trite and tedious moralizing'. This leads to the conclusion – an amusing one coming from the author of an unpublished 440-page dissertation on Victor – that 'it might be thought more difficult to summon up enough enthusiasm to write a whole book on his life and work'.[100] Enthusiasm has indeed been in short supply: articles have since continued to trickle out on a variety of topics, but there has been surprisingly little sustained work.[101] It is fair to say that the appearance of Dufraigne's creditable French translation in 1975 and Bird's rather less satisfactory English version in 1994 failed to spark a renaissance in Victorine studies.[102] Neither was widely reviewed, and such reviews as were written spared neither Victor nor the scholars of his text.[103] Work on him remains a rather minor province in the great Empire of late antiquity, one still dominated by Enmann's invention, which crowds the pages (for instance) of Nickbakht and Scardino's recent text, German translation, and commentary.[104] In fact, it is striking that Victor as an individual has often attracted more attention than Victor as an author – it is repeated almost as a mantra that he is interesting only as a specimen 'of the political and moral mentality of his age'.[105] Ammianus would perhaps be disappointed.

There is, in short, a contradiction between what Victor's contemporaries thought of him and what we believe that we know about him. For them, he was *the* historian of the middle of the fourth century – for us, he is closer to a footnote. That contradiction, never explored, never even articulated, might make us curious about the man and his work, might make us wonder about who he was and what he wrote. To understand Victor, to understand why Ammianus and Julian held him in such high regard, it is necessary to assemble the evidence for the man and his work, examine it without the preconceptions which have so often clouded its study, and pursue it wherever it leads. The path it takes is often faint, often difficult to discern, but traced with care it will transform our understanding of ancient attempts to write the history of Rome's empire. This book begins that work.

---

98 Bird 1984: 4.
99 Wankenne 1986: 468.
100 Nixon 1985: 410–411. The dissertation is Nixon 1971.
101 *e.g.* Nixon 1991 (on his relations with Julian), Christ 2005 (Victor's ideas), Mollea 2018 (the text).
102 It is telling that the first English translation published was privately printed in 200 copies (Echols 1962). Note also the Spanish translation by Falque 2008 and the German by Groß-Albenhausen and Fuhrmann 2009.

103 Dufraigne: Tarrant 1978, Colledge 1977. Bird: Ando 1995, Muhlberger 1996, Wardle 1995.
104 Nickbakht and Scardino 2021.
105 In Cameron 2011, a magisterial treatment of life and letters in the later fourth century, Victor figures fairly often as an individual and office-holder (517–519 *e.g.*), but much less frequently as an author. The quotation is from Colledge 1977: 287.

Chapter II

The Works Attributed to Victor

Two works of Roman history survive today with the name of Aurelius Victor attached to them in the manuscripts, the texts commonly (but, as we shall see, inaccurately) referred to as the *Liber de Caesaribus* and the *Epitome de Caesaribus*, or *Caesares* and *Epitome* for short. The *Caesares* is a short (*ca.* 11,000 words), intermittently scrappy, and often perplexing history of the Roman Empire from Augustus down to AD 360.[1] In the manuscripts, it is merely the imperial part of a longer but rather superficial compendium, which aimed to sweep the reader from Saturn and Janus to Constantius and Julian in some 25,000 words – the so-called *Corpus tripertitum* (another inaccurate title).[2] The *Caesares* is certainly derived from a fourth-century text and the *Corpus* of which it forms a part may be roughly contemporary.[3] The *Epitome*, in contrast, is a coherent, readable, and very concise (*ca.* 9,500 words) account of the emperors from Augustus to the death of Theodosius I (395).[4] It circulated in manuscripts as a free-standing text. It is generally, though wrongly, supposed to have been written at the end of the fourth or beginning of the fifth century.[5]

So, the *Epitome* and the *Caesares* are both works of imperial history, both cover the period from Augustus to the latter part of the fourth century, and both are attributed to Aurelius Victor in the manuscripts. What exactly is their relationship to one another? At first sight, it seems rather more limited than their shared characteristics might imply. The two works have different end-points: some thirty years separates the *terminus* of the *Caesares* from the end of the *Epitome*. They are very different in literary and intellectual ambition. The *Caesares* is written in 'an idiosyncratic and excessively didactic style', filled with the author's 'own opinions and moralizing judgements', as a standard work of reference puts it.[6] 'More the work of a moralist than a historian' is the deflating judgement of another modern commentator.[7] The *Epitome* is much more impersonal, its wording plain and generally factual, but at points the work is judged 'far superior to Victor' in the information it provides and the coherence of its narrative.[8] Whether or not it really derives from a 'complex mix' of different sources, it seems far removed from the *Caesares*.[9] Victor's career, as we have seen, seems to have taken place largely in the western, or at any rate Latin-speaking, parts of the Empire.[10] Scholars have arrived at no consensus on where the anonymous author of the

---

1 See Dufraigne 1975 for an edition with French translation and commentary; the most recent edition, with a German translation and commentary, is Nickbakht and Scardino 2021.

2 On the compilation, see further below. The three texts are edited together in Pichlmayr's Teubner edition (initially published in 1911, revised 1970), but that is deeply flawed: Ando 1995 called Teubner's decision to republish it in an uncorrected paperback 'most bizarre' (if anything an understatement). The Budé trio of Richard

1983, Martin 2016, and Dufraigne 1975, though not perfect, are much preferable.

3 On the date of the *Corpus tripertitum* see below.

4 Again in Pichlmayr 1970, but see Festy 1999a.

5 See below.

6 *ODLA*, 'Victor, Sextus Aurelius' (Burgess).

7 Festy 1999a: liii.

8 Barnes 1976a: 263.

9 *ODLA*, 'Epitome de Caesaribus' (Burgess).

10 See Chapter I.

Epitome was located, but no one has seriously thought that the work reveals a career similar to Victor's. Composition in Constantinople has been canvassed recently.[11] Most importantly, while it is generally accepted that the author of the *Epitome* made some use of the *Caesares* in his first eleven chapters (and there are clear overlaps), after the life of Domitian that link is supposed to have been abruptly broken.[12] It is for these and similar reasons that today the uniform scholarly consensus is that 'the *Caesares* and the *Epitome* are entirely dissimilar works, which were both fortuitously ascribed to Aurelius Victor'.[13]

★ ★ ★

This conclusion is, however, rather more fragile than the weighty support that it has attracted would suggest, resting as it does on *a priori* assumptions about the nature of each text. The most important of these in discussions of the relationship between the *Caesares* and the *Epitome* is that both are roughly contemporary with their terminal dates. In modern scholarship, the *Epitome* has until very recently been universally thought to date from between 395 and 408 (the death of Arcadius).[14] This would mean that the text of the *Epitome* offers us unmediated access to the thoughts of an author of the 390s or early 400s writing about his own day. Such a date of composition has played a crucial role in most attempts to understand the text, framing discussion of the author's circumstances, sources, and agenda. That dating – and the analysis of connections between the two Victorine texts that depends on it – is mistaken.

The date of the *Epitome*

In an article published in 2021, we showed that the *Epitome* is an early-medieval text. Sections towards its end – from Valens to Theodosius – overlap verbatim with the *Historia Romana* of Jordanes, the famous historian of the Goths active in Constantinople in the 550s. Those scholars who have considered these passages have generally assumed that they show that Jordanes used the *Epitome* in his own work, directly or through an intermediate source. As we demonstrate, however, this cannot be so. Some historical details and stylistic quirks strongly suggest the priority of Jordanes: phrases that he used repeatedly, but which never otherwise appear in the *Epitome*; ideas that were almost unimaginable in 395, but commonplace in 550. Moreover, the shared sections are written in prose with an accentual rhythm, a consistent characteristic of Jordanes' style, but otherwise not a feature of the *Epitome*. In other words, the *Historia Romana* is a source for the *Epitome*.

If the *Epitome* drew on Jordanes, that means the work must be dated, at the earliest, to after the middle of the sixth century. It was put together by someone who lived long after the events he described and drew on pre-existing works: besides Jordanes, the compiler made considerable use of Eutropius in

---

11 Cameron 2011: 670. On earlier theories of the *Epitome's* authorship, see Stover and Woudhuysen 2021: 150–151.

12 Use of Victor: *e.g.* Cohn 1884: esp. 27–28; Schlumberger 1974: 63–66; Barnes 1976a: 261–262; Festy 1999a: xxi–xxii; Cameron 2011: 759; *ODLA*, 'Epitome de Caesaribus' (Burgess). Abrupt break: *e.g.* Schlumberger 1974: 66; Baldwin 1993: 82; Festy 1999a: xxiv–xxv; Cameron 2011: 759.

13 Den Boer 1972: 110; *cf.* Barnes 1976a: 259.

14 For this and what follows, see the extended treatment in Stover and Woudhuysen 2021.

his account of the second and third centuries AD. As we further showed, one other clause in the *Epitome* is taken verbatim from the *Etymologies* of Isidore of Seville (d. 636), a work of the early seventh century, which moves our *terminus post quem* later still. The first point at which we can be certain the *Epitome*, as we have it, existed is in *ca.* 770, when Paul the Deacon drew a great deal from it for his own *Historia Romana* (a work that also made extensive use of Jordanes).[15] This gives us a secure *terminus ante quem*. The material taken from Isidore relates to an obscure point of geography: the question of which Italian town named Adria had given its name to the Adriatic Sea. The circulation of Jordanes in the early Middle Ages has a heavily Italian flavour. Paul the Deacon, the first individual who certainly knew and used the *Epitome*, was also obviously active south of the Alps. All this points to early-medieval Italy as the place of the *Epitome*'s composition, at some point between the mid-seventh century and the mid-eighth.

This late date for the *Epitome* should not obscure its enormous value for Roman history: there is a reason that it has invariably been taken for the work of someone writing under the house of Theodosius. In fact, if anything, the date rather helps to clarify the source of all the rich and often precise evidence contained in the *Epitome*. Scholars have generally supposed that the work had a complex origin, drawing on multiple sources in Greek and Latin, most of them now lost. It seems, however, vanishingly unlikely that an author writing in Italy between roughly the 630s and 760s had access to all of these rarities. Instead, we ought probably to be looking for a single lost work of Roman history, which was the *Epitome*'s predominant source, supplemented intermittently from the epitomes by Eutropius and Jordanes. If we strip away the material taken from the latter to bolster the end of the work, then we find that the *Epitome* describes no historical events after the defeat of the usurper Magnus Maximus by Theodosius in 388. In fact, it has not all that much to say about events after the death of the Emperor Gratian in 383, beyond sketching out the character of his colleague Theodosius. We are looking, in other words, for a source composed probably at the very end of the 380s, perhaps in 389 itself, since the aftermath of a civil war was otherwise an odd point to pause. An early-medieval compiler took this work of *ca.* 389 as his major source, adding some material from Jordanes to bring the *terminus* of his work down to the death of Theodosius. As a result, our text of the *Epitome* is not in any straightforward way a view of Rome's imperial past by a contemporary of Theodosius.

If the *Epitome* is *derived from* a fourth-century work, not a work *of* the fourth century, then the whole question of its relationship to the *Caesares* needs to be revisited. The two texts – separated as they are by at least some 300 years – cannot be compared in the way that all prior scholarship has compared them. The interesting question is not whether they diverge, but rather how much they agree: the relationship not between the *Epitome* and the *Caesares*, but between the *Epitome*'s source and the *Caesares*. If we undertake this analysis afresh, then we will see that, crucially, the divergence of the two works after the first eleven chapters – the single most important reason to reject the *Epitome*'s attribution to Victor – has been drastically overstated. In fact, they show considerable agreement through to the *terminus* of the *Caesares* in 360. Further, even when there is not direct textual correlation, there is sometimes a definite parallelism and complementarity between the two texts that emerges from close study, even in material in the *Epitome* describing events after 360.

15 Chapter V.

17

Caes. [*HAb*] 5.2	*Epit.* [*LB*] 5.2–4
Qui cum longe adolescens dominatum parem annis vitrico gessisset, **quinquennium** tamen tantus fuit, augenda urbe maxime, uti merito Traianus saepius testaretur **procul differre cunctos principes Neronis quinquennio**; quo etiam **Pontum in ius provinciae Polemonis permissu redegit**, cuius gratia **Polemoniacus Pontus appellatur, itemque Cottias Alpes Cottio rege mortuo.**	Iste **quinquennio** tolerabilis visus. Unde quidam prodidere Traianum solitum dicere procul **distare cunctos principes Neronis quinquennio**. Hic in urbe amphitheatrum et lavacra construxit. **Pontum in ius provinciae Polemonis** reguli **permissu redegit**, a quo **Polemoniacus Pontus appellatur, itemque Cottias Alpes Cottio rege mortuo.**
He [*sc.* Nero], although he held power for as many years as his stepfather, albeit younger by far, was nevertheless so great for five years – during which the city was especially increased – that rightly Trajan quite often used to claim that all emperors fell far short of the five years of Nero. In this period he also reduced Pontus into the legal condition of a province, by the permission of Polemon (on his account it is called Pontus Polemoniacus) and so too the Cottian Alps, when King Cottius had died.	He seemed to be bearable for five years. For this reason some men have asserted that Trajan used to say that all emperors fell far short of the five years of Nero. He built an amphitheatre in the city, baths too. He reduced Pontus to the legal condition of a province, by the permission of Polemon its prince (after whom it is called Pontus Polemoniacus) and so too the Cottian Alps, when King Cottius had died.

The *Caesares* and *Epitome* compared

Comparison of the types of connections, before and after Domitian, between the two works shows this clearly. It would be otiose to print in their entirety the parallels which connect the *Caesares* and *Epitome* in their first eleven chapters. One example from the life of Nero (**TABLE 2.1**) suffices to demonstrate quite how closely they are linked. Despite their close parallelism, some differences are immediately apparent. The diction is significantly simpler in the *Epitome* than in the *Caesares*: compare *testaretur* to *dicere*, *differre* to *distare*, and the Sallustian *cuius gratia* to the colourless *a quo*.[16] At the same time, however, there is remarkable overlap between the two texts, including in some very obscure details, like the idea of the *quinquennium Neronis*.[17] Significantly, the relationship between the two texts here is of precisely the same character as their strong verbal overlap on the death of Constantius I, which almost all scholars acknowledge (**TABLE 2.2**).[18]

Such are the substantial and obvious overlaps between the two texts: at the very least, they demonstrate that they share a significant connection. What has largely escaped attention is that the passage on the death of Constantius is far from the only such link between the two works after the death of Domitian. There is a subtle but relentless series of connections between them in the intervening thirty

---

16 For *cuius gratia*, *cf. Cat.* 45.1. Hegesippus, Victor, and Dictys were all fond of the phrase: on these *Sallustiani* see Stover and Woudhuysen 2022b.

17 For the *quinquennium*, see, briefly, Drinkwater 2019: 27, with reference to earlier literature.

18 Barnes 1976a: 262; on the other side, Birley 2005: 409 sees a common source, the *KG*, on which see Chapter VI.

Table 2.2 – The *Caesares* and *Epitome* on the death of Constantius I

Caes. [HAb] 40.2–4	Epit. [LB] 41.2–3
Quod tolerare nequiens Constantinus, cuius iam tum a puero ingens potensque animus ardore imperitandi agitabatur, **fugae commento, cum ad frustrandos insequentes publica iumenta, quaqua iter egerat, interficeret, in Britanniam pervenit**; nam is **a Galerio religionis specie** ad vicem obsidis tenebatur. **Et forte iisdem diebus ibidem Constantium** patrem [vel parentem] vitae ultima urgebant. **Quo mortuo cunctis, qui aderant, annitentibus imperium capit**.	Constantinus, Constantii imperatoris et Helenae filius, imperavit annos triginta. Hic dum iuvenculus **a Galerio** in urbe Roma **religionis specie** obses teneretur, **fugam arripiens atque ad frustrandos insequentes publica iumenta, quaqua iter egerat, interfecit** et ad patrem **in Britanniam pervenit**; et **forte iisdem diebus ibidem Constantium** parentem fata ultima perurgebant. **Quo mortuo cunctis, qui aderant, annitentibus**, sed praecipue Croco, Alamannorum rege, auxilii gratia Constantium comitato **imperium capit**.
Constantine was unable to bear this, since his huge and powerful spirit was already from his boyhood driven by a passion to rule. He devised a scheme for his flight to thwart his pursuers, he would kill the public beasts, wherever his journey took him, and he made it to Britain. All this was because he was held as a hostage by Galerius, on the pretext of religion. By chance, in those very days, the end of life was pressing hard on Constantius, his father. When he died, at the urging of all those who were present, he seized imperial power.	Constantine, the son of the Emperor Constantius and Helena, reigned for thirty years. While still a young man, held as a hostage by Galerius, on the pretext of religion, he took flight and, to thwart his pursuers, killed the public beasts, wherever his journey took him, and he made it to his father in Britain. By chance, in those very days, the end of life was pressing very hard on Constantius, his parent. When he died, at the urging of all those who were present, but especially by that of Crocus, the king of the Alamanni, who accompanied Constantius as an ally, he seized imperial power.

chapters: verbal resonances, shared facts of considerable obscurity, and peculiar details. Many of these links are individually inconspicuous, but the cumulative case that *something* is going on is overwhelming. Most importantly, their relationship goes beyond that commonly acknowledged between the works of the fourth-century breviarists (so-called), as comparison to the text of Eutropius shows very clearly.

These less obvious overlaps start in the period immediately after the death of Domitian and continue down through the Severan emperors. Both *Caes.* [HAb] 13.8 and *Epit.* [LB] 13.8 list *patientia* among Trajan's virtues. There is nothing corresponding in Eutropius, and yet this is a telling detail, since it was a particular theme of Pliny's *Panegyricus*.[19] Both use a form of *lascivia/lascivus* in the catalogue of Hadrian's vices (*Caes.* [HAb] 14.6 and *Epit.* [LB] 14.6). Eutropius (8.6–7) has no comment on the emperor's sexual morality, somewhat surprisingly, for he was not in general a fan of his. Both Victorine texts say that Marcus Aurelius died at Vindobona (*Caes* [HAb] 16.14 = *Epit.* [LB] 16.12); of all other sources, only Tertullian is so specific as to give a place, and he says Sirmium.[20] There is also a clear intertext at the end of the life of Marcus: *Caes.* [HAb] 16.15 *patres ac vulgus soli omnia* **decrevere, templa columnas sacerdotes** ~

---

19 *Pan.* 59.3: *diceris iustissimus humanissimus patientissimus fuisse*, 'you are said to have been the most just, the most kind, and the most patient' (*cf.* also *Ep.* 10.106.1). See Kaster 2002: 143 and Benferhat 2015.

20 Tertullian, *Apol.* 25.5. Birley 1987: 210 splits the difference by having him die at Bononia on the Danube, a little north of Sirmium.

TABLE 2.3 – THE *CAESARES* AND *EPITOME* ON GALLIENUS' AMOURS

Caes. [*HAb*] 33.6	*Epit.* [*LB*] 33.1
expositus **Saloninae coniugi** atque **amori** flagitioso filiae Attali Germanorum **regis**, **Pipae nomine**.	**amori** diverso pellicum deditus **Saloninae coniugis** et concubinae, quam per pactionem concessa parte superioris Pannoniae a patre, Marcomannorum **rege**, matrimonii specie susceperat **Pipam nomine**.
he abandoned himself to his wife Salonina and his disgraceful passion for the daughter of Attalus, King of the Germans, called Pipa.	given to the opposing loves of his consorts, his wife Salonina and his concubine, called Pipa, whom he had taken under the guise of marriage after part of Upper Pannonia had been granted by her father the king of the Marcomanni as part of an accord.

Epit. [*LB*] 16.14 ***templa columnae** multaque alia **decreta** sunt.*[21] No other ancient text ever speaks of someone having temples and columns decreed them. There is another close link on the death of Commodus: *Caes.* [*HAb*] 17.8–9 *in **palaestrum** perrexit. Ibi per ministrum unguendi . . . **faucibus** . . . validius **pressis expiravit*** ~ *Epit.* [*LB*] 17.6 *ab . . . **palaestrita compressis faucibus exspiravit**.*[22] Eutropius (8.15) says blandly only that the emperor was *strangulatus vel veneno interfectus*. In his *Apologeticum* (35), however, Tertullian mockingly asks whence, if the Romans are so loyal to their emperors, come those 'who drill themselves in the art of wrestling, to squeeze his neck?' (*unde qui **faucibus** eius exprimendis palaestricam exercent*). Though he does not name him, the apologist is clearly thinking of Commodus, so once again the two Victorine texts mirror the language of a contemporary. There is yet another overlap between them on the treatment of the corpse of Caracalla: *Caes.* [*HAb*] 21.6 ***Corporis** reliqua luctu publico **relata Romam*** ~ *Epit.* [*LB*] 21.7 ***Corpus** eius **Romam relatum** est*. Strange as it may sound, no other ancient text ever uses this combination of words to describe the return of someone's remains to Rome.[23]

This close connection continues in the generally short lives of the numerous emperors of the third century. The full name of the emperor commonly known as Maximinus Thrax was Gaius Julius Verus Maximinus, but most literary texts were ignorant of anything but Maximinus.[24] It is only the *Caes.* [*HAb*] 25.1, which calls him Gaius Julius Maximinus, and the *Epit.* [*LB*] 25.1, which calls him Julius Maximinus, that show any awareness of his full nomenclature. Both also make clear that Maximinus was made emperor *e(x) militaribus* (*Caes.* [*HAb*] 25.1 and *Epit.* [*LB*] 25.1); Eutropius has the idea, but different wording (9.1.1: *ex corpore militari*). The *Caes.* [*HAb*] 28.1 and *Epit.* [*LB*] 28.1 are also the only literary texts to know the full name of Philip the Arab: Marcus Julius Philippus.[25] They alone show any sustained interest in his

21 'The senators and the people decreed to him alone everything: temples, columns, priests' ~ 'temples, columns, and many other things were decreed to him'. Throughout, we use intertext as a neutral term to mean a verbal relationship between two (or more) texts, without seeking to imply anything more theoretically adventurous.

22 'He went out onto the wrestling ground. There at the hands of the servant who oils people up . . . his neck was strongly squeezed and he died' ~ 'his neck squeezed tight by a wrestler, he died'.

23 *cf. Epitome* [*LB*] 13.11 on the death of Trajan (where it is the ashes, *exusti corporis cineres*, of his body that are so conveyed).

24 *PIR*[2] I.619; Peachin 1990: 106–107.

25 *PIR*[2] I.461; Peachin 1990: 198 ff.

TABLE 2.4 – THE *CAESARES* AND *EPITOME* ON AURELIAN'S CONSTRUCTION OF WALLS AT ROME AND CHANGES TO THE *ANNONA*

Caes. [HAb] 35.7	Epit. [LB] 35.6
. . . **muris** urbem quam **validissimis laxiore** ambitu **circumsaepsit**; simulque **usus porcinae carnis**, quo plebe Romanae affatim cederet, prudenter munificeque prospectavit . . .	Hic **muris validioribus** et **laxioribus** urbem **saepsit**. **Porcinae carnis usum** populo instituit.
. . . he fenced round the city with a more expansive circuit of the strongest possible walls; and at the same time he prudently and munificently provided for the supply of pork, so that he might grant it abundantly to the Roman people.	He fenced the city with stronger and more expansive walls. He organised the supply of pork for the people.

son, who plays a disproportionate and rather sinister role in their accounts of Philip.[26] The Victorine texts use the same words to describe Decius' elevation of his son, Q. Herennius Etruscus Messius Decius, each mentioning one of his many names: *Caes.* [HAb] 29.2 *filium Etruscum nomine* **Caesarem facit** ~ *Epit.* [LB] 29.1 *Decium filium suum* **Caesarem fecit**. The corresponding passage in Eutropius (9.4.1) makes no mention of any of the son's names.[27] A usurper called Valens, active in the short reign of Decius, appears only in the *Caes.* ([HAb] 29.3: *Iulius Valens*) and *Epit.* ([LB] 29.5: *Valens Lucinianus*), but a reference in a contemporary letter of St Cyprian (*Ep.* 55.9.1), which mentions an *aemulus princeps*, makes it very likely that such an individual did exist.[28] Both *Epitome* and *Caesares* say that Hostilian died from *pestilentia* (*Caes.* [HAb] 30.2 and *Epit.* [LB] 30.2); in contrast Eutropius (9.5.1) mentions the general *pestilentia* of the times, but suggests that Hostilian died by violence.

It is particularly revealing that there is a string of links between the two texts in their accounts of the era of Gallienus and his successor Claudius, one of the most obscure periods of Roman history. First, significant parallels can be found in the discussion of Gallienus' *amours*, as shown in **TABLE 2.3**.[29] The entire story is omitted in Eutropius (who also does not reveal the name of the emperor's wife) and Gallienus' barbarian consort is transmitted as *Pipara* in the *Historia Augusta* (*Gall.* 21.3). Second, only the *Epitome* [LB] 33.2 and *Caesares* [HAb] 33.18 tell us of a battle against the general-turned-usurper Aureolus, at a bridge which was then named the *pons Aureoli* after him. The *Itinerarium Burdigalense*, written well before 360, gives the name of just such a bridge on the road from Milan to Bergamo – the nearby commune is still called Pontirolo.[30] Third, the Victorine texts then also use the otherwise unparalleled phrase *a(b) suis*

---

26 *Caes.* [HAb] 28.3 ff.; *Epit.* [LB] 28.3; *PIR*[2] I.462.

27 His names vary a good deal in surviving coins and inscriptions (see *PIR*[2] H.106; Peachin 1990: 253–255), but these appear to be the authentic ones (*n.b. e.g. CIL* 6.1101, from Rome).

28 *PIR*[2] I.610. The *HA, Tyranni Triginta* 20, mentions a third-century usurper called Valens, but is patently pulling the reader's leg and does not place him under Decius. Greater caution in identifying the two is needed than has sometimes been shown (*e.g.* Syme 1971a: 202). *cf.* also Polemius Silvius (19). On Cyprian's letter, the

meaning of which is not pellucid, but which can most plausibly be interpreted as a reference to Valens, see Clarke 1986: 179–180.

29 See Bray 1997: 31–32.

30 *Itinerarium Burdigalense* (ed. Wessling 558). The text mentions the consulship of Dalmatius and Zenophilus in AD 333 (Wessling 571) and was presumably written not long after that. The bridge is mentioned by the *HA Tyr.* 11.4, as the site of a battle between the Emperor Claudius and Aureolus.

TABLE 2.5 – THE *CAESARES*, *EPITOME*, AND EUTROPIUS ON GALERIUS

Caes. [*HAb*] 39.24–25	*Epit.* [*LB*]39.2	Eutropius 9.21.1–2
His de causis Iulium Constantium, **Galerium Maximianum, cui cognomento Armentario erat, creatos Caesares** in affinitatem vocant. Prior **Herculii privignam**, alter Diocletiano editam sortiuntur, **diremptis prioribus coniugiis**, ut in Nerone Tiberio ac Iulia filia Augustus fecerat . . .	. . . Constantium et **Galerium Maximianum, cognomento Armentarium,** Caesares creavit, tradens Constantio Theodoram, **Herculii** Maximiani **privignam, abiecta uxore priori.**	. . . Diocletianus Maximianum Herculium ex Caesare fecit Augustum, Constantium et Maximianum Caesares . . . Atque ut eos etiam adfinitate coniungeret, Constantius privignam Herculi Theodoram accepit . . . Galerius filiam Diocletiani Valeriam, ambo uxores quas habuerant repudiare conpulsi.
For these reasons, they [*sc.* Diocletian and Maximian] called into kinship with them those who had been appointed Caesars, Julius Constantius and Galerius Maximianus, whose nickname was 'Armentarius'. The former chose the stepdaughter of Herculius, the latter Diocletian's offspring as wife, after their former marriages had been dissolved, as Augustus had done in the case of Nero Tiberius and Julia his daughter.	[*sc.* Diocletian] appointed Constantius and Galerius Maximianus, nicknamed 'Armentarius', as Caesars, handing over to Constantius Theodora, the stepdaughter of Herculius Maximianus, after he had cast aside his former wife.	Diocletian made Maximianus Herculius Augustus from Caesar, Constantius and Maximian Caesars. And so that he might connect them to himself by kinship, Constantius received the stepdaughter of Herculius, Theodora, as a wife, Galerius the daughter of Diocletian, Valeria; both were forced to renounce the wives that they had already.

interiit to describe Gallienus' demise at the hands of his own men (*Caes.* [*HAb*] 33.19 and *Epit.* [*LB*] 33.1), whereas Eutropius notes only that he was killed (9.11.1). Fourth and finally, that Gallienus, with his dying breath, had made Claudius his successor is a notion found only in the *Caesares* [*HAb*] 33.28 and *Epitome* [*LB*] 34.2; the two texts also share a remarkably parallel account of the circumstances that led to Claudius' final campaign (*Caes.* [*HAb*] 34.3 = *Epit.* [*LB*] 34.3).[31]

The links between the two texts persist through the late third and early fourth centuries. There is a clear intertext in the description in both works of Aurelian's construction of walls at Rome and changes to the *annona* (TABLE 2.4). Eutropius (9.15.1) talks of the wall in very different language (*muris firmioribus cinxit*) and says nothing of pork. The *Historia Augusta* talks of the wall (*Aurelian* 39.2) and of the pork (35.2), but separately and (in both cases) in rather different language.[32] The *Caesares* and *Epitome* have the same account of the period after the death of Aurelian: 'what seemed to be an interregnum took place' (*Caes.* [*HAb*] 35.12 *interregni species obvenit* ~ *Epit.* [*LB*] 35.10 *interregni species evenit*). Both the wording and the concept of something that was 'like an interregnum', but not actually one, are exclusive to these two texts. Only the *Epitome* [*LB*] 39.2 and the *Caesares* [*HAb*] 39.24 give Galerius the nickname 'Armentarius' ('cowboy', appropriate for one 'born to peasant parents' as the *Epitome* [*LB*] 40.15 says). With a few

31 On the *devotio* of Claudius, see Chapters IV and X.   32 Chapter VIII.

TABLE 2.6 – THE *CAESARES* AND *EPITOME* ON CONSTANTIUS II'S CHARACTER

Caes. [HAb] 42.23	Epit. [LB] 42.12
laboris patiens ac destinandi **sagittas mire** promptus; **cibi somni** libidinis atque omnium **cupidinum** victor.[159]	**mirus** artifex in **sagittis**; a **cibo** vinoque et **somno** multum temperans, **patiens laboris**, facundiae **cupidus**.
Enduring of hardship and marvellously skilled at directing arrows, a victor over food, sleep, lust, and all the passions.	Marvellously talented with arrows, very temperate in food and wine and sleep, enduring of hardship, passionate for eloquence.

significant verbal overlaps, this is enough to show that the Victorine works are textually linked here, where Eutropius has most of the same facts but very different wording (**TABLE 2.5**). Only the *Caesares* makes the comparison to Tiberius and Julia, but, significantly, the *Epitome* [LB] 2.1 is the only other late-antique historical work in Latin to show knowledge of the names of the second emperor, before his adoption by Augustus in AD 4: Claudius Tiberius Nero.[33] The minor harmonies stretch up to the very end of the *Caesares*, the assessment of Constantius II's character, where there are clear parallels (**TABLE 2.6**).

Language and style

As small as some these resonances are individually, as a mass they show that the conventional picture of the relationship between the *Caesares* and the *Epitome* needs refinement: it is not the case that the compiler of the latter stuck closely to Victor for eleven chapters, only to discard him for the next thirty-nine, and finally to copy two sentences towards the end of the text. For the history of the emperors from Trajan to Constantius II, the two works are linked by a strand – sometimes thin, but always present – of common language and common information. Of course, some of the less conspicuous overlaps might be explained by positing the use of a now-lost common source, that favourite refuge of the modern student of late-Roman historiography. That, however, there are so many unique convergences between the two texts ascribed to Aurelius Victor should perhaps give us pause – they might plant the idea that the man and his work merit further investigation.

Moreover, there is one connection between the two texts that a common source is ill-equipped to explain: the *Epitome* has a substrate of language similar to that of the *Caesares* running through it, well beyond the first eleven chapters and despite their considerable superficial differences of style. Take for example the *Epitome*'s obituary of Gratian (47.5): *Parcus cibi somnique et vini ac libidinis victor.*[34] This is even closer to the *Caesares*' ([HAb] 42.23) description of Constantius' habits than the directly parallel passage in the *Epitome* quoted in Table 2.6. Similarly, both texts use the same words to speak of Tiberius' cruelty, relating how he punished *insontes noxios, suos pariter externosque*, 'the guilty and the innocent, his own

---

33 *PIR*² C.941; *cf.* Ausonius, *Caesares* l. 54.

34 'He was sparing of food and sleep, and a victor over wine and lust'.

people and strangers alike' (*Caes.* [*HAb*] 2.1~ *Epit.* [*LB*] 2.8), but then the *Epitome* goes on to use a very similar expression regarding Maximinus Thrax's targeting of the wealthy, *insontes pariter noxiosque* ([*LB*] 25.2). The two texts use virtually the same phrase to describe the origins of two mid-fourth-century usurpers: *Caes.* [*HAb*] 42.15 says Silvanus was 'born to barbarian parents in Gaul' (*in Gallia ortus barbaris parentibus*) while the *Epit.* [*LB*] 42.7 says that Magnentius was 'born to barbarian parents, who dwelt in Gaul' (*ortus parentibus barbaris, qui Galliam inhabitant*). No other works use the phrase *ortus barbaris parentibus*. So too *Caes.* [*HAb*] 11.3 describes Domitian as 'pretending clemency' (*clementiam simulans*), as does the parallel line in the *Epit.* [*LB*] 11.2. The same phrase is used in the description of Hadrian in the *Epit.* [*LB*] 14.6, and nowhere else in ancient literature.

Both texts also use the vanishingly rare pleonastic expression *vix aegreque* (*Caes.* [*HAb*] 11.10 ~ *Epit.* [*LB*] 13.2): before Victor, it is found only once, in Plautus (*Poenulus* 236). Both use *absque* in temporal calculations – no other extant ancient text does the same.[35] Other uncommon turns of phrase are found in both texts:[36]

> *morbo consumptus*, 'killed by illness' (*Caes.* [*HAb*] 1.2, 16.9 ~ *Epit.* [*LB*] 16.12, 41.15)
>
> *ingens scientia*, 'vast knowledge' (*Caes.* [*HAb*] 37.2 ~ *Epit.* [*LB*] 43.5)
>
> *senecta aetas*, 'senescent age' (*Caes.* [*HAb*] 5.15 ~ *Epit.* [*LB*] 40.20)
>
> *grandaeva aetas*, 'grand old age' (*Caes.* [*HAb*] 13.11~ *Epit.* [*LB*] 41.25)
>
> *luctu publico*, 'with public mourning' (*Caes.* [*HAb*] 21.6, ~ *Epit.* [*LB*] 16.13)
>
> *fato quodam*, 'by a certain fate' (*Caes.* [*HAb*] 20.6 ~ *Epit.* [*LB*] 9.16)
>
> *iisdem diebus*, 'in those same days' (*Caes.* [*HAb*] 40.3 ~ *Epit.* [*LB*] 41.2, 41.4)

Victor was quite taken with the archaic *quis* for *quibus*, using it on some twenty occasions in the *Caesares*. Despite the relative normality of the *Epitome*'s diction, it occurs three times in passages not otherwise parallel to the *Caesares* ([*LB*] 9.4, 13.10, and 39.7).[37] A couple of other favourite Victorine expressions also occur in the *Epitome,* such as *pari modo* (*Caes.* [*HAb*] 21.1, 29.5, 39.39 ~ *Epit.* [*LB*] 32.4) and *haud dubie* (*Caes.* [*HAb*] 5.15, 15.5, 40.12 ~ *Epit.* [*LB*] 15.2, 45.5, 48.16). While these expressions are not that rare, they occur substantially more frequently in the *Caesares* and the *Epitome* than average. Obviously, one might attempt to explain these parallel idiolects by the idea that the author of the *Epitome* was influenced by Victor's style, even when he was using other sources. Nonetheless, like the parallels of content, they suggest that the relationship between the two texts is more complex and much closer than the standard account would allow.

Indeed, in light of this mass of evidence, the whole question could be turned around: why do we think that there is no relationship between the *Caesares* and the *Epitome*, both works transmitted with an association with Victor, beyond the first eleven chapters? There are certainly differences in content and

35 *Caes* [*HAb*] 14.12 *anno imperii absque mense vicesimo secundo*; *Epit.* [*LB*] 9.17 *Itaque annum agens vitae absque uno septuagesimum.* No mention is made of temporal *absque* in the *TLL* 1.185.56–1.188.49 (Lommatzsch) and a search of *CDS* confirms its rarity.

36 By 'uncommon', we mean expressions that, while hardly unprecedented and occasionally found in a handful of

major authors, are statistically unlikely to independently occur in two texts of around 10,000 words.

37 It is interesting to note that on one occasion where we have parallel passages from the two texts, the *Epitome* used *quibus* where the *Caesares* had *quis*: *Caes.* [*HAb*] 10.4 *quis perculsis et constantiam mirantibus* ~ *Epit.* [*LB*] 10.10 *quibus perculsis et constantiam mirantibus diceret.*

wording between them, but they are not so pronounced as has been asserted. None of the other obvious reasons to disassociate the two texts is particularly convincing. The different terminal points of the *Caesares* and of the *Epitome*'s main source both probably fall within Victor's lifetime, and thirty-five years is a rather shorter interval than the one that separates Augustine's or Jerome's first works from their last. The different styles and emphases of the two texts, the different backgrounds and world-views at which they might hint, could be no more than the outcome of an intervening three decades of thought and experience in the life of a single individual. Even the existence of two distinct works is no *prima facie* reason to pull them apart: late-antique authors were far from averse to revisiting what they had already written.[38]

All of the points that we have raised here are not designed to deny the obvious – that these are two distinct works with significant differences – but rather to query why contemporary scholarship simply assumes that they have nothing to do with one another, once we get beyond some shared material at the beginning. There is more than enough preliminary evidence to warrant reopening the question without prejudice. To do this – to try to understand the precise relationship between the *Caesares* and the *Epitome* – it is necessary to go back to fundamentals, and fundamentals means manuscripts.

Whatever the parallels and similarities between the *Caesares* and *Epitome* in phrasing and content, their *fortunae* diverge sharply: the former comes down to us by only the most slender of threads, while the latter enjoyed a robust medieval circulation. Since this is a topic of considerable obscurity and some confusion, it is worth setting down the rough outline of both what we know and what we can reasonably deduce about the transmission of the two works, with an eye for what it tells us about them and their author(s).

The *Corpus tripertitum*

In the manuscripts, the *Caesares* is only the imperial part of a longer compilation that was designed to cover all of Roman history down to AD 360. This compilation is, in spite of its creator's division of it into two parts, commonly referred to as the *Corpus tripertitum*, or *CT* (for short). To make this collection, the *Caesares* was combined with two other texts: the *De viris illustribus urbis Romae* (*DVI*), which covers regal and republican history, and the so-called *Origo gentis Romanae* (*OGR*), which deals with the mythical and mysterious era before Rome's foundation. Like the *Caesares*, the *Origo* survives only as part of this corpus, but the *De viris illustribus* has an independent transmission as well: in the *CT*, the text has eighty-six chapters, whereas in the independent tradition it has only seventy-seven (the result of medieval mutilation of the archetype), but it is clear that both are versions of the same text.[39] That is significant, for, together with what the compiler says about the *CT*, it confirms that rather than writing anything himself, he

---

38 See the Conclusion to Part 1 of this book.

39 *DVI*: *T&T* '*De viris illustribus*' (Reeve and Tarrant); Stover and Woudhuysen 2017; Stover forthcoming a.

took pre-existing works and manipulated them to create a new compilation.[40] The fact that these three texts are parts of a single compilation is often obscured by their being edited as separate works, but it is important to keep in mind that someone at some stage had put them together.[41]

When and where this act of assembly took place is a tricky question, one to which various answers have been given, none totally satisfactory. The *CT* is most probably a late-antique production, but when exactly in late antiquity should its compilation be placed? Puccioni and Richard, two of the *OGR*'s more recent editors, opted separately for the latter half of the sixth century. In both cases, the grounds are weak and the idea that Cassiodorus and his circle were the sort to make such compilations, and so this must be a compilation that they made, plays an over-large role.[42] A more, if by no means totally, secure argument might be made by noting first that the *Caesares* was completed by AD 360, which gives us a *terminus post quem* for the corpus.[43] That year was not an obvious historical punctuation mark, falling as it did just before the death of Constantius II and his cousin Julian's rise to sole power in 361. That could simply have been a calque from his source, but it might also point to a compiler working soon after 360, when the date seemed less strange than it would in the future.[44] Moreover, it is hard to understand why someone would have set themselves the task of creating the *CT* after Eutropius' *breviarium* (*ca.* 370) had covered the same ground in only *ca.* 20,000 words and with rather greater coherence, especially given the rapid and widespread success of his work.[45] For these reasons, it seems most economical to suppose that the *CT* was produced not long after its terminal date, though that is more a reasonable assumption than a firm conclusion.[46] There are plenty of late-antique parallels for the creation of a collection of pre-existing works: the *Chronography of 354*, a lavishly illustrated collection of historical, administrative, and calendrical texts put together for the use of one Valentinus, the *Panegyrici Latini*, a collection of twelve Latin speeches, the *Corpus agrimensorum*, Marcellus' *De medicamentis*, the Donatist compendium that preserves the stichometric lists of Cyprian's works, the so-called 'Ravenna corpus' (transmitted as a collection of texts), the *Anthologia Latina* (in the Codex Salmasianus), a collection of poems made in Vandal North Africa, the

40 See below for the activities of the compiler.

41 Their separation is obvious in the three separate Budé volumes, but even Pichlmayr 1970, who has them under one cover, treated them as effectively separate. On the compilation, Momigliano 1958a remains indispensable.

42 Puccioni 1958c: 222–223 and 1958b: 32–33 rests his case on little more than the assertion that 'a Cassiodoro o a un dotto della sua cerchia' would be a good fit as author (that the compiler of the *CT* does not give the name of the author of the *OGR* – which, *pace* Puccioni, is not the same as his being ignorant of it – signifies little; certainly it does not prove that some centuries had elapsed after its putative fourth-century composition). Richard 1983: 19 opted specifically for the 580s, but his view rests also on a misunderstanding of the form in which John the Lydian and Paul the Deacon encountered the work of Victor (Chapter V); he later changed his mind (1993) and preferred a date in the later part of the fourth century. D'Elia 1965: 27 wondered more cautiously whether the fact that John the Lydian knew the *Caesares* and Isidore of Seville knew the *DVI*, but not the *OGR* or *Caesares*, suggested that the *CT* was

compiled later than them. Unfortunately, the first point rests also on an incomplete understanding of what John the Lydian had read and, given that Isidore knew the *DVI* in its independent transmission (see below), the second carries little weight.

43 Chapter I.

44 On the one hand, even an inept compiler could have added a few details to have brought the narrative to a more natural stopping point, or alternatively cut short the *Caesares*. The compiler of the *CT* was quite willing to do the latter elsewhere, albeit for the purpose of harmonising his texts (see below). On the other, the sixth-century *Historia tripertita* of Cassiodorus terminates in AD 439 (12.16.5: *consulatu septies decies imperatoris Theodosii*), a point taken over from its source material.

45 For Eutropius: Droysen 1879. His *fortuna* is treated in greater detail in Chapters VI and VIII.

46 For a compiler working soon after 360, *cf.* Momigliano 1958a: 59; Braccesi 1973: 81–86; *HLL* 5.532.1 (Schmidt); D'Anna 1992: xiii–xiv.

47 For the *Chronography of 354*, the edition of Mommsen 1892: 13–148 remains fundamental. The *Panegyrici Latini*

Scholia Bernensia to Vergil, the *De orthographia* of Cassiodorus, and the *Historia tripertita* (which combines the Greek ecclesiastical histories of Socrates, Sozomen, and Theodoret in Latin translation) with which he was associated.[47] Perhaps the closest parallel would be the gathering of Eutropius and Festus into a single corpus, made in late antiquity for one Censorinus.[48]

There is no evidence that anyone in antiquity or, for that matter, anyone much in the Middle Ages knew the *CT*: there are no secure references to the collection *qua* collection. For this reason, attempts to trace its transmission rely on finding texts that show knowledge of one or more of its components. This is not an easy task and the effort put into it has perhaps generated more heat than light, along with depressingly few concrete results.[49]

The *Caesares*

While there are numerous references to the work of Aurelius Victor in late antiquity, there is no proof that anyone had read the *Caesares* as we have it.[50] The text was, on current evidence, simply unknown for most of the Middle Ages and the Renaissance.[51] In extensive research, the closest we have come to finding readers of the *Caesares* are two possible reminiscences in medieval works. One, in the twelfth-century account of King Stephen called the *Gesta Stephani*, is very close to Victor but isolated.[52] The other, in the eleventh-century *vita* of St Hiltrud, is weaker, but of considerable interest, for the life was written at Waulsort in modern Belgium, not so far from where one manuscript of the *CT* later surfaced.[53]

were probably compiled by Pacatus towards the end of the fourth century (see Pichon 1906: 244–249; Rees 2012). For the *Agrimensores* see (briefly) the entry in *T&T* (Reeve). Marcellus *Praef.* 2 makes clear the composite nature of his work. On the Donatist compendium, see Rouse and McNelis 2001. On the 'Ravenna corpus', the best starting point is *T&T* 'Censorinus' (Rouse and Tarrant): 48. On the *Anthologia Latina*, see (briefly) the entry in *ODLA* (McGill) and at greater length Zurli 2017. *Scholia Bernensia, praef. ad Georg.*: *Haec omnia de commentariis Romanorum congregavi, idest Titi Galli, et Gaudentii et maxime Iunii Flagrii Mediolanensis* (Hagen p. 839). Cassiodorus' *Preface* to the *De orthographia* mentions the *duodecim auctorum opuscula* which he has combed to make his collection (see also O'Donnell 1979: 229–237, perhaps a touch too pessimistic). On the *Historia tripertita*, see Van Hoof and Van Nuffelen 2017: 285–288.

48 As argued by Reeve 1997; *cf.* Cameron 2011: 432, who casts doubt on whether this was the Censorinus known to Symmachus.

49 D'Elia 1965: 15–27, 45–51 for the medieval fortunes of all three texts in the *CT*, esp. 49–50 concluding that there is effectively no secure evidence for medieval knowledge of the *Caesares* or *Origo* (drawing heavily in the latter case on Puccioni 1958a). *cf.* Schmidt 1978: I.5, II.4, III.4, IV.4, summarised at 1584: 'Das Corpus führt in Rezeption, handschriftlicher Überlieferung und früher Editionsgeschichte eine wahrhaft prekäre, gleichsam schattenhafte Existenz'.

50 See Chapter V for discussion of Victor's reputation in late antiquity. Lapidge 2018: 529, 532 suggests that sections 2–5 of the possibly seventh-century *passio* of Pope Urban (preserved in the A-recension of the text) show knowledge of Victor, as well as the *Historia Augusta*. In fact, the text here (Mombritius 1477/1478: ii, f. 346v) is verbatim from the *Historia miscella* of Landolfus Sagax (9.24–25; Crivellucci 1912: 1.245–247). We hope to explore the implications of this elsewhere. On the basis of an annotation in the edition of Arnold 1879: 20, Manitius 1892: 152 alleged that Henry of Huntingdon used the work in his *Historia Anglorum* (1.17), on the Emperor Tiberius. This is a compound error: Arnold almost certainly meant the *Epitome*, which is indeed close to Henry's text, but he in turn likely took this from Landolfus (*HM* 7.22; Crivellucci 1912: 1.195–196), since there is nothing in Henry from the *Epitome* that is not also in Landolfus. As Momigliano 1958b: 254–255 showed, the work *De Caesaribus* which Flavio Biondo found in the 1420s is vanishingly unlikely to have been Victor.

51 *cf.* Dufraigne 1975: lii–liii.

52 *Caes.* [*HAb*] 28.9: *Etenim quamvis rerum omnium prospero successu, pudore amisso tamen fortunatus esse quis potest ~ Gesta Stephani* 1.28: *. . . nec prospere eis aliis in factis succedere, qui, reverentia et pudore amisso . . .*

53 The key phrase is the extremely rare *immodice grassari*, found only in *Caes.* [*HAb*] 20.13 and the *Vita Hiltrudi Lesciensis* (*AASS, Sept, VII*, 466). The question is slightly

The *Origo gentis Romanae*

The *Origo* is equally elusive. In a series of characteristically acute publications, Mommsen argued that Jerome, Paul the Deacon (in the eighth century), and Landolfus Sagax (in the early eleventh) had all read a (fuller) version of the text.[54] Mommsen was really making three distinct arguments: that the *OGR* was an abbreviated version of a longer text; that Jerome, Paul, and Landolfus had read that longer text; and that Jerome referred to it as a *Latina historia*. The first of these is, as we shall see, very likely to be true; the third is based on an unfortunate misunderstanding of what Jerome meant when he referred to *Latina historia*.[55] It is the second with which we are directly concerned here. In subsequent scholarship, the issue has perhaps been somewhat confused by the elision of the idea that there was once a fuller *OGR*, which Jerome and later authors knew, with the idea that they knew the *Origo* as it survives in the *CT*, so one has to treat the circulation of both the *Origo* and the *Origo plenior* (so to speak) together.[56] For Jerome, the case is rather weak and has been heavily criticised.[57] Clearly, Jerome had some source for the history of Italy before the foundation of Rome, which covered much of the same ground as the *Origo*.[58] Since, however, the verbal overlaps between Jerome and the *OGR* are not so close, nor so exclusive, as to require that he knew the text, it seems very unwise to argue for a direct relationship between the two. We ought also to keep in mind the sheer quantity of antiquarian material lost to us that was still available in the fourth century – much of it in the form of commentaries to Vergil – before assuming that Jerome used something that has happened to survive.

If we turn to Paul the Deacon, the eighth-century Lombard historian, the case for knowledge of the *OGR* is superficially rather stronger. One of Paul's works was a *Historia Romana*, an extended cut of the *breviarium* of Eutropius, supplemented (as we shall discuss in detail in Chapter V) from other sources – and the idea that he might have incorporated material from the *Origo* is, on the face of it, quite plausible. There are similarities of both fact and wording between the opening of the *Historia Romana* (I.1ᵃ – sometimes called the 'archaeology', a swift survey of Italy's mythical prehistory) and the *OGR*.[59]

complicated by the obvious influence of Sallust, who used *grassari* thrice (*Iug.* 1.3, 64.5; *Hist.* fr. 53R = 14M), on both Victor and the *Vita* (compare *Cat.* 5.1: *fuit magna vi et animi et corporis* ~ *Vita* p. 461: *hic enim quia ad id dignitatis idoneus erat utpote magna vi et animi et corporis*).

54 Mommsen 1850: 680–681, 684, 689–691 posited a lost *Latina historia de origine gentis Romanae* as Jerome's source for some notices in his *Chronicle*. It was only in Mommsen 1877: esp. 407–408 that he identified that text as a fuller version of the *Origo gentis Romanae*, to which he suggested both Paul and Landolfus had also had access. He later extended the case to Jordanes (Mommsen 1882: xxviii–xxix) .

55 On *Latina historia*, see Chapter VI.

56 As Richard 1983: 28–32 does. For elision, see *e.g.* Momigliano 1958a: 64 ('there is nothing in St. Jerome to imply that he had before his eyes either the present text of the "Origo" or a longer text of it'), 65. In the latter case, it is not clear why suggesting that Landolfus shows knowledge of the *OGR*, but has additional details

and therefore knew a fuller version of the text, is necessarily to 'argue in a circle', especially when Mommsen (*e.g.* 1877: 407 on the death of Romulus) had argued from internal features of the text that it must be abbreviated.

57 Helm 1927a: 147–149 with 1927b: 303–305, for whom Jerome's source for the period before 753 BC was folded already into the first part of a *Latina historia* covering all of Roman history, which was his main source; Puccioni 1958a: 135–153; Momigliano 1958a: 64; D'Elia 1965: 19–20.

58 The passages in question are in Mommsen 1850: 689–691. See also Helm 1927a: 148–149 (with some parallels).

59 Easily grasped through the notes to Crivellucci 1914: 5–10.

60 It is accepted in the editions of both Droysen 1879: xxxix (and the annotations) and Crivellucci 1914: xxxix–xli and annotations (rejecting use of an *OGR*

For this reason, the idea that Paul did indeed have access to the *Origo*, or something like it, has attracted more support.[60] It is also, however, not ultimately convincing. As Momigliano showed, Paul's history of mythical Italy diverges factually from the *Origo* on some crucial points and, where they do share information, it can be found in other ancient sources, so there is no particular reason to assume that the former derived from the latter.[61] It is also very hard to understand why, if Paul indeed had a copy of the *Origo* to hand, he did not make much greater use of it. The whole point of the *Historia Romana* was to expand the narrative offered by Eutropius, and Paul noted specifically that he had added an account of the period before the *breviarium* began.[62] The *Origo* is full of rare and recondite information on that period and it offers a fairly continuous narrative of it. To have used it for only one or two points in an account derived primarily from Jerome, Orosius, and Jordanes seems distinctly odd.[63]

What then explains the *Historia Romana*'s account of earliest Italy? In probing whether Paul possibly knew one very rare ancient text, scholars seem to have forgotten that he certainly had access to another: the *De verborum significatu* of the Roman lexicographer Festus, a massive repository of information on people, places, and words.[64] That work, which mostly survives only in Paul's slimmed-down epitome, contained by its very nature a good deal of information about Rome's most distant past.[65] It is a more plausible source than the *Origo* (let alone a hypothetical fuller text than extant) for the fragments of Roman pre-history in the *Historia Romana*. An example can perhaps illuminate this point. Mommsen was much impressed by the fact that Paul and the *Origo* coincided in making Saturn the first to coin money, though he was wrong to think the idea peculiar to them.[66] Where might this notion have come from? It seems most likely that it was a back-formation from the fact that the treasury of the Roman people was the *aerarium Saturni*, located in a temple of Saturn: most of the sources which make him the inventor of money also mention this building, often connecting the two facts.[67] Sure enough, this is precisely what the *OGR* 3.6 says: 'Also the building beneath the Capitoline hill, in which he [*sc.* Saturn] kept the money he had made, is even today called the treasury of Saturn (*aerarium Saturni*)'. Paul's epitome of Festus contains an (obviously abbreviated) entry which explains that the Roman treasury was in the temple of Saturn.[68] What other information might Festus' original entry (which does not survive in manuscripts of that work) have contained? It seems very likely that it also explained that some people thought that Saturn himself invented coinage.[69] In general, then, the otherwise unexplained information in Paul's 'archaeology' of

plenior but accepting use of the *OGR*), as well as in a series of studies by Brugnoli 1958, 1960.

61 Momigliano 1958a: 64. See also, at much greater length, Puccioni 1958a: 63–104 and Puccioni 1960.

62 See his letter to Adelperga (Crivellucci 1914: 4): *ac primo paulo superius ab eiusdem textu historiae narrationem capiens* ('And first, beginning the narrative a little further up from the text of the same history [*i.e.* Eutropius] . . .').

63 See the notes in Crivellucci 1914: 5–16. Brugnoli 1958 was aware of this, but attempted to explain it by chalking up the, at best extremely selective, use of the *OGR* to Paul's critical acumen.

64 See below, Chapter V.

65 See, for example, its long fragmentary entry on *Roma* (Lindsay 1913: 326, 328–330).

66 Paul, *Historia Romana* 1.1ᵃ (Crivellucci 1914: 6); *OGR* 3.4; Mommsen 1877: 404–405. As Momigliano 1958a: 64 and n. 34 pointed out, Tertullian, Minucius Felix, and the pseudo-Cyprianic *Quod idola dii non sint* also have the idea. So does Isidore, *Etymologies* 16.18.3–4 and pseudo-Maximinus in the *collectio Veronensis* (ed. Gryson 1982: 125) (drawing on pseudo-Cyprian?).

67 Pseudo-Cyprian, *Quod idola dii non sint* 2.20; Isidore, *Etymologies* 16.18.3; Tertullian, *Apologeticum* 10.39. They (unsurprisingly) tend to derive the name of the treasury from the act of minting coins, not the other way around.

68 Paul, *Excerpta* (Lindsay 1913: 2): *Aerarium sane populus Romanus in aede Saturni habuit.*

69 See further Chapter V.

early Italy probably comes from Festus, whose antiquarian information occasionally overlapped with material that also found its way into the *Origo*. At the very least, scholars should be cautious about positing that Paul used a lost source for any information that might reasonably have come from Festus.

Landolfus Sagax, who was most likely writing in southern Italy in the early eleventh century, at first glance also seems to show knowledge of the *Origo* in his *Historia miscella*, an expanded and extensively supplemented version of Paul's *Romana*.[70] In particular, he tells the story of how, on the death of Proca, his sons Numitor and Amulius each chose one part of his property as their inheritance: Numitor took his money, Amulius his kingdom.[71] Here again, however, there are reasons to be sceptical. Momigliano pointed out two serious obstacles to the idea that *Historia miscella* drew on the *Origo*. First, Landolfus generally copied his sources verbatim, but if he was using the *Origo* here, then he was engaged in a very loose paraphrase. Second, Landolfus knew at least one 'authentic' ancient detail (the name of Numitor's son) which is not in our *Origo*.[72] Momigliano suggested, following Crivellucci, that Landolfus had in fact used some (Vergil) *scholia* as his source for this material, which does rather suit its fragmentary and limited nature.[73] It might be added, that, as with Paul, it is very hard to understand why, if Landolfus had had the *Origo* (let alone a more expansive text of the same), he did not make greater use of it. The whole *raison d'être* of his *Historia miscella* was that Paul the Deacon had not expanded Eutropius enough – the work needed to be bulked out still further.[74] An obvious place to do that was in the narrative of Italian pre-history, where the *Historia Romana* was relatively concise. In fact, however, Paul and Landolfus devoted roughly the same amount of space to the period, both well under 1,000 words.[75] Were the *Origo* at his fingertips, then Landolfus missed a trick.

What then explains those details in the *Miscella*'s narrative of early Italy that overlap with the *Origo*? As with Paul the Deacon, in wondering whether Landolfus had access to one very rare ancient text, scholars have ignored the fact that he certainly knew another equally obscure work. Landolfus was in possession of Januarius Nepotianus' epitome of Valerius Maximus' *Memorable Deeds and Sayings*, a text not used by Paul the Deacon in his *Romana*.[76] Today, this valuable work is preserved only down to Valerius Maximus 3.2.7, but Landolfus had access to the complete original.[77] This was a very useful thing to have. Nepotianus' epitome was based on the full text of Valerius Maximus (including sections lost in the manuscript tradition of that work).[78] It was also in some ways closer to a reworking of the *Memorable Deeds and Sayings* than a plain summary: the text has been recomposed and its author was not afraid to supplement

---

70 For Landolfus, about whom we know very little, see Crivellucci 1912: 1.xxvii–xxix. Interests, sources, and manuscripts all combine to suggest his date and rough location. For passages identified as coming from the *OGR* see Mommsen 1877: 402 and Droysen 1879: 227. *Historia miscella* is not the authentic title of his work, but a convenient way to distinguish it from Paul's.

71 Landolfus, *HM* 1.4 (Crivellucci 1912: 1.4), *OGR* 19.1–3. Lengthy analysis suggested to Puccioni 1958a: 205 that Landolfus knew the *OGR*, as well as Cassius Dio and perhaps Plutarch and Dionysius of Halicarnassus. This seems somewhat unlikely.

72 Momigliano 1958a: 65.

73 Momigliano 1958a: 65; Crivellucci 1912: 1.xxviii–xxix.

74 See the *titulus* to the work (Crivellucci 1912: 1.3).

75 Paul, *HR* 1.1ᵃ (Crivellucci 1914: 5–10), down to the opening of Eutropius (1.1.1) is *ca*. 700 words. Landolfus, *HM* 1.1–4 (Crivellucci 1912: i.3–7) is *ca*. 800 words.

76 On Januarius Nepotianus, see *HLL* 5.534.2 (Schmidt); Briscoe 1998: 1.xxi–xxv; Briscoe 2018: 22–23; Raschieri 2020. The text can be found in Briscoe 1998: 2.800–846.

77 Vat. lat. 1321 (s. XIV) is the only manuscript. For Landolfus' use of Nepotianus, see Droysen 1879: lxv; Ihm 1894; Crivellucci 1912: 1.xxiii–xxiv.

78 In Briscoe 1998, these are helpfully marked with an initial *(Par.)* or *(Nep.)* to indicate whether they come from Nepotianus or Julius Paris, the other epitomator of Valerius Maximus (below).

the original with things that he found interesting.[79] Landolfus made heavy and generally verbatim use of Nepotianus, so much so that Hans Droysen felt confident that he could, in effect, reconstruct parts of his text by comparison of the *Miscella* with Valerius Maximus.[80] It should, however, be obvious that – keeping in mind Nepotianus' method in making his epitome and the mutilated state of that text – there may be passages of *Nepotiana* in the *Miscella* that we cannot identify, because they were additions to the material in Valerius Maximus, not derived from him. Since the *Memorable Deeds and Sayings* mentions Romulus quite often and even Numitor on one occasion, it seems reasonable to wonder whether Nepotianus added a few details about the period before Rome's foundation which Landolfus then used to expand his work.[81] At the very least, scholars should be cautious about positing a lost source for any information that Landolfus might have drawn from Nepotianus, or from some more limited source like *scholia* to the *Aeneid*. There is thus every reason to think that the *OGR*, like the *Caesares*, was quite unknown for most of late antiquity, the Middle Ages, and the Renaissance.

The *De viris illustribus*

The *DVI*, because of its independent transmission, is a tougher nut to crack. It certainly was a text that attracted readers in late antiquity and the Middle Ages – not numerous, but not undistinguished either. There are some suggestive links between entries in Jerome's translation of Eusebius' *Chronicle* and the *DVI*, but, once again, they are neither so close nor so exclusive as to require that one was drawing on the other: where they share similar wording, Jerome often has more information than his putative source.[82] Again, it seems wise to keep in mind the sheer quantity of antiquarian material that was available in the fourth century, before assuming that Jerome must have used a text that happens to have survived. On the other hand, Isidore of Seville in the seventh century certainly knew the *DVI* and used it in both his *Chronicle* and *Etymologies*.[83] There is also some slight but persuasive evidence that material from the *DVI* found its way into some of the non-Servian *scholia* to Vergil.[84] Godfrey of Viterbo in the twelfth century also shows knowledge of the text, though his use of it has attracted rather less attention than that of Isidore. He deployed it in extensive notes attached to the account of the kings of Rome in his *Speculum regum* (written *ca.* 1183, but never seemingly disseminated), a work that boldly traced the ancestry of the

79 For Nepotianus' working method and additions, see Chapter III. The passages not derived directly from Valerius Maximus are marked 'nou.' in the edition of Briscoe 1998.

80 Droysen 1878. See also Ihm 1894. An edition along these lines is being prepared by Rainer Jakobi (forthcoming).

81 Romulus: Valerius Maximus 1.8.11, 2.2.9 (which also features Numitor), 2.4.4, 2.8, 3.2 *passim*, 4.4.11, 5.8.1, 9.6.1.

82 D'Elia 1965: 19–20 was suitably cautious. As an example, compare *DVI* 28.4, *Consul bello Latino filium suum, quod contra imperium pugnasset, securi percussit*, with Jerome, *Chron.* 123[c], *Romanorum consul Mallius Torquatus filium suum, quod contra imperium in hostes pugnaverat, virgis*

caesum securi percussit. There are some verbal overlaps with both Aulus Gellius, *NA* 9.13.20 and the *Periochae* to Livy 8.14. It seems unlikely that something so simple as Jerome reading the *DVI* is going on here.

83 Accepted even by the (rightly) cautious D'Elia 1965: 26–27 on the strength of the *Chronicle*.

84 See Ottaviano 2013: 243–244, who cautiously suggests a common source. The question deserves further study. The *scholia* are pre-Carolingian (found in manuscripts of s. IX), but of uncertain date. Crivellucci 1914: xxxviii, 12–13 argued that Paul the Deacon drew on the *DVI* in *Historia Romana* 1.2. The first example he provides (*pepigere . . . efficerentur*) covers the same events as *DVI* 2.4–11 (not merely 2.10 as he suggests), but with no verbal overlaps, while the second (*quod ad tutelam*

Hohenstaufens back to pretty much anybody of note mentioned in either the Bible or classical myth.[85] For those interested in Victor and the *CT*, the crucial question is: in what form were Isidore and Godfrey reading the *De viris illustribus*?[86]

The text of the *DVI* in the *Corpus tripertitum* (generally referred to as the 'A' version) varies a good deal from that in the independent transmission (known as 'B') — many of these variants are very minor, but some are fairly significant.[87] Because of this, by examining what Isidore and Godfrey say with an eye to the significant variants between the A and B texts of the *DVI*, we can work out to which family their manuscripts belonged. In his *Etymologies* (10.1.28), Isidore borrowed from the text for his account of Brutus, the foundational figure of the Roman Republic. The bishop of Seville says that Brutus' brother had been executed by their uncle Tarquinius Superbus 'on account of his riches and his foresight' (*ob divitias et prudentiam*). That curious wording is found in the B text of the *DVI* (10.1), but the A version says that he was killed 'on account of his riches and because of his lack of foresight' (*ob divitias et de imprudentia*). There is no small difference between being executed as a tall poppy and because of a lack of political nous. Isidore's text of the *DVI* clearly belonged to the independent transmission, not that of the *CT*: this sits well with the fact that he shows no knowledge of either the *Origo* or the *Caesares*, texts which 'God's librarian' would surely have devoured.[88]

Godfrey of Viterbo was similarly drawn to the *DVI*'s account of Romulus and excerpted it extensively for his notes to the *Speculum*.[89] On one very significant point (where Tarpeia was to lead the Sabine army in its attack on Rome), Godfrey specifically mentions the Capitol. Only the B text of the *DVI* mentions the Capitol by name.[90] Like Isidore, then, Godfrey was not reading the *DVI* as part of the *Corpus tripertitum*, but instead in the independently transmitted text. Even those who at first glance seem to hint at knowledge of the *CT* reveal on examination precisely how little that text was known.

The only conclusion from this review of evidence for knowledge of the *Corpus tripertitum* and its constituent parts can be that the former was entirely unknown and the latter almost equally without readers.[91]

. . . *transilierit*) is almost verbatim Jordanes, *Romana* 89 (perhaps from Florus 1.7.16).

85 Godfrey's use of the *DVI* (he never cites the work explicitly) was noted by Waitz (1872: 4, 56–59) in his edition (in marginal notes to the text, where it is unhelpfully attributed to Aurelius Victor), but does not seem to have attracted subsequent attention (no mention of him in Martin 2016, *e.g.*). That the prose commentary attached to the *Speculum* does go back to Godfrey was demonstrated by Schulz 1926: 90–91. That the work was never published is the argument of Weber 1994: 182–184, an accurate and faithful guide to a topic of (at times) mind-numbing complexity.

86 The evidence of the *scholia* is too slight (as yet) to answer this question.

87 On the two traditions, see further below.

88 D'Elia 1965: 27. Other points at which Isidore used the *DVI* are *Etymologies* 15.3.6 (= *DVI* 2.2–3) and 5.1.3 (= *DVI* 21.1). See also below on his *Chronicle*. On Isidore in general, see now Barrett 2019.

89 Godfrey, *Speculum Regum* (Waitz 1872: 56–57) = *DVI* 2. Godfrey (Waitz 1872: 58) also drew on *DVI* 4 for his account of Tullus Hostilius.

90 Godfrey, *Speculum Regum* (Waitz 1872: 56) ~ *DVI* (B) 2.5: . . . *si exercitum suum in Capitolium perduxisset* . . .

91 One possible exception is the somewhat speculative belief that a reader of the *CT* interpolated its text of the *DVI* from Landolfus Sagax, the continuator of Paul the Deacon, who wrote during the joint reign of the Byzantine emperors Basil II and Constantine VIII, between 976 and 1025 (see the list of emperors in Crivellucci 1912: 2.296, who elsewhere, 1.xxxvii–xxxviii, gives the date of Basil's death as 1023, which has occasionally misled the unwary). The idea goes back to Wijga 1890: 7, who attributes it to Opitz 1874: 207 (which does not in fact appear to say this, though *cf.* 223, n. 31). It was stated most influentially by Momigliano 1958a: 59–60, who was followed by D'Elia 1965: 97–105; D'Elia 1973: 59; D'Anna 1992: xxxvi; Festy 1994: 100. Though Momigliano's case has been widely accepted and formed the basis of elaborate theories,

The manuscripts of the *Corpus tripertitum*

What we know of the *CT* thus rests, and rests solely, on the manuscripts that transmit it. The *CT* survives in only two fifteenth-century witnesses: Oxford, Bodleian Library, Canon. class. lat. 131 and Brussels, Bibliothèque Royale, 9755–9763, conventionally referred to as **o** and **p**. Neither manuscript, it must be said, gives away much about itself.[92] In **o**, produced probably in Italy and written on paper in a fine, clear humanistic hand, the *CT* is bound together with a translation of Xenophon's *Memorabilia*.[93] That translation was made by Cardinal Bessarion and, as the characteristic ownership inscription in Greek on f. 2r that lists both it and the *CT* reveals, he also owned the book.[94] The script of the translation is an Italian Gothic *hybrida* (using Derolez's terminology) and is prefaced (as frequently) by a letter, to Giuliano Cesarini, the cardinal bishop of Frascati, killed at the battle of Varna in 1444.[95] It also has an *explicit* (f. 84ar) that dates it to 1453 and shows that it was made for Cardinal Colonna, though it seems it was never handed over. It is certain that it was Bessarion who combined this translation of his own with the *CT*, before adding his ownership inscription, with its résumé of the contents. We might thus situate the production of the *CT* portion of the manuscript in roughly the middle of the fifteenth century, perhaps during the period when Bessarion was papal legate at Bologna (1450–1455).[96]

A paper manuscript, offering a rather more cramped humanist script, **p** was probably produced in Flanders or Germany in the mid- to late fifteenth century.[97] Besides the *CT*, **p** contains works of Cicero (the *De officiis* and *Pro Sulla*) and speeches taken from Sallust, Livy, and the *Historia* attributed to Hegesippus.[98] As an ownership inscription on f. 156v shows, it was owned by Johannes de Loemel, chaplain of the church of St Denis at Liège. This is significant, for one 'Ioannes de Lumel' is reasonably

his proofs are not all that convincing and his theory cannot explain all the evidence. In particular, some of the 'interpolations' he identifies in the *CT* must come from a version of Eutropius' *breviarium* different to the one used by Landolfus. Subsequently manuscripts of just the *DVI* (not the *CT*) with some of the 'interpolations' have turned up: see Sherwin 1972 and Stover and Woudhuysen 2017. This suggests that a rather different explanation is required.

92 On the MSS, see the short, though very valuable guide in *T&T 'De viris illustribus'* (Reeve and Tarrant) and (at greater length) D'Elia 1965: 53–59, 125–139. The discussion that follows is indebted to both of these, but is based also on inspection of both manuscripts.

93 There is an extremely useful description in the catalogue by Hunt 1975: 86–87.

94 *cf.* Omont 1894: 50 (no. 239), which shows that it was among those works donated by him to St Mark's in Venice in 1468.

95 *Hybrida*: Derolez 2003: 163–175. Comparison with his plates would be enough to secure the scribe's geographical background, even if the provenance did not survive.

96 This is consistent with the watermark: similar to Briquet 3668, which was used at Rome in 1454. On Bessarion in Bologna, see Mohler 1923: 258–269. Bessarion was closely connected to Niccolò Perotti, scholar of Martial *extraordinaire*, and it has been alleged that the

latter knew the *OGR*: see Pade and RammINger 1994: 115–116, who identify similarities between *Cornu copiae* 5.141–142 and *OGR* 5. There is, however, nothing that secures a textual connection here and the facts relayed are relatively widely disseminated. Perotti did certainly know the *DVI* (e.g. Charlet *et al.* 1998: 38, for use of *DVI* 23 in *Cornu copiae* 53.19) and it has been suggested that he read the A version (Charlet *et al.* 1998: 13, for *DVI* 12 = *Cornu copiae* 50.1). The agreement with A is, however, very slight (*a rea* B, *ab* (*ob* o) *ea* A and Perotti) and there are much stronger indications of a link with the D family of MSS in the B version, such as the omission of the word *hoc* at *Cornu copiae* 53.18 = *DVI* 33.7 (Charlet *et al.* 1998: 37) and (in the same passage = *DVI* 33.8) *gutum* A vs *cadum* B and Perotti.

97 For the rough date and location, *T&T 'De viris illustribus'* (Reeve and Tarrant): 150 and n. 5, who point out that the text of the *Pro Sulla* suits the area. The watermark Briquet 26 (Chiny 1467, noted by Reeve and Tarrant) can be seen on the blank f. 155r; on f. 1v the watermark is a unicorn, which does not precisely match any single entry in Briquet, but is very similar to types often used in the Low Countries and north-eastern France. The entry in Thomas 1896: 35–37 remains useful.

98 For Hegesippus and the true title of the work ascribed to him, see Stover and Woudhuysen 2022b: esp. 7–8.

well attested as a professional copyist active in the 1450s-1470s, working at least partly in Italy.[99] Of his manuscripts, the most important for our purposes is Vat. lat. 1815, which contains Poggio's translation of Diodorus Siculus and a neat colophon (f. 129r) explaining that 'de Lumel' wrote it in 1459 for Pius II. A little later, it was in the hands of the bishop Giovanni Andrea de Bussi, for whom it was apparently decorated by Andrea da Firenze.[100] The hand of this manuscript is identical to that in **p**: evidently de Loemel was responsible for copying both manuscripts and owned one of them.[101] Identifying him as the scribe of **p** has important implications, because the fact that he had connections in both the Low Countries and Italy significantly lessens the apparent distance between the two places in which the *CT* was copied in the fifteenth century. In fact, de Loemel has been identified as the second scribe of a copy of Bessarion's *In calumniatorem Platonis*, produced for the cardinal himself, so he was on the scene as **o** was being copied.[102] That manuscript does not seem to have been written by him, but it is possible that some of the slightly cramped contemporary annotations in its margins are his work.[103] de Loemel's connection to Giovanni Andrea de Bussi is also tantalising, for the latter was both in the circle of Bessarion and the former secretary of Nicholas of Cusa.[104] Nicholas was, of course, himself a friend of Cardinal Bessarion and had in fact been on the embassy to Constantinople that first brought him to Italy.[105] He was also a great finder of manuscripts: he made a number of important discoveries at Cologne, most famously the plays of Plautus, which Poggio desperately desired and Cardinal Orsini wisely refused to give him.[106] In the sixteenth century, **p** came into the hands of Theodor Poelman, who left neat little notices *sum Theod. Pulmanni* scattered through it (f. 52r *e.g.*). In short, **o** and **p** look at first sight rather different, but they emerged in precisely the same circles.

---

99 de Lumel is named as copyist by the colophons to Vat. lat. 1815 (f. 129r) of 1459, 434 (f. 391v – the hand of this MS is interestingly different) dated to 31 October 1460 (Augustine, *De civ.* written for Theodore de Lellis), and part of Naples, BN 'Vittorio Emanuele III' IV.B.2 (Quintilian on ff. 233r-299r, with the arms of both Nicholas of Cusa and Giovanni Andrea de Bussi) of 1460 (per Winterbottom 1967: 335 and n. 4 with Caldelli 2006: 116). Winterbottom also (1993: 236) identifies him as the scribe of Brussels 9756 (Cicero, *De officiis*; second half of s. XV). Another colophon by him is (per the online catalogue) found in St Louis, Missouri, Washington University Library, MS *s.n.* (LC PA6231.C8 1476) (Boethius, *De consolatione*) dated to 25 July 1476 (f. 84r). If the general pattern of survival here were not enough to secure his Italian connections, then the provenance of Vat. lat. 1815 would guarantee it. The discussion of de Loemel in Caldelli 2006: 116, while useful, is hobbled by the belief that **p** was written a little after 1453. This would indeed be rather hard to reconcile with his career (a problem Caldelli explores at some length), but no evidence is provided for it and it would seem to be contradicted by the evidence of the paper (could it simply be a mistake in which the date of **o** has been substituted for that of **p**?). The assumption derived from this date for **p** – that its less neat hand is automatically early (rather than, say, informal) – is also dubious.

100 Ruysschaert 1968: 256, pl. 17.

101 Earlier scholarship (*e.g.* D'Elia 1965: 138) identified the owner of **p** as Jean Huybrechts, from Lommel in Limburg, an ecclesiastic active in the Low Countries in the late fifteenth and early sixteenth centuries (see Thomissen 1886–1887: col. 726). The identification is still repeated (D'Anna 1992: xxxv; Martin 2016: xxviii *e.g.*), but should be dismissed.

102 Hunt 1975: 87. The manuscript in question is Venice, Marc. Lat. VI 60 (2591).

103 As Hunt 1975: 87 suggested. The long annotation in **o** f. 123r (*DVI* 84, which had been missed out by the primary scribe) is especially intriguing. While the individual letter forms are sometimes different from other instances of de Loemel's script, the *ductus* is rather similar. As a professional scribe, we would expect de Loemel's hand to vary a good deal, especially when comparing a commissioned MS (were the corrections to **o** made at Bessarion's direction?) to one written for himself (as perhaps **p** was). John Monfasani (personal communication) has, however, suggested *per litteras* that the hands are not the same.

104 On Bussi, see Miglio 1972; on his connections to Bessarion, see Monfasani 2011.

105 Vansteenberghe 1920: 61–63.

106 The manuscript of Plautus is Vat. lat. 3750. On the discovery see Vansteenberghe 1920: 19–21; Ullman 1960: 66–67.

Though closely affiliated and descended from the same archetype, it has generally been held that **op** were not copied from the same exemplar.[107] This belief emerged in a context where their close connection was unknown and rested in large part on the lengths of skipped lines. There are a number of these in **o**, easy to spot because they have been added in the margin: they are all in the range of forty to fifty characters.[108] There are seven in **p** – two later supplemented, five not – and they are all of seventy to eighty characters.[109] This does point to different exemplars, but not definitively: agnosticism is perhaps wise. At any rate, the text of the *CT* was first printed by the energetic Jesuit Andreas Schott in 1579, from **p**.[110] In one of those moments of happenstance that can profoundly shape the way a text is read, Schott divided the *Caesares* into chapters based on those used in editions of the *Epitome*, already in print for seven decades.[111]

There was, in the sixteenth century, still extant at Cologne an (allegedly) older manuscript of the compilation, which belonged to the scholar Jean Matal (hence the siglum **M** and the name often used in modern scholarship, *codex Metelli*).[112] Matal had obtained it from Cornelius Wouters, who had moved to Cologne in 1549.[113] It thus seems likely that it was at Cologne that the *CT* had survived in the Middle Ages. We have evidence for the text of this manuscript for only the *OGR* and the *DVI* (which represents a special case that we do not need to go into in detail here) and it is limited to some quotations in an undated letter of Matal to the Dutch historian Steven Winand Pigge.[114] It is also possible that Antoine le Conte of Noyon had consulted the text, though he says little of interest.[115] Nothing survives of the *Caesares* in Matal's letter. The text of the quotations of the *OGR* and *DVI* is often very different to that in the manuscripts **op** – and rarely better.[116] How much of this difference ought to be attributed to haste and error on Matal's part and how much to the manuscript itself is an open question. At the very least, we can be reasonably sure that the note that came just before Victor's text in the manuscript (or so Matal tells us), *expliciunt nomina principum Romanorum*, could hardly have been invented. Since there is no trace

---

107 That **op** go back to the same archetype is proved by the shared lacuna at *Caes.* [*HAb*] 34.7. Not the same exemplar: Festy 1994: esp. 94–99; Mariotti 1961.

108 **o**: f. 91r, 109v, 111v, 140r, 143v, 151v, 153v.

109 Later supplemented: *OGR* 9.5, *Caes.* [*HAb*] 32.5. Omitted altogether: *DVI* 2.2–3, 7.6–7, 51.2–3; *Caes.* [*HAb*] 2.4 and 17.7. Most easily found in Festy 1994: 97.

110 Schott 1579: 14–15 mentions that Poelman lent him the manuscript. He had already used **p** for his edition of just the *DVI* published at Douai in 1577; see in general Solaro 2022: esp. 151.

111 On the *Epitome*, see below.

112 On Matal see in general Heuser 2003, who has a commendably cautious discussion of his codex (276–289).

113 This is revealed by Matal's letter to Pigge (preserved only in later printed editions, beginning with Schott 1609: 21–23; it can be conveniently consulted in Sepp 1885: 40–45) and the note to Victor in Schott 1579: 202: *Asterico notare satis habui dum iactura sarciatur, et lacunae Victoris impleantur ex alio exemplari, quale in Ubiis Coloniae Agrippinae apud Jo. Metellum Sequanum esse audio ex bibliotheca Corn. Gualtheri V.C.* On Wouters, see briefly van de Schoor 2016: 2.

114 Sepp 1885: 40–45.

115 In the notes to his edition of Anastasius Bibliothecarius (1573, reprinted in *PL* 129), le Conte discusses the length of Tiberius' reign. He says (ff. 15v/17r – no f. 16 appears): *et Sextus Aurelius Victor, non quidem impressus sed manuscriptus, ei 23 annos tribuunt* (*cf. Caes.* [*HAb*] 3.1, *Epit.* [*LB*] 2.1). His other references to Victor, for the lengths of the reigns of Claudius, Nero, and Vespasian (f. 19v), all seem to be drawn from the *Epitome* (*Epit.* [*LB*] 4.1, 5.1, 9.1), but his statement in the first that the text is unprinted should give us pause (the *Epitome* had been in print since 1504 – see below). Nothing explicit seems to link le Conte to either Matal or Poelman, so it is not obvious how he would have read the *Caesares*. That said, both le Conte and Matal were deeply involved in the publication of Roman law texts (especially the *Corpus iuris civilis*) and it seems possible that they perhaps met or corresponded in that context. Savelli 2018 offers an overview of this activity.

116 Festy 1994 offers a very maximalist interpretation of the evidence for **M**. Momigliano 1958b was rightly more circumspect.

of something similar in **op**, it looks as if Matal's manuscript offered a rather different version of the *CT*: that is about as much as we can say with certainty. At any rate, as Tarrant has shown, the *codex Metelli* has had no impact whatsoever on our text of the *Caesares*.[117]

In both of the extant manuscripts, as well as in the *codex Metelli*, at the head of the collection of three works, of which the *Caesares* is only one part, is found the following title:

> Aurelii Victoris historie abbreviate ab Augusto Octaviano id est a fine Titi Livii usque ad consulatum decimum Constantii Augusti et Iuliani Cesaris tertium.[118]

> The *Abbreviated Histories* of Aurelius Victor from Augustus Octavian, that is from the end of Titus Livy, up to the tenth consulate of Constantius Augustus and the third of the Caesar Julian.

This is obviously not a description of the collection as a whole, which (on even the most cursory of inspections) starts long before Augustus. Though comprising three texts, the compilation seems to have originally been divided into two parts: **o** (f. 123v) has a notice reading *EXPLICIT PRIMA pars hui(us) operis*, while **p** (f. 68v) has *FINIT PRIMA PARS HUIUS OPERIS // INCIPIT SECUNDA: AURELII VICTORIS*. It seems most likely that this chronological description was extracted from the point of transition between the first and second part of the collection and placed at its head: that is, it was originally set before the part of the *CT* that contained the *Caesares*.[119] The manuscript title of that work is thus *Historiae abbreviatae* (or *Historia abbreviata*), so henceforth we will refer to it as such (*HAb* for short). *Abbreviatus* means – and the ancient evidence is unanimous on this point – that the work in question is an epitomised version of some full text.[120]

The role that Aurelius Victor's work played in this compilation is clarified by the short passage found in both manuscripts immediately after this heading (**o** f. 85r, **p** f. 82r), which seems in fact to have been the original preface to the work:

> Origo gentis Romanae a Iano et Saturno conditoribus, per succedentes sibimet reges usque ad consulatum decimum Constantii, **digesta ex auctoribus** . . . atque ex omni priscorum historia, proinde ut quisque neotericorum asseveravit, hoc est Livius et Victor Afer.[121]

> A history of the Roman people, from Janus and Saturn their originators, through the kings who succeeded them, up to the tenth consulship of Constantius, excerpted from the following authorities . . . [a list of Republican historians and antiquaries] . . . and from every history written by the men of old; thereafter as each of the modern authorities has affirmed it, that is Livy and Victor the African.

---

117 Tarrant 1978: 358–359.

118 The texts are identical (**o** f. 85r; **p** f. 82r; **M** Sepp 1885: 40), though capitalisation varies a little between them.

119 *cf.* T&T 'De viris illustribus' (Reeve and Tarrant): 149. It is not, however, entirely clear how the title at the beginning can be reconciled with the undoubtedly authentic *incipt secunda* [*sc. pars*] *Aurelii Victoris*. One might note that the preface at the beginning describes the first text as derived *ex omni priscorum historia*, while the bridge passage between the *OGR* and *DVI* calls the latter a *historia Liviana* (most easily consulted in

Richard's edition of the *OGR*, 1983: 9), and Victor's work was known in antiquity as the *Historia* (see Chapter V). Might the bare title of the whole *CT* have been *Historiae abbreviatae*, to reflect that it is a corpus of three separate 'abbreviated histories'?

120 On this point, see Chapter III.

121 The preface is most easily found in Richard 1983: 76. On the meaning of *neoterici*, see Cameron 1980: 140–141. For *proinde* in a temporal sense, as must be the case here, *cf.* Commodianus, *Instructiones* 1.5 l. 3.

Whoever assembled this collection of texts here asserts that it was compiled by abbreviating a large number of texts, of which one (the source for the imperial period) was the work of Victor.[122] Such notices of the sources used in compiling a work are not unparalleled in antiquity – they are found, for example, in the digests of the contents of each book of Pliny the Elder's *Natural History* (Book I). Read straight, the title in the manuscripts is telling us that what we have is not Victor's original work, but only some fraction of it. This has obvious significance for our evaluation of Victor's work, and that significance only grows when we consider in the context of the transmitted titles of the other text attributed to him, the *Epitome*.

The transmission of the *Epitome*

The transmission of the *HAb* is a rather complex and involved subject, primarily because we are without the evidence that would clarify crucial points in it. In contrast, the *Epitome* is a much simpler case (because the evidence is richer), but not necessarily always more helpful for that simplicity. The text's origins are a little murky.[123] As we have demonstrated elsewhere, the *Epitome* makes extensive use of the *Historia Romana* of Jordanes (*ca.* 550) and also seems to draw on the *Etymologies* of Isidore of Seville (d. 636). The work first seemingly surfaces in *ca.* 770, when Paul the Deacon made extensive use of it in his *Historia Romana*.[124] Its composition can thus be dated to some point between the middle of the seventh century and the middle of the eighth: it was probably produced in Italy. This late date for the creation of the *Epitome* as we have it should not (to reiterate) obscure its enormous importance for Roman imperial history. The sheer density of information that it offers in a rather small frame strongly suggests that whoever compiled it had access to (probably) a single excellent source, composed late in the fourth century. That perhaps explains its remarkable success after its first emergence with Paul. In the decades after 800, it was rapidly disseminated and much used in the Carolingian world. Quite a few ninth-century scholars – Frechulf of Lisieux, Lupus of Ferrières, Sedulius Scottus, Christian of Stavelot, and Hincmar of Rheims – knew the text.[125] Intriguingly, it was also quarried for lexical items in a glossary that might have been composed in the region of Paris in the first decades of the ninth century, perhaps with a connection

---

122 Momigliano 1958a: 58 suggested that the title of the whole *CT* was *Origo gentis Romanae*, which has its attractions, but is hard to reconcile with the discursive nature of the preface in which it appears. The words *id est a fine Titi Livii* in the first title, nonetheless, make clear that Victor is the sole source for the imperial section.

123 We consider the date of the *Epitome* in greater detail above, but see Stover and Woudhuysen 2021.

124 See Chapter V.

125 Frechulf took over roughly a quarter of the *Epitome*'s text verbatim in his *Histories*, completed in 829 (see e.g. Frechulf, *Histories* 2.1.4 = *LB* 1.2–12 on Augustus; for the date Allen 2002: 1.13★–16★). Lupus sent a copy to Charles the Bald in 844 (*Ep.* 37, ed. Levillain 1964) – *pace* Innes 1997: 271, n. 22, the reference

to Trajan and Theodosius all but guarantees that this must be the *Epitome*. Sedulius made use of the *Epitome* in his *Collectaneum miscellaneum* (78.1, 80.7, 16, 20, 21, 22, 24 *e.g.*). Christian of Stavelot used at least one anecdote (on Diocletian's cabbages) from the *Epitome* in his commentary on St Matthew (*PL* 106.1323d–1324a): see Laistner 1927: 135. Hincmar, *De divortio* 6 (ed. Böhringer 1992: 248) mentions a *Vita Caesarum*, which is probably the *Epitome* (the editor suggests this is Suetonius, but the idea Hincmar mentions – *successio paterna* – is hardly appropriate to him). The dissemination of the *Epitome* is discussed by Festy 1999a: lx–lxvi, D'Elia 1965: 31–45, though the relationship of Orosius and Jordanes to the text is rather different to that supposed by Festy (see Stover and Woudhuysen 2021).

to Hilduin of Saint-Denis.[126] Unfortunately, none of these authors offers us much of an insight into the nature or history of the *Epitome*: to understand it, we must turn to the manuscripts.

In contrast to the *Corpus tripertitum*, the *Epitome* has a relatively extensive manuscript tradition; it was also printed much earlier than the *CT*, for the first time in 1504 (twice).[127] The text survives in some twenty different copies, including three from the ninth century and two neglected scraps of a fourth of the same era.[128] All of these give it (more or less) the same title:

> Libellus de vita et moribus imperatorum breviatus ex libris Sexti Aurelii Victoris a Caesare Augusto usque ad Theodosium.[129]

> The little book on the life and manners of the emperors abbreviated from the books of Sextus Aurelius Victor from Caesar Augustus up to Theodosius.

The *Epitome*'s transmitted title, by which we will henceforth refer to it, is thus the *Libellus breviatus* (or *LB* for short). Again, this title has largely been ignored and again it provides precise and interesting information.[130] The work is a short one (a *libellus*) and the information in it has been summarised from a longer, multi-book work (note the plural *libris*) written by Aurelius Victor. No other source ever refers to Victor as having written a history in several books (or says anything remotely similar), and no one could mistake the *HAb* for such a work: simple confusion cannot explain the clear statement that Victor wrote a *Historia* of some length. As for what happened to it, like *abbreviatus*, *breviatus* in this context means to 'summarise' or 'condense' something longer.[131] Lactantius, in epitomising his own *Divine Institutes*, said he had striven 'to tighten up what is diffuse and shorten what is prolix' (*et diffusa substringere et prolixa breviare*) and later explained that 'the proof-texts which I cannot shorten I have omitted' (*testimonia, quia breviare non poteram, praetermisi*).[132] Orosius (1.12.1) announced his intention (in writing history) to *praeterire plurima, cuncta*

126 Paris lat. 7651, which is a famous manuscript containing the Graeco-Latin glossary of ps-Philoxenus, followed after the *explicit* (f. 218r) by a set of *glossae collectae* which contain a number of *lemmata* from the *Epitome*, some of them in text order. The manuscript dates to the third quarter of s. IX (*cf.* Bischoff, *Katalog* 4490). For the connection to Hilduin of Saint-Denis, *cf.* Lapidge 2013: 414–415; for the localisation we thank Franck Cinato for sharing his impressions of the script.

127 An edition by Astemio was printed at Fano by Soncino (*USTC* 824102); another by Josse Bade at Paris (*USTC* 142941).

128 The manuscripts are surveyed by Festy 1999: lxvii–lxxi, with additions by Stover forthcoming c. The imprecision and vagueness with which short historical texts have often been catalogued makes it far from impossible that others lurk undetected in libraries. The three ninth-century manuscripts are Wolfenbüttel, Herzog August Bibliothek, 84 Gud. lat. (ff. 66r–93v, with Vegetius; see Koeheler and Milchsack 1913: 131–132; Bischoff, *Katalog* 7312, northern France, first/second quarter of s. IX); Paris lat. 6121 (ff. 2r–38v, with the *Epistola Alexandri magni ad Aristotelem de situ Indiae*; Bischoff, *Katalog* 4398, northern France, second quarter of s. IX); Vat. lat. 3343 (ff. 101r–125v only

down to 48.16; with Solinus; Bischoff, *Katalog* 6875, Saint-Amand 'oder nächstverwandt', middle or second half of s. IX). Though their texts are distinct, it is a curiosity worth noting that the capitalisation in the first chapter of the *Epitome* in the Vatican manuscript (the letters are nicely coloured) seem very close to that in the Paris codex. The fragments are Soest, Stadt-bibliothek fr. 26, identified in Michael 1990: 249, who says '9. Jh., 2. Hälfte, wohl Frankreich' (*cf.* Bischoff, *Katalog* 5992). The Soest fragments are not included in Festy 1999a and seem never to have attracted scholarly comment: we intend to treat them in detail elsewhere.

129 Variations (see the *apparatus* in Festy 1999: 2) are trivial.

130 It was dismissed by Barnes 2002: 27 as 'a librarian's attempt to describe its contents for a catalogue'. For Callu 1985: 104 and n. 49 (relaying a suggestion of Dolbeau) it was a mangling of a lost preface or title to the work that described its sources, of which Victor was one (the same solution adopted by Festy 1999: x–xi, who traces it back to Hankius in the seventeenth century).

131 *TLL s.v.* 'brevio' 2.2171.13–45 (Münscher). See further Chapter III.

132 Lactantius, *Epit. praef.* 4, 5.4.

breviare. The anonymous translator of 2 Maccabees into Latin rendered that work's claim to be an epitome of a lost text by Jason of Cyrene: 'I have attempted to shorten what Jason of Cyrene covers in five books to a single volume' (*itemque ab Iasone Cyreneo quinque libris conprehensa temptavimus nos uno volumine breviare*).[133] Lactantius, Orosius, and the anonymous translator were not saying that they had merely written short works: they were explaining that they (or their sources) had drastically summarised much longer ones. As with the *Historiae abbreviatae*, to call something a *libellus breviatus* is not a loose way of saying that it is a 'very short introduction' to some topic: it means precisely that it has been summarised from some longer work. Read straight, the title in the manuscripts is – once again – telling us that the text which follows is summarised from a longer original work by Aurelius Victor.

On the basis of the manuscript titles, there are solid grounds for thinking that both the *HAb* and the *LB* are condensed versions of a more ambitious composition. Were that true, the obstacles to assigning them both to Victor – or better, making them both witnesses to an otherwise lost work by him – would melt away. The process of epitomisation, of hacking down Victor's work, would naturally introduce variations of style and might easily change the chronological range of its coverage, a phenomenon discussed in the next chapter. Depending on the length and complexity of the original and the comprehensiveness of the summaries, they might also reveal rather different sources and emphases. If we have only fragments of Victor's original work, then that might explain the discrepancy between his fourth-century reputation and the tattered works that survive today under his name. At a stroke, abbreviation resolves the apparent contradictions in our evidence. But are the titles trustworthy?

The evidence of the titles

It is always difficult to assess the origins and reliability of mere scraps of information and some of what turns up in manuscripts of classical texts is little more than medieval and Renaissance guesswork (or scholarship, as we might more charitably term it, with James Hankins).[134] As it happens, however, the paratexts of both *Historiae abbreviatae* and *Libellus breviatus* offer detailed and precise information which could not straightforwardly have been extracted from the texts themselves. The preface to the *CT* offers two crucial facts about the *Historia* from which it claimed to have derived its imperial history: that Victor was from (North) Africa (*Afer*) and that his history went down to the tenth consulship of Constantius and the third of Julian (360). Both seem to be true and neither is obvious. Victor's (qualified) praise for Septimius Severus darts into a confused and very difficult-to-understand digression that mixes a *paean* to the benefits of a liberal education with some information about the historian's humble background.[135] Next, with an abrupt change of direction, the text describes *gens nostra* as *bonorum . . . parce fecunda* ('not

---

133 2 Maccabees 2:24, in the Vulgate text – the variant versions in de Bruyne and Sodar 1932: 114–117 if anything make the point clearer. On the books of Maccabees, see the papers in Xeravits and Zsengellér 2007.

134 See Hankins' remark, quoted in Tarrant 2016: 15. On the complex titles transmitted in manuscripts, and the manifold difficulties in working with them, see Sharpe 2003.

135 *HAb* 20.1–5. See Chapter I.

particularly productive of good men') and offers Severus (*velut Severum*) as an example of this.[136] This must mean that, like Severus, Victor was from Roman North Africa, but the sentence is so badly mangled and complex that it is not safe to assume that it was the source of the information in the title.[137] Similarly, as we have seen the *HAb* was completed in 360. It concludes with an assessment of the Emperor Constantius 'who has ruled the empire as Augustus for three and twenty years': he had been proclaimed Augustus on 9 September 337.[138] The year 360 indeed saw the emperor's tenth consulship, one which he shared with his cousin Julian.[139] Yet there is no way to arrive at the precise consular date from the text itself. In other words, whoever wrote the paratextual material for the *CT* appears to have had accurate information about Victor and his work that was not derived from the text as we have it.

The title of the *LB* offers less information, but it is equally revealing. It says that Victor had a *praenomen*: Sextus.[140] Phantom *praenomina* in medieval manuscripts are not unknown: scholarship still occasionally labours under the misapprehension that the North African philosopher and rhetorician was called Lucius Apuleius.[141] In Victor's case, however, there is external evidence confirming that he indeed had the *praenomen* Sextus. In 1563, a statue base honouring the Emperor Theodosius for having 'surpassed the gentleness, holiness, and liberality of ancient emperors' was discovered at Rome, not far from Trajan's column.[142] It had been erected by one 'SEX · AUR · VICTOR · V·C · VRBI · PRAEF' (see Figure 1.1). This, as was realised as late as the seventeenth century, by when both Victorine works had long been in print, can only be the Victor described by Ammianus, historian and urban prefect: a nice touch for the *scriptor historicus* to have included an historical judgement in such a dedication.[143] Whoever composed the title of the *LB* thus had access to authentic information about Victor that was not derived from the text of that work (or the *HAb* for that matter) and that could not have been discovered by anyone between the end of antiquity and 1563. In sum, the paratextual material of the *HAb* and *LB* makes four claims about Victor not derived from the texts: that he was from North Africa, that he had the *praenomen* Sextus, that his work of history (at least in one version) finished in Constantius' tenth consulship, and that that *Historia* had been summarised to produce the two works that survive. Three of those four claims can be tested against other evidence and confirmed. This offers sound reasons to lend some credence to the fourth.

That there are strong grounds to think that abbreviation has indeed been at work can be confirmed by taking a closer look at the *Corpus tripertitum*. One consequence of treating the constituent parts of the *CT* as objects of discrete study has been a lack of attention to what the compiler did to them when he

---

136 *HAb* 20.6. See the Appendix to the present book, section V.

137 *cf.* Momigliano 1958a: 59.

138 *HAb* 42.20: *annos tres atque viginti Augustum imperium regens.* See Chapter I for more detail.

139 For the consulship, see *CLRE* 254–255.

140 *cf.* Chapter I.

141 *e.g.* Barchiesi and Hardie 2010: 70, 78; Lucius is even accepted in *HLL* 4.457 (Sallmann and Schmidt). On the name, see Harrison 2000: 1.

142 *CIL* 6.1186. For a full text and translation, see Chapter I.

143 The story of the inscription in scholarship is a little complex: it was first associated with a historian called Aurelius Victor by Vossius 1627: 207. Vossius, however, believed in three separate historians of that name, the authors of the *HAb* and *LB* (respectively), as well as another individual referred to in the *HA* (Chapter VI) – he associated the inscription only with the second. It was not until the preface to Dacier 1681 that they were united. Tillemont 1701: 302 may have made the discovery independently (it is enigmatically concealed in the marginal reference to a discussion of Victor, where 'Grut. p. 286, 5' is the entry for the inscription in Gruter 1602).

assembled the collection.[144] His preface, as we have seen, says that the text was condensed (*digesta*) from a large number of authors: the compiler makes clear that he has intervened in the materials that he had at hand. Because the *DVI* survives in a version transmitted independently (the 'B' text) from the *CT*, we can test his claim. The independent version of the *DVI* begins with Proca and has seventy-seven chapters, terminating abruptly mid-sentence in the life of Pompey the Great, suggesting that a mutilated archetype was the source of all extant manuscripts.[145] The version in the *CT* (the 'A' text) begins after Proca and is in eighty-six chapters, ending with Cleopatra.[146] The different start-point is very probably the result of the compiler fitting together the *Origo* and the *DVI*, for the former text had discussed Proca and his progeny at some length.[147] The insertion of a bridge passage between the two, which casts doubt on what the *Origo* has just said, all but guarantees this: it must be an editorial comment by the compiler.[148] It is also worth noting that both **o** and **p** do not have chapter 16 of the *DVI*, which may also be an excision from the *CT*.[149]

Because the independent tradition of the *DVI* survives only in a mutilated form, it is more difficult to compare the end-points, but counter-intuitively it seems that here the compiler of the *CT* actually cut material. We saw above that Isidore of Seville used the independent tradition of the *DVI*, but his copy of the work also included the chapter on Cleopatra, which he used in his *Chronicle*.[150] The additional chapters of the *DVI* found only in the *CT* are thus not the composition of the compiler, but go back to his source.[151] What did that original *DVI* look like? In the early fourteenth century, Giovanni de Matociis, *mansionarius* of the cathedral of Verona and as industrious a pre-humanist as ever existed, saw a version of the *DVI* in ninety-eight chapters, running from Proca to Cleopatra. It seems most likely that this manuscript, mutilated, was the source of the independent transmission of the *DVI*, and that the work originally went down to the last queen of Egypt, with a fistful of biographies that survive in neither the *CT* nor the independent transmission.[152] So, the creator of the *CT* trimmed material at the end, perhaps because of an overlap with what was covered at the start of the *HAb* (which picks up after the battle of Actium), or perhaps because he felt that the work was rather too long for his compilation. The extent to which he also modified the text that he kept is difficult to discern. Modern editions of the *DVI* offer a chimerical blend of the *CT* and the independent transmission, reconstructing a text that never existed, which considerably obscures things. There is also the difficult question of the possible interpolations from the *Historia miscella* of Landolfus Sagax, which makes it hard to divine whether differences between the A

---

144 To this general rule, Momigliano 1958a is an honourable exception. It is shocking, for example, that it is virtually impossible to read the *CT* with its bridge passages and transitions intact in a modern edition.

145 Many manuscripts complete the sentence on Pompey (*illud plurimis et pretiosissimis odoribus cremandum curavit*), but the wording is a medieval insertion from Valerius Maximus (5.1.10) (*T&T* 'De viris illustribus' (Reeve and Tarrant): 151) and it seems most likely that the archetype was mutilated.

146 For this sketch, see Pichlmayr 1970: xv; *T&T* 'De viris illustribus' (Reeve and Tarrant); Martin 2016.

147 *Origo* 19–23.

148 As Momigliano 1958a: 57, saw. D'Elia 1965: 108–111 alleged on stylistic grounds that the bridge passage was

medieval, but it seems very unwise to subject so short a passage in corrupt manuscripts to such an exacting analysis.

149 Festy 1994: 115 and 120 (accepted by Martin 2016: xxxi) suggested that this loss was the result of physical damage in transmission, because the *Codex Metelli* contained the chapter. The grounds are weak (two readings transmitted by Schott, both bad and neither certainly from Matal's MS of the *CT*) and it seems more likely that this short and not especially biographical chapter was deliberately cut from the *CT*.

150 Isidore *Chronicle* 232a = *DVI* 86.1

151 *cf.* also Martin 2016: xxxiv–xlix.

152 See Stover and Woudhuysen 2017: 126–128.

and B versions of the *DVI* are original or not.[153] Even so, it is clear that the *CT*'s text of the *DVI* has some small but important differences from the independent transmission, which may well reflect intervention by the compiler throughout, not just at the start and the end.[154] He was no passive transmitter of material: he manipulated what he incorporated.

The text of the *Origo* in the *CT* points in precisely the same direction. Here there is no independent transmission against which we can compare the work, but we can turn once again to the words of the *CT*'s preface:

> . . . digesta ex auctoribus Verrio Flacco, Antiate, ut quidem idem Verrius maluit dicere quam Antia, tum ex Annalibus Pontificium, dein Cincio, Egnatio, Veratio, Fabio Pictore, Licinio Macro, Varrone, Caesare, Tuberone atque ex omni priscorum historia . . .

> . . . excerpted from the authors Verrius Flaccus, [Valerius] Antias (the form that Verrius himself prefers over [the first-declension] Antia, from the Pontifical Annals, from Cincius, Egnatius, Veratius, Fabius Pictor, Licinius Macer, Varro, Caesar, Tubero, and from every history written by the men of old.

It is of course extremely unlikely that the compiler of the *CT* had genuinely extracted the text of the *Origo* from a laborious review of these Republican historians: more plausibly, he abbreviated a work that leant on their expertise.[155] There are several signs in the text itself that what we have is an abbreviation. The surest of these is that while some of the historians mentioned in this preface are cited in the text of the *Origo*, not all of them are: Verrius Flaccus, Veratius, and Varro are exempted. It is hard to claim that they lent an authority that the other authors did not and so were haphazard insertions into the preface, especially given that *omnis priscorum historia* was pled in aid as well, and (as Momigliano pointed out) the *Origo*'s citations are surprisingly reliable.[156] They are there because they were probably the sources of

---

153 See above. A partial exception is the edition of Sherwin 1973, which, however, is based on the curious theory that the mutilated version is in fact the original.

154 For example (B vs A): 2.5, *si exercitum suum in capitolium perduxisset* ~ *si exercitum suum in arcem perduxisset*; 4.10, *quod bellum sola trigeminorum certatione finisset, ut rem corrigeret . . .* ~ *quod bellum sola trigeminorum certatione finisset . . .*

155 The identity and nature of this original source has occasioned a good deal of debate. Frier 1979: 43–44 and Schmidt 1978: 1611 opted for Verrius Flaccus (*cf. HLL* 5.532.1 (Schmidt)). Richard 1983: 40–48 was more sceptical (*cf.* D'Anna 1992: xxviii and n. 1), but Cameron 2004a: 331 offered a cautious endorsement. In favour of the identification would be Verrius' prominent position in the preface and the attribution to him of a view on the name of Valerius Antias (it seems also that none of the sources named are certainly later than him). Momigliano 1958a: 71–72 rejected speculation on this point as 'useless'. The precise relationship of this original source to the *OGR* as we have it has been equally controversial and a good deal muddier. Momigliano 1958a: 57 (*e.g.*) distinguished between original source(s), author of the *OGR*, and

compiler of the *CT* (to whom he tended to attribute signs of abbreviation in the text). In contrast, Schmidt 1978: 1587, 1594 and D'Elia 1965: 106–107 identified the compiler of the *CT* with the author of the *OGR*. Richard 1983: 11–12, 36–37 returned to a sharp distinction between author and compiler (accepted by Schmidt in *HLL* 5.532.1; endorsed by Smith 2005: 98). The position taken by Cameron 2004a: 331–332 is rather murky: he holds that the compiler of the *CT* was most likely 'abridging an abridgement, in all probability a text already abridged more than once', but also rejects the idea that the compiler intervened in the text much (partly out of a mistaken belief that the A and B versions of the *DVI* are 'essentially the same'). For our purposes, the question of whether the compiler of the *CT* was working with a pre-existing epitome (which is certainly possible) is less important than the fact that he clearly intervened in whatever his source was.

156 In the few places we can test them: Momigliano 1958a: 66–70, whose conclusions were accepted by Schmidt 1978: 1604 ff. and Richard 1983: 19–28. The very plausible inclusion of Egnatius (with a citation in the text itself), a figure nowhere else listed as a historian, demonstrates the value of the *Origo*'s source; see now,

whatever text the compiler had adapted, but, in adapting it, he had omitted explicit references to them.[157] There is also internal evidence that the text has been abbreviated.[158] For example, Janus reigns (3.1), but we are never told that he was made king. Perhaps the strongest proof comes at the rather creaky hinge of *OGR* 3–4. Here, after what may be a lacuna or clumsy abbreviation (3.8), the *OGR* says (3.9) that the Trojans came to Italy, and then, in a very confusing fashion, asks how Sallust can say what he does about the *aborigines* (the original inhabitants of Italy), quoting *Cat.* 6.1. The text moves on (4.1) to give an account of the etymology of *aborigines*, which is introduced by the nonsensical *quidam autem tradunt* ('However, some say'): there has been no preceding account of the same issue to which this could be contrasted. None of this really makes sense as written, but it is perfectly explicable if an original account that claimed the Trojans came to Italy and met the *aborigines* – whose name was variously explained – has been clumsily hacked down. Just like the *DVI*, the *Origo* was probably abbreviated for its inclusion in the *CT*.

Two works that the manuscripts attribute to Aurelius Victor survive today. While superficially quite different and treated as entirely distinct, they are in fact very closely connected: they share a good deal of text, a remarkable number of facts and the formulations for them, and a substrate of common language. One of these works, the *HAb*, survives only as part of a corpus of texts on Roman history. There is no sure evidence that either this collection or its constituent parts were known before they emerged in the fifteenth century. To understand it, we must rely entirely on the evidence of the *CT* and the manuscripts that transmit it. The other, the *LB*, was better known in the Middle Ages, but surfaces first in the eighth century: again, to understand what the text is, we must rely on the manuscripts. The titles of both the *HAb* and the *LB* say, very plainly, that they are summaries of a longer work by Aurelius Victor. Where we can test the information that these titles provide, it turns out to be both accurate and obscure, not easily derived from the texts in their transmitted form. Moreover, when we examine the *CT* as a corpus of texts, it is clear that its compiler intervened extensively in his source material and that he generally did so to abbreviate it. In short, the evidence of the manuscripts and titles presents a strong *prima facie* case that the *HAb* and *LB* are exactly what they claim to be: remnants of the historical work of Aurelius Victor. More proof is certainly required, but it is at least now possible to begin asking the right questions. The first of these, concerning the nature of epitomisation and the process of making abbreviated works, will be the topic of our next chapter.

briefly, *FRH* 105 (Smith). Cameron 2004a: 328–334 offers a partial challenge to the reliability of the *OGR*'s citations (though not alleging deliberate imposture; he focused largely on the author of the *OGR* having no direct access to the sources that he mentions). It is not clear, however, that Cameron's conclusions are as different from Momigliano's as their vigorous statement would suggest. *cf.* Smith 2005, who is more optimistic (based on careful comparison to other works, not least

Macrobius) and who calls (98) Cameron's remarks 'a case for the defence' of the *OGR*.

157 All this is as Momigliano 1958a: 65–70 astutely discerned.

158 On this see Momigliano 1958a: 65–66 (a minimalist case); Behrens 1917: 6–9 (a more expansive one); Richard 1983: 32–38 (somewhere in the middle).

159 This uses Rudoni's conjecture of *somni* for the MS *omnis* (2010: 313–314).

CHAPTER III

THE GENRE OF EPITOME

Epitomes, understood broadly, were everywhere in antiquity.[1] Literary, historical, philosophical, geographical, technical, medical, and theological works were all epitomised. The whole system of later-Roman legal writing and scholarship revolved around the making and use of epitomes. Texts and their epitomes circulated side by side; in fact, sometimes they even shared an author. We might be tempted to think that such works were second rate – of interest only to students and tiros – yet serious scholars and *litterateurs* had no problem with using and even creating epitomes.[2] Cicero had to hand two epitomes, made by Brutus, of the historians Fannius and Coelius Antipater.[3] If we are to believe Plutarch, Brutus in fact occupied himself before the battle of Pharsalus by making an epitome of Polybius.[4] Sallust apparently requested that his teacher Ateius the Philologist make an epitome of Roman history.[5] The omnivorous antiquarian Varro made an epitome of his own work, *De lingua latina*.[6] Apuleius was also the author of a now-lost epitome, the nature of which is not clear from the two surviving *testimonia*.[7] The Christian Bible itself contains an epitome: 2 Maccabees. Lactantius, the Christian Cicero, like Varro made an epitome of one of his own works, the *Divinae Institutiones*.[8] The great Vergilian scholar Servius made an epitome of Donatus for his friend Aquila, the *De finalibus*.[9] The making of epitomes ought to be understood as a central feature of the intellectual life of the ancients, even if they are reduced to mere footnotes in our histories of their literature. For that reason alone, exploring how they were made and what they were made for is a worthwhile endeavour. More to the point, however, our manuscripts of the two Victorine works both purport to be epitomes, or 'condensed texts'. To understand what that means, it is worth devoting some time and space to bringing out the key features of the Latin epitome.[10]

1 This chapter necessarily invokes a large number of texts, often merely to point to their existence. We have provided citations for the more obscure of these works and references on important points, but the genre as a whole is sorely neglected and we have not always cited when there is little to cite. Throughout the chapter, we quote approximate word counts, because more precise figures would be actively misleading: differences between editions and various electronic and print texts lead to statistically insignificant variations.

2 See in general Mülke 2010.

3 Cicero, *Ep. Att.* 12.5b; 13.8.

4 Plutarch, *Brutus* 4.7.

5 Suetonius, *De Grammaticis* 10.6.

6 Jerome, *Ep.* 33.2.

7 See Harrison 2000: 24.

8 Galdi 1922: 262–269.

9 *GLK* 4.449–455.

10 Such texts have only recently received a substantial guide, in Horster and Reitz 2010a (there is now also Boehm and Vallat 2020, a very useful collection of papers). The collected volume edited by Horster and Reitz has both strengths and weaknesses: see the penetrating review by Pontani 2012. Among the omissions he points out (853–854) are lack of attention to the terminology for condensed works and to their manuscript transmission, deficiencies that we attempt to address here. Before Horster and Reitz 2010a, the main works were the long essay by Bott 1920 and the monograph of Galdi 1922, effectively a series of short studies of different epitomes, which remains useful as a synthesis; *cf.* Opelt 1962, short, but with useful lists of epitomes. See also the discursive analysis of Brunt 1980, specifically devoted to historical epitomes. We have not seen MacLachlan 2004 (an unpublished thesis) and Sacchi and Formisano 2022 appeared after our manuscript had been submitted.

★ ★ ★

The main problem bedevilling this study is the apparently almost limitlessly flexible nature of the 'genre': texts of wildly different characters, with different subjects, and different titles all fall within its bounds.[11] Much of the vast quantity of evidence has been neglected, and lies buried in critical *apparatus* or obscure manuscripts. It can seem as though very little links epitomes together and that any attempt to draw general conclusions about them is doomed to fail. Even so, with careful attention to terminology, the nature of the source texts, and the methods of condensation, we can detect some important continuities. In what follows, we aim not to offer a comprehensive treatment of ancient Latin epitomes (a monograph in itself), but rather a survey of the genre, which will in turn cast a revealing light on the works ascribed to Aurelius Victor. We can begin with the important and neglected issue of terminology.

Terminology

A recent account of the genre of 'condensed text' divides it into four categories: (1) an abbreviation of a single text, (2) of a single text with additional material, (3) of several texts by one author, and (4) of several texts by several authors.[12] This is a useful framework. While ancient usage was far from uniform, it was not random and we can detect patterns (if not rules) in the names given to epitomes in each of these four categories.[13] We can begin with the most general.[14] Some works are actually transmitted with the title *epitome* or *epitoma*: examples include Florus' *Epitoma de Tito Livio bellorum omnium*, Julius Paris' *Epitoma* of Valerius Maximus' *Facta et dicta memorabilia*, Vegetius' *Epitoma rei militaris*, and Lactantius' *Epitome divinarum institutionum*.[15] We also have works which were referred to as epitomes in late antiquity. Jerome (*DVI* 70), for example, calls Novatian's *De trinitate* a 'sort of epitome of the work of Tertullian' (*quasi epitomen operis Tertulliani*). Since it is in fact longer than the opuscule of Tertullian which goes under the name *De trinitate* (*Adversus Praxean*), Jerome is probably saying that Novatian's work, certainly influenced by that most original theologian, is really a sort of summary of his output more generally. This is a heterogenous group: one is an author's condensation of his own lengthy work (Lactantius), one is a condensation by one author of a long work by another (Julius Paris), one is largely a summary of a single author's work, but with some additional material (Florus), one consists of brief synopses of a topic taken from a number

---

11 We use the term 'genre' here in a general sense – a type of textual production – and not in a more specific one, as epitomes could be made of texts of very different genres. Van Hoof and Van Nuffelen 2020b prefer the term 'form' instead of 'genre'.
12 Dubischar 2010: 44–45.
13 *cf.* Horster and Reitz 2010b: 8.
14 *cf.* Galdi 1922: 17–22. Compare the account that follows with Blaudeau 2015: esp. 73–75, which is less precise than the discussion here.
15 Julius Paris: the sole significant manuscript of the text (Vat. lat. 4929 f. 79v – on this MS, the 'Ravenna corpus', see below) offers no *titulus*, but Paris' letter to Cyriacus

refers to the work as an *epitoma*, as does the *explicit* (f. 148r). On Paris, see *HLL* 5.534.1 (Schmidt); Briscoe 2018: 21, 22–23; Raschieri 2020; the text can be read in Briscoe 1998: 2.638–793. Vegetius: Reeve 2004: v–vi. Lactantius: Heck and Wlosok 1994: xxxiii–xxxiv. Florus is a more difficult case. It is possible the title of his work is not authentic to the original (see Reeve 1988: 480, n. 13), but the manuscript tradition is unanimous as to the central point, *Epitoma de Tito Livio*, and John Malalas (8.28: καθὼς ὁ σοφώτατος Φλῶρος ὑπεμνημάτισεν ἐκ τῶν Λιβίου τοῦ σοφωτάτου συγγραμμάτων) shows that it was known by something like that in late antiquity.

of sources (Vegetius), and the last (at least as Jerome imagined it) is an *in extenso* summary of the works of a single author. It thus seems that *epitome* can certainly describe at least three of the four categories – Julius Paris' and Lactantius' work representing the first, Florus' the second, and Vegetius' the fourth – and, depending on how we interpret Jerome, it may well apply to the third also.

Some other terms were also flexible, if perhaps somewhat less so than the all-encompassing *epitome*. *Excerpta*, which we find as part of the title in the manuscripts of the epitome of Calpurnius Flaccus for instance, are just that: excerpts.[16] Normally they were made from a single work (category 1), but the title could also be used for an epitome of multiple works by one author (category 3), as in the *Excerpta ex operibus S. Augustini* made by Eugippius in the early sixth century.[17] It is hard to tell how typical this last was, part of a broader problem that for category 3 we have no consistent terminology. This is largely because relatively few works fall into it and those that do are often rather curious. It is possible, for instance, that the mysterious collection of legal material dubbed the *Tituli ex corpore Ulpiani* in the manuscripts is one such, but the nature of the text (along with pretty much everything about it) remains under debate.[18] More secure extant Latin examples include the summary of some of Plato's dialogues by Apuleius, called in one manuscript a sort of compendium (*expositio compendiosa*) and the pseudo-Ausonian *periochae* to the *Iliad* and the *Odyssey*.[19] The Greek title *Periochae* is also famously used for an epitome of Livy (that is, for a category 1 work).[20] It too, however, seems to have been flexible, for it turns up as the heading of summaries prefixed to Terence's comedies in the manuscripts, attributed to one C. Sulpicius Apollinaris, and similarly of summaries of individual books of Lucan's *Bellum civile* in one important manuscript of the *scholia* to him.[21]

In contrast to this flexibility, other titles for condensed works were somewhat more precise: *breviarium*, for instance, is a straightforward term. It was appropriate to texts which provided a summary of a topic (category 4): Eutropius and Festus (the historian) offer the best-known examples.[22] There is, however, no sense whatsoever that this was a title confined to works of history. That this was the word's general sense explains why Augustus left at his death a *breviarium* outlining the military-fiscal state and

---

16 Edited by Håkanson 1978; for the title see p. 1.

17 In his *Epistula ad Probam*, which prefaces the work, Eugippius calls it an *excerptorum codicem*. The same title is used in a remarkable note about a manuscript of the work copied during the siege of Naples by the Lombards in 581 (Knoell 1885: 25–26).

18 See in general Mercogliano 1997.

19 Apuleius: Stover 2016. Pseudo-Ausonius: Green 1991: 677–695.

20 Only Paris lat. 7701 features the word as a title, but Heidelberg, Pal. lat. 894 and Π (Pithou's lost manuscript) offer it at the *explicit*.

21 Sulpicius Apollinaris: Fleckeisen 1898: 2, 52, 106, 162, 216, 260. Lucan: Bern, Burgerbibliothek cod. 370.

22 For the definition of *breviarium* cf. Van Hoof and Van Nuffelen 2020b: xxxiii–xxxiv. One important manuscript (Gotha Memb. I 101) calls Eutropius' work a *Breviarius* though that is not otherwise common in the manuscript tradition (the modern dominance of the title *Breviarium* is probably due to Mommsen 1866). If

Reeve 1997 is correct, Festus also referred to Eutropius' work as a *breviarium*, though he does not explicitly draw this conclusion. Even so, there is no evidence that it is a title, rather than a description. The authentic title is *Historia Romana*, which is found in the B family of manuscripts; it is also in the securely transmitted title of Paeanius' Greek translation (p. 9 Droysen; the authoritative manuscript is Florence, BML Plut. 70.5, f. 198r) and in the notice in the *Suda* (E.3775); finally, it is what Paul the Deacon calls the work. Even so, there is no doubt that *breviarium* is an appropriate description of the work, and so we use it in this study for convenience. The evidence that *Breviarium* is the title of Festus' work is much stronger (Eadie 1967: 13). cf. the title added to the *Chronicle* of Fredegar (which, however we might categorise it, is clearly derived from multiple sources) in Paris lat. 10910 ff. Av-1r, the earliest manuscript of the text, by a roughly contemporary hand: *Breviarium scarpsum ex chronici eusebi hieronimi aliorumque auctorum a quodam adatio.*

Tertullian could call the Lord's Prayer the *breviarium totius evangelii*.[23] Equally, it makes sense of the claim by the author (whoever that might have been and however interested he was in astrology) of the *Questions of Zacchaeus* that in his work 'learning collected from many different volumes will yield a sort of *breviarium*, which does not work through every topic in every detail'.[24] St Cyprian, who had assembled a collection of *praecepta dominica et magisteria divina* into what he called a *breviarium*, had a just view of such works' utility, noting that the things they collected could be both read swiftly and often reviewed.[25] Because they were a summary of a topic, *breviaria* could also be drawn from a single author or text. The compiler of the *Medicina Plinii*, for instance, calls his own collection of medical recipes a *breviarium*, even though the vast majority of them come from Pliny's *Historia naturalis* (albeit with occasional additions from elsewhere), a fact which probably explains why it circulated as a work of his homonymous nephew Pliny the Younger.[26] Augustine mentions one of his own (sadly lost) books in his *Retractiones*, with the splendid title *Contra nescio quem Donatistam* ('Against some Donatist, I forget which'), the *incipit* of which references a *breviarium* of proofs against that sect.[27] In both cases, it was form rather than source that made these *breviaria*.

Abbreviatio or *liber abbreviatus* was, similarly, rather limited in its range of reference: generally, it was used for texts of the first two categories. The closest analogues to the transmitted titles associated with Victor are the *Ars breviata*, a grammatical work attributed to Augustine that is certainly a condensation of an original text (probably Augustine's lost *De grammatica*), the *liber abbreviatus* of Faventinus (based on Vitruvius), and the *De divisione definitionum ex libro Marii Victorini abbreviata* (sic), a severely compendious treatment of Victorinus' *De definitione* incorporated into Isidore's *Etymologies* and transmitted independently in a Bamberg manuscript.[28] In line with these, Servius describes his own *De finalibus* as material excerpted (*aliqua ex his decerpsimus*) from Donatus, 'for the sake of abbreviation' (*breviandi causa*).[29] So too Orosius called Justin the *breviator* of Pompeius Trogus (1.8.1) and Augustine described St Mark as the *pedisequus et breviator* of St Matthew (*De consensu evangelistarum* 1.3.6).[30] Hence to *abbreviare* a work was to summarise it and a work *abbreviatus* had been abbreviated, epitomised, summarised, or gone through some equivalent process of diminution. This is the only attested sense of the word in the secular literature of antiquity.[31] Rufinus, describing his object in summarising the work of Origen, said (*Orig. in Rom.*, praef.):

23 Suetonius, *Aug.* 10.4; Tertullian, *De oratione* 1.
24 *Consultationes Zacchaei* 2.3: *Ita instructio ex multis collecta voluminibus breviarii vicem dabit, non omnia in singulis elaborans.*
25 Cyprian, *Ad Quirinum* 3.praef.: *in* **breviarium** *pauca digesta et velociter perleguntur et frequenter iterantur.*
26 *Medicina Plinii, praef.*: *undique valitudinis auxilia contraherem et* **velut breviario** *colligerem.* Ascription: see Doody 2009: 95–96 (a useful article on the work in general).
27 *Retract.* 2.28: *probationes rerum necessariarum quodam breviario collectas promisimus.*
28 Augustine: see most recently Zetzel 2018: 284–285. The second editor of the text, Crecelius, suggested that Cassiodorus was responsible for the epitome (1857: 2, n. 3). This is very likely, since Cassiodorus was a reader of Augustine, a well-known maker of epitomes, and the only other user of the phrase *mediocritas fratrum* (*Exp. Psalm.* 101), which crops up in the *Ars breviata*. He is

also the first person to refer to the text: *sed et sanctum Augustinum propter simplicitatem fratrum breviter instruendam aliqua de eodem titulo scripsisse repperimus* (*Instit.* 2.1.1). See also Pizzani 1985. Faventinus: Plommer 1973: 1, n. 1, 86. Victorinus: Stover forthcoming b.
29 *GLK* 4.449: *Quamquam rationem litterae et syllabae in Donati artibus habeamus, tamen breviandi causa aliqua ex his decerpsimus, quae ad scientiam metrorum proficere credimus.*
30 Orosius: *cf.* Jerome, *In Dan.*, prol. Augustine *De civ.* 4.6. On Trogus and Justin, see Yardley 2010.
31 See *TLL s.v.* 'abbrevio' 1.51.23–35 (Bannier): 'in brevius redigere'; *cf. s.v.* 'abbreviatio', 'abbreviator' (Bannier). It is worth noting that there is no evidence for the word *abbreviare* in the sense of shortening a work before Ambrosiaster, whose activity took place during the papacy of Damasus I, 366–384; and indeed the earliest evidence for the word at all is in the *Vetus* translation of the Bible.

That I may abbreviate (*adbreviem*) this whole corpus of fifteen volumes, which the Greek language has stretched out to almost forty thousand, or even more, lines.

An anonymous piece of pseudo-Augustiniana, probably composed in the 430s, which denounces the Pelagians and Caelestians, is advertised as both a *libellus abbreviatus* and a sort of *hypomnesticon* (i.e. ὑπομνηστικόν, or memorandum), the latter being the title under which it is conventionally known.[32] While it does not specifically claim to have been epitomised from other works, the bizarre miniature books of which it is composed strongly suggest that it is an *aide-mémoire* to the anti-Pelagian works of Augustine.[33] The only partial exception to this otherwise really consistent pattern, a case where *abbreviare* is used to describe a text condensed from multiple authors, is found in Vegetius. He boasted that he had been ordered to *abbreviare* the lore of war *per diversos auctores librosque dispersa* ('scattered through many different authors and books').[34] Even so, this suggests more a process of serial abbreviation of individual works than the topical summary that the title *breviarium* would imply.[35]

In short, while it seems that any condensed text might be called an *epitome*, and *excerpta* or *periochae* had a flexible range of reference, it was not the case that all the names for such works were interchangeable: some had more or less specific meanings. *Breviarium*, for instance, referred to a summary treatment of a topic. Most importantly, for our purposes, *abbreviatio* (*vel sim.*) almost always referred to a text condensed from a single work by a single author.

Authorship

So much for the terminology; let us turn to the ways in which authorship was denoted in epitomes. Condensed texts are unusual in that most of them have two authors: the creator of the original and the maker of the epitome. How to best explain this was something of a problem for those in antiquity who mentioned epitomes by name, a problem to which there were various solutions. Cicero used a genitive for the epitomator and an adjective for the original author: *epitome Bruti Fanniana* (*Ep. Att.* 12.5b), *Bruti epitoma Fannianorum* [*sc. librorum*] (*Ep. Att.* 12.5b), and *epitomen Bruti Caelianorum* (*Ep. Att.* 13.8). Pliny the Elder preferred a more cumbersome formula, with a prepositional phrase for the author of the original: 'Diophanes who made epitomes from Dionysius' (*Diophane qui ex Dionysio epitomas fecit, HN* 1, *externi auctores* for books 8, 10, *etc.*). Ausonius also used a prepositional formulation to describe Paulinus' epitome of Suetonius, 'an epitome from the three books of Suetonius' (*Ep.* 19: *de tribus Suetonii libris . . . epitomen*). So too the title of an epitome of Augustine's *De musica*: 'The precepts of the art of music collected from the six books of Augustine *On music*' (*Praecepta artis musicae collecta ex libris sex Augustini De musica*).[36] This

32 On the date, see most recently Hwang 2009: 22–26.
33 See Chisholm 1967: 178.
34 Vegetius 3.*praef.*4.
35 There is only one other sense of the word *abbreviare*, found in Christian texts, specifically quotations of the Bible from a *Vetus* version, translating the Greek συνεσταλμένος (at 1 Cor. 7:29) and ἐκολοβώθησαν (at

Matt. 24:22 or Mark 13:20), in both cases for shortening days.
36 The *Praecepta artis musicae* survives in the Ravenna corpus (Vat. lat. 4929), on which see Billanovich 1956 and 1993. It was first printed by Mai and re-edited twice by Vecchi 1950 and 1986.

formulation was particularly popular in the early Middle Ages, as witnessed, for example, by a condensed version of Martial's epigrams in the *Florilegium Thuaneum*, dubbed *Ex libris M. Valeri Martialis Epigrammaton breviatum* and a collection of historical epitomes in a ninth-century Lyons manuscript under titles such as *Ex libris Hystoriarum Pauli Horosii*.[37] Victorinus of Pettau makes reference to some *epitomae Theodori*.[38] If this refers to 'excerpts of Theodotus' used by Clement of Alexandria (a trivial orthographic change), as argued by Morin, then Theodotus would be the author of the original and the epitomator unnamed.[39] Similarly, Augustine's grammatical work is transmitted simply as the *Ars Augustini pro mediocritate fratrum breviata*, 'the *Ars* of Augustine, abbreviated according to the modest ability of the brethren', that is, with only the name of the original author in the genitive. Jerome with *epitome operis Tertulliani* used the name of the original author in the genitive together with the genitive of *opus*. The same is true of the *Abbreviatio Braulii*, which purports to be a condensation of Braulio's life of Isidore.[40] The original title of Faventinus' work, by contrast, used a simple genitive for the name of the abbreviator, with no mention of the source: *M. Ceti Faventini artis architectonicae privatis usibus abbreviatus liber* ('The abbreviated book of M. Cetius Faventinus on the art of architecture for private purposes').[41]

As these examples show, there was great flexibility in the way that the authorship of epitomes was delineated in the ancient world. That was true both within and between works and authors. The *Digest* is perhaps our richest source for ancient references to epitomes. Often the original author and title are mentioned first, usually then qualified with *epitomatus a* and the name of the epitomator, *e.g.* 3.5.42: *LABEO libro sexto posteriorum epitomatorum a Iavoleno*. Sometimes, however, it goes the other way, with the original author in the genitive, as in 5.4.9: *PAULUS libro tertio epitomarum Alfeni digestorum*, where Paulus is the epitomator and Alfenus the author of the original. The same text is described elsewhere with the opposite formulation, *e.g.* 19.2.30: *ALFENUS libro tertio a Paulo epitomarum*. Sometimes we even get just the original author, with no mention of the epitomator, as in 48.22.3: *ALFENUS libro primo epitomarum*.

This flexibility continued right through the Middle Ages, where we see similar patterns and solutions. In one place, Hrabanus Maurus copied Orosius' careful delineation of the nature of Justin's epitome of Pompeius Trogus: *Pompeius Trogus eiusque breviator Iustinus* (*Comm. Macc.* 1.10). Later on in the same work, however, he refers to Justin's *Epitome* as simply the *Historia Pompeii Trogi* (1.15). The manuscripts of Justin's epitome show just how varied practice could be. Most entitle the work simply *Pompei Trogi Epitome historiarum* (*e.g.* Florence, BML Plut. 66.20, f. 7v, or Laon 400, f. 1v, among many others); the two manuscripts (Florence, BML Plut. 66.21 and Vat. lat. 1860) that transmit Justin's full name, M. Junianus Justinus, do not mention Trogus at all, calling the text *(M.) Iuniani Iustini epithoma historiarum*. Similarly, in the thirteenth century, Gottfried von Franken's epitome of the agricultural work of Palladius went under the title *Palladii liber per Godefridum abbreviatus* (*e.g.* St Gall 827), *Palladii liber*

---

37 Martial: Paris lat. 8071, f. 24r; Lyons: Vat. lat. 3852 (see Turcan-Verkerk 1999: 189–190 for the contents).

38 *Commentarii in Apoc.* 4.5.

39 Morin 1906: 456–457. Dulaey 1993: 1.271–272 makes no identification.

40 This curious text, of uncertain date, is edited in Anspach 1930: 56–64 and Martín-Iglesias 2016: 99–105. On it,

see Henriet 1997: 55 and n. 14 and Carlos Martín, 2005: 200–202. The latter says that the text is attributed to Braulio, something Henriet is concerned to deny. In fact the title tells us that it is not a work by Braulio, but rather an epitome of one.

41 See Plommer 1973: 1.

breviatus per Godefridum, excerpta librorum Palladii (in Amplonius' catalogue), and *Palladius abbreviatus* (in the 1483 catalogue of Melk).[42]

The broad conclusion from these examples is that, in both antiquity and the Middle Ages, the complex authorship of condensed texts was expressed with various formulae. The more specific point that we might take away is that, in general, it is the original author who was given pride of place. In most instances, both figures necessary for the production of an epitome were named, but if only one features, then (just as one might expect) it is much more likely to be the person whose work has been condensed. This, we might note, seems also to be true of both of the Victorine texts.

Originals and epitomes

What works were condensed? To start with the obvious, an epitome was only worth making for a work of some length, which, in the fourth century and earlier, meant one in multiple books. The shortest work which was condensed seems to have been Suetonius' three-book *De regibus*, from which Paulinus of Nola composed a verse epitome, but that is hardly a typical case.[43] There is also an extant epitome of the three-book work on Alexander that Julius Valerius Alexander was born to write, but that was produced in the Middle Ages, from a surviving manuscript, and provides no sure guide to ancient practice.[44] These two outliers, however, help to establish the minimum number of books required for a work to be worth epitomising: normally, it had to be longer. We have epitomes of the six books of Augustine's *De musica*, the seven books of Lactantius, the nine books of Valerius Maximus (by Julius Paris, but also Januarius Nepotianus), the ten books of Vitruvius (Faventinus), the ten of Seneca the Elder's *Controversiae*, the forty-four of Pompeius Trogus (by Justin), and the 142 of Livy.[45] So, even when we have only the epitome of a work surviving, we can still be pretty certain that the original was in not fewer than five books.[46]

Epitomes were often made for works which had only very recently been produced: Lactantius' epitome of his own *Divine Institutes* and Augustine's *breviculus* to the *City of God* show that very clearly.[47] We also have the works of the bishop of Hippo's contemporary Prosper of Aquitaine, four of which are (arguably) epitomes of Augustine: the *Expositio Psalmorum*, the *Sententiae* (transmitted as an epitome) and its verse derivative, the *Epigrammata*, and the lost *Excerptio ex libris de trinitate S. Augustini*, all of which were produced within a decade or two of Augustine's originals.[48] Eucherius, the fifth-century bishop of

42 For the second, see *CTC* 3.196 (Rodgers), for the last two, see Manitius 1935: 186.

43 Ausonius, *Ep.* 19: *poema . . . de tribus Suetonii libris, quos ille de regibus dedit, in epitomen coegisti*. See also Trout 1999: 57.

44 See Rosellini forthcoming.

45 For the elder Seneca, see Håkanson 1989. For Januarius Nepotianus, see Chapter II.

46 Of course, in the codex era the length of books could vary enormously: the five books of Hegesippus are longer than the thirteen of Augustine's *Confessions* (see Stover and Woudhuysen 2022b: 11).

47 Augustine refers to the *breviculus* in his letter to Firmus (*Ep.* 1a.3).

48 The surviving portion of the *Expositio* (Psalms 100–150) was edited by Callens 1972; he describes Prosper's practice as *pauca ad litteram excerpens, plura ad sensum in compendio redigens* (vii). The *Epigrammata* were edited critically for the first time by Horsting 2016. The *Excerptio* is mentioned in the Lorsch catalogue with an extensive index of its contents; see Gorman 1997: 66 and n. 15.

Lyons, epitomised some of the works of his friend and contemporary John Cassian.[49] At the very end of antiquity, we have Paterius' *Liber testimoniorum*, which is a rearranged epitome of the exegetical works of Gregory the Great, produced within a decade of their publication *at Gregory's own request*.[50] Similarly, the existence of an epitome of a work was seemingly little impediment to anyone thinking of making another: that explains why we have so many Livy epitomes and two for Valerius Maximus. It is a pattern that is very noticeable with the works of Augustine. His vast corpus unleashed an enthusiasm for epitomisation which would extend from the fifth century into the Carolingian period and beyond, with literally dozens of extant examples. Some of these are reasonably famous: Eugippius, *Excerpta ex libris S. Augustini* (*ca.* 520), and the *Praecepta artis musicae ex libris sex S. Augustini de musica*, plausibly from the sixth century as well, for instance.[51] Many of them, however, have not yet been studied or even edited, including an epitome of the *Enarrationes* in Lyons MS 426 (+Paris, NAL 1629, ff. 7r–14v), written in uncials probably in the sixth century.[52] The works of Gregory the Great had a similar, if not quite so expansive, reception: besides Paterius, there are two other seventh-century epitomes, by Lathcen and Taio of Saragossa.[53]

Works in many different genres were condensed. For handbooks and encyclopaedia, we have the epitomes of Valerius Maximus and Pliny the Elder, as well as the extract on the Roman calendar from Macrobius' *Saturnalia*, which circulated as the *Disputatio Chori et Praetextati*.[54] We have technical *breviaria* as well: Vegetius epitomised a range of sources for military science in his *Epitoma* while the *Mulomedicina Chironis* condensed a wealth of earlier (and lost) hippiatric material into its eighth book, which it dubs an *epitoma*.[55] For theological works, we have Lactantius' own epitome of the *Divine Institutes*, Augustine's *breviculus* to the *De civitate Dei*, Prosper's works, and Paterius' *Liber testimoniorum*, *inter alia*. The Bible itself could also be the source of epitomes, as in the anonymous compilation *Prophetiae ex omnibus libris collectae*, which was incorporated into the Donatist compendium.[56] It is worth noting, however, that works of history were perhaps especially prone to epitomisation.[57] For Livy, we have the *Periochae*, the *Oxyrhynchus Epitome*, Florus, Julius Obsequens, and the *De viris illustribus*.[58] For Pompeius Trogus, we have Justin's *breve corpusculum*. For Suetonius' *De regibus* we know of Paulinus' verse epitome. We may not have as much as

---

49 Gennadius, *DVI* 64: . . . *et sancti Cassiani quaedam opuscula lato tensa eloquio, angusto verbi revolvens tramite in uno coegit volumine aliaque tam ecclesiasticis quam monasticis studiis necessaria*, 'certain writings of the holy Cassian, works stretched out by his broad eloquence, he [*sc.* Eucherius] also gathered into one volume (along with other things necessary as much to the education of churchmen as of monks), wending his way along a narrow path of words'. The punctuation we adopt reflects the fact that Gennadius seems to write his prose with an accentual rhythm (*tensa eloquio* and *coegit volumine* both offer a *cursus tardus* and *studiis necessaria* is an *octosyllabicus*). The work does not seem to have survived: Stewart 1998: 24 and n. 222. Cassian dedicated *Collationes* 11–17 to Eucherius (and Honoratus): Petschenig 1886: 311–312.

50 Paterius' preface (*PL* 79.683a–686b) reveals the encouragement (*verbis* . . . *suasoriis*) of Gregory. See in general on the *Liber testimoniorum* and its transmission Castaldi and Martello 2011.

51 The text's modern editor Vecchi (1950 and 1986) considers it an early-medieval product.

52 *CLA* 6.773a.

53 See Wasselynck 1962: 5–15. Another patristic author whose work circulated in epitome is Apponius, whose commentary on the Song of Songs was epitomised at some stage by the mysterious Burginda and also in a series of twelve homilies attributed to Jerome (ed. De Vregille and Neyrand 1986).

54 On the latter, see Holford-Strevens 2019.

55 *Mulomedicina Chironis* 8.743 (p. 232 Oder): *propter quod multis auctoribus inspectis et quae ad equorum genus pertinuit secretis singulorum sensus et motus animae in unum contuli et ex his epitoma feci et omnia, quae dispersa fuerant in eis, naturali ingenio plenius per hunc librum docui, ne quo errore pastor generis equini decipi possit.*

56 Chapter II. See Rouse and McNelis 2001: 213. The text is edited in Zahn 1916.

57 As Galdi 1922: 21–22 noted.

58 On the Livy epitomes, see Galdi 1922: 31–93 (a general chapter, then individual studies of the different epitomators/epitomes). The *Oxyrhynchus Epitome* is *P. Oxy.* 4.668.

we would wish of Sallust's *Historiae*, but we do have the miniscule compendium of Julius Exuperantius (who probably also made use of Livian materials).[59] We have *breviaria* from multiple sources as well: Eutropius and Festus, not to mention the mythical history in the *Origo gentis Romanae*. This tradition of epitomising historical works continued right down to the very end of late antiquity: Gregory of Tours' monumental *History* was rearranged into a much more economical six-book version very soon after he had laid down his pen (and against his explicit instructions).[60]

It is not hard to understand why long discursive works of history were particularly prone to condensation: their style almost cried out for it. As Ambrose explained at the start of his *De Tobia*, his reading in the book of Tobit had prompted him to think that 'those topics which the scripture laid out at length in the historical style, we might cover more concisely'.[61] Epitomes were for readers who mainly valued the 'facts' that they could garner from their historical reading. Indeed, one historical *breviarium*, that of Ampelius, is called the *Liber memorialis*, or 'Book of Things One Ought to Commit to Memory'.[62] The preface of Eutropius, addressed to the Emperor Valens, conveys exactly the same general idea:

> By the order of Your Gentleness, I have gathered together in a brief account in chronological order from the founding of the city to our own era Roman affairs which were important in matters of either war or state, with the addition only of those things which have been of marked importance in the life of princes . . .[63]

In writing to the same emperor, Festus takes the idea of brevity even further, in the process confirming that his work is a *quasi*-epitome of Eutropius' *breviarium*. He suggests that dealing with his account was more like doing sums than reading:

> Your Clemency has ordered me to produce from the *breviarium* of the history of the Roman people a summary. I will willingly obey your command, even though I lack the ability to discourse at length. And following the custom of the accountants, who express gigantic sums in small figures, I will point out events, not discourse upon them. Receive, therefore, something which is worked out more briefly, from what was already said briefly: so that, most glorious of princes, it may seem that you do not so much read about years gone by and previous eras of the *res publica* and the deeds of times past, as count them.[64]

---

59 Zorzetti 1982.

60 On this, see Reimitz 2016: 528–540. Gregory's orders are in *Histories* 10.31.

61 Ambrose, *De Tobia* 1.1: *ut ea quae scriptura historico more digessit latius nos strictius conprehendamus.* Of course, the *De Tobia* is in fact longer than the book of Tobit, but the relevant point here is about the nature of the historical style.

62 Arnaudt-Lindet 1993: despite Ampelius' transmission only in an edition, the title is secure, for it features in the prologue (p. 1).

63 Eutropius, *praef.*: *Res Romanas ex voluntate mansuetudinis tuae ab urbe condita ad nostram memoriam quae in negotiis vel bellicis vel civilibus eminebant per ordinem temporum brevi narratione collegi, strictim additis etiam his quae in principum vita egregia extiterunt . . .* Droysen 1879 was wrong to punctuate after *strictim* (*cf.* Bleckmann and Groß 2018:

46); note that *narratione collegi* yields a *cursus planus*, which suggests it is the end of a clause (*collegi strictim* has no particular rhythm).

64 Festus 1: *De breviario rerum gestarum populi Romani brevem fieri clementia tua praecepit. Parebo libens praecepto, quippe cui desit facultas latius eloquendi; ac morem secutus calculonum, qui ingentes summas aeris brevioribus exprimunt, res gestas signabo, non eloquar. Accipe ergo, quod breviter dictis brevius conputetur, ut annos et aetatem rei publicae ac praeteriti facta temporis non tam legere tibi, gloriosissime princeps, quam numerare videaris.* The text here is adapted from Eadie 1967, with the all-but-certain reworking of the first line suggested by Reeve 1997: 508–509, based on reconsideration of the manuscript evidence. *Quod breviter dictis brevius conputetur* has attracted little attention, but would seem to confirm that Reeve is right.

In thinking about why epitomes were popular, we should not discount the expense in producing or obtaining long books (a vice to which works of history are particularly prone), nor the resources required to house and preserve them: *Livius ingens / quem mea non totum bibliotheca capit* ('huge Livy, whom my library does not hold entire'), wrote Martial at the end of the first century (*Epig.* 14.190). Whatever the reasons for the ubiquity of historical epitomes, posterity should be grateful for them. The fact is that no long work of history written in Latin survives from antiquity in its entirety.[65] We have less than a quarter of Livy, just fragments, speeches, and letters from Sallust's *Histories*, and nothing but quotations from all the Latin historians preceding them.[66] Only Pompeius Trogus' prologues survive. Seneca the Elder's history of Rome from the beginning of the civil wars is entirely lost, unless a book of it is to be found in a carbonised roll from Herculaneum (*P. Herc.* 1067).[67] Suetonius' *Caesares* is mostly complete, but the dedication to Septicius Clarus and the beginning of the life of Julius Caesar do not survive; of his *De viris illustribus*, only one section, on grammarians, survives in full, the rest piecemeal. Of Tacitus' large-scale histories, only eleven of the original books survive entire and five more in part. The *Historia Augusta* is missing (at least) the lives of Decius and Philip the Arab.[68] Only books 14–31 of Ammianus' *Res gestae* survive.[69] Indeed, the first long work of history written in Latin to survive in its entirety is either Hegesippus's adaptation of Josephus (of uncertain precise date but probably composed late in the fourth century), or else Rufinus' translation and supplementation of Eusebius' *Historia Ecclesiastica* (402 or 403).[70] For two of these authors, Livy and Trogus, epitomes give us some reasonable sense of what we have lost. For the rest, we have no way of knowing the scope and structure of the original, since, as Brunt put it, 'short extracts can in any case tell us little of the *scope, manner,* and *quality* of the historian'.[71]

So, while all sorts of texts might be epitomised, we can detect some interesting patterns in those selected for condensation. They had to be reasonably lengthy. That they were a recent work was no bar to creating an epitome, nor was the existence of a previous short version of the text. Historical texts were particularly popular candidates for summary and, strikingly often, we are dependent on those summaries for our knowledge of the lost originals. All this casts an interesting light on the Victorine works, which purport to be two epitomes of a multi-book historical work, itself lost.

The function and use of epitomes

The most basic, indeed the obvious, function of an epitome was simply to shorten a work: such was Varro's own condensation of his twenty-five-book *De lingua Latina* into a nine-book epitome, or Sex.

65 For the transmission of the works mentioned in the following, see generally the entries in *T&T*. The *Commentarii* of Caesar might be thought a possible exception, but there is (1) the question of whether they are history by ancient generic standards, and (2) the fact that they are transmitted as a heterogenous corpus (Kestemont *et al.* 2016), which was in antiquity believed to be incomplete and supplemented (Suetonius, *Iul.* 56.1), and (3) that the close of *BG* 8 and opening of *BC* 1 are lost. See in general Gaertner 2018.

66 See Cornell 2013 for a magisterial collection of the fragments of the Roman historians.

67 See Piano 2017.

68 On the codicological nature of the lacuna, oft supposed to be 'authorial' 'artistry', see Stover 2020.

69 On the slight transmission of Ammianus' work, see Kelly and Stover 2016.

70 Hegesippus: Bell 1987; Stover and Woudhuysen 2022b. Rufinus: Murphy 1945: 158–174.

71 Brunt 1980: 483, emphasis in the original.

Pompeius Festus' trimming of Verrius Flaccus' forty books into twenty.[72] In general, the point of such cutting down was to make the result more useful and more usable, in a word, more *utilis*.[73] Around this central aim, however, there was a good deal of variation. Some epitomes aimed to cover roughly the same field as the work from which they were derived, but at a shorter length. Julius Paris and Januarius Nepotianus, for instance, drew from all of Valerius Maximus to create their epitomes. Others aimed to extract only a single category of information from a much larger work: Julius Obsequens was only interested in Livy's prodigies, while Florus focused just on his wars. As his title shows, Faventinus sought in Vitruvius only what was useful for private architecture. The excerptor of the elder Seneca was interested only in the declamations. The magnitude and heterogeneity of Pliny's *Historia Naturalis*, in particular, encouraged such specialisation: Solinus' *Collectanea rerum memorabilium* covers only Pliny's geography, while the *De remediis salutaribus*, the *Medicina Plinii*, and Gargilius Martialis' *Medicina ex holeribus ex pomis* cover his medical books.[74]

In line with this variation, some epitomes were meant as stand-alone texts for independent reading, replacements or even substitutes for the original. That was seemingly how Lactantius envisaged his epitome of the *Divine Institutes*, as can be seen from its rather defensive preface, in which he explains that 'it seems difficult to gather in one volume those things which have been explained in seven of the greatest size'.[75] The work also has a more obviously Christian flavour than its parent, perhaps a reflection of its different audience.[76] In a similar fashion Julius Paris makes clear in his preface that he had squeezed from Valerius Maximus the material that those engaged in declamation or legal oratory might need.[77]

Other condensed texts, however, were probably meant as a reading guide or index to the longer original.[78] The *Periochae* to Livy or Augustine's *breviculus* to the *De civitate* are examples. In his introductory letter to Proba, Eugippius is explicit that she had the unabridged works of Augustine in her library already, but still wished to make use of his epitome.[79] As early as the first century, Seneca the Younger admitted that 'what is now commonly called a *breviarium*, though once it was known as a *summarium*, when we used to actually speak Latin' was useful for reminding the reader of something they had encountered already.[80] Hence, while epitomes could replace originals, they were also used alongside them. We can see this in practice in the compendium of Julius Obsequens, where it seems that his prodigies were drawn directly

72 Festus and Flaccus: Glinister *et al.* 2007: 1–2; *T&T* 'Sex. Pompeius Festus' (Marshall). Festus' twenty books were themselves further reduced by Paul the Deacon in the eighth century (Chapter V).

73 See, for instance, Januarius Nepotianus, *praef.*: *opera eius utilia esse, si sint brevia.* Julius Paris: *ut et facilius invenires, si quando quid quaereres.*

74 Galdi 1922: 157–166 on epitomes of the *HN*. On Solinus, see also Brodersen 2011. On Martialis, see now Zainaldin 2020.

75 Lactantius, *Epit. praef.* 2: *difficile videtur ea quae septem maximis voluminibus explicata sunt in unum conferre.*

76 A point well made by Perrin 1987: 32.

77 Paris, *Praef.*: *Exemplorum conquisitionem cum scirem esse non minus disputantibus quam declamantibus necessariam, decem*

Valerii Maximi libros Dictorum et factorum memorabilium *ad unum volumen epitomae coegi.* This passage would seem to suggest something rather important about who was not in the audience for the *Facta et dicta*.

78 On the idea of index epitomes, by which we mean epitomes designed to point to the position of a *locus* within a text or corpus, see Stover 2015: 62.

79 Eugippius, *Epistola ad Probam*: 'and although the multitudinous riches of your library contain entire the works from which I have reaped a few things, nevertheless it has pleased you to possess the reapings' (*et cum bibliothecae vestrae copia multiplex integra de quibus pauca decerpsi contineat opera, placuit tamen habere decerpta*).

80 Seneca, *Ep.* 39.1: *quae nunc vulgo breviarium dicitur, olim cum Latine loqueremur, summarium vocabatur.*

from the text of Livy, and his historical notices from an epitome.[81] Take his second chapter, drawn from the thirty-eighth book of Livy:

> M. Messala C. Livio coss. luce inter horam tertiam et quartam tenebrae ortae. In Aventino lapidum pluviae novendiali expiatae. In Hispania prospere militatum.

> In the consulship of M. Messala and C. Livius [188 BC] during the daytime, between the third and fourth hour, darkness arose. On the Aventine there was a rain of stones, expiated by a *novendialis*. In Spain, the campaigns went well.

The prodigies and expiation are drawn almost verbatim from Livy's text (38.36.4: *quod luce inter horam tertiam ferme et quartam tenebrae obortae fuerant. Et novemdiale sacrificium indictum est, quod in Aventino lapidibus pluvisset*), while the historical notice is a very broad generalisation, which may well have come from another epitome (*cf.* the very frequent occurrence of *prospere res gestas* and *prospere pugnavit* in the *Periochae*). What is interesting here is that not only must Obsequens have had both a copy of Livy and an epitome open as he worked, but that we can see him switching techniques of epitomisation depending on the subject. His method makes perfect sense: whatever the precise aim of Obsequens' work, the exact wording of the prodigies and the expiations was clearly critical to it, whereas the historical notices required nothing more than broad summary. We can find this pattern of epitomes and originals being used side by side elsewhere. Gorman has uncovered one particularly interesting medieval case where a later hand copied the omitted material into the manuscript of an Augustine epitome, making it whole once more.[82]

Depending on the needs or ideas of its creator and users, an epitome could be as much a *complement* to an original text as a rival. That should cause us to think carefully about the interaction between epitomes and originals in transmission. An oft-repeated idea in the scholarship is that epitomes came to eclipse originals, but there is very little evidence that this is true.[83] We might have only a few decades of Livy's history, but most of the Livy epitomes have a much more tenuous transmission than the main text.[84] We have many manuscripts of Valerius Maximus, and very few of Julius Paris and Januarius Nepotianus.[85] The *Historia Naturalis* of the elder Pliny survives in so many manuscripts and a tradition of such complexity as to make editing the text a Herculean labour.[86] Solinus has a robust transmission, but the *De remediis*

81 This was the plausible argument of Schmidt 1968, picking up on a suggestion by Rossbach 1897: 4 (the objections of Bessone 1982: 1241 are weak). It is also possible that Obsequens was using not two sources but two approaches to the text of Livy: direct excerption for the prodigies, and paraphrased summary for the history.

82 Gorman 1997: 68–69. The manuscript is Berlin Phillipps 1657.

83 The idea is so widely accepted, indeed assumed, that it might seem invidious to single out instances where it is stated clearly, but see *e.g.* 'Epitome, Latin', *OCD*[4] (Kaster); Rose 1996: 14. As always, Syme is especially elegant (1992: 11): Livy 'had been sunk by his bulk long since, replaced by epitomes'.

84 Julius Obsequens survives only in an edition (*T&T* 'Julius Obsequens' (Winterbottom)); the *Oxyrhynchus Epitome* is a chance survival; for the *DVI* see Chapter II;

the *Periochae* survive entire in only two manuscripts of the twelfth century or earlier (Paris lat. 7701, s. XII; Pal. lat. 894, s. IX). It is true that Florus has a more secure transmission (*T&T* 'Florus' (Marshall)), but the others are swamped by Livy (*T&T* 'Livy' (Reynolds)).

85 Valerius Maximus: Schullian 1981; *T&T* 'Valerius Maximus' (Marshall). Julius Paris: fully extant only in Vat. lat. 4929 (a fragment in Reg. lat. 314 and all of the text in its apograph Ottob. Lat. 1549; Lupus of Ferrières and Heiric of Auxerre knew the lost exemplar of Vat. lat. 4929, see *CTC* 5.253–254 (Schullian)). Januarius Nepotianus: only extant in Vat. lat. 1321 (also above, Chapter II).

86 Reeve 2007 both gives a sense of the editorial history and lists manuscripts; see now also the more comprehensive Reeve 2021.

salutaribus (for instance) survives in a single manuscript.[87] Lactantius' *Epitome* survived complete in only a single manuscript, whereas the *Divine Institutes* has a much more robust transmission.[88] None of the Augustine epitomes have anywhere near the circulation of Augustine's originals – they are generally found in one or at most a handful of manuscripts.[89] Hence, had Justin not made his epitome of Pompeius Trogus, it is not as if we would have instead had the original: we simply would have nothing but a name and a few stray quotations. If anything, epitomes – created for particular times and contexts – enhanced interest in their source texts. As those times and contexts changed, a particular epitome might lose its relevance, while its source could remain as fresh as ever.

★ ★ ★

All this serves to demonstrate that, in thinking about any single epitome, it is vital to keep in mind the function that it was meant to serve. This determined much about how it was put together and the nature of the end result. That is something that it will be important to remember when we turn back to the Victorine texts – it also leads neatly to our final topic (in two parts) in this chapter: the way that epitomators went about their work.

The mechanics of epitomisation I: Structure, order, length

Epitomes come in a wide variety of forms and vary significantly in their textual and material relationship to the works from which they were derived. In the era before the codex, when books were limited by the amount of text that could be fitted onto a papyrus roll, an epitome would always consist of a reduced number of them compared with the original.[90] Varro reduced his twenty-five books to nine, Florus reworked Livy into (probably) four books.[91] The more capacious codex offered a much greater degree of flexibility. Some codex epitomes reproduced the structure of the original – consider the forty-four miniature books of Justin's epitome of Trogus, or the ten books of *excerpta* of the elder Seneca. Others reworked the original material into a new format, such as Faventinus' single book derived from the ten books of Vitruvius, or Solinus' adaptation of four books of Pliny (*HN* III-VI) into a continuous text. Eutropius chose a novel format, with his ten miniature books, as if his work were an epitome of some

---

87 Solinus: *T&T* 'Solinus' (Rouse). *De remediis*: Paris lat. 10318 (where it is attributed to Apuleius).

88 *Epitome*: Turin, Archivo di Stato, Biblioteca Antica, I B. II. 27. *DI*: Heck and Wlosok 2005: xiv–xxiv.

89 Prosper's works are a notable exception, although the number of their manuscripts still pales in comparison to Augustine's.

90 Stover and Woudhuysen 2022b; Stover 2021a, forthcoming e.

91 The four-book structure of Florus is widely attested in manuscripts, including the earliest (Heidelberg, Pal. lat. 894; Bischoff, *Katalog* 1514, second third of s. IX), which also transmits an ancient subscription at the end of the *Periochae* (f. 104v), a text that long circulated together with the *Epitoma de Tito Livio* – a significant detail; *cf.* Reeve 1988: 479. The two-book structure is found only in Bamberg Class. 31 (E.III.22) (Bischoff, *Katalog* 208: s. IX/X or beginning of s. X), but contemporary editions have generally adopted it (*cf. T&T* 'Florus' (Marshall): 164).

imaginary ten-book Roman history. Paeanius, who made a Greek translation of it just a decade after it was produced, evidently found this a baffling decision and eliminated the book divisions entirely.[92]

Many, perhaps most, epitomes followed the order of material in the original, but some fitted it into a different *schema*. The *Medicina Plinii*, for example, adopted the sensible idea of arranging Pliny's botanical remedies by disease rather than by species of plant.[93] After all, it was made to be a practical text, suitable for bringing on journeys to avoid being swindled by charlatan doctors, as the author explains in the prologue.[94] Doody argues that this new arrangement was designed to implicitly argue for the epitome's superiority to the original.[95] Brodersen has made a similar claim about Solinus: that his rearrangement of Plinian materials displays a more sophisticated concept of geography.[96] Equally, it was possible for an epitome to follow the rough order of the original, but still make significant structural changes. The *DVI*, which our only ancient *testimonium* (the bridge preceding it in the *Corpus tripertitum*) declares to be a *Historia Liviana*, adapts Livy's discursive history into a biographical format.[97] Florus turns the same original text into an epitome arranged by individual wars. Julius Obsequens, in contrast, opted for an annalistic format, providing a year-by-year account of prodigies, expiations, and notable events. It is worth keeping in mind that had we only these three epitomes, we would no doubt have a completely warped sense of how Livy structured his history.

Abbreviation could be extremely severe, as in the case of index epitomes, such as the *Periochae* to Livy or Apuleius' compendium of Plato. Such texts are less than three per cent of the original in length.[98] It could also be rather more expansive: Julius Paris' epitome (*ca.* 24,000 words) is about thirty per cent the length of Valerius Maximus (*ca.* 80,000), as is Januarius Nepotianus' for the portion it covers. In between, we have Lactantius' epitome of his own *Divine Institutes* at fourteen per cent of the original (*ca.* 19,000 vs *ca.* 120,000) and Faventinus at ten per cent of Vitruvius' text (*ca.* 5,500 vs *ca.* 58,000). Similarly, where Seneca's original survives, we can determine that the *excerpta* of the *Controversiae* represents between ten and eighteen per cent of the original.[99] Indeed, where we have two extant independent epitomes of the same non-extant source, one can use standard statistical analysis to judge the length of the original with some degree of accuracy.[100] Nepotianus, for example, provides sixty-four *exempla* for Book II of Valerius Maximus, whereas Paris gives eighty-one. By our count, forty-six of the *exempla* are shared between the two epitomes. The standard formula (the product of the two populations divided by their overlap) would lead us to believe that the second book of Valerius Maximus contained 112 *exempla* (the product of 64 and

92 See the text in Droysen 1879, which added book numbers back in (understandably, for ease of reference), where the manuscripts omit them.

93 Doody 2009: 94.

94 *Med. Plin. praef.*: *frequenter mihi in peregrinationibus accidit ut aut propter meam aut propter meorum infirmitatem varias fraudes medicorum experiscerer.*

95 Doody 2009: 95.

96 Brodersen 2011: esp. 87–88.

97 For the bridge passage, see Chapter II.

98 Books I–X and XXI–XXXVIII of Livy come to almost 420,000 words, while the *Periochae* for those books are a mere 6,200, or 1.5 per cent. Apuleius: see the commentary of Stover 2016 on each dialogue, which provides per cent coverage.

99 Electronic versions of both texts are available on the *PHI* 'Classical Latin Texts' database, from which comparisons can be made.

100 A recent use of this method to estimate authors in general circulation in the second century, along with a clear and engaging description of its workings, can be found in Netz 2020: 548–551.

81 divided by 46). In fact, it contains 102 (including introductions). In this case, however, we know that six of Nepotianus' *exempla* are not found in our text of Valerius Maximus: that gives us an astonishingly accurate prediction of 102 *exempla*.

What determined how much of the original made it into the summary? Obviously, the purpose that it was designed to serve must have been the major influence on the length of the end-product: if an epitome was designed to function as a short index to a massive text like Livy's, to help the reader search through it, then it was hardly helpful to take over ten per cent of the original (well over 100,000 words). It is worth noting, however, that a number of condensed texts cluster at around or a little over 20,000 words: Julius Paris (*ca.* 24,000), Januarius Nepotianus (probably *ca.* 19,000 words in its original form), Lactantius (*ca.* 19,000), Eutropius (*ca.* 19,000 words), and the combined edition of Eutropius and Festus made for Censorinus (*ca.* 24,000 words).[101]

Interestingly, both Lactantius and Julius Paris say in their prefaces that they reduced the original work *in/ad unum volumen.*[102] It may be that they were not speaking figuratively and that *ca.* 20,000–25,000 words was the most that could be crammed into a single-quire papyrus codex. That was the cheap, convenient, portable, and ultimately consumable format of late antiquity.[103] It was ideally suited to the epitome (a text meant to be used), whereas the luxury codex, which contained the work epitomised (a text meant to be read), was monumental, unwieldy, lavish, and (in theory, but lamentably not in practice) eternal.[104] It is worth remembering that there was a dramatic difference in price between these formats, a difference due not only to the contrast in materials, but also explained by the quality of their writing: the swift and functional script of everyday against a luxurious and laborious bookhand.[105] That external constraint, as much if not more than the character of the original work, may have determined how epitomators operated: what they chose and how much of the original they included. It might also be pointed out that the *CT* runs to just above 25,000 words.

One other feature of the length of epitomes is also worth noting. Epitomators seem often to have started out full of enthusiasm for their source text, keen to take over a great deal of it. As they went on, that enthusiasm waned and they became more selective. We see this again and again in extant epitomes. Compare, for instance, the first book of the *Periochae* (*ca.* 450 words) with the last ten taken together (*ca.* 430 words). This pattern where the first book is much longer than later ones can be seen also in Januarius Nepotianus (Book I, *ca.* 3,100; Book II *ca.* 2,160) and Lactantius (Book I, *ca.* 3,700 words;

---

101 On the edition for Censorinus, see Reeve 1997: 510–511. Nepotianus: taking Book II as typical (*ca.* 2,160 words for the *ca.* 9,000 of Valerius Maximus); Book I is longer (*ca.* 3,100 words for the 8,000 of the original), but many epitomes start comprehensively, before becoming more selective (see below). It is noteworthy that both the *Getica* (*ca.* 20,000 words) and *Historia Romana* (*ca.* 18,000) of Jordanes fall into this range. Vegetius (*ca.* 27,000 words) falls a little above the line, but his work had a complex gestation in which Book I appears to have been issued first and then supplemented (see Conclusion to Part 1).

102 Lactantius, *Epit. praef.* 2; Julius Paris *praef.* (in both cases, the text is quoted above, notes 75 and 77). Compare Gennadius on Eucherius's epitome of Cassian, above. Augustine (*Retractationes* 1.22) says of his *Contra Adimantium* that *quod opus uno volumine conclusi*: the work is *ca.* 18,000 words.

103 Stover forthcoming e.

104 Gameson 2019: 8. In this connection, Isidore, *Etymologies* 6.12.1 is interesting: *At vero historiae maiori modulo scribebantur, et non solum in carta vel membranis, sed etiam et in omentis elephantinis textilibusque maluarum foliis atque palmarum.*

105 See, *e.g.*, the cost of having something written *scriptura optima* vs *scriptura libelli vel tabularum* in the *Prices Edict* of Diocletian (7.39, 41 ed. Giacchero 1974).

Book VII, *ca.* 1,800).[106] Sometimes, however, the prospect of finishing seems to have revived flagging interest, so that it is the middle parts of the work that are shortest: Julius Paris, for instance, has a long first book (*ca.* 2,900 words), four shorter middle ones (*ca.* 2,600, 2,200, 2,400, 2,350), and then three longer ones at the end, the last being the longest in the work (*ca.* 2,900, 2,800, 3,200). It is worth noting that this in no way reflects the structure of the original: the second shortest in Julius Paris, Book V, is actually the longest in Valerius Maximus. The key point here is that, once again, it was not necessarily the nature of the original that determined the length of the epitome.

So, as is by now familiar, epitomes varied a great deal in their approach to structure, order, and length. We should not expect them to have preserved the structure of their original: it might easily have been arranged in books, where they opted for continuous prose. Nor did they necessarily keep its ordering totally intact. They might rearrange it entirely, but they also might keep it roughly in the original order, while changing the structure around that: converting history into biography, for example. Finally, while length was obviously largely dependent on function, it is striking that format (a single-quire codex) seems to have primarily determined the length of some epitomes, rather than the number of words in the original. Equally, epitomators seem often to have begun with greater enthusiasm than they were able to sustain through the whole work.

The mechanics of epitomisation II: Adapting the original

Epitomes varied also in *how* they adapted the text of the original work. Some simply took over the wording of the source verbatim, cutting out material to make it shorter. This, for example, is what we find generally in Roman law codes. Where, for instance, we have epigraphic evidence for the original text of the constitution, we find that the version of the law in the codes consists of extracted sentences, with some very minor additions for sense (in the example in **Table** 3.1, the addition of a discourse particle). This was far from the only approach to epitomisation, however. Other epitomes adapted the source text into a very different style: we have seen above in several cases that stylistic simplification was one major reason for making an epitome. Still other condensed texts used some hybrid of these two methods: Julius Obsequens, for instance, with his mixture of verbatim Livy and what we might think of as epitome-speak.

The simplest way to appreciate the variety of different modes of epitomisation is to look at cases where we have multiple epitomes of the same extant work. The two epitomes of Valerius Maximus neatly illustrate the two contrasting approaches (**Table** 3.2). Julius Paris has hacked his summary out of the *ipsissima verba* of Valerius Maximus, while Januarius Nepotianus has rephrased and reworked the same passage, trying to convey its crucial information at rather shorter length.[107]

Another example can be drawn from the thirty-eighth book of Livy, where he tells the shocking story of the wife of the chieftain Orgiago, Chiomara.[108] Here we are fortunate to possess four epitomes – the

---

106 *cf.* on Lactantius Heck and Wlosok 1994: xviii–xix.
107 *cf.* Raschieri 2020, who comes (165–166) to compatible conclusions on the basis (158–161) of different passages.

108 Her name is found only in Plutarch, *Mulierum virtutes* 22.

TABLE 3.1 – LEGAL EPITOMES

CTh 1.16.8, 28 July 362 (= *CJ* 3.3.5)	Feissel 2000: 323 (= *CIL* 3.459 + p. 982 and 3.14199)
IMP. IULIANUS A. SECUNDO PPO – Quaedam sunt negotia in quibus superfluum est moderatorem exspectari provinciae: ideoque pedaneos iudices, hoc est qui negotia humiliora disceptent, constituendi damus praesidibus potestatem. DAT. V. KAL. AUG. ANTIOCHIAE MAMERTINOS ET NEVITTA CONSS.	E(xemplum) s(acrarum) l(itterarum). Ovoriri solent nonnul[le] controversie que not[io(nem)] re{i}quirant et ex{t}amen iudici{i}s celsioris, tum autem **quedam negotia sunt in quivus superfluum sit moderatorem exspectare provincie.** Quod novis{u}utrumque penden<t>ivus rectum admodum visuṃ est <u>t **pedane<o>s iudices, <oc es>t eos qui negotia umiliorạ discepten<t>, constituendidaremus presidivus potesta<t>e<m>.** Ita enim et sivi partem qurarum ip<s>i den{s}-p<s>erint et tamen niilom<i>n{i}-us quas{s}i ipsi oc munus adme-nestravunt, qum illi quos legere admenestreṇ[t]. Quius rei consci (?) ani[. . .] adque eminente[m ex-]cellentiam tuaṃ [san-]cimus, Secunde pareṇ[s ca-][ri]ss[ime ad]qu[e] amạ[nti-] [ssime, - - -]★
The emperor Julian Augustus to Secundus the Praetorian Prefect. There are certain matters in which it is superfluous to await the governor of the province, therefore we grant to *praesides* the power to appoint petty judges, that is those who may arbitrate more lowly affairs. Issued on the fifth day of the Kalends of August at Antioch in the consulship of Mamertinus and Nevitta.	Copy of the Imperial Letter. Some controversies habitually arise which require the judicial investigation and examination of a loftier judge, but there are on the other hand certain matters in which it is superfluous to wait for the governor of the province. And it seemed quite right to us, when we weighed both <facts>, that we grant to *praesides* the power to appoint petty judges, that is those men who arbitrate humbler matters. For in this way they may cut away a part of their own cares, and nevertheless likewise <it will be> as though they themselves will administer this office, while those, whom they have chosen, administer it. Aware of this matter . . . we have ordered that . . . and your excellence, Secundus, our most dear and beloved father . . .

★ We have reproduced Feissel's edition of the first part of the Amorgos inscription here, though we have not marked the trivial orthographic slips (*v* for *b passim e.g.*) as he does. The second (lost) part of the inscription was much more heavily damaged when discovered and the text is very uncertain. For the comparison of the inscription to the texts found in the law codes, *cf.* Feissel 2000: 334–337.

Oxyrhynchus Epitome, the *Periochae*, Florus, and the *De viris illustribus* – as well as an account in Valerius Maximus (itself derived from Livy), alongside the full text (**TABLE 3.3**). Not one of these epitomised versions attempts to replicate the style of the original, and indeed only the *Periochae* consistently uses Livy's vocabulary. The condensed texts vary considerably in how much they have compressed the 215 words of the original, with forty per cent coverage in Valerius Maximus and ten to twelve per cent coverage in the remaining four.[109] In addition, this story represents a very small part of Livy's thirty-eighth book, one per cent of its 17,000 words, yet it plays a disproportionately prominent role in the epitomes: it is ten per cent of the *Periochae*'s treatment of the book, fifteen per cent of Florus', twenty per cent of the *Oxyrhynchus Epitome*'s, and more than half of the *DVI*'s. We do not need to posit any kind of *ur-epitome*

109 Of course, this was further compressed by Valerius Maximus' epitomator Julius Paris 6.ext.2, which is fifty-four words long (about half the length of Maximus' epitome).

TABLE 3.2 – EPITOMES OF VALERIUS MAXIMUS

Julius Paris 2.5.1	Valerius Maximus 2.5.1	Januarius Nepotianus 2.5.1
Statuam inauratam nec in urbe nec in ulla parte Italiae quisquam prius vidit quam a Manlio Acilio Glabrione equestris patri poneretur in aede Pietatis, quam aedem ipse dedicaverat.	Statuam auratam nec in urbe nec in ulla parte Italiae quisquam prius aspexit quam a M. Acilio Glabrione★ equestris patri poneretur in aede Pietatis. eam autem aedem P. Cornelio Lentulo M. Baebio Tamphilo consulibus ipse dedicaverat compos voti factus rege Antiocho apud Thermopylas superato.	Marcus Acilius Glabrio ex voto aedem dedicaverat ob id quod regem Antiochum apud Thermopylas felici vicisset eventu. In aede statuam auratam patri posuit. Nec in Italia nec Roma cuiquam prius inaurata statua fuit.
Nobody saw a gilded statue, either in Rome or in any other part of Italy, until an equestrian one was placed in the temple of Piety by Manius Acilius Glabrio in honour of his father, which temple he himself had dedicated.	Nobody beheld a gilded statue, either in Rome or in any other part of Italy, until an equestrian one was placed in the temple of Piety by M. Acilius Glabrio in honour of his father. The latter had himself dedicated that temple in the consulship of P. Cornelius Lentulus and M. Baebius Tamphilus, for the granting of his vow when king Antiochus was defeated at Thermopylae. (Trans. Shackleton Bailey 2000: 1.161, adapted)	Marcus Acilius Glabrio had dedicated a temple in fulfilment of a vow, because he had defeated king Antiochus at Thermopylae with a successful outcome. In the temple he placed a golden statue for his father. Neither in Italy nor in Rome was there a gilded statue dedicated to anyone before this.

★ The praenomen of Manius Acilius Glabrio caused some confusion at this point. The MSS of Valerius Maximus read M. (i.e. Marcus), corrected by Kempf to M'. (i.e. Manius). Julius Paris' text reads Manlius (Vat. lat. 4929, f. 93r), corrected by Halm to Manius, while Nepotianus has Marcus (Vat. lat. 1321, f. 152v), which seems not to have attracted editorial attention.

to explain this – and indeed the lack of overlap in wording between the different summaries rules one out. Instead, this is an engaging story, which Livy himself calls a *facinus memorabile*: it is no surprise that four different readers over several centuries would be drawn to it independently. Confirmation of this independence comes with Julius Obsequens, who – unflinching in his devotion to prodigies – makes no mention of the event at all in his second chapter (quoted above), since it was not germane to his purposes.

This offers an important qualification to the claim above that where we have multiple independent epitomes of the same work we can gauge the size of the original: while we obtained excellent results in predicting the *number* of *exempla* in Valerius Maximus through analysis of the two epitomes, the same method gives slightly misleading results if we look at word counts. Given the number of words in the second books of Nepotianus and Paris (*ca.* 2,160 and 2,600, respectively) and considering their overlaps (approximately 1,020 words), we would expect Book II of Valerius Maximus to consist of 5,500 words. In fact, it contains almost 9,000. This is because both epitomators *independently* were drawn to copy the first lines of each *exemplum* and much less likely to include the later lines. The crucial consequence of this is that where we try to estimate the length of a source text from two (or more) surviving epitomes, the figure produced is likely to be an underestimate: a lower bound, rather than an accurate approximation.

TABLE 3.3 – EPITOMES OF LIVY

Livy 38.24.2–11	*Oxy. Epit.* 38 (486 Hillen)
Facinus memorabile a captiva factum est. Orgiagontis reguli uxor forma eximia custodiebatur inter plures captivos; cui custodiae centurio praeerat et libidinis et avaritiae militaris. Is primo animum temptavit; quem cum abhorrentem a voluntario videret stupro, corpori, quod servum fortuna erat, vim fecit. Deinde ad leniendam indignitatem iniuriae spem reditus ad suos mulieri facit, et ne eam quidem, ut amans, gratuitam. Certo auri pondere pactus, ne quem suorum conscium haberet, ipsi permittit, ut quem vellet unum ex captivis nuntium ad suos mitteret. Locum prope flumen constituit, quo duo ne plus necessarii captivae cum auro venirent nocte insequenti ad eam accipiendam. Forte ipsius mulieris servus inter captivos eiusdem custodiae erat. Hunc nuntium primis tenebris extra stationes centurio educit. Nocte insequenti et duo necessarii mulieris ad constitutum locum et centurio cum captiva venit. Ubi cum aurum ostenderent, quod summam talenti Attici (tanti enim pepigerat) expleret, mulier lingua sua, stringerent ferrum et centurionem pensantem aurum occiderent, imperavit. Iugulati praecisum caput ipsa involutum veste ferens ad virum Orgiagontem, qui ab Olympo domum refugerat, pervenit; quem priusquam complecteretur, caput centurionis ante pedes eius abiecit, mirantique, cuiusnam id caput hominis aut quod id facinus haudquaquam muliebre esset, et iniuriam corporis et ultionem violatae per vim pudicitiae confessa viro est, aliaque, ut traditur, sanctitate et gravitate vitae huius matronalis facinoris decus ad ultimum conservavit.	Origiagontis <uxor> capti*va* nobilis [*centuri*] onem, cuius vim pass*a* erat, aurum ad <se> /[*mittendam*] poscentem occidit caputque eius ad virum / [*secum tulit*]
While they were established in camp there, a memorable deed was done by a captive woman. The wife of the petty king Orgiago, a woman of surpassing beauty, was held under guard among a large number of prisoners; the commander of the guard was a centurion, characterised by both the lust and the greed of the soldier. At first he tried her disposition; when he found it shrinking from voluntary fornication, he did violence to her body, which fortune had made a slave. Then, to quiet her indignation at the injury, he held out to the woman the hope of a return to her own people, but not even that, as a lover might have done, did he grant her for nothing. Having stipulated for a definite quantity of gold, to avoid taking one of his own men as an accomplice, he allowed the woman herself to send as a messenger to her people whomsoever of the prisoners she should choose. He designated a spot near the river to which not more than two of the kinsmen of the captive were to come with the money the following night to receive her. It happened that one of the woman's own slaves was among the prisoners under the same guard. The centurion brought him as the messenger out of the camp. The following night both the two kinsmen of the woman and the centurion with the prisoner came to the appointed place. While they were displaying the money, which was to amount to an Attic talent – for so great had been the sum agreed upon – the woman in her own language ordered them to draw sword and kill the centurion as he was weighing the money. When they had slit his throat and cut off his head, the woman herself wrapped it in her garment and carried it on her return to her husband Orgiago, who had escaped home from Olympus; before she embraced him she dropped at his feet the head of the centurion, and, when he wondered whose head this was and what this act meant, so unlike that of a woman, she confessed to her husband the violence done to her person and the vengeance exacted for her forcibly violated chastity, and, as the story goes, by the purity and dignity of her life in other respects maintained to the end the glory won by a deed that marked her as a true matron. (Trans. Sage 1936, adapted)	The noble wife of Orgiago, taken captive, killed a centurion who had raped her, since he asked for gold for her return, and brought his head back with her to her husband.

Val. Max. 6.1.ext.2	Periocha 38 (44 Rossbach)	Florus 2.11	DVI 55.2
Orgiagontis reguli uxor mirae pulchritudinis a centurione, cui custodienda tradita erat, stuprum pati coacta, postquam ventum est in eum locum, in quem centurio misso nuntio necessarios mulieris pretium, quo eam redimerent, adferre iusserat, aurum expendente centurione et in eius pondus animo oculisque intento Gallograecis lingua gentis suae imperavit ut eum occiderent. Interfecti deinde caput abscisum manibus retinens ad coniugem venit abiectoque ante pedes eius iniuriae et ultionis suae ordinem exposuit. Huius feminae quid aliud quisquam quam corpus in potestatem hostium venisse dicat? Nam neque animus vinci nec pudicitia capi potuit.	Exemplum quoque virtutis et pudicitiae in femina traditur. Quae cum regis Gallograecorum uxor fuisset, capta centurionem, qui ei vim intulerat, occidit.	Nam Orgiacontis regis uxor a centurione stuprum passa memorabili exemplo custodiam evasit, revolsumque adulteri hostis caput ad maritum reportavit.	Inter captivos uxor regis Orgiagontis centurioni cuidam in custodiam data; a quo vi stuprata de iniuria tacuit et post impetrata redemptione marito adulterum interficiendum tradidit.
The wife of the petty king Orgiago, a woman of extraordinary beauty, was forced to suffer rape by a centurion to whose custody she had been consigned. When they came to the place to which the centurion had told the woman's relations by messenger to bring the ransom money and the centurion was weighing the gold, his mind and eyes intent on that operation, she commanded the Galatians in her native tongue to kill him. That done, she went to her husband with the severed head in her hands, threw it at his feet, and told him the story of her injury and vengeance. Would anyone say that aught but the body of this woman came into the enemies' power? For her soul could not be vanquished nor her chastity captured. (Trans. Shackleton Bailey 2000: 2.13)	An example of virtue and modesty in a woman is also related. She was the wife of the king of the Gallograeci, and she killed a centurion who had raped her.	For the wife of the king Orgiago was raped by a centurion, and in a memorable example, escaped her captor, tore off the head of the enemy who violated her, and brought it back to her husband.	Among the captives, was the wife of the king Orgiago, who was put in the custody of a certain centurion. He raped her, and she was silent about the crime she suffered, and when a ransom was offered for her, she handed her violator over to her husband to be killed.

TABLE 3.4 – EPITOMES OF AUGUSTINE

Augustine, *Enarrationes in psalm.* 100

Facientes praevaricationem odio habui. Intendite, fratres mei . . . [40 words] . . . qui sunt praevaricatores? Qui oderunt legem Dei; qui audiunt illam, et non faciunt, praevaricatores dicuntur. Facientes praevaricationem odio habe, repelle illos a te. Sed odisse debes praevaricatores, non homines. Unus homo praevaricator, videte quia duo nomina habet, homo et praevaricator: hominem Deus fecit, praevaricatorem ipse se fecit; ama in illo quod Deus fecit, persequere in illo quod ipse sibi fecit. Cum enim persecutus fueris praevaricationem eius, occidis quod homo fecit, et liberatur quod Deus fecit. *Facientes praevaricationem odio habui. Non adhaesit mihi cor pravum.* Quod est cor pravum? Cor tortum. Quod est cor tortum? Cor non rectum. Quod est cor non rectum? Vide quod est cor rectum, et ibi invenis quod est cor non rectum. Rectum cor dicitur hominis, qui omnia quae vult Deus, non ipse non vult. intendite. Orat aliquis ut nescio quid non eveniat . . . [127 words] . . . *non adhaesit mihi cor pravum. Cum declinaret a me malignus, non cognoscebam.* Quid est: non cognoscebam? Non approbabam, non laudabam, non mihi placebat. Cognoscere enim invenimus in scripturis aliquando dici, pro eo quod est placere nobis. Quid enim latet Deum, fratres? Numquid novit iustos, et non novit iniustos? Quid cogitas quod ille nesciat? Non dico: quid facis; sed: quid cogitas quod ille nesciat? Non dico: quid cogitas; sed: quid cogitaturus es quod ille non ante viderit? Omnia ergo novit Deus; et tamen in fine, id est in iudicio post misericordiam, de quibusdam dicit: in illa die multi venturi sunt, et dicent . . . [30 words] . . . ille non novit aliquem? Sed quid est: non novi vos? In regula mea non vos agnosco. Novi enim regulam iustitiae meae: non illi congruitis, declinastis ab illa, distorti estis. Ideo et hic dixit: non cognoscebam. Cum declinaret a me malignus, non cognoscebam . . . [126 words] . . . Non quia nesciebam, sed quia non adprobabam.

I hated the workers of iniquities. Listen, my brothers . . . [40 words] . . . Who are the 'workers of iniquities'? Those who hate the law of God, who hear it, and do not act, are called workers of iniquities. Hate the workers of iniquity, drive them from you. But you ought to hate them as workers of iniquity, not men. A man is a worker of iniquity: see how this has two terms, man, and worker of iniquity. God made the man; but the man made himself a worker of iniquity. Love in him what God made, persecute in him what he did to himself. For when you persecute his iniquity, you kill what the man has made and set free what God has made. *I hated the workers of iniquities. The perverse heart did not cleave to me.* What is 'the perverse heart'? A twisted heart. What is a twisted heart? A heart that is not upright. What is a heart that is not upright? See what an upright heart is and there you will find what a heart that is not upright is. The heart of a man is said to be upright, when he wants everything that God wants, not what he wants. Listen. Someone prays for something not to happen . . . [127 words]. *The perverse heart did not cleave to me. And the malignant that turned aside from me, I did not know.* What does 'I did not know' mean? I did not approve, I did not praise, it did not please me. For we find 'to know' in Scripture sometimes meaning 'to please us'. For what escapes God, brothers? Surely he knows the just and does not know the unjust? What do you think he does not know? I do not say 'what do you do?', but 'what do you think he does not know?' I do not say 'What do you think?' but 'What are you going to think that he has not already seen before?' Therefore, God knows all, and nonetheless, at the end, that is, in judgement after mercy, he will say about some people, *In that day many will come and say* . . . [30 words] . . . Does he not know someone? But what is *I will not know you.* 'I do not recognise you in my rule. For I know the rule of my justice. You have not conformed to it, you have fallen short of it, you have twisted it'. Therefore he has also said: *And the malignant that turned aside from me, I did not know* . . . [126 words] . . . Not that I was unaware, but that I did not approve.

Prosper, *Expositio ps.* 100.31–38 (Callens)	Lyons Epitome (Paris NAL 1629 f. 14r)
Facientes praevaricationem odio habui. Diligendi sunt homines, ut odio habeantur praevaricationes, quia aliud est amare quod facti sunt, aliud odisse quod faciunt. *Non adhaesit mihi cor pravum, declinantem a me malignum non agnoscebam.* Pravo, inquit, cordi consensum non praebui et ab immaculata via declinantem malignum non cognoscebam, hoc est propter dissimilitudinem non probabam.	*Facientes praevaricationem odio habui.* Qui sunt praevaricatores? Qui oderunt legem Dei, qui audiunt illam et non faciunt. *Facientes praevaricationem odio habui, non adhaesit mihi cor pravum.* Quod est cor pravum? Cor tortum. Quod est cor tortum? Cor non rectum. Quod est cor non rectum? Vide quod est cor rectum et ibi invenis quod est cor non rectum. Cor rectum dicitur hominis, qui omnia quae non vult Deus, ipse non vult. Ergo *non adhaesit mihi cor pravum. Cum declinaret a me malignus, non cognoscebam.* Quid est: non cognoscebam? Non approbabam, non laudabam, non mihi placebat. Cognoscere enim invenimus in scripturis aliquando dici, pro eo quod est placere nobis. Quid enim latet? Non enim latet Deum, et tamen dicturus est in finem impiis: non novi vos. Numquid ille non novit aliquem? Sed quid est: non novi vos? In regula mea non vos agnosco. Novi enim regulam iustitiae meae: non illi congruitis, declinastis ab illa, ergo cum declinaret a me malignus, non cognoscebam. Non quia nesciebam, sed quia non adprobabam.
I hated the workers of iniquities. Men are to be loved, so that their iniquities might be hated, since it is one thing to love the fact that they were made and another to hate what they make. *The perverse heart did not cleave to me. And the malignant that turned aside from me, I did not know.* 'I did not offer', he says 'consent to a perverse heart and I did not know the malignant one who fell from the spotless path, that I did not approve on account of our unlikeness'.	*I hated the workers of iniquities.* Who are the 'workers of iniquities'? Those who hate the law of God, who hear it, and do not act, are called workers of iniquities. *I hated the workers of iniquities. The perverse heart did not cleave to me.* What is 'the perverse heart'? A twisted heart. What is a twisted heart? A heart that is not upright. What is heart that is not upright? See what an upright heart is and there you will find what a heart that is not upright is. The heart of a man is said to be upright, when he wants everything that God wants, not what he wants. *The perverse heart did not cleave to me. And the malignant that turned aside from me, I did not know.* What does 'I did not know' mean? I did not approve, I did not praise, it did not please me. For we find 'to know' in Scripture sometimes meaning 'to please us'. For what escapes him? It does not escape God and nonetheless, at the end, he will say to the impious, *I will not know you.* But surely there is not someone he does not know. What does 'I will not know you' mean? 'I do not recognise you in my rule. For I know the rule of my justice. You have not conformed to it, you have fallen short of it', and therefore: '*when the malignant that turned aside from me*, I did not know them, not that I was unaware, but that I did not approve'.

TABLE 3.5 – EPITOMES OF PLINY

Pliny *HN* 20.67

In cholera quoque coctas [*sc.* lactucas] patinis dederunt, ad quod utilissimae quam maximi caulis et amarae. Quidam et lacte infundunt. Defervefacti hi caules et stomacho utilissimi traduntur, sicut somno aestiva maxime lactuca et amara lactensque, quam meconidem vocavimus. Hoc lacte et oculorum claritati cum muliebri lacte utilissimum esse praecipitur, dum tempestivo capite inunguantur oculi, et ad vitia, quae frigore in his facta sint.

For jaundice lettuces have been given, cooked in a pan, in which case it is those with the largest stalk and which are bitter that are the best: some persons infuse them in milk. These stalks boiled are remarkably good, it is said, for the stomach: the summer lettuce, too, more particularly, and the bitter, milky lettuce, of which we have already made mention as the *meconis*, have a soporific effect. This juice, in combination with breast milk, is said to be extremely beneficial to the eyesight, if applied to the head in good time; it is a remedy, too, for such maladies of the eyes as result from the action of cold. (Trans. Bostock and Riley 1855–1857, modified)

Another example of a text with multiple ancient epitomes is Augustine's *Enarrationes in psalmos*, mentioned above. The *Enarrationes* is an enormous text – the current critical edition sits in three large volumes – and hence was, in Gorman's words, 'an especially popular object for those who practised the epitomist's craft'.[110] Prosper produced an epitome of it, probably in the 420s or 430s, while another is extant, albeit unedited, in a sixth-century manuscript. Compare their versions with Augustine on vv. 3–4 of Psalm 100 (TABLE 3.4). These two condensations represent two very different approaches to epitomisation. Prosper is exiguous, at nine per cent of the original, where the *Lyons Epitome* is relatively generous at twenty-seven per cent. Prosper rewords and rephrases everything; the *Lyons Epitome* keeps to Augustine's own words, and where it innovates (as in *et tamen dicturus est in finem impiis*) it uses very Augustinian language.[111] The two epitomators were also interested in different parts of the main text. If one compares their comments on v. 3, *facientes praeuaricationem odio habui*, they have used different parts of Augustine's exegesis: the *Lyons Epitome* on the meaning of *praevaricator* and Prosper on the distinction between the *praevaricatio* and the person who does it.

A penultimate comparison is from Pliny epitomes. At *HN* 20.67, Pliny discusses the (surprising) medicinal uses of lettuce, and we can compare the original with the *De remediis salutaribus*, the *Medicina Plinii*, and Gargilius Martialis (TABLE 3.5). Yet again we see contrasting approaches to epitomisation. The *De remediis* gives us Pliny's own words, reduced to about thirty per cent of the original. The *Medicina* and Gargilius Martialis, in contrast, rephrase and simplify. They also clarify, giving more detail on the method of cooking. These differences correspond to different purposes. The *Medicina* and Martialis' work were practical texts – Cassiodorus recommends the latter as a useful reference work for a monastery (*Inst.* 1.28.5). Their purpose is not to provide a point of access for readers interested in Pliny, but rather to offer useful information for readers who had neither need of nor interest in delving into the massive

---

110 Gorman 1997: 67.

111 *cf.* Augustine, *Enarrationes in psalmos* 103.3: *et tamen dicturus est in fine quibusdam: non novi vos.*

De rem. sal. p. xxxvi Sillig	*Medicina Plinii* 2.7	Garg. Mart. *Med. ex holer.* 11.8–9
In colera quoque coctas patinis dederunt, ad quod utilissime quam maximi caulis et amare. Quidam et lacti [ḷẹti *cod.*] infundunt defervefacti[s].	Adversus quam [*sc.* choleram] lactucae caules quanto maiores et amariores in patina coquuntur ex aqua et sic eduntur.	Coctae [*sc.* lactucae] in patina aliorumque holerum more condita cholera laborantibus utilissime offeruntur. Quidam eas ad eandem causam cum lacte coxerunt.
For jaundice, lettuces have been given, cooked in a pan, in which case it is those with the largest stalk and which are bitter that are the best: some persons infuse them boiled in milk.	Against jaundice, the larger and more bitter stems of lettuce are cooked in a pan with water and are thus consumed.	Lettuce cooked in a pan, in the way other vegetables are, is very useful when offered to people suffering from jaundice. Some people cook them with milk for the same purpose.

Historia naturalis. For the same reason, both also occasionally include non-Plinian materials, even though the vast bulk of the two works comes directly from Pliny. The *De remediis*, however, despite the title, is clearly a direct condensation of Pliny, of use for readers who wanted to read him, but not quite at full length. This condensation comes at the expense of medicinal clarity: while the *De remediis* seems to imply that the lettuce infused in milk ought to be boiled, as a remedy against jaundice, Pliny actually says that heating or boiling lettuce is beneficial for the stomach. This means that, despite the manuscript title, this epitome is not actually about medicine at all: throughout the text, medical information is curtailed and obscured, while antiquarian material is reproduced at length. Indeed, sometimes the process of producing an epitome could even introduce error into a text. At 2.6.13, Valerius Maximus adduces the *exemplum* of the Lycians who put on women's garb when they were mourning. When Nepotianus hacked this down for his epitome he removed the opening phrase, which has the effect of attributing the custom to the Thracians, who are in fact the subject of the previous entry (2.6.12).

We can see from this, and indeed from other examples, how some epitomes drew only from a single source (category 1), while others incorporated other relevant material to supplement what they had found in the original (category 2). Again, the epitomes of Livy, Augustine, and Valerius Maximus are useful evidence of this. It is well known that Florus includes non-Livian material, even though his work is securely transmitted as an epitome of Livy, 'as if', Erasmus once said derisively, 'one could deny that Florus wrote an epitome of Titus Livy's *Histories*, just because he added something of his own'.[112] Likewise, Prosper also used external material in his epitomes of Augustine. His well-turned *aliud est amare quod facti sunt, aliud odisse quod faciunt* gets at the heart of what Augustine says about the verse, but is actually drawn from his own *Sententiae*.[113] Similarly, Martialis and the *Medicina Plinii* include material from outside Pliny. This phenomenon was by no means limited to those working with texts that others

---

112 Erasmus, *Apologia ad Fabrum, resp.* 1 n. 4 (trans. Rummel 2005: 91).

113 See Horsting 2016: 78.

TABLE 3.6 – ADDITIONS TO AN EPITOME

Valerius Maximus 2.5.5	Januarius Nepotianus 2.5.nov.5– 2.5.5
Fuit etiam illa simplicitas antiquorum in cibo capiendo humanitatis simul et continentiae certissima index: nam maximis viris prandere et cenare in propatulo verecundiae non erat. Nec sane ullas epulas habebant, quas populi oculis subicere erubescerent. Erant adeo continentiae adtenti, ut frequentior apud eos pultis usus quam panis esset, ideoque in sacrificiis mola quae vocatur ex farre et sale constat. Exta farre sparguntur et pullis, quibus auspicia petuntur, puls obicitur. Primitiis enim et libamentis victus sui deos eo efficacius quo simplicius placabant.	Nobili cuique quaestum facere turpe erat Romae. Apud Poenos vero vel turpiter lucrum facere honestum putabatur. Veteres Romani ad frugalitatem probandam pro foribus vescebantur et crebrius pulte quam pane.
The simplicity of the men of old in the taking of their meals is another sure sign both of good nature and of self-restraint. The greatest among them were not ashamed to take luncheon and dinner in the open. To be sure, they had no feasts that they blushed to expose to public gaze. So intent were they on self-restraint that they used more gruel than bread, and that is why the cake (*mola*, as it is called) at sacrifices consists of flour and salt, entrails are sprinkled with flour, and gruel is fed to the chickens from which the auspices are sought. For they placated the gods with first offerings and tastes of their own diet, the more simply, the more effectively. (Trans. Shackleton Bailey 2000: 1.163)	At Rome it was disgraceful for any noble to make a profit. Among the Carthaginians, however, it was thought honourable to make a profit, even in a disgraceful way. The ancient Romans, to demonstrate their frugality, ate out of doors and more often gruel than bread.

had written. In producing the *Epitome* of his own *Divine Institutes*, Lactantius took the opportunity to add a significant amount of material. This included substantial new quotations to illustrate his argument, some of them drawn from works that he had not used in the original – perhaps a reflection of his ongoing reading.[114]

A final example can illustrate this neatly. In his second book, Valerius Maximus offered readers a little resumé of the simple diet of the ancients. In his epitome, Januarius Nepotianus provided an economical summary of this, but added a telling little observation about the difference between prominent Romans and their Carthaginian counterparts (**TABLE 3.6**). Contrasting attitudes to commerce form no part of Valerius Maximus' text: it is an additional bit of material that Nepotianus thought useful to his readers. That does not make the result less of an epitome.

So, when it came to actually working through the text of the original, epitomes once again show themselves many and varied. Here, however, it is perhaps easier to fit them into a framework. There was, in essence, a spectrum of approaches to adapting the source, with the *ad verbum* method at one end (taking over the wording of the original) and the *ad sensum* at the other (rewriting entirely), with more mixed approaches in between. Each had different advantages and flaws. The *ad verbum* method ensured that the reader of the epitome got the full flavour of the style of the original: they were reading Pliny, for instance, just in shorter form. It ran the risk, however, of making the epitome hard to follow, even

114 Heck and Wlosok 1994: xxi–xxii collect these passages.
    See also Perrin 1987: 31–36.

incoherent: it is not easy to select a handful of individual sentences from a text, run them together and end up with a free-flowing and representative summary. The *ad sensum* approach, in contrast, guaranteed (or ought to have) a smooth and easy read. It could, however, lapse into a facile paraphrase, which left the reader with no sense of the style, vocabulary, and even ideas of the original. Besides these two methods, the parallels above show that epitomes varied a great deal in how much of the original they took over: some summarise a particular passage brutally, others give it much more space. They might also, however, be drawn independently to the same dramatic episode and give it a disproportionate place in their text. In the example above from Livy, Orgiago's wife plays a minor but dramatic role in the thirty-eighth book of the history. If we had only the epitomes, however, we might think she was its major character. Finally, the parallel passages also neatly illustrate the way that some epitomators were profoundly relaxed about adding a little here and there to their dominant source.

All this is very helpful for thinking about the two Victorine texts. We should be unsurprised that they are stylistically so different and consider it no impediment to their being derived from the same source. Equally, while it makes sense that they have often very different accounts of the same events (one will have summarised more drastically than the other), we can also see why they frequently coincide in what they have chosen to cover: epitomators' eyes were evidently often drawn to the same dramatic episodes. We ought also to accept that some material from other sources might have made its way into them, without in any way impugning their claim to be epitomes of Victor.

This means we can even say something about the text from which they were derived, at least for the first eleven chapters, where their overlaps are obvious and verbal. For this chunk, the *HAb* contains approximately 2,750 words while the *LB* has 2,600. Their verbatim overlaps consist of around 635 words. Hence, if they are epitomes, the text from which they were derived ought to have covered the emperors from Augustus to Domitian in an absolute minimum of 11,260 words (the product of 2,750 and 2,600, divided by 635). Such a number, as we have seen with the Valerius Maximus epitomes, is probably a substantial under-count (although likely by no more than a factor of two) since even two independent epitomators would be drawn to some of the same material, such as the basic biographical facts of origin, reign, and death. More likely, we are looking at a text of 18,000–20,000 words in length – *i.e.* quite a bit shorter than Suetonius on the same emperors (*ca.* 60,000 words) but still substantial.

In this chapter, we have been concerned with condensed works in Latin: they are obviously the relevant framework for the Victorine texts. It is worth noting, however, that much, perhaps all, of what we have said above could be extended to Greek texts. If study of Latin epitomes has been retarded by the forbidding quantity of evidence and its obscurity, then those are even greater obstacles to approaching condensed texts in Greek: it is simply not possible here to give them even the kind of survey we have attempted above. We might, however, note some particularly important continuities. Greek historical works also have a fragile transmission. We are lucky to have Herodotus and Thucydides more or less complete, but we have only parts of Polybius, Dionysius of Halicarnassus, Diodorus Siculus, Nicolaus of Damascus, and Cassius Dio, not to mention the serried ranks of Hellenistic historians whose works barely survive at all. For some of these lost histories, we have surviving epitomes: Cassius Dio is partially preserved in Xiphilinus, for instance, and portions of Polybius in the so-called *Excerpta antiqua*.[115] Where we can compare original and epitome, much of what we have said above applies: Xiphilinus' choices, for example, are sometimes idiosyncratic and his coverage is patchy; he was also not averse to adding material.[116] Above all, he has recast Dio's annalistic history from Rome's foundation to his own day into a basically biographical account of the period from Pompey onwards, as though the era of the first triumvirate marked a transition, after which only biography could capture the nature of events.[117] For the grand historians who followed Dio (besides Herodian) – Dexippus, Eunapius, Priscus, and others – what we know of their work is substantially derived from the Byzantine *Excerpta* prepared for Constantine VII Porphyrogenitus in the middle of the tenth century.[118] As with Latin historical texts, Greek epitomes served as a complement as often as a replacement: there is a good case to be made that the Emperor Julian, for instance, read his Plutarch at least partly through the moralising *breviarium* of Damophilus of Bithynia.[119] The Greek epitome is a subject that deserves more leisurely attention than we can give it, but it seems likely that that study would reinforce much of what we have said here.

Even for Latin epitomes, this survey has been able to discuss only a fraction of the very rich evidence for them and it has generally found that that evidence supports the (rather uncontroversial) idea that the genre of epitome was extraordinarily varied. That said, while none of this allows us to lay down hard-and-fast rules for what the average epitome might have looked like, it does allow us to establish what we might call the range of plausible variation for such texts: the limits and some of the common features of the genre. While any condensed text might be an *epitome*, a *liber (ab)breviatus* was a summary of a single longer work by a single author. Epitomes had to be produced from multi-book works: three *libri* at an absolute minimum, five or six more generally the lower bound. They might be created for things which had only very recently been written, and two (or more) might coexist for the same original. Histories were particularly prone to being condensed. Epitomes might be designed to replace the original, supplement it, or provide a guide to it. They were unlikely to represent less than about three per cent of a very long work or more than thirty per cent of a somewhat shorter one, falling (most plausibly) somewhere in the middle: the main constraint on their length in late antiquity seems often to have been the need to cram them into a single-quire codex, or the degree to which the epitomator could keep enthusiasm for the project aflame. Finally, they need to be handled with care. 'Ability to pick out the essential elements in a story or a description and to condense it accurately was as rare among them as among the less talented students we may teach today', Brunt wrote of the writers of historical epitomes:

> They were therefore at their best when they chose to excerpt or paraphrase their authorities. Unfortunately their choice was too often determined not by the importance of the matters they enlarged on but by their value for entertainment.[120]

---

115 On the *Excerpta antiqua*, see part II of Moore 1965.
116 For the supplemental material, see Brunt 1980: 489.
117 On Xiphilinus, see Mallan 2013. On Dio's annalistic structure, see Rich 2016. See also Mallan 2017 on the book indices, which would give us a sense of the structure of the original, even if we were reliant on Xiphilinus alone.
118 See Németh 2018.
119 Van Hoof and Van Nuffelen 2013, and below, Chapter V.
120 Brunt 1980: 493.

As valuable as epitomes sometimes are as witnesses to their source texts, they can conceal as much as they reveal. Some adopt the wording of their model entirely; some rework it extensively. Some hew closely to their source; some are peppered with information from elsewhere. Some maintain the structure of the original; some recast it entirely according to a different scheme. Some offer a general and fair sampling of their source's scope; others focus on small parts, obscuring the thrust of the original. We can see all of these practices in cases where we have the original to compare. Where we do not, we should be clear-eyed about the limitations of the epitomes we do have and recognise that our access to their sources is necessarily limited, in ways that we cannot always accurately gauge. In other words, we should be cautious in making confident judgements about lost texts on the basis of epitomes alone.

A survey of the Latin epitome has taken us a little way from the ostensible subject of this book. Yet an understanding of the genre of epitomes is vital to any attempt to make sense of the two Victorine texts. Going all the way back to the first attempts to systematically analyse and categorise them (which we will delve into later), a consensus developed that neither text could be an epitome because they did not fit correctly into the generic category.[121] By analysing the genre at greater length and breadth here, it is easy to see that it offers no *a priori* reason to say that the texts are not exactly what they purport to be. The titles they are known by in the manuscripts, *Aurelii Victoris Historiae abbreviatae* and *Libellus breviatus ex libris Sex. Aurelii Victoris*, find ample parallel in other condensed texts. Moreover, they both mean the same thing: a multi-book work by one Aurelius Victor, entitled either *Historiae* or dealing with history, presented in condensed form. Neither should be understood as a *breviarium*, or a summary treatment of history, authored by Aurelius Victor. The differences between them – differences of content, coverage, style, and wording – are of the same order as that found in other cases where we have multiple epitomes of the same work. Indeed, thinking of them as epitomes might pay even greater dividends: can epitomisation explain why the two texts attributed to Victor, the *Historiae abbreviatae* and the *Libellus breviatus*, are so unsatisfactory as works of history (especially the former), and why both are peculiar productions in different ways? All we have shown here is that there is no reason to reject their self-description as epitomes. To make progress on the deeper question, we need to delve more deeply into the texts themselves.

121 Chapter VI.

CHAPTER IV

THE NATURE OF VICTOR'S *HISTORY*

Reading Victor is a challenge, which the first English translator of the *Historiae abbreviatae* described as 'a fascinating, and admittedly often frustrating, bout with the innumerable non sequiturs, trivial details, inexplicable hints and allusions characteristic of the epitomes'.[1] The task is rendered slightly easier by the progress made so far on the transmission of the Victorine works (Chapter II) and on the broader genre of epitome (Chapter III). First, we have established that the *Historiae abbreviatae* and *Libellus breviatus* are both presented in the manuscripts as condensed texts: epitomes of a longer, multi-book work by Aurelius Victor. Second, we have seen that there are some strong reasons to accept these claims, principally that whoever composed the titles and paratexts of both works had access to recondite information about Victor that could not have been deduced from study of the *HAb* or *LB* as we have them. Third, we have shown that the notion that both works are condensed texts is entirely compatible with what we can deduce about the genre of epitome in the Latin literature of antiquity.

With these considerations firmly in mind, we can now turn to examining the two works themselves in greater detail. In this chapter, we attempt to set out to what can be deduced from them about the literary culture, in the broadest sense, of Sextus Aurelius Victor and the extent to which that aligns with or modifies the conclusions we have so far drawn. We begin with, and devote the most attention to, the *HAb*, both because the text is universally acknowledged to have been written by Victor and because it has never received the kind of systematic analysis that it deserves. We then turn to the *LB*, a very different kind of text and one that has been more intensively studied, to see what we can learn from its nature and how it compares to that of the *HAb*.

The *Historiae abbreviatae*

For a supposedly minor Roman historian, Victor is an unusually chatty author: Festus and Eutropius are largely devoid of personality.[2] In contrast, throughout the *Historiae abbreviatae*, a distinct and consistent picture of Victor emerges, as he repeatedly explains to the reader both what he is doing and why he has done it.[3] At a minimum, Victor assumes the persona of someone writing a grave and learned work of proper history: someone who took research seriously, gloried in the recondite and the pedantic, and aspired to Latin style. Close attention to what Victor wrote does indeed reveal traces of considerable

---

1 Echols 1962: vi–vii.
2 Outside of the prefaces that we have discussed (Chapter III). See further below.
3 There are twelve first-person pronouns in the *HAb*, nine of them clear references to Victor himself. Singular: *HAb*

5.9, 11.13, 20.5, 13, 28.9, 39.7. Plural: 14.9, 20.10, 39.48. *HAb* 39.37 is in the sense 'we the Romans'; at 13.9 *mihi* and *me* are in the direct speech of Trajan. This is of course without even broaching the considerable number of verbs in the first person (both singular and plural).

erudition and intricate style. Yet, none of what he says about his project, none of the signs of the careful and deliberate historian its author aspired to be, suits the text we actually have. Read straight, the *HAb* is a work whose many infelicities, obscurities, and abrupt changes of direction should long have made scholars suspicious about its nature.

That it has generally not stirred up doubts is explained by the way in which it has customarily been read: as part of a broader tradition of texts that can be lumped together or split apart as needed to create a reasonably coherent narrative.[4] In modern discussions of fourth-century historiography, the individual contributions of the breviarists (so-called) tend to blur one into the other (a pernicious consequence of the *Kaisergeschichte*). Even so, Eutropius, Festus, and the *Libellus breviatus* have all been the subject of studies that paid close attention to their idiosyncrasies and information.[5] Victor, universally regarded as the oddest of the bunch, has in contrast never received such treatment. 'A need exists for a proper elucidation of Aurelius Victor', T.D. Barnes wrote in 1976.[6] The situation has scarcely improved since then.[7] That neglect has done much to obscure the strangeness of the *HAb*. We can see what is really going on only if we read the text as it actually is, resisting the historicising impulse to fill in the blanks and solve the problems which its current condition presents. Put bluntly, close examination reveals that there is a radical incompatibility between what the *HAb* is and what Victor clearly meant his history to be.

Victor's claims about his *History*

The first glaring example of this incompatibility comes just a few pages in. After relating the grisly fate of Vitellius, Victor turns aside to ruminate on what the end of the Julio-Claudians revealed about Roman history (*HAb* 8.7–8):

> Hi omnes, quos **paucis attigi,** praecipueque Caesarum gens adeo litteris culti atque eloquentia fuere, ut, ni cunctis vitiis absque Augusto nimii forent, tantae artes profecto texissent modica flagitia. Quis rebus quamquam satis constet praestare mores, tamen bono cuique praesertim summo rectori, utroque (si queat) iuxta opus: sin aliter, vitae proposito immensum regrediente elegantiae saltem atque eruditionis sumat auctoritatem.

> All these, whom **I have touched upon in a few words**, especially the race of the Caesars, were so cultivated in letters and eloquence that, if they had not been excessive in all their vices (apart from Augustus), such great skills would have doubtless veiled modest disgraces. In these matters, although it is well enough agreed that morals are important, nevertheless it is necessary for each good man, and especially for the highest ruler, to be both – if he is able. Otherwise, at least they might enjoy the authority of elegance and learning, when their mode of life declines to a great degree.

This is one of the most explicit historiographical statements that Victor makes: it prepares the reader for the work's moralising themes and almost obsessive interest in literary culture.[8] Victor is quite clear that he

---

4 Chapter I.
5 For Festus, see *e.g.* Eadie 1967, Kelly 2010. Eutropius is widely regarded as the author closest to the supposed *Kaisergeschichte* and has been extensively studied in that context (Chapter VI). For the *LB*, see below.

6 Barnes 1976a: 258. *cf.* in general Müller 1998–1999, who calls for a radical reassessment of Victor's literary culture.
7 Bird 1984 is little more than an extended article and barely scratches the surface. See also Hayashi 2017.
8 On which see *e.g.* Bird 1984: 116–121, 71–80.

has cantered through these emperors (whose lives were already well known from a variety of sources) at a fast clip, because his primary interest lies in drawing out moral lessons, not narrating events. He is setting the stage for the *principes* to follow, who will (by implication) receive much more detailed treatment. Hence, he says, he has touched upon the Julio-Claudians 'in a few words' (*paucis attigi*). Yet, this statement flatly contradicts the text of the *HAb*. It is specifically wrong, for the lives of Caligula, Claudius, and Nero are among the longest in the work (*ca.* 480, 400, and 420 words), each exceeding those given to all the subsequent emperors down to the Tetrarchy, with the exception of Septimius Severus and Gallienus (the two longest, at *ca.* 770 and 790 words). It is also generally incorrect, for the lives down to AD 69 represent just under twenty per cent of the entire work (a little under 2,000 words). The considerably more numerous emperors from Vespasian to Carinus are covered in the next fifty-five per cent (*ca.* 5,900 words). The Tetrarchs to Constantius II consume in the final sections twenty-five per cent of the whole (*ca.* 2,700 words). In other words, the nine emperors down to Vitellius receive proportionately more coverage than the (approximately) thirty-five who followed them until Diocletian and only slightly less than the emperors of Victor's own lifetime. For the emperors from AD 69 to 284 the disparity is even greater than these raw numbers suggest, because, between them, Septimius Severus, Gallienus, and Aurelian make up eighteen per cent of the whole work (*ca.* 1,900 words). This means that those first nine emperors receive considerably more attention than thirty-two of the following thirty-five. As pedantic as these calculations might seem, what they demonstrate very clearly is that Victor's explicit statement of what he is doing and the nature of the work as we have it are incompatible.

The same conclusion emerges from everything else that Victor tells us about his methods and his approach. As is obvious from his discussion of the Julio-Claudians, Victor is one of history's great advocates for a liberal education, idiosyncratically using education (and sometimes education alone) as the yardstick for measuring emperors, rather than (say) political effectiveness or moral character.[9] He was proud that his intellectual achievements had raised him from a humble background to a position of some prestige, as a reflection on the unsuccessful attempt of Septimius Severus to erase the memory of the jurist Salvius Julianus reveals (*HAb* 20.2–5):

> The influence of a liberal education is so strong, that not even brutish characters prevent writers from being remembered. Moreover, a memory of this sort is the cause of glory to those who have it, and of blame to those who have attacked it, since everyone, and especially posterity, believes that such talents could not have been destroyed except by public lawlessness and through madness. All good men should have confidence in this, and especially I myself, who though born on a farm to a poor and uneducated father, have in these times achieved a more honourable mode of life, thanks to liberal studies such as these.[10]

It is no surprise that an educated man would produce an educated history. Victor is quite clear that he conducted considerable research to assemble the work. When he comes to the two Macrini, he says (almost apologetically) (*HAb* 22.3): 'I have discovered (*reperimus*) nothing about them, except that they

---

9 For instance, *HAb* 41.26, where Vetranio is described as 'the worst (*pessimus*) on account of his peasant stupidity'. Few others in antiquity thought that Vetranio (for all his faults) was the worst emperor.

10 On this passage see Müller 1998–1999: 415–417; Chapter I.

had savage and uncivil spirits'. *Reperio* suggests more than casual inquiry – it implies an active process of hunting for source material, which here came up short.[11]

This is far from the only such claim in the work. When discussing the achievements of Constantius II, close to the end of the *HAb*, Victor says (*HAb* 42.22) that he has 'discovered' (*conperimus*) that Pompey the Great restored the Armenian king Tigranes to his throne, something that scarcely even a few of the ancients did. The fact about Pompey is not particularly recondite – it is in Florus (2.32), for instance – so Victor's emphatic statement here might seem rather surprising. On closer inspection, he is making a very precise point:

> When by his [*sc.* Constantius'] arms the tyranny of such formidable men had been driven out and meanwhile an attack by the Persians had been endured, he appointed a king for the Sarmatian people, sitting among them (*considens apud eos*) with great honour. I have discovered that Gnaeus Pompey did this when he restored Tigranes, but very few other of our ancestors.

Constantius made Zizais king of the Sarmatians while they were actually gathered before him.[12] Similarly, the restoration of Tigranes to his throne (like his surrender) was a personal act in the presence of Pompey himself.[13] This initially rather colourless claim turns out to be an example of real erudition and careful investigation.

Victor's research was not, however, limited to hunting down recondite details. At the death of Domitian, he paused to consider the question of whether the integration of foreigners into the Roman polity had strengthened or weakened it. What he says asserts that he had done careful and general research to write his *Historia* (*HAb* 11.13):

> And indeed to me, *based on the many things I have heard and read*, it is completely obvious that the city of Rome has in particular grown great by the virtue and transplanted talents of outsiders.

These are not the words of a man who had lightly skimmed a few recent summaries of Rome's past as preparation for his own unambitious work.

What is particularly striking about these three claims to detailed investigation of Roman history is that none relates to Victor's primary concerns as a historian of the Roman Empire. The Macrini were, even by third-century standards, short-lived emperors.[14] Pompey the Great is obviously important but, equally obviously, he is rather outside the scope of an imperial history. The question of Rome's greatness and the role of foreign transplants in it is an interesting one, but the story of the city's rise was largely one of the Republic. If Victor carefully probed things that were peripheral to his project, what does that imply about his study of more central topics? There are no similar claims of research in Eutropius or Festus, so in this respect Victor's work resembles those of the great historians of antiquity and indeed the *Res gestae* of his contemporary Ammianus.[15] The *HAb* is clearly not that.

---

11 Hence, for instance, why Jerome was so keen on using the word in his commentaries: *In Isaiam* 4.10.28, 4.11.1, 5.23.1, 15.54.11, 17.63.8 *e.g.*

12 Somewhat unwisely; *cf.* the account in Ammianus 17.12.17–20 (see further Chapter IX).

13 Appian, *Hist. Rom.* 12.104–105.

14 Kienast 2004: 169–171.

15 *cf.* for *conperimus* AM 25.10.13 (comparison of the deaths of Jovian and Scipio Aemilianus), 31.2.1 (prefacing the lengthy digression on the Huns), 31.13.17 (the fate of one of the Scipios); Tacitus, *Ann.* 6.10.3. *Repperi*: Tacitus, *Ann.* 4.53.2, 6.7.4. As we have said, Eutropius and Festus generally avoid first person statements of this kind.

Victor's facts

One might riposte that Victor exaggerated the seriousness of his work and the depths of his research – that he was different from his peers in tone, but not in fact. That, however, would be a mistake, for close examination shows that Victor was telling the truth, at least in part, about the pains he had taken to research his work. If we bring the *HAb* into sharper focus, we can make out a large number of independently verifiable facts unique to it.

Names are a good place to start. Well-born Romans of the third and fourth centuries generally had complex names reflecting a variety of family connections, blending what would earlier have been examples of the *nomen gentile* and the cognomen. Our best evidence for these full names is provided by honorific inscriptions (and, for emperors, coins). For most purposes, however, high-status individuals were referred to by only one, or at most two, names: in his letters, Symmachus almost always refers to people by a single name, but in consular *formulae* two appear to have been standard. The name that was always used was the final one, sometimes referred to as the diacritic (that is, the individuating name): that an individual was always referred to by at least this name was as close as later-Roman onomastics came to an iron law.[16] This was supplemented occasionally by one of the numerous family names that elite Romans bore, always placed before the diacritic.[17] In our literary sources, reference is almost always by the diacritic alone and dual names are few and far between. Most fourth-century historians use only a handful of them, often for figures from Rome's past dragged in as *exempla*, amidst a sea of individuals referred to by single names. Reference to actual figures of the third and fourth centuries by more than one of their names is rare indeed.[18]

Victor cuts against many of these trends. Set against the fourth-century Latin historians, the *HAb* is unusual both in the number of dual names that it uses and in how often it uses them for individuals of the third and fourth centuries. For example, of the Augusti from Macrinus to the first Tetrarchy that the text mentions and presents as such, around half are introduced by two or more names.[19] Nor was this simply a mark of formality at their first appearance. Victor was perfectly happy, when describing the cut and thrust of events, to revert to the more typical single name, but occasionally an emperor suddenly appears again with two. So, for example, Constantius II is generally Constantius in the *HAb*, but is called Julius Constantius (*HAb* 42.20) as the work draws to a close.[20] Victor has a still stranger quirk than this: he varied the single name by which he referred to an individual, using sometimes their last (diacritical) name and sometimes one of their other names (normally a *gentilicium*). So, the emperor whose full name was C. Aurelius Valerius Diocletianus is sometimes just plain Diocletianus (*HAb* 39.11, 25), but is actually

---

16 *Signa*, and other nicknames, present a limited exception to this rule (see Woudhuysen 2019), but it was in general strictly obeyed. On the rarity of oscillation of the diacritic, as it has been termed, see Cameron 1985.

17 For this simplified sketch, see Woudhuysen 2019; Stover and Woudhuysen 2022a.

18 Stover and Woudhuysen 2022a.

19 Two or more: Opilius Macrinus (*HAb* 22.1), Marcus Antoninus (23.1), Aurelius Alexander (24.1), Gaius Julius Maximinus (25.1), Antonius Gordianus (26.1),

Clodius Pupienus and Caelius Balbinus (26.6), Marcus Julius Philippus (28.1), Aemilius Aemilianus (31.1), Licinius Valerianus (32.1), Licinius Gallienus (33.1), Valerius Diocletianus (39.1), Julius Constantius and Galerius Maximianus (39.24). One: Gordian III (27.1), Philippus (the Younger, 28.1), Decius (29.1), Gallus and Hostilianus (30.1), Claudius (34.1), Aurelian (35.1), Tacitus (36.1), Florianus (36.2), Probus (37.2), Carus, Carinus, and Numerian (38.1), Maximian (39.17).

20 Compare Julius Maximinus at *HAb* 27.3.

more often referred to as Valerius (39.8, 13, 18, 29, 30, 36, 46).[21] Constantine is generally Constantinus, but sometimes Flavius (*HAb* 40.26, 41.2, 6, 42.6). Septimius Severus and Opilius Macrinus (as Victor called him) receive the same treatment.[22] It is difficult to overstate how atypical this was: it looks back to the era of Tacitus, if not of Cicero and Caesar, when an individual might naturally be referred to in different contexts by their cognomen or the *nomen* alone.[23]

It is not merely the case, however, that Victor had slightly archaising tastes in the way that he used names. His enthusiasm for dual names shows off a remarkable knowledge of onomastic obscurities. Pupienus and Balbinus, the elderly senatorial chaperones to Gordian III in the great crisis of 238, were, in full, Marcus Clodius Pupienus Maximus and Decimus Caelius Calvinus Balbinus.[24] The manuscripts of the *HAb* (26.7) call them Clodius Pupienus/Cupienus and Caecilius Balbinus – mangled, but clearly reflecting knowledge of their genuine nomenclature, knowledge that no other source shows.[25] The emperor Gallienus was, properly, P. Licinius Egnatius Gallienus, and Victor, alone of Latin literary sources, calls him Licinius Gallienus.[26] Only Victor knew that the *nomen* of Diocletian was Valerius. Still more impressive is the *HAb*'s awareness that the ephemeral emperor Aemilianus, on the throne for mere months in 253, had the *nomen* Aemilius.[27] Nor was Victor's interest in names confined to those who held imperial power: he knew that the jurist Ulpian was a Domitius, information preserved in Greek and in the *Digest*, but scarcely elsewhere in Latin.[28] The *HAb* is the only Latin literary text to know that the prominent senator Volusianus, servant of Maxentius and then Constantine, had the *nomen* Rufius (*HAb* 40.18).[29] Victor is also the only author who shows any awareness that Constantius II bore the name Julius. These are small details, but they are also very learned touches.[30]

This onomastic interest extended beyond a slightly pedantic desire for fullness and precision: Victor was extremely sensitive to the use and interpretation of names. Consider his introduction of the emperor Nero: 'Lucius Domitius, for that certainly was Nero's *nomen*, since his father was Domitius'.[31] Here, Victor shows a typically pedantic attention to the details of nomenclature, for no other fourth-century author

21 *PLRE* 'Diocletianus 2'.

22 Septimius: *HAb* 20.1, 24.8. Opilius: 23.3.

23 For Tacitus, the best guide remains Fabia 1900 (see *e.g.*, 60, Antistius Sosianus, who appears under that dual name, but also as Antistius and Sosianus). For Cicero, see Adams 1978. For Caesar, see the pair highlighted by Steele 1918: 113, L. Aurunculeius Cotta and Q. Titurius Sabinus, who appear as both Aurunculeius and Titurius (*BG* 6.32.4) and Cotta and Sabinus (5.52.4).

24 Peachin 1990: 150–156; *PIR*² C.126, 1179.

25 The reading of Pupienus' name is a problem: in both **o** and **p** it is Cupienus, but **o** (f. 140r) has a gap and what appears to be an erased initial 'p'. A variant in or correction to the archetype might explain this. *cf. HAb* 27.6: 'Clodio Caecilioque'. The *HA Gord.* calls them *Maximinus sive Puppeienus et Clodius Albinus* (10.1, *sic*) and *Puppienum sive Maximum et Clodium Balbinum* (22.1). The error of Caeculius for Caelius in the *HAb* may have arisen through contamination with the Caecilius Balbus, who features prominently in the immensely popular *Policraticus* of John of Salisbury.

26 *PLRE* 'Gallienus 1'; *HAb* 33.1. In Greek, the heading of a letter preserved in Eusebius, *HE* 7.13.1 gives the name, as does Malalas 12.38.

27 *HAb* 31.1; Peachin 1990: 292–295; *PIR*² A.330.

28 *HAb* 24.6, *cf. Digest* 19.1.43; Cassius Dio 80.1.1, Zonaras 12.15. The *HA Alex.* 68.1 also knew the name, but is widely acknowledged to have drawn on Victor for that *Vita* (*e.g.* Chastagnol 1967). Lactantius, *DI* 5.11.19 does refer to the *De officio proconsulis* of Domitius, but never calls him Ulpian.

29 *PLRE* 'Volusianus 4'.

30 Victor appears to make one howler in saying that the emperor Pertinax was called Aulus (not Publius) Helvius Pertinax. The explanation for this is, however, almost certainly palaeographical corruption in transmission: see the Appendix to the present book.

31 *HAb* 5.1: *L. Domitius, nam id certe nomen Neroni, patre Domitio, erat*. For the text here, see the Appendix to the present book, no. I.

refers to the emperor by his birth name. He also, however, demonstrates (with a rather casual parenthesis) that he understood the principles on which the traditional system of *tria nomina* worked, with children receiving the *gentilicium* of their father, even though it was antiquated by the fourth century, of interest primarily to grammarians.[32] In the same vein, Victor refers to both Marcus Aurelius and Lucius Verus by their *praenomina* in his discussion of their dealings with each other (16.5–8).[33] In the most traditional form of the *tria nomina*, brothers might share a *gentilicium* and cognomen, being distinguished only by their *praenomen*.[34] This pattern was completely archaic by the fourth century, but Victor was clearly aware of it.

The names of Nero, Marcus Aurelius, and Lucius Verus were matters of some complexity, because they had of course all been adopted.[35] As is well known, Roman adoption often involved the person adopted taking over the nomenclature of their new parent.[36] It has largely escaped notice, but Victor took extraordinary care over such cases. That is why, when alluding to the marriage of Tiberius and Julia, he called Augustus' successor Tiberius Nero (*HAb* 39.25), for the couple married in 11 BC, but Tiberius was adopted only in AD 4. It is for the same reason that Victor calls Antoninus Pius 'T. Aelius Antoninus' at his accession (*HAb* 15.1), for he had been adopted by the emperor Hadrian.[37] Similarly, he introduces Marcus Aurelius as M. Boionius (*HAb* 16.1), a reminder of his adoption by Antoninus Pius, who as a *privatus* had borne that name.[38] In line with this interest in how names changed, Victor alone among Latin sources explains how and why Diocletian and Maximian took the *signa* 'Jovius' and 'Herculius' (respectively), names also given to the army's crack regiments (*HAb* 39.18).[39] Maximian is termed 'Herculius' in many other Latin works, but none of them ever stops to explain why: Eutropius, for instance, uses the name throughout his Books IX and X without any gloss whatsoever.

Another indication of Victor's close attention to names and their significance is a curious quirk that Gavin Kelly first identified in Ammianus: his use of *nomine* after some names that could in any way be mistaken for a normal Latin word.[40] No other fourth-century historian, however, not even Ammianus, does this with the consistency of Victor: it looks very much like his innovation.[41] So, Trajan's praetorian prefect is *Suburanum nomine*, lest anyone mistake him for an inhabitant of the valley in Rome (*HAb* 13.9). A gladiator who boldly stood up to Commodus was *Scaeva nomine* to avoid confusion with being on the

---

32 See Salway 1994: esp. 127–128. Nero's father was Cn. Domitius Ahenobarbus (*PIR*[2] D.127), but in antiquity there were those who believed his *praenomen* to have been Lucius: Suetonius, *Galba* 6.1 (if the text is sound), Josephus, *Antiquitates* 20.149 (who says Nero was ὁμώνυμον τῷ πατρί), *Scholia in Iuvenalem* 1.155 (Wessner 16). Traditionally, the eldest son received both the *nomen* and the *praenomen* of his father. It seems that the Domitii Ahenobarbi, who famously had few sons (Velleius 2.10.2), in fact alternated between Lucius and Gnaeus down the generations, as Suetonius says (*Nero* 1.2) – the error may have arisen from the assumption that they followed the more usual custom. It is thus possible that Victor too thought Nero's father was L. Domitius and was making an even more precise (though erroneous) point about Nero's names than is obvious.

33 On this passage, see further Chapter IV.

34 Salway 1994: 127.

35 *PIR*[2] D.129 for basic details.

36 The most detailed study of this phenomenon is Salomies 1992, who assembles a vast mass of evidence for the late Republic and Principate.

37 See the Appendix, no. III.

38 Salomies 1992: 75–76.

39 On *signa* see Woudhuysen 2019. Zosimus 3.30.2 has the same idea (see Chapter X for their relationship).

40 Kelly 2015 (a blog-post – a fuller study is in preparation). It also seems likely (as Kelly has suggested to us) that Ammianus sometimes uses *nomine* merely to point out a noteworthy name, or at a name's first appearance in the text.

41 Festus never uses *nomine*. Ammianus does very frequently, but not always in the same fashion as Victor (*e.g.* 17.10.5: *Hortari nomine*). Eutropius offers one possible example (4.6.2: *Gentium nomine*).

left (*HAb* 17.5).[42] The son and co-emperor of the ephemeral Macrinus is *Diadumenus nomine* (*HAb* 22.1), possibly just to show off Victor's knowledge of the very rare word meaning 'wearing a diadem' – his name was really Diadumenianus.[43] The mother of Severus Alexander was *nomine Mammaea* (*HAb* 24.5), to avoid the unwary reader thinking Victor was commenting on her appearance.[44] Examples could easily be multiplied.[45] The phenomenon even crossed the linguistic divide between Greek and Latin, so Carinus' (possibly treacherous) praetorian prefect is *nomine Aristobulus*, lest one think Victor regarded him as a wise counsellor (*HAb* 39.14). Of course, it seems most unlikely that Victor seriously thought his readers were at risk of confusion when confronted by many of these names: the point was, presumably, to illustrate his own free-wheeling erudition. It is curious to note that Diadumenus became established as the name of Macrinus' son in the Latin tradition, though no other text ever even winks at its falsity.[46]

Victor knew more than names, however. At the hinge between the reigns of Caligula and Claudius there was a failure of the *annona* (food supply) at Rome: Victor is the only Latin source to record this.[47] Victor gives the *nomen*, the background, and the rank of the soldier – Vimius, a centurion from Epirus – who found the cowering Claudius after the assassination of Caligula. The detail he offers contradicts and supplements the information available in Josephus (who says he was a στρατιώτης and gives a cognomen, Gratus) and Suetonius (who gives no name, but says he was a *miles gregarius*).[48] That Plotina, Trajan's wife, was responsible for Hadrian being made her husband's heir is attested only by Victor and Cassius Dio.[49] Numerous sources mention an *Athenaeum* at Rome, but only Victor says that Hadrian built it. Excavations in anticipation of the construction of Line C of Rome's Metro have turned up a building plausibly identified with the *Athenaeum*: brick stamps give a Hadrianic date.[50] In his description of Septimius Severus' campaigns in Britain, Victor calls York a *municipium* (*HAb* 20.27). By AD 237 at the latest, it was a *colonia*, but there are very good reasons to think that it had indeed obtained municipal status before its promotion.[51] Victor says that Caracalla defeated the Alamanni near the river Main (*HAb* 21.2). Cassius Dio clearly said something about the campaign, for fragments survive, but an inscription confirms Victor's location.[52] Victor is the only late-antique source to correctly locate the city founded by Philip the Arab, Philippopolis, in Arabia: a cluster of inscriptions secures the site.[53] That that emperor's son was killed in

---

42 The use of *nomine* almost by itself guarantees the correctness of Schott's conjecture here.

43 The common noun *diadumenus* is a vanishingly rare Hellenism for 'crowned', found only in Seneca, *Ep.* 65.5 and Pliny the Elder, *HN* 34.55.5; see *TLL* 5.1.947.12–15 (Gudeman). Diadumenianus: amply attested in inscriptions despite many efforts to delete it, *e.g. CIL* 11.6116 (Umbria); *PIR*[2] O.107. On Diadumenus, see further Chapter VIII.

44 The actual adjectives are *mammeata* and *mammosa*; but *cf.* for example, Servius, *Ad Georg.* 2.5: *Pampineo pro pampinoso, ut 'nemus frondeum' pro 'frondosum'.*

45 *HAb* 29.1: *Etruscum nomine*; 33.6: *Pipae nomine*; 39.4: *Allectus nomine*; 41.13: *Constans nomine.*

46 Eutropius 8.21; Orosius 7.18.3; *HA passim. cf.* Chapter VIII.

47 *HAb* 4.3; Cassius Dio 60.11.1 (*cf.* Suetonius, *Claud.* 18.1). *n.b.* that only Victor links this to Caligula's activities in the Bay of Naples

48 *HAb* 3.16; Josephus, *Antiquitates* 19.217; Suetonius, *Claud.* 10.2. In fourth-century usage, a *centurio* was not a *miles gregarius*: Jerome, *In Isaiam* 17.60.17. The name may perhaps be Vin(n)ius, for Vimius is extremely rare (Lőrincz 2002: 170).

49 *HAb* 13.13; Dio 49.1.1–4.

50 *HAb* 14.3; Dio 64.17.4; *HA Pert.* 11.3; Sidonius, *Ep.* 2.9.4, 9.14.2. Excavations: Egidi 2010.

51 *Colonia*: Courteault 1921. Municipal status: Mason 1988: 187–188.

52 Dio 78.13.4–6. *CIL* 6.2086: *per limitem Raetiae ad hostes extirpandos.*

53 *HAb* 28.1. *IGRRP* 3.1196 (dedicated to Philip; year 1 of the city), 1999, 1200 (both seemingly in honour of Marinus, father of Philip). Jerome, *Chron.* 217[g] places the city in Thrace (confusion with the more famous Philippopolis). There is a much later Greek tradition (Zonaras 12.19 *e.g.*) that locates his foundation near Bostra in Arabia.

the camp of the Praetorian Guard appears only in Victor and the *Chronography of 354*.[54] Victor tells us that the short-lived emperor Decius spent some time at Rome early in his reign in order to dedicate buildings there (*HAb* 29.1). No other literary source reveals this visit, but coins of Decius minted at Rome with the legend *ADVENTUS AUGUSTI* survive.[55] Famously, Victor alone claims that Gallienus forbade senators from holding military commands, a measure he perhaps once terms an edict.[56] He may have exaggerated the finality and legal character of this measure, but it is absolutely true that senators generally ceased to hold important military commands suddenly during the reign of that most unfortunate emperor.[57] Only Victor and Zosimus record that Aureolus was a commander in northern Italy or Raetia before his attempt to seize power, the usurpation that ultimately brought down Gallienus.[58]

Victor alone gives the name of the killer of the Gallic usurper Victorinus – Atticianus, rare but attested.[59] He knew that the emperor Tacitus had been consul before he obtained the purple (*HAb* 36.1). Inscriptions show that he must be right.[60] Victor is the only author to tell us that, after the death of Carinus, Diocletian kept his predecessor's praetorian prefect Aristobulus in office and honour – the evidence of the *fasti* and epigraphy confirms that he is right.[61] He implies that the leniency shown to Aristobulus was part of a general amnesty for the supporters of Carinus and a snippet in a law code suggests that this was indeed issued.[62] Victor and Zosimus are the only sources to tell us that the Tetrarchic usurper L. Domitius Alexander was *vicarius* in North Africa before he became emperor, and that Maxentius dispatched Rufius Volusianus to suppress him.[63] Victor has other rarities about the history of Maxentius. He describes a massacre of civilians at Rome by the Praetorian Guard (*HAb* 40.24). This is a story told also by Eusebius, but in Latin we otherwise get only a notice in the *Chronography of 354*, which mentions the massacre but not the Praetorians.[64] Victor and Zosimus are alone in mentioning that Constantine disbanded the Praetorian Guard after his victory.[65] After Constantine had entered Rome, Victor says that he magnificently adorned the Circus Maximus, something otherwise described only in a near-contemporary panegyric.[66] The usurpation of one Calocaerus late in the reign of Constantine is

54 *HAb* 28.11; *Chron. 354* (p. 147, l. 30). In an article (2012) and a book (2014), Burgess has provided a very speculative reconstruction of the protohistory of the corpus generally known as the *Chronography of 354*. In this he has argued that the text we refer to here, which Mommsen called the *Chronica urbis Romae*, is actually an unrelated work, to which he refers as the *Breviarium Vindobonense*. There is no need here to engage in a detailed discussion of his arguments as they relate to transmission but, given the fact that the lost Luxembourg manuscript of the *Chron. 354* shows patent evidence of descending from a disordered exemplar, it seems most likely that its archetype had lost texts at the end, which could have included the *Chronica*. On the title, while Burgess is correct that Mommsen simply came up with the customary appellation for convenience, based perhaps on a tendentious interpretation of the text's genre, the same criticism applies also to his own preferred term of *breviarium*, which is equally invented and equally tendentious. Since all is in doubt, we refer to the text here simply as the *Chronography of 354*, without particular prejudice as to when it was written and whether it was originally part of the corpus or not.

55 *RIC* 4.3: 120–121.

56 *HAb* 33.34, 37.6: *Gallieni edicto*.

57 See Davenport 2019: 533–549.

58 *HAb* 33.17; Zosimus 1.40.1 (*cf.* Chapter X).

59 *HAb* 33.12; Lőrincz 2005: 89. The name is Atticianus in **o** and Attitianus in **p**, but the latter is hyper-correction.

60 *ILS* 591 (Narbonensis); *CIL* 17.2, 433 (Aquitainia). He was not, as is sometimes said, the consul of 273: Christol 1986: 111–113, 183–184.

61 *HAb* 39.14; *PLRE* 'Aristobulus'.

62 *HAb* 39.14; *CJ* 9.43.2, on which see Corcoran 1996: 51.

63 *HAb* 40.17; Zosimus 2.12.2. *HAb* 40.18; Zosimus 2.14.2–3. The *Chron. 354*'s list of urban prefects (p. 67) has the *nomen*. On Victor and Zosimus, see Chapter X.

64 Eusebius, *HE* 8.14.3 = *Vita Constantini* 1.35.1. *Chron. 354* (p. 147, ll. 33–34) – the massacre is carried out *a militibus*.

65 *HAb* 40.25; Zosimus 2.17.2.

66 *HAb* 40.27; *Pan. Lat.* 4.35.5.

mentioned in a number of sources, but only Victor records that he was *magister pecoris camelorum* before opting for a career change.[67] Of course, all this detailed, specific, and largely unique information could derive from a lost source common to a number of authors, but it would still be true that Victor was the only one to exploit it properly.

Victor claims that in the course of his research he has read a great many things. At several points, he invokes his researches to explain the significance of some act or to apologise for not being able to say more. The obscurity of some of the historical facts he provides would seem to support his boasting about the lengths to which he had gone to dredge up information from the depths of Roman history. Small touches bespeak an author who cared a lot about precision and accuracy (as we have seen already with names). He knew that the word *familia* was a technical term in gladiatorial matters – rare in literary texts after Cicero, common in inscriptions.[68] He used *conficere* for gravely wounded gladiators, a rare sense of that flexible verb attested only by Donatus' commentary on Terence.[69] He knew that the precise term for founding a colony was *coloniam deducere*.[70] Victor knew (as did Pliny the Elder) that the North African city was most properly *Carthago Poenorum* to avoid confusion with other Carthages.[71] All this is, at the least, very suggestive. Fortunately, we can subject Victor's claim to research to a different, but equally revealing test, by examining his learned and literary sources and models.

Sallust

Victor, in sharp contrast to Eutropius and Festus, was self-consciously literary. There was one figure in particular who occupied the most space in his mental library. It is clear from any page of the *HAb* that Sallust was the dominant influence on Victor's style: his prose is larded with Sallustian expressions and collocations.[72] Indeed, Victor's Sallustianism can take almost ludicrously subtle forms. Let us look at a single example of extremely recondite Sallustian usage to illustrate the point. Twice in the *HAb*, Victor uses the preposition *cis* as part of a temporal expression.[73] Perhaps because temporal phrases starting 'within' are so natural in English, the peculiarity of this usage in Latin has escaped notice – Victor is one of only a handful of Latin authors to deploy it.[74] The others are Plautus (once or twice), and Sallust, at least once in his *Histories*, but never in the monographs.[75] This is a minute point of style, but Victor had clearly read Sallust with sufficient attention to pick up on it. Yet in spite of the work that has been done on Victor's use of Sallust, it has largely escaped notice that his engagement was much deeper than the merely stylistic. Unlike the superficial and posturing devotee of Sallust so memorably described by Aulus Gellius, Victor

---

67 *HAb* 41.11; *PLRE* 'Calocaerus'.
68 *HAb* 27.2. For the term, see *TLL* 6.1.239.31–56 (Hey). In late antiquity, Symmachus, *Ep.* 2.46, lamenting the suicide of his Saxons (*nihil igitur moror familiam Spartaco nequiorem*), used it in the same sense.
69 *HAb* 17.5–6, describing Commodus' gladiatorial contests. *cf.* Donatus, *Ad Eun.* 5.926: *nam proprie hoc verbum convenit gladiatoribus his, qui gravissimis vulneribus occuberint.*

70 *HAb* 13.4. *TLL* 6.1273.27–80 (Störger).
71 *HAb* 16.12; Pliny, *HN* 3.21.1.
72 See in particular La Penna 2004–2005: 377–384, who offers a catalogue; Bird 1984: 90–94.
73 *HAb* 37.4: *cis sextum annum*; 42.1: *cis mensem decimum.*
74 *TLL* 3.1190.53–58 (Spelthahn).
75 Sallust, *Hist.* fr. 21R = 1.70M. *cf. Pan. Lat.* 3.15.1 – it is curious that an author who had presumably recently met Victor should use it. Plautus: *Truculentus* 349 *e.g.*

TABLE 4.1 – SALLUST AND VICTOR ON ROME'S CONQUEST OF FOREIGN PEOPLES

Sallust (*Cat.* 53.2 and 10.1)	*HAb* 11.12–13
But to me, when I was reading and hearing about the many noble deeds (*multa legenti, multa audienti*) which the Roman people did at home and on campaign, at sea and on land, there came by chance the desire to turn my attention to those factors in particular which had supported such great achievements.	Up to this point, those born at Rome or in Italy ruled the Empire; from it, foreigners did also: probably, as in the case of Priscus Tarquinius, they were much better. And indeed to me (*mihi*), based on the many things I have heard and read (*audienti multa legentique*), it is completely obvious that the city of Rome has in particular grown great (*crevisse*) by the bravery of foreigners and transplanted skills of outsiders.
But when the state grew great (*res publica crevit*) through hard work and justice; when great kings had been subdued in war, when wild nations and vast peoples had been conquered by violence, when Carthage, the rival of Rome's empire, perished at the root, when all seas and lands lay open, Fortune began to rage and to confound all things.	

really could claim to be the historian's true expositor: he was interested in his ideas as well as the way he conveyed them.[76]

Let us look first at Sallust's famous monographs, the *Catiline* and the *Jugurtha*. We have shown elsewhere that Victor alluded to the lost ending of the *Jugurtha* – with its description of Marius' triumph and his fraught decision to enter the Senate House still in the garb of a *triumphator*.[77] He used this both to contextualise his description of Diocletian's various sartorial innovations (the purple robe, the jewels, the generally magnificent appearance) as the characteristic behaviour of the low-born man raised to high office, but also to suggest that (*pace* Sallust) it was wrong to think arrogance (*superbia*) a peculiar characteristic of the *nobiles*. In the *Catiline* too, Victor found much food for thought. We have already seen him grappling with the question of foreigners and Rome's rise.[78] Here, he is also engaging with the work of Sallust both intertextually and intellectually. Memorably, Sallust described how Rome's conquest of foreign peoples had sowed the seeds of moral decline. Victor did not necessarily disagree, but he wanted to point out that this was only part of the story. Rome had also been renewed *externorum virtute atque insitivis artibus*, 'by the bravery of foreigners and transplanted skills' (TABLE 4.1).[79] The quotation from Sallust alerts the reader to the engagement with Sallust, an engagement that is simultaneously compliment and criticism. At the same time, it provides tangible proof of Victor's claim: he is not just saying he has read a lot, he is showing it. This is far from the only such instance. Victor uses a significant intertext to link Severus to Pompey the Great, both important but ambiguous figures in Roman history (TABLE 4.2). The subtlety of Victor's engagement with Sallust is often remarkable. In his *Catiline* (2.2), Sallust had famously described how the 'lust for mastery' (*libido dominandi*) had driven mankind to build empires from the era of Cyrus onwards. At the death of Severus Alexander, Victor identifies that same lust as the catalyst for Rome's descent into repeated civil war in the middle of the third century AD (TABLE 4.3).

76 Gellius, *NA* 18.4. On this point, see Stover and Woudhuysen 2020 [2015] *passim*, 2022b.
77 Stover and Woudhuysen 2020 [2015].
78 See above.
79 *cf.* Penella 1983a: 234.

TABLE 4.2 – SALLUST AND VICTOR: POMPEY AND SEVERUS

Sallust, *Cat.* 16.5	*HAb* 19.4
In Italy, there was no army; Gnaeus Pompey was waging war in faraway lands (*in extremis terris bellum gerebat*); he [*sc.* Catiline] had great hopes of seeking the consulship; the Senate was in no way paying enough attention; all things were safe and calm, but that was entirely advantageous for Catiline.	When he learnt what had happened in that place, Septimius Severus, who by chance was then in Syria as legate waging war in faraway lands (*in extremis terris bellum gerebat*), was made emperor; he defeated him [*sc.* Didius Julianus] in a battle very near the Milvian Bridge; those sent to pursue him as he fled butchered him in the palace at Rome.

TABLE 4.3 – SALLUST AND VICTOR ON LUST FOR MASTERY

Sallust, *Cat.* 2.2–3	*HAb* 24.9–11
However, after Cyrus in Asia, the Lacedaemonians and Athenians in Greece, began to subjugate (*subigere*) cities and nations, to consider lust for mastery (*lubidinem dominandi*) a cause of war, to think that the greatest glory was in the greatest dominion, then at last it was discovered through danger and through trouble that in war cleverness can be most valuable of all. If, however, the strength of spirit of kings and generals were as powerful in peace as in war, then human affairs would be more uniform and steadier, and you would not see all things carried to-and-fro, nor changed and confounded (*mutari ac misceri omnia*).	From this point, while they desired more (*cupientiores*) to exercise mastery (*dominandi*) over their own people than to subjugate (*subigendi*) foreigners and were, rather, armed against themselves, they cast headlong, as though from a precipice, the Roman state . . . Indeed, when all things are in confusion (*confusaque omnia*) everywhere and do not proceed on their proper course, everyone thinks it is right – as though they are in a riot – to seize other people's offices, which they cannot command, and they shamefully spoil knowledge of the liberal arts. In this way the power of fortune gives birth to licence and drives mortals to destructive lust (*libidine*); for a long time indeed this was prevented by virtue, as though a wall; afterwards almost all men were subdued by shameful things, and that same power entrusted public affairs to those who were basest by birth and education.

Victor was also quite capable of using a Sallustian tag or two to sharpen his point. Catiline had committed acts *contra ius fasque* (*Cat.* 15.1), of which the most notable was *stuprum* with a Vestal Virgin. He also possessed a 'savage spirit' that was driven on 'more and ever more' (*magis magisque*) by consciousness of his family's poverty and his own crimes (*Cat.* 5.7). According to Victor, Nero had also defiled a Vestal Virgin (*HAb* 5.11), one of the many acts by which he had trampled (*trivisset*) on *omne ius fasque*, just as he had raged *magis magisque* against the nobility (5.13). The subtle juxtaposition of Nero and Catiline – achieved by a few relatively unobtrusive words – is designed to lead the reader to compare them.

On occasion, Victor uses allusion to Sallust to lend a subversive element to his prose (a phenomenon that we will see with other authors as well). The *HAb* closes with a quasi-obituary for the not-yet-deceased Constantius II, a daring move in a time of latent civil war.[80] It tempers its praise with a

---

80 On the obituary, see further Chapters V and IX.

TABLE 4.4 – SALLUST AND VICTOR ON PIMPS AND WINE-DEALERS

Sallust, *Historiae* 1.55R = 1.63M	*HAb* 33.6
In truth, pimps (*lenones*) and wine-dealers (*vinarii*), and butchers and those in addition of whose services the common people make daily use, collected together for a price.	Amidst these events, he frequented taverns and dives; he clung fast to the friendship of pimps (*lenonum*) and wine-dealers (*vinariorum*).

stinging critique of his ministers and concludes by seeming to juxtapose the admirable emperor and his wicked servants (*HAb* 42.24):

> And to sum up the truth briefly (*uti verum absolvam brevi*): just as nothing is more outstanding than the emperor himself, so there is nothing more savage than most of his civil servants.

The four key words appear rather insignificant, but the only remotely similar collocation is found in Sallust's *Catiline* (38.3):

> For to sum up the truth in a few words (*uti paucis verum absolvam*): after that time, whoever shook the state counterfeiting the public interest on noble pretexts – some as though they were protecting the rights of the people, a part so that the influence of the Senate would be as great as possible – each was really striving for his own power.

Sallust's whole point here was that both sides were out for themselves: whatever they said about their motives, they were equally bad. Victor's conclusion is superficially balanced, but the allusion tips the reader off that the appearance is deceptive.

Sallust's monographs have always been classics of Latin historiography: to show that an ancient or a medieval historian knew them is not that remarkable, even if the sophistication of Victor's use of them is. His engagement, however, extended beyond the *Catiline* and the *Jugurtha* to the *Historiae*, Sallust's (lamentably fragmentary) *magnum opus*. Victor and Sallust, very unusually, speak of a war being redoubled with *bellum duplicare* – a phrase sufficiently evocative that Tacitus also imitated it.[81] Victor used the rare word *quaesitissimus*, first in Sallust's *Historiae*, then in Tacitus (again clearly inspired by Sallust).[82] Victor and Sallust are the only extant ancient authors to have used the phrase *post memoriam humani*.[83] These lexical overlaps, which have been called *flosculi Sallustiani*, make plausible the kind of involved engagement with the *Histories* that we have already seen in the case of the *Jugurtha* and the *Catiline*. We can find confirmation in a passage where Victor uses Sallust to make a point about Gallienus (one of his least favourite emperors). Sallust described how Lepidus bought the support of pimps, wine-dealers, and butchers – the kind of individuals with whom only the *vulgus* would normally have commercial dealings, but whom an aristocrat should not treat with *amicitia*. Victor says that Gallienus clung to the *friendship* of pimps and wine-dealers (**TABLE 4.4**).

81 *HAb* 33.2; Sallust, *Hist.* 1.33R = 1.36M; Tacitus, *Hist.* 4.54.1. *cf.* La Penna and Funari 2015: 158.

82 *HAb* 2.1; Sallust, *Hist.* 3.10R = 2.70M; Tacitus, *Ann.* 2.53.3, 15.44.2.

83 *HAb* 39.15; Sallust, *Hist.* 1.49.6R = 1.55.6M. See below.

The depth of Victor's engagement with Sallust is particularly striking, given that (because of their different chronological *foci*) neither the *Historiae* nor his monographs could serve as source material (*strictu sensu*). Instead, like Tacitus, Victor found in Sallust – *rerum Romanarum florentissimus auctor* – a model for how to think about history and how to write it.[84]

Tacitus

Victor and Tacitus shared more than an admiration for Sallust.[85] Victor exploited the *Annales* and *Historiae*: the two works have left a deep verbal impression on the *HAb*.[86] Only Tacitus and Victor (to AD 361) use the unwieldy comparative *formidolosior*.[87] The description of Maximinus Thrax as *e militaribus* is very rare: it probably comes from Tacitus and is specifically meant to describe someone below the rank of general.[88] The unusual temporal phrase *adulta aestate* (for springtime or the first part of summer) is common to Victor and Tacitus.[89] The words *plus quam civilia* for aspirations beyond what was proper to a citizen is another such link between the two.[90] Victor also certainly used Tacitus as a historical source for this account of the first century: his characterisation of Tiberius, for example, as *subdolus et occultior* (*HAb* 2.1), 'treacherous and secretive', clearly harks back to *Annales* 6.51.3 *occultum ac subdolum*, and his given reason for Tiberius' self-exile to Capri (*HAb* 2.2) *dum urbes et conventus exsecratur* ('since he hated the cities and the assemblies') to *Annales* 4.67.1 *perosus . . . municipia et colonias* ('he loathed . . . the towns and colonies').[91]

As with Sallust, however, Victor looked to Tacitus for more than words and historical information: he took ideas as well. Famously, Tacitus begins the *Histories* with a sweeping statement taking in the whole duration of the period from the foundation of the city, through the one-man rule of Augustus, down to the accession of Nero.[92] The *HAb* opens with the identical idea in very similar language, announcing the work's sympathies at its very beginning (**TABLE 4.5**). The sequel in Victor, describing how Octavian effected this, then alludes to the beginning of the *Annales* (**TABLE 4.6**). This is an extraordinary double allusion to the openings of both of Tacitus' works. From the outset, Victor is preparing his audience to expect a work in the Tacitean tradition, with much attention to the process of constitutional change. For

---

84 Tacitus *Ann.* 3.30.2. Tacitus and Sallust: Syme 1958: 1.144–156, esp. 149, 196–199, 353–356.

85 The reception of Tacitus' works in late antiquity is a curiously neglected subject. Though it has been invoked in the context of Marius Maximus (Chapter VII) and given more serious attention by students of Ammianus (Chapter IX), the most comprehensive overview remains Cornelius 1888, now seriously dated (see also Ramorino 1898; Haverfield 1916; Tenney 1935, who mentions (341, n. 7) her 1931 Cornell Ph.D. thesis, 'Tacitus in the Middle Ages and the Early Renaissance and in England to about the Year 1650', but it seems never to have been published). A more up-to-date study is a major *desideratum*.

86 See Bird 1984: 94–96 for an incomplete list; also Callu 1996; Cornelius 1888: 22–25; Wölfflin 1874: 302–308.

87 *HAb* 17.6; Tacitus, *Ann.* 1.62.2.

88 *HAb* 25.1; Tacitus, *Ann.* 4.42.2. Birley 2000: 101.

89 *HAb* 32.3; Tacitus, *Ann.* 2.23.1. For the meaning, see Servius Danielis, *In Aen.* 3.8.

90 *HAb* 39.2; Tacitus, *Ann.* 1.12.4. Both were perhaps inspired by Lucan 1.1. One other possible allusion to Lucan is *HAb* 38.5: *Proinde arduum fatalia devertere, eoque futuri notio superflua* vs *BC* 6.590–593: *O deus Haemonidum, populis quae pandere fata / quaeque suo ventura potes devertere cursu, / te precor ut certum liceat mihi noscere finem / quem belli fortuna paret.*

91 These were identified by Wölfflin 1874: 304.

92 On Tacitus' view of the nature of Rome's constitutional evolution, see Malloch 2022.

TABLE 4.5 – THE OPENINGS OF TACITUS' *HISTORIES* AND VICTOR'S WORK

Tacitus, *Histories* 1.1.1	*HAb* 1.1
For many authors have described the eight hundred and twenty years of the earlier era, after the foundation of the city, while recounting the history of the Roman people with equal eloquence and freedom; after the battle of Actium, it was in the interest of peace that all power be granted to one man (*omnem potentiam ad unum conferri*), those great talents ceased.	In almost the seven hundredth and twenty-second year of the city, the custom arose at Rome of obeying one man absolutely (*mos Romae incessit uni prorsus parendi*).★

★ See Baldwin 1993: 83.

TABLE 4.6 – THE OPENINGS OF TACITUS' *ANNALES* AND VICTOR'S WORK

Tacitus, *Annales* 1.2.1	*HAb* 1.1
When he seduced (*pellexit*) the soldier by bribes (*militem donis*), the people with the food supply (*annona*), all men by the sweetness of peace.	When the soldiers had been enticed with bribes (*illectis per dona militibus*) and the common people by the pretence he was seeing to the food supply (*annonae*), he subdued the rest without difficulty.★

★ Wölfflin 1874: 303.

this reason, what Victor says (*HAb* 41.10) about Constantine's position in AD 324, when he became the sole ruler of the Roman world, is highly significant:

> In this way the state was governed by the will of one man (*unius arbitrio*), his children keeping the distinct title of Caesar.

This is a window allusion: Victor is looking back to the start of his own work and through that to Tacitus on Octavian.[93] Constantine as a new Augustus was hardly a novel idea – indeed, the emperor himself encouraged it – but it was not Tacitus' Octavian to whom he would have wished to be compared.[94] Victor is thus using Tacitus on the final victor of the civil wars to make a point about Constantine, one which subverted the emperor's own self-presentation: subtle but devastating.

The engagement with Tacitus continues throughout the whole work. At *HAb* 24.3, Victor describes the ominous consequences of Alexander Severus' suppression of some rebellious legions: 'in that moment, this deed was accounted to his glory, but soon thereafter to his downfall' (*quod in praesens gloriae, mox exitio datum est*). In Victor's telling, it was the disaffection created by new measures of discipline imposed after this rebellion that would lead to Alexander's assassination and the accession of Maximinus

---

93 On the terminology, see the essays collected in Burrow *et al.* 2020.

94 For Constantine as Augustus, see Rodgers 1980, 1989. Note also the exchange of letters between the emperor and Optatian (p. 5 Polara), with the allusion in *Saeculo*

*meo scribentes dicentesque non aliter **benignus auditus** quam lenis aura prosequitur* to Suetonius, *Aug.* 89.3: *ingenia **saeculi sui** omnibus modis fovit; recitantis et **benigne** et patienter **audiit**, nec tantum carmina et historias, sed et orationes et dialogos.*

Thrax, whose rise set the stage for the civil war of 238, the year of the six emperors. The key phrase imitates a line in Tacitus, who describes the rapturous reception of Vitellius by the citizens of Cremona, after the internecine slaughter at Bedriacum in AD 69 (*Hist.* 2.70.2): 'their joy at the moment was soon thereafter the cause of their ruin' (*quae laeta **in praesens mox** perniciem ipsis fecere*).[95] That ruin was the massacre at Cremona perpetrated a few months later by the legions loyal to Vespasian after the second battle at Bedriacum (described at *Hist.* 3.33), a downfall that would soon be followed by that of Vitellius himself. Victor's allusion to Tacitus here invites his readers to meditate on a number of themes. Imperial murder was one: both events would swiftly lead to the assassination of an emperor. Military discipline was another: both events were precipitated by the failures of leaders to curb their soldiers. The unintended consequences that give history its ironies were the third and broadest: Alexander was murdered by the very legions who had assisted him in putting down the rebellion of others; the people of Cremona would be slaughtered by one of the legions (XIII) they were rapturously applauding. All the while, the comparison quietly foreshadows the consequences of Alexander's death, offering an implicit parallel between the chaos of the years 69 and 238. For Victor, the reign of Alexander represented a turning point. All the way from Rome's beginning – from Romulus up to the reign of Caracalla – he claims that Roman power had expanded: 'that it did not immediately slip was due to Alexander' (*HAb* 24.9). At this point, the historian pauses his narrative to provide a complex analysis of the causes of greatness and decline (*HAb* 24.9–11). Victor's use of Tacitus to analyse the events of the 230s is of a piece with the intertext on Augustus and Constantine: at moments pregnant with significance, both historical and historiographical, he turns to the *Annales* and *Histories*.

The calamity foreseen with the death of Alexander came to a head in the 250s. After a chaotic sequence of emperors, from Philip the Arab to Aemilianus, a man of a somewhat distinguished lineage (*genere satis claro*) was raised to the purple: Licinius Valerianus (*HAb* 32.1–2). With Valerian came a son who was soon after named Caesar, Gallienus, whose sole reign would bring the Roman Empire (in Victor's telling) to its lowest point. Besides persecuting Christians, Valerian is primarily known for campaigning against the Persians, being captured by Shapur I and subjected to various indignities before dying in captivity. The *HAb* (32.5) notes that he was 'foully mutilated' (*foede laniatus*) and died still 'hearty in his old age' (*senecta robustiore*). The only earlier occurrence of the phrase *foede laniare* is in Tacitus, describing the fate of Galba, the first of four emperors of the year 69 (*Hist.* 1.41.3):

> The rest foully mutilated (*foede laniavere*) his legs and arms (for his chest was protected) and in their cruelty and savagery they kept on adding many wounds to his body, even after it had been torn apart.

Like Valerian, Galba was an old man (in Victor's words, *senecta aetate*, *HAb* 5.15) and also from a distinguished family (*e gente clarissima*, *HAb* 6.1). Indeed, Galba and Valerian are the only two people in the *HAb* described as coming from a *gens clara*. Victor uses the resonance with Tacitus' description of the riot in which Galba was slain in January 69 – presaging the chaos of the year to come which would see the rapid accession and deaths of Otho and Vitellius, before Vespasian won unchallenged mastery of the city

---

95 *cf. Hist.* 3.6.1: *unde infami gratia primum pilum adepto laeta ad praesens male parta mox **in perniciem vertere*** with *HAb* 41.20 ***verteratque** gratiam muneribus **in perniciem** posterorum dissimulatio.*

and empire by December. In a similar way, Valerian's capture, mutilation, and eventual death at the hands of Shapur presaged the dark days of Gallienus' reign, when the empire would be torn apart by usurpers on every side.

A further significant example of Victor's engagement with Tacitus comes in the discussion of the aftermath of Gallienus' death. In Victor's telling, Gallienus designated Claudius II as his successor as he lay dying. In return, Claudius coerced the reluctant Senate to deify his predecessor, despite their hatred for him. This prompts a wry observation on deification (*HAb* 33.30):

> By dint of honourable living rather than titles sought after and contrived, princes and the best of mortals (*principes atque optimi mortalium*) enter heaven, as far as one is permitted to guess, or at least are celebrated as gods by their reputation (*fama*) among men.

The scepticism and rationalism here is striking: Victor suggests (if tentatively) that the real force of deification is to be remembered as a god by other men, and not necessarily to attain literal divinity. *Optimi mortalium* is the key phrase: it links Victor's idea to one of the more significant imperial deifications in earlier literature. In *Annales* 4.38.5, Tacitus relays what people were saying about the fact that Tiberius declined the offer of divine cult in Spain:

> The best of mortals (*optimos . . . mortalium*) long for the loftiest things: in such a way were Hercules and Liber added to the number of the gods by the Greeks, and Quirinus by us . . . Princes (*principibus*) have everything else at their fingertips, but there is one thing they should insatiably seek to procure: to be remembered favourably, for to have contempt for reputation (*famae*) is to despise the virtues.

What we see here is Victor's engagement with Tacitus not just as a historiographic model, but also as a source of ideas. He draws out what is at most a muted implication in Tacitus: that divinisation is a merely human affair.[96]

So Victor used Tacitus extensively throughout his work, for substance as much as for style. It is worth noting, however, that this sophisticated engagement with the *Annales* and *Histories* does not imply slavish devotion to the opinions of a predecessor. Just as with Sallust, Victor was not afraid to depart from Tacitus' judgements, an allusion nodding to the disagreement. In his *Germania* (14.2), Tacitus had remarked on how Germans would seek out warfare, if their *civitas* 'became lethargic through extended peace and tranquillity' (*longa pace et otio torpeat*). The theme of *longa pax* as enervating also surfaces in the *Agricola* (11.4). In describing the reign of Antoninus Pius, than which few were more peaceful, Victor praised the emperor (*HAb* 15.3):

> He was so fair and so upright in character, that he plainly showed that minds freed from care are not corrupted by continuous peace and extended tranquillity (*iugi pace ac longo otio*).

Tacitus was wrong about the effects of peace: virtue was virtue. It shows a striking independence of mind to depart from antiquity's general suspicion that when things were quiet, they were usually too quiet. At other times, in a pattern we have seen before with Sallust, Victor uses an unobtrusive allusion to Tacitus

---

96 See the discussion of the passage in Tacitus and its
    context in Pelling 2010.

to twist the knife a little. We have already looked at the conclusion to the *HAb*, with its barbed praise of Constantius II and contempt for his officials. One of the things for which Victor reprimands the latter is their 'uncouth customs', or *absurdi mores* (*HAb* 42.24). This collocation is found otherwise only once in extant Latin literature. Famously, Book V of Tacitus' *Histories* opens with a digression on the Jews, their past and customs. He was particularly riled by what he saw as their separatism and self-conscious distinctiveness. He noted that some of their rites resembled those of Liber Pater, but the appearance was deceptive, for the rites of Liber were joyous, unlike the 'foul and uncouth custom of the Jews' (*Hist.* 5.5.5: *Iudaeorum mos absurdus sordidusque*). Read straight, one could believe that Victor was objecting to the lack of culture in court circles under Constantius, but anti-Christian polemic lurks just below the surface.

Suetonius

From Tacitus, let us turn to his very different contemporary, Suetonius. The grammarian and imperial biographer has never been considered a stylistic lodestar in Latin prose, unlike Tacitus, and there is little pronounced stylistic imitation of Suetonius in Victor. What there is, however, is sophisticated engagement with the *Lives of the Caesars*. As is already widely acknowledged, Victor used Suetonius as a source for the emperors from Augustus to Domitian.[97] What has attracted less attention is that we also find significant intertexts with Suetonius' biographies in the *HAb*'s accounts of later emperors. Victor's narrative of the aftermath of Gallienus' demise, when his family members and supporters were executed and thrown down the Gemonian steps (not a moment too soon, per Victor), pointedly recalls Suetonius' account of Tiberius' death (**TABLE 4.7**) *and not his own narration of the same event*. This intertext was first spotted by Syme, but he regarded it as evidence only for Victor's laziness and fraudulence.[98] This is quite wrong – Victor is doing something much more sophisticated, drawing his readers to consider the parallelism between two emperors who at first glance have little to do with one another.

We see the same technique in the treatment of Diocletian. Broadly speaking, he emerges from the pages of the *HAb* as a good emperor, but things are rarely quite that simple with Victor. In describing Diocletian's decision to abdicate, Victor uses (*HAb* 39.48) the phrase *curam rei publicae abiecit*, 'he cast aside the cares of state'. The idea is very rare and, in descriptions of the emperors, found only in Suetonius on Tiberius: *regressus in insulam* **rei publicae** *quidem* **curam** *. . .* **abiecit**, 'having retired to the island, he indeed cast aside the cares of state'.[99] Victor's superficially factual description takes on sinister and selfish connotations in the light of Suetonius.

Victor thus uses Suetonius in some remarkably clever ways to convey complex ideas on a large scale. At other times, he takes only a little from the *Lives of the Caesars*, but uses it to add subtle colour to his portrait of a later emperor. In his discussion of Trajan, for example, Victor explains that 'he applied the remedy of the *cursus publicus* to swiftly learn news brought from everywhere in the *res publica*'

---

97 Dufraigne 1975: xxviii–xxxi; Baldwin 1993 (though with a greater focus on the *LB*). Bird 1984: 20–23 did attempt to deny direct recourse to Suetonius (positing instead use of Suetonian material through other channels), but even on its own terms the case is unconvincing.

98 Syme 1980b: 271.

99 *Tib.* 41.1. *cf.* Cicero, *Ep. Fam.* 9.24.4: *Sed cave, si me amas, existimes me quod iocosius scribam abiecisse curam rei publicae.*

TABLE 4.7 – SUETONIUS AND VICTOR ON THE GEMONIAN STEPS

Tib. 75.1	*HAb* 33.31
The people rejoiced so at his death, that at the first news of it some ran about shouting 'Tiberius to the Tiber!', some beseeched the Mother Earth and the infernal deities to allot to the dead man no place other than one among the impious (*pars Terram matrem deosque Manes orarent, ne mortuo sedem ullam nisi inter impios darent*), while others – enraged by the recent barbarity over and above the memory of his earlier cruelty – threatened his corpse with the hook and the Gemonian steps.	But the Senate, when his demise became known, decreed that his retainers and relatives be thrown headlong down the Gemonian steps. It is well known that they were punished by having their eyes gouged out, when a fiscal advocate had been brought [? †*perduci*] into the Senate House, as the common people rushed in, supplicating with equal din both Mother Earth and the gods below that Gallienus be allotted the place due to the impious (*pari clamore Terram matrem, deos quoque inferos precaretur, sedes impias uti Gallieno darent*).★

★ The passage is perplexing, but Den Boer 1972: 82–83 adopts Olivarius' conjecture *perducto*. Perhaps we might read *perduci iusso* (something suggested to us by Gavin Kelly). Porena 2021 places the episode in the context of various (unpopular) changes to fiscal structures in Italy initiated by Valerian and Gallienus.

TABLE 4.8 – SUETONIUS AND VICTOR: POMPEY AND CONSTANTIUS

Suetonius, *Iul.* 35.1	*HAb* 42.10
per quattuor paene menses maximis obsessum operibus, **ad extremum** Pharsalico **proelio** fudit et **fugientem** Alexandriam **persecutus**, ut occisum deprehendit . . .	Ipsi inter se acrioribus **proeliis per** triennium congressi; **ad extremum** Constantius **fugientem** in Galliam **persecutus** vario ambos supplicio semet adegit interficere
When he had besieged him with enormous fortifications for almost four months, at the end he routed him in the battle of Pharsalus and having pursued him as he fled to Alexandria, when he discovered he had been killed . . .	They met each other in bitter battles for three years; at the end, after Constantius had pursued the one fleeing into Gaul, he forced both to kill themselves, each by a different method.

(*HAb* 13.5: *simul* **noscendis ocius**, *quae ubique e republica* **gerebantur**, *admota remedia publici cursus*).[100] This recalls Suetonius' description of Augustus' establishment of the *cursus*: 'and so that he could swiftly learn news from each province . . .' (*Aug.* 49.3: *Et quo* **celerius** *. . .* **cognoscique** *posset, quid in provincia quaque* **gereretur** *. . .*). This is a delightfully understated way to nod to the ubiquitous comparison of Trajan to Augustus in late antiquity.[101]

A final example well illustrates the various ways that Suetonius is used in the *HAb*. Whenever Victor was confronted with a period of civil war when writing his history, he often seems to turn back to earlier episodes of civil strife. The reign of Constantius II – wrapped in the purple, as Victor wrote – was marked by several such episodes. The most notable were the usurpation of Magnentius from 350 to 353

---

100 *cf.* the Appendix, no. II.

101 The comparison between Trajan and Augustus was a commonplace in antiquity, *cf. e.g.* Eutropius 8.5.3.

and the incipient war with the Caesar Julian, cut short by Constantius' death in 361. We have already seen how Victor compared Constantius explicitly with Pompey, Caesar's adversary. What is interesting is that he also uses Suetonius to make parallel Constantius' war with Magnentius and Caesar's with Pompey, but this time with Constantius cast as Caesar (**TABLE 4.8**). This intertext primes the reader to consider the wars of Constantius in terms of the final wars of the Republic, only to twist that notion later by comparing the emperor not to Caesar, but to Pompey.

Livy

There has been one significant omission among the canonical Latin historians discussed so far: Livy. At first sight, Victor's work has little in common with the massive history *Ab urbe condita*: subject matter, approach, and style appear radically different. The influence of Sallust on Victor is transparent at a glance, that of Tacitus or Suetonius detectable with a little more work, but Livy is superficially very different. The compiler of the *CT*, however, clearly thought that Victor was comparable to Livy, indeed that (in some sense) he continued his work (*a fine Titi Livii*).[102] Close attention does indeed reveal a substrate of Livian language in the *HAb*. One of Livy's favourite temporal expressions was *sub idem (fere) tempus*: 'at (almost) the same time'. Other historians of the late Republic and early Empire do deploy this phrase (though significantly Sallust does not), but Livy uses it thirty-seven times in what survives of his work.[103] Victor (*HAb* 33.1) is one of only a handful of late-antique authors to deploy it.[104] Livy twice describes something as happening *foedum in modum* (9.31.2, 23.7.3: 'in a shameful manner') – Victor is one of only two other authors ever to use the phrase (*HAb* 6.1).[105] Livy used the phrase *ductu atque/et auspicio* or *ductu auspicioque* (of a commander) some twenty-five times, the overwhelming majority of ancient instances.[106] Victor was one of two late-antique authors to deploy it (*HAb* 42.19).[107] These are small indications, but they hint at a deeper acquaintance with Livy.

Sure enough, if we probe we can find evidence of the sort of sophisticated engagement that we saw above with Sallust and Tacitus. Victor's account of the emperors from Aurelian to Carinus systematically compares them to the kings of Rome and specifically to Livy's kings. A demonstration of this requires too many supporting theses to expand on it here, but it shows extended rumination on Livy's account of the regal period.[108] Elsewhere, Livy is used in a more limited way to sharpen a particular point. One of the themes of the *HAb*'s account of Septimius Severus is his harshness to enemies internal and external, a harshness that Victor both censured and defended as sensible *Realpolitik*, necessary to root out the grave threat of factionalism (*HAb* 20.13). Even as his power grew more assured and he made greater

102 See Chapter II.
103 So a search of *CDS* suggests. It occurs eleven times in Tacitus, six times in Suetonius, five times in the *Bellum Alexandrinum* (but nowhere else in the Caesarian *corpus*), and once in Velleius.
104 Before him, only in Lactantius, *DI* 7.24.5. After, in AM 27.10.1 and Sulpicius Severus, *Vita Martini* 9.1,

14.1. It also appears in Julius Obsequens 12 (probably verbatim from Livy, whose text is lost at this point).
105 Suetonius, *Claud.* 36.1 is the third.
106 Per a search of *CDS*. There is one instance in the *Bellum Alexandrinum* 43.1 and two in Fronto (*De Bello Parthico* 2, *Ep. ad Verum* 2.24, cf. 2.3).
107 See also *Pan. Lat.* 8.5.4.
108 Chapter VIII.

use of rewards, Severus remained 'unforgiving towards crimes' (*HAb* 20.19: *implacabilis delictis*). This is a surprisingly rare phrase, one that crops up elsewhere only in Livy. He describes how (25.16), during the Second Punic War, the Roman general Tiberius Gracchus was lured to his death in an ambush by the Lucanian traitor Flavus (in one version of the story at least). Flavus told Gracchus that he had persuaded the Italians who had defected to Carthage to return their allegiance to Rome, encouraging them by saying that 'the Romans would not be unforgiving of their former crime' (25.16.12: *veteri delicto haud implacabiles Romanos fore*). This was enough to persuade Gracchus to attend a meeting with the Lucanians, the pretext that brought him to the ambush. The story is a cautionary tale about the costs of forgiveness and is used in Victor as implicit justification of Severus' harshness. Another example is equally rich. In his account of the enormities of Caligula, Victor says that 'the whole world was befouled by the manifold slaughter' of senators and nobles (*HAb* 3.9: *multiplici clade terrarum orbis foedaretur*). The only other author to say anything remotely similar is Livy, who in his description of a year early in the Republic (453 BC) says that it 'was befouled by numerous disasters' (3.32.4: *multiplici clade foedatus annus*), among which he singles out the deaths of senators and nobles. There may be more going on here than a simple comparison by Victor of one grim period to another. Livy is careful to note that the year was free from enemy attacks (*ab hoste otium fuit*): it was plague and famine that did the damage. Victor describes Caligula as like a beast that had tasted blood (*beluae hausto sanguine ingenium exercuit*), another kind of natural disaster. Moreover, in Livy this year serves as a prelude to the constitutional experiment of the *decemviri*, the board of ten that briefly and unhappily governed the Republic. In Victor, too, Caligula's reign marks a point when there might have been a fundamental constitutional evolution – the end of the *principes* and the restoration of a republic – but ultimately there was not.[109]

These are not Victor's only allusions to significant moments in Livy's narrative. In his account of the emperor Constans (a figure towards whom he was at best ambivalent), Victor noted that he had become more arrogant (*tumidior*) after defeating his brother (Constantine II) in the civil war of 340. A reckless young man with a violent soul (*animi vehemens*), Constans won the hatred of his subjects through the wickedness of his ministers and his rash inclination to greed (*praeceps in avaritiam*) (*HAb* 41.23). This seemingly inconspicuous collection of words is actually used by only one other author: Livy. In his description of the period of fluctuating fortunes after the battle of Cannae, Livy relates how Hannibal, frustrated at the way that the Roman siege of Capua had cost him Italian support, turned from trying to protect his allies to ravaging territory. The cause of this disastrous decision was his 'spirit, rashly inclined to greed and cruelty' (26.35.3: *praeceps in avaritiam et crudelitatem animus*). The comparison between two leaders, puffed up by their victories and plunging through their greed into the hatred of those who ought to have supported them, is both savage and effective. It casts an interesting light on another Livian reminiscence in Victor. Describing the year 350, when the emperor Constantius II had deposed the usurper Vetranio and made himself master of the Balkans, Victor says that he would 'at once' (*statim*) have invaded Italy to confront his other enemies, but 'the harsh winter and blocked Alps delayed him' (*hiems aspera clausaeque Alpes tardavere*) (*HAb* 42.5). A few years after the fall of Capua, Hasdrubal was about to enter Italy, bringing Hannibal reinforcements. The Senate received an intelligence report that he would

---

109 *HAb* 3.14 is quite explicit, mentioning the example of Brutus. See further below, Chapter IX.

do so in the coming spring and that 'nothing else delayed him than that the Alps were blocked by winter' (27.36.3: *nec tum eum quicquam aliud morari nisi quod clausae hieme Alpes essent*). Hannibal and Hasdrubal, like Constantius and Constans, were brothers.[110]

Of course, the early history of Rome and the war with Hannibal were among the most famous parts of Livy's work – there is a reason (after all) that they survive entire. There is, however, evidence that Victor's consultation of the *Ab urbe condita* reached close to the end of that voluminous work. In his account of Severus, Victor noted that, at the emperor's death, men said that 'it was not at all fitting for this man to have been born or to have died' (*illum nasci aut emori minime convenisse*).[111] On the testimony of Seneca (for the relevant part of the original is lost), Livy reported a remarkably similar *dictum* about either Marius or Caesar (the text is corrupt): *in incerto esse utrum magis nasci an non nasci reipublicae profuerit*, 'that it was uncertain whether the state benefited more from his being born or not being born'.[112] It took a true student of Livy to allude to a passage that must have fallen after his sixtieth book.[113]

Velleius Paterculus

Victor's knowledge of the Latin historians is both deeper and more sophisticated than has generally been acknowledged, but it is, in a way, not that surprising to find a fourth-century historian who looked to the works of his greatest predecessors for inspiration. What is much more interesting is that the *HAb* also shows evidence of a broader range of historical reading. Perhaps the best evidence for this lies in its connections with the work of Velleius Paterculus, never acknowledged as one of the canonical Latin historians. There is no earlier historian whose style so closely resembles that of Victor as Velleius.[114] This could, of course, be chalked up to shared imitation of Sallust, the major historiographical model of both authors.[115] There are, however, indications of a more direct influence. Velleius says that in assassinating Caesar, Brutus and Cassius 'perpetrated a monstrous crime' (2.58.1, *patravere facinus*). This collocation was likely inspired by Sallust's famous description of the evil Catiline intended for Rome (*Cat.* 18.8). Victor uses the same phrase as Velleius to describe the death of another Caesar who was formidable in civil war and slaughtered by those in whom he had put his trust – the emperor Aurelian (*HAb* 35.8). Velleius and Victor are both alone in describing an individual as possessing *antiquissimi mores* (Aelius Lamia and Pertinax, respectively), a shared twist on a famous line of Ennius.[116] Both use the otherwise unattested characterisation 'far excelling by their eloquence' when comparing two related individuals.[117]

---

110 They were also both two out of three significant brothers: Constantine II, Constantius II, and Constans vs Hannibal, Hasdrubal, and Mago.
111 *HAb* 20.6; on this passage see further below.
112 *NQ* 5.18.4. On the text, see Toher 2009: 232. Badian 1993: 36, n. 51 favoured Marius.
113 Though it cannot be ruled out that Victor took the line from Seneca directly.
114 On the style of Velleius, see Oakley 2020.
115 Stover and Woudhuysen 2022b.

116 Velleius 2.116.3 (the name is a plausible restoration); *HAb* 18.1. Ennius: *Moribus antiquis res stat Romana virisque* (Vahlen l. 500; preserved in Augustine *De civ.* 2.21, he got it from Book V of Cicero's *De re publica*, which is not otherwise extant). The line is quoted (without attribution) in the *HA Avid. Cass.* 5.7.
117 Velleius 2.6.1: *ingenio etiam eloquentiaque longe praestantiorem* (of the Gracchi). *HAb* 16.1: *philosophandi vero eloquentiaeque studiis longe praestantem* (Marcus Aurelius against Antoninus Pius).

TABLE 4.9 – THE USAGE OF -*ANNUS* COMPOUNDS BY LATIN HISTORIANS

Compound	Sallust	Livy	Tacitus	Suetonius	Velleius	Victor	
						HAb	LB
biennium							
Total	0	42	5	10	13	10	1
Per 100,000 words		8.4	3.6	14	50	90	
triennium							
Total	1	18	8	9	15	4	3
Per 100,000 words	2.8	3.6	5.7	13	56	36	
quadriennium							
Total	0	6	3	1	5	0	2
Per 100,000 words		1.2	2.1	1.4	19		
quinquennium							
Total	1	12	8	8	4	2	3
Per 100,000 words	2.8	2.4	5.7	11	15	18	
sexennium							
Total	0	0	0	0	0	3	0
Per 100,000 words						27	
septennium							
Total	0	0	0	0	1	0	0
Per 100,000 words					3.8		
decennium							
Total	0	0	0	0	0	1	1
Per 100,000 words						9	
Overall total	2	78	24	28	38	19	10
Per 100,000 words	5.6	15	17	40	135	180	111

There are also more subtle and pervasive signs of Velleius' influence on Victor. In the expression of the duration of time, Victor has a marked preference for *annus* compounds: *biennium*, *triennium*, *quadriennium etc.* While these expressions are not themselves rare, no Latin historian uses them with the same frequency as Victor, except Velleius (TABLE 4.9). Even with the loss of the *Histories*, we can be reasonably certain that this is not a Sallustian feature. Nor is it Tacitean, since he used such words at roughly the same frequency as Livy. If Victor took this stylistic tic from anywhere, then it ought to have been from Velleius.

These traces of Velleius' style and language in Victor suggest that he might also have had a deeper and more intellectual influence. For example, in his narration of Caligula's abortive German campaign, Victor describes how 'the legions were drawn together into one' (*HAb* 3.11: *contractis ad unum legionibus*). The source is quite clearly Suetonius (*Calig.* 43.1), but the closest parallel in phrasing is in Velleius (2.113.1): *contractisque in una castra decem legionibus.* This too was in the context of a German campaign (that of Tiberius, Caligula's predecessor, in 6 BC), and Velleius goes on to note that this was the largest single force mustered together since the civil wars (*tanto denique exercitu quantus nullo umquam loco post bella fuerat civilia*), just as Suetonius notes that the provisioning for Caligula's campaign was unprecedented (*omnis generis commeatu quanto numquam antea*). Or take the account of Caracalla. Victor records what the emperor's mother – or as Victor would have it, his stepmother – Julia Domna said to him as she attempted to seduce him: 'It is your pleasure? Obviously it is permitted' (*HAb* 21.3: *Libet? plane licet*). Den Boer has already suggested that in the background of Victor's portrayal of Julia Domna is an *exemplum* of the two Augustan Juliae, whose 'name . . . became synonymous with the traditional idea of a wanton woman'.[118] Augustan *exempla* would have been at the front of Victor's mind as he wrote on Severus, Caracalla's father, whom he consistently portrayed as a new Augustus.[119] This, however, is no general insinuation, as Den Boer implies, but rather an intertextually rich linking of Julia Domna with the elder Julia. In Suetonius, Victor would have found Caligula's allegation that Augustus had committed incest with his daughter Julia (*Calig.* 23.1), providing an appropriate reversal of the situation between Caracalla and Julia Domna. Victor combined this idea with a description of the elder Julia in Velleius Paterculus (2.100.3):

> For his daughter Julia, in everything forgetful of her great father and her husband, neglected nothing whatsoever stained with lust or wantonness that a woman could either do or experience wickedly and used to measure the size of her good fortune by her license to sin, claiming as lawful whatever pleased her (*quidquid liberet pro licito vindicans*).[120]

While wordplay on *libere/licere* is attested elsewhere, the context makes Victor's direct dependence on Velleius unavoidable.[121]

In fact, the evidence for Victor's engagement with the Tiberian historian is still more extensive. We can turn, for instance, to Velleius' description of the reforms of Tiberius Gracchus (2.2.3):

> pollicitusque toti Italiae civitatem, simul etiam promulgatis agrariis legibus, omnibus †statum† concupiscentibus, **summa imis miscuit** et **in praeruptum** atque anceps periculum adduxit **rem publicam**.

> Having promised citizenship to the whole of Italy, at the same time as the agrarian laws were also promulgated, with all men intensely desiring the †. . .†, he mingled the highest things with the lowest and brought the state into extreme and unpredictable danger.

Victor uses the same language to describe what happened due to the barbarian incursions under Gallienus (*HAb* 33.4):

> Ita quasi ventis undique saevientibus parvis maxima **ima summis orbe toto miscebantur**.[122]

> So, as though the winds were raging on every side, the highest things were mingled with the lowest, the greatest with the least through the whole world.

Slightly earlier, in a passage projecting forward to those same invasions, Victor detailed what would happen (*HAb* 24.9):

118 Den Boer 1972: 66.
119 See below.
120 Noted without any discussion by Bird 1994: 113.
121 *e.g.* Cicero, *Quinct.* 30.94 and Persius, *Sat.* 5.83–84; *cf.* Weyman 1904: 387 and Woodman 1977: 123. Only a handful of Weyman's parallels predate Victor.

122 Noted by Klebs 1890: 303, without comment. A similar expression is found in Tacitus, *Hist.* 4.47 (*summaque et ima miscentis*), but Victor's formulation is far closer to Velleius in both form and context.

Romanum statum quasi abrupto praecipitavere, immissique in imperium **promiscue** boni malique, nobiles atque ignobiles, ac barbariae multi.

They cast the Roman state headlong, as though from a precipice, and there were allowed into the imperial office without distinction good men and bad, well-born and humble, and many from barbarian lands.

For Velleius, the extension of Roman citizenship to all of Italy, the land redistributions, and the mingling of high and low that they entailed, brought the Roman state to the edge of the precipice; for Victor, the barbarian incursions and the subsequent admixture had exactly the same effect.

There are reasons why Velleius – one of the first genuinely imperial Latin historians – might have been a particularly attractive choice for Victor. Like Victor, he was given to providing character sketches, with a pronounced interest in the *mores* of the figures he covered. Like Victor, Velleius is an unusually opinionated historian, one whose admiration and condemnation are often explicit, who talks to and at the reader.[123] Even more significantly, Velleius did not close his history with a significant terminal date, concluding in the insignificant year of the consulship of his dedicatee, M. Vinicius (AD 30), in the middle of the reign of Tiberius. This contrasts with Livy, who (according to the *Periochae*) published his books on Augustus only after his death, and concluded with the death of Drusus, as well as Suetonius and Tacitus, who both closed their narratives with the death of Domitian.[124] The *Historiae abbreviatae* concludes with the tenth consulate of Constantius and the third of Julian (AD 360), in a year whose significance was as yet unclear, and with coverage of still-reigning emperors. In this Victor is quite alone among his peers: Eutropius concludes with the death of Jovian, Ammianus with the death of Valens and the aftermath of the battle of Adrianople, Jerome with the same events, and even the *Historia Augusta* with the death of Carinus (the last emperor before its putative era of composition). In seeking to do something different, Victor seems to have looked to Velleius as a model for how to structure a narrative of imperial history.

Velleius was not widely read in antiquity. There is only slim evidence for knowledge of his history circulating, at least among grammarians and those with serious antiquarian interests: one citation in Priscian, two in the *scholia* to Lucan, and evidence that Sulpicius Severus imitated him in his *Chronicon*.[125] Victor's use of Velleius as a model might cause us to question his taste, but it certainly puts him in select company. It gives us some idea of how wide his historiographical frame of reference was.

Lactantius

Indeed, Victor's frame of reference was wide enough even to accommodate Christian sources. We have no extant secular history written in Latin from the century before Victor; what we do have is a quasi-historical work written by a Christian rhetor, the *De mortibus persecutorum* of Lactantius (composed *ca.* 315). Victor and Lactantius are linked by more than genre: they were both confirmed imitators of

---

123 Something well brought out by Oakley 2020: 214.
124 *cf.* Conclusion to Part I.

125 Priscian, *Institutiones* 6 (*GLK* 2.248). *Adnotationes super Lucanum* 8.663 and 9.178. Sulpicius Severus: Klebs 1890.

Sallust.[126] Their backgrounds were also parallel: both were North Africans, both achieved prominence in the Empire through education.[127] Compelling similarities in their accounts of the rise of Constantine provoked the author of the most thorough treatment of Lactantius *qua* historian, Arne Søby Christensen, to raise the question of whether Victor used Lactantius as a source:

> But how to explain the connection? There can hardly be a direct link between Lactantius and Aurelius Victor, if only because no pagan writer in the fourth century used Christian works in his writing of history.[128]

As it stands, this is mere assertion, and Søby Christensen retreated to the tired excuse that they must have had some lost common source. If we look, however, at a different episode, Diocletian's abdication, we can find strong evidence for direct engagement. In Lactantius' account, the instigator of this momentous decision was Galerius. The fearsome Caesar first tried to convince Maximian to resign, terrifying him by 'sowing fear of civil strife' (*DMP* 18.1 *iniecto armorum civilium metu*). *Iniecto metu* was not a common phrase – before Lactantius, it is found twice in Cicero, and once each in Livy (at least what survives), Frontinus, and Suetonius – but it would later become a favourite of Victor's, occurring twice in the *HAb*.[129] One of those instances is in the account of Diocletian, right before Victor turns to the topic of his abdication.[130]

In Lactantius' telling, Galerius next assailed Diocletian himself, adducing the example of Nerva, who (he said) had abdicated in favour of Trajan (*DMP* 18.2). The idea that Nerva abdicated is probably not itself true – Dio says that he considered such a move (68.3.4) and Pliny the Younger hints at the idea in his *Panegyricus* (6.3), but there is no evidence that Nerva actually went through with it. Besides Lactantius (*DMP* 18.4), our only historical sources to state explicitly that Nerva abdicated is Victor (*HAb* 12.2–3). Moreover, the language Victor uses to describe Diocletian's abdication is, intriguingly, almost the same as that of Lactantius on Nerva – *Nervam . . . **abiecisse gubernaculum rei publicae** atque ad privatam vitam redisse* (*DMP* 18.4, 'Nerva . . . had cast aside the direction of the state and returned to private life') ~ *curam reipublicae abiecit . . . **ad communem vitam** spreto ambitu descendisse* (*HAb* 39.48, 'he cast aside the cares of the state . . . and having scorned desire for power came down to ordinary life').[131] Victor also, with his *spreto ambitu*, links his account back intratextually to his own discussion of Nerva (*HAb* 12.3: *neque ambitione praeceps agi*, 'not to be driven headlong by ambition'). All this strongly suggests that Victor had Lactantius' account of these events before him as he worked.

One very significant detail confirms that that was indeed the case. Victor gives a curious reason for Diocletian's abdication. As a devotee of divination, a *scrutator imminentium*, Diocletian could see the troubles and calamities that lay ahead for the Roman state (*HAb* 39.48): wanting no part in them, he renounced imperial office. Lactantius offers the same characterisation of Diocletian, in a rather different context, 'a *scrutator* of things to come, out of fear' (*DMP* 10.1: *pro timore scrutator rerum futurarum*). *Scrutator* was a very rare and rather poetic word: it is never used in the context of divination before Lactantius and

---

126 Stover and Woudhuysen 2022b.
127 Victor: Chapter I. Lactantius: Jerome, *DVI* 80.
128 Søby Christensen 1980: 56.
129 Cicero, *Ver.* 2.2.67 and *Ep. Quint.* 2.1.3; Livy 38.34.1; Frontinus, *Strat.* 2.4.11; Suetonius, *Calig.* 38.2.

130 *HAb* 39.45; the other is 4.9.
131 The modification of *gubernaculum* to *curam* perhaps recalls Suetonius' description of Tiberius (above).

Victor.[132] It is found most commonly in Christian authors, in a tag confected from several biblical passages (*Ps.* 7:10, *Sap.* 1:6, and *Apoc.* 2:23): *scrutator cordium et renum dominus*, 'the Lord who trieth the hearts and reins'.[133] This is what inspired Lactantius' acid characterisation. Diocletian styled himself *dominus*, as Lactantius reminds us in the next line (*DMP* 10.2; *cf. HAb* 39.3). Like the Lord, this *dominus* is a searcher of the inner parts, but only of the viscera of animals in a vain attempt to learn the future: 'in their livers he sought what was to come' (*DMP* 10.1: *in iecoribus earum ventura quaerebat*). All in all, Lactantius is offering a sophisticated mockery of the persecutor for his Christian readers, implicitly contrasting the *dominus scrutator rerum futurarum in iecoribus pecudum* with the *dominus scrutator cordium et renum*. In Victor, obviously, we have none of this engagement with Christian Scripture, yet we still have Diocletian described as a *scrutator imminentium*. This cannot but be, then, engagement with Lactantius.

Taken by themselves, any of the reminiscences mentioned above might be dismissed, but to reject them all is to posit an impossible series of coincidences. That in turn suggests why Victor closed off his account of the abdication on a defensive note (*HAb* 39.48):

> And although the good deed of Valerius has been twisted – others giving different explanations – it seems to me at least fitting for an excellent nature to have scorned desire for power and to have come down to ordinary life.[134]

Who are these others, who attributed the worst motives to an honourable man? The obvious answer is that they were Christians, like Lactantius, for whom the abdication was yet another sign of Diocletian's weakness and timidity. Victor's *History* was, in other words, in dialogue with Lactantius. In a way, this should not be surprising. A would-be Latin historian in the 350s seeking to write about the previous 200 years or so would have had to range widely for source material. Surely it would have been a dereliction of duty to avoid Christian works entirely, especially when they provided rich historical evidence.

Josephus and Cassius Dio

It would have been an even more serious omission, especially for a scholar working at the crossroads of east and west in the praetorian prefecture of Illyricum and in the ambit of the 'sophistic prefect' Anatolius, to avoid the Greek historians who together provided a continuous narrative of Roman history up to the final decades of the third century: Josephus, Cassius Dio, Herodian, Asinius Quadratus, and Dexippus.[135] Josephus, for example, was certainly enjoying something of a vogue in the second half of the fourth century – quoted by Ambrose, and translated into Latin in a highly Sallustian mode by an author the manuscripts call Hegesippus.[136] According to the current consensus, this fashion was confined to

---

132 Lucan, *BC* 4.298, 5.122; Statius, *Silvae* 3.1.83, 3.3.89; *Thebaid* 6.880, 7.720. In non-Christian prose before Victor: Suetonius, *Claud.* 35.1; ps.-Quintilian, *Declamationes maiores* 18.11.

133 The *Vetus Latina Database* published by Brepols offers an extraordinary collection of versions of these verses.

As a result, it is not clear to which one individual citations of the tag refer, as *e.g.* Cyprian, *Ep.* 10.5.1: *Dominus scrutator est renis et cordis*.

134 On the text here, see the Appendix, no. XV.

135 Chapter I.

136 Ambrose, *Ep.* 6.34.2; on Hegesippus, see Stover and Woudhuysen 2022b.

Christian circles, but, as we have seen above, this should not cause us to prejudge the question of whether Victor knew his works, and both Suetonius and Dio knew and used Josephus.[137] We do, in fact, have some intriguing evidence that Victor used Josephus as a source. Consider Victor's account of Chaerea, the killer of Caligula (*HAb* 3.14):

> For this reason, at the instigation of Chaerea, those in whom Roman virtue was present were moved to free the state from such a great disaster (*tanta pernicie rempublicam levare*) by running him [*i.e.* Caligula] through; and the noble deed of Brutus, when Tarquin was driven out, would have been brought back . . .

Both Suetonius and Dio have Chaerea taking vengeance for a private slight, as does the contemporary observer Seneca (*De const.* 18.3), but Victor here makes him into a freedom-fighter. Tacitus' account of Caligula's demise is lost, but his forward reference to Chaerea's action (*Ann.* 1.32.2) betrays no obvious hint of that characterisation. The only other source to depict Chaerea as a liberator is Josephus (*Antiquitates* 19.18–211).[138] This is not the only link: Victor notes that Galba 'was cut down in the seventh month and day of his reign' (*HAb* 6.3: *caesus est mense imperii ac die septimo*). He could not have obtained this information from Suetonius, who notes only that Galba was killed in the seventh month (*Galba* 23), nor from Tacitus, who gives the same duration in an oblique fashion (*Hist.* 1.37.5). The only other source to give the same exact duration (and with a very parallel expression) is Josephus (*BJ* 4.499: ἀναιρεθεὶς μετὰ μῆνας ἑπτὰ καὶ ἴσας ἡμέρας). In both these cases, of course, both Victor and Josephus could have had recourse to a common, now lost, source, but given the popularity of Josephus during Victor's lifetime, direct acquaintance should not be ruled out.

Cassius Dio provides an even more clear-cut case. We have already discussed the opening of Victor's work, with its richly allusive reference to the battle of Actium, when *mos Romae incessit uni prorsus parendi* (*HAb* 1.1), and its connection to Tacitus' *Histories*. Among the other links we have pointed out, both works begin with an AUC date. Crucially, however, the dates are different: Tacitus refers to the 820th, Victor to the 722nd year of the city (the year of Actium). What explains this divergence? After his description of the battle of Actium, Dio departs from his usual habit (as he tells us explicitly) and provides the day, 2 September, on which engagement took place. He is clear about why he has done this: 'then for the first time Caesar held all power alone, so that the counting up of the years of his monarchy is done exactly from that day'.[139] This is exactly what Victor is doing as well: he is telling the story of monarchy, 'obeying one man' (*uni parendi*), and so, in a nod to Dio, begins with the date of Actium.

This significant intertext should inspire us to look for further evidence of Dio in Victor. An obvious place to turn next would be the reign of Trajan, where there was a distinct shortage of other Latin or Greek source on which Victor could draw.[140] Dio appears to have thought Nerva's appointment

---

137 See Schreckenberg 1972: esp. 69–70 and 71–72.

138 On the vexed question of the sources of Josephus's account of the events, see Goud 1996 and Wiseman 2013.

139 Dio 51.1–2: Τοιαύτη τις ἡ ναυμαχία αὐτῶν τῇ δευτέρᾳ τοῦ Σεπτεμβρίου ἐγένετο. τοῦτο δὲ οὐκ ἄλλως εἶπον (οὐδὲ γὰρ εἴωθα αὐτὸ ποιεῖν) ἀλλ᾽ ὅτι τότε πρῶτον ὁ Καῖσαρ τὸ

κράτος πᾶν μόνος ἔσχεν ὥστε καὶ τὴν ἀπαρίθμησιν τῶν τῆς μοναρχίας αὐτοῦ ἐτῶν ἀπ᾽ ἐκείνης τῆς ἡμέρας ἀκριβοῦσθαι.

140 The one generally acknowledged exception would be the 'consular biographer' Marius Maximus, who is alleged to have written on the emperors from Nerva to Elagabalus. On him, see Chapter VII.

of Trajan as his heir particularly significant because he became the first emperor from outside Italy: 'since before this no foreigner had held power over the Romans'. Victor remarked on this transition in very similar terms: 'up to this point, those born at Rome or at least somewhere in Italy, ruled the Empire; from this time onwards, foreigners also did'.[141] More minor details also speak to a connection. Victor describes Trajan's construction of military camps in terms very close to Dio's (*HAb* 13.4: **Castra suspectioribus aut opportunis locis exstructa** ~ Dio 68.21.1: φρουρὰς ἐν τοῖς ἐπικαίροις καταλιπών).[142] Even more interesting is an incident, described by both authors, in which Trajan handed a blade to his new praetorian prefect, telling him to use it for him if he ruled well, and against him if ill. Not only are the two accounts closely parallel, but Victor also reproduces half of Dio's epigrammatic play with prepositions (κατ᾽ἐμοῦ ~ *in me magis*).[143] We could equally turn to Victor's description of Trajan's relationship to Hadrian, his 'fellow citizen and kinsman' (*HAb* 13.11: *Hadriano civi propinquoque*), since they both came from Italica in Spain.[144] Before Victor, this pair of relationships is found only in Dio, in terms absolutely parallel: 'For Hadrian was his Trajan's fellow citizen (πολίτης), had been under his guardianship, and came from the same family (γένους θ᾽οἱ ἐκοινώνει)' (69.1.1).[145]

Points of exact verbal contact continue beyond Trajan. Consider, for example, the brief comment in Dio on Marcus Aurelius' decision to share power with Lucius Verus at the death of Antoninus Pius (71.1.1):

ἐπειδὴ τοῦ ποιησαμένου αὐτὸν τελευτήσαντος Ἀντωνίνου τὴν ἀρχὴν ἔσχε, προσειλήφει ἐς κοινωνίαν τοῦ κράτους εὐθὺς τὸν τοῦ Λουκίου Κομόδου υἱόν.

When he took up imperial rule at the death of Antoninus who had adopted him, he had once taken as his partner in power the son of Lucius Commodus.

This is found in almost exactly the same words in the *HAb* (16.3): 'When his father-in-law had died, he swiftly took his brother Lucius Verus as a partner in power' (*socero . . .* **mortuo confestim fratrem Lucium Verum in societatem potentiae accepit**). Such touches may be subtle, but are nonetheless revealing, particularly since Victor approaches the delicate constitutional question of the relationship of the two emperors

---

141 Dio 68.4.2: ἐπειδὴ μηδεὶς πρόσθεν ἀλλοεθνὴς τὸ τῶν Ῥωμαίων κράτος ἐσχήκει ~ *HAb* 11.12: *Hactenus Romae seu per Italiam orti* **imperium** *rexere, hinc advenae quoque.*

142 Signalled by Dufraigne 1975: 102.

143 *HAb* 13.9: *usque eo innocentiae fidens, uti praefectum praetorio Suburanum nomine, cum insigne potestatis, uti mos erat, pugionem daret, crebro monuerit: 'Tibi istum ad munimentum mei committo, si recte agam; sin aliter,* **in me magis**'; Dio 68.16.1–2: ἀλλὰ καὶ ὅτε πρῶτον τῷ μέλλοντι τῶν δορυφόρων ἐπάρξειν τὸ ξίφος, ὃ παραζώννυσθαι αὐτὸν ἐχρῆν, ὤρεξεν, ἐγύμνωσέ τε αὐτὸ καὶ ἀνατείνας ἔφη 'λαβὲ τοῦτο τὸ ξίφος, ἵνα, ἂν μὲν καλῶς ἄρχω, ὑπὲρ ἐμοῦ, ἂν δὲ κακῶς, κατ᾽ἐμοῦ αὐτῷ χρήσῃ. The incident is alluded to in Pliny, *Pan.* 67.8: *ego quidem in me . . . etiam praefecti manum armavi.* Of the three sources, only Victor gives the name of the new prefect, Suburanus, though Dio survives here only in epitome.

144 *cf. HAb* 13.1: *Ulpium Traianum Italica, urbe Hispaniae, ortum.* Appian, *Hisp.* 38.153 says of Italica: πατρίς ἐστι Τραϊανοῦ τε καὶ Ἁδριανοῦ.

145 Hadrian's origins are a slightly murky subject (*PIR*² A.184). Besides Victor, Dio, and Appian, Gellius also says he was from Italica (*NA* 16.3.4: *unde ipse ortus est*), while Eutropius (8.6.1) and Jerome (*Chron.* 197ᵇ) say he was actually born there. The *LB* (14.1) has his father born at Adria, in Picenum. The *HA* says that his ancestors came from Adria and moved to Italica in the age of the Scipios (*Hadr.* 1.1, *cf.* 19.1 for service as a *quinquennalis in patria sua*), but that he was born at Rome (1.2). Syme 1964b: 142–143 defended the veracity of the *HA* on this point (its precise date does match that in the calendars of Philocalus and Polemius Silvius). *cf.* Chapter VII. At the same time, however, in *Sev.* 21.3, the *HA* describes Hadrian as the *municeps ac nepos* of Trajan.

in terms identical to Dio's. These links continue throughout the entire period covered by Dio, all the way up to the accession of Alexander Severus, which Dio says happened immediately (80.1.1: εὐθὺς) on the death of Elagabalus, where Victor uses *statim* for the same event (*HAb* 24.1).[146]

Herodian and Asinius Quadratus

Victor also seems to have known the work of Herodian, that inferior chronicler of the Severan age.[147] The evidence here is more subtle than was the case with Dio, but certain echoes are significant, particularly for the period after the terminal point of Dio's history. Herodian characterises Maximinus Thrax, Alexander's successor, as the 'first from the lowest class' (7.1.1: πρῶτος ἐξ εὐτελείας τῆς ἐσχάτης) to become emperor; Victor notes that he was the *primus e militaribus* (*HAb* 25.1).[148] Both historians describe how Gordian I sent letters promising rewards to the Praetorians:

> He sent a public letter to the people of Rome and the Senate . . . To the soldiers, he promised a cash donative as great as any before. (Herodian 7.6.3–4)

> Indeed Gordian, after he learnt that imperial power had been bestowed upon him, holding out the prospect of rewards in generous measure had sent ambassadors and letters to Rome. (*HAb* 26.6)

Both Herodian and Victor emphasise the haste with which Maximinus made for Italy on learning of the accession of the Gordians (7.8.11: αἰφνιδίου γὰρ γενομένης τῆς ἐπ᾽ Ἰταλίαν ὁδοῦ; 7.12.8: τῆς ἐπ᾽ Ἰταλίαν εἰσβολῆς εἴχετο ~ *HAb* 27.3: *Italiam propere petunt*).[149] Victor's discussion of the arrival of the news of the Gordians' demise at Rome could well be a translation of the corresponding line in Herodian (7.10.1: ὡς δὲ ἐς τὴν Ῥώμην ἐδηλώθη ἡ τοῦ πρεσβύτου τελευτή . . . ~ *HAb* 26.5: *Interim Romae comperto Gordiani interitu . . .*). As noted centuries ago, Victor also shares with Herodian the detail that young men were conscripted to form a force to defend the city from the disaffected Praetorians, and in very similar terms (7.12.1: ἥ τε νεολαία πᾶσα ἠθροίζετο ~ *HAb* 26.7: *conscriptis iunioribus*).[150] Finally, only Victor among Latin sources describes the riots against the Praetorians after the appointment of Pupienus and Balbinus, events covered extensively by Herodian (7.11). Both historians single out the role played in these by the gladiatorial schools (7.11.7: τὰ τῶν μονομάχων καταγώγια ~ *HAb* 27.2: *gladiatorum familiae*). All of this suggests that Victor had recourse to Herodian, despite the marked differences between their respective accounts of the chaos of the year 238.[151]

It is also possible that Victor knew the works of the shadowy Greek historians of the third century, the successors of Dio. Their writings are generally preserved for us only in fragments, so it is difficult to be certain, but there are some suggestive links. The work of Asinius Quadratus, who was active perhaps

---

146 Signalled by Dufraigne 1975: 137.
147 Van Hoof and Van Nuffelen 2020b: 493 list Herodian among Victor's sources.
148 This is usually chalked up to the supposed common source of Victor and Eutropius, since the latter notes that he was *ex corpore militari primus* (9.1), but see Chapter VI.

149 'For the journey into Italy was sudden'; 'They launched an invasion of Italy' ~ 'hastily, they made for Italy'.
150 By Anne Dacier 1681, *ad loc* (on whom, see Chapter VI).
151 On which, see Chapter VIII.

under Severus Alexander, unfortunately survives only in snippets.[152] In the sixth century, the historian Agathias quotes him on the Alamanni (1.6.3):

> The Alamanni, if indeed one ought to follow Asinius Quadratus, a man of Italian extraction who recorded German affairs (τὰ Γερμανικά) with some precision, are a promiscuous (ξύγκλυδες) and thoroughly mixed-up group of men, and this is what their name means.

By the standards of ancient etymology, the accuracy of this is positively scientific: there is a reasonable case to be made that 'Ala-manni' means something like 'all-men'.[153] The only other author to offer some commentary on it is Victor (*HAb* 21.2): *Alamannos, gentem populosam, ex equo mirifice pugnantem*, 'the Alamanni, a very numerous people, wonderfully skilled at fighting from horseback'. Victor has generally been understood to be making some specific claim about Alamannic demography, but it is much more likely that this is a discreet etymology, glossing the two elements of the name.[154] Whether or not Victor had read Quadratus' work, this etymological note speaks at the least to his unusually wide-ranging learning.

Dexippus

Victor's connections to Dexippus, the Athenian aristocrat and contemporary historian of the darkest period of the third century AD, are more numerous and more secure. In its discussion of the events of 238, the *HAb* notes very elliptically how the first step the Senate took was the establishment of an 'alternation of powers' (*HAb* 26.7: *senatus . . . primo potestatum vices . . . constituit*). This is a very obscure reference to events themselves very obscure, but it must have to do with the 'board of twenty' established by the Senate. That this emergency vigintivirate existed is beyond doubt – we have inscriptions attesting to six of its members – but it is not in Herodian.[155] The only other reference to it in Latin comes in the *Historia Augusta,* where the fact is explicitly attributed to Dexippus (*Maximin.* 32.3): 'Dexippus adds that such was the hatred for Maximinus that, when the Gordians were killed, the Senate appointed twenty men (*viginti viros*) who would oppose Maximinus'. Obviously, every citation in the *HA* deserves careful scrutiny, but the author must have obtained this one from somewhere (because it is not fiction) and it is not unreasonable to think that Victor found it in the same source.

Even more suggestive is an anecdote from the life of Decius (*HAb* 29.5). Victor tells us that Decius' son, Herennius Etruscus, was killed in battle against the barbarians after a bold sortie, whereupon the stricken soldiers began to try 'to console their emperor' (*ad solandum imperatorem*). He would have none of it, forcefully declaring that 'the loss of a single soldier seems a small matter' (*detrimentum unius militis parum videri*). The only other source for this story is the *Getica* of Jordanes (103):

152 Much about Quadratus is uncertain, though a date some time between Severus Alexander and the middle of the third century is not in doubt. See *FRH* 102 (Levick and Cornell) for a careful discussion.

153 Which is not to claim that the interpretation is uncontroversial: see Drinkwater 2007: 63–70, for a survey

of opinions. Servius, *Ad Georg.* 2.478 seems to have derived the name from Lac Leman.

154 Numbers: briefly, Drinkwater 2007: 141.

155 On the *vigintiviri*, see Dietz 1980: 326–340 (with a list of the known members).

When his father noticed this, it is related that he said (even if it was to strengthen the spirits of the soldiers) 'let no one be sad at this: the loss of one soldier does not diminish the commonwealth' (*perditio unius militis non est rei publicae deminutio*).

No other text (not even Jordanes' own *Romana*) includes this anecdote, but we have some idea of his ultimate source, since a closely parallel account (without the dictum) is attributed to Dexippus by the Byzantine chronographer George Syncellus, and the Vienna Dexippus finds prove that Jordanes' account of Decius is (at times closely) related to that of the Athenian historian.[156] It is not impossible, of course, that Jordanes got this saying from Victor – we have other evidence that he was being read in sixth-century Constantinople – but the fact that they have so little verbal overlap makes it likely that these are two different Latin adaptations of a single Greek source.[157]

Obviously these examples are far from conclusive: both historical works of Dexippus are mostly lost and so we will not find definitive proof that this saying of Decius was indeed in his account unless the right palimpsested leaf turns up. Nevertheless, the evidence is extremely suggestive, as a final example neatly demonstrates. Victor connects the appearance of the Phoenix in Egypt to the eight-hundredth anniversary of the city in AD 47, during the reign of Claudius. Dio and Tacitus both put the event a decade earlier, in 36 (58.27.1) and 34 (*Ann.* 6.28) respectively, in the reign of Tiberius. George Syncellus, however, once again citing Dexippus, also mentions its appearance under Claudius (*BNJ* 100 fr. 11 (McInerney)). Since Victor drew on both Tacitus and Dio, his agreement with Dexippus against them provides a strong indication that he was drawing directly on the Athenian's work.

Victor's Latin literary culture

Victor's reading ranged far wider than the historians. He knew his Cicero, for one, very well indeed. Numerous turns of phrase and peculiarities of expression reveal his many minor debts to the man from Arpinum. Some are very small – two- or three-word phrases.[158] Others are more significant, such as his version (*HAb* 15.3) of the famous Platonic *sententia* about philosopher kings (*Rep.* 473c-d), which seems closely related to Cicero's in *Ep. Quint.* 1.1.29. It is clear, however, that Victor liked using Cicero, rather than just reading him: he was looking for ideas as well as for style in the orator's works. As with Sallust and Tacitus, Victor at times engages in a sophisticated intertextual way with Cicero's works. Take his description of the aftermath of the death of Septimius Severus: 'although he died having reached old age (*exacta aetate mortuum*), they nonetheless decreed public mourning for him' (*HAb* 20.6). The key phrase is

---

156 George Syncellus p. 376a–b = *BNJ* 100 fr. 22 (McInerney). On the Vienna Dexippus, see Mitthoff et al. 2020; Brodersen's paper in that volume treats Jordanes and Dexippus.
157 On Victor's readers, see Chapter V.
158 A small selection: Cicero, *Phil.* 11.6: *pro rerum atrocitate* ~ *HAb* 39.8: *atrocitatem rerum*; only Ammianus in antiquity otherwise used the phrase (28.1.14). *De sen.* 26.13: *ad virtutum studia* ~ *HAb* 39.45: *virtutum studia*. *HAb* 40.12 uses *insulsitas*, a Ciceronian coinage (e.g.

Brut. 284) – in the interval only in Quintilian 5.13.38. *HAb* 42.24: *tam tantaque inclita*, cf. Cicero, *tam tantaque praeclara* (e.g. *De nat.* 1.56). *HAb* 15.5: *quod longe secus est*, a Ciceronian peculiarity (*De div.* 1.105; *Lael.* 29), otherwise only in Lactantius, *DI* 7.1.6. *HAb* 8.8: *quamquam satis*, cf. Cicero, *De orat.* 1.160, *Ep. Att.* 14.14.1, *Part. orat.* 109, *Pro Cluentio* 114, otherwise once in Apuleius (*Met.* 4.23), once in Augustine (*Contra Cresconium* 3.57.63), and once in a (counterfeit?) letter of Jerome (*Ep.* 148.1).

taken from a discussion of death in Cicero's *Tusculans*: 'but those who die having reached old age (*exacta aetate moriuntur*) are praised for their good fortune' (1.39.93). The broader context in both is even more illuminating. Victor's Severus reflects at the end on how little all his accomplishments meant at the point of death (with a sophisticated Sallustian intertext): 'as if a testament of mortal life, he said, "I was all things. It availed me nothing"'.[159] In Cicero, the conclusion of the argument is much the same. For an insect that lives only a day, making it to the eighth hour would be a long and full life; so too appears the longest human life *sub specie aeternitatis*.

Victor also uses Cicero for significant historical parallels. For example, Cicero deploys the ominous sobriquet *miserum fataleque bellum* for civil war (*Pro Marcello* 31, *Pro rege Deiotauro* 13), while Victor calls the conflict in which Constantine II was killed by his brother a *fatale bellum* (*HAb* 41.22). Besides the fact that this phrase is hardly found outside these two authors, Victor makes the borrowing obvious by the slight exaggeration of describing the conflict between the brothers – mostly consisting of a single chaotic and lethal ambush – as a *bellum*.

In both of these cases, as with other authors, Victor uses the intertext to provide an undertext: another layer of meaning beneath the surface. This can be subversive and that seems to be a particular feature of Victor's use of Cicero. In the *Philippics* (11.13), Cicero mocked Antony's supporter Decius, who had to auction off his property: 'I saw as well the auction of P. Decius, a distinguished man, who, following the example of his ancestors (*qui maiorum exempla persequens*), devoted (*devovit*) himself for his debt'. Cicero clarifies this mocking allusion two speeches later (13.27):

> There is also [in Antony's camp] a Decius, descended from, I believe, the Decii Mures . . . After a long space of time, by this famous man the memory of the Decii of old has been renewed (*Deciorum quidem multo intervallo . . . memoria renovata est*).

The reference is to the Republican P. Decii Mures, who performed a *devotio*, or the sacrifice of their life for victory on the battlefield, in the fourth and third centuries BC. This Decius performed a *devotio* too: he devoted himself to Antony to make good his debts. Victor has a *devotio*, of the emperor Claudius II, who allegedly vowed his life for victory over the barbarians. His description of it mirrors Cicero exactly (*HAb* 34.2): *quippe ut longo intervallo Deciorum memoriam renovaverit*.[160] While the *devotio* of Claudius – the putative ancestor of Constantine – has often been taken rather seriously as a bit of Constantinian propaganda, Victor is our earliest source to mention it and considering his reference in its Ciceronian frame gives the whole episode a darkly comic tinge.[161]

This is not the only instance where Cicero's words are put to a subversive purpose. Sometimes the target is a character in Victor's pages, as (possibly) with Claudius II. Sometimes it seems as though it is Cicero himself, perhaps unsurprisingly given Victor's Sallustianism. In a letter to Atticus, Cicero mentions having received a work from him on his own consulship.[162] He offers some slightly underhand criticism, a nice jab at his friend's composition, by which he manages to praise his own discernment:

---

159 *HAb* 20.29; *cf.* Chapter VIII.
160 See the Appendix, no. X, on this passage. As the intertext makes clearer still, the Decii here are the Decii

Mures (Livy 8.9, 10.28.12–18), not the emperors of the third century (as De Jonge 1972: 113).
161 See below.
162 Cicero, *Ep. Att.* 2.1.1.

> Although your work (for I read it gladly) seemed to me somewhat frightful and unpolished (*horridula mihi atque incompta visa sunt*), nevertheless it was adorned by the very fact that it had disregarded adornment and, like women, seemed to smell pleasant because it smelt of nothing.

The collocation of *horridus* and *incomptus* is very rare.[163] Only one other author uses it in a literary context, Victor in a description of the virtues of princes (*HAb* 40.13):

> From this it is clear that learning, grace, and taste are especially necessary for princes, since without these the benefits of nature are (so to speak) unpolished and even frightful to look at (*quasi incompta aut etiam horrida despectui sint*), and on the contrary they won for Cyrus, king of the Persians, eternal glory.

Victor's point is that without polish, things are just ugly: the discernment on which Cicero vaunted himself was simply self-deception. Another example points in the same anti-Ciceronian direction. In one of his more implausible passages in the *Philippics*, Cicero defended Aricia (the *patria* of Octavian's mother) against an alleged sneer by Antony (3.16):

> **Hinc** Voconiae, **hinc** Atiniae leges; **hinc** multae sellae curules et **patrum memoria** et **nostra**; **hinc** equites Romani lautissimi et plurimi.

> From here [Aricia] came the Voconian and Atinian laws; from here came many curule chairs, both in the memory of our fathers and our own; from here came Roman knights, very noble and very numerous.

In his account of Diocletian, Victor offered a comparison of that emperor to Marius which more than nods to Cicero (*HAb* 39.6):

> **Hinc** Marius **patrum memoria**, **hinc** iste **nostra** communem habitum supergressi, dum animus potentiae expers tamquam inedia refecti insatiabilis est.

> For this reason, Marius in the recollection of our ancestors and this man in our own exceeded the common style of dress, since a mind without experience of power, as though suffering from starvation, cannot be satisfied by refreshment.

Victor's point is, however, precisely the opposite of Cicero's. Where the latter was defending the respectability of great men from Aricia, Victor held that people from modest, non-metropolitan, backgrounds were likely to be arrogant when they reached power.[164]

From Cicero, let us turn to Vergil. Vergil was the most widely read poet of the fourth century (and indeed of every era of Latin literature after his own), and other historians, including Victor's predecessor Tacitus and successor Ammianus, engaged deeply with his work.[165] So too did Victor, but what is interesting is the extremely subtle and allusive use to which he puts the *Aeneid* (in particular). Three examples can demonstrate the point. First, Victor says in the *HAb* (24.8) that Rome's dominion had expanded

---

163 Tacitus, *Hist.* 2.11.3; Apuleius, *Met.* 5.28. Neither of these contain a verbal form derived from a verb of seeing.

164 On this see Stover and Woudhuysen 2020 [2015].

165 On Tacitus and Vergil see Joseph 2012; Ammianus: Kelly 2008: 13–20 and O'Brien 2006. *cf.* Foucher 2000.

TABLE 4.10 – VERGIL AND VICTOR

Aen. 6.811–812	*HAb* 24.9
Curibus parvis et paupere terra **missus in imperium** magnum	There were allowed into the imperial office (*immissique in imperium*) without distinction good men and bad, well-born and humble, and many from barbarian lands.
From the little town of Cures and its poor territory, he entered into a great command.	

continuously 'from Romulus to Septimius [Severus]'. Alexander Severus managed to keep it stable, but after his assassination, the Empire was plunged into chaos, with the result that imperial office was now open to individuals from all backgrounds, including barbarians.[166] He drives the point home with a subtle Vergilian touch, taken from the *Aeneid*'s description of Romulus' successor Numa (**TABLE 4.10**). Of course, the reputation of Numa in antiquity was almost uniformly positive. By using this Vergilian hemistich here, Victor adds a level of ambiguity to his otherwise negative portrayal of the crisis of the third century. Second, in *HAb* 41.11, Victor describes how the *magister pecoris camelorum*, one Calocaerus, attempted a usurpation: 'he seized the island of Cyprus in a fit of madness as if it were a kingdom' (*specie regni demens*). This picks up Dido's lament in the fourth book of the *Aeneid*: 'I took in the man cast up on my shore with nothing, and gave him a share of my kingdom in fit of madness' (*regni demens*).[167] Like Dido, Calocaerus met a fiery end: he was burnt alive after his capture, so there is (again) perhaps a slightly dark humour to the intertextuality here.[168] Third, after discussing the emperor Constans' dalliances with barbarian boys and subsequent death at the hands of the usurper Magnentius, Victor turns to an account of the latter with a curious exclamation: 'would, nonetheless, that such vices had endured!' (*HAb* 41.24: *Quae tamen vitia utinam mansissent!*). This too comes from Vergil. Achaemenides, a sailor left behind by Odysseus on Polyphemus' island, is telling Aeneas his story: that he was born at Ithaca and that his father was poor. As bad as that was, his lot was only made worse by joining Odysseus: 'would that such fortune had endured!' (*Aen.* 3.615: *mansissetque utinam fortuna!*). *Fortuna* here comes unexpectedly: normally we would not think of being born in squalor as an example of good luck, but compared to what followed, such a state was positively blessed. In the same way, for Victor, Constans' behaviour was not exactly what one would normally want in an emperor, but it was more than tolerable compared with the disasters that followed.

Cicero and Vergil give some sense of the extent and the sophistication of Victor's knowledge of Latin literature. It is, however, important to stress that he was not merely interested in the 'classics'. He read widely in works that had never attained that truly canonical status of being school texts: the famous *Quadriga Messii* of Vergil, Terence, Cicero, and Sallust that drove Roman schoolboys round the *circus* of their education.[169] We have already seen this with the historians, but it is not a phenomenon confined to

---

166 For the passage, *cf.* above.

167 *Aen.* 4.373–374: *eiectum litore, egentem / excepi et regni demens in parte locavi.*

168 The precise fate of Calocaerus is only in Theophanes AM 5825.

169 The appellation is from Cassiodorus, *Institutiones* 1.15.7. For the work of Arusianus Messius (active in the 390s), the *Exempla elocutionum*, see *GLK* 7.449–514.

historical literature. Victor knew the works of the younger Seneca well. He appears to have combed them for facts. In his *Natural Questions* (6.21.1), Seneca speaks of an island that 'in our time' appeared 'in the Aegean Sea' (*in Aegaeo mari*) 'when we were watching' (*spectantibus nobis*).[170] Among the prodigies towards the end of its account of Claudius, the *HAb* mentions that 'in the Aegean Sea (*in Aegaeo mari*) swiftly at night a huge island emerged'.[171] No other source speaks of this event and it seems almost certain that Victor lifted it from Seneca.[172]

In a way, it is unsurprising that a historian would turn to Seneca for historical colour in his account of the middle of the first century AD – yet Victor also made more subtle and allusive use of his works. In his account of the civil war of 350–353, he describes two of the usurpers, Nepotian and Vetranio, as having a *stolidum ingenium*, or 'brutish character'.[173] This is a very rare characterisation in late antiquity and the only classical author to use it is Seneca, who deploys it twice.[174] In one of these instances, in his *De Clementia*, Seneca characterises L. Cinna as *stolidi ingenii virum* (1.9.2). Cinna was a young nobleman who conspired against Augustus when the latter was in Gaul (1.9.2–3). The plot was revealed to the emperor, who, having first resolved to execute him, was tormented by doubt. Eventually, after meditating on the threats of civil war and bloodshed, Augustus resolved to show clemency: confronting Cinna, he spared his life and thereafter found him a loyal friend (1.9.4–12). A usurpation by a young nobleman of brutish character, planned when the emperor was in Gaul: the parallels to Nepotian – a princeling who usurped in the aftermath of Magnentius' bid for power in Gaul – are uncanny.[175] Yet, where Seneca's story has a happy ending, Nepotian's revolt was ruinous to the Roman Senate and people, the cause of a promiscuous massacre at the hands of Magnentius' troops, something that Victor explicitly attributed to his *stolidum ingenium*. Not for the first time, there is a dual meaning here: outward criticism of Nepotian, but also a sense of the road not taken by Magnentius.

Of course, a historian as widely read as Victor might turn to Seneca's *De Clementia* – a great repository of historical anecdotes. What is perhaps more surprising is that Victor can also be seen also using his tragedies. We discuss one very significant instance of this in a later chapter, but there is another that we wish to single out here.[176] The *Phoenissae* opens with a long speech by Oedipus, addressed to his daughter Antigone. In this, he describes a vision of his dead father Laius 'bearing the blood-soaked emblem of his plundered royal power' (ll. 40–41: *sanguineum gerens insigne regni . . . rapti*). Reference to a singular *insigne regni* is rare, though not unparalleled.[177] Victor, however, uses it for Caligula (*HAb* 3.13): *insigne regni nectere capiti tentaverat*, 'he had attempted to fasten on his head the emblem of royal power'. In Victor's telling, Caligula was perhaps responsible for the death of Tiberius and had certainly engaged in incest with his sisters (*HAb* 3.1, 10).

There is another particularly intriguing case of wide and obscure reading, found in the *HAb*'s account of the emperors Carus, Carinus, and Numerian. Victor was interested in clothing and what it

170 This island is distinct from the one that appeared in the Aegean at an earlier date, which Seneca mentions on the authority of Posidonius (*NQ* 2.26.4); *cf.* Henry 1982.
171 *HAb* 4.9 (*cf. LB* 4.9).
172 *cf. Pan. Lat.* 9.18.2, which describes the appearance of the island of Delos in the Aegean Sea.

173 *HAb* 41.26, 42.7; *cf.* 4.1.
174 Ambrose, *Expositio psalmi cxviii* 17.14; Martianus Capella, *De nupt.* 4.360. Seneca, *De ira* 3.30.2.
175 *PLRE* 'Nepotianus 5'.
176 Chapter VII.
177 Cicero, *Phil.* 3.12 (the diadem). Silius Italicus, *Pun.* 16.240 (the *chlamys*).

might say about powerful people.[178] In his description of Carus and his sons, he uses a very unusual periphrasis to say that the father was made Augustus and his sons Caesars (*HAb* 38.1): 'they were clothed in the raiment of emperors (*augusto habitu*)'. Awkwardness of phrasing like this often suggests that something is going on and, sure enough, it is here. Unusually for the third century, we have a surviving literary work which tells us at least a little about these emperors: a rather fine poem, the *Cynegetica* of Nemesianus. In this, the poet fancies that he can already see the 'imperial raiment' (*augustos habitus*) of the brothers Carinus and Numerian, on whom he has not yet actually laid eyes.[179] No other surviving Latin work before Victor uses this striking phrase.[180] One of the few authentic details known of the reigns of Carus, Carinus, and Numerian was that under them Nemesianus had written poetry, and it found some readers in late antiquity.[181] Such rare phrasing in conjunction with such obscure emperors cannot be coincidental: Victor knew Nemesianus and he thought that some of his readers would as well.

Pliny the Younger is another author with whose work Victor engaged. We have already suggested that it is possible he used the *Panegyricus* for facts about Nerva and Trajan, but he also engaged with Pliny's ideas. At *Pan.* 2.2–3, Pliny reflects on how much has changed from the time of Domitian:

> Let us say nothing of the sort we used to say, for we suffer nothing of the sort we used to suffer. Let us not proclaim publicly (*palam*) what we did before, for we do not say privately what we did before. Let the difference of the eras be marked in the way we speak, and from the way in which we give thanks let it be clear to whom and when we are so doing. Nowhere ought we flatter him like a god (*ut deo*), nowhere like a divinity, for we do not speak about a tyrant, but a citizen, not of a master but a parent (*non de domino sed de parente*).

In his discussion of the *ambitio* of (Valerius) Diocletian, Victor picks up on this idea, with explicit reference back to Domitian (*HAb* 39.4–8):

> For he was the first of all the emperors after Caligula and Domitian who allowed himself to be publicly (*palam*) called 'master' (*dominus*), and to be worshipped and acclaimed as a god (*uti deum*) . . . But in Valerius these faults were overshadowed by other good qualities; and especially by the fact that, though he allowed himself to be called 'lord', he played the part of a parent (*dominum dici passus parentem egit*). And the fact that he willed this, it is generally agreed, teaches the prudent man that savagery in reality is more damaging than savagery in words.

Beyond the compelling textual parallels and the shared context, Victor is subverting Pliny's claim.[182] For Pliny, words matter, and how to talk about an emperor and what to call him was important; for Victor, the ostensible point is precisely that what an emperor was called, whether he was referred to as 'master', was much less important than how he acted, whether he behaved like a parent.

It would be wrong, however, to get the impression that Victor read only *belles-lettres*. We saw above that he was browsing the *Natural Questions* of the younger Seneca. There are other hints of his reading

---

178 For instance, he offers a detailed comparison of the dress of Marius and Diocletian (*HAb* 39.6) (on which, see Stover and Woudhuysen 2020 [2015]); *cf.* 3.10 on Caligula, 21.1 on Caracalla, and 21.3 on Julia Domna.

179 Nemesianus, *Cyn.* 76–81.

180 *cf.* AM 20.4.22 for a later use.

181 See Stover and Woudhuysen 2022a: 190–191.

182 This single *locus similis* between the two texts is more compelling than the handful of parallels Burgersdijk 2013 gathered between Pliny and the *HA*.

in more technical literature. Victor describes Carthage as the *terrarum decus* (*HAb* 40.19); the only other occurrence of this phrase is in the (third-century?) compendium by Solinus, where it is also used for Carthage: 'the second city after Rome, earth's glory' (27.11: *alterum post urbem Romam terrarum decus*). We do not know whence Solinus drew this phrase – it is not from either Pliny or Pomponius Mela – and so it is not clear whether Victor was reading Solinus or his source. Something similar may be said about his evocative description of Augustus' reign, *quiescentibus bellis*, 'when wars grew still' (*HAb* 1.3). The only other occurrence of this absolute is in Solinus, describing the same period (1.33): 'This time is almost the only one to be found in which arms gave way and talents blossomed . . . when wars grew still (*bellis quiescentibus*)'. What is striking about the latter example is that the shared context suggests this is more than Victor simply lifting an evocative phrase.[183]

Grammar, philosophy, law, and rhetoric

Victor clearly had unusually broad tastes in Latin literature and the skill to use what he read to good effect. His wide reading – knowledge of Cicero, Sallust and Vergil, above all – points at the very least to a thorough grammatical training, but Victor also shows signs of a much deeper knowledge of the technicalities of grammar. In his account of the Tetrarchy, Victor says that after Galerius' defeat of the Persians (*HAb* 39.36):

> He was so victorious that had Valerius, at whose nod all things were carried out (*cuius nutu omnia gerebantur*), not declined to assent to it (his reason is uncertain), the Roman *fasces* would have been carried into a new province.

There is a sort of joke concealed here, one that emerges only if one turns to Varro's *De lingua Latina*, where the polymath explains a quotation from Accius with the following comment:

> They say that *numen* (divine will) is *imperium* (power), derived from *nutus* (nod), because the one at whose nod all things are, his power seems to be the greatest: so Homer <uses the word> for Jove and Accius (?) does sometimes too.[184]

Diocletian adopted the *signum* 'Jovius' and Jupiter as his special patron, so, of course, all things were done at his nod.[185] Another example is less elaborate but equally revealing. Victor says that Domitian was 'deranged (*amentior*) by a crime both private and public' (*HAb* 11.1), the murder of his brother Titus. Victor has a mania for using comparative adjectives where we might expect a positive, but in this case it seems that the comparative makes a point. As Donatus explained: 'a man is out of his mind [*amens*] when

---

183 On Solinus, his date, and sources, topics on which there is not much certainty, see the essays in Brodersen 2014. Were he drawing directly on Solinus, then Victor would be his first attested reader.

184 *De ling. lat.* 7.5.85: *numen dicunt esse imperium, dictum ab nutu, <quod cuius nutu> omnia sunt, eius imperium maximum esse videatur: itaque in Iove hoc et Homerus et † alius † aliquotiens.* It would make sense for the other author mentioned to be Accius, doubtful though the text is.

185 On the *signum*, see above.

he does not know what he is saying; he is deranged [*amentior*] when his deeds do not cause him regret'.[186] Superficially, Victor seems to be saying that Domitian regretted his crimes, but a closer reading shows him making precisely the opposite point.

The grammatical tradition was, of course, central to Roman schooling, but there is also evidence in the *HAb* of higher education. Victor evinces technical philosophical knowledge. We have already mentioned the Platonic *placitum* on philosopher-kings, but even more significant is his veritable obsession with fate. Victor knew that the technical term for the kind of knowledge we can have of future events is *notio* (*HAb* 38.5).[187] His description of how present events can influence future ones 'by a certain law' (*HAb* 34.6: *ratione quadam*) seems to engage with the doctrines of Chrysippus, on how all things are 'subject to an inevitable and fundamental law (*ratione quadam*) and are closely linked to fate', as reported by Gellius.[188] Similarly, Victor discussed how even after exchanging a vicious ruler for a good one, people have their hopes dashed, since 'the force of their troubles endures' (*HAb* 40.30: *vis aerumnarum manet*). The only other occurrence of the phrase *vis aerumnarum* is in another one of Gellius' discussions of Chrysippus, where he argues that unphilosophical people consider that the 'force of their troubles and evils' (*vim aerumnarum et malorum*) is inconsistent with the existence of providence.[189] Victor also believed in a specifically cyclical model of historical change (*HAb* 35.13), not much different from the conception of Marcus Aurelius (*Med.* 10.27). He held that what drives history is *vis naturae*, the power of nature. On the other side is the *vis Fortunae*, 'the power of Fortune', against which mortals are protected by virtue, 'as if by a wall' (*uti muro*) (*HAb* 24.11).[190] This notion of virtue as a wall has more of a Greek than a Roman pedigree. Plutarch reports in his *Apothegmata Laconica* the Spartan idea that their virtue was the real wall of their city (210e).[191] The precise notion, however, of virtue as the city wall that protects the individual from the incursion of vice (in Victor, the *libido*, or desire, with which the *vis Fortunae* drives mortals) is not common, coming specifically from the Socratic Antisthenes of Athens.[192] All of this is not necessarily meant to suggest that Victor was using specific philosophical texts, but rather that his comfort in deploying philosophically fraught terminology suggests a certain level of technical education in the discipline.

Victor also displays technical knowledge of law, broadly considered. He religiously distinguishes between *prodigia* and *portenta* and uses the traditional pontifical terms for describing them.[193] Victor speaks of Hadrian establishing *initia Cereris* at Rome: this was a technical term, used previously only by Livy and Varro.[194] There are even hints of an actual training in the law. Victor was clearly interested in the technicalities of imperial government: he cared about the precise bureaucratic position that the jurist

---

186 Donatus, *Ad And.* 5.877.1. Of course, the transmitted commentaries of Donatus do not always give his original phrasing. Another instance: compare Victor's description of Crispus as *natu grandior* (*HAb* 41.11) with Donatus, *Ad Phorm.* 2.362.4 on the same phrase: *hic comparativus non est, sed habet significationem a positivo minus.*

187 *cf.* Marius Victorinus, *Def.* p. 18 Stangl.

188 Gellius, *NA* 7.7.2 *ratione quadam necessaria et principali coacta atque connexa sint fato omnia*. The translation is from Rolfe's Loeb.

189 Gellius, *NA* 7.1.2. This passage has been lost in the manuscript tradition of Gellius, but was fortuitously preserved by Lactantius, *Epit.* 24.5.

190 The idea of the opposition of Fortune and Virtue has a long history (*cf.* Hinard 1987; Balmaceda 2017), and is also found, for example, in Ammianus (e.g. 14.6.3: *cf.* Marié 1989).

191 The same idea underlies Strabo 5.3.7.

192 Fr. 90 Caizzi; *cf.* Prince 2015: 346–348.

193 In particular, see *HAb* 28.3, 41.14 (*caeli facies conflagrauit igni continuo*), 47.2.

194 Varro, *Res Rusticae* 2.4.9, 3.1.5; Livy 31.14.7, 31.47.2; *cf.* Justin 5.1.1.

Papinian had occupied and had strong views about the *cursus publicus*.[195] His knowledge of this topic encompasses some very obscure subjects: Victor, alone of fourth-century authors, tells us in so many words that Diocletian's reforms included the imposition of taxes on Italy (*HAb* 39.31). He is surely correct, for Lactantius' detailed account (*DMP* 26.2) of the usurpation of Maxentius makes clear that this was a significant cause of the revolt, though it presents it in a (characteristically) fiery and general fashion. More than what he knows, however, it is the language that Victor uses that is suggestive. He speaks of *vectigalium pensiones*, 'the payment of taxes', and *adventiciae praebitiones*, or 'extraordinary payments': the former term is a piece of legal bureaucratese, while *praebitio* was a standard official word for payment in late antiquity.[196] Of course, Victor's time in the entourage of Anatolius might have given him plenty of indirect exposure to the fiscal machinery of the state and its terminology, but there are signs of a more wide-ranging interest in the law. In discussing the legal reforms of Marcus Aurelius, Victor shows detailed and specific knowledge of the laws surrounding bail and summonses, using technical terms like *vadimonia* and *denuntiatio litis*.[197] His wording for Salvius Julianus' codification or quasi-codification of the praetorian edicts has a technical flavour to it, particularly with the phrase *edictum . . . composuerit*.[198] We have already seen that Victor was very careful when it came to adoption and that care extended beyond names. He explains that Tiberius was 'by adoption brought back among the number of Augustus' children from having been his stepson' (*HAb* 2.1: *in Augusti liberos e privigno redactus arrogatione*). This is technical language. Tiberius was *redactus* because he returned to Augustus' *patria potestas* (Suetonius, *Tib.* 15.2).[199] The arrangement was *arrogatio*, because, as the jurist Gaius explains, 'we adopt by the authority of the people those who are legally independent: this type of adoption is called *adrogatio*'.[200] Victor is one of only two literary authors to ever use the word, which is the almost exclusive preserve of legal works – he deploys it again when describing the adoption of Trajan (*HAb* 13.1).[201]

As we have already mentioned in passing, Victor took considerable interest in – and had strong opinions about – eloquence, especially its importance for emperors. His remarks on the Caesars (*HAb* 8.7–8) are a good example of this, but it is a recurring theme: he covers at some length, for instance, the rhetorical skill Constantius II had shown in the civil wars of the 350s (*HAb* 42.1–4).[202] It is unsurprising therefore that we can find signs of some technical rhetorical training in Victor. A rich intertext

---

195 *HAb* 20.33–34; 13.6. On Papinian, see further Chapter VIII.

196 *Vectigalium pensiones*: *HAb* 9.6 (*LB* 9.7); *CTh* 5.15.14; *Digest* 39.4.10, 11; Paulus, *Sententiae* 5.1a.15. *Adventiciae praebitiones*: *HAb* 41.19. The only literary use of *praebitio* from before late antiquity is a fragment of Varro, preserved in Nonius Marcellus p. 152M. On 'bureaucratese', see the classic paper by MacMullen 1962.

197 *HAb* 16.11: see Metzger 2000, though Victor's dating of the reforms under Marcus Aurelius has been criticised.

198 *cf. Digest* 1.2.2.44 (Pomponius, quoting Ofilius). *cf.* Cicero, *II Verr.* 1.116, 119. Cancelli 2010: 130–131.

199 For the legal flavour, *cf. Digest* 1.6.11: *Inviti filii naturales vel emancipati non rediguntur in patriam potestatem. TLL* 11.2.534.26–50 (Spoth).

200 *Institutiones* 1.99.27: *Populi auctoritate adoptamus eos, qui sui iuris sunt: quae species adoptionis dicitur adrogatio . . . cf. Digest* 1.7.1: *Quod adoptionis nomen est quidem generale, in duas autem species dividitur, quarum altera adoptio similiter [simpliciter ?] dicitur, altera adrogatio. Adoptantur filii familias, adrogantur qui sui iuris sunt.*

201 The other literary source is *HA Aurel.* 11.1, 12.3. Gellius, *NA* 5.19 could perhaps be added as a third.

202 For the Caesars, see above. It is curious that what Victor says about their rhetorical abilities rather recalls the comments of Fronto, *Ep. Ver.* 2.10, which also have the Sallustian *pudere/pigere* wordplay of which Victor was fond (Chapter V).

TABLE 4.11 – SENECA THE ELDER, SUETONIUS, AND VICTOR

Seneca 2.7.1	*HAb* 33.23	Suetonius, *Iul.* 86.2
Quamquam eo prolapsi iam **mores** civitatis **sunt**, ut nemo ad suspicanda adulteria nimium credulus possit videri . . .	**Quamquam eo prolapsi mores sunt**, uti **suo quam reipublicae** magisque **potentiae** quam **gloriae** studio plures agant.	. . . non tam **sua quam rei publicae** interesse, uti salvus esset: se iam pridem **potentiae gloriae**que abunde adeptum.
Although the morals of the city have already so far decayed that no man can be considered too ready to believe when it comes to suspecting adultery.	Although morals have so far decayed that more men act in their own interest than for the state and more out of zeal for power than for glory.	. . . that it was not in his own, but in the state's interest that he remain unharmed; that he had already long before won more than enough power and glory.

combines the *Controversiae* of the elder Seneca with Suetonius (**TABLE 4.11**). Engagement with Seneca the Elder shows that Victor was imbued with the precepts of a rhetorical education. Other turns of phrase he uses are paralleled only in imperial declamation, such as *fere vix* (*HAb* 42.3; *cf.* pseudo-Quintilian, *Decl. mai.* 1.4) and the evocative *atrocitas nominum* in a passage discussed above (39.8; *cf. Decl. mai.* 11.8). His deep familiarity with the rhetorical and oratorical works of Cicero points in the same direction.

All of this is hardly surprising: Victor was, as he said himself, intensely proud of his education.[203] As we have seen, he also seems to compare himself to Septimius Severus, as another example of a North African who made it in the Roman world through education (*HAb* 20.5–6). Severus was, he says, 'given to philosophy, declamation and all liberal pursuits', 'though of humble origin, he was first immersed in literature, and then in the law courts' (*HAb* 20.22, 28). Whether or not Victor meant to describe his own education here, literature, philosophy, rhetoric, and law seem to offer a portrait of his intellectual background. Everything we know about his milieu points in the same direction: the circle of Anatolius was specifically a place in which literary culture, law, rhetoric, and philosophy were all held in particularly high esteem.

Victor's Greek literary culture

Victor's literary culture was, however, by no means limited to Latin, as was that of so many of his contemporaries, some from rather more privileged backgrounds.[204] We have already seen that he used the works of Greek imperial historians and that he seems to have had some acquaintance with Greek philosophy, but his Hellenism was more extensive still. A curious episode shows the extent to which Victor positively revelled in obscure Greek knowledge. He describes the notorious seaside excursion – the outcome of the German campaign mentioned above – of the emperor Caligula, wherein (clad as Venus) he ordered his

203 Chapter I.

204 Symmachus, who had some pretensions to literary culture, seems to have known remarkably little Greek: see Cameron 2011: 535–542.

soldiers to collect the shells of molluscs (*conchae* and *umbilici*), which he described as 'spoils from the gods' (*HAb* 3.11–13). The use of *umbilicus* for a seashell is in itself extremely rare.[205] What follows the *umbilici* in Victor's account of Caligula's grand day out is, however, even more *recherché*. Victor explains (tongue-in-cheek) that the reason Caligula spoke of heavenly spoils is that the Greeks call 'fish of this sort . . . the eyes of nymphs (*nympharum lumina*)'. There is no evidence beyond this that the Greeks called anything beyond the ocular organs of immortals 'nymphs' eyes', but a fragment of Speusippus, who directed the Academy after Plato, mentions that a kind of sea-creature, similar to a number of other shelled ones, was indeed called a νύμφη.[206] Victor's joke is so obscure as to be almost lost on us, but it seems to come from the most recondite of Greek usage.

That Victor did indeed know and use Greek literature is beautifully demonstrated by his account of the loving, perhaps too loving, relationship between Caracalla and Julia Domna (*HAb* 21.3), an episode on which we have already touched:

> For he desired to have his stepmother Julia, whose crimes I have mentioned above, as a wife, captivated by her beauty, after she, rather slyly, had presented herself with bared body to his youthful gaze, as if she were unaware of his presence, and when he said 'I would wish, if it were permitted, to have use of that', she replied much more naughtily (*for she had taken off her modesty with her clothes*) 'It is your pleasure? Obviously it is permitted'.

Unlike the common run of stripteases, this one is literally Herodotean, clearly based on the story of Gyges and his lord, Candaules, the king of Lydia (1.8–12). In a brilliant but neglected article, Friedhelm Müller has demonstrated that Victor must have taken this story directly from Herodotus' Greek text.[207] Alone of all the Latin retellings of this unsurprisingly popular tale, Victor includes the sententious comment 'for she had taken off her modesty with her clothes (*quippe quae pudorem velamento exueret*)'. This is a verbatim translation of a line from Herodotus' account: ἅμα δὲ κιθῶνι ἐκδυομένῳ συνεκδύεται καὶ τὴν αἰδῶ γυνή (1.8). The key point here is not the question of how Julia Domna passed the long winter evenings, but the clear proof that Victor was engaging in a sophisticated way with literature in Greek, as well as in Latin.[208] In this, he is very unusual among fourth-century historians – only Ammianus is comparable.[209]

That Victor was indeed engaged with Greek literature in a sophisticated way should long have been obvious, for on one occasion he practically footnotes it. We have already seen him opining on the necessity of *eruditio*, *elegantia*, and *comitas* for princes, with a swipe at Cicero mixed in (*HAb* 40.13). His illustration of the point is the career of Cyrus, most famous of the Persian monarchs. This ought to make us curious about the possibility of an allusion to the *Cyropaedia* of Xenophon and, as Anne Dacier pointed out centuries ago, there is a passage that Victor seems to have had in mind (1.2.1):

---

205 Once in Cicero (*De orat.* 2.6.22) and once in Valerius Maximus (8.8.1, derived from Cicero). The *TLL* has not yet reached *umbilicus*, but a review of the slips it holds for the entry suggests that these are the only two usages in this sense.
206 Athenaeus, *Deipnosophistae* 3.105b.
207 Müller 1998–1999.
208 For the Greek flavour of this episode, compare Herodian 4.9.3 (on jibes at Julia as 'Jocasta') and Heliodorus,

Aethiopica 1.10 (signalled by Dufraigne 1975: 133), which describes a remarkably similar incident. Marasco 1996 points out the extent to which the family drama of the Severans is described by ancient authors in terms reminiscent of Greek tragedy.
209 For Ammianus and Greek, see Fornara 1992b; Barnes 1998: 65–78; Ross 2016a: 207–218.

φῦναι δὲ ὁ Κῦρος λέγεται καὶ ᾄδεται ἔτι καὶ νῦν ὑπὸ τῶν βαρβάρων εἶδος μὲν κάλλιστος, ψυχὴν δὲ φιλανθρωπότατος καὶ φιλομαθέστατος καὶ φιλοτιμότατος ὥστε πάντα μὲν πόνον ἀνατλῆναι, πάντα δὲ κίνδυνον ὑπομεῖναι τοῦ ἐπαινεῖσθαι ἕνεκα.

Even today it is still mentioned in the barbarians' songs that Cyrus was most handsome in appearance, most generous in spirit, most fond of learning and most ambitious for distinction, so that he endured every hardship and patiently submitted to every danger for the sake of praise.[210]

Immediately after the mention of Cyrus, Victor goes on to meditate on the role of ambition in Constantine's life (*HAb* 40.15). This is more than a nod to a classic work – it is a rumination prompted by reading it.

Further evidence for Victor's reading in the literature of Greece can be found in his account of the bizarre rumour that Marcus Aurelius poisoned Lucius Verus, his adoptive brother and co-emperor (*HAb* 16.5–7):

Lucius paucis diebus moritur, hincque materies fingendi dolo consanguinei circumventum; quem ferunt, cum invidia gestarum rerum angeretur, fraudem inter cenam exercuisse. Namque lita veneno cultri parte vulvae frustum, quod de industria solverat, eo praecidit consumptoque uno, uti mos est inter familiares, alterum, qua virus contigerat, germano porrexit.[211]

A few days later Lucius died and this offered an opportunity for concocting the story that he was betrayed by the deceit of his kinsman. They say that Marcus, since he was tormented by envy at Lucius' accomplishments, practised a wicked act of deceit at dinner. For he smeared one side of a knife with poison and cut off part of the womb of a sow, which was carefully separated from the other. When he had eaten that part, as is the custom among family members, he offered the other, which the venom had touched, to his brother.

As Schott pointed out in the notes to his *editio princeps*, this agrees almost word for word with the story of Parysatis and Stateira from Plutarch's *Artaxerxes* (19.3). Parysatis was the mother of Artaxerxes II Mnemon, king of Persia from 404 to 358 BC; Stateira was his wife. The mother was resentful of her daughter-in-law's influence, and such an atmosphere of distrust arose between them that they took to sharing their meals to forestall attempts at poisoning. This did not stop Parysatis, armed with a bird and a gift for deception:

τοῦτό φησιν ὁ Κτησίας μικρᾷ μαχαιρίδι κεχρισμένῃ τῷ φαρμάκῳ κατὰ θάτερα τὴν Παρύσατιν διαιροῦσαν, ἐκμάξαι τῷ ἑτέρῳ μέρει τὸ φάρμακον· καὶ τὸ μὲν ἄχραντον καὶ καθαρὸν εἰς τὸ στόμα βαλοῦσαν αὐτὴν ἐσθίειν, δοῦναι δὲ τῇ Στατείρᾳ πεφαρμαγμένον.

Ctesias says that it was this sort of bird that Parysatis divided with a small knife, smeared with poison on one side, so as to wipe the poison on one of the portions of it. Putting the undefiled and clean part in her mouth, she ate it and gave to Stateira the poisoned one.

This was not a widely discussed story in Latin literature: not only was Victor reading Greek, he was also showing remarkable independence in what he chose to read.[212] To understand why Victor chose

---

210 Dacier 1681 *ad loc.*
211 On this corrupt passage, see the Appendix, no. IV.

212 No extant Latin text from antiquity appears to discuss it. Significantly, it is not in Justin 10.1–2, nor is it mentioned in the *prologi* to the *Historia Philippica* 9–10.

to imitate Plutarch in this particular instance, we need to go back to Cassius Dio.[213] In the remnants of Book LXXI, Dio makes a brief reference to the story of Marcus and Verus (71.3.1): 'For he [*sc.* Verus] is said after this to have plotted against his father-in-law Marcus, and to have been killed with poison before he could do anything'.[214] In both Victor and Dio, this is connected with Lucius' return from his Persian campaign, which might explain why Victor chose a Persian case of poisoning. Even more significantly, Dio emphasises a different aspect of the relationship of the two emperors: not only was Marcus the brother of Verus – they were both adopted by Antoninus Pius – he was also his father-in-law (πενθερῷ), due to Verus' marriage to Marcus' daughter Lucilla. Hence a story about the troubled relationship of a Persian mother-in-law and daughter-in-law must have seemed doubly *apropos*. Like Plutarch, Victor stresses that the cause of the discord was envy (*invidia* ~ 19.1: ζηλοτυπίας).

There is, however, one key difference between the two accounts: in Plutarch the dish in question is a particular kind of bird, a *rhyntaces*, eaten whole, like an ortolan.[215] In Victor it is a sow's womb (*vulva*). In general, sow's womb in Latin literature is an ostentatious and opulent dish, one that makes frequent appearances in satire.[216] The appearance of this delicacy at the dinner of Marcus and Verus could have been inspired by the latter's reputation for extravagance, but we know of that reputation solely from the *Historia Augusta* (e.g. *Verus* 5.1–5). Victor is probably making a subtler point. In the span of sixty-five words in the *HAb*, three different terms are used to describe their relationship: *frater* (16.3), *consanguineus* (16.5), and *germanus* (16.7). The significance of the first, *frater*, is broad and uncontroversial. While the second was generally reserved for blood relations, late-antique legal sources are explicit that adoption also makes those adopted *consanguinei*.[217] *Germanus* is what poses a problem: it was usually thought to apply only to full, biological brothers.[218] A minority tradition, however, defended by Servius (*In Aen.* 5.412) on the authority of Varro, defined *germanus* as 'one who shares the same mother (*genetrice*)', and this does indeed seem to be how Vergil used the word.[219] The occurrence of the word in this passage in Victor seems to be the only instance in which it is applied to an adoptive brother.

Why would Victor choose to use the only word for brother which ought not apply to the relationship of Marcus and Verus? Marcus himself had no problem describing Verus as his ἀδελφός (*Med.* 1.17.4), but this is because ἀδελφός has a similar semantic range to Latin *frater*, despite its etymological association with δελφύς, 'womb'.[220] Victor may well have known this passage from Marcus directly, but regardless of whether or not he had the Marcus' book before his eyes, it is likely that ἀδελφός and its etymology were in the back of Victor's mind as he put together this episode and specified that the dish they ate was sow's

213 It is of course possible that Victor had the story directly from Ctesias, whose work was still available to Photius (*Bibliotheca*, cod. 72).

214 Interestingly, Herodian also makes brief reference to the story in a speech he puts into the mouth of Caracalla (4.5.6).

215 The word appears to be only here in ancient literature, though Photius, *Bibliotheca* cod. 72 (44b) confirms that it was indeed in Ctesias.

216 Gowers 1993: 121.

217 Paschoud 2006a [2001]: 415–416. *TLL* 4.359.14–4.360.22 (Gudeman). *Collatio legum* 16.6.1: *consanguineos*

et adoptio facit. Institutiones 3.2.2: . . . *inter filios naturales et eos, quos pater eorum adoptavit (nec dubium est, quin proprie consanguinei appellentur)* . . .

218 *TLL* 6.2.1915.10– 6.2.1916.5 (Meyer).

219 In *Aeneid* 5.412, Entellus addresses to Aeneas the words *germanus Eryx . . . tuus*. According to at least one tradition, Aphrodite was the mother of Eryx (Diodorus Siculus 4.23.2), but no one thought him the son of Anchises.

220 It was probably for this reason that the ancient glossaries defined *germanus* as ἀδελφός, *cf. TLL* 6.2.1914.55–60 (Meyer).

womb.[221] Before the meal, Marcus and Verus had been *fratres* and *consanguinei*, but by sharing a womb, *vulva*, they became *germani*.[222]

With the mere scraps of Dio's Book LXXI that Xiphilinus has preserved, it is difficult to evaluate Victor's account of the fate of Verus. The only other text to even mention the story of his poisoning is the *Historia Augusta*, but it (as we discuss later) derived its telling of this incident wholly from Victor.[223] Even so, it seems very likely that Dio's full work provided more detail as to the allegation that Verus was poisoned. Victor's exact verbal parallels with Plutarch suggest, however, a direct relationship:

> μικρᾷ μαχαιρίδι (~ cultri) κεχρισμένη (~ lita) τῷ φαρμάκῳ (~ veneno) κατὰ θάτερα τὴν Παρύσατιν διαιροῦσαν (~ solverat) ἐκμάξαι τῷ ἑτέρῳ μέρει τὸ φάρμακον (~ alterum qua virus contigerat)· καὶ τὸ μὲν ἄχραντον καὶ καθαρὸν εἰς τὸ στόμα βαλοῦσαν αὐτὴν ἐσθίειν (~ consumptoque uno), δοῦναι (~ porrexit) δὲ τῇ Στατείρᾳ πεφαρμαγμένον.

Victor thus shows a broad and deep knowledge of Greek prose, from Herodotus, through Xenophon, down to Plutarch. He makes sophisticated use of that reading, in precisely the same fashion in which he deploys his extensive knowledge of Latin literature: as a tool for interpreting history, as much as a way to adorn his writing. All of this makes Victor a figure of considerable, indeed unusual, literary culture. He claims to have read widely and deeply in the course of researching his history: there is plenty in the text to suggest that he was telling truth.

Compound allusions

To illustrate this, and to bring to a close this survey of Victor's learning, let us look at a few significant examples of compound allusions, where he weaves together material from two different sources to fashion something new. We have elsewhere explored one of these in detail: the way that Victor uses Cicero and Sallust in concert to discuss the impact of Diocletian's humble origins on his conduct as emperor.[224] Another comes just a few lines later, when Victor touches on how Diocletian conducted himself after his victory over Carinus (*HAb* 39.15):

> Quae res **post memoriam humani** nova atque inopinabilis fuit civili bello *fortunis fama dignitate spoliatum* neminem . . .

> This situation was in all the memory of man novel and inconceivable, that in a civil war no one was despoiled of his wealth, reputation, and dignity . . .

---

221 We have seen that Victor was interested in philosophy and his description of Marcus' estimation of Hipparchus at *HAb* 41.20, *praestanti ingenio*, seems to go back to *Med.* 6.47.1, Ἵππαρχος . . . ἄλλαι φύσεις ὀξεῖαι. On this episode, see Haake 2016, who cites earlier literature extensively. Based on what we have shown about Victor's use of names above, Pékáry 1993 was correct to argue that the imposition of the fine on Nicaea should date to before Marcus' accession as emperor.

222 Juvenal too plays on the double meaning of *vulva* as a part of human anatomy and a rich dish: Gowers 1993: 198. We ought to note that Victor explicitly rejects this tale, which may well have licensed his embellishment of it.

223 Chapter VIII.

224 Stover and Woudhuysen 2020 [2015].

The first part of this recalls a significant moment in Sallust's *Histories*, the speech of Lepidus, where he excoriates Sulla for punishing people yet to be born by forbidding the children of the proscribed to hold office:

> He alone of all men in all the memory of man (*post memoriam humani*) devised torments against those yet to come, for whom injustices were fixed before life itself was.[225]

Sulla's brutal measure was, in a word, unprecedented and, for Victor, just as unprecedented was the lack of customary retaliation after Diocletian's victory. The second part of his description of 283/284 engages with a passage from Cicero's speech in defence of P. Cornelius Sulla, nephew of the dictator, who was deprived of the consulship to which he had been elected in the aftermath of the so-called 'first Catilinarian conspiracy' (*Pro Sulla* 91):

> How swiftly all of these things turn from happiness and pleasure to lamentation and tears, so much that one who before had been consul-designate suddenly retains no trace of his former dignity (*dignitatis*)? What misfortune might he seem to be lacking after being robbed of his reputation, his honour, his fortune (*huic spoliato fama, honore, fortunis*)?

It is no surprise that Victor was drawn to this passage, with its invocation of the variability of Fortune, a favourite theme of his. The coincidence of name and family between the subjects of the lines in Sallust and Cicero might have recommended the conjunction, along with the fact that Sulla's own nephew, though not guilty, ended up suffering in the same way as the innocent children of the proscribed. Both authors meditate on the ways in which the innocent suffer in civil war, real or potential, and its aftermath. In Victor's telling, this was Diocletian's historically unprecedented policy: not to make the innocent suffer the loss of fame, fortune, and office.

Perhaps there was something about crisis and civil strife that particularly moved Victor to this richly allusive mode. We have already looked separately at his deep engagement with Tacitus and Suetonius when he details the aftermath of Gallienus' death: what is striking about their conjunction is that both passages are about Tiberius. This double allusion crowns a whole series of comparisons between Gallienus and Tiberius, made through subtle intratextual links and historical parallels: both emperors had good beginnings to their reigns (*HAb* 2.1, 33.3), both were given to indolence and luxury (*HAb* 2.2–3, 33.6), both became known for simulation (*HAb* 2.1, 33.15), and, most significantly of all, both displayed excessive indulgence to the army, with ruinous and long-lasting consequences for the Roman state (*HAb* 2.4, 33.33–34). Having rolled the pitch throughout his account of Gallienus, Victor uses the terminal allusions to two of his predecessors to bring the point devastatingly home. Similarly, at *HAb* 42.7, a passage on which we have touched before, he describes the effects of Nepotian's short-lived rule at Rome:

> Cuius stolidum ingenium adeo plebi Romanae patribusque exitio fuit, uti passim domus fora viae templaque cruore atque cadaveribus opplerentur bustorum modo.

> His brutish character was so destructive to the Roman people and Senate that everywhere the houses, fora, streets, and temples were filled up with gore and dead bodies, as though they were tombs.

---

225 Sallust, *Hist.* 1.49.6R = 1.55.6M. The intertext with Victor, which has not received sufficient attention, all but guarantees that Orelli was wrong to supply *generis* after *humani*.

As we have seen, the first part of this is an allusion to Seneca, but the vivid description of carnage is striking and has been taken as evidence of autopsy.[226] In fact – like so many other supposed autopsies in ancient works – it is also literary.[227] Describing the aftermath of the death of Vitellius in AD 69 (*Hist.* 4.1.1), Tacitus recounts how 'the roads were full of corpses, the forums and temples with gore, people cut down here and there' (*plenae caedibus **viae**, cruenta **fora templaque, passim** trucidatis*). No one would seriously hold this as evidence for the youthful Tacitus' autopsy of these events: just like Victor after him, he presumably had recourse to a book.

Here, however, Victor does not glance merely to Tacitus. In Sallust's *Catiline*, the historian has Cato the Younger give an account of what happens during civil war (51.9):

> . . . young women and boys are seized, children are ripped from their parents' embrace, matrons endure the victors' pleasure, shrines and houses (*domos*) are despoiled, there is slaughter and fire, and (at last) everything is filled with arms, corpses, and lamentation (*cruore atque luctu omnia conpleri*).

Victor uses the three passages in tandem to encapsulate the horrors of civil war: the character of Nepotian from Seneca; the gore and corpses filling the houses from Sallust; the forums, roads and temples from Tacitus. What we have here in Victor is something much more exciting than autopsy: a telescoping of republican, Julio-Claudian, and later imperial history through the lens of the constant fact of civil strife. This is not to deny the possibility that Victor did in fact witness these events, but rather to suggest that the way that he interpreted even what happened in his own lifetime was through the books that were his constant companions.

The result of this detailed excavation of Victor's erudition and literary culture is a portrait of an author remarkable in his intellectual sophistication, a worthy heir of Tacitus and fitting predecessor for Ammianus. Victor provides a great deal of recondite factual information, much of it unique to his pages. He shows a deep knowledge of the Latin historians and of those works in Greek which chronicled Roman history. He was clearly an omnivorous reader of Latin literature, from the canonical works of Cicero and Vergil to items of considerable obscurity. At points, he shows clear signs of having been steeped in various disciplines: grammar, philosophy, law, and rhetoric. He seems besides all this to have read a good deal of Greek literature, across a similarly broad range of topics. These qualities alone would make Victor one of the most learned men of his age, but his erudition and reading were not simply acquisitive, designed to heap up rarities for their own sake. Victor used what he knew and what he had read to interpret Roman history, to undercut a superficial reading of events, to discreetly signal his own views, and (one suspects) for sheer devilment.

All this might come as a surprise to scholars of Roman history – unaccustomed as they are to detecting Latin literary genius at work in the middle of the fourth century – but it should not be *that much of a surprise*, considering that Victor vaunts his own education and claims to have done extensive research. The reason it has never been noted before is that it is only through minute and careful excavation of the *HAb* that we can recover the ambition of Victor's intentions and the remains of his literary culture, that is to say the nature of his historical work. For the fact is that the *HAb as a whole* is quite incompatible with both that ambition and the cultivation that underlies it.

---

226 *e.g.* Bird 1994: vii.   227 *cf.* Kelly 2004.

The nature of the *Historiae abbreviatae*

The *Historiae abbreviatae* is a work full of humiliating mistakes, bizarre omissions, and sophomoric confusions. Augustus' only significant act is dying and it offers not even a cursory account of his reign, but an obituary (1.2). The emperor Vespasian receives quite extensive treatment in the *HAb*, but does not die (9). Victor sets up Nerva's accession with great fanfare as a pivotal moment in Roman history, but then the text moves swiftly on with no intervening detail (11.12–12.2). The life of Marcus Aurelius, read straight, is positively baffling: it is primarily devoted to the sexual deviance of his wife (14.2), how he absolutely did not kill his brother Verus (3–9), and how the philosophers became distraught at his departure for the front (9–11) during the Marcommanic wars. Besides these, we have only his obituary and less effort than one might hope is put into connecting these topics. There is no life of Pertinax (17.10–18.2). Victor clearly knew much about the jurist Papinian's career, but he is introduced into the narrative only to be murdered (20.33–34). The Syrian libertine known to history as Elagabalus is never made emperor: one moment he is cowering in the temple of Elagabal in Emesa, after his supposed father Caracalla has been murdered by Macrinus, and the next he is moving his cult statues into the palace (23.1). The emperor Gordian I looms surprisingly large in the *HAb*, but his death is never narrated, even though great importance is attached to its announcement at Rome (26.5–6). Philip the Arab is never made emperor either: the lengthy (by the work's standards) account of his reign is almost entirely taken up by an incoherent discussion of a prodigy (28.3–10). The emperor Decius materialises with no introduction, wins a battle at Verona, and then appears at Rome without explanation (28.10, 29.1). The *HAb* devotes considerable attention to the age of Gallienus, but tells us almost nothing about the emperor himself: half of its account is devoted to usurpers (33.2–21) and the other half to reflections on the role of history (33.23–34). We meet the most formidable of these would-be emperors, Postumus, as he is about to seize power in Gaul (*imperium ereptum ierat*); the next moment he is dead at his own soldiers' hands (33.8). Postumus actually ruled in Gaul for almost ten years.

Counter-intuitively, the *HAb* seems to get less accurate and more garbled as it approaches Victor's own day. Without parallel accounts, we could never extract a coherent history of the Tetrarchy from the text, even though it is very detailed (39). Bafflingly, almost the only concrete thing Diocletian does in its pages is refuse to expand the Roman Empire (39.36). He also retires, but (like Vespasian) remains undead (39.48). The emperor who has hitherto been called Constantine begins to be referred to as Flavius partway through the story of his rise (41.2). Unlike in the other instances of this odd usage in the *HAb*, it is never explained that this was one of his names.[228] Victor lived through the civil war of the early 350s and it could hardly have escaped the notice of his readers in 360, yet the *HAb*'s account of events is hopelessly wrong. It puts the usurpation of Nepotian (an account of extraordinary intricacy, as we have seen) in 351, not 350, and wrongly asserts that the elevation of the Caesar Gallus came before it, even as it gets the duration of Vetranio's rule correct almost to the day.[229] The *HAb* entirely omits the battle of Mursa, perhaps the largest clash of any of the fourth-century civil wars, extensively covered in all other

---

228 On onomastics, see above.

229 *HAb* 42.6, 9; *PLRE* 'Nepotianus 5', 'Constantius 4'. Vetranio: *HAb* 42.1, *cis mensem decimum*; per the *Consularia Constantinopolitana* p. 237 Burgess 1993b, he was proclaimed on 1 March and deposed on 25 December, so he reigned for ten months less eight days.

surviving accounts of the period, including those contemporary with Victor.[230] Attempts might be made to explain away individual problems by special pleading, but their number, regularity, and distribution throughout the entire work indicates that something else must be going on. Victor, noted one of the best early-modern commentators, is scarcely able to be understood unless one already knows the history his work purports to relate.[231] That makes the notion that the *HAb* as it survives was intended as a standalone work of history impossible. The nature of the text poses a fundamental problem.

The *Historiae abbreviatae* as *abbreviatio*

The obvious solution lies in abbreviation. Once one starts reading the *HAb* – really reading it – the signs are everywhere. To understand *why* abbreviation is an obvious answer, one which has left so many signs in the text, it is worth casting back to what was said in Chapter III about techniques of epitomisation in late antiquity. When our anonymous compiler came to put together the *Corpus tripertitum*, his method, like that of Julius Paris, was to hack whole chunks out of his source and recombine them into a new text.[232] This might seem a rather clumsy approach, but it had one great virtue, for its product kept at least some of the stylistic and intellectual character of the original. The reader can encounter Victor's words and Victor's thoughts without reading Victor's work (in any straightforward sense). Its principal vice, however, was that, unless the epitomator was very careful, the abbreviated text he had produced ran the risk of incoherence. So, we might expect the abbreviation to move around seemingly at random, to miss things out and forget their omission, and to pay insufficient attention to the careful arrangement of the original. We have already seen that the *HAb* has all the positive features of an epitome made on such lines: it also has more than its fair share of the weaknesses. Once one starts looking for the small yet tell-tale signs of abbreviation, they come thick and fast, something which has perhaps often been obscured by reading what should be in the text, not what is actually there.

It is true that, at a very basic level, the abbreviator was minimally competent. There are no straight-forward missing cross-references, though there are several points where it takes more faith than reason to conclude that nothing is wrong. For example, in the story of Caracalla and Julia Domna (on which we have touched several times), Victor says that he has mentioned (*memoravi*) her crimes before, implying some detail was given about them (*HAb* 21.3). Yet in the *HAb* all we find is a bare reference to the fact that they existed (20.23). If the abbreviator managed generally to avoid more flagrant inconsistencies than this, then we ought still not to overrate his abilities. There is a severe *anacoluthon* at the start of the account of Philip the Arab, where 'they came (*venere*)' to Rome, even though Philip alone is the subject (*HAb* 28.1). The original presumably had both Philip and his son (who is mentioned in an ablative absolute in the same sentence) arriving at the capital. There are also several points where the text illogically mentions a

230 See Julian, *Or.* 1.35d–37b; Zosimus 2.50.1–53.1 (the longest and most detailed account); Eutropius 10.12.1; Sulpicius Severus, *Chron.* 2.38.5; Orosius 7.29.12.

231 Dacier 1681, *praef.*: *Vix enim ab iis intelligi poterit qui non aliquam Historia Romanae notitiam prae se ferant.*

232 This assumes the identity of the compiler of the *HAb* with the compiler of the *CT*, which is by no means certain (see the Conclusion to Part I), but that does not affect our argument here.

story about one emperor only in its coverage of another.[233] The most egregious example of this is found in the *HAb*'s account of Aurelian, which refers glancingly to an invasion of Italy that occurred during the reign of Gallienus. Victor says that the Aurelian walls were built 'to avoid what had happened because of Gallienus ever coming to pass again' (*HAb* 35.7). Yet a reader would turn to the text's lengthy treatment of Gallienus in vain to discover this event.

There are also points where the text of the *HAb* is missing some crucial part of a story that it was clearly keen to tell. Its account of Diocletian is dominated by the way that his humble origins shaped his career, an idea it develops at some length and with a good deal of elaboration.[234] Yet nowhere in the text are we told anything of Diocletian's origins, beyond the fact that he was in charge of the *domestici* when he was made emperor (*HAb* 39.1). Or consider the account of the succession of Hadrian (*HAb* 13.11–12):

> Trajan died at a grand old age, not before he had associated in imperial power Hadrian, his fellow-citizen and relative. From this point onwards, the titles of Caesar and Augustus were divided and the practice was introduced into the state that two or more were unequal partners in supreme power, differing in title and authority.

All the text tells us is that Trajan, before dying, adopted his compatriot and kinsman Hadrian *ad imperium*; it then launches into a discussion of how this was the first time that the name Caesar was separated from that of Augustus. Something is obviously missing: a middle term, so to speak, which explained how Hadrian was called Caesar, and not Augustus, when adopted. Such a claim may or may not be true – there is numismatic evidence supporting it, of dubious provenance but intriguing – but it is the only way that the narrative can make sense.[235]

Indeed, taken as a whole, the narrative of the *HAb* is frequently incoherent, changing scene, subject, and point with almost no notice and for no clear reason, or saying something flagrantly absurd if read without preconceptions. To give even a representative sample of instances of these phenomena would require a substantial chapter in itself, but a few choice pieces can give a sense of the problem. The emperor Titus is said to have surpassed someone he was imitating, but we are never told on whom he wished to model his behaviour (*HAb* 10.1). After being informed that Lucius Verus overmastered the Parthians, we learn that 'a few days later' (*paucis diebus*) he passed away, even though Victor knew that he died at Altinum in Venetia, not a city very close to Parthia (16.4, 5, 9). It is perhaps particularly revealing that such slips cluster in the fourth century, when an abbreviator might have taken background knowledge too much for granted as he cut the text down. Constantine is said in the *HAb* to have been buried in the city named after him (41.17). Naturally, we infer that his corpse was taken to Constantinople for burial (as in fact happened: Eusebius, *Vita Constantini* 4.66.1). The text, however, never mentions Constantinople by name, nor does it suggest that the emperor named it for himself (*HAb* 41.12). What it does say is that Cirta in North Africa was renamed Constantina when Constantine re-founded it (40.28). Examining the

---

233 *e.g. HAb* 4.3 on Caligula's attempt to bridge the Bay of Naples, but in the account of Claudius; 10.5, the life-span and regnal duration of Vespasian in the life of Titus, not the emperor himself; 20.10, Severus showed a parsimony 'similar' to Pertinax, but no such restraint was mentioned in the notice of that emperor;

29.2, Jotapianus, a usurper under Philip the Arab, appears only (*sans tête*) in the account of Decius; 36.2, Mucapor, the killer of Aurelian, shows up only in the life of Tacitus.

234 See Stover and Woudhuysen 2020 [2015].

235 Roman *et al.* 2009.

text of the *HAb* as it stands, the logical reader would have to conclude that Constantine was buried in North Africa. The *HAb* mangles the death of Crispus, saying merely that the unnamed *natu grandior* of Constantine's sons was executed (the last of them mentioned was actually Constantius II). After this, it then explains (41.11) that 'suddenly' (*repente*) the usurper Calocaerus made a bid for power, even though nearly a decade separated his revolt from the execution of Crispus. To round things off, it finally connects the death of Calocaerus (in 334) with Constantine founding the (unnamed) Constantinople (41.12: *condenda urbe*), something we know happened several years beforehand. At *HAb* 42.9, Victor tells us how Constantius made Gallus Caesar and put him in charge of the east, while the usurper Magnentius made his brother Decentius Caesar and put him in charge of Gaul. For three years, these two rival pairs clashed and, 'at the end, after Constantius had pursued the one fleeing [*fugientem*] into Gaul, he forced both to kill themselves'.[236] Not only is this a passage where the *HAb* manages to make an utter hash of the most significant events of the middle of the fourth century – the bloody civil war between Constantius and Magnentius – but it is specifically problematic in the word *fugientem*. The only plausible deduction from the text is that the one fleeing into Gaul is Decentius, who had just in the line before been entrusted with affairs there. Yet it must actually be Magnentius and refer to the aftermath of the omitted battle of Mursa, from which he fled into Italy, then Gaul, before suffering a final defeat at Mons Seleucus in 353. These are not mere clumsy slips by an incompetent and slap-dash author: this is what happens when a complex and intellectually sophisticated work is put through the mincing machine of abbreviation.

Particles and conjunctions

Particles, unobtrusive but significant, are a particularly revealing trace element for the process of hacking the text down. Causal connections which have not been made are signalled; concessives appear in the text baldly stated without any contrasting idea; new thoughts which are in no sense adversative are firmly stated by an intrusive *sed*. The fate of the Caesar Dalmatius in 337 can serve as an example. After a complex sentence on the perverse significance of vices in men of real ability, the *HAb* (41.22) says: '*Igitur*, Dalmatius was swiftly killed, at whose urging it is not certain'. The natural conclusion from *igitur* ('consequently', 'therefore' *etc.*) is that Dalmatius was killed by a moralising digression. Similarly, the text says (39.12) that Carus and his sons reigned for a *biennium* and 'therefore' (*igitur*) Diocletian gave his first public address (*prima contio*) to the army, which (incidentally) he had already led from Anatolia to the Balkans in the course of a bloody civil war.[237] We are told (4.13) that Agrippina 'although (*quamvis*) considered more absurd than Messalina . . . feared an equal fate', the *quamvis* dangling unexplained. The fragment *nisi forte triumphorum expertem socordiae videtur* ('unless by chance that he was without triumphs seems to be due to sluggishness') intrudes into the life of Antoninus Pius (15.5), but no properly contrasting idea is expressed before or after it, sandwiched as it is between a chronological note on his reign and a justification for his lack of triumphs. With no logical connection, we are then told that 'moreover' (*quin etiam*) he entrusted

---

236 See above on the literary allusions here.

237 This closely corresponds with a passage in Eutropius (see Chapter VI), who, despite using the same phrase, puts the speech at the correct time.

the *res publica* to his daughter's husband. In the account of Macrinus, the *HAb* (22.2–3) says the soldiers called his son 'Antoninus', because they missed Caracalla, before revealing that 'meanwhile (*interim*) I have discovered nothing about these two'. Meanwhile what? We see something similar in the life of Gordian I (26.4–5), where *interim* joins his role in interpreting an omen, still very much alive, with the (presumably posthumous) announcement of his death at Rome, and in the life of Aurelian, where it links the plotting against the emperor *before* he was struck down with the actions of the soldiers *after* his death (35.8–9). In the account of the Tetrarchy (39.32), the same adverb connects a moralising digression on taxation to Galerius' campaigns against the Persians.

Once again, examples such as these might be explained, or at least explained away, but cumulatively what they reveal is a radical incompatibility between the demonstrable intellectual and rhetorical sophistication of Victor's work and the sorry state of the *HAb*. On the standard view, we have to suppose Victor an extremely ambitious but ultimately incompetent author. Indeed, picking up on a suggestion of Wölfflin and contemplating the absurd *nam* in *HAb* 20.23, Den Boer actually declared that:

> . . . this and similar conjunctions do not necessarily stand for any logical links in Victor's work, since as many examples show,[114] conjunctions originally indicating causality have frequently lost this function in his writings . . . Indeed, in my opinion, it is quite possible that many causal conjunctions have lost their meaning . . .
> [n. 114] With respect to Victor, I noted, among others, the following instances: igitur (39,13; 11,1; 14,1; 28,1; 31,1; 36,1; 38,1; 40,1); hinc denique (39,31); idcirco (11,4); ceterum (21,1).[238]

There can be no justification for assuming some kind of idiolect: that *nam*, *igitur*, and the like do not mean the same thing in Victor that they do in all of his contemporaries, what they mean in every Latin literary author. We need an alternative explanation: abbreviation can, should, provide that.

That the features of the *HAb* we have discussed are a product of epitomisation emerges most clearly when we compare them to other abbreviated texts. Consider the following, from a Christian author writing a century or so after Victor's death:

> But think how it is that we believe that God operates with human wills to establish earthly kingdoms and that men operate their own wills to seize a heavenly kingdom. *Ergo* grace precedes faith as well (*praevenit ergo et fidem gratia*).[239]

If one thinks about it, one can see some distant implicit connection between the two statements, but nothing to justify something definitive like an *ergo*. There is, however, a reason for this incoherence: this passage comes from the *Excerpta ex operibus S. Augustini* of Eugippius, that sprawling epitome of Augustine's works arranged roughly by topic. The first sentence is actually from Augustine's *De praedestinatione sanctorum* (*PL* 44.991), while the second is from an entirely different work, his *De dono perseverantiae* (*PL* 45.1018), where it follows upon a discussion of the prevenience of grace to will. The particle usage in this case, and in many other instances in Eugippius, presents no particular difficulty to the reader, because the epitome is derived from works that still survive and we have paratextual features which clearly differentiate the separate excerpts: in this case, a title that precedes the second sentence, telling us

---

238 Den Boer 1972: 52 and n. 114.　　　　239 Eugippius, *Exc. op. S. Aug* 313–314 (p. 931 Knoell).

its theme and source (QUOD GRATIA PRAEVENIAT FIDEM PRAESTETQUE PERSEVERANTIAM. EX LIBRO DE DONO PERSEVERANTIAE).[240] The 'oddity' of Eugippius' use of particles is entirely a product of the way his work was hacked out of Augustine.

Victor therefore needs no special pleading. The particles in the *HAb* are a remnant of the process by which the text was created. The compiler of the *CT* has reworked his source – a complex and discursive work of history – into a cruder biographical epitome, hacking his way through the source material. That explains the *HAb*'s curious combination of extraordinary erudition, stylistic ambition, and basic incompetence. The radical incompatibility between what Victor says about his work and the actual condition of the *HAb* exists because the *HAb is a witness to that work, not the work itself.* In approaching the text, we would do well to keep that in mind. We do not, on observing the Forum Romanum today, conclude that the Romans were shoddy builders – it would be wise to apply the same logic to the ruins of Victor's *Historia*.

The *Historiae abbreviatae* is both extremely sophisticated and at the same time rather crude: a consequence of the method by which it was produced. The *Libellus breviatus*, on the other hand, is a much smoother and superficially more satisfying production. Whatever the ancient source(s) on which it drew, its early-medieval compiler worked hard to integrate everything into a reasonably uniform style. If it is what the title claims, a *libellus breviatus*, then it is a product of the other main technique of abbreviation that we encountered: reformulating material (sometimes from one text, sometimes from several) into a new and coherent work.[241] That makes it much harder to apply to the *LB* the sorts of analysis to which the *HAb* is susceptible: hunting for the combination of intellectual complexity and compositional incoherence that argues so strongly that it is an abbreviation of a much longer work. Yet we have already seen that the *LB* shares a good deal with the *HAb*: specific wording, odd facts, interesting ideas.[242] If we investigate further, we can find a good deal of evidence that it, too, is an abbreviation of a longer text of considerable complexity.

Facts in the *Libellus breviatus*

The *Historiae abbreviatae* is crammed with information of considerable obscurity: in particular, it is a rich source of often unique information about the names of important Romans. The *Libellus breviatus* shares

---

240 An early manuscript in which the paratextual features can be easily observed is Paris, NAL 1575 (s. VIII), where the main text is written in minuscule and the headings in uncials. Other examples include: 41 (204 Knoell) *sequitur ut videamus* (a literal non sequitur) from *De Gen. ad litt.* 8.6.12; 44 (204 Knoell) *itaque* from *De Gen. ad litt.* 8.19.38; 124 (383 Knoell) *ergo* from *Serm. ad pop.* 9; *ergo* again at 131 (403 Knoell) from *Serm. ad pop.* 71; 132 (423 Knoell) *enim* from *Ep.* 54.6;

and so on. A combined example can be seen in 133b, which consists of excerpts from *Ep.* 55, ripped from their original context but with particles intact: *igitur* (434 Knoell) from *Ep.* 55.13; *ideoque* (437 Knoell) from 55.20; *ergo* (438 Knoell) from 55.19; *unde* (438 Knoell) from 55.20; and *itaque* (442 Knoell) from 55.30.
241 Chapter III.
242 Chapter II.

this characteristic. Alone of Latin sources, it knew that the emperor Julian was 'Claudius Julianus' (42.12). With Zosimus, it gives us the name of Gaiso, killer of the emperor Constans on the orders of Magnentius: we know from *consularia* that the usurper made a man with that name consul in 351, which would fit admirably his important role in the *LB*.[243] Of late-antique sources, only the *LB* gives Constantine the nickname 'Trachala' (it re-emerges in later Byzantine texts).[244] Its information, however, was not limited to the fourth century. The emperor Probus is called 'Equitius Probus' in the *LB* (36.2) – the legend *AEQUITI* or *EQUITI* appears on a number of his coins from Pavia.[245] The ruler of the Gallic Empire in the middle of the third century was M. Cassianius Latinius Postumus, as coins and inscriptions reveal. The *LB* (32.3) calls him 'Cassius Labienus Postumus' – mangled, but clearly related to his real names – while all other sources call him plain Postumus.[246] The full name of one son of Gallienus was P. Licinius Cornelius Valerianus, but of literary sources only the *LB* knew that he was a Cornelius.[247] No other source names the man, Gallonius Basilius, supposedly sent by Gallienus to take the *indumenta regia* to Claudius II.[248] The *LB* alone calls Hostilianus, the short-lived emperor of 251, 'Perpenna' (30.2), an Etruscan name: his parents were the emperor Decius and Herennia Cupressenia Etruscilla, whose nomenclature is 'patently Etruscan' according to Syme, a connoisseur of such things.[249] No other literary source gives Trebonianus the name Vibius (*LB* 31.1: 'Vibius Gallus'), but inscriptions record his full name as C. Vibius Trebonianus Gallus.[250] Only the *LB* (of our extant sources) connects the given name of the emperor Caracalla, Bassianus, with his grandfather, Julius Bassianus, whom it knows (23.2) was a priest of the sun.[251] It also says that Caracalla took the name 'Magnus', something that only the *Chronography of 354* otherwise tells us among texts.[252] Besides Cassius Dio, it is the only text which transmits the *praenomen* of Vindex, the famous rebel of the first century AD: Gaius (*LB* 5.6).[253]

The *LB* has a particularly important role to play in providing evidence for imperial women, who are otherwise largely anonymous. Of literary texts, the *LB* alone gives us the *gentilicium* of Plotina, wife of Trajan: Pompeia.[254] The *LB* is the only Latin source to offer something properly resembling the real name of the mother of Elagabalus, 'Soemea' (23.1, 2): Dio (79.30.2) and Herodian (3.3.2) call her Σοαιμίς.[255] It provides the name of Diocletian's mother, Dioclea, which she apparently shared with the city of her son's birth.[256] Lactantius also knew that the mother of Galerius was Romula, but only the *LB* tells us that the emperor named a city after her, a fact dramatically confirmed by excavations at modern Gamzigrad, which turned up an inscription reading *Felix Romuliana*.[257] The *LB* and Zosimus know the name of Crispus'

243 *LB* 41.23; Zosimus 2.42.5; *CLRE* 236.
244 Bruun 1995.
245 *RIC* 5.2: 2–3, 68–73.
246 *LB* 32.3; *PLRE* 'Postumus 2'.
247 Peachin 1990: 339–343; *PIR*² L.184.
248 *LB* 34.2, *cf.* below Chapter VIII.
249 Syme 1971a: 197.
250 *PIR*² V.579. The manuscripts of the *LB* have *virium*, but that is clearly related to his real name.
251 *PIR*² I.202.
252 *Chron. 354* (p. 147, l. 13).
253 *PIR*² I.628.
254 *LB* 42.21, indirectly confirmed for us by the names of her freedmen (*AE* 1958, 184; *cf. ILS* 1912); *PIR*² P.679.

255 The best Eutropius could manage seems to have been 'Symia sera', but the MSS offer some interesting variations in spelling (B's Sumia Syra is particularly note-worthy) and Paeanius has Symia Severa (see Droysen's *apparatus ad loc.*). The *HA* has Symiamira (*e.g. Heliog.* 2.1).
256 *LB* 39.1. Constantine Porphyrogenitus knew of a κάστρον by this name in Dalmatia, the foundation of which he attributed to the emperor (*De administrando imperio* 29).
257 *LB* 40.16; Lactantius *DMP* 9.9; *AE* 1986, 625. On the site in general, see Popović 2011, with a fine illustration of the relevant inscription on 67.

mother, Minervina, and that Eutropia was the mother of the short-lived usurper Nepotian.[258] The *LB* (42.20) also knew the names of some of the attendants of Eusebia, wife of Constantius II: Adamantia and Gorgonia, otherwise completely unattested. Only the *LB* gives Thermantia as the name of Theodosius' mother (48.1). Theodosius had a niece with that (rare) name, seemingly derived from that of a Spanish town, and it would fit snugly onto a fragmentary inscription in honour of *m]atri d(omini) n(ostri) Theodosi* ('the mother of our master, Theodosius').[259] Names like these are far from the only thing for which the *LB* is useful, but they are a striking illustration both of the detailed and precise information it can provide and of its similarity to the *HAb*.

It is, however, not merely the many rare names of which *LB* has knowledge that connect it to the *HAb*: it is the way it uses them. Like the *HAb*, though to a lesser degree, the *LB* has a partiality for dual names. For the Augusti from Macrinus to the first Tetrarchy, about one-third are introduced by more than one name.[260] As in the *HAb*, the dual name is not confined to introductions, so Maximian, the colleague of Diocletian, appears first under one name, but crops up a little later (40.10) as Aurelius Maximianus. The *LB* also has the very curious habit of referring to individuals by a name other than their diacritic: the emperor Galerius Maximianus is generally Galerius (39.6, 40.1, 40.14, 15, 41.2), while Cornelius Valerianus (the son of Gallienus) is called Cornelius (33.1). Marcus Aurelius Antoninus (16.1) appears variously as Marcus Antoninus (16.7), Marcus (16.14), and Antoninus (17.1). The *LB* also has that idiosyncratic use of *nomine*, superficially to avoid confusion between names and words: *Regulum nomine* (12.10, 'petty king'), *Pipam nomine* (33.1), *nomine Aureolus* (33.2, 'golden'), *Crispum nomine* (41.4, 'curly'). It also shows great precision in cases of adoptive nomenclature. We have already seen that the *LB* refers to Tiberius by his names before adoption: Tiberius Claudius Nero (2.2). It specifies that Augustus acquired the names 'Gaius Caesar' through adoption (1.2). The *LB* also preserves the name Boionius, in this case for Antoninus Pius himself (15.1). In this respect, one name in the *LB* deserves particular attention: the text asserts that Alexander Severus was called Marcellus before he was appointed Caesar (23.4). We can rule out an idiosyncratic textual mistake, since this same identification occurs in one other source we discuss later.[261] Instead, the significant fact is that even though we do not know the full birth name of Elagabalus – Alexander's cousin, predecessor, and ultimately adoptive father – we do know that his father was named Sex. Varius Marcellus.[262] The only reason, then, why Alexander (of whose full birth name we are equally ignorant) would have been called Marcellus is because of his adoption by Elagabalus.[263] This situation is exactly parallel to the way that Victor refers to Marcus Aurelius as M. Boionius and Antoninus Pius as T. Aelius Antoninus: it suggests that the *LB* was keen on using adoptive nomenclature in an unusually precise and literal fashion.

258 *LB* 41.4; Zosimus 2.20.2. *LB* 42.3; Zosimus 2.43.2. Athanasius, *Apol. ad Const.* 6.5 puns on the name, but does not give it.

259 Niece: *PLRE* 'Thermantia 2'. Town: Matthews 1975: 108 n. 3. Mother: *CIL* 6.36960. None of the standard repositories (the *Onomasticon Provinciarum Europae Latinarum*, Kajanto 1965, Solin and Salomies 1994) list the name, but see *AE* 1983, 885 (Macedonia).

260 Two or more names: Aurelius Antoninus Varius (23.1), Severus Alexander (24.1), Julius Maximinus (25.1), Marcus Julius Philippus (28.1), Gaius Julius Saturninus (28.3 – the son of Philip the Arab), Vibius Gallus (30.1),

Hostilianus Perpenna (30.2), Licinius Valerianus (32.1), Equitius Probus (36.2), Galerius Maximianus (39.2). One: Macrinus and Diadumenus (22.1), *Gordiani duo* (26.1), Pupienus and Balbinus (26.2), Gordian III (27.1), Decius (29.1), Aemilianus (31.1), Gallienus (32.2), Claudius (34.1), Quintillus (34.5), Aurelianus (35.1), Tacitus (36.1), Florianus (36.2), Carus, Carinus, and Numerian (38.1–2), Diocletianus (39.1), Maximianus and Constantius (39.2).

261 Polemius Silvius, *Laterculus* 31. See Chapter X

262 *PIR²* V.273, 282.

263 *PIR²* A.1610.

In the round, it is extraordinary how two texts that are so superficially different as the *HAb* and *LB* prove so similar when it comes to names. There is a substrate of facts that they share in matters onomastic, but more than that they betray the same very unusual habits of usage. It is simply impossible that an early-medieval compiler could have had direct access to so many rare names, let alone that he could so effortlessly mimic the idiosyncratic way one fourth-century author deployed them, unless he was drawing directly on an unusually well-informed fourth-century source. Whatever that source was, it seems to have been remarkably similar to Victor.

Literary culture in the *Libellus breviatus*

As we have seen, however, the *HAb* offers much more than mere facts. It has a style and substance deeply informed by the classics of Latin literature, especially Sallust, Tacitus, and Cicero, but also by deep reading of authors who never attained canonical status. The very first lines, with their careful allusions to the *Histories*, the *Annales*, and Cassius Dio, make this plain. Its author (or at least his source) must have had recourse to a wide range of texts – Latin and Greek – for the raw material out of which he fashioned its narrative. The same is true of the author of the *LB* (or at least his source). This fact is already known to scholarship: indeed, the *LB* has received much more detailed treatment than the *HAb*. While both texts have benefited from typically thorough Budé commentaries, the *LB* was also the subject of a detailed monographic treatment by Schlumberger in 1974, a chunky and thorough review article of Schlumberger's work by Barnes 1976(a), and a stand-alone treatment of its first eleven chapters by Baldwin in 1993, to name only some of the more prominent analyses.[264] As a result, it is not especially controversial to say that historical material in the *LB* ultimately goes back to at least Tacitus and Suetonius, as well as to a host of disputed and often more vaguely defined Greek and Latin sources, although the exact vectors of influence remain controversial.

What has attracted less attention is that the *LB* also reveals a substrate of allusive and literary language, evidence of surprisingly wide reading. Take, for instance the descriptions of two banquets gone wrong set out in **TABLE 4.12**. *In multam noctem* is a rare phrase, occurring twice in Suetonius, once in Curtius Rufus and Cicero, but the context here links it closely with Tacitus.[265] This corroborates the suggestion of Baldwin, who found evidence in the use of the word *cupitor* that the author of the *LB* was a 'devotee of Tacitus'.[266] There are other signs of this enthusiasm, as in the two texts' descriptions of individuals who rashly aimed at greater power. Tacitus said that he found it hard to credit the elder Pliny's account of the notoriously uxorious Piso's plans (as part of the eponymous conspiracy) to appear with Antonia, the daughter of Claudius, as though he were to marry her (*Annals* 15.53.4): *nisi si cupido dominandi cunctis adfectibus flagrantior est*, 'unless lust for power blazes more fiercely than all other affections'. The *LB* says (43.8) that 'a blazing lust for glory' (*cupido gloriae flagrantior*) had so overmastered the emperor

---

264 Mention might also be made of the McGill doctoral dissertation by Gauville 2005, the Romanian translation and commentary of Paraschiv and Zugravu 2012, and the Budapest dissertation of Sólyom 2018 (in Hungarian).

265 Suetonius, *Tib.* 74.1, *Nero* 20.1; Curtius Rufus 6.11.12; Cicero, *De Rep.* 6.10. *cf. Querolus* (p. 41, l. 22 Ranstrand 1952).

266 Baldwin 1990: 294.

TABLE 4.12 – TACITUS AND THE *LIBELLUS BREVIATUS*: TWO BANQUETS

Tacitus, *Ann.* 2.65.3	LB 41.22
Rhescuporis added a banquet for the ratification, as he said repeatedly, of the agreement and when the celebration had been dragged out long into the night (*in multam noctem*) by feasting and intoxication, loaded the heedless Cotys with chains, who, after he had understood the treachery, appealed to the sacred rites of kingship, the shared gods of their family, and the tables set for guests.	Therefore when the banquet had been celebrated long into the night (*in multam noctem*), Magnentius, as though going out to attend to the stomach's usual business, put on an emperor's dress.

Julian that he ignored various heavenly signs not to invade Persia. A *cupido* that was *flagrantior* occurs only in these two works.[267]

The *LB* almost certainly also transmits materials derived from Cassius Dio. Take *LB* 2.4 on the character of Tiberius: 'Pretending that he wished for those things that he did not want, appearing as though hostile to those whose advice he desired, but to those whom he hated seeming friendly (*quasi benivolus apparens*)'. This is very close to the corresponding passage in the *HAb* (2.1), and both of them are more closely linked to Dio (57.1.1) than to either Suetonius or Tacitus. Even so, one phrase that occurs in the *LB* (*quasi benivolus apparens*) is much closer to Dio than the *HAb* (ἐπιεικὴς . . . ἐδόκει εἶναι).[268] Likewise, the *LB* is the sole Latin work to assert that the soldiers plotted against Macrinus because he reined in their excessive bonuses (22.1). The only other text to suggest this is Dio's history (78.28) – Herodian offers the considerably less likely suggestion the soldiers were disgusted by Macrinus' indulgent and unphilosophical lifestyle (5.2.6). Yet, at other times, the *LB* offers very close parallels to Herodian, such as the description of the character of the emperor Severus in **TABLE 4.13**.[269] What is interesting here is that the *LB*'s characterisation of the African emperor also picks up on what Sallust had said about the African king Jugurtha (*Jugurtha* 20.2): *ipse acer, bellicosus* (cf. 7.4 and 28.5 *acri ingenio*).

There are other learned literary touches as well. The 'wheel of fortune' is one of the most famous ideas of antiquity (perhaps also the only one to have inspired a gameshow). There was a much rarer variant, in which Fortune was atop a sphere that rolled, rather than having a wheel that she span.[270] This was primarily known to Greek authors and it seems to have dropped out of common use as early as the Hellenistic age.[271] In Latin, it is an even rarer idea, occurring only in a fragment of Pacuvius preserved in the *Rhetorica ad Herennium* (2.23.36):

Fortunam insanam esse et caecam et brutam perhibent philosophi
saxoque instare in globoso praedicant volubili.

267 Compare Apuleius, *De Platone* 2.18: *flagrantiores cupidines furoresque*.
268 *cf.* Festy 1999a *ad loc.*
269 *cf.* Festy 1999a *ad loc.*
270 Robinson 1946: 213 (who appears rather indebted to the uncited Smith 1913: 306–307); Den Boeft *et al.* 2008: 234.

271 Dio Chrysostom (*Or.* 63.7) includes Fortune on a ball in his list of the ways she is portrayed, but that list is described as comprising the τὰ τῶν παλαιῶν αἰνίγματα. It does not include Fortune with a wheel.

TABLE 4.13 – HERODIAN AND THE *LIBELLUS BREVIATUS* ON THE CHARACTER OF SEVERUS

Herodian	*LB* 20.5
3.15.2: ἐνδοξότατα βιώσας, ὅσον πρὸς τὰ πολεμικά, τῶν πώποτε βασιλέων 2.9.2: νοῆσαί τε ὀξὺς καὶ τὸ νοηθὲν ἐπιτελέσαι ταχύς.	fuit bellicosissimus omnium ante eum fuerunt, acer ingenio, ad omnia quae intendisset in finem perseverans.
3.15.2: having lived a life of higher repute in affairs of war than any emperors ever yet. 2.9.2: quick to devise and quick to carry out what he had devised.	He was the most warlike of all those emperors who were before him, sharp in his character, steadfast to the end in all those things in which he had exerted himself.

The philosophers hold that Fortune is mad and blind and stupid; they declare that she stands on a spinning ball of rock.

This is thus a quite extraordinarily recondite item to find in a text like the *LB*, in reference to the career of Pertinax, compared to the *fortunae pila* or 'ball of Fortune'. There are other, somewhat more conventional literary touches. The *LB* discusses how Severus' son Caracalla murdered his brother and was subsequently afflicted by the Furies (*Dirae*), 'who are not inappropriately called the avengers (*ultrices*)' (*LB* 21.3; he later recovered). This story finds no direct parallels, but it seems to relate to a brief hint in what remains of Dio's account of the emperor, where it is mentioned that Caracalla dedicated the sword with which he had killed his brother in the temple of Serapis at Alexandria (78.23.3). It is also worth mentioning that *Dirae ultrices* is a Vergilian collocation (*Aen.* 4.465 and 607).[272] Even more Vergilian is the *LB*'s discussion (39.4) of the suicide of the Diocletianic usurper Julianus, who drove a dagger through his ribs (*per costas*) and threw himself into a fire. Dubious, perhaps, as a historical event, but surely redolent of the death of Dido in the *Aeneid* (4.646–689).[273] What is puzzling, however, is that only Victor in the *HAb* puts Julianus' rebellion in Africa (39.22), whereas the *LB* puts it in Italy. The Vergilian flavour, however, is actually confirmed by the words *per costas*, a genuine tag from the *Aeneid* in the context of Aeneas' contemplated suicide (10.682).[274] A more learned example of literary culture and grammatical education is found when the text discusses how the Romans were 'garbed in hideous black' (*veste tetra amictus*) in response to the death of Marcus Aurelius. The only other occurrence of the phrase *veste t(a)etra* (or anything similar) is in a line of Accius quoted by Nonius Marcellus.[275]

There are also verbal traces of Ciceronian and Sallustian influence. The Ciceronian exclamation *incredibile dictu est* (42.21), rare in antiquity, crops up in the text and Baldwin also noted the Ciceronian noun *oppressor* (1.29).[276] The signs of Sallust's influence are a little more substantial and there are occasional

272 *cf.* Festy 1999a *ad loc.*
273 Pointed out by Edgeworth 1992.
274 The only other ancient occurrence, outside of Vergil commentaries, is in Livy 8.7.10, in a rather different context.
275 Accius l. 374 Ribbeck, *apud* Nonius Marcellus p. 184M.

276 *Incredibile dictu est*: Cicero, *Verr.* 2.3.128, 4.124; *Pro Cluentio* 195. Justin 12.9.8. Arnobius, *Adv. nat.* 1.62; Jerome, *Vita Hilarionis* 29 (presumably in one of his more Ciceronian and less Christian moments). AM 25.3.10, 31.10.18. Orosius 3.19.7, 4.21.7. Baldwin 1993: 88.

hints of an intellectual connection. Famously, Sallust thought that the defeat of Carthage had opened the road to civil strife at Rome, something stated programmatically early on in the *Histories* (1.12R = 1.12M):

> After fear of Carthage had been removed, there was time to engage in strife (*simultates*); very numerous tumults (*turbae*), riots, and – in the end – civil wars (*bella civilia*) began.

Contrast the *LB*'s characterisation of Augustus in the aftermath of civil war (1.1):

> Indeed, he so detested tumults, wars, and strife (*turbas bella simultates*), that he never made war on any people whatsoever without a just cause.

These three terms are linked together only in these two texts, placed at either end of Rome's late-Republican descent into chaos. Evidence for the *LB*'s debt to Sallust's style are more numerous. Compare his characterisation of Catiline with the *LB* on Hadrian (**TABLE 4.14**). The point is not necessarily that there is a cutting comparison of the emperor and the renegade here – it is that this is a Sallustian phrase. The only other author to use it in antiquity was Augustine, always in allusion to Sallust's famous characterisation.[277] Both Sallust and the *LB* (3.9) speak of things being *in spatio milium*, the only ancient authors so to do – a minute Sallustianism.[278] There is a vague reminiscence in their respective descriptions of Marius and the emperor Licinius, each explaining why they favoured the humble classes (**TABLE 4.15**) Again, it matters much less whether this is the ghost of a comparison between the two (an interesting idea), than that the phrasing shows the impress of Sallust. There may also be a hint of Velleian influence in the *LB*. In the peculiar lexicon for time periods discussed above (Table 4.9), the text uses -*annus* compounds at a rate far beyond any other Latin histories (at ten times in just over 9,000 words, or 111 per 100,000 words), besides the *HAb* (180) and Velleius (135).

Finally, there is good evidence for the *LB*'s engagement with Lactantius. Take the fate of Decius, for example, in the *De mortibus* (4.3): 'he was not even able to be honoured with burial (*ne sepultura quidem potuit honorari*), but he lay stripped bare, as befits an enemy of God, fodder for beasts and for birds'.[279] The *LB* also suggests that the unfortunate emperor received no burial, but for a slightly different reason: because 'he sank in the swirls of a swamp, so that not even his body was able to be found' (29.3: *gurgite paludis submersus ita ut nec cadaver eius potuerit inveniri*). This directly contradicts Lactantius, with a specificity that suggests polemical engagement. Instead of lying unburied to be violated by animals, the *LB*'s more sympathetic Decius suffered a fate like that of Romulus, who disappeared at a swamp (*palus*), never to be seen again.[280] Instead of evidence of divine punishment, this might be construed as a sign from heaven of exceptional favour. Similarly, with the story of the even unluckier emperor Valerian, both the *LB* and Lactantius say that his conqueror, Shapur, used the poor man as a mounting block (**TABLE 4.16**). The intertextual links between these two versions are clear: indeed, they are significantly closer to each other than to the other accounts of the same story.[281]

---

277 Augustine, *Contra Iulianum* 4.3.19, *De Patientia* 5.4, *Ep.* 167 (*bis*).

278 Sallust, *Iug.* 75.2.

279 On this passage in Lactantius and its parallel with the *LB*, see Søby Christensen 1980: 66.

280 *cf.* Livy 1.16.1; Florus 1.16; *DVI* 2.13.

281 *e.g.* Orosius 7.22.4: *donec vixit, damnatione sortitus, ut ipse adclinis humi regem semper, ascensurum in equum, non manu sua sed dorso attolleret.* Given the vanishing rarity of the *DMP* in the early Middle Ages, and the fact that this is not a verbatim overlap, we can rule out the idea that the compiler of the *LB* incorporated the passage directly from Lactantius.

Table 4.14 – Sallust and the *Libellus breviatus*: Catiline and Hadrian

Cat. 5.3	*LB* 14.3
His body was capable of enduring starvation, cold, wakefulness, more than any man can believe (*supra quam quoiquam credibile est*).	He had a memory better than any man can believe (*supra quam cuiquam credibile est*), able to review by their names places, matters, soldiers, even those who were absent.

Table 4.15 – Sallust and the *Libellus breviatus*: Marius and Licinius

Iug. 86.2–3	*LB* 41.9
He meanwhile enrolled soldiers, not in the manner of our ancestors nor according to their census grades, but just as each man desired, the majority of them rated only for their persons [*i.e.* in a very low census class]. Some relate that he did this because of the shortage of better-off men, others out of ambition for the consulship, because he had been honoured and exalted by that class of men (*quod ab eo genere celebratus auctusque erat*).	He was very helpful to the farmers and the country folk, because he was sprung from and supported by that class of men (*quod ab eo genere ortus altusque*).

Table 4.16 – Lactantius and the *Libellus breviatus*: Shapur and Valerian

DMP 5.3–4	*LB* 32.6
Si quando libuerat aut vehiculum **ascendere** aut **equum**, inclinare sibi Romanum iubebat ac terga praebere et **imposito pede super dorsum eius** . . . Ita ille dignissime triumphatus **aliquamdiu vixit** . . .	Nam **quamdiu vixit**, rex eiusdem provinciae incurvato eo **pedem cervicibus eius imponens equum conscendere** solitus erat.
Whenever he wanted to mount his carriage or his horse, he ordered the Roman to bend down and offer his back: with his foot on his raised back . . . So, after he had been triumphed over as he entirely deserved, he lived for long enough . . .	For as long as he lived, the king of the same region was accustomed to mount his horse by placing his foot on Valerian's neck, when he was bent down.

In brief, the *Libellus breviatus* is not so ambitious a work, in literary or historiographical terms, as the *Historiae abbreviatae*. Its style is plain and generally factual, not florid and obscure. Yet, here and there, one can find little verbal tics and inconspicuous phrases that hint at wider research and subtle literary influences: Suetonius, Tacitus, Dio, Herodian, and even Lactantius, for historical material; Sallust, Tacitus again, Cicero, and Vergil, for literary reference. The *LB* also produces here and there individual items – like the ball of Fortune – that were obscure even in antiquity. At a glance, one can see that the *LB*'s intellectual milieu is not that of seventh- or eighth-century Italy, but instead mirrors the world of the *HAb* very closely indeed.

Authorial personality in the *Libellus breviatus*

The *Historiae abbreviatae* is a work full of personality: Aurelius Victor was a man with views, views that he was unafraid to share with his readers. The *Libellus breviatus* is much more restrained. It mostly lacks the complex digressions, the personal reflections on history and what it means, that fill the pages of the *HAb*. Yet it is not so totally devoid of character as it might at first seem: comparison to epitomes which it superficially resembles makes this obvious. The works of Eutropius and Festus *are* very largely impersonal: the authors intrude only very occasionally and usually at significant moments, despite the fact that both had active and consequential careers in public life.[282] They avoid saying that they saw this, or heard that, or think the following – first-person verbs are few, limited to cross-references and the opening and close of their works.[283] In contrast, the author of the *LB* is not afraid of the perpendicular pronoun.[284] Some of these authorial intrusions, it is true, are generalising, cross-references, or explanations. Others, however, are more revealing, like this knowledgeable and rather pointed consideration of the literary culture of the emperor Theodosius (48.11):

> He was moderately knowledgeable (*mediocriter doctus*) about literature, if we consider (*contemplemur*) those who are very accomplished in it; clearly sharp and very industrious in finding out about the deeds of men of old.

Mediocriter doctus is a Ciceronian phrase.[285] Likewise, in cataloguing the disasters during the reign of Marcus Aurelius, the author expresses his own belief about the importance of wise rulers (16.4):

> I believe (*credo*) it has been granted by heaven that, when the law of the universe, or nature (*mundi lex seu natura*), brings forth something that is unknown to men, they are mitigated by the deliberations of those in power, as though by the cures of medicine.[286]

There is much one could discuss here, but let it suffice to note that the evocation of the quintessentially Stoic idea of the *lex mundi* as *natura* is a particularly erudite touch for a discussion of Marcus Aurelius.[287] Victor himself was quite taken with the idea of these 'natural laws' that govern history and human behaviour, such as that parents bear children of opposite proclivities *quasi naturae lege* (*HAb* 3.5: 'as though by some law of nature'), or that people who do not indulge during adolescence are more likely to commit even worse excesses as adults *quasi lege* (*HAb* 5.3: 'as though by law'), or that 'nothing happens which the power of nature (*naturae vis*) cannot bring back once more after the interval of an age' (*HAb* 35.13).

Another of these first-person moments in the *Libellus* is particularly important, because it hints at the life and career of the author behind the source on which it drew. It comes in the account of Septimius Severus, as the emperor's behaviour towards his friends and supporters is described (20.6):

---

282 Eutropius 10.16.1 *e.g.*, telling the reader he was part of Julian's Persian expedition.

283 Eutropius 5.4.2, *de quo diximus*; 10.17.2, *quae commemoravi*; 10.18.3 (*bis*), the *sphragis* of the work. Festus does use first-person plural verbs, but they are generally for 'we the Romans' (*e.g.* 5.7 on the defeat of the Lusitani), rather than for the author himself.

284 In this section we are using 'author' in the sense of the author of the source text on which the *LB* drew, not the text itself. Below, we present a definitive case that licenses this usage (*LB* 8.6).

285 Cicero, *De fin.* 3.1.3; *De leg.* 3.14; *Pro Rabirio* 23.

286 See the Appendix, no. XVI.

287 *cf. Meditations* 4.4 and Lucan, *BC* 2.2–3.

> He was equally ardent towards friends and enemies, inasmuch as he enriched Lateranus, Cilo, Anullinus, Bassus, and several others with houses also worthy of mention; we see today (*videmus*) the most outstanding of these, which are called 'the house of the Parthians' and 'the Lateran'.

The precise details of which buildings Severus was giving to his friends are less important than the fact that they were at Rome and the author of the *LB* (or rather of its source) had seen them. This is not the only piece of local knowledge that can be found in the text. In describing the origins of the emperor Maximian, the *LB* says (40.10):

> For even now there is, not so far from Sirmium, a place prominent on account of the palace built on that very spot, where his parents worked for a wage.

Now there was certainly a palace *at* Sirmium in the fourth century, for Ammianus mentions it twice (26.5.4, 30.5.16), but the *LB* is the only work to locate one *near* there built by Maximian. The ongoing excavations at Glac in Serbia seem likely to prove that its author knew whereof he spoke.[288] It hardly needs saying that it is vanishingly unlikely that this is the personal reminiscence of whoever redacted the *LB* in early-medieval Italy. This is his source speaking.

Where do these reminiscences lead? The 'author' of the *Libellus breviatus*, that is, the 'I' of its first-person verbs, emerges a little in the text, to an unusual degree for such a short work of history. He was widely read in Greek and Latin sources, he was interested in the education and culture of emperors, and he knew both Rome and Sirmium well. Aurelius Victor was an author with personality. He certainly read voraciously in Latin and Greek and was interested in, indeed obsessed with, imperial culture. He spent time in Sirmium, where Julian found him in 361, and he knew Rome well.[289] Given all that, it seems not over-bold to suppose that the two texts share all these features because they ultimately go back to the pen of the same individual.

That the first person of the *Libellus breviatus* is indeed the first person of the *Historiae abbreviatae* would seem to be confirmed by a sentence we have touched on already, one extremely significant for understanding Victor. It occurs in both texts in identical wording (*HAb* 8.7 = *LB* 8.6):

> All these, whom I have touched upon (*attigi*) in a few words, especially the race of the Caesars, were so cultivated in letters and eloquence, that, if they had not been excessive in all their vices (apart from Augustus), such great attainments would have doubtless veiled modest disgraces.

Read straight, the 'I' of the *LB* is the same as the 'I' of the *HAb*.

The *Libellus breviatus* and the *Historiae abbreviatae*

Can it actually be shown that the *LB* is an abbreviation and that it was epitomised from a text very similar to the source of the *HAb*? If there is not quite a smoking gun, then there is certainly a whiff of

---

288 The results have not yet been published, but see https:// glac-project.sydney.edu.au.

289 Chapter I.

cordite in the air. We have already seen that the *HAb* and *LB* share a remarkable number of unusual facts, a substrate of common language, recourse to uncommon sources like Lactantius, and a good deal of material verbatim – but there is more than that.[290] Three examples make the case separately for abbreviation and derivation from the work of Victor. They show that the *LB* and *HAb* make most sense when we treat them both as witnesses to a lost and more extensive work.

The death of Marcus Aurelius, our sources agree, caused considerable consternation: 'the greatest groan of all mortals', as the *HAb* puts it (16.14). The text goes on (16.15) to describe how:

> The senators and common people (*patres ac vulgus*), who were divided in other matters, decreed to him alone every honour, temples, columns, priests (*omnia decrevere templa columnas sacerdotes*).

We have already seen that this passage has an intertextual link to the *LB*, but the broader context is revealing (*LB* 16.14):

> Et quod de Romulo aegre creditum est, omnes pari consensu praesumpserunt Marcum caelo receptum esse. Ob cuius honorem **templa columnae multaque alia decreta sunt**.

> And all with unified agreement assumed that Marcus was received into heaven, which was scarcely believed of Romulus. Temples, columns, and many other things were decreed in his honour.

On the one hand, the *HAb* clarifies the *LB*: the unclear *omnes pari consensu* makes sense with the specification of the *patres ac vulgus*. More importantly, however, the *LB* clarifies the *HAb*. Why note that the 'senators and common people' were 'divided in other matters'? If one turns to the first book of Livy, where the apotheosis of Romulus is discussed, one finds a sharp division between the common people and the Senate.[291] This was overcome by universal agreement that Romulus was a god (1.16.3):

> Then, when a start had been made by a few men, all together (*universi*) saluted Romulus as a god and a god's son, as the king and father of the city of Rome.

The *HAb* is missing Romulus and the *LB* lacks the Senate and the people. Only together do their separate accounts make a single story, which necessitates derivation from a common source containing all the requisite elements. This source was like the Victor we know from the *HAb*: interested in Livy and the regal period, in understanding how the age of kings might shed light on the age of emperors. It even sounded like Victor, making use of one his favourite adverbs, *aegre*.

There is another episode that points in the same direction – it takes us from brightly lit age of the Antonines deep into the darkness of the third century. We have already briefly discussed the *devotio* of the emperor Claudius II, his self-sacrifice to win victory over the Goths. In the *Historiae abbreviatae*, the story is told as follows (34.3–5):

> Nam cum pellere Gothos cuperet, quos diuturnitas nimis validos ac prope incolas effecerat, proditum ex libris Sibyllinis est **primum ordinis amplissimi** victoriae vovendum. Cumque is qui esse videbatur

---

290 Chapter II.

291 Livy 1.15.8: *multitudini tamen gratior fuit quam patribus*; 1.16.6: *sollicita civitate . . . et infensa patribus*

semet obtulisset, sibi potius id muneris competere ostendit, qui revera senatus atque omnium princeps erat. Ita nullo exercitus detrimento fusi barbari summotique, postquam imperator **vitam reipublicae dono dedit**.

For when he desired to drive out the Goths, whom long duration had made very strong and nearly inhabitants [*sc.* of the Empire], it was revealed from the Sibylline books that the man who had first place in the most honourable order needed to be vowed to the victory. And when the one who seemed to be that man had offered himself, he [*sc.* Claudius] showed that that duty was fitting to himself, who in truth was the first man in the Senate and among all. So, when the barbarians had been routed and driven off with no loss to the army, afterwards the emperor offered his life as a gift to the state.

This is a dramatic story, with a range of historical and literary resonances. It occurs almost nowhere else in accounts of the emperor Claudius, an omission which should make us pause before assuming that it was merely part of the 'official' Constantinian myth of descent from the conqueror of the Goths.[292] Eutropius, the *Historia Augusta*, Festus, Zosimus, Zonaras, Jerome, Orosius, the *Panegyrici Latini* all know nothing of it. The *only* other source to include something resembling the *HAb*'s story is the *Libellus breviatus* (34.3):

Claudius vero cum ex fatalibus libris, quos inspici praeceperat, cognovisset **sententiae in senatu dicendae primi** morte remedium desiderari, Pomponio Basso, qui tunc erat, se offerente **ipse vitam** suam haud passus responsa frustrari **dono reipublicae dedit**, praefatus neminem tanti ordinis primas habere quam imperatorem.

However, Claudius, when he had learned (from the books of fate, which he had ordered to be examined) that the cure needed was the death of the man who spoke his opinion first in the Senate, although Pomponius Bassus, who was that man at the time, was offering himself, did not permit the answer to be rejected, but himself offered his own life as a gift to the state having said that no man other than the emperor had the primacy of so great an *ordo*.

These passages are fascinating, for their style (remarkably similar in its ambition) as much as for their content, but four points are particularly worth discussion. First, the two texts are drawing on a common source: the shared phrase – *vitam rei publicae dono dedit* – is used nowhere else in antiquity. Second, they are both incomplete. The *HAb* lacks the name of the *princeps senatus* who offered himself for the safety of the state, though it clearly assumes that his identity is important. The *LB* does not provide context for the episode: it fails to explain that this momentous exchange took place during a war with the Goths and that that was why the *devotio* was needed. This renders the emperor's act of self-sacrifice heroic, but bizarre. It also lacks the literary context provided by the *HAb*'s slightly subversive intertext with Cicero.[293] Third, they share an important omission: neither of them actually specifies that Claudius was killed on the battlefield. It is widely assumed, through over-reading, that the two texts explicitly claim that Claudius fell in battle and are in error, because it is well known that he died of disease.[294] In point of fact, fulfilling a *devotio* was not incompatible with a death from natural causes.[295] The two texts thus share an amazingly

292 On which, see Syme 1974.
293 See above.
294 Error: Dufraigne 1975: 168; Bird 1997: 11–12; Festy 1999a *ad loc. e.g.* Disease: Eutropius 9.11.2, Zosimus

1.46.2, Zonaras 12.26, and the *HA Claud.* 12.2 all say he died of the plague (*cf. Chron.* 354 (p. 148, l. 6)).

295 Versnel 1976: 391–392. What matters is the act of *devotio*: the way it turns out is not in the power of whoever makes the vow.

recondite piece of religious-*cum*-historical lore and both convey it in a way that is susceptible to a rather comic misreading. Fourth, combined, they complete each other. The *HAb* provides the context for the *devotio* of Claudius, the *LB* gives the name of the man who was spared by the emperor's decision. Pomponius Bassus, it is worth noting, was a real and prominent figure under the emperors from Gallienus to Aurelian.[296]

In this case, if we read the text of two works which claim to be summaries of Victor's *History* in parallel, then combined they give the definitive account of an event that separately they reproduce incompletely or incoherently. Further support for the obvious conclusion can be found in Ammianus. The book(s) of the *Res gestae* that covered the reign of Claudius II are lost, but – while working himself into a high dudgeon at the visit of Constantius II to Rome in 357 – Ammianus reminds his readers of the better example set by *veteres principes*. One of these (16.10.3): 'vowed his life for the state's sake according to the example of the Decii' (*ad Deciorum exempla vovisse pro re publica spiritum*). Of whom could Ammianus be thinking? The text of the *HAb* (34.1–2) gives the answer, when it says that Claudius was 'a man dedicated to the republic, such that he renewed the memory of the Decii after a long stretch of time' (*viri . . . dediti reipublicae, quippe ut longo intervallo Deciorum morem renovaverit*).[297] As we have seen, Ammianus knew and admired Victor's work. When searching for an *exemplum* with which to belabour Constantius II, he reproduces what is very specifically one of Victor's ideas, using Victor's words, in a way that implies it was common knowledge. Moreover, Ammianus' rewording – *exempla* instead of *memoria* and cutting both *longo intervallo* and the verb *renovare* – obscures the original Ciceronian allusion: this demonstrates the intellectual priority of Victor and almost requires derivation. The unavoidable conclusion is that behind this tangled mass of *testimonia* to the fate of Claudius lies a complex and involved account of that emperor – an account produced by Victor.

Final confirmation of this line of argument can be found in a brief passage in the *HAb*'s life of Septimius Severus (20.6):

> They decreed (*sanxere*) official mourning for Severus with a public holiday, and an inscription, bewailing (?) that it was not at all fitting for this man to have been born or to have died (*illum nasci aut emori minime convenisse*).[298]

Why does Victor include this curiously gnomic statement, which, as we have seen, seems to be ultimately derived from Livy?[299] The explanation lies in his desire to draw comparisons between emperors. Like Constantine, Severus was set up by Victor as a new Augustus, drawing on a contemporary tradition that compared the two men.[300] Here, Victor puts into the mouths of Severus' contemporaries a famous saying about Rome's first emperor: that either he should have never been born or never died. The *HAb*,

296 *PLRE* 'Bassus 17'; Christol 1986: 221–224.
297 *HAb* 34.2: note also *vovendum*/*vovisse* in the two texts.
298 The precise identity of the subject here is not explicit, but since they have 'decreed (*sanxere*)' Severus honours, they ought to be the Senate. On the textual difficulties of this passage, see Den Boer 1972: 47–48.
299 See above.

300 For Severus as a new Augustus: Barnes 2008. See besides Dio 76.8.1 (a speech of Severus to the Senate after his victory over Albinus, in which he praised the severity and fierceness of Augustus, among others) and Herodian 3.7.8 for comparison of Severus to Augustus, among other victors in civil wars, again after the defeat of Albinus (the two passages may not be unconnected).

however, never uses this *sententia* in its coverage of Augustus. We know that it relates to him only because the *LB* tells us so, the only Roman history to transmit it (1.28): 'everyone taking up the common cry, "Would that either he had not been born or not died!"' (*cunctis vulgo iactantibus: 'Utinam aut non nasceretur aut non moreretur!'*). The *HAb*'s inclusion of this saying makes sense only as a reference back to what was said about Augustus; yet it is nowhere to be found in the *HAb*'s biography of the first emperor. Once again, the texts of the *LB* and the *HAb* complete each other.

The *Libellus breviatus* claims to be a summary of the longer, multi-book work of Aurelius Victor. It shares a good deal with another work that makes the same claim: language, information, ideas. Its author's literary tastes, philosophical views, and personal experiences are very close to those of Victor. That the two works are so similar when they were produced by such different methods of epitomisation is striking. The *HAb* and the *LB* are, as we have seen, plausibly genuine abbreviations of longer work. If that is so, then the account of the funeral of Marcus Aurelius, the *devotio* of Claudius II, and the comparison of Severus to Augustus shows that their sources were the same. There is, thus, every reason to believe that the *Libellus breviatus* is, like the *Historiae abbreviatae*, exactly what the manuscripts say it is: an epitome of Victor's *Historia*.

A reconsideration of the connections between the *Historiae abbreviatae* and the *Libellus breviatus*, an analysis of their transmission, and an exposition of the genre of epitome in Latin literature all suggested that both texts were summaries of a much more substantial work produced by Aurelius Victor. Were that so, we ought to be able to recover some sense of that original history from which they were derived. That is what we have sought to do in this chapter and the results are richly rewarding. A detailed examination of the *HAb* – the first one undertaken without preconceptions about the nature or value of the work – has made some points incontestable. The work is a mine of obscure factual information on Roman history. It has an obvious historiographical debt to a number of Latin and Greek historians and shows a remarkably broad range of cultural reference: from Vergil and Cicero to Herodotus and Plutarch, from grammar and rhetoric to law and philosophy. It systematically uses the material to which it alludes as a tool for historical analysis and interpretation, wielding literary references like a bludgeon or a scalpel as the occasion demands. All this speaks to an author of deep learning and serious intellect, one with ambition and the skill to effectuate it. Yet, that is simply incompatible with the more obvious signs of incompetence and incompleteness in the text. That yawning chasm between what we see and what we can recover is explained by abbreviation. Once one knows what to look for, the signs are obvious on every page of the *HAb*. As we read the work, we are encountering Sextus Aurelius Victor, but only in fragments. A more selective analysis of the *Libellus breviatus* points in precisely the same direction. Whatever its differences from the *HAb* – differences explained by the techniques of epitomisation – they share a common frame of factual information, literary reference, and compositional technique. When they are read in parallel, key episodes that are garbled or confused in each of them become clearer and more complete. We have explained already that the *LB* is a production of the early Middle Ages: based on an excellent source, certainly, but not itself an ancient work. Could that source be the work of Victor? Obviously, it cannot be identical with the work from which the *HAb* was derived, since that terminates in 360 and must have been published shortly thereafter. As we have already seen, however, the terminal date of the ancient source of the *LB* is 388, and that still sits comfortably with what we know of Victor's lifetime and career. After all, there are no good reasons to think that a man of serious literary inclinations and historical interests would have simply stopped writing in the last thirty years of his life, especially given that we have no evidence he was occupied with an official career.[301]

This chapter has ranged far and wide, delved into questions of sometimes considerable obscurity, and at points made arguments of some complexity. It is worth pointing out, however, that its conclusions are in the main part simplifying. The *HAb* and *LB* are so intimately linked because they go back to a common source. That source was the work of Sextus Aurelius Victor, which is exactly what the manuscripts of both works claim. The marked peculiarities of both texts are neatly explained by what we know about both the nature of epitomes in antiquity and the way that they were produced. Above all, it is only on the thesis of epitomisation that we can reasonably explain the sharp divergence between Victor's elevated reputation in antiquity and the meagre remains of his work that we have today. It is to this reputation – and its implications – that we must next turn.

301 Chapter I.

Chapter V

Victor's Readers

Manuscripts, literary context, and the texts of the *HAb* and *LB* themselves all point towards the same conclusion: Aurelius Victor wrote a long, discursive work of history, of which we today have only a remnant. This is a radical idea in the context of current academic opinion, but it is entirely logical in the light of the evidence, indeed demanded by it. Crucially, moreover, it is only on the assumption that Victor wrote a major work of history that what was said about him in late antiquity makes any sense at all. Victor has much the most extensive *Nachleben* of any fourth-century historian writing in Latin. His later reputation is one impossible to square with the *Historiae abbreviatae*, but it makes plenty of sense if he was the author of a *Historia* of serious literary ambition and deep research. It is thus to the *testimonia* that we must turn next. They stretch from the middle of the fourth century down into the eighth and offer crucial new evidence, evidence that decisively confirms the thesis advanced in the previous chapters.

In what follows, we continue to assess Victor's reputation in late antiquity primarily against the evidence of the *Historiae abbreviatae*, since all scholars acknowledge that that is his work and because, as we have seen, it preserves some portion of what he wrote in his own words. We also, however, examine the degree to which those who can be shown to have had some knowledge of Victor's work, as the *HAb* preserves it, share details, emphases, or wording with the *Libellus breviatus*. Though the *LB* is a work of the early Middle Ages and was not provably known to any individual before Paul the Deacon in the later eighth century, it clearly preserves material from an excellent fourth-century source. Since authors of the fourth, fifth, and sixth centuries could not read the *LB* as we have it, those who combine awareness of Victor as a historian with knowledge of material also found in both the *HAb* and *LB* offer particularly strong evidence for the thesis advanced so far in this book: that both texts are epitomes of Victor's much more substantial *Historia*.

Julian

We have already seen that, by 361, Victor seems to have acquired a considerable reputation as a historian: enough of one for the Emperor Julian to promote him to high office on its strength and honour him with a bronze statue. The governorship of Pannonia Secunda was a plum position, making Victor not just an *iudex* but a *consularis*, which brought with it senatorial position.[1] The statue was also a mark of considerable intellectual distinction. Ammianus (14.6.8) makes fun of the aristocratic non-entities who coveted statues,

---

1 Chapter I.

when they ought to have thought them of little importance, so it is striking that he clearly believed Victor deserved his monument. Other literary and scholarly recipients of such an honour were major 'cultural' figures: Themistius, C. Marius Victorinus, Prohaeresius, and Claudian, for example.[2] Indeed, the regard shown Victor seems all the greater if we fix it in the context of 361/362. At the time, Julian's patronage of intellectuals seems largely to have been confined to philosophers or rhetoricians in the Greek tradition, several of whom he had known (in person or by reputation) for some time. Such were the men to whom he wrote after the death of Constantius had made him ruler of the Roman world, informing them of his altered situation or charging them to come to him at Constantinople.[3] In their company, Victor was triply unusual in being a historian, writing in Latin, and having no prior connection to the emperor (so far as we know). The act of favouring him so lavishly would seem to presuppose some famous scholarly achievement. The *HAb* is not that; a longer *Historia* might have been sufficient. It is also worth noting that Julian's letters from the time betray some concern to shape the historical record.[4] One can see why he might have taken an interest in Victor, if he was the author of a recent and weighty work of scholarship.

Did Julian's acquaintance with Victor extend beyond their fleeting encounters at Sirmium and Naissus in 361? The last pagan emperor has left us an extensive corpus of extant writings and, though they are in Greek and Julian's Latin was not that strong, it is natural to wonder whether there is anything of Victor in them. We need not envisage Julian poring over the *Historia*: the work was probably circulating among his entourage and ideas could easily have been transmitted indirectly. The place to hunt for them is the *Caesares*, Julian's survey of his predecessors, purportedly (*Caes.* 306a) written for the Saturnalia in 361 or 362.[5] Julian imagines that, on Mt Olympus, Romulus plays host at a banquet for the gods and the Roman emperors (307b). A competition is held to judge who was the best of Rome's rulers (316a–317b), with Alexander the Great thrown in for comparison. Much 'humorous' reflection on their characters and achievements follows, partly in Julian's own voice, partly through Silenus, the class clown of the heavenly host. While author, time, and topic might all make some connection seem likely, scholarship has generally been rather dismissive of the possibility. In his classic treatment of the *Caesares*, G. W. Bowersock remarks that: 'it is obvious that if Julian had read Victor's work . . . it had made no impression whatever'.[6] This conclusion is, however, somewhat hasty.

Throughout the *Caesares*, the view that Julian takes of his predecessors often matches the emphasis of Victor's account. We can start with Augustus: famously, Julian compares Rome's first emperor to a chameleon (309a), but he also pays particular attention to the effect that philosophy had had on him.

---

2 Themistius: *Or.* 4.54b, 17.214b (*inter alia*). Victorinus: Jerome, *Chron.* 239ᵉ, Augustine, *Confessions* 8.2.3. Prohaeresius: Eunapius, *VS* 10.7.3–4. Claudian: *CIL* 6.1710, *De bello Gothico* 7–9.

3 See Julian, *ELF* 26–39, esp. 26 (to Maximus), 27 (Chrysanthius), 31 (Prohaeresius, though *cf.* Watts 2006: 64–67 on the possibly sarcastic nature of the letter), 34–36 (Eustathius), 37 (Priscus, Chrysanthius, Melite), 38 (Himerius); see Elm 2012: 90 ff. for Julian's connections to these figures. *cf.* AM 22.7.3 on Julian's over-warm welcome of Maximus to Constantinople.

4 Julian, *ELF* 25 (Eunapius, *ES* 16 = Blockley fr. 23.2), 31.

5 The year is disputed, but must be one of these two: see Elm 2012: 286 and n. 68 (with reference to earlier scholarship). Greenwood 2021: 45–54 makes a persuasive case for 361.

6 Bowersock 1982: 166. That Julian might have used Victor has been canvassed by others (Bouffartigue 1992: 401–407 has a good discussion; see also Alföldi 1968), but always with the assumption that the *HAb* is the totality of his work and that borrowing was therefore somewhat limited. In general, the cultural background of the work is assumed to be Greek, as *e.g.* in Quiroga Puertas 2017.

Early on (309c) Zeno the Stoic recites some of his teachings over Octavian and makes him 'prudent and self-controlled' (ἔμφρονα καὶ σώφρονα). Later, Augustus himself boasts (326b):

> I showed myself so amenable to philosophy that I patiently bore the freedom of speech of Athenodorus, not irritated but rather delighted by it, and I respected the man as my teacher (παιδαγωγόν), or rather my father.

Whence came this complex of ideas? We might expect it to have a Greek source and Athenodorus, the Stoic philosopher, does indeed appear in Plutarch (*Apoth.* 207c) and Cassius Dio (52.36.4; 56.43.2).[7] The former is in roughly the same area as Julian – Athenodorus advises Augustus to recite the twenty-four letters of the Greek alphabet when he gets angry (Zeno's incantations?) – but cannot be his direct source, since there is no reference to Athenodorus as the emperor's teacher, nor to his 'freedom of speech'. In fact, the text that comes closest is the *LB* on Theodosius (48.14):

> He had in his nature what Augustus obtained from his teacher in philosophy (*philosophiae doctore*). He, when he had seen that Augustus was easily provoked, admonished him (lest he should decree something harsh) that when he had begun to grow angry, he ought to recite from memory the four and twenty letters of the Greek alphabet, so that that passion, which is momentary, would mellow with a little interval of time, his mind transported elsewhere.

What is interesting here is not so much the *prima facie* impression that (once again) Victor has made use of a Greek source, but the reference to Athenodorus (unnamed, but that is surely the result of abbreviation) as Augustus' *doctor*, his teacher. That is, of course, very close indeed to Julian's terming him a παιδαγωγός, an idea perhaps implicit in Plutarch and Dio, but expressed by neither.

Theodosius reigned (of course) long after Julian had died, but it seems likely that this is a back-reference to what Victor had said in his earlier account of Augustus. We have seen elsewhere how Victor liked to think about more recent history through the lens of Rome's past, so it would have been natural for him in describing the 380s to look back to what he had already written about Rome's first emperor. We can perhaps confirm that Julian was influenced by Victor's description of Augustus from one other significant detail. When the latter enters the contest in the *Caesares*, Julian says (309b):

> He wished the glance of his eyes to resemble that of great Helios himself, for he thought no man who encountered him fit to look him in the face.

This anecdote recalls a point made generally in Suetonius' *Augustus* (79.3), which also compares Augustus' gaze *ad fulgorem solis*, but the same idea is found in the *LB* (1.20), which speaks of his *fulgor oculorum*. Julian was clearly using a source that both remarked on the effect of philosophy on Augustus and the glare of his gaze: Victor's *Historia* would seem to fit the bill.[8]

The resemblances between Victor and Julian continue throughout the emperors of the first and second centuries. Tiberius, about whom Julian knows a remarkable amount that comes from the Latin

---

7 Other references at Dio Chrysostom 33.48; Aelian 12.25; Lucian, *Macrobii* 23.

8 On this passage in the *LB*, see further Chapter IX.

tradition, is presented as a dissimulator.[9] He enters with an 'august and solemn' demeanour, looking both self-controlled and warlike (309c–d), but his back was covered in wounds from his 'licentiousness and cruelty'. Victor emphasised that Tiberius was *subdolus et occultior* and acted often *simulando* (*HAb* 2.1, *cf. LB* 2.4).[10] Trajan, while undoubtedly heroic in Julian's eyes, is criticised for his φιλοποσία, or love of drinking (327c, *cf.* 318c), which made him seem ἀμβλύτερος (more sluggish) than he was. Victor had noted his *vinolentia* (*HAb* 13.10, *cf. LB* 13.4), with a particular attention to its effect on his decision-making. It is not a detail unique to him, but again it is striking that Julian's emphasis coincides so neatly with Victor's.[11] Julian also has Trajan describe the empire on his accession as ναρκῶσαν ('growing stiff') – Victor has 'the ruined and exhausted Roman order' restored by him (*LB* 13.10: *perdito atque prostrato statu Romano*). Julian says little about Hadrian, but characterises him as 'meddling in forbidden things' (311d: πολυπραγμονῶν τὰ ἀπόρρητα) and notes his obsession with Antinous. Victor, with his detailed coverage of the emperor's favourite and tale of his possible human sacrifice, 'Hadrian desiring to bring forth an oracle' (*HAb* 14.8: *Hadriano cupiente fatum producere*), is remarkably close. Marcus Aurelius receives more extensive and positive coverage, but is introduced by Julian as making mistakes over his wife, who was not κοσμίαν, or 'well behaved' (312a–b). Victor, in his own introduction of the emperor, praised his conduct of affairs, but censured his 'lack of judgement in controlling his wife' (*HAb* 16.2: *imprudentia regendae coniugis*), giving lurid details of Faustina's affairs.

Julian continues to echo Victor on the third-century emperors. Severus is described as 'a man full of bitterness, given to punishing' (313d: ἀνὴρ πικρίας γέμων, κολαστικός). Victor is more positive, but notes his excessive harshness in correcting morals (*HAb* 20.7) and his tendency to punish even small misdeeds (20.21). Julian subtly alludes to Caracalla's Alexander-mania by making the Macedonian take his seat when he is expelled for fratricide (316c) – Victor made much of the same subject (*LB* 21.4) and also devoted a great deal of attention to his murder of Geta (*HAb* 20.32–34, *cf. LB* 21.3). Alexander Severus is mocked by Silenus for his hoarding of wealth, much of it entrusted to his mother – both his parsimony and his mother's role in it come up in the *LB* (24.5). Julian is also dismissive of Gallienus (313b–c), cast as soft and effeminate in his gait and dress, in a fashion similar to Victor's account of the debauched emperor (*HAb* 33.6). Claudius II is introduced (313d) both as the ancestor of the imperial house and as an extraordinary φιλοπάτρις ('lover of his country') – the latter looks decidedly like an oblique reference to his *devotio*.[12] Probus is teased by Silenus for driving his men too hard (314c) – Victor has him murdered by legionaries sick of public works (*HAb* 37.4). Even for the fourth century, when the common conversation of the educated classes and family legend might have been expected to shape Julian's coverage of the emperors, there are telling links to Victor. Maxentius is called 'unwarlike and soft' (329a: ἀπόλεμόν τε καὶ μαλακόν) – this is an odd and unparalleled collocation in Greek, but it is remarkably close to the *HAb*'s characterisation of him as *pavidus et imbellis* (40.20), itself never otherwise used in Latin literature. Magnentius is denied entrance to the feast, because though he did much that looked good, none of it was really done from virtue (315d–316a). His talent for dissimulation, his fundamental falseness, appears to have been one of Victor's themes (*LB* 42.7).

---

9 *Caes.* 310a: pulling the ears of a grammarian (*cf.* Suetonius, *Tib.* 56); Capri as his residence; story of the mullet and the fisherman (*Tib.* 60).

10 On Tiberius' simulation, see Chapter IV.

11 See also Fronto, *De feriis Alsiensibus* 3.5; Cassius Dio 68.7.4–5.

12 Chapter IV.

This is by no means an exhaustive overview of the connections between Julian and Victor: a detailed examination of both would no doubt yield still more. Even so, it is striking how much the abbreviated text of Victor and Julian's festive satire share, not in factual details, but characterisation and emphasis. It is true that, in some cases, what Julian says can be found in a source besides Victor and it might also fairly be pointed out that we lack, for instance, most of Plutarch's *Caesares* – an obvious repository of information, at least for the early emperors, by an author whose works Julian certainly used.[13] Still, it seems unwise to suppose that Julian's *jeu d'esprit* was based on wide reading in Greek and Latin historians – given what it shares with Victor through its entire course, it is much more plausible that his *Historia* lies behind it. That is obviously significant for our understanding of Victor's reception – what he had produced was something qualitatively superior to what had existed before. The *HAb* is not that.

The *Corpus tripertitum*

Our next *testimonium* hangs uncertainly, perhaps in the middle of the fourth century: the prefatory material to the *Corpus tripertitum*. As outlined in Chapter II, there are reasons to think that this was put together not so very long after 361, before Eutropius' work entered wide circulation, though later dates certainly cannot be ruled out. We have already examined the testimony of this preface in some detail and seen that it explicitly states that Victor wrote a longer work from which the *HAb* has been epitomised, something which there is good reason to believe. There is one more point in the compiler's remarks that deserves to be picked out. Having given a lengthy list of authorities for the mythical prehistory of Rome, the *CT*'s compiler then says (in a more business-like fashion) that thereafter he used *Livius et Victor Afer*, the former for republican, the latter for imperial history.[14] The two authors are clearly meant to enjoy some sort of equivalence, yet the juxtaposition is, on the face of it, absurd. Livy, as everyone knows, wrote a history *ab urbe condita* in 142 books. The extant parts alone run to somewhere north of half a million words. The *HAb* is, in comparison, a bantamweight 11,000 words or so. In spite of that, the compiler of the *CT* clearly thought of Victor and Livy as in some sense engaged in a similar endeavour. That we do not have all of Victor's work would neatly explain the discrepancy between his opinion and the state of the *HAb*. We need not imagine that Victor wrote at the same length as Livy (few can have dared), but the evidence of the *CT* would make a good deal more sense if his work was a long, learned, and discursive history in the Roman tradition.

13 It was long a commonplace that Julian owed a great deal to Plutarch, *e.g.* Bowersock 1982: 171: 'If we should wish to hazard a guess as to one author whose works on historical subjects had actually made a substantial impression on Julian, Plutarch would be the best candidate' (with specific reference to the *Caesares*). Bouffartigue 1992: 285–293 took a much more sceptical approach, arguing for limited acquaintance with the *Parallel Lives* alone, perhaps largely through the compilation of Damophilus of Bithynia. His case is both strengthened and complicated by Van Hoof and Van Nuffelen 2013 (esp. 215 ff.), who argue for parallel use of Damophilus and Plutarch in one instance. Scepticism about Julian's reading is always wise, but Bouffartigue perhaps goes a little too far. Since the advent of the *TLG*, it is easier to find examples that meet the standard he set (287: textual resemblance) and it is striking how many quotations turn up in both Plutarch and Julian (the common coin of rhetoric or evidence of derivation?). The topic merits further investigation.

14 His later reference to the *DVI* (in the bridge passage from the *OGR* to that work) as *Liviana historia* confirms this point.

Jerome and Rufinus

We next hear of Victor by name in a letter which Jerome sent to Paul of Concordia in the years before AD 380.[15] It is a rather playful, perhaps even teasing missive, touching on the general decline of mankind's strength since the days of Adam and its recipient's great age, but undimmed vigour. Its real purpose, however, is a request for books, in return for which Jerome offered his own *Vita Pauli*, specifying that he wanted:

> . . . *Commentarios* Fortunatiani et propter notitiam persecutorum Aurelii Victoris *Historiam* simulque *Epistulas* Novatiani . . .[16]
>
> . . . the *Commentaries* of Fortunatian, and the *Historia* of Aurelius Victor, on account of its information on the persecutors, and the *Letters* of Novatian as well . . .

Jerome wanted the *Historia* (*n.b.* not *Historiae abbreviatae*) of Victor. Even if that is not the original title of Victor's work, but rather Jerome's own coinage, then his other uses of the word in the context of classicising history generally refer to lengthy and serious works: Josephus, for instance.[17] It is interesting that while Jerome included a slightly apologetic parenthesis about this non-Christian work, he assumed that his correspondent would both know and have access to a work published little more than a decade earlier: he certainly does not imply that this is a particularly obscure or *recherché* thing for which to ask. We know relatively little about Paul beyond what Jerome tells us in one place or another. He had been in Rome as a young man, where he had met St Cyprian's secretary, who had remarked on his master's enthusiasm for reading Tertullian (*DVI* 53). He came from Concordia, for he was a compatriot of Rufinus of Aquileia, who was born in that city (*Ep.* 5.2). That is about as much as we can say with certainty. Even from this limited evidence, however, Paul appears to have been quite a bibliophile: besides his request for Victor (*i.a.*), in *Ep.* 5.2 Jerome mentions that Paul was aggressively seeking after (*vehementer poposcit*) a copy of Tertullian (a peculiar interest of his?) that he had lent Rufinus. Evidently, Paul was a man with a fine library and a willingness to lend (but never more) from it. It is worth noting, however, that in every case but one Paul's literary interests were Christian. That he had a copy of Victor's *History* is perhaps itself a testament to its importance.

Jerome says he wished to read the *Historia* for what it said about the persecutors. By *persecutores*, he normally means those emperors, primarily of the third and early fourth centuries, who had persecuted the Church: Nero, Decius, Valerian, and Maximian are the names that keep coming up, but Diocletian, Maximinus (*saevissimus omnium*), and Julian occur as well.[18] It is also worth noting that Jerome refers to

---

15 Jerome, *Ep.* 10. On Paul and Jerome, see Rebenich 1992: 48, 101, 131. The date of the letter is not completely certain but would appear to fall in the latter half of the 370s: see Cavallera 1922: 2.16; *cf.* the more recent synthesis of Williams 2006: 273–276.

16 Jerome, *Ep.* 10.3. Capitalisation ours, on the basis of Dorfbauer's edition (2017: 62–65).

17 Josephus (*e.g.*): Jerome, *In Zach.* 3.14, one of very many such instances. *cf.* the long list of historians necessary to understanding the book of Daniel (*In Dan., prol.*). On the title of Victor's work, see below.

18 *e.g.* Jerome, *In Zach.* 3.14.473 ff.: *omnes persecutores*, who are then listed as Valerian, Decius, Diocletian, Maximianus, Maximinus, and Julian; *Ep.* 109.1 (Julian); *Tractatus LIX in Psalmos* 137.33 (Nero, Maximian, Decius), 143.30 (Julian, Nero, Decius); *Vita Pauli* 2 (Decius and Valerian). *cf.* his use of *persecutio*: *DVI* 9, 17 (Nero), 54, 62, 69 (Decius), 83 (Decius and Valerian), 67 (Valerian and Gallienus); *In Naum* 1.474 ff. (Valerian, Decius, Maximian); *In Ezech.* 11.36.671 (Diocletian and Maximian).

HAb 21.1	Jerome, *Chronicon* 213[d]
Ceterum Antoninus incognita munerum specie plebem Romanam adficiens, quod indumenta in talos demissa largiretur, Caracalla dictus, cum pari modo vesti Antoninianas nomen e suo daret.	Antoninus Caracalla cognominatus propter genus vestis, quod Romae erogaverat, et e contrario Caracallae ex eius nomine Antoninianae dictae.
But Antoninus, influencing the Roman people with unheard of show of munificence, was called 'Caracalla' because he bountifully distributed garments that hung down to the ankles; in the same fashion he gave this style of dress the name *Antoninianae*, from his own.★	Antoninus, nicknamed 'Caracalla' from the sort of clothing which he disbursed at Rome; on the other side, *Carcallae* were called *Antoninianae* after him.

★ The awkwardness of *ceterum* and *cum* are both excellent signs of abbreviation.

Lactantius' *De mortibus persecutorum*, a work very largely about the era of the Tetrarchy, as a single book *de persecutione* (*DVI* 80). One can see why Jerome, in the process of composing his *Chronicon*, might have had need of such information and some of the persecutors, lost in the mists of the third century, had reigns of considerable obscurity.[19] Yet, the request is very strange in the context of the *HAb*. That text does offer quite a lot on Nero, though much less than Suetonius (whose works Jerome knew), and it does have information about the Tetrarchs, though it is considerably less informative than Lactantius and puny against the mass of material in Eusebius – both authors well known to Jerome.[20] It has, however, really very little to say specifically about Decius and Valerian, and almost nothing about Maximinus and Julian.[21] In asking that Paul send him Victor's *Historia* so that he might learn about the 'persecutors', Jerome implies that Victor had written a work of serious history, full of recondite details about less-well-known emperors – a work that went beyond the material he could access in Suetonius, Lactantius, and Eusebius. That implication is totally at odds with the text of the *HAb*.

Was Jerome's request for reading successful? In general terms, the answer is clearly in the affirmative. Lukas Dorfbauer's discovery of Fortunatian's *Commentaries on the Gospels* has dramatically confirmed that Jerome did indeed use them in his own work.[22] That he had read the letters of Novatian also seems likely: Jerome gives an unusually detailed biography of the schismatic in his *De viris illustribus* and claims good knowledge of his style.[23] Did Jerome know Victor's work? Given that his request to Paul of Concordia was otherwise entirely successful, the presumption ought probably to be that he did. There are several tantalising hints in the *Chronicon* to this effect. Take the emperor Caracalla, named for a sort of Gallic cloak that he liked to wear (**TABLE 5.1**). That Caracalla was so named for the garment was known

19 Jerome concludes the *Chronicon* with the sixth consulate of Valens and the second of Valentinian II (378) and the work was written by 380 or so; see Cavallera 1922: 2.20.
20 Suetonius and Jerome: *Chron.*, *praef.* (Helm 6); *DVI*, *Prologus*. Eusebius: *DVI* 81. Lactantius: *DVI* 53.

21 The treatment of Decius is short, *HAb* 29; Valerian briefly features at 32.1–2, and then 33.2; Maximinus occurs only at 40.1 and 41.1; Julian is mentioned once at 42.17.
22 Dorfbauer 2017: 50–51.
23 Biography: Jerome, *DVI* 69. Style: *Ep.* 36.1; *Apologia adversus libros Rufini* 2.19.

TABLE 5.2 – VICTOR AND JEROME ON PHILIP THE ARAB AND HIS SON

HAb 28.1	Jerome, *Chronicon* 245[c]
Therefore Marcus Julius Philippus, an Arab from the Traconitis, after he had taken his son Philip into partnership (*consortium*). . .	Philip made his son Philip the partner (*consortem*) of his rule.

TABLE 5.3 – THE *LIBELLUS BREVIATUS*, JEROME, AND RUFINUS ON THE DEATH OF CONSTANTINE II

LB 41.21	Jerome, *Chron.* 235[a]	Rufinus, *HE* 10.16
Constantinus latrocinii specie dum incautus foedeque temulentus in aliena irruit, obtruncatus est proiectusque in fluvium, cui nomen Alsa est, non longe ab Aquileia.	Constantinus bellum fratri inferens iuxta Aquileiam Alsae occiditur.	Igitur ubi Constantius orientis regnum solus obtinuit, Constantino fratre non longe ab Aquileia apud Alsam fluvium a militibus interfecto, Constans utriusque germanus occidentem satis industrie gubernabat.
Constantine, when like some bandit he recklessly and with shameful drunkenness invaded the territory of another, was butchered and cast into a river called the Alsa, not far from Aquileia.	Constantine, making war on his brother, was killed on the Alsa, near Aquileia,	Therefore when Constantius achieved sole rule of the east, Constantine his brother was killed by the soldiers at the river Alsa, not far from Aquileia; Constans, the brother of them both, governed the west with adequate diligence.

to other writers, but Victor and Jerome are unusual in explaining that the garment came to be named for the emperor (Marcus Aurelius Antoninus) and they do so in a remarkably similar way.[24] It is also worth noting some shared phrasing in their accounts of Philip the Arab and his son (**TABLE 5.2**). There is nothing remotely similar in Eutropius.[25]

There are also connections to the *Libellus breviatus*. That text and Jerome's *Chronicon* are two of only three Latin sources (the other being Rufinus of Aquileia) to tell us that the obscure emperor Constantine II was killed near the river Alsa (**TABLE 5.3**). The phrasing shows that the *LB* is not in any straightforward sense derived from either the *Chronicon* (which does not say that the Alsa was a river) or Rufinus, whose interpretation of the incident is much more neutral. If anything, it would make more sense for there to be a common source for all three texts.[26]

Nor was it only in the *Chronicon* that Jerome found use for Victor. The *HAb* (39.44), in describing the reforms of Diocletian, mentions that he abolished a class of government agents:

> And with no less zeal for peace the government departments were bound by the fairest laws and the destructive breed of *frumentarii* was withdrawn; today (*nunc*) the *agentes in rebus* are extremely similar to these (*quorum nunc agentes rerum simillimi sunt*).

---

24 *cf. HA Carac.* 9.8: *unde hodieque Antoninianae dicuntur caracallae huiusmodi, in usu maxime Romanae plebis frequentatae*. Importantly, the detail is not in Dio 79.3.3.

25 Eutropius 9.3: *Philippi duo, filius ac pater, Gordiano occiso imperium invaserunt.*

26 That the Alsa was a river is confirmed only by Pliny, *HN* 3.126. That it was the scene of the battle between

The rather barbed point here is that Diocletian got rid of the *frumentarii*, but they have returned in the form of the *agentes in rebus*, the feared agents of the central government.[27] In explaining a point of translation in one of his Biblical commentaries (*In Abdiam* ll. 573–575), Jerome says something very similar:

> This is the word which the Septuagint translated πυροφόρον, *which we have turned into frumentarius*, as fits the diction of the old-time speech; for those whom they today (*nunc*) call *agentes in rebus* or *veredarii*, the ancients used to call *frumentarii*.

No other ancient author ever connects the *frumentarii* and the *agentes* – it is just the kind of bureaucratic detail in which Victor luxuriated and it seems likely that the comparison is his invention.[28] Jerome was clearly exploiting Victor's work for the detailed and often technical information it could provide.

Details, however, were not all Jerome took from Victor: on occasion, he also borrowed a well-turned phrase. In the 390s, after he had settled into a quasi-monastic life in Bethlehem, Jerome was drawn into a bitter dispute with John, the bishop of Jerusalem, who (at one stage) tried to have him and his fellow ascetics expelled from the region.[29] Theophilus, the bishop of Alexandria, was called into mediate and worked away at both parties. In response to one of his missives, Jerome sent his *Ep. 82*, a rhetorical masterwork that brilliantly combines an ostensible longing for reconciliation with a series of wounding attacks on John. As part of this, Jerome offers a description and a defence of the attitude that he and other ascetics took to churchmen who stood in authority over them. He then characterises how bishops ought to behave (*Ep.* 82.11):

> Sed contenti sint honore suo et patres se sciant esse, non dominos, maxime apud eos, qui spretis ambitionibus saeculi nihil quieti et otio praeferunt.

> But let them be content with their own honour and let them know that they are fathers, not masters, especially to those who despise the desire for worldly power and prefer nothing to peace and tranquillity.

These are resonant words – Jerome's flattering description of Theophilus' 'artful eloquence' (*Ep.* 82.1) is barely disguised self-praise – so we might expect them to be drawn from elsewhere. Only one other Latin author says something similar in prose: Victor (*HAb* 39.48), who praises Diocletian because he 'scorned desire for power (*spreto ambitu*) and came down to ordinary life'.[30] Earlier on (*HAb* 39.8), Victor had also described how although Diocletian 'allowed himself to be called master (*dominum*), he played a father's (*parentem*) part'. If *spretis ambitionibus* was too *juste* a *mot* for Jerome's omnivorous literary appetite, then there is a barb in his description of bishops as fathers, not masters. Even Diocletian had managed that – was John of Jerusalem worse than him?

In sum, Jerome's works – from the *Chronicon*, through his commentaries, to his letters – show that he has made a good deal of use of Victor's work, a work that we know he was keen to read. He expected

---

Constantine II and Constans seems to crop up also in a pre-metaphrastic *Vita* of Athanasius (*Bibliotheca Hagiographica Graeca* 185, *PG* 25.233d).

27 Their activities were famously condemned a few years after 361 by Libanius, *Or.* 18.135–140.

28 *cf.* Paschoud 1983: esp. 223–232. Bureaucracy: *e.g. HAb* 20.33–34. On the critique of bureaucrats in Victor, see Hayashi 2017: 239–268 and Bird 1984: 41–59.

29 Kelly 1975: 195–209.

30 *cf.* Paulinus of Nola, *Carm.* 21.484: *spreta ambitione*.

TABLE 5.4 – VICTOR AND RUFINUS ON THE DEATH OF CONSTANS

HAb 41.4	Rufinus, HE 10.20
In the tenth year after his triumph, Constans was overcome by the conspiracy of Magnentius (*Magnentii scelere*).	But when the emperor Constans had been removed at the same moment from royal power and his life by the conspiracy of Magnentius (*Magnenti scelere*) . . .

to learn from Victor more about the persecutors than could be found in Lactantius or Eusebius. He has information, obscure points of antiquarian detail or bureaucratic nomenclature, which we see in fragmentary form in the *HAb*. He also shares facts with the *LB*. He respected Victor's Latinity enough to rifle it for a few choice phrases. This tangle of conclusions makes sense if Victor was the author of a learned and lengthy *Historia* – it does not fit with the *HAb* as we have it.

That Jerome can be shown to have known Victor's work might make us take a second look at his nearest and dearest enemy: Rufinus of Aquileia. We saw above that Rufinus was – besides the *LB* and Jerome – the other Latin author to know that the river Alsa was the scene of Constantine II's death. A detail of local, Aquileian, history is not by itself the strongest of links to Victor, but three factors lend it some additional weight. First, Rufinus was also part of the Jerome/Paul of Concordia network, indeed had borrowed books from the latter, so we might reasonably lower the bar for proof that he too knew Victor's work. Second, the nature of his work as a continuation of Eusebius means that it overlaps chronologically with a mere fraction of the *HAb* and only a little more of the *LB*.[31] Third, and most importantly, Rufinus' phrase – *regnum solus obtinuit* – reflects a characteristically Victorine fascination with periods of sole rule and echoes verbatim what Victor says about Gordian III (*HAb* 27.6). The only earlier author who used the words was Sallust (*Iug.* 5.6).[32] One clear factual link between such different texts, in other words, is more significant than it might first appear.

A final telling connection between the *HAb* and the *Historia Ecclesiastica* clinches the case that Rufinus had read Victor's work. No other source deploys the crisp formulation in TABLE 5.4 when describing the fate of Constans. Surprising as it may seem, the use of the ablative *scelere* preceded by the name of the miscreant in the genitive is rare and rather literary in Latin – intensive searching yields only a handful of examples and suggests the influence of Cicero.[33] Victor used a very similar formula once elsewhere, when describing the death of Aurelian *ministri scelere* (*HAb* 35.8) – Rufinus, for what it is worth, did not. Moreover, the sense of *scelus* in both texts is perhaps more specific than general 'wickedness' – it means besides something like 'plot', or 'conspiracy'. This was a sense that Victor used often, but Rufinus rarely (if at all), though he used the word *scelus* frequently.[34] Small as this detail is, it strongly

---

31 As he explains in his preface, Rufinus omitted much of the material in the tenth book of Eusebius' *HE*, conjoining it to Book IX. His own tenth book thus begins with an account of the Arian controversy.

32 *cf.* Augustine, *De civ.* 3.13 (on Romulus, intriguingly).

33 Sallust, *Iug.* 104.4; Cicero, *Ep. Brut.* 1.12.1, *scelere* preceded by a genitive was a favoured construction of Cicero (*cf. e.g. De orat.* 3.10); Eutropius 8.16.

34 *HAb* 9.3, 10.3, 16.8 (where it perhaps has a dual sense of 'minds prone to wickedness/conspiracy theories'), 39.1. Rufinus, *Apologia* 1.19, 21; 2.45; *De adulteratione librorum Origenis* 9, 11, 12, 13; *HE* 10.16, 18 (*bis*), 20 (*bis*); 11.22 (*ter*), 24 (*bis*), 25, 31 (*bis*), 33.

suggests that the *Historia Ecclesiastica*'s account of secular events was influenced by Victor. One Christian intellectual reading and using Victor's work might be regarded as happenstance – two begins to suggest that his *Historia* was *the* history of the era.

Symmachus

The enthusiasm with which Jerome exploited the work of Victor might make us curious about how that other (inferior) epistolographer, Symmachus, received his work. Disappointingly, Symmachus never seems to have referred to Victor by name.[35] Famously, however, one of his letters was written to a contemporary historian (*Ep.* 9.110), whose name (unfortunately) does not survive – the date is equally mysterious, but probably fell later in Symmachus' career (380s–390s), along with most of the other letters in Book IX, rather than earlier (the 360s).[36] It is a fascinating missive, worth reproducing in full:

> (1) You ought indeed to pay attention to the opinion of *others*, for whom it is proper to make some judgement about their peers. The meagreness of my talent admires even small things, and, for this reason, I wish you to believe that no honour whatsoever accrues to you from my testimony. For, although there is an old saying 'to be praised by a praised man' nevertheless my limited powers do not much help the brilliance of your reputation. But since your wish ought to be granted, I will set out, as ordered, what I think about your speeches, one man out of the crowd. (2) It is nearly the case that I ought to bring a suit against you, because, so sparing of your style, you have denied to our age something Ciceronian. You will reply that you have allotted all your labour to composing history (*condendae historiae*) – forgive my greed, if I want both. For you have polished with equal elegance and seriousness the business of the Senate and a memorial for the Roman state (*Romanae rei*), so that clearly, to use a Homeric tag [*cf. Iliad* 21.163], I should declare you to be ambidextrous. Therefore, I beg you, proceed and strive to leave this gift to posterity, that what in the past has given pleasure divided up in separate authors, the same may now, joined together in you, be praised.

The question of who received this elaborate compliment is extremely controversial – multiple identifications have been proposed and all are open to serious challenge.[37] The letter was long believed to have been sent to Ammianus Marcellinus, but Alan Cameron showed decisively in 1964 that that cannot be so. Not only is there no evidence Ammianus was a senator (as the recipient clearly is), but Symmachus was careful to avoid inflicting his shaky Greek on those fluent in the language, so the lumbering Homeric allusion here would actually seem to rule out the *miles quondam et Graecus*.[38] Cameron noted that there were plenty of other contemporary historians who might have been the addressee. He was most tempted by Naucellius, another correspondent of Symmachus, whose *Tullianum aurum* is elsewhere praised (*Ep.* 3.12) and who translated a Greek work which had something to do with *prisca res publica* (3.11.2), a suggestion endorsed by *PLRE* and by Roda in his detailed commentary on the letter.[39] More recently, Callu has criticised this

---

35 *PLRE* 'Victor 4' identified the Victor, *vir spectabilis*, as the historian during his urban prefecture, but the title ill suits someone of that rank (who ought to have been *vir inlustris* – Jones 1964: 2.528).

36 Seeck 1883: ccii–ccix.

37 There is a balanced overview in Van Hoof and Van Nuffelen 2020a: 74–76.

38 Cameron 1964a: 15–18.

39 *PLRE* 'Anonymus 159'; Roda 1981: 242–245.

identification, arguing that Naucellius in fact translated an epitome of Aristotle's work on constitutions, and suggested that the recipient was Nicomachus Flavianus.[40] Cameron accepted the condemnation of Naucellius but – in his general assault on the Flavian thesis – pointed out that the tone is far too distant for a close friend of Symmachus, like Flavianus, that there is no evidence the latter was a distinguished orator, and that the letters to him are grouped in Book II, so it seems odd for an acephalous one to appear here.[41] He proposed, courageously, that the author of the *Libellus breviatus* might have been the recipient.[42]

Scholarship has thus arrived at something of an impasse. Cameron is certainly correct that the recipient cannot be Ammianus or Flavianus. Equally, Callu has a point that Naucellius is a weak candidate. For one thing, surely it was not beyond even the wit of Symmachus to praise two separate people for resembling Cicero in eloquence. For another, the description of Naucellius' work in *Ep.* 3.11 makes clear that it was a translation and an *opusculum* – hardly the major Roman history (written in Latin) of *Ep.* 9.110.[43] Naucellius' epitaph, moreover, makes no allusion to his historical work, but, even in its fragmentary form, makes clear his poetic credentials and perhaps his translations.[44] Other potential identifications are equally open to criticism. The letter tells us that the recipient had 'polished . . . a memorial to the Roman state' (*Romanae rei monumenta limasti*). *Monumenta* implies some very substantial work: Livy (*praef.* 10) compared the study of history to gazing on an *illustre monumentum* and he was not talking about a *breviarium*.[45] Symmachus himself (*Ep.* 4.24.1) called the *Jugurtha* 'Sallust's monument' – a work of over 20,000 words on the career of one man.[46] *Limare*, to polish or refine, suggests a history that had serious stylistic ambitions.[47] *Condere historiam* points in the same direction: a well-known barb against Sallust called him the *Iugurthinae conditor historiae* (quoted in Quintilian, *Inst.* 8.3.29), Quintilian called Cato an *historiae conditor* (*Inst.* 12.11.23), Solinus called Xanthus, Hecataeus of Miletus, and Herodotus *historiae conditores* (40.6), as did Ammianus Polybius (24.2.16), and Cassiodorus puts into the mouths of those who urged him to assemble the *Variae* the claim *Gothorum historiam condidisti* (*Var. Praef.* 11). We are thus looking for a major and literary Roman history: that alone ought to have long ago ruled out Eutropius (already a correspondent of Symmachus), Festus (dead by *ca.* 380), the *Origo Constantini imperatoris*, the *LB* (even before its early-medieval date was established), the *CT* itself, and any other short and summary work that might be canvassed.[48] There is a reason that Ammianus – though quite impossible – was long the popular solution: he alone seems to fit the bill.

What about Victor? Read without preconceptions, the letter suits him very well indeed. To judge by his general absence in Symmachus' letters, Victor was not a close friend, so a single stray missive like this would hardly be surprising. His career, spanning the period from the 360s to the 380s, overlapped very nicely with that of Symmachus. Victor was a senator and he had enormous interest in (and respect

---

40 Callu 1999: 95–96. The identification with Naucellius was challenged also by Paschoud 2010: 318.
41 For the Flavian thesis (the idea that the lost *Annales* of Nicomachus Flavianus were the historical masterwork of the later fourth century), see Chapter IX.
42 Cameron 2011: 564–565, 635 and n. 34.
43 See Van Hoof and Van Nuffelen 2020a: 69–72.
44 Champlin 1982: the word *Latinis* suggests a complement of *Graecis*.

45 Eigler 2003: 195–197 is correct to see a Livian allusion here, but while that might incline us to envisage a work Livian in scope, it need imply nothing about its style.
46 Symmachus, *Ep.* 3.11 does speak of *peregrina monumenta*, but that would seem to be the content of Naucellius' work, not its nature.
47 *TLL* 7.1421.82–1422.15 (Balzert).
48 All examples from Cameron 1964a: 17, though not seriously entertained for the letter. On the *Origo*, see Chapter X.

for) eloquence (*HAb* 8.7, *e.g.*), so one can well believe he put great effort into his speeches. If he was not Cicero's biggest fan, then he certainly knew and alluded to his works – the subversive purpose to which they were sometimes put might well have been lost on Symmachus, seemed merely *Tullianus*.[49] Victor knew Greek sources and Greek literature, but he was not himself Greek – hence why Symmachus could safely allude to Homer in a letter to him. Victor certainly had style, however rebarbative it may sometimes seem (*cf. limasti*), and (as we have seen) his reputation suggests that he produced a major work of history (a *monumentum*?). Symmachus' correspondent had worked 'with equal elegance and seriousness' – the word he used for the last quality, *gravitas*, is rather close to Ammianus' praise of Victor's *sobrietas*. Victor even liked the expression *res Romana* for the Roman state (*HAb* 33.3, 33.11). In the fourth century, that was a popular locution, but only Arnobius (*Adv. nat.* 7.50) and the Gallic panegyrists (*Pan. Lat.* 7.2.2, 8.11.3, 9.19.4) used it before Victor – its efflorescence post-dated his work.

The final point is perhaps a matter of mere typography. What Symmachus' letter shares with nearly every other testimonium to Victor's work is the word *historia*, which – singular or plural – is everywhere attested as the title. It is possible, of course, that Symmachus was using the noun in the common sense, but elsewhere he does deploy it as a title (*e.g. Ep.* 1.24, of Pliny's *Historia naturalis*). It is entirely feasible, then, that Symmachus does not mean, 'you have allotted all your labour to composing history', but rather 'you have allotted all your labour to composing your *Historia*' (*omnem te operam condendae* Historiae *deputasse*).

Everything about the letter makes sense with Victor as its recipient and his *Historia* its subject. The only real obstacle to so identifying him has been the idea that the meagre *HAb* is the totality of Victor's historical work, which was thus finished in 360, somewhat too early to expect a letter from Symmachus. We have seen already that neither assumption is really tenable. If Victor were the recipient of this letter – a letter that presupposes a monumental work of Roman history – it would speak to his pre-eminent reputation.

Theodosius and Ammianus

After Jerome, we next encounter Victor by name in *ca.* 389, when he was made prefect of the city of Rome by the emperor Theodosius. We know nothing certain of his career between being appointed *consularis* in 361 and this date, but it seems very likely that this was only the second major office he had held.[50] What then recommended him to Theodosius? On the standard interpretation, his appointment is rather baffling – hence, perhaps, the attraction of hypothesising a long career to which the prefecture was a sort of capstone. If such a career did not exist – and it seems that it did not – then the only real alternative is to assume that Victor was made prefect on the strength of his literary reputation, considerable by the date in question. Again, the *HAb* seems frankly inadequate as the cause of elevation to so prestigious a position. It is hard to believe that the reputation of the work would have been improved by thirty or so years of close examination. It is much easier to imagine Victor's fame justifying high office if he were the author of a lengthy *Historia*, in an era when Latin historiography was largely the province of the epitomator.

49 Chapter IV.

50 Chapter I.

Victor's prefecture leads neatly to the testimony of Ammianus Marcellinus, for it is one of the latest events mentioned by the author of the *Res gestae*.[51] What Ammianus says about Victor, and what it implies, has already been examined in some detail but the central point perhaps bears repetition.[52] In the pages of the *Res gestae*, Victor is treated as though he were the author of a work of real importance: he is a *scriptor* (*historicus*), a term elsewhere always applied to authors of equal antiquity and authority. The closest comparison to what is said about him would seem to be Herodotus (the other historian described as a *scriptor*), also the author of a *Historia*. As has already been pointed out, the *HAb* makes such a high opinion of Victor seem hyperbolic. Conventionally, it has been thought that Ammianus did not use Victor's work and that might offer a way out of this conundrum – ugly, but effective. In fact, it can be shown in considerable detail that Ammianus did not characterise Victor in total ignorance of the contents of his work. We will discuss Ammianus' debt to Victor at much greater length later on, but here suffice it to mention his glancing invocation of the *devotio* of Claudius II, every word of which betrays its derivation from Victor.[53] It is also well known that Ammianus' *Res gestae* shares a number of details with the *Libellus breviatus*.[54] Hence his high opinion of Victor as a historian must be based on at least some acquaintance with the latter's work. That almost demands a history more substantial than the *HAb*.

After Ammianus, reference to Aurelius Victor as a living person suddenly ceases. As we have discussed, there is no firm evidence for the date of Victor's death. Given, however, that he was alive early enough to remember Constantine, it is unlikely that he lived long past 389. Even so, his work continued to find readers.

Sulpicius Severus and the *Historia Augusta*

At the beginning of the fifth century, the Christian author Sulpicius Severus completed his *Chronicle*, an ambitious two-book *breviarium* of universal history, from the Creation to his own day, in a Sallustian mode.[55] As he tells us in the preface, he made use of secular or pagan historians (*Praef.* 2: *historicis mundialibus*). He does not identify these writers, but we know from fairly extensive borrowings that Tacitus was one and Velleius Paterculus another; in fact, Severus is the latter's hitherto only securely identified imitator.[56] In 1971, C.E.V. Nixon brought forward nearly conclusive evidence that Victor was also one

---

51 See Matthews 1989: 22–27 for allusions to events after 378 in the *Res gestae*, supporting a date of publication around 390–391.
52 Chapter I.
53 See Chapter IX for a more extended analysis of Ammianus' relationship to Victor. *Devotio*: Chapter IV.
54 Chapter IX.

55 For the date, see de Senneville-Grave 1999: 12–16. For the work's nature as a condensed text: *Praef.* 1: *ea, quae permultis voluminibus perscripta continebantur, duobus libellis concluderem.* For Sallust's influence on Severus, see Stover and Woudhuysen 2022b: 2, 10.
56 Tacitus: Cornelius 1888: 28–29; Barnes 1977; Stancliffe 1983: 59; de Senneville-Grave 1999: 41. Velleius: Klebs 1890: 288–298.

Table 5.5 – Victor and Severus on Nero

HAb 5.4–12	Chron. 2.28.2–3
For he conducted the rest (*reliquum*) of his life in such disgrace that I am disgusted and ashamed to mention (*pigeat pudeatque memorare*) anyone of this sort, much less a ruler of nations. He, when he had begun to sing in public gatherings to compete for a crown (a Greek invention), advanced so far that (*eo progressus est uti*) he spared neither his own modesty, nor that of others . . . finally they advanced (*processerint*) to crime with each other . . . the mother, foiled, was slain . . . (*cf. LB 5.5*).	The subject suggests that I ought to set out his vices more fully, if it were not unsuited to this work to enter so monstrous a matter. I am content to have recorded one thing only: through all deeds most shameful and savage this man advanced so far that (*eo processisse ut*) he killed his own mother . . . It is uncertain whether it is more disgusting or more shameful to discuss the rest of his actions (*reliqua vero eius incertum pigeat an pudeat magis disserere*).

of these *historici mundiales*.[57] Compare the two on Nero (**Table 5.5**). It is simple enough to chalk up these resonances to a shared model, given both authors' fondness for Sallust, Tacitus, and Velleius. A glance at the *Jugurtha* (95.4, on Sulla) would seem to settle the question:

> For I consider it uncertain whether it is more disgusting or more shameful to discuss (*incertum habeo pudeat an pigeat magis disserere*) what he did afterwards.

The problem with such a solution is that the parallels between Victor and Sulpicius go beyond just *pigeat* and *pudeat*, and that both are talking specifically about Nero. Hence what we have here is a window-allusion in Sulpicius: he looks back to Victor on Nero, and beyond that nods to Sallust, Victor's model. Nixon found further corroboration in the remainder of the vanishingly slight treatment of Roman imperial history in Sulpicius, such as *HAb* 5.15 *Galba . . . imperio correpto* ~ *Chron.* 2.30.1 *Galba imperium rapuit*, and in the style of Sulpicius' treatment of the early emperors, which verges at times on Victorine pastiche.

Nixon's *trouvé* has not been followed up – this is probably because he was unsure if it should actually be chalked up to use of a common source.[58] It is, however, supported by other evidence for Sulpicius imitating Victor's style, just as he imitated other earlier Roman historians. Take his mention of the elation of the 'Arians' at 2.45.1: 'things were moving on exceedingly successfully, as they hoped' (*rebus nimium prospere et secundum vota fluentibus*). The only earlier author who has anything remotely similar is Victor (*HAb* 33.3): *his prospere ac supra vota cedentibus, more hominum secundis* ('these events were proceeding favourably and beyond his hopes, in the manner of men in fortunate circumstances'). Here we cannot rule out the possibility that they are both imitating some lost bit of Sallust or Tacitus but a direct connection is worth considering. Indeed, the stylistic aims that make Sulpicius' work unique among his Christian contemporaries – his constant, unrelenting imitation of Sallust, his use of Velleius and Tacitus – make it eminently likely that he would also turn to the work of a later historian writing in the same tradition. The

---

57 Nixon 1971: 141–143.
58 Bird, for example, in his monograph (1984) on Victor, ignores it entirely. A similar case was later made (apparently independently) by Bessone 1980, but rejected by de Senneville-Grave 1999: 42 precisely because of the problem of Sallust.

fact that Victor and Sulpicius are the *only* two later figures whom we can be sure used and drew inspiration from Velleius makes the existence of a direct link between them more likely.

Before we depart the fourth and fifth centuries, there is one more reader of Victor who demands brief discussion. We do not know this reader's name, nor do we know when he was writing, beyond the fact that it was some time after 370.[59] His work we know as the *Historia Augusta* (*HA*). Even the most basic facts about this text are mired in controversy, occluded by perverse and deliberate obfuscation.[60] The *HA* is presented in the manuscripts as the *Vitae diversorum principum et tyrannorum a Divo Hadriano usque ad Numerianum a diversis conpositae* ('The lives of various different emperors and usurpers, from the deified Hadrian up to Numerian, written by divers hands'). The text as we have it is just that: individual biographies of the emperors, junior emperors, and usurpers from Hadrian to Carinus, each attributed to one of six authors: Aelius Spartianus, Julius Capitolinus, Aelius Lampridius, Vulcacius Gallicanus, Trebellius Pollio, and Flavius Vopiscus.[61] The lives are mostly dedicated to the emperors Diocletian and Constantine, and the first five of the six *scriptores* never quote or refer by name to the others. At the same time, all six refer to a passel of other historians who are entirely unknown outside the collection. On the surface, the *HA* looks like an anthology of independent biographies, written *ca.* 285–320 and put together some time in the reign of Constantine. All is, however, not as it seems. In one of the landmark achievements of nineteenth-century scholarship, Hermann Dessau demonstrated that the collection must date to at least fifty years after its putative *terminus* and that, instead of being written by six *scriptores*, it was actually composed by a single inventive individual.[62] Further work has shown just how deeply the fraud penetrates the text: the otherwise unattested historians cited are as fictitious as the six authors who cite them; many of the historical figures were probably made up; the documents with which the collection abounds – acts of the Senate, letters, speeches, ephemera – were likely forged.

In this morass of uncertainty and confusion, one thing about the *HA* at least is clear: its author knew the work of Victor. As is almost universally accepted, a long passage from Victor's treatment of Septimius Severus is lifted wholesale and adapted by the author of the *HA* for his own life of that same emperor.[63] A little later in the work, in the life of Opellius Macrinus, the author explicitly quotes someone named Aurelius Victor (4.2):

> Verba denique Aurelii Victoris, cui Pinio cognomen erat, haec fuerunt: Macrinum libertinum, hominem prostibilem . . .[64]

> These are the words of Aurelius Victor, who had the cognomen Pinius: 'Macrinus was a freedman and a prostitute . . .'

---

59 For this *terminus post quem*, which hinges on dependence on Eutropius, see Chapter VIII.

60 The bibliography on the *HA* is vast; suffice it here to note that the many volumes of *Colloquia* on the text offer treatment of a vast range of individual subjects. The nearly complete Budé series, in progress since 1992, offers useful commentary on almost all of the individual lives. Three recent monographs include Thomson 2012, Rohrbacher 2016 and Savino 2017. While we do not necessarily endorse their larger conclusions, especially regarding sources and authorship, all of them provide an entrée into the text and its nature.

61 On the names of the *scriptores*, see Stover and Woudhuysen 2022a.

62 Dessau 1889. We discuss this is in detail in Chapter VII. On single authorship, see Stover and Kestemont 2016.

63 Chapter VIII.

64 Identified as an oblique reference to our Victor by Syme 1972c: 284–285, Chastagnol 1970: 36, Lippold 1991: 89, Turcan 1993: 122, among others.

TABLE 5.6 – THE *LIBELLUS BREVIATUS* AND THE *HISTORIA AUGUSTA* ON HADRIAN

LB 14.2–3	HA Hadr.
Hic Graecis litteris impensius eruditus a plerisque Graeculus appellatus est. Atheniensium studia moresque hausit potitus non sermone tantum, sed et ceteris disciplinis, canendi psallendi medendique scientia, musicus geometra pictor fictorque ex aere vel marmore, proxime Polycletus et Euphranoras. Proinde omnino ad ista et facetus, ut elegantius umquam raro quicquam humanae res expertae videantur. Memor supra quam cuiquam credibile est, locos negotia milites, absentes quoque, nominibus recensere.	1.5: imbutusque inpensius Graecis studiis, ingenio eius sic ad ea declinante, ut a nonnullis Graeculus diceretur 14.8–9: Fuit enim poematum et litterarum nimium studiosissimus. Arithmeticae, geometriae, picturae peritissimus. Iam psallendi et cantandi scientiam prae se ferebat. 16.10: grammaticos, rhetores, musicos, geometras, pictores, astrologos habuit 20.7–10: Fuit memoriae ingentis, facultatis inmensae . . . Nomina plurimis sine nomenclatore reddidit, quae semel et congesta simul audiverat, ut nomenclatores saepius errantes emendarit. Dixit et veteranorum nomina, quos aliquando dimiserat.
He was lavishly educated in Greek letters and was called by many the 'Greekling'. He had lapped up the pursuits and the morals of the Athenians. He was well versed not only in speech, but also in the other disciplines – the knowledge of singing, playing instruments, and practising medicine. He was also a musician, a geometer, a painter, as well as a sculptor in bronze and marble, practically a Polycletus and a Euphranor. In addition to these things, he was also very witty, such that human experience rarely ever seems to have known something more elegant than him. He had a memory better than any man can believe, able to review by their names places, matters, soldiers, even those who were absent.	He was lavishly imbued with Greek pursuits, his character was so pulled down by them that he was called by some 'Greekling'. For he was excessively enthusiastic for poetry and literature. He was most expert in arithmetic, geometry, and painting. He used to flaunt his knowledge of playing instruments and singing. He had around him grammarians, rhetors, musicians, geometers, painters, and astrologers. His memory was vast, his ability huge . . . He could recall the names of most people without the aid of an assistant, though he had heard them only once and in a mass, so that he often corrected the assistants when they made mistakes. He could say the names of the veterans whom he had discharged some time ago.

These words do not occur in Victor, nor do we know what the cognomen means, nor even if the transmitted text is sound, but this cannot but be a reference to the famous historian.[65] There are also suggestive links between the *HA* and the *LB*. Compare their accounts of the emperor Hadrian (**TABLE 5.6**). The two accounts are exceptionally close, and both share (for example) a reminiscence of Juvenal (3.76–78).[66]

---

65 Could it be a corruption for something derived from *Poenus* or *Punicus* (*Punius e.g.*), riffing on Victor Afer? See Prag 2006: 28–29 on names with *Poenus* and its variants, and their relation to *Afer*. On the name Pinius (not Pinio as often supposed), see Stover and Woudhuysen 2022a

66 Cameron 2011: 760 has argued that the *LB* is the debtor here, even though it has an additional Juvenalian reminiscence that the *HA* does not pick up (Polycletus

and Euphranor, from *Sat.* 3.217). Obviously, the early-medieval date of the *LB* makes this vanishingly unlikely, but it can be shown on internal grounds as well. Logically speaking, it is much more likely that the author of the *HA* has failed to pick up one in run of allusions to Juvenal's third satire, than that a later author supplied an additional allusion. Further, having shown that the *LB* is in fact an early-medieval product, we need not share Cameron's concern about the nominative *Euphranoras*.

The *HA* will loom large in the remainder of this study, and we will subject many of its features to searching scrutiny. Here, however, let it suffice to note that the author of the text mentions a figure named Aurelius Victor, used the *HAb*, and has material cognate with the *LB*. This testifies once again to the enormous *cachet* and prestige of Victor and his *Historia* in late antiquity.

John the Lydian

Even if the number of references diminishes after Victor's lifetime, his work clearly continued to circulate. Over a century after his death a reference to it appears in the *De magistratibus* of John the Lydian, noted sixth-century bureaucrat and servant of Justinian's regime.[67] Running through various minor administrative positions (as is his wont), John reaches the σιτῶναι, of whom he says (3.7):

> οὓς Οὐΐκτωρ ὁ ἱστορικὸς ἐν τῇ Ἱστορίᾳ τῶν ἐμφυλίων φρουμενταρίους οἶδε τὸ πρὶν ὀνομασθῆναι, ὅτι τῆς τοῦ παλατίου εὐθηνίας τὸ πρὶν ἐφρόντιζον.[68]

> Victor the historian in his *History* on the civil wars knows that formerly they were called *frumentarii*, because in the past they were responsible for the grain supply of the *palatium*.

This is an important and rather complex citation, but its key features can be swiftly identified. This is clearly a reference to Aurelius Victor, who, as we have seen already, offered a learned discussion of the *frumentarii*, comparing them to the *agentes in rebus* of his own day in a way that Jerome found useful. Victor is called a 'historian' (ἱστορικός): John applies the same label to Sallust and to Sammonicus, an otherwise unknown historian of Tetrarchic date.[69] His work is described as a *Historia* (that significant title). John qualifies this with the description 'on the civil wars' (for so ἐμφυλίων seems to mean).[70] The precise significance of that qualification is not totally clear, but it is worth remembering that the best literary precedent for the title *Emphylia* lay in the work of Appian. Appian's *Roman History* contains five books called *Emphylia*, as part of its broader account of Rome's rise and interactions with foreign peoples.[71] Perhaps John was thinking of only a part of Victor's work: in the *HAb*, the *frumentarii* are mentioned in the account of Diocletian and the era of the Tetrarchy was certainly a period marked by numerous civil wars.

The reason that John cites the evidence of the *Historia* is that Victor apparently revealed that the σιτῶναι had once been called *frumentarii*, because they supplied food to the palace. Now, the *frumentarii* are

---

67 For the date of John's work, see Maas 1992: 8.

68 It is not totally clear from what John says who the σιτῶναι were (not a common word, it had originally been used for public grain-buyers) and whether he connected them to the *agentes in rebus*. At *De mag.* 2.26, in a discussion of the *magister officiorum*, he says that the *frumentarii* are now called *magistriani* (*i.e.* men of the *magister*), while at *De mens.* 1.30 he again puts the σιτῶναι under the *magister* and links them to the *curiosi*. The *agentes* were under the *magister* and the *curiosi* were drawn from their number (Jones 1964: 1.369, 578–582), so clearly the σιτῶναι were in the same general area.

69 John the Lydian, *De mag. prologue*, 3.32. In the latter, the name Sammonicus is a restoration (but surely the only plausible reading of the MS σαμωκον); the title (?) of Sammonicus' work (περὶ ποικίλων ζητημάτων, 'on manifold questions') itself indicates its very varied character.

70 *cf. De mag.* 3.46, where the work of Lucan is so called.

71 Appian sets out the titles and structure of his work in its *Preface* (14), but see also the helpful table in Brodersen 1993: 342–343.

TABLE 5.7 – VICTOR AND JOHN THE LYDIAN ON DIOCLETIAN

HAb 39.4	De mens. 1.26
Namque se **primus** omnium Caligulam **post** Domitianumque **dominum** palam **dici** passus.	πρῶτος ὁ Διοκλητιανὸς μετὰ Δομετιανὸν δεσπότης καὶ βασιλεὺς Ῥωμαίων ὠνομάσθη.★
For he, first of all after Caligula and Domitian, allowed himself to be called 'master' openly.	For Diocletian was the first after Domitian to be called 'master' and 'king of the Romans'.

★ On the basis of *De mens.* 4.20 (Τὸν Δομετιανὸν δεσπότην ἐκάλουν, ἀλλ᾽οὐ βασιλέα, διὰ τὸ τυραννικὸν αὐτοῦ), we might wonder if we ought to read οὐ rather than καὶ. After the quotation at 1.26 come the words λίθοις ἀντὶ δάφνης τὴν κεφαλὴν καὶ τοὺς πόδας ψηφώσας, ὥς φησιν Εὐτρόπιος. Eutropius does indeed say (9.26): *Ornamenta gemmarum vestibus calciamentisque indidit*, but has nothing about titles.

certainly mentioned in the *HAb*, but the detail about why they were called by that name is nowhere in the text – it is not even hinted at. Yet it is absolutely clear that John knew the work of Victor and specifically his account of the Tetrarchy. He explained how the model of the *civilis princeps* persisted down to Diocletian, who adopted the diadem, bejewelled clothes, and gem-studded sandals with which later emperors were adorned (*De mag.* 1.4). Victor probably originated this characterisation and description of the first Tetrarch (*HAb* 39.2), but other sources also transmit the details.[72] John goes on to say, however, that Diocletian 'surveyed the mainland and oppressed it with taxes'.[73] He does not specify which 'mainland' he means, but the passage comes early on in his account of the development of Rome's political institutions and the natural assumption is that he is referring to Italy. As we have seen, it is Victor alone who tells us explicitly that Diocletian imposed taxation on that peninsula.[74] At another point, John seems almost to quote Victor (**TABLE 5.7**). That Diocletian had introduced a new kind of imperial ceremonial was not an uncommon idea in late antiquity, but that he had specifically adopted the title *dominus* is something only Victor says.[75] If John the Lydian certainly knew the work of Victor, but cited it for details that the *HAb* does not contain, then there is only one logical conclusion: he had a text of Victor with more information than is found in the *HAb*. He had the *Historia* of Victor before it had been *abbreviata*.

Further confirmation of this can be found in an example that connects the *De magistratibus* with both the *HAb* and the *LB*. John the Lydian reproduces an interesting remark (*De mag.* 2.3) made by 'the Romans' (which ones is not totally clear) about the emperor Augustus: *utinam nec natus nec mortuus fuisset*, 'would that he had neither been born nor died'. The idea (as John explains) was that though they disliked his establishment of imperial rule, they appreciated the peace and order he had brought. That John had taken this from a Latin source is guaranteed by the fact that the words appear in a (slightly garbled) form of Latin in his Greek text.[76] What was that Latin source? As we have seen, Victor borrowed a very similar

72 See Stover and Woudhuysen 2015 [2020]: esp. 93–96.

73 *De mag.* 1.4: ἀνεμετρήσατό τε τὴν ἤπειρον καὶ τοῖς φόροις ἐβάρυνεν. Bandy 1983: 15 translates τὴν ἤπειρον as 'the continent' (as indeed he does elsewhere). This is an attested sense of ἤπειρος, but the word really means the mainland as distinct from the sea and islands, which is how John uses it, *e.g. De mag.* 2.14 (of crossing the straits from Constantinople), *cf.* 4.61 (of Asia, that is Asia Minor), *De mens.* 4.95 (of Sicily, before the ancient flood separated it from Italy).

74 Chapter IV.

75 Eutropius 9.26, Jerome, *Chron.* 226ᶜ, AM 15.5.18.

76 See the apparatus to *De mag.* 2.3 (Bandy 1983: 86).

phrase from Livy for his obituary of Septimius Severus. Describing the honours offered to him in death, he noted that the senators said: *illum iustum nasci aut emori minime convenisse* (*HAb* 20.6: 'it was not at all fitting for this man to have been born or to have died').[77] The idea was that he was too severe in correcting morals, but that once his subjects had returned to virtue, they found him clement (*HAb* 20.7). This curious sentiment was applied to Severus because he went to some lengths to present himself as a new Augustus: a man who had brought peace to a *res publica* bleeding from the civil wars. Something very like it had originally been said of Rome's first emperor. We know this only from the *LB* (1.28), which, in recounting the honours paid to Augustus after his death, relates a contemporary remark: *utinam aut non nasceretur aut non moreretur*, 'would that he either were not born or did not die'. The text goes on to explain that this reflected his villainous rise to power and virtuous reign (*LB* 1.29). We thus have three interlocking pieces, which when combined strongly suggest that a common source, one that dealt with public comment after the deaths of both Augustus and Severus, stands behind the *HAb*, the *LB*, and the *De magistratibus*. That source can only be the *Historia* of Aurelius Victor.

John was a formidably learned individual, fluent enough in Latin to be asked to deliver a panegyric of Justinian in the language before some visitors from Rome (*De mag.* 3.28).[78] He cited a wide range of Latin texts, of many different periods and genres.[79] Late-antique Constantinople, it ought also to be borne in mind, was a major centre for Latin literary culture and the production of Latin manuscripts.[80] Even so, it is a remarkable testament to Victor's stature that his work was being read and cited in the Greek east, by a native son of Philadelphia, nearly two centuries after it had first appeared.

Victor's reputation

Three things are worth drawing out from this extended discussion of the *testimonia* for Victor. First, they are actually rather numerous: we are told a good deal about Victor and his work. No contemporary historian received nearly as much attention for their historical writing in late antiquity. Second, the *testimonia* are fairly consistent in suggesting that the title of Victor's work was *Historia* – a title which looks back, inevitably, to Sallust and to other authors of lengthy and discursive works of history.[81] Third, all the *testimonia* imply that Victor himself wrote a *major* work of history, one that offered rich material for later authors. Those who used him used him for obscure or recondite information, but they also took ideas from him: the comparison of the *frumentarii* and the *agentes in rebus*, or the *devotio* of Claudius II. Taken as a group, the *testimonia* to Victor are simply incompatible with the text of the *HAb* – they suggest, like all the other evidence assembled so far, that it is a mere summary of the *Historia* which Victor himself wrote.

Victor's greatest misfortune is to have survived. If we did not have the *HAb* or the *LB*, one can only imagine the rapturous reconstructions of the *Historia* of Ammianus' *scriptor historicus*, its author honoured with a statue by Julian, its text sought after by Jerome, read even by Greeks in Constantinople two centuries

---

77 For this and what follows, see Chapter IV.
78 For John and Latin, see Maas 1992: esp. 27–28.
79 Most easily grasped from the appendix in Maas 1992: 101–134.

80 A few tantalising pages in Cameron 2004b: 521–525 assemble some of the evidence. See also Horsfall 1993 (with copious citation of earlier literature); Schamp 2009.
81 On the title, see also Stover and Woudhuysen 2022b: 8.

later. There is here a stark contrast to the other Latin historians of late antiquity. Lactantius' monograph *On the Deaths of the Persecutors* is referred to only once (and glancingly) by Jerome – from the reference, we would have no idea of the historical nature of this gloriously Sallustian take on the Tetrarchy.[82] The *Itinerarium Alexandri* (which originally covered Trajan as well) is known to us only because the text happens to survive.[83] There are no explicit fourth-century references to Eutropius or Festus as historians: we have every reason to believe that their successful political careers were not primarily due to their writings.[84] Ammianus is famously anonymous outside the pages of his own work, his *testimonia* restricted to a single quotation in the grammarian Priscian (*Inst.* 9.51).[85] That there were later Latin historians similar in style and approach – Sulpicius Alexander and Renatus Profuturus Frigeridus – is known to us only because Gregory of Tours quotes them at length (for his own, peculiar, purposes).[86] Other supposed historians have been assumed to be figures of major, even central, importance on much slighter evidence than that which we have for Victor. The work of Nicomachus Flavianus, for example, is attested only by two inscriptions, both erected by his own family.[87] The evidence for Marius Maximus (outside the *HA*) amounts to single a dismissive comment by Ammianus and an exiguous quotation in a Juvenal *scholion*, neither of which implies he was a historian.[88] The (lost) *Historia Romana* of Q. Aurelius Memmius Symmachus is known only from Cassiodorus and a quotation in Jordanes.[89] The only sure *testimonium* for Eusebius of Nantes is in a fourteenth-century description of a lost work by Ausonius.[90] The slightness and mediocrity of the surviving works attributed to Victor have blinded us, preventing us from seeing what his contemporaries thought about him. On *Nachleben* alone, we would judge him by far the most significant of fourth-century historians.

So far, we have presented a *theory*, one that accounts for the existing evidence much better than the currently accepted view. Following the medieval trail of Victor's work leads to a set of *facts* which offer decisive proof that it is correct. That trail goes cold until the eighth century and the career of one of the most important scholars of the entire Middle Ages: the extraordinary Italian polymath Paul the Deacon.

---

82 Jerome, *DVI* 80: *de persecutione librum unum.*

83 Tabacco 2000.

84 Eutropius: Orosius does twice cite him by name (7.11.1, 7.19.4) (so too does John the Lydian, *De mag.* 1.26 *e.g.*). The letters of Symmachus (*Ep.* 3.46–53) speak perhaps to a literary reputation, but there are no straightforward references to him as a *historicus, vel sim.* The title of Paeanius' translation naturally alludes to Eutropius as a historian (p. 9 Droysen).

85 Ammianus: some attempt has been made to identify him with the recipient of Libanius, *Ep.* 1063 (Matthews 1989: 8), but also resisted (Fornara 1992a). Barnes 1998: 54–58 rejects the identification, attempting to find a reference to the historian in the Ammianus who appears in Libanius, *Ep.* 233.4 (61) – this is very unlikely on onomastic grounds, for Ammianus Marcellinus, if he appears by a single name, ought to be Marcellinus, not Ammianus. Other readers of Ammianus have been detected, but the case always rests on allusion (sometimes rather slight): Jerome (*e.g.* Maenchen-Helfen 1955), the *HA* (*e.g.* Syme 1968a, esp. chapters X–XIII), Claudian (*e.g.* Cameron 1970: 333–334, Maenchen-Helfen 1955: 394–395), Cassiodorus (*e.g.* Heather 1993).

86 Gregory, *Hist.* 2.8, 9.

87 *CIL* 6.1782 (= *ILS* 2947) and 6.1783 (= *ILS* 2948). Let it suffice here to reference Cameron 2011: 627–658. See below, Chapter IX.

88 On the evidence, see *FRH* 101 (Levick and Cornell) and Chapter VII.

89 See the balanced discussion in Van Hoof and Van Nuffelen 2020a: 146–165; or, *e.g.*, Festy 2003.

90 On Eusebius, see Chapter VI.

Paul the Deacon

Paul's biography has more mysteries than landmarks, but the rough outline is clear.[91] Born to a noble Lombard family in Friuli in *ca.* 730, Paul was educated at the court in Pavia – he recalled once seeing king Ratchis (r. 744–749) handling a cup made from a human skull.[92] In the 760s, he was in contact with Adelperga, daughter of the Lombard king Desiderius and wife of the *dux* of Lombard Benevento, Arichis.[93] Slightly later (*ca.* 770), Paul wrote his *Historia Romana* at her prompting.[94] It is possible that their association shows he was already resident in southern Italy.[95] In the early 780s, he left his native land to join the court of Charlemagne – one of several foreign scholars recruited to add a scholarly lustre to the Frankish monarch.[96] He returned a few years later, but his links with Francia continued – he received several literary commissions from north of the Alps.[97] It is to this later period that his *magnum opus*, the *Historia Langobardorum*, belongs, along with several other works, including his epitome of Festus' *De verborum significatu*.[98] The likely scene of at least some of these scholarly endeavours was Monte Cassino, than which few places were more important for the transmission of Latin literature.[99] Precisely when

91 For a basic overview of Paul's life, see Goffart 1988: 333–347; *cf.* McKitterick 1999: 324–326, who differs on several important points. The fullest study remains Menghini 1904.

92 Birth and education: see the epitaph by his pupil Hilderic (ed. Waitz 1878: 23–24), ll. 15–18 and *cf. HL* 6.7. Skull: *HL* 2.28.

93 On Adelperga, see Paul's poem to her from 763 (Neff 1908: 7–10); in general, Nelson 1998.

94 The *Historia Romana* was edited by Crivellucci 1914, but is perhaps more accessible in Droysen 1879. Adelperga's request to Paul (on which see further below) is revealed by his prefatory letter (Crivellucci 1914: 3–4 = Droysen 1879: 4–5). The date of the *HR* is, within relatively narrow bounds, uncertain and the subject of a good deal of confused discussion (the best overview is still Crivellucci 1914: xxviii–xxxvi; *cf.* the cautious Mortensen 2000: 358, n. 10). The work's preface offers no date, but does say that Adelperga had three children at the time (Goffart 1988: 337 suggests she was also pregnant, but that seems to be a misunderstanding of the closing *utere felix*, not a reference to her womb). Since Dahn 1876: 14–15, many scholars have held that Adelperga's first child was born in 763, which seems to establish a *terminus post quem* (Goffart 1988: 337, Nelson 1998: 177, and McKitterick 1999: 324). This is based on a misunderstanding of Paul's earlier poem to Adelperga (l. 3, Neff 1908: 10): *Adelperga cum tranquilla stirpe nata regia*, which is a reference to her royal descent, not her children. In fact, Adelperga's first child, Romuald, seems to have been born in 761/762: he died at the age of twenty-five in July 787 (*Chronicon Salernitanum* 21–22, Westerbergh 1956: 25–27, *cf.* Paul's epitaph for Arichis l. 43, Neff 1908: 149). A *terminus post quem* of 765 or so for the *HR* (at the very earliest) is thus likely to be correct. Most scholars have, for varying reasons, accepted a *terminus ante quem* of 774, the fall of the Lombard Kingdom (Crivellucci 1914: xxxii–xxxiii; Goffart 1988:

337; Nelson 1998: 177; and McKitterick 1999: 324 opt for 773 as the date of composition). It does seem unlikely (as Dahn pointed out) that Paul would have promised Adelperga that he would extend the *HR* to their own day, after these traumatic events had occurred. On the other hand, Paul seems to refer to Arichis as a *princeps* in his prefatory letter (*qui nostra aetate solus paene principum sapientiae palmam tenet*) as does the notice at the start of Book XI in most manuscripts of the *HR* – he took this title only in 774 (Kaminsky 1974). A date of *ca.* 770 for the *HR* is thus likely correct, but by no means certain. The title, *Historia Romana,* is conventional and convenient. It is, however, also probably the original title of Eutropius' work (see Chapter III), so Paul's use of it is not meant to distinguish his own production but rather to affiliate it with that of Eutropius: he so titled the work to indicate that it is a *Eutropius auctus*.

95 Goffart 1988: 336; McKitterick 1999: 325 is unpersuaded.

96 Goffart 1988: 341 argues for departure in 781.

97 Goffart 1988: 342–343 (arguing for a return to Monte Cassino in 785); McKitterick 1999: 273–274.

98 Goffart 1988: 343–344.

99 For Paul at Monte Cassino, see Goffart 1988: 344, 382–424; *cf.* Costambeys 2000: 130 for the same conclusion from very different premises. In contrast, McKitterick 1999: 334–337 argues forcefully for the possibility that the *HL*, at least, might instead have an origin in northern Italy, at the court of Pippin. Her case rests on the provenance of early MSS and the evidence for the early circulation of the text, but this seems a somewhat dubious method: applying it to Isidore of Seville's *Etymologies*, for example, might lead us to the conclusion that he wrote the work in Ireland. Monte Cassino and transmission: see, for instance, Bloch 1972; Cavallo 1975; Loew 1980: 2.16–18; *T&T*: xxiii, xxxiii, xl; Reynolds and Wilson 1991: 109–110; Bischoff 1994: 152–153.

Table 5.8 – Eutropius and Paul the Deacon

Eutropius 10.18.3	Paul, *Liber de episcopis Mettensibus* (p. 269 Pertz 1829)
For what remains ought to be described in a grander style (*stilo maiore dicenda sunt*), which we do not now so much pass over as keep back for grander craftsmanship in writing.★	But not unmindful of my own insignificance, I do not dare to approach the events of the praiseworthy course of your life in a style less fitting to them: they ought to be published in a grander style (*maiori stilo promenda sunt*).

★ Paul the Deacon would not have put a full stop after *dicenda sunt* (*contra* Droysen 1879, Santini 1979, *et al.*).

Benedict's monastery had welcomed Paul is a disputed and disputable question: estimates vary from as early as the 750s down into the 780s and are complicated by the very real possibility that he was associated with the place before he formally became a monk.[100] It was certainly where he was buried when, before 800 in all likelihood, he died.[101]

Paul's was a career that showed a deft ability to navigate the courts of princes and produced a body of scholarly work enviable for both its range and bulk. It is not the least sign of his achievements that he was so remarkable in fields beyond Lombard history and lexicography. Indeed, it is no exaggeration to describe Paul as the cardinal figure in the transmission of Roman history in the Middle Ages: his *Historia Romana* is the hinge which links late-antique historical compilations with the sprawling medieval tradition that follows them.[102] We can date his first serious interactions with Roman historical texts to the 760s at the latest.[103] At some point in that decade, Adelperga had written to him to ask for guidance on what to read in Roman history. Sensibly enough, he recommended Eutropius. His was a work very important to Paul, for style and content, but also for his own conception of what he was doing. For example, at the close of his (later) history of the bishops of Metz, addressing the then bishop Angilram, he imitated the conclusion of Eutropius (**Table 5.8**). Adelperga was, however, a demanding student, and a slightly more discerning reader than the 'beer-swilling' (*sabaiarius*) emperor Valens, Eutropius' dedicatee.[104] Upon reading his *breviarium*, she pronounced herself dissatisfied with its *immodica brevitas* and (in particular) with its lack of attention to Christian history. Prompted by her complaints (or so he said), Paul set to work remedying the defects of Eutropius' work. He took over the entirety of the text as a framework into which he could weave other materials, both Christian and pagan, to fill out its account of Roman history, supplementing it at the end to take the narrative up to the sixth century. For the period from Augustus to Theodosius, the principal non-Christian source he used to bulk out Eutropius was something like

100 Goffart 1988: 336–338 favours a date in the 750s. McKitterick 1999: 325–326 dissents. The case is complex and there is no definitive evidence for or against. The epitaph by Hilderic (ll. 26–32) is often said to state that he did not enter the monastery until after his return from Francia (McKitterick 1999: 325; even Goffart 1988: 335, n. 25, 346 accepts this, so is forced to impute error to it). While it might be thought to imply this, it is perhaps unwise to read such a poem so literally. A letter Paul wrote to Theudemar, abbot of Monte Cassino, while in Francia (Neff 1908:

69–73) and normally dated to 783 (McKitterick 1999: 326) suggests in any case that he was already closely associated with the place. In general on Paul and the monastery, see Costambeys 2000.
101 Goffart 1988: 346.
102 For Paul's importance, see the papers collected in Chiesa 2000.
103 For this and what follows see Paul's letter to Adelperga (note 94 above).
104 For the description, see AM 26.8.2 (*cf.* Dzino 2005).

TABLE 5.9 – THE *LIBELLUS BREVIATUS* AND THE *HISTORIAE ABBREVIATAE* ON THE ALPS

LB 5.4	*HAb* 5.2
Pontum in ius provinciae Polemonis reguli permissu redegit, a quo Polemoniacus Pontus appellatur, itemque Cottias Alpes Cottio rege mortuo.	Quo etiam Pontum in ius provinciae Polemonis permissu redegit, cuius gratia Polemoniacus Pontus appellatur, itemque Cottias Alpes Cottio rege mortuo.
He reduced Pontus into the legal condition of a province, by the permission of Polemon its prince (on his account it is called Pontus Polemoniacus) and so too Alpes Cottiae, when king Cottius had died.	In this period he also reduced Pontus into the legal condition of a province, by the permission of Polemon (on his account it is called Pontus Polemoniacus) and so too Alpes Cottiae, when king Cottius had died.

the *Libellus breviatus*. There are significant, often verbatim, overlaps between the *LB* and Paul's *Historia Romana*, though he never spells out in what form he was using the text. Paul's *Historia Romana* provides our only secure *terminus ante quem* for the *LB*: it was produced at some point between the seventh century and *ca.* 770.[105] For this reason, working out the precise relationship of Paul to the *LB* is a matter of some importance for understanding the nature and origin of that text.

Before we turn to that subject, however, it is vital to note that the use of something like the *LB* in the *Historia Romana* was not Paul's only acquaintance with Victor. In the *Historia Langobardorum*, he makes reference to a *Historia Victoris* in his geographical digression on the provinces of Italy (2.18):

> There are those who say that the Alpes Cottiae and the Alpes Appenninae are a single province, but the *Historia* of Victor, which calls Alpes Cottiae a province in its own right, refutes them.[106]

That he could indeed have found in Victor information about the Alps can be confirmed from the *LB* and *HAb* (**TABLE 5.9**). Paul thus knew a historical work by Victor, which contained material related to that in both the *LB* and the *HAb*. This is intriguing.

There is, however, one small problem to tidy away first. A long geographical section in Book II of the *Historia Langobardorum*, which includes the discussion of the Cottian Alps, circulated independently under the title *De terminatione provinciarum Italiae* in three manuscripts from centuries after Paul's lifetime (Vat. lat. 1361, s. xii; Brussels 3897–3919, s. xii; and Milan Ambros. A 226 inf., s. xiv).[107] This has occasioned a *Prioritätsproblem* (a question of priority), the subject of a lengthy and surprisingly passionate debate between Carlo Pascal and Amadeo Crivellucci early in the twentieth century.[108] At issue was the

---

105 For the *terminus post quem* of the *LB*'s compilation, see Chapter II.

106 There was, of course, no Roman province of *Alpes Appenninae*, though there was *Alpes Poeninae*. Paul is clear in what he says that he is talking about the Apennines (*Hae Appenninae Alpes per mediam Italiam pergentes, Tusciam ab Emilia Umbriamque a Flamminia dividunt*), but he also derives their name from *Punicis*, because Hannibal had led his army through them towards Rome (*dictae sunt a Punicis, hoc est Annibale et eius exercitu, qui per easdem Romam tendentes transitum habuerunt*). Isidore of Seville provides the same etymology explicitly linked

to the *Alpes Poeninae* (*Etym.* 14.8.13: *Appenninus mons appellatus quasi Alpes Poeninae, quia Hannibal veniens ad Italiam easdem Alpes aperuit*), clearly based on Servius, *In Aen.* 10.13. It looks very much as though Isidore has confused two different sets of mountains (which he himself had never seen) and Paul has then matched this erroneous description to his own (much more accurate) geographical knowledge.

107 On the manuscripts, see Milani 2009. The text is edited in Glorie 1965: 349–363.

108 Pascal 1906; Crivellucci 1906; Pascal 1907; Crivellucci 1908.

question of whether the *De terminatione* was Paul's source or derived from Paul's description of the Italian peninsula in the *HL*. The issue remains unsettled in recent scholarship.[109] This debate is relevant to Victor, because the *De terminatione* includes the reference to his *Historia*.[110] It is at least theoretically possible that Paul's citation of that text was taken from the *De terminatione*, rather than being evidence for his own reading: that, in other words, he knew of Victor's *Historia* only indirectly.

There are, however, several points strongly in favour of Paul's priority. The most important is the fact that information in the *De terminatione* derives from the *LB*. This can be seen most clearly in the etymology of the Adriatic Sea. The *LB* claims that it was named for a town called Adria (*LB* 14.1): *Adriae . . . quod oppidum agri Piceni etiam mari Adriatico nomen dedit*.[111] There are two towns named Adria: one very ancient in the Veneto, still called Adria, and the other, modern Atri, much more recent, in the Abruzzo (ancient Picenum), which is the one referred to here.[112] It is certain that it is the ancient Venetic Adria that gave its name to the sea. Adria in Picenum first appears in our sources in around 282 BC (*Periochae* 11.5). It cannot have given its name to the Adriatic, known by that name at least since Herodotus (5.9). The only other ancient or medieval instance of this mistaken etymology is found in the section of the *Historia Langobardorum* that circulates as the *De terminatione* (*HL* 2.19):

> sunt civitates Firmus, Asculus et Pinnis et iam vetustate consumpta Adria, quae Adriatico pelago nomen dedit.

> There are the cities Firmus, Asculus, and Pinnis, as well as Adria, now swallowed up by great age, which gave its name to the Adriatic Sea.

No one between the age of Isidore and the Carolingian Renaissance shows any knowledge the *LB* except for Paul, so it multiplies entities beyond necessity to suppose that another anonymous Italian author of unknown date had also read it.

That being so, the natural conclusion is that the *De terminatione* is derived from the *Historia Langobardorum*: it is a product of Paul's text, not its source. Further confirmation of this thesis can be found in the fact that the *De terminatione* makes use of Paul's epitome of Festus in its etymology of *Samnites*.[113] Pascal, the originator of the theory that Paul used the *De terminatione*, acknowledged the link, but tried to suspend judgement on what it meant, leaving open the idea that the *De terminatione* might have used Festus directly.[114] Evidence has, however, since turned up that shows that the *De terminatione* was drawing directly on Paul, not on the text of Festus' work itself.[115] That means that the reference to the *Historia* of Victor in the *Historia Langobardorum* is original to Paul: he had used the text of a *Historia* by Victor and he knew the *Libellus breviatus*. This on its own would make Paul a very significant witness to Victor's *Nachleben*. As it turns out, however, it does not particularly matter if the *De terminatione* precedes Paul, because, as we shall see, Paul also cites the name of Victor elsewhere.

---

109 In favour of Paul's priority is Iasiello 2007: 43, 100.

110 *De terminatione* 9: *Sunt qui Alpes Cottias et Apenninas unam dicunt provinciam, sed hos Victorini revincit hystoria qui Alpes Cottias per se provinciam appellat.*

111 On this, see Stover and Woudhuysen 2021: 169.

112 See Briquel 1990: 315; Festy 1999a *ad loc.*

113 *De terminatione* 49–51. The passages are quoted and discussed below. It is also significant that the reference to *Alpes Appeninae*, which the *De terminatione* shares with the *HL*, seems to arise from a mistake by Isidore, of whose works Paul was a devoted student.

114 Pascal 1906: 303–304.

115 See below.

The use of the *LB* in the *Historia Romana* and the *Historia Langobardorum*, small as it is, combined with Paul's reference to Victor, is extremely important, for it is the first evidence we have – outside the manuscript title – that can firmly associate the name of Victor with the text. Even so, there is something slightly curious about Paul's citation of Victor's *Historia*. Why does he quote Victor for the point when Eutropius (7.14.5), a text that Paul knew intimately, says exactly the same thing in almost exactly the same words as can be found in the *HAb* and *LB*?

> Duae tamen sub eo provinciae factae sunt, Pontus Polemoniacus concedente rege Polemone et Alpes Cottiae Cottio rege defuncto.

> Two provinces were created under him: Pontus Polemoniacus when it was relinquished by king Polemon and Alpes Cottiae, when king Cottius died.

Further, the *LB's* text (like that of the *HAb*) does not quite say what Paul claims for it: that the *Alpes Cottiae* was a province *per se*. One could draw from it the inference that the Cottian Alps were their own province, but there is nothing here that says explicitly that they were distinct from the other Alpine provinces. The reason this might have mattered is that there was some controversy over the province's status, for the *Alpes Cottiae* came to be a province by a very unusual route.[116] It is worth noting also that the whole story of their eponymous monarch, King Cottius, was narrated in detail by Ammianus (15.10.1–7). In other words, despite appearances, this was a question worth wrangling over. Paul wanted more than an inference: he wanted hard evidence and he found it in Victor's *Historia*. So, on the surface this looks rather similar to the case of John the Lydian: Paul seems to be referring to something related to the text of Victor that we have, but which contained more information than survives. Yet, there is one crucial difference. For John, we have only the citation of Victor and the snippets derived from his work. With Paul, we know for a fact that the text he used in the *Historia Romana* to supplement Eutropius was the *Libellus breviatus*. How then to explain his apparent access to both *Historia* and abbreviation? One possible solution to this conundrum is that Paul had a rather greater role in the shaping of the *LB* than has been generally realised.

Paul and the *Libellus breviatus*

Five factors closely associate the *Libellus breviatus* with Paul the Deacon. First, as we have seen, the text was likely compiled in Italy at some point between the middle of the seventh and the middle of the eighth century, by someone with access to recondite materials from antiquity. Besides being the earliest author whom we can say with certainty knew and used the text, Paul also fits this Italian and intellectual context perfectly. Second, transmission: the medieval dissemination of the work begins in the early ninth century, *after Paul's lifetime*, in centres closely connected to the Carolingian court, to which Paul travelled in the 780s.[117] Third, genre: writing epitomes was one of Paul's specialities. The history of Latin lexicography would be considerably poorer if he had not epitomised the massive twenty-book work of Sex. Pompeius

---

116 Roncaglia 2013; Cornwell 2015. 117 Chapter II.

Festus.[118] Fourth, the title: *Libellus de vita et moribus imperatorum breviatus ex libris Sex. Aurelii Victoris* is very close in form and wording to *Excerpta ex libris Pompeii Festi de verborum significatu*, which is Paul's title for his epitome of Festus, while Paul's history of the bishops of Metz circulated as a *libellus*.[119] The titles of the two epitomes are structurally closer to each other than to any of the other transmitted titles for epitomised texts.[120] Fifth, the text of the *Libellus breviatus* we have is dependent on Isidore.[121] We have already had occasion to mention the bizarre notion that Adria in Picenum is the source of the name of the Adriatic, an idea found only in Paul and the *LB*. Tellingly, the text of the *LB* is identical to Isidore, *Etymologies* 13.16.6, which is, however, speaking of the other Adria: *Nam Adria quaedam civitas Illyrico mari proxima fuit, quae* ***Adriatico mari nomen dedit***.[122] Far from being an ancient variant account, the idea that Adria in Picenum gave its name to the Adriatic is a medieval innovation by someone after Isidore who knew his work. Paul, as we shall see, is just such a person, and he expressed his belief in the origin of the name (in somewhat different terms) in the *Historia Langobardorum*. He would have had reasons to think the Picene city more important: Adria in Paul's day was in one of the central parts of the Lombard world, the Duchy of Spoleto, while the more ancient Venetic Adria was at the margins of the Lombard Kingdom, with links to the Byzantine exarchate of Ravenna, and later the Venetians and the Franks.[123]

These five considerations strongly suggest that Paul had some role in the creation of the *LB*: that supposition is rendered a certainty by textual evidence from Eutropius. It is well known that – like Paul's *Historia Romana* – the *LB* has extensive verbatim overlaps with Eutropius. We have argued elsewhere that these probably do not reflect use of a common source, but rather come directly from his work. The way that material from Eutropius is incorporated into the *LB* closely mirrors the way that portions of Jordanes have been woven through it: they are clearly the work of the same individual who compiled the text.[124] It can be demonstrated on textual grounds that Paul was that compiler. Many of the late-antique and early-medieval readers of Eutropius give us some notion of their text of his *breviarium* by including distinctive readings, which are transmitted in one branch or other of our manuscript tradition.[125] When we look *textually* at the *LB*'s quotations of Eutropius, we find that they consistently affiliate only with Paul's Eutropius (*i.e.* the text incorporated almost wholesale into the *HR*, Droysen's C tradition). At 8.15, on Commodus, most of Eutropius' manuscripts read *privatus*, where Paul and the *LB* correctly have *depravatus*. Both the *LB* and Paul omit *saepe* with the A family before *dimicavit* in the same chapter. In 8.19, both the *LB* and Paul make the length of Severus' wall in Britain thirty-two miles (*XXXII passuum milia* in Paul, *per triginta duo passuum milia* in the *LB*), where Eutropius' manuscripts record 132 miles (*CXXXII* in A, the trivial corruption *ĒXXXII* in the B family); both also use the verb *deduxit* with the A tradition against B's

118 Paul's epitome: *T&T* 'Sex. Pompeius Festus' (Marshall), Cervani 1978. There is also the possibility that Paul made an epitome of the *Institutiones* of Cassiodorus. Some *Excerpta ex libro breviario Pauli abbatis* survive in a manuscript now at Erfurt (Amplon. 2° 10) and were (before 1944) also to be found in one at Chartres (†92 (47)). There are reasons to associate the collection of material in these more generally with Paul. On all this, see Holtz 1986: 286 ff.

119 See the apparatus to the edition of Pertz 1829: 261.
120 Chapter III.
121 On this, see also Stover and Woudhuysen 2021: 169–170.
122 It could theoretically also come from Isidore's source, Justin 20.1.9.
123 On the Lombards in the Abruzzo, see Staffa 2010.
124 Stover and Woudhuysen 2021, which prints the overlaps.
125 On the tradition of Eutropius, see Stover and Woudhuysen forthcoming a and *T&T* 'Eutropius' (Reynolds).

reduxit. At 9.14, Paul and the *LB* have the word order *in urbe monetarii* with A, against B's *monetarii in urbe.* At 9.19, on Carinus, both Paul and the *LB* read *verbi fatigatione taxaverunt* where Eutropius' manuscripts read *levi fatigatione taxaverant* (*relaxaverunt* B). This is an error, and not just with respect to the tense of the verb: while *verbi* might be technically construable ('with verbal banter [?]'), it is clearly inferior to *levi* ('with light-hearted banter'). Only Hartke seems to have actually confronted the implications of all this, attempting to explain the *LB*'s readings as evidence that a text of Eutropius related to Paul's was in circulation already in the last decade of the fourth century.[126] Given, however, that the *LB* is a post-sixth-century text and that Paul is the first one to cite it, how plausible is it that the same otherwise unattested strand of Eutropius just happens to show up in both? At the very least, this means that the *LB* must have been produced in a milieu so close to Paul's as to be almost identical. The economical solution is the one indicated by all the other evidence: we have a text which Paul seems to have been the first to know, the dissemination of which tracks his career closely, in a genre which we know he favoured, which circulated under a title that is very similar to that which he gave to another work, and which is interpolated from two of Paul's favourite texts, in one case with an idea that seems to have been Paul's own invention. That is, Paul himself is responsible for the *LB* as we have it.

Paul's own testimony points in precisely this direction. In his dedication to Adelperga, he writes (*Ep. ad Adelpergam*):

> And since Eutropius brought the sequence of his narrative only up the reign of Valens, I have followed him with six further books in my own style (*meo . . . stilo*) using ancient writings.

A note in most of the manuscripts of the *Historia* at the beginning of Book XI restates this point:

> Up to this point, Eutropius has composed the history to which Paul the Deacon added some materials, at the wish of the Lady Adelperga, most Christian duchess of Benevento, spouse of the Lord Arichis, most wise and Catholic prince; henceforth, what follows the same Paul stitched together from various authors in his own style (*proprio stilo*).

In other words, Paul reproduced Eutropius almost exactly for the first ten books, with a few additions from other authors: a quick glance at the two in Droysen's 1879 or Crivellucci's 1914 edition will confirm that this is true. For the remaining six books, material from other authors has been reshaped by Paul, as he says 'in my own style'. Paul says virtually the same thing in the dedication of his Festus epitome to Charlemagne – 'laying out certain deeply concealed things in my own style (*stilo proprio*)' – and we can judge from the extant parts of Festus' original that this is a fair description of his method.[127] This statement by Paul of his method in compiling the *Historia Romana* is extremely interesting for understanding the *LB*. In the *HR*, the use of materials from it does not stop at Book X but continues, and becomes more prominent, through Books XI and XII.[128] Most of Paul's sources for these books survive – besides the *LB*, he used Orosius, Jordanes, and Jerome – and one can clearly see that, while sometimes he does copy

---

126 Hartke 1932: 16.
127 For an example, see below.
128 See Gauville 2005: 34 for the following very handy list: *HR* 11.1 = *LB* 45.2–3, 4; *HR* 11.5 = *LB* 45.8–9; *HR* 11.6 = *LB* 45.5–6; *HR* 11.11 = *LB* 46.2; *HR* 11.14 = *LB* 47.3; *HR* 11.16 = *LB* 47.6–7; *HR* 11.17 = *LB* 47.4–5; *HR* 12.1 = *LB* 48.1; *HR* 12.5 = *LB* 48.2–5, 8–19; *HR* 12.8 = *LB* 48.19.

Orosius and Jordanes verbatim, at least half the time he paraphrases.[129] His text, however, almost always matches the *LB* precisely. That would seem to suggest that the *LB* was written in what Paul regarded as his own style, or something very close to it.

There are a few points where Paul's *Historia Romana* diverges in wording from the text of the *Libellus breviatus*. In the most recent edition of the *LB*, by Festy, two short passages he prints are not found in the manuscripts of that text, but only in Paul's *Historia*. At *LB* 1.16, describing the emperor Augustus, Festy prints *diligebat praeterea Virgilium **Flaccumque poetas***, with the last two words supplied from Paul. At *LB* 31.2, listing the martial feats of Claudius II, Festy opts for Paul's version, which has the emperor fight *adversus trecenta millia Alamannorum*, where the two manuscript families of the *LB* read *adversum gentem Alamannorum* and *adversus autem* (!) *Alamannorum*.[130] Bleckmann has argued that Paul's reading in the latter case, at least, must be original, since the *LB* is the only source to mention this engagement and Zonaras mentions the same number of Alamanni in a battle he puts two years earlier, during the reign of Gallienus (12.24).[131] One might add that the variant readings in the MSS of the *LB* make it look very likely that a textual issue is involved. Further, where the text of the *LB* offers the bizarre error *patre Honorio* for the father of Theodosius I, Paul offers the correct *patre Theodosio*.[132] Festy and Bleckmann thus treat Paul as a witness, at some points a very superior witness, to the text of the *Libellus breviatus*.

That, however, is not a totally a satisfactory explanation of what is going on here. As noted, the *LB* is the *only* ancient source which mentions Claudius' engagement with the Alamanni, yet Paul not only has a superior text to our MSS of the *LB*: he provides more information than they do. He knew not just the numbers involved but also the location: *adversus trecenta milia Alamannorum haud procul a lacu Benaco **in silva, quae Ligana dicitur*** (*HR* 9.11). The bolded words are nowhere to be found in the manuscript tradition of the *LB*. Ligana (or Lugana) was a real wood near Lake Garda, though our first other mentions of it do not come until charters written centuries later.[133] How could Paul possibly have had additional information about an engagement mentioned in no other ancient source? Similarly, Paul knew that the emperor Gallienus was killed *fraude Aureoli ducis sui* (*HR* 9.11).[134] Eutropius makes no mention of Aureolus at all and the *LB* (33.2, which does name him) does not explain that he was a general of Gallienus, nor could *fraude* be straightforwardly deduced from its oblique statement that a *commentum* (a stratagem or invention) lay behind the emperor's death. The logical explanation of these curious episodes is that, in the *HR*, Paul shows knowledge not only of the *LB*, but also of its source, the *Historia* of Victor: that was how he knew where Claudius had fought, or that Augustus had favoured Vergil and Horace, or that one of Gallienus' generals conspired to kill him; it was also why he had good information about the Cottian Alps.

---

129 A glance at any page of *HR* 11–12 (down to the death of Theodosius) in Droysen 1879: 185–195 or Crivellucci 1914: 151–175 will confirm this.

130 Other additions not printed by Festy 1999a, albeit not an exhaustive list, can be found in Bleckmann 1999: 143–146.

131 Bleckmann 1999: 146–149. This conclusion is disputed by Gauville 2005: 239–241.

132 *HR* 12.1. Bleckmann (1999: 146) considers this a case of mere textual corruption in our manuscripts of the *LB*. He fails, however, to explain the genesis of the

manuscript reading in a convincing manner, since he chalks it up to an incorporated gloss referring to Theodosius' son *Honorius*. This cannot explain how the bare ablative *Honorio* ended up in the text of all of our manuscripts. If it is a manuscript issue, perhaps a word like *avo* has dropped out.

133 *e.g. Diplomata Heinrici IV* D 876 (Gladiss and Gawlik 1941–1978: 2.375–376); *Diplomata Friderici I* D 876 (Appelt 1990: 116).

134 On these events, for which there is a rich historical tradition, see Chapter X.

To sum up so far, Paul seems to have known the *Historia* of Victor, he says that the *LB* was written in 'my own style', and there are compelling reasons to think that he had some active role in shaping and disseminating the text. The simplest and most convincing explanation of these data is that Paul himself was the *breviator* who had formed the *Libellus breviatus ex libris Sex. Aurelii Victoris*.

Scholia Vallicelliana

Fortunately, confirmation of this modest thesis is at hand. In 1913, A.E. Anspach announced the discovery of some *Scholia* to the *Etymologies* of Isidore of Seville in the twelfth-century portion of a manuscript in Rome, Bibliotheca Vallicelliana, MS A 18, a copy of one written for Grauso, who was bishop of Ceneda (modern Vittorio Veneto) around the year 1000.[135] These scholia contained new *testimonia* to the work of Sex. Pompeius Festus. Three years later, W.M. Lindsay published a selection of these in *Classical Quarterly*, and a full edition by J. Whatmough followed in 1925 in *Archivum Latinitatis Medii Aevi*.[136] In their use of Festus, sometimes the scholia matched Paul's *Epitome*, sometimes they matched Festus himself, and sometimes they attributed material to Festus of which we have no other trace.[137] Besides, they contained a remarkable amount of material from other authors, much of it of a very recondite kind. This ought to have made the *Scholia* of central interest to scholars of both classical and medieval Latin literature, but they were somewhat neglected in the decades after Whatmough's edition. In 1984, however, Claudia Villa made a brilliant advance in the study of the *Scholia*, by showing that they derived from Paul the Deacon himself.[138]

Villa's case must be among the strongest ever made for the attribution of anonymous marginalia to a known individual. After showing how the evidence of the *Scholia* pointed to an origin in southern Italy (in part through a painstaking comparison of their discussion of birds to dialect terms), Villa showed quite how closely the material in them tracked Paul's interests and writings.[139] In addition to the use of Festus, of whose work he was the most important medieval reader, the *Scholia* exploit authors who were particular favourites of Paul's, right down to reproducing portions from them for which he evinced an especial fondness.[140] Moreover, they contain material that overlaps with Paul's works: the *Historia Langobardorum* in particular, but more obscure writings as well.[141] Recent work has strengthened Villa's case still further. In 2012, Veronika von Büren showed that material found in the *Scholia* is also present in a Cava manuscript of the *Etymologies* of mid-eighth-century date, closely associated with Monte Cassino, perhaps even produced under Paul's instruction.[142] In 2014, Michael Reeve demonstrated that at least some of the extracts from Pliny's *Natural History* contained in the *Scholia* must go back to a manuscript

---

135 Anspach 1913. For this and what follows, see Stover and Woudhuysen 2023.

136 Lindsay 1916, Whatmough 1925.

137 Lindsay 1916.

138 Villa 1984. See further on the *Scholia* Lanciotti 2000 (tracing possible connections with Anglo-Saxon glossaries); Lendinara 2000 (examining the way in which Paul used Festus); Petoletti 2019; Fravventura

2020. On Paul and Isidore, see Heath 2016, though he omits the *scholia*.

139 Birds: Villa 1984: 63–64.

140 It seems almost invidious to choose a single one of Villa's examples, but the appearance (1984: 73) of *Aeneid* 7.759 (a line that Paul particularly liked to imitate in his own verse) is especially revealing.

141 Villa 1984: 67–69.

142 Von Büren 2012.

(probably Italian) of that work earlier than 800.[143] Michael Crawford has also shown that the legal knowledge displayed in the *Scholia* matches Paul's interests very closely.[144] We might add that at least one entry (on Apulia) from the *Scholia* also appears in Vat. lat. 1469, a south-Italian glossary collection of the eleventh century.[145] Another was incorporated into an eleventh-century manuscript of Hrabanus Maurus' *De universo* copied at Monte Cassino. Yet another was incorporated into a twelfth-century manuscript of the *Gynaecia* of Vindicianus, the ultimate origins of which may be traced back to Monte Cassino.[146] All this makes Villa's attribution of the *Scholia* to Paul absolutely secure.

The importance of the *Scholia* can be seen easily by comparing the various witnesses for what Festus said about the Samnites. First, Festus' mutilated entry for *Samnites* in the codex Farnesianus:

> **********]mnitibus nomen
> **********]s propter genus
> **********]α appellent
> **********]. Sabinis vere
> **********r] hominum
> ********** C]omio Castronio
> **********]ollem cui nomen
> ********** . . . (p. 135 Moscadi)[147]

Whatever this originally said, Paul must have drastically cut it down to produce the gloss in his *Excerpta*:

> Samnites ab hastis appellati sunt, quas Graeci σαύνια appellant; has enim ferre adsueti erant; sive a colle Samnio, ubi ex Sabinis adventantes consederunt. (Lindsay 1913: 437)

> Samnites were named from their spears, which the Greeks call *saunia*, for they were in the habit of bearing them, or else from the hill Samnium, where they took residence upon arriving from the Sabines.

The *Scholia*, however, reveal a text very close to what must have been Festus' original:

> Samnites: Samnitibus nomen est inditum propter genus hastae quas Graeci saunia appellant, quibus uti solebant. Alii dicunt ex Sabinis vere sacro natos circiter hominum septem milia duce Comi[ni]o Castronio profectos occupasse collem cui nomen erat Samnio indeque traxisse vocabulum. (Whatmough 1925: 154)

> Samnites: The name was given to the Samnites on account of the kind of spear, which the Greeks call *saunia*, which they used to wield. Others say that about seven thousand men set out from the Sabines in the sacred spring, led by Comius Castronius, and took over the hill, which is called Samnium, and got their name from there.

Incidentally, this immediately makes obvious that what the *De terminatione* (14) says about the Samnites is derived directly from Paul, not from Festus:

---

143 Reeve 2014.
144 Crawford 2019.
145 A connection spotted by Pirie 1926: 190.

146 Stover and Woudhuysen 2023.
147 On the Farnesianus, see *T&T* 'Sex. Pompeius Festus' (Marshall).

Quartadecima Samnium . . . Samnites nomen sumpsere ab astis olim quas ferre solebant, quas Greci samnia appellant.

The fourteenth province is Samnium . . . the Samnites take their name from the spears they used to bear, which the Greeks call *samnia*.

The precise origin of etymologies for the Samnites is far from the only point of uncertainty that the *Scholia* can help us to resolve.

Attentive readers may remember that one item invoked in support of the idea that Paul knew the *OGR* was the fact that they both make Saturn the first individual to coin money.[148] We have already expressed some scepticism about this point, but it can in fact be shown that Paul instead took it from Festus. In his epitomised lexicon, Paul includes an entry on the *Aerarii tribuni*:

a tribuendo aere sunt appellati. Aerarium sane populus Romanus in aede Saturni habuit. (Lindsay 1913: 2)

They are named after 'paying out *aes* [bronze]'. Certainly, the Roman people had their *aerarium* [treasury] in the temple of Saturn.

The *Scholia*, however, reveal that Festus offered a much more extended discussion of the *aerarium*:

Aedem Saturni a publica pecunia aerarium appellarunt, quia pauperes adhuc Romani aere utebantur et quod debebant aes alienum, quod possidebant aes suum dicebant. Unde et adhuc, quamvis mutatis speciebus nomina tamen ipsa perseverant. In nummis antiquis ideo **ex una parte Ianus bifrons pungitur, ex alia navis quia Ianus Saturnum dicitur excepisse cum navigio venit** . . . (Whatmough 1925: 158)

They called the temple of Saturn the *aerarium* [treasury] from the public money, since poor Romans still use *aes* [bronze; *aes, aeris*] and call what they owe another's *aes* and what they own their own *aes*. For this reason even to this day, although the appearance has changed, the names themselves nevertheless persist. On ancient coins, therefore, on one side is stamped Janus with two faces, on the other a ship, since Janus is said to have greeted Saturn when he came on a vessel . . .

This cannot be the full extent of Festus' entry, but at the very least it shows that he did discuss the early history of coinage in some detail: that, and not the *OGR*, was what had given Paul the notion that Saturn first struck coins. In fact, if we now examine the *OGR*'s text again (3.4–6), it looks very much like a garbled derivative of information ultimately taken from Festus:

He is said to have also demonstrated the use of stamped bronze and of money struck into an image, in which on one side his head was stamped and on the other the ship on which he had sailed there (*ab una parte caput eius imprimeretur, altera navis, qua vectus illo erat*). For this reason, even today, when a coin has been put down and covered over, gamblers impose on their fellow-players the choice of what they think is underneath: the head, or the ship (which now they generally mangle, calling it a *naviam*). Also the building beneath the Capitoline Hill, in which he kept the money he had made, is even today called the treasury of Saturn.

148 Chapter II.

Though one can work it out, the *OGR* does not actually make explicit that it was the face of Janus on those early coins, nor does it tell us that Saturn arrived on a (presumably single and therefore significant) ship, one that Janus met – Festus, did, however. It is possible that between the *Scholia* and the *OGR* we can gain a sense of the original scope of the entry in Festus or his source.[149]

The *Scholia Vallicelliana* thus confirm, were confirmation needed, that Paul had access to and had read the full text of Festus and that he was interested in some of the things it said, even if he chose not to include them in his *Excerpta*. Just occasionally, as with the Samnites, they allow us to recover material that Paul knew, but which does not otherwise survive. That is what makes a scholion on f. 117v, a note to *Etymologies* 18.8 (*De sagittis*), so exciting:

> Victor historiographus: ego vitas principum pertractans, raro quemquam repperi studio saggitandi deditum utilem fuisse rei publicae. Quod unde accidat, nequeo intellegere, nisi forte conici datur, dum arduum magis quam utile negotium plusque eventu oblectans, ac ne[c] in ipso quidem bello satis validum sectantur, mittere imperialia officia †consultando salutaria. Idem Domitianus imperator sagittarum tam doctus fuit, ut inter patentes digitos extentae manus viri procul positi spicula transvolarent. (Whatmough 1925: 160)

> Victor, the writer of history: As I examine the lives of the emperors, rarely have I found that any of them who was devoted to the pursuit of archery was also useful to the state. I am not able to understand the reason for which this happens, unless perchance one is given to conjecture that while they pursue a pastime that is more difficult than it is useful, and gives more pleasure in its successful completion (?), and is not even very effective in battle itself, they neglect imperial duties and vital counsels. This same emperor Domitian is said to have been so skilled in archery that his arrows could sail between the outstretched fingers of a man stationed a considerable distance away.[150]

This is an extract, a chunky one by the standards of scholia, from the work of a historian called Victor, who treated the Roman emperors. The noun *historiographus* in Paul is reserved for ancient historians (*cf. HL* 1.15 and 2.23), so we are looking for a Roman historian. The style is elevated, even literary, incorporating a Horatian tag.[151] The last line of this scholion is found verbatim in the *LB* (11.5): *Sagittarum tam doctus fuit, ut inter patentes digitos extentae manus viri procul positi spicula transvolarent.* The rest is entirely unknown.[152]

There is more. Consider this passage on the emperor Theodosius:

> Constat aliquotiens longo intervallo latentem in seminibus vim quandoque erumpere, sicut de Theodosio imperatore factum est, qui de Traiani imperatoris stirpe post plurimos annos progenitus eidem simillimus fuit. (Whatmough 1925: 140)

---

149 The information on *aleatores*, or dice-players, looks in particular like the kind of item to bring joy to the heart of the lexicographer.

150 *Consultando* is certainly corrupt; perhaps read *consultaque* (cf. *HAb* 16.2 *domi militiaeque facta consultaque*). The translation reflects this conjecture.

151 *cf.* Horace, *Sat.* 1.1.115–117: *raro . . . reperire queamus.*

152 Villa 1984: 71–72 attempts to explain this scholion as a scribal error, which moved *Victor historiographus* from before *idem Domitianus* to before *ego*, with the result that the first-person statement belongs to Paul himself. There are, however, no other first-person statements of Paul in the *Scholia*, and the content of this one is hardly the sort of thing that Paul would say; his own great grandfather Lopichis, for example, was evidently a bowman (*cf. HL* 4.37).

It is well established that sometimes the power which lies hidden in seeds bursts forth after a long period of time, just as happened with the emperor Theodosius, of the line of Trajan, who, though born many years after, was extremely similar to him.

A single word links this to the *LB* (48.1, 8), *simillimus*, but that is enough to secure a link based on the parallel ideas:

> [*sc.* Theodosius] genere Hispanus, originem a Traiano principe trahens . . . moribus et corpore Traiano **similis**, quantum scripta veterum et picturae docent.

> Theodosius was of Spanish origin, tracing his descent from the emperor Trajan . . . he was similar in manners and body to Trajan, as far as the writings and paintings of men of old show them.

In the *Historia Romana*, Paul combined these two passages into one (12.5):

> Fuit autem Theodosius . . . moribus et corpore Traiano similis, quantum scripta veterum et picturae docent, a quo et originem traxit.

> Theodosius was . . . in habits and body like Trajan – as much as can be surmised from old writings and pictures – from whom he also was descended.

The idea contained in the scholion is vastly richer: again, Paul seems to have had access to a late-antique work of Roman history that preserved information reflected in the *LB*, but otherwise lost.

On *Etymologies* 5.33.3, there is this extract, which is likewise not attributed, but must come from the same text:

> Commodus imperator Ianuarium mensem Amazoneum, Septembrium Commodum `censuit appellari. (Whatmough 1925: 70)

> The Emperor Commodus decreed that the month of January should be named Amazonius, and September Commodus.

Then, next to 5.33.11:

> Domitianus Septembrem Germanicum, Octobrem suo nomine censuit appellari. (Whatmough 1925: 70)

> Domitian decreed that September should be named Germanicus, and October from his own name.

Villa attempts to attribute these lines to Prosper's *Chronicon*, but Prosper (who is simply copying Jerome in this passage) does not mention the month of January.[153] Eutropius does not either (8.15). Instead, it almost certainly comes from the same source as Paul's other imperial material.

The only plausible explanation of these data is that the relationship of the *Scholia Vallicelliana* on Roman history to the *LB* is the same as that of those on lexicography to Paul's *Epitome* of Festus. They

---

153 Villa 1984: 73. Prosper, *Chron.* p. 432 Mommsen 1892:
  Commodus Septembrem mensem nomine suo appellavit (cf.
  Jerome, *Chron.* 208[k]).

draw on the fuller text from which the abbreviated versions were derived. That, in turn, entails that the relationship of the *Libellus breviatus* to Paul is the same as that of the *Epitome* of Festus: Paul cut it out of an existing text, reworked much of it in his own style, and probably brought it north to the Carolingian world, where it was rapidly disseminated.

The *Scholia* and the *Historiae abbreviatae*

So, what was that text from which Paul worked? Here the title of the *LB* becomes crucial again: *Libellus . . . breviatus ex libris Sex. Aurelii Victoris.* That is, Paul had access to the full text of the *Historia* of Aurelius Victor. The scholion on emperors and archery proves this. It is attributed to one *Victor historiographus*, a description which matches the *Victoris Historia* of the *Historia Langobardorum* and is entirely compatible with our other evidence for Victor's *opus*, which is normally titled *Historia*. It also further justifies the title of the *LB*. The statue base has already shown that the name *Sexti* is authentic: the scholion now confirms that *breviatus* and *Victoris* are also correct, because it transmits a longer version of material that appears in the *LB*, which it attributes to Victor. Only obstinance would prevent one from giving credence to the penultimate word of the title: *libris*.

We have every reason to believe that this Victor is the Aurelius Victor from whose work the manuscripts say the *Historiae abbreviatae* was derived. The scholia sound like the author of the *HAb*, every page of which betrays an unmistakable (and deeply idiosyncratic) authorial voice. This contrasts with the *Libellus breviatus*, which has no strong authorial personality and no first-person pronouns.[154] Lexical peculiarities confirm this: the phrase *conici datur* is rare in antiquity.[155] As Heraeus saw a century ago, it must also lie behind the corrupt text of *HAb* 33.30: *quantum coniciatur*, that is *quantum conici <d>atur*.[156] In combination with the mass of other evidence, the scholion confirms that Victor wrote a long discursive work of history – the *Historia* – to which the *HAb* and *LB* are witnesses. It also demonstrates that Paul the Deacon was the last individual to show knowledge of that full *Historia*, from which he himself extracted the *LB*. Moreover, it also confirms what Paul himself says in his letter to Adelperga: that the *LB* was written in a style quite different to that of its source, that it was in Paul's own style. The observation ascribed to Victor *historigraphus* in the scholion is not the voice of the *LB*, nor indeed the voice of Paul himself, but the distinctive voice of an imperial historian who was interested in general axioms, arising from comparing multiple emperors across centuries, and teasing out moral lessons. In other words, it is the voice of Victor.

The other scholia – though not explicitly attributed to Victor – point in the same direction. First, Theodosius' supposed descent from Trajan. The idea in the scholion is much richer than that which is found in the *LB*: that there are certain seeds of greatness which inhere in certain lines of descent and can blossom into flower after dormant centuries, something Theodosius proves. Characteristic of Victor, the

154 Chapter IV.
155 Jerome, *In Ezech.* 14.48; Augustine, *Ep.* 102.1; Orosius 1.12.10, 3.6.3. Eugippius, *Excerpta* 86.101b has *quantum conici datur de scripturis sanctis*, where Augustine,

Enarrationes in Psalmos 85.17 (its source text) has *quantum conceditur de scripturis sanctis*.
156 Heraeus 1899: 311.

TABLE 5.10 – SUETONIUS, VICTOR, AND JEROME ON DOMITIAN'S RENAMING OF THE MONTHS

Suetonius, *Domitianus* 13.3	*HAb* 11.4	Jerome, *Chron.* 274[k]
Septembrem mensem et Octobrem ex appellationibus suis Germanicum Domitianumque transnominavit.	Septembrem Octobremque menses Germanici superiorem, e suo nomine alterum appellaverat.★	Duo menses aliter appellati, September Germanicus, et October Domitianus.
He altered the names of the months of September and October from his own titles, calling them Germanicus and Domitianus respectively.	He renamed the months September and October, the former Germanicus, the latter from his own name.	Two months were named in a new way: September Germanicus, and October Domitianus.

★ *cf.* also Macrobius, *Sat.* 1.12.36, which must be derived from Victor: *Mensis September principalem sui retinet appellationem: quem Germanici appellatione, Octobrem vero suo nomine Domitianus invaserat.* Note in particular the distinction between *appellatio* and *nomen*, not drawn by Suetonius.

idea of *vis in seminibus* is both precise and *recherché*, found in those terms only in Cicero's *De divinatione*, where his brother Quintus is justifying the existence of fate on the analogy of seeds (1.128):

> And as there lies within seeds the power (*in seminibus vis*) of those things which are produced from them, so future events have been stored up in causes.

Everything about this scholion fits Victor: the interest in Trajan and Theodosius (after all, he did erect a statue to Theodosius close to the Forum of Trajan), the engagement with the works of Cicero, and the pause in the narrative for learned reflections on the meaning of history. The vocabulary of the scholion confirms this. The expression *longo intervallo* is not especially common outside Cicero (who used it twenty-eight times) and Augustine (nine times), with a handful of other attestations in Suetonius (four), Paulinus of Nola (three), Calcidius (three), Quintilian (two), and Ammianus (two), for a total of about seventy instances in all of antiquity up to the fifth century.[157] In the 11,000 words of the *HAb*, Victor uses it twice (34.12 and 42.13). *Constat* expressions are another favourite of Victor's, with seven examples in the *HAb* (8.8, 9.6, 16.9, 20.34, 33.31, 39.8, 39.27), compared with fourteen in all the extant works of Tacitus, for example, or two in Caesar, or seventeen in Suetonius.

The emperors Domitian and Commodus and the names of the months clinch the case. While Suetonius and Jerome do mention Domitian's calendric activities, the phrasing is much closer to Victor's in the *HAb* (TABLE 5.10). The case of Commodus is even more telling. Besides the *HAb*, Eutropius, Jerome, and Prosper say that he renamed September *Commodus*, but the only Latin source to mention *Amazonius* is the *Historia Augusta* (*Comm.* 11.8). There is no good evidence that Paul knew the *HA*, a text with a limited circulation in the early Middle Ages, which in any case assigns the name to December, not January (as in the scholion).[158] Cassius Dio, however, does provide a complete list of the names of the twelve months (73.15.3):

157 A conclusion based on *CDS*.

158 On the dissemination of the *HA* see Bertrand *et al.*, 1986: 97–101.

> The months were all named after him, so that they were reckoned in this way: Amazonius, Un-conquered [*sc.* Invictus], Fortunate [*sc.* Felix], Pius, Lucius, Aelius, Aurelius, Commodus, Augustus, Herculeus, Romanus, Most Excellent [*sc.* Exsuperatorius].[159]

While Dio does not explicitly link individual names to months, it is logical to suppose that his list represents the sequence from January to December: that is also consistent with our only non-literary evidence for the Commodian months.[160] That would make January Amazonius, as it is in the scholion, the only Latin or Greek text surviving to explicitly contain this authentic second-century detail. The simplest solution is that Paul also derived this from his text of Victor, an author who knew, used, and appreciated Greek history-writing, and who was used (and abused) in turn by the author of the *Historia Augusta*.

This inquiry into Victor's contemporary and posthumous reception confirms what we have already deduced from the texts, paratexts, and literary contexts of the *HAb* and *LB*: his work was considered a major history, and was widely read even in his own lifetime and in the centuries that followed. That work was not identical to either the *HAb* or the *LB*. The *HAb* is an abbreviation put together at some point probably in late antiquity, perhaps in Victor's lifetime, and inserted into the *Corpus tripertitum* as the imperial portion of that compilation. Yet the original *Historia* from which it was derived remained available to John the Lydian in the sixth century in Constantinople and to Paul the Deacon in southern Italy in the eighth. Paul quoted from the text in his lectures on Isidore and cited it in his *Historia Langobardorum*. He also used it as the fundamental source for the *LB*: a handy epitome of Roman history, which both followed and supplemented Eutropius, and which he in turn used in his *Historia Romana*. Victor is thus finally revealed as a later Roman historian of the first rank.

This book opened with a fundamental paradox: the contrast between Victor's background and reputation and the meagre work that circulates under his name. Subsequent investigation confirmed the genuine nature of this paradox and deepened its strangeness. New evidence allows it to be resolved. The *Scholia Vallicelliana* put the study of Victor on an entirely new footing.

---

159 Dio survives here only in Xiphilinus' epitome, but Zonaras confirms the details.

160 Speidel 1993.

CONCLUSION TO PART ONE

TWO EDITIONS OF VICTOR'S *HISTORIA*

The first part of this book has made a cumulative argument. In Chapter I, we outlined what is known and what might reasonably be deduced about the life of Victor, showing that his career and standing among his contemporaries seemed fundamentally incompatible with the work today widely attributed to him, the *Historiae abbreviatae*. In Chapter II, we compared the *HAb* to the other work that was transmitted from antiquity under Victor's name, the *Libellus breviatus*, illustrating how intimately they were connected. We then reviewed the transmission of both works, showing that they are presented in the manuscripts as epitomes of a longer *Historia* by Victor and that this claim deserves to be treated with utmost seriousness. In Chapter III, we surveyed the genre of the epitome in Latin literature, demonstrating that both *HAb* and *LB* are entirely compatible with what we otherwise know about condensed texts. In Chapter IV, we set out to provide the first sustained analysis of the *HAb* from a literary and intellectual standpoint. We probed the exceptional richness of the literary imagination visible in the work, the broad frame of cultural reference that it reveals, and the many internal signs that it is indeed an epitome of some longer and more complex original. We surveyed the *LB* more briefly, detecting many of the same literary and intellectual influences that can be seen more clearly in the *HAb*. We then showed that at several points the two texts offer different fragments of the same original story: details or interpretations presupposed in one version appearing only in the other, as we would expect with two epitomes of the same work. In Chapter V, we then followed the thread of references to Victor from his own day into the early Middle Ages. His work, invariably referred to as a *Historia*, attracted admiration and attention from a remarkable range of contemporary and later readers: admired by Ammianus, perused by St Jerome, pilfered for facts by John the Lydian. Victor's *Nachleben* is the most extensive and impressive of any of the fourth-century Latin historians: it cannot be reconciled with the idea that the *HAb* is the totality of his work. Crucially, those who know of Victor and who can be demonstrated to have had direct acquaintance with material found in the *HAb* usually also show knowledge of the content of the *LB*. Towards the end of Chapter V, we analysed the evidence of Paul the Deacon – the last individual to refer to Victor's *Historia* and the first to certainly show knowledge of the *LB*. We suggested that the evidence pointed towards Paul himself being the early-medieval compiler of the *LB*. Finally, we presented new fragments of Victor – preserved in Paul's annotations to Isidore, the *Scholia Vallicelliana* – which decisively confirmed the arguments advanced thereto.

The *Scholia* show that Paul the Deacon had access to the complete work of Aurelius Victor: he used that work to create the *Libellus breviatus*. This was exactly what it claimed to be: a *Libellus de vita et moribus imperatorum breviatus ex libris Sex. Aurelii Victoris*. The fact that the scholion on Domitian overlaps with, but contains more information than, the *LB* demonstrates very clearly that the text is an epitome. The *Scholia* are also closely connected by idiom, style, facts, and ideas with the *Historiae abbreviatae*, that work universally ascribed to Victor, the *scriptor historicus*. Like the *LB*, the *HAb* must be precisely what its manuscript title suggests: the *Historia* of Victor abbreviated, cut down by the compiler of the *Corpus tripertitum* to produce the third part of his Roman history.

There are very real differences between the *HAb* and the *LB*, differences of style and of substance that we have remarked upon already. Most importantly, whoever compiled the *CT* was working with a version of Victor's history that terminated in AD 360, where Paul's material seems to have ended with the triumph of the Emperor Theodosius in 388 – both significant moments in Victor's career. None of these differences should, however, obscure the fundamental fact that the *HAb* and *LB* are both epitomes of a longer, sophisticated, and discursive work written by one Sextus Aurelius Victor. We cannot know the full scope and content of this original *Historia*, but we have every reason to believe that it was of an ambition and quality that justified the high opinion of Victor's contemporaries.

Not the least of the virtues of the solution provided by the *Scholia* is how neatly it aligns with the arguments made in Chapters I–IV, arguments advanced from quite different premises and with quite other evidence. Victor's career and reputation seem so out of kilter with the text of the *HAb* because it is not the totality of his work. The *HAb* and the *LB* are so closely connected through the entire period to AD 360 because they are both epitomes of a longer and more sophisticated *Historia* by Victor: the manuscript titles are (not for the first time) correct. That we have two separate epitomes is hardly surprising: historical works were particularly prone to epitomisation and multiple epitomes of the same work were not uncommon in antiquity. The obtrusive stylistic difference between the *HAb* and the *LB* is unremarkable in view of the very different ways that epitomators might go about their work, some opting to preserve the *ipsissima verba* of the original, others preferring a smoother and less faithful rendering. The *HAb* is written in a grand and vastly ambitious style because it is a remnant of a grand and vastly ambitious work – qualities reflected less brilliantly in the *LB*, but visible all the same. That the two works so often complement each other in recounting some complex episode is because they offer only a partial view of the richness of the original. Many authors in late antiquity refer to a *Historia* by Victor in admiring tones, and seem to know material found in both the *HAb* and the *LB* – because they were reading Victor's complete work. The case advanced in this book has been complex, even intricate at times, but it is also fundamentally simplifying: hosts of unanswered questions and difficult problems vanish at a stroke.

The first part of this book has ranged far and wide, made arguments both large and small on a vast number of topics. Some of these may be uncontroversial – others ought to provoke debate. We can hardly anticipate which ideas will cause the greatest controversy, let alone what specific objections might be advanced in detail. There are, however, certain *prima facie* problems with the broad argument advanced here: that both the *HAb* and the *LB* are epitomes of a longer *Historia* by Aurelius Victor. Three loom particularly large: the question of multiple editions, the issue of the superficial dissimilarity of the *HAb* and the *LB* after the first eleven chapters, and the fact that the two texts diverge on some points of detail. We call these problems merely *prima facie*, because closer examination suggests that they are not really problems at all.

Multiple editions in antiquity

The *HAb* is derived from a source that terminated in AD 360. This is demonstrated by a remarkable variety of evidence: it is obvious from the text itself, is stated explicitly in the title in the *CT*, and can be inferred from Ammianus' account of Victor's encounter with Julian in 361. The *LB* terminates in 395, but (as we have shown elsewhere) the core of historical material from the fourth century stops somewhat earlier, in 388.[1] Paul's copy of Victor's *Historia* certainly went up to the reign of Theodosius, as one of the *Scholia Vallicelliana* proves. It is an inescapable conclusion of the evidence presented in Part 1 of this book that there existed in antiquity at least two versions of Victor's history, with slightly different terminal dates. This might inspire some scepticism, since the issue of multiple editions in antiquity has been rather controversial, so it is worth briefly treading this treacherous ground.[2] The whole subject faces the conceptual problem that the 'edition' (and its publication) is really a phenomenon of the print, rather than the manuscript era: we are perhaps better off thinking of different versions of the same text, without the cumbersome intellectual apparatus that the word 'edition' implies.[3] It has also perhaps been somewhat distorted by a reaction against two tendencies in scholarship that were keen to detect multiple editions everywhere in the ancient world. First, in the nineteenth and early twentieth century, it was common to posit multiple editions, with authorial revisions, as a way of explaining textual variants.[4] In 1941, Hilarius Emonds turned a sceptical eye to these postulated editions, but the attractive title of his work, *Zweite Auflage im Altertum*, has perhaps lent its conclusions a more general application than the author intended.[5] It seems possible that mistrust of editions hypothesised from variants – what Pasquali called the *ultima ratio* of the textual critic – has bled over into treatments of revision and serial publication more generally.[6] Second, it was once common to use ancient subscriptions – little notices tacked on the end of manuscripts showing that one or another individual had read and reviewed the text at such and such a time – as evidence for systematic editorial activity.[7] As Alan Cameron has convincingly shown, however, this is a misconception: the subscriptions mostly testify to a fairly basic *recensio* of the text, making sure it was not erroneous.[8]

These two demonstrations, more limited than is perhaps generally realised, have encouraged scholars to be parsimonious in accepting the existence of ancient editions, continuations, and revisions. Yet, given the fluid publication context which prevailed before print, multiple authorial versions were probably closer to the norm than the exception. The papyri offer very rich evidence for the revision of

1 Stover and Woudhuysen 2021: 172–175.
2 Scepticism: *e.g.* Cameron 1995: 114; Cameron 2011: 671.
3 As a result, we use the words 'edition', 'publication', 'publish' and so on in only a loose sense. On the topic of authors revising their own work, see in general the lucid articles 'Revision in Greek and Latin Literature' in *OCD Online* (Gurd) and 'Editions, Second' in *BNP* (Heyworth and Wilson).
4 As, *e.g.*, W.M. Lindsay (1903) did for Martial (though the view was not his alone) and Lindsay (1904) did for Plautus. On Martial, see the sceptical treatment of *T&T* 'Martial' (Reeve): 243-244; there are still believers, *e.g.*

Velaza 2016b (*cf.* Stover 2019). In general, see also *BNP* 'Authorial Variants' (Heyworth and Wilson).
5 Emonds 1941. As 1–4 and the extensive first section devoted to such cases (24–135) makes clear, Emonds' starting point was editions hypothesised on the basis of variants. Work subsequent to Emonds has tended to reject evidence of authorial variants: *e.g.* Reeve 1969 on Longus; Green 1991: xlii–xlix on Ausonius.
6 Pasquali 1952: 419.
7 On the subscriptions, see now Wallenwein 2017.
8 Cameron 2011: 421–497.

literary works in the ancient world.[9] It would be unwise to assume that this can all be tidied into a box marked 'pre-circulation drafts'. Medievalists, with access to vastly more abundant contemporary material, have been able to document this kind of authorial re-edition in detail in cases such as Godfrey of Viterbo, *Piers Plowman*, and Chaucer, to give only three examples.[10]

For most ancient authors, in contrast to those in the Middle Ages, we are simply in the unfortunate position that we can document such a textual history in only a very small number of cases, where we happen to have the right manuscript evidence surviving. Most of our extant texts yield proof of only a single post-classical archetype.[11] There is, however, a wealth of ancient evidence for multiple versions, outside the texts themselves. Plenty of historical works show signs of revision or serial issue. It seems likely that Polybius' *History* reflects two main periods of effort: Books I–XXIX, written largely before 146, and XXX–XL, after that year.[12] Cornelius Nepos (*Atticus* 19.1) says explicitly that he wrote something about Pomponius Atticus that circulated before his subject's death, then extended his efforts after it. Livy seems to have put out his work in multiple tranches, with Books I–V issued before 25 BC, VI–X after 9 BC, the final twenty or twenty-two books after AD 14, and the intervening eleven decades in the twenty-three years between.[13] Velleius Paterculus seems to have planned to return to many of the events he covered in his history and treat them in greater detail.[14] Whether or not Jerome was right to conceive of Tacitus' works as a single thirty-book history from Augustus to Domitian, the *Annals* and the *Histories* are at least linked historical works published at different times.[15] The structure and publication history of Plutarch's *Parallel Lives* are a rather murky subject, but cross-references make clear that some of them were published before others.[16] Cassius Dio had gathered materials for his history down to the death of Septimius Severus, but kept its limits undetermined, as though he might keep going and going (73.23.5).[17] Before he embarked on his monumental Roman history, he had already written one account of the dreams and portents that encouraged Septimius Severus to hope for supreme power and another of the struggle for mastery after the death of Commodus (73.23.1–2). Eusebius of Caesarea extensively revised his own historical works, the *Chronicle* and the *Historia Ecclesiastica*, though the precise dates of different editions remain controversial.[18] How many editions of his history Eunapius published (and when) is a very vexed question, but his own testimony at the very least shows that he had produced and circulated an earlier version of the work, which he intended to update or supplement.[19] In the early fifth century, Prosper of Aquitaine released at

9 For a thought-provoking introduction, see Gurd 2014

10 Godfrey: Chapter II. *Piers Plowman*: Warner 2011. Chaucer and *Piers Plowman*: Hanna 1996.

11 A point amply demonstrated by perusal of the entries in *T&T*.

12 Dreyer 2011: 58–68 is a reasonable discussion of this controversial topic.

13 *Periochae* 121: *Ex libro CXXI qui editus post excessum Augusti dicitur.* On the authenticity of this heading, see Reeve 1988, and for a reconstruction of the publication history, see Barnes 1998: 209–212 and the still valuable Luce 1977.

14 At several points, Velleius alludes to a more expansive work that he intended to write (often but not always a *iustum opus* or *iusta volumina*): 2.48.5, 96.3, 99.3, 103.4, 114.4, 119.1. There has been doubt over how seriously

to take these statements, but they seem unusually numerous and emphatic to be purely the product of literary convention – see Woodman 1975: 287–288.

15 Jerome, *In Zach.* 3.14. The second Medicean manuscript (Florence, BML Plut. 68.2) does number the books of the *Histories* and the *Annals* continuously. See further Conte 1994: 530–531.

16 *e.g. Theseus* 1.2. For the authenticity of the cross-references (assailed in the nineteenth century), see Mewaldt 1907; on the Plutarchan book, see Duff 2011.

17 On the composition of Dio's history, see Millar 1964: 28–72, and Barnes 1984.

18 Barnes 1981: 111, 128–129, 149–150, 191–194; Burgess 1997.

19 Eunapius, *VS* 8.2.3, 7.3.5. See further on this question Chapter X.

least three editions of his chronicle over the course of some twenty-two years, in 433, 445, and 455 (and probably in 451 as well), each subsequent edition bringing the earlier up to date.[20] In the sixth century, Count Marcellinus initially composed his continuation of Jerome from 395 to 518, but then added entries for 519–534, as he describes in his preface.[21] A little later still, Procopius would supplement his seven-book history of Justinian's *Wars* with both the scandalous *Secret History* and a more staid eighth book.[22]

Outside historiography, multiple versions were also common in all periods and genres of ancient literature. Cicero originally wrote his *Academica* in two books, then subsequently revised and expanded it, dividing the second edition into four books. What we have surviving is the second book of the first edition (the *Academica priora* or the *Lucullus*) and most of the first book of the second edition (the *Academica posteriora*).[23] He also sent a copy of his *De gloria* to Atticus 'somewhat more carefully revised – and it is indeed the original itself with interlineations and corrections in many places'.[24] Indeed, Cicero had a habit of submitting drafts to friends for comments – some of these seem to have escaped into wider circulation.[25] Whatever the truth of Servius' claim (*In Buc.* 10.1, *In Georg.* 4.1) that Vergil revised the *Georgics* after the suicide of Cornelius Gallus, it makes sense only in an environment where revision and reissue were common. Ovid originally wrote his *Amores* in five books, and then issued a second edition in three, which is what survives.[26] While the evidence for ancient editions of Martial is extremely tenuous, we do know that his epigrams were issued serially (and some of them revised and reissued) between 84 and 102: one of Martial's poems (*Epig.* 7.17.6–7) mentions seven earlier volumes of his work, annotated by his own pen, in a friend's library.[27] As only he can, Tertullian describes how the extant text of his *Adversus Marcionem* is the third iteration, the work having first been rushed (*properatum*) and then mendaciously interpolated by an apostate (1.1). Solinus too makes clear, in a second preface to his work, that it circulated in more than one version (*Praef.* II).

Famously, Porphyry produced an edition of the works of Plotinus, for which he provides an extensive rationale – they circulated independently under fluid titles and there were rival arrangements.[28] While the manuscript evidence for Lactantius' *Divine Institutes* is complex, the simplest explanation for it is that the work had two editions: a first issued before 311 and a second, with praise of Constantine, in 324.[29] Victor's contemporary, the Christian exegete unfortunately dubbed Ambrosiaster, issued his

20 See Mommsen 1892: 345–347; Muhlberger 1986; Muhlberger 1990: 56–57. Mommsen thought there was also an edition of 443, but Muhlberger shows that to be an unnecessary supposition.

21 ed. Mommsen 1894: 60.

22 The chronology of Procopius' works is controversial (Greatrex 2014: 97–104 is a helpful guide), but that *Wars* I–VII was later supplemented is not in doubt.

23 Hunt 1998 surveys the textual history of the *Academica*: see esp. 10–16 on their complex gestation.

24 Cicero, *Ep. Att.* 16.3.1 (trans. Shuckburgh): *retractatius, et quidem ἀρχέτυπον ipsum crebris locis inculcatum et refectum.* It is impossible to know in what form the text circulated as it is now lost, although it was certainly available in late antiquity (see Freund 2015 for some *testimonia*). Petrarch claims to have had a manuscript of the *De gloria*, which he unfortunately deposited with a penurious tutor of

his; it was never seen again – see the full discussion in De Nolhac 1907: 1.260–267.

25 Gurd 2007 studies this practice.

26 Ovid, *Amores* I, *epigramma*. See Cameron 1968 for a minimalist account of what this involved.

27 On ancient editions, see above.

28 Porphyry, *Vita Plotini* 24–26 (for his edition and its rationale); 4 (for independent circulation – interestingly Porphyry offers *incipits* for the text because the titles varied; Augustine also gives *incipits* in his *Retractationes*); the scholia to *Enneads* 4.4.29 (Henry and Schwyzer 1959: 118) attest an edition by Eustochius (a contemporary of Porphyry). Henry 1935 argued forcefully that Eustochius' edition was used by Eusebius of Caesarea.

29 See briefly Heck and Wlosok 2005: viii and (at greater length) Heck 1972. The issue of two editions ought to be separated from the question of whether the two editions can be recovered from the extant manuscripts.

commentaries on Paul in three editions over a twenty-year period, reworking and updating his earlier material in response to criticism and subsequent debate.[30] The poet Ausonius refers on one occasion to the *opusculorum meorum seriem* (*Epiced. praef.* 12), which conjures up an image of a stream of publications that formed a (more or less) coherent *oeuvre*. Vegetius, whenever in the fourth or fifth centuries he was writing, appears to have issued the first book of his *Epitoma rei militaris* as a separate *libellus*, before adding to it.[31] There is evidence for serial publication of at least one multi-book work roughly contemporary with Victor, Augustine's *De civitate Dei*.[32] Another of Augustine's works, the *De doctrina Christiana,* was written over decades and there are reasons to think that the first two books were circulated long before the third and fourth had been completed.[33] In fact, there are reasons to believe that serial publication was something like Augustine's normal habit. In a letter on the *De Trinitate*, part of which had been issued without his authorisation, Augustine remarks that he had decided to publish the books of that work 'not one by one, but all together', as though that were something that called for commentary and explanation (*Ep.* 174). A little later, still in the first half of the fifth century, Sedulius tells us that the Tetrarchic jurist Hermogenianus had issued three separate editions of one of his works: *Cognoscant Hermogenianum, doctissimum iurislatorem, tres editiones sui operis confecisse.* Sedulius cited this to justify his own substantially reworked prose edition of the *Carmen Paschale*.[34] In the sixth century, Boethius wrote two versions of his commentary on Porphyry's *Isagoge*, one based on Victorinus' translation and one based on his own, as well as two editions of a commentary on Aristotle's *De interpretatione*.[35] Dionysius Exiguus produced multiple versions of his canonical collections, with prefatory letters explaining his rationale for each of them.[36] Cassiodorus' *Divine Institutes* has an unusually complex manuscript transmission, with Book II (if that is what it is) surviving in three separate versions.[37] It seems likely that all three reflect versions of the text written or adapted in Cassiodorus' own lifetime.[38] In his list of his own writings, Gregory of Tours makes clear that, in some sense, he thought of his hagiographic works – written at different times and often revised – as a collection (*Hist.* 10.31). He also expresses a vivid abhorrence of the idea that what he had written might be altered and reissued. Whether or not an annotation in the *propria manu* of Gregory the Great survives in a contemporary manuscript of the *Regula pastoralis*, that work certainly circulated in two different authorial recensions.[39] Gregory is probably the ancient author for whose compositional habits our evidence is richest – his example ought to carry considerable weight.

30 *cf.* Cooper and Hunter 2010.
31 Vegetius 2.*prol*.8–9. Reeve 2004: viii–x is a sensible discussion of the limited evidence for Vegetius' precise date.
32 *Ep.* 1a★. The letter concerns how twenty-two separate *quaterniones*, presumably meaning booklets here instead of literal quaternions, could be bound into two volumes. This makes sense only with some kind of serial publication, in which a devoted fan of Augustine might have collected each book as it became available.
33 Augustine, *Retractiones* 2.4 gives a good sense of the work's complex gestation. The precise chronology of composition is slightly murky, but it seems likely that the first stage of work took place in the 390s and the last in the 420s: Green 1996: xii–xiii. On the basis of a very early manuscript of the work containing only Books I

and II of *De doctrina Christiana* (St Petersburg Q.v.I no. 3), Green 1959 argued that they circulated before the work was completed.
34 Sedulius, *Ep. ad Maced.* (Huemer 1885: 172). See briefly, Corcoran 1996: 36–37.
35 Marenbon 2003: 17–42.
36 The prefaces are collected in Glorie 1972: 39–42, 45–47, and 51.
37 The introduction to Mynors 1937 summarises the manuscript evidence.
38 Halporn 2004: 39–42 offers an overview of interpretations.
39 Clement 1985: it is difficult to think of another explanation for the facts there adduced than that it is Gregory's annotation.

Confronted by two texts attributed to the same author, with different end-points, our instinct should be not 'this is a red flag', but 'this is very much in line with what we know of literary publication in antiquity'. Obviously, we do not have firm evidence for the composition process and publication of the *Historia*, beyond the fact that one edition was available in 361, while another went up to 388, and that both are linked to crucial points in Victor's career. Nonetheless, one can easily imagine various scenarios. Victor could have published a first edition in 360, subsequently releasing additional instalments on more recent history, with a second and third tranche of new material, like Livy. He could just as well have released a fully revised and updated new edition *ca.* 388. Agnosticism about Victor's specific publishing arrangements is perhaps wise – we offer one tentative hypothesis in our overall Conclusion – but the fact that his work entered circulation at different points and displays two different terminal dates is very much of a piece with ancient publication practice – it is, if anything, almost the norm for historiographic texts.

Divergences and discrepancies

The *HAb* and the *LB* are very different texts, though (as we have seen) they share a great deal more than first impressions might suggest. We have argued that this divergence – most marked in style – is best explained by the different techniques through which these epitomes were created: excerpting Victor's own words against rewriting them.[40] It is, however, noteworthy that the *HAb* and *LB* are much more similar to each other – including in their wording – from Augustus to Domitian. Thereafter, they diverge rather sharply. In the nineteenth century, when the idea that both texts might be epitomes of a longer work by Victor was still occasionally canvassed, this was regarded as a major argument against it.[41] Yet, far from being impeded by it, the idea of epitomisation actually helps to explain this divergence. The narrative of events from the Julio-Claudians to the Flavians was, as Victor himself tells us (*HAb* 8.7 = *LB* 8.6), relatively concise. Two epitomators working from the same brief work are likely to produce very similar texts, even if they have rather different approaches: there is only so much from which they can select their gleanings. From Nerva onwards, Victor's *History* grew more expansive and discursive: two epitomators with different techniques working from a rather longer text are likely to produce very different abbreviations. Epitomes are also rarely uniform – as we have seen, they generally start expansively and then peter out as the task drags on and the initial impetus fades. The epitomator of the *LB*, Paul the Deacon, seems to have laboured to produce a careful and accurate epitome for the first several chapters, judiciously selecting material from the original and keeping a flavour of its style. Soon, however, his enthusiasm waned, and he began picking out (often fairly random) facts and rewriting them in his own plainer idiom (inspired by Eutropius). Given all this, and contrary to expectations, it is actually remarkable how much the *HAb* and the *LB* share in entries of such brief compass. That undoubtedly has something to do with the fact that independent eyes were likely to be drawn towards the same sections of the lives as

---

40 Chapter III.

41 See *e.g.* Cohn 1884: 23. On nineteenth-century developments in the study of the two works, see Chapter VI.

they tried to crunch the text down: the opening of an emperor's reign (with its details about background) and his obituary, with its waspish judgements on deeds and character.

The *HAb* and the *LB* differ, however, in more ways than mere style. At various points, they seem to offer different, sometimes even mutually exclusive accounts of the same events. These cases are not nearly so numerous as has sometimes been supposed, especially when one takes into account the obscurity of Victor's style and the miserable state of the text of the *Historia abbreviata*. Still, they do exist and at first sight they seem to constitute an objection to the idea that both texts are epitomes of an original source that shared most of its content. Part of an explanation for these divergences might be found in the existence of multiple authorial versions of the *Historia*. If Victor revised his history for a second edition, for example, then it would have been perfectly possible for him to change aspects of his narrative: to reflect new research or reading that he had done, to shift the emphasis in light of later events, or simply because he had changed his mind about something. That would have the effect of making the *LB* diverge from the *HAb* and vice versa. Perhaps the most compelling example of this is *LB* 40.20, on the usurper Domitius Alexander: 'Alexander was Phrygian by birth (*Phryx origine*), timid by nature, and not equal to hardship by the fault of his old age'. That this line must represent roughly an ancient original is guaranteed by its close proximity to the Greek historian Zosimus' assessment of the same man (2.12.13), describing how the purple was bestowed 'on Alexander, Phrygian by birth (Φρυγί τε ὄντι τὸ γένος), timid, soft, unable to endure any hardship, and already very old'. These two are far closer to each other than to the *HAb* (40.17): 'Alexander . . . of feeble old age, gutless, born to rustic Pannonian parents' (*Alexander . . . debili aetate, agrestibus ac Pannonicis parentibus vecordior*).[42] We will discuss the relationship of Victor with the later Greek tradition in Chapters IX and X: here it suffices to note that both the structure of the sentence and the individual detail about Alexander's origins in the *HAb* and *LB* are not compatible with each other. Could this reflect revision?

In most cases, however, dissensions can be chalked up to several other factors, such as Victor's habit of including competing interpretations and variant facts in his original account. This feature of his *Historia* is still occasionally visible in the *Historiae abbreviatae*. For example, for the death of the two Decii, Victor gives two separate versions of events (*HAb* 29.4–5):

> Decii barbaros trans Danubium persectantes Abruti fraude cecidere, exacto regni biennio. Sed Deciorum mortem plerique illustrem ferunt. Namque filium audacius congredientem cecidisse in acie. Patrem autem, cum perculsi milites ad solandum imperatorem multa praefarentur, strenue dixisse detrimentum unius militis parum videri sibi. Ita refecto bello cum impigre decertaret interisse pari modo.

> The Decii, when they were pursuing the barbarians fleeing across the Danube fell by treachery at the Abritus, after a full *biennium* of their rule had been completed. Most men, however, say that the death of the Decii was glorious. For the son fell fighting boldly in the battle line. The father, however, when the soldiers in dismay had first uttered many things to console the emperor, forcefully declared

---

42 The considerable difficulty of construing what the *HAb* says here may suggest that there are deeper textual problems. It cannot be ruled out that the divergence is the result of incompetent epitomisation or perhaps corruption.

that the loss of one soldier seemed to him a trivial matter. So, when battle was rejoined, although he fought vigorously, he perished in the same manner.[43]

Compare *LB* 29.3–4 on the same events:

> [*sc.* Decius] in solo barbarico inter confusas turbas gurgite paludis submersus est, ita ut nec cadaver eius potuerit inveniri. Filius vero eius bello exstinctus est.

> In barbarian territory, in the midst of the chaotic mêlée, Decius sank in the swirls of a swamp, so that not even his corpse could be found. His son was also killed in that war.

Victor gives a simple factual notice of their death (perhaps abbreviated), and then provides what he claims is one popular embellishment of it, from which he distances himself through sustained *oratio obliqua*. Someone using Victor's text could go with either version: it is interesting that Eutropius (9.4) gives only the bare fact, where Ammianus offers the glorious explanation with almost verbatim overlap with the *LB* (31.13.13: *abiectumque in paludem nec emergere potuisse nec inveniri*). These sorts of competing explanations and facts are extremely common in the *Historia Augusta*, for example: if two unlucky scholars were set the task of producing epitomes of that work, it would be extremely likely that they would vary constantly in detail.[44]

Differences might equally be a result of the way that complex discussions were infelicitously epitomised. Consider the origin of the emperor Trajan as an example: the *HAb* places his birth correctly in Italica in Spain (13.1).[45] The *LB* (13.1), by contrast, seems to make it Todi:

> Ulpius Traianus, from the city of Todi (*ex urbe Tudertina*); called Ulpius after his grandfather, named Traianus from Traius, the origin of his father's family, or from the name of Traianus his father; he was emperor for twenty years.

As Syme has pointed out, we have decent epigraphic evidence that the *gens Ulpia* was indeed originally from Todi, where the rare name Traius is also attested.[46] One can easily imagine that in the source of the *HAb* and the *LB* there was a detailed discussion of Trajan's ancestry and birthplace (of the sort often found in the *Historia Augusta*) and that Paul, in producing the *LB,* omitted the information about Italica since he already knew that from Eutropius (8.2.1). So, this could well be an example of a complex narrative reduced into two competing epitomised versions. Indeed, in this particular case, we have confirmation that something like this happened in the fact that *LB* 48.1 makes the Spaniard Theodosius (*genere Hispanus*) a descendant of Trajan, something otherwise at odds with its account of the latter emperor.

---

43 On this difficult passage, see the Appendix, no. VIII.

44 This actually happened in the Middle Ages, where we have a ninth-century abbreviated version of the text up to Alexander Severus (Pal. lat. 866) and a complete abbreviated paraphrase which was probably made in the fifteenth century (the *Excerpta Patavina*; unpublished but for a brief reference see Marshall 1977: 4).

45 *PIR*[2] V.865: of sources before Victor, this information is found only in Appian, *Hisp.* 38.153.

46 Syme 1958: 2.785–786. This seems a much more likely solution than the suggestion in Schlumberger 1974: 81 and n. 22 (following a conjecture by Dierauer) that we should read *Turdetana*, the Turdetani being the local Iberian tribe in whose territory Italica was founded. No Latin source after Livy appears to mention the Turdetani, where *Tudertinus* was a reasonably common word from late antiquity onwards: *e.g.* Gregory the Great, *Dialogi* 1.10 (five times).

The death of the Emperor Titus offers a parallel case. The *Libellus breviatus* clearly states that he died of a fever, *i.e.* from natural causes (*LB* 9.15). This was the standard account, found also in Suetonius (*Tit.* 11) and Eutropius (7.22.1), among many others. The *HAb*, however, alleges poisoning (10.5 *veneno periit*).[47] There is another ancient source that also suggests poison: Philostratus in his *Life of Apollonius of Tyana* (6.32).[48] According to Philostratus, Domitian poisoned his brother Titus with a sea hare. Sea hares are normally considered neither edible nor toxic, but the ancients firmly believed in their toxicity.[49] It is easy to imagine in this case a long source text which discussed the different theories as to Titus' demise. The two epitomators ended up including different accounts in their respective versions of the story. Again, there are hints in the *LB*'s portrait (10.11) of a scheming Domitian, set on the murder of members of his family (*parricidium*), that its source had a more complex version of what had happened.[50]

None of these *prima facie* objections – the different end-points, the divergence in coverage, and the apparent discrepancies of fact in the two texts – are as compelling as they might seem at first glance. They are certainly not sufficient to outweigh the preponderance of evidence we have uncovered, a preponderance that more than warrants us to take the manuscript titles of the two works at face value. Any challenge to the arguments advanced in Part 1 of this book will require a rather different foundation.

Two epitomes

Since our two epitomes both represent a single moment in Victor's reception, future work should pay close attention to their differences. For example, was the *HAb* a pre-existing epitome which the compiler of the *Corpus tripertitum* further trimmed and adapted, or did he work directly from Victor's *History*? The *DVI* is a Livy epitome independent of the *CT* and the *OGR* may well also have already been an epitome before its incorporation. If the *HAb* were derived from a pre-existing epitome, then that might go some way to explaining how it came to be incorporated into a historical compendium, when it is fairly dire as a work of history in its own right. Perhaps the original epitomator had little interest in history *per se*, but rather more use for historical narrative as a bare structure into which he could fit what really commanded his attention: Victor's many and varied opinions, his digressions and judgements? On this theory, the compiler of the *CT* took this text and fitted it to the Procrustean bed of imperial biography. While such a process might explain why the *HAb* is quite so unsatisfactory as it is, we would not claim that it fundamentally misrepresents the character of Victor's *Historia*. After all, of the three extracts from Victor in the *Scholia Vallicelliana*, two are moralising reflections and one of those, on Domitian, occurs in the period covered by the *HAb* but is not contained in it. This gives us independent evidence that this sort of rumination was a significant part of Victor's *History*. Yet the fact that the *Scholia* also include the Commodian months suggests there was quite a bit more actual historical information contained in the original than the *HAb* on its own might indicate.

---

47 On Titus' death, see Bastomsky 1967.
48 Dio 66.26.2 and Herodian 4.5.6 both mention the possibility of foul play, but neither has anything about poison.

49 Costantini 2019: 129–133.
50 *Parricidium* for murder of a brother: *HAb* 20.33, *cf. e.g.* Livy 40.24.6.

There are similar goads to further work in the *LB*. The title tells us explicitly that we should not expect a neutral or general epitome, but one specifically focused on a single category of information: the *vita et mores imperatorum*. It is no surprise, then, that the work is so rich in anecdotes and character sketches, but comparatively poor in the historiographic reflections which are so prominent in the *HAb*. Identifying it as Paul's handiwork might well explain some of its particular historical *foci*. Paul was far removed from the events he was summarising and from the living historiographic traditions of the fourth century. His knowledge depended almost entirely on books and on a relatively restricted number of them: Victor's *Historia*, Eutropius, Jordanes, Orosius, Jerome, and the ecclesiastical historians. Excelling as a summariser and populariser, his stylistic aims – and the expectations of his audience – stand in stark contrast to those of Victor and the compiler of the *HAb*. Hence why a *Libellus breviatus ex libris Sex. Aurelii Victoris* in his *proprio stilo* reads and feels so very different to the lines from the *Victor historiographus* that he quotes in the *Scholia* and whose style we better understand from the *HAb*. There are other ways that the specific context in which Paul worked may be reflected in the text. Consider the role of women, for example. Of all the Roman imperial histories, the *LB* is surely the one which mentions by name the largest number of women in proportion to its length: twenty-seven in its 9,000 words, almost four times as many as in the *HAb* and three times as in the imperial section of Eutropius. Some of them, such as Thermantia, the mother of Theodosius, appear nowhere else. Naming and discussing women was evidently a feature of Victor's *Historia*, even though there is scant evidence for it in the *HAb*.[51] That we can see this only in the *LB* might tell us something about Paul himself: the tutor of Adelperga was perhaps particularly keen to highlight the role of women in his historical narrative. Perhaps the production of the *LB* itself was part of the commission from the duchess: in the earliest manuscript to transmit Paul's letter to her, it comes not before the *Historia Romana* but instead directly preceding the *LB* itself (Bamberg, Msc.Hist.3). These and other aspects of the two epitomes of Victor's work – understood as epitomes – would certainly repay further study.

Let us turn our attention back to Victor himself. As it turns out, Victor's greatest misfortune was not to have survived, but rather to have been *thought* to have survived. Freed from that misconception, he is restored to a central position among the historians of the fourth century. The history of Roman attempts to write history will need to be rebuilt from the ground up – the second part of this study makes a first foray.

---

51 The fact that the *HAb* (33.14) does transmit the name of
    one very obscure woman – Victoria, the mother of the
    Gallic emperor Victorinus – is telling

PART TWO
LATE-ROMAN HISTORIOGRAPHY RECONSIDERED

Hos Victoris Revincit Historia
(Paul the Deacon, *Historia Langobardorum* 2.18)

In some ways, the most remarkable element of Victor's historical work is its date. Looking backwards, it is easy to assimilate the edition of the *Historia* that gave rise to the *HAb* into the general trend of history-writing over the last decades of the fourth century and the first of the fifth: Eutropius, Festus, Jerome, Ammianus, the *Historia Augusta* (perhaps), Rufinus, and Orosius. Such hindsight distorts: when Victor began his work, the landscape of Latin historiography was remarkably barren. On the surface, the tradition of writing history in Latin had lain dormant for two centuries: we have no incontrovertible proof that any work of history was written in Latin between the age of Hadrian and that of Julian. Such evidence we do have falls into three categories:

1. authors about whom we have certain information, but for whose date we have no sure evidence, conjecturally assigned to the period 138–360;
2. hypothesised lost sources for which we have no direct evidence beyond their supposed impact on later texts;
3. texts whose existence or nature is attested only by the *Historia Augusta*.

Let us examine these in turn.

The first category is very diverse, but broadly falls into two groups: those who certainly wrote history, or something like it, and those who may never have composed anything strictly historical at all. Granius Licinianus was certainly a historian, as the surviving fragments of his work in a palimpsested manuscript of the fifth century attest.[1] He could, however, have written at any date before that manuscript: the consensus that he belongs to the age of Hadrian or the Antonines, though by no means implausible, has only rather thin evidence in its support.[2] Ampelius, if one can consider his jejune *Liber memorialis* a work of historiography, has been dated to the late second century, largely because the name of his dedicatee is Macrinus, identified with the future emperor.[3] This is dubious: Macrinus was a rather

---

1 London, BL Add. MS 17212 (*CLA* 2.167).
2 See Criniti 1993: 151–153. Besides a general resemblance to Florus, the case for the date really rests on the idea that 28.13 refers to Hadrian's dedication of the temple of Jupiter Capitolinus at Athens in 131/132. Yet, the text – <*a*>*edes nobilissima Olympi Iovis Atheniensis diu inperfecta permane | |* – is at best suggestive.

3 Arnaud-Lindet 1993: xxi–xxii, xvii–xx, who accepts the identification and date (with references to earlier work), *cf. eadem* 1997. It is perhaps not reassuring that the *terminus post quem* she advances (66) is also based on Hadrian's building work at Athens.

common cognomen and there are numerous stylistic and intellectual reasons to prefer a considerably later date.[4] The quotation of Aemilius Sura's *De annis populi Romani* at Velleius 1.6.6 has occasionally been considered an interpolation and therefore hypothetically assigned to our period, but the date is nothing more than supposition standing on a supposition.[5] Sidonius mentions a Juventius Martialis as a historian who wrote about Julius Caesar, alongside Livy, Suetonius, and Balbus (*Ep.* 9.14.7).[6] Bardon put him in the Antonine period but again there is no evidence for the date.[7] The order of historians in Sidonius' letter – Martialis is listed after Suetonius but before Balbus, Caesar's contemporary – implies nothing.

Then there are those whose claim to be historians – let alone historians writing between Hadrian and the 360s – is still weaker. We know that Fronto *planned to write* a history of Verus' Parthian war, but we have every reason to believe that he never actually wrote it.[8] The magnificent *Fragments of the Roman Historians* cautiously lists several others whom it does not consider historians, but who might or actually have been held to be such – they are even more dubious.[9] Antonius (Antoninus in the MS) Julianus is cited as an authority on the Jews by Minucius Felix (*Oct.* 33.4), along with Josephus.[10] An Antonius Julianus was in Titus' *consilium* at the fall of Jerusalem (*BJ* 6.236–238) – he could be Minucius' Antoni[n]us, but Gellius mentions a Spanish rhetor of the same name (*NA* 15.1), so some have preferred a second-century date. One Pescennius Festus is quoted by Lactantius (*DI* 1.21.13) on child sacrifice at Carthage, and he has been identified with an aristocrat killed in 197 by Septimius Severus (*HA Sev.* 13.6).[11] Not only does this identification depend on the *HA*, but he was in any case probably more an antiquarian than a historian: Lactantius cites his work as the *historia per saturam*. Someone named simply Valens is cited by John the Lydian (*De Mens.* 4.102) for the meaning of the name Caesar, from a work he calls the τὰ Καίσαρος.[12] We obviously have no way of dating or determining the nature of this work, and the only reason he has been assigned to our period is that a Statius Valens appears as a source for the life of Trajan in *HA Alex.* 48.6.

This is a miserable body of evidence, and so it is no wonder that scholarship has attempted to bulk out the slim record of historical writing in this period by positing lost sources: our second category. These are of different sorts: for example, the *Origo Constantini Imperatoris* in its surviving form must absolutely date from after Orosius, but that has not stopped scholars from suggesting that it derives from an *Ur-Origo* which was written in the late 330s.[13] The sound historical information in the lives up to Alexander Severus in the *Historia Augusta* was attributed by Sir Ronald Syme to a reliable biographical source written perhaps in the 230s who is never named or quoted: he has been lumbered with the sobriquet Ignotus.[14] The most famous of all the hypothesised lost sources, however, is the *Kaisergeschichte* of Alexander Enmann: a terse and scrappy summary of imperial history down to either 337 or 357, which has allegedly left extensive evidence in our surviving historical texts. As we shall show, this (extremely popular) hypothesis

---

4 Macrinus: Lőrincz 2000: 43 (Aßmann 1940: 213–214 was right to be sceptical). Date: Aßmann 1940: esp. 213–221 opted for the fourth century, with some very persuasive arguments (linguistic, stylistic, rhythmical) against an earlier date. *cf.* Holford-Strevens 1995 (an implicit but persuasive case for a later date).
5 See in general *FRH* 103 (Levick).
6 *FRH* 106 (Levick).
7 Bardon 1952–1956: 2.206.

8 Briefly, see Champlin 1980: 115–116, 141–142.
9 Cornell 2013: 1.629–649.
10 *FRH* A5 (Levick).
11 *FRH* A30 (Levick).
12 *FRH* A38 (Levick).
13 See Stover and Woudhuysen 2021: 152 and n. 8; and see Chapter X.
14 See Chapter VII.

was produced at a particular time, under the influence of specific historical and intellectual traditions: it is sorely in need of a reassessment.[15] In any case, the identification of the *Historia* of Aurelius Victor has profound ramifications for our understanding of all of these hypothetical sources.

The final category is that of works for whose existence or nature we are dependent on the *Historia Augusta*. Most of these phantoms – from Junius Cordus to Fabius Marcellinus – have been (rightly) exorcised – the *Fragments of the Roman Historians* makes a real advance on previous collections by regarding (almost) all of them as pure invention.[16] Even so, the shadow of the *HA* remains. As we have seen, historical figures known only from the text have been used to anchor undated historians in our period. At the same time, Syme's Ignotus derives entirely from the *HA*, which was also crucial to Enmann's hypothesis of the *Kaisergeschichte*. The most influential *HA* historian, however, is Marius Maximus. As we discuss in Chapter VII, *a* Marius Maximus was certainly a real person and *a* Marius Maximus was certainly a real author. He belongs in the third category, however, since it is only from the *HA* that we think these two Marii Maximi are the same and consider him a writer of imperial biography. There are reasons to be dubious about Marius Maximus the 'consular biographer'.

The result of this brief survey is a stark conclusion: we have almost no evidence that history was written in Latin after Hadrian's day and before Victor's. It is the combination of the absence of any extant works of history and the absence of any sure *testimonia* to historians that makes the period from *ca.* 138 to 360 so distinctive, contrasts it so sharply to the other periods of Roman history from which we have little surviving historiography. While we cannot read any historical texts from before Sallust in full, we do have a vast roster of Republican annalists and historians who can be securely placed and dated.[17] The same is true of the fifth century AD. While few historical works from it survive entire, we have very good evidence for a number of active historians, recently surveyed by Van Hoof and Van Nuffelen.[18] The third century is, of course, famous for its lack of Latin literature, but the lacuna in Latin historiography is both greater in duration and more total in extent than in any other genre: no works, no names, no titles.

Because the nature and importance of Victor's *Historia* have been generally misunderstood, it has not been recognised quite how revolutionary it was for Victor to write history. The possibility that his work might have inaugurated and inspired a revival of Latin historiography has scarcely been considered. In the second part of this study, we attempt a first foray into the impact of the discovery of Victor's *Historia* on our understanding of the historical works of late antiquity and their relation to one another.

We do this by surveying briskly the modern history of later-Roman historiography, from the time that Victor first appeared in print in the sixteenth century up to the present day. In Chapter VI, we begin by considering the developing awareness of the links between the various extant texts. We examine how these links became interpreted as evidence not of the impact of Victor's *Historia* but of that of a lost *Kaisergeschichte* (*KG*), similar to Eutropius in scope and style, if slightly fuller in detail. In Chapter VII,

15 Chapter VI.
16 Cornell 2013: 1.650–651.
17 As the rich entries in Cornell 2013 demonstrate.
18 Van Hoof and Van Nuffelen 2020a.

we begin to look at the question of the *Quellenforschung* of the *Historia Augusta* and particularly its earlier lives. Through twentieth-century scholarship a consensus has emerged that these depend on a supposed third-century imperial biographer, Marius Maximus, in conjunction (in some accounts) with another unknown biographer of roughly the same date, Ignotus – we show how ill-founded the case for these shadowy authors is. In Chapter VIII, we approach the *Historia Augusta* itself and show just how deep its debt to Victor is, concluding with a new theory on why a text written by one author after 370 purports to be written by six authors before 330. In Chapter IX, we pursue more deeply the question of Ammianus Marcellinus' relationship to Victor, and consider how to approach the resonances between Ammianus, later Greek histories, and the *Libellus breviatus*. Far from being a reflection of the lost *Annales* of Nicomachus Flavianus – a theory that has gained increasing traction in some circles in the past few decades – these resonances are better explained by Victor's *Historia*. In Chapter X, we show that Victor's influence extended beyond Latin authors, with distant echoes of his work still to be discerned across the whole breadth of the later Byzantine historiographical tradition. We then show that two orphan works of history in Latin are actually dependent on Victor. In the Conclusion, we offer a brief consideration of Victor as a historian, offering a first hypothesis on the structure of his work and its relation to his project.

A new star changes the whole constellation. Identifying a new source, as we have done in the first part of this study, requires us to reanalyse what we think we know about all of our other sources and their relationships to one another. We present here a model of what that might look like, without asserting that it is the only one possible. What is clear is that Victor's *Historia* requires the history of writing history in Latin be entirely reconsidered.

CHAPTER VI

ENMANN AND THE *KAISERGESCHICHTE*

On the face of it, what we have presented in Part 1 of this book is a very new theory, one radically at odds with how both the *Historiae abbreviatae* and the *Libellus breviatus* are treated in the scholarly literature, down to the very titles by which we refer to them. It might then come as a surprise to learn that an enthusiast for Roman history who picked up the latest edition of Victor's *HAb* in 1681 would have found this written in the preface:

> One matter, dear reader, could give rise to a scruple: namely why, if Aurelius Victor lived under Arcadius and Honorius, he did not go beyond Julian in his lives of the Caesars. Many reasons could be adduced as to why Aurelius Victor stopped his work with Julian. Perhaps he did not so much omit the lives of the remaining emperors, as reserve them for grander craftsmanship in writing (*ad maiorem scribendi diligentiam*), as Eutropius writes about himself. In order to say what I actually think, I believe that the little book on the Caesars was once more expansive (*auctiorem*), and included the life of Theodosius. But a little while later, in almost the same period, someone made an Epitome [*i.e.* the *LB*], either for his own use or for circulation, from this book and others, including Suetonius, Eutropius, and Ammianus, and it came to pass that the little book on the Caesars was gradually neglected and came into people's hands disfigured by many errors and even mutilated of part of it. This unjust fate many authors have experienced at the hands of their abbreviators, Trogus Pompeius, for example, at the hands of Justin, and Livy, at the hands of Florus.[1]

Such was the judgement of Anne Le Fèvre, better known as Madame Dacier. In the top tier of classical scholars of her day (and still under-appreciated), she produced a string of editions of Latin texts *Ad usum Delphini* in the decade from 1674 to 1683, including (besides Victor) Florus, Dictys, and Eutropius.[2] Her edition of the *HAb* appeared almost exactly a century after the text was first published by Schott in 1579: her theory about the *De Caesaribus* – important because she regarded Victor as an *optimus historicus*, better than Florus or Eutropius – shows just how rapidly scholars came to understand that something was amiss in Victor's text and began to work towards the theory we have demonstrated in the first part of this study. The crucial question this raises is why classical scholarship abandoned this approach.

---

1 Dacier 1681: *praef.*: *Illud tibi, lector, scrupulum movere possit, cur si Aurelius Victor sub Arcadio et Honorio vixerit, idem in Caesarum vitis ultra Julianum non pergat : verum multa etiam in causa esse potuerunt, cur Aur. Victor in Juliano operi suo modum dederit. Nam fortasse reliquorum imperatorum vitas non tam praetermisit, quam eas ad majorem scribendi diligentiam reservavit, quod de se scribit Eutropius. Ut vere dicam quod sentio, libellum de Caesaribus auctiorem olim fuisse reor, et Theodosi vitam amplexum. Sed paulo post quum aliquis* ejusdem fere ætatis ex hoc libello, et aliis nempe Suetonio, Eutropio, Ammiano, Epitomem, vel in sui ipsius, vel in aliorum usum texuisset, ita factum esse ut libellus de Caesaribus paulatim neglectus in manus hominum venerit, et multis mendis inquinatus, et parte sui etiam mutilus. Hanc iniquam sortem per Abbreviatores suos multi alii experti sunt, ut Trogus Pompeius per Justinum, Livius per Florum.*

2 On Dacier's life and work, see Farnham 1976.

193

In this chapter, we follow the trail of Victor's reception – and that of his fellow fourth-century Latin historians – from the seventeenth century to the end of the nineteenth. We show how the idea of the Victorine texts as epitomes was both widespread and never properly refuted. We then investigate the development of the standard model of late ancient historiography in Latin in the later nineteenth century, with a particular focus on two monuments in the history of scholarship. The first of these is Alexander Enmann's theory of a lost imperial history, a *Kaisergeschichte* (*KG*), which supposedly underlies our extant texts, from Victor to the *Historia Augusta*.[3] The second is Hermann Dessau's masterful demonstration that the *HA* is not what it purports to be – the work of six authors writing under Diocletian and Constantine – but the composition of a single individual active as much as a century later. These two theories are the bedrock on which twentieth- and twenty-first-century scholarship on the secular Latin historiographic tradition of the fourth century has been built. Yet, as we will show, they are far from compatible with each other. We will then demonstrate that there are fundamental flaws in Enmann's theory of the *Kaisergeschichte*, both in its original formulation and in more recent adaptations. Insofar as Enmann had identified a real problem in the textual relationship(s) between the *HAb*, the *HA*, and Eutropius, the solution lies in Victor's *Historia*.

In 1627, Gerrit Vos (Gerardus Vossius) published his *De historicis Latinis libri tres*, a bold attempt to synthesise all that was then known of the Latin historians. It was also the first major study of Latin historiography *in toto* to appear after Schott's publication of the *Historiae abbreviatae* in 1579. In it, Vossius introduced the adventurous idea that there was not one, but rather three historians named Aurelius Victor.[4] The first was Aurelius Victor Primus, cited by the *HA* at *Macr.* 4.2, who must have been active before the time of Diocletian.[5] The second was Sextus Aurelius Victor Afer, who was the author of the *De Caesaribus* (what we call the *HAb*) and the *De viris illustribus*. This Victor was the one mentioned by Ammianus, wrongly identified by Vossius with the consul of 369 who shared the honour with the two-year-old son of Valens, Valentinian Galates.[6] Finally, there was Sextus Aurelius Victor, the historian who was urban prefect under Theodosius, and the author of the *Epitome* (our *LB*). Vossius was a very fine scholar, but this was not his finest moment: while we might forgive him for stepping into the *HA*'s snare and misidentifying the consul of 369, overlooking the fact that Ammianus' Victor was later urban prefect is a serious blunder. So, in 1669 Martinus Hankius proposed a new theory: the author of the *LB* was not in fact named Sextus Aurelius Victor at all; rather, this was a scribal error.[7] Originally, he suggested, the title of the *LB* listed a string of authors, the first of whom was Victor, *i.e. breviatus ex libris Sex. Aurelii Victoris, Suetonii, Eutropii*

---

3 Throughout, we refer to the *Kaisergeschichte* by the abbreviation *KG* – in the scholarship, *EKG* (= *Enmannische Kaisergeschichte*) is also found, often for something rather far removed from Enmann's ideas.

4 Vossius 1627: 183–184 (2.8) and 207–208 (2.15).

5 See Chapter V: Vossius read *Primus* for *Pinius*, as was common in editions of the *HA* from the *editio princeps*.

6 The consul named Victor in that year was actually the Sarmatian *magister equitum* (*PLRE* 'Victor 4').

7 Hankius 1669: 304–305 (1.2.5.1).

etc. The other names were excised to produce the manuscript attribution as we have it.[8] Both Vossius' and Hankius' theories found adherents over the next two centuries: indeed one, can still find references to *Victor iunior*, *Victor alter*, and *Victor Schotti*, even in such authors as Gibbon, all the way up to the 1860s.[9]

Amidst these rather haphazard attempts to systematise the evidence, there remained some more interesting approaches: the work of those who simply read the two texts and offered their opinion, even if they had not made a systematic inquiry. One student in Altdorf, named Wilhelm Bechmann, composed a short *disputatio* on Victor in 1685. Dacier's Paris edition seems not to have yet made it to Altdorf – Bechmann does not include it in his otherwise comprehensive list of editions – but his feeling from reading the texts was not so different from hers:

> The fourth text usually attributed to our Victor [the *LB*] certainly, as present opinion goes, did not issue from him, but was excerpted by someone – whoever he was – from a book of the sort that Sex. Aurelius Victor wrote on the Caesars, with the idiosyncratic character of its diction (it was written earlier on the same subject at greater length), which perished, along with many other volumes of ancient writers, through the depredations of time.[10]

In the middle of the eighteenth century, in his vast history of the ages of the Latin language, Johann Funck makes much the same point (with reference to Hankius), albeit with a broader knowledge of the manuscript titles afforded both the *LB* and the *HAb*:

> To state my opinion candidly: *Sexti Aurelii Victoris* [in the title of the *LB*] does not designate the author of this little book, but rather the writer of the longer book, from which it was drawn and excerpted, just as the epitomes of Livy and Trogus Pompeius acknowledge very different authors, such that we search in vain for another author of the same name. Let him be whosoever he was: he gives us an epitome of Victor, from that larger work, which has perished through the depredations of time, and of which Victor himself has left behind a more abbreviated history. This is clear enough from its title in the old manuscripts.[11]

---

8 This theory has been defended in recent years: see Chapter II above. It also seems to partially underlie Dacier's theory of the *LB* outlined above.

9 Gibbon, *Decline and Fall* ch. 18, n. 90 (ed. Womersley 1994: 1.681): 'the elder Victor'; and, *e.g.*, Görres 1868: 7, with a careful delineation of 'Victor senior' in the 350s and 'Victor iunior' in the 390s.

10 Bechmann 1726: 11: Quartum *Victori nostro adiungi solitum* Scriptum, *non quidem, uti nunc habetur, ab ipso illo profectum est, ab aliquo tamen, quisquis etiam ille fuerit, ex libro ejusmodi excerptum, qualem* Sex. Aurel. Victor *de Caesaribus, peculiari dicendi charactere, & majori ac prior de iisdem conscriptus erat amplitudine exaravit, qui tamen cum aliis multis veterum Scriptorum voluminibus injuria temporum periit.* We have done our best with the Latin here, but it seems likely that there is some error in the text (perhaps *enim* for &). It is not totally clear whether Bechmann or his professor Daniel Moller actually wrote this disputation. In 1874, Richard Jakobi pointed out that another disputation under Moller from two years later, credited to one Johan Jakob Sturm (1687), makes reference to

Disp. mea de Sex. Aur. Victore, which would seem to imply that Moller wrote both disputations (Jacobi 1874: 4–5). However, the *BnF* online catalogue (http://www.gallica.bnf.fr/) lists a total of 100 disputations submitted to Moller, on a stunning variety of subjects. Since they tend to be shorter than twenty pages, it is possible that he wrote all of them, but it seems more likely that Moller added the reference before publication, and the *mea* refers to the fact the *disputatio* was done under his supervision.

11 Funck 1744: 741–742: *Vti vero, quid sentiam, ingenue fatear, Sexti Aurelii Victoris, illius libelli non auctorem designat, sed eum operis diffusioris scriptorem, vnde fuerit haustus atque decerptus; quemadmodum Liuii, et Trogi Pompeii epitomae diuersos longe auctores agnoscunt: vt frustra de alio eiusdem nominis scriptore laboremus. Esto, quisquis ille fuerit: epitomen exhibet Victoris, ex illo maiori opere, quod temporum iniuria periit, et cuius ipse historiam magis abbreuiatam reliquit. Satis clara in veteribus libris inscriptio.* We have reproduced the curious inconsistency of *v/u* in the original.

What Funck makes clear is that, in his view, both works were epitomes of Victor. The difference was only that the *HAb* was made by Victor himself, while the *LB* was produced by someone else. The same essential notion was mooted in a footnote by Hermann Ulrici in his 1833 study of ancient historiography:

> On Sextus Aurelius Victor we have preferred to remain silent . . . That the book *De Caesaribus* and its so-called *Epitome* are both excerpts of one and the same older work made by different hands is very clear, when one sees how some things in both writings correspond verbally, while quite a few others are contained in the *Epitome*, which the main work does not have at all . . . Furthermore, these writings are not history, but a collection of historical notes. The same applies to Eutropius . . .[12]

Both *HAb* and *LB* were, for Ulrici, epitomes and both were derived from one and the same prior work, since sometimes they agree word for word and sometimes the *LB* has material that the *HAb* does not. Once again, however, one gets the sense that this is only an instinctive feeling. Even so, the instinctive feelings of a scholar who had really mastered vast swaths of ancient historiography should carry some weight, or at least push us to question our own assumptions where they differ.

Opitz and Cohn

After these relatively perfunctory treatments, the Victor question suddenly exploded into scholarly controversy in 1872. The spark was provided by a twenty-one-year-old at Leipzig named Moritz Theodor Opitz, a student of Friedrich Ritschl, who obtained *summi in philosophia honores* in the summer of that year with a dissertation entitled 'Quaestiones de Sex. Aurelio Victore'.[13] Making connections with a range of eminent scholars – including Ludwig Jeep, Eduard Wölfflin, and Friedrich Nietzsche – to obtain manuscript collations and advice, Opitz looked at the whole subject of Victor with fresh eyes and from the ground up.[14] This study afforded him a crucial insight:

> The book *De Caesaribus*, which survives to this day, does not seem to be the history of the Caesars written by Sex. Aurelius Victor, but rather both the *Caesares* and the first eleven chapters of the *Epitome* were excerpted from that work.[15]

Most of Opitz's study is dedicated to a chapter-by-chapter analysis of the two texts, where he highlights the constant breaks in sense and *non sequiturs* of the *HAb*, and (at least for the first eleven chapters) the

12 Ulrici 1833: 156–157 n.: 'Von Sextus Aurelius Victor haben wir es vorgezogen zu schweigen . . . daß aber das Buch de Caesaribus und dessen s.g. Epitome beides Excerpte aus einem und demselben älteren Werke von verschiedenen Händen verfertigt sind, ist ziemlich deutlich, wenn man sieht, wie Einiges in beiden Schriften wörtlich übereinstimmt, Anderes und nicht weniges in der Epitome enthalten ist, was das Hauptwerk gar nicht hat . . . Außerdem sind diese Schriften keine Geschichte zu nennen, sondern eine Sammlung von historischen Notizen. Dasselbe gilt von Eutropius . . .'. For some

perceptive comments on Ulrici, see Momigliano 1946: 163.

13 Opitz's dissertation was completed in 1872 and published in part in that year by Teubner; in 1874 a fuller publication followed in the *Acta Societatis Philologae Lipsiensis* (edited by Ritschl). Throughout, we refer to the extended 1874 version.

14 Opitz 1874: 199–200.

15 Opitz 1874: 210: *Is liber de Caesaribus, qui nunc superstes est, non videtur esse historia Caesarum a Sex. Aurelio Victore conscripta, sed potius et Caesares et Epitomae capita XI priora ex illa excerpta sunt.*

complementarity between it and the *LB*. For the rest of the *LB*, Opitz held (like most contemporary scholars) that it drew on a range of others sources, which he identified as Marius Maximus and Eutropius for Nerva to Elagabalus (*cc.* 12–23), an unknown source and Eutropius for Alexander Severus to Carinus (*cc.* 24–38), and Ammianus Marcellinus, with a (hypothetical) continuator, for Diocletian to Theodosius (*cc.* 39–48).[16] As a hypothesis, strictly speaking, he then makes the final suggestion that all the chapters from *LB* 12–48 could in fact derive from Ammianus, who began his history with Nerva, even though the first fourteen books, which treated the emperors before Constantius II, are lost.[17] Hence, he suggested, the whole of the *LB* could perhaps just be explained as the combination of Victor and Ammianus. This is a seductive theory, which has the virtue of actually trying to account for why the constant correspondences between the *HAb* and the *LB* apparently break off after chapter 11. It has, however, two major weaknesses: that it needs to conjure up a continuator of Ammianus to make sense of the relationship between the texts, and that it can only explain the correspondences between the *LB* and *HAb* after Nerva by recourse to a common source.

Opitz's work did not pass unnoticed. Two other scholars, Ludwig Jeep and Eduard Wölfflin, had evidently both already been engaged in working on the Victor problem. The appearance of Opitz's dissertation gave them the impetus to publish their findings. Jeep, who had written a dissertation (on Claudian) at Leipzig in 1869 and was a teacher at the prestigious Thomasschule in the same city, got his work out the next year in 1873.[18] He argued that Victor had in fact written *two* works of history, the *Historia abbreviata* we have now, and then, decades later in Rome, a much longer history of the emperors from Augustus to Theodosius, which was epitomised to produce our *LB*.[19] In 1874, a more penetrating study by Wölfflin, professor of Latin at Zurich, appeared.[20] He supported Opitz's theory almost entirely, with one additional wrinkle: that the compiler of the *Epitome* had himself contaminated Victor's original in the first eleven chapters with Suetonian material, which is why the pronounced Sallustian character of the *HAb* is missing from the *LB*.[21] Along the way Jeep and Wölfflin touch on many of the points we have developed in this study, although generally in an off-hand fashion. Jeep, for example, wondered whether Ammianus' epithet *scriptor historicus* implies that Victor must have written something more substantial than the *HAb*.[22] Wölfflin demonstrated, to a degree never before seen, the literary characteristics of Victor's style and his constant imitation of Sallust and Tacitus.[23] Along the way, he also showed just how much *less classical* the diction of the *LB* is.[24] The fact that two established figures of classical scholarship in the German-speaking world had thrown their weight behind Opitz's position was not insignificant. An 1888 Marburg dissertation on Tacitus, for example, could state baldly that Victor's works on the emperors were handed down to posterity as excerpts in the *De Caesaribus* and the *Epitome*, citing Wölfflin, as well as Opitz. [25]

---

16 Opitz 1874: 228, 229, 243, 245, 254, 260.

17 Opitz 1874: 265.

18 Jeep 1873. On Jeep, see Tolkiehn 1913 – he married Ida Warburg (from a minor branch of the famous Hamburg family) and went on to be a professor at Königsberg.

19 Jeep 1873, summary at 513–514.

20 On Wölfflin, see Dill 2013. Wölfflin would soon move to Erlangen and then to Munich, where he would inaugurate the *Thesaurus Linguae Latinae*.

21 Wölfflin 1874: 283 (a warm endorsement of Opitz) and 294–299 (Suetonius in the *LB*)

22 Jeep 1873: 511.

23 Wölfflin 1874: 285–288 (Sallust), 302–308 (Tacitus).

24 Wölfflin 1874: 292–293, *cf.* Wölfflin 1902, which reaches much the same conclusion.

25 Cornelius 1888: 22.

This apparent consensus – that both works were connected to Victor and that the title of the *LB* was a reliable indicator of its nature – did not last long. In 1884, a little over a decade after Opitz's work, Arthur Cohn – another young scholar and a student of Mommsen – obtained his doctorate at Berlin with a *dissertatio inauguralis* on the sources of Aurelius Victor (*i.e.* the *HAb*) and the first eleven chapters of the *LB*.[26] Cohn argued that not only were neither the *HAb* nor the *LB* epitomes of larger works, they were not even related to each other.[27] Instead, their shared material in the first eleven chapters was explained by the fact that they were both drawing on a now lost work: a *Suetonius auctus*, that is, a text of Suetonius enriched with additional materials.[28] Cohn made his case with some vigour: 'Therefore all those careful constructs, built on the weakest of foundations by learned men, crash to ruin'.[29]

Cohn's work has its virtues: it is rigorously comparative, for example, and really does attempt (for the first time) a systematic analysis of the sources of the texts (in its fourth and seventh chapters). What concerns us here, however, is Cohn's attempt to demolish the idea that either Victorine text is a condensation of a longer original: ultimately, this is very far from convincing. While he offers a number of arguments, at their base lies a series of ideas about the nature of the genre of condensed texts. He sets these out with high-flown rhetoric:

> For if it is inquired whether the book [the *HAb*] is whole or not, I think that the most certain evidence – than which there can be nothing more trustworthy – is the book itself, of which those learned men [Opitz and Wölfflin] have an insufficient understanding. But if in this there appear clearly defined clues that the book is complete – that is, if we are taught about the life of the author to whom it is attributed, if a great number of opinions appear, if the author makes judgements – certainly no one will consider that that book has been excerpted.[30]

When Cohn was writing, Latin epitomes were an even more obscure topic than they are today. So, unlike those whose work he attacked, his thesis really did rest on 'the weakest of foundations'. His argument here is simple nonsense. If the original contained such material and the method of condensation was to extract whole sentences, then of course an epitome might have all these features: that was the point.[31] In no way do any of the items listed by Cohn guarantee that a book was not excerpted. If they did, we would have to think that Xiphilinus authored Book LXXIV of Dio, for example, since it contains all of those features.[32]

Most of Cohn's other objections cannot withstand rigorous scrutiny. He dismissed the evidence of the manuscript titles as worthless, 'interpolated by some scribe (*librarius*)' – an attitude to *tituli* which would not stand today and which is demonstrably wrong in this case.[33] Similarly, he claimed that *abbreviata*

26 Cohn 1884. There is a brief *vita* of him at the end of the dissertation.
27 Cohn 1884: 14–26.
28 Cohn 1884: 26–37 (*LB* using *Suetonius auctus*), 54–57 (Victor using the same); 59 offers a useful diagram of the source relationships as Cohn saw them.
29 Cohn 1884: 26: *corruunt igitur omnia illa artificia a viris doctis in fundamento debilissimo exstructa.*
30 Cohn 1884: 16: *Nam si quaeritur, utrum liber integer sit necne, certissimum testem, quo locupletiorem nullum existere*

posse credo, libellum ipsum, cuius illi viri doctissimi parum rationem habuerunt, esse puto. Quodsi in hoc expressa apparent vestigia, librum integrum esse – id est, si de vita scriptoris, cui tribuitur, instruimur, si sententiarum occurrit multitudo, si auctor iudicia facit ; – certe nemo librum excerptum ducet.
31 Chapter III.
32 74.5.2–3: favourable judgement of Pertinax (with details); 12.2, personal anecdote (with first-person verbs).
33 Cohn 1884: 9 and n. 10. Chapter II.

in a title was generally just equivalent to *breviarium*, which is (as we have seen) untrue.[34] Cohn simply denied that the *HAb* showed traces of the verbal and intellectual disorder that epitomisation would produce, claiming that in contrast numerous examples could be detected in the *LB*.[35] This is the opposite of the truth: the *HAb* is extremely hard to understand, every page showing evidence of clumsy excisions, where the *LB*, whatever its faults, is generally a smooth and easy read.[36] Cohn also argued that the *HAb* and *LB* are works of a very different character, as though that proved they could not be epitomes.[37] Yet every difference of style, of selection, and of interest between the two summaries of Victor's work can be paralleled in other epitomes of other works produced in late antiquity: the *HAb* is an epitome like that of Julius Paris, consisting of extracts cut out of the original but left internally intact, while the *LB* is like that of Januarius Nepotianus, constantly reworded and sometimes intermixed with material from other sources.[38] Of course, as a result the *HAb* is littered with personal judgements and *sententiae*, where the *LB* is more staid and less full of character, but that is simply irrelevant to the question of whether they are condensed texts. Cohn's attempt to explain the overlap between the *HAb* and the *LB* is also simply impossible on statistical grounds. When two texts overlap because they share a common source, the lower limit of the size of that common source can be calculated. In the first eleven chapters, the *HAb* and the *LB* share 635 words out of 2,750 and 2,600 words, respectively. Their common source must thus have been a work that consisted of at least 11,260 words and was probably not much longer than 20,000 – a quarter of the length of Suetonius. There is simply no way, statistically speaking, that these two texts were independently derived from a work that was even longer than Suetonius, that is, a *Suetonius auctus*.

Cohn's argument is thus fundamentally flawed – based on a series of misconceptions about the core question it set out to tackle. Even so, it would take us far afield to trace the contours of this debate in its entirety: the points Jeep makes against Opitz, the arguments Wölfflin deploys against Jeep, the objections Cohn raises to all three. This exercise, while useful and instructive, would have a primarily antiquarian interest: none of these scholars actually proposed the theory that we advance here, nor do they have any contemporary disciples.[39] This is because the debate was undercut almost as soon as it began. In 1884, a work was published which would go on to the lay the foundation for the next thirteen decades of scholarship on Victor and late Roman Latin historiography more generally: Alexander Enmann's *Eine verlorene Geschichte der römischen Kaiser und das Buch De viris illustribus urbis Romae* (1884). The subtitle is instructive: *Quellenstudien*.

---

34 Cohn 1884: 9–10. Chapters II and III.
35 Cohn 1884: 18–19, 25.
36 Chapter IV.
37 Cohn 1884: 14–18.
38 On Paris and Nepotianus, both epitomators of Valerius Maximus, see Chapter III.
39 This is not to say that cognate ideas have not occasionally been mooted: Tarrant and Reeve in *T&T* ('*De viris illustribus*'), for example, could say simply about the *HAb*: 'It may of course be either the original or an adaptation by the compiler. A work that too simply proclaims itself

an epitome of the original, *Libellus de vita et moribus imperatorum breviatus ex libris Sexti Aurelii Victoris,* survives in about twenty manuscripts' (149). Baker briefly entertains this idea, citing Tarrant and Reeve, and gives some references to scholarship on Victor before Enmann (2014: 91–92). His subsequent analysis, however, conducted in the service of the idea that the *HA* was Victor's source, assumes throughout the identity between Victor's work and the *HAb*, with some possible 'interpolation' by the compiler of the *CT* (see especially 101).

Alexander Enmann

The 1870s were an exciting time in the University of Dorpat, present-day Tartu, Estonia. Though then located in Russian Livonia, 400 miles north-east of Königsberg, the university was a central part of the German intellectual landscape. At the time, Dorpat's leading light was the theologian Theodosius Harnack (d. 1889), a moderate Lutheran, and specialist in liturgy, with an extraordinary family. He had four sons: one would become a famous mathematician, another a chemist, and a third a literary historian.[40] More famous than all of these, however, was the son who followed in his father's intellectual footsteps: Adolf von Harnack (1851–1930), who studied theology in Dorpat from 1869 to 1872, before moving on to Leipzig.[41] There, in 1873, he completed his doctorate, really the fruit of his time at Dorpat and dedicated to his father. His dissertation investigated the sources for ancient Gnosticism: *Zur Quellenkritik der Geschichte des Gnosticismus*.[42] Harnack argued that the earliest detailed source for Gnostic thought, Justin Martyr's *Syntagma against all heresies* (Σύνταγμα κατὰ πασῶν τῶν γεγενημένων αἱρέσεων), though lost, could be partially reconstructed through a minute comparison of parallel passages in later sources, such as Tertullian and Irenaeus of Lyons.[43] This was very much of a piece with cutting-edge theological scholarship of the day, in which the intellectual energies of liberal and moderate Protestant circles were devoted above all to *Quellenkritik* of the New Testament.[44] It was in 1863 that Holtzmann published his *Die synoptischen Evangelien: ihr Ursprung und geschichtlicher Charakter* at Leipzig, which set forth in influential and definitive terms the two-source hypothesis for the synoptic Gospels, *i.e.* that Mark's Gospel was prior to Matthew and Luke, and that it, along with an unknown *Quelle* (later dubbed Q) consisting of Christ's sayings, was their source. Adolf von Harnack would himself in 1907 publish at Leipzig a reconstruction of this Q: *Sprüche und Reden Jesu: die Zweite Quelle des Matthäus und Lukas*. These were heady notions, particularly seductive in an intellectual world where philology reigned supreme and there was general confidence that sound *Methode* would give historical studies the kind of certain knowledge available in mathematics and physics, that what had been lost in the messy and complicated process of transmission could be recovered through scientific scholarship. It was inevitable that such methods would also be applied to ancient historical texts. Biblical studies, theology, and Church history, on the one hand, and classical studies and ancient history, on the other, were not in separate siloes, as they are today.[45] Harnack himself engaged deeply with the Roman world to understand the rise of Christianity and exchanged a series of letters with the greatest Roman historian of his day, Theodor Mommsen.[46]

Dorpat was an important centre for the study of ancient history, so it is hardly surprising to see source-criticism also occupying a place of prime importance there. In 1872, Franz Rühl came to Dorpat from Leipzig, bringing with him a specialism in the *Quellenkritik* of Plutarch, the subject of his 1867 Marburg dissertation. His new project was on Justin, the epitomator of Trogus (whose medieval reception

---

40 On Theodosius, see Grundmann 2015.
41 For Harnack's early career, see Nowak 1996: 2–5.
42 Harnack 1873.
43 Smith 2014: 49–86 argues against the idea that it was a work of Justin at all.

44 The classic work on this period is Schweitzer's *The Quest of the Historical Jesus*, first published in 1906 (translated 1910).
45 A full sense of the range of Harnack's interests, *e.g.*, can be found in the papers in Nowak and Oexle 2001.
46 Edited, with an extensive and helpful contextual introduction, by Rebenich 1997.

had been the subject of his 1871 Leipzig *Habilitation*), and was particularly focused on his sources – it was published in 1872. Rühl would later go on to edit Eutropius (1887). In 1876, he left to take up a chair at Königsberg and was replaced at Dorpat by the celebrated Ludwig Mendelssohn, who would be promoted to *professor ordinarius* two years later.[47] His energies were devoted to editing ancient and late-ancient Greek historians: Appian in two volumes (1879–1881), Herodian (1883), and Zosimus (1887). At the same time, Mendelssohn was interested in biblical questions, leaving an edition of the *Letter of Aristeas* – a document of fundamental importance for the Septuagint Bible – unfinished at the time of his death in 1896.[48]

It was into this world that Alexander Enmann stepped in 1874. For six years he was in Dorpat, obtaining a degree of *magister historiae universalis* in 1880, for a thesis on the *Quellenkritik* of Pompeius Trogus, doubtless inspired by Rühl, who (along with Mendelssohn) supervised him.[49] This was a difficult subject and one that remains challenging to this day.[50] Pompeius Trogus' history does not survive; we have only an epitome made by Justin at some unknown date.[51] Though Trogus wrote in Latin, he focused not on Roman and Italian history, but on the rest of the world, clearly centred on Greece, for which he used Greek materials. Both these facts conspired to make the usual methods of source-criticism unusually difficult. What Enmann ended up doing was triangulating Justin's epitome with Cornelius Nepos and Diodorus Siculus, using parallel passages to identify where they shared a common source. This is not the place to go through his arguments: it suffices simply to note that he identified Timaeus of Tauromenium (d. *ca.* 260 BC), whose celebrated thirty-eight-book history is almost entirely lost, as one of Trogus' principal sources. What is important for our purposes, however, is that the methods he employed on Trogus were the same as those that he would use in his next work, *Eine verlorene Geschichte der römischen Kaiser* (1884).[52] By this point, Enmann had left Dorpat to take up a position as librarian at the Imperial St Petersburg Academy of Sciences, although he would continue his formal studies at the university, gaining a doctorate in 1886 with a dissertation on archaic Greek history.[53]

'Eine verlorene Geschichte' is a work of genius, but not quite in the way that it is made out to be in modern scholarship. Enmann was not, as is commonly stated or implied today, primarily concerned with the rather narrow issue of how a number of fourth-century historical epitomes (alleged or actual) share certain words, ideas, and errors, though he certainly had something to say on that topic.[54] His lengthy and involved essay has a much broader frame of reference. Enmann's starting point was the events of AD 238, the year of the six emperors.[55] He noted that Aurelius Victor (*HAb* 26) and Eutropius (9.1.2)

47 On Mendelssohn, see Sandys 1903–1908: 3.198.
48 It was published in 1900 by Wendland.
49 Enmann 1880.
50 On Trogus' sources see, briefly, Forni and Angeli Bertinelli 1982: 1312–1353.
51 On Justin, see Chapter III. On the manuscripts of his work, see briefly *T&T* 'Justinus' (Reynolds).
52 Enmann 1884: 337 (the first page) specifically locates his work in the tradition of *Quellenforschung*, noting the search for Plutarch's and Tacitus' sources as its primary object. Enmann's essay actually appeared in 1883 (see Barnes 1978: 91), though published in the 1884 volume of *Philologus*' supplementary series.
53 For more on Enmann's career, see Gilliam 1980.

54 'Alexander Enmann argued that certain shared errors in the fourth-century epitomes written by Aurelius Victor, Eutropius, and the anonymous *Epitome de Caesaribus* could best be explained by positing a common, now-lost source' (Rohrbacher 2013: 149). 'The *Kaisergeschichte* (KG) was first postulated in 1883 by Alexander Enmann. He noticed that the epitomators Aurelius Victor (writing in mid-361) and Eutropius (ca. 369) wrote (especially about the third century) in such a way as to necessitate a single common source' (Burgess 1995b: 111). 'Close on a century has now elapsed since ENMANN came out with his Kaisergeschichte, the common source of Victor and of Eutropius' (Syme 1980b: 267, *cf.* Syme 1981: 282).
55 On this, see Chapter VIII.

share a cluster of errors (so he judged them) about this turbulent period and suggested (really assumed) that they must have had a common source, which originally made all these mistakes. The existence of that source, Enmann argued, could be demonstrated from a series of passages in the *Historia Augusta* which attacks the views found in Victor and Eutropius.[56] He was particularly impressed by the resemblance between a passage of Victor (*HAb* 27.1) and these extracts from the *HA* (allegedly written by one 'Julius Capitolinus'):

> The similarity is so striking that one would have to assume that Capitolinus almost had Aurelius Victor before his eyes, if one did not know that the former wrote under Constantine and the latter only under Constantius I [*sic*, for II].[57]

Enmann saw, correctly, that this passage and the *HA* were closely linked and, also correctly, that any direct relationship between them could be explained only by 'Capitolinus' using Victor. He took it for granted, however, as most scholars at the time did, that the *HA* had been written by six different authors under Diocletian and Constantine, so it obviously pre-dated the *HAb*. As a result, something else, something much more complex, must be at work: this was a puzzle which required examination of the relationship between Eutropius, Aurelius Victor, the *HA*, and the *Libellus breviatus*.[58] The conclusion of Enmann's study was that the data could be explained only by the existence of a common source to which all these various authors had access: the *Kaisergeschichte*, a lost Latin text that underlay the surviving works of later Roman historians.[59] This work must have had an extraordinary circulation, despite the fact that it was never referred to by those who quarried it: traces of it were widely scattered in the literature of the fourth and fifth centuries.[60]

Enmann found in the *HA* and Victor (in the first instance) an apparent problem; in the techniques he had previously used for Pompeius Trogus, and those being applied in contemporary New Testament criticism, he thought that he saw a solution. His methods should be, by now, entirely familiar. In essence, what he did was assemble long lists of parallel passages, from which he tried to deduce a common source, making allowances for the way in which that source has been treated by different writers. This was an endeavour very much in the spirit of late-nineteenth-century German philology. Compare von Harnack in 1907 talking about the fate of Q, the supposed lost source for Matthew and Luke:

> The final blow to the independent existence of Q was dealt when it was incorporated in the gospels of St. Luke and St. Matthew. In St. Luke it exists, split up and dispersed throughout the gospel in subservience to the historical narrative; in St. Matthew it was treated in more conservative spirit, though in some important passages it has suffered more from revision and shows clearer traces of the particular bias of the evangelist. In most skilful fashion – often only by means of an accent or by an arrangement of the context which seems quite insignificant – the first evangelist has made this

---

56 Enmann 1884: 334–335. The *HA* passages are: *Gord.* 2.1; *Max. Balb.* 15, 16.7; *Maximini duo* 33.2.

57 Enmann 1884: 339–340: 'Die ähnlichkeit ist so frappant, dass man annehmen müsste, Capitolinus habe geradezu den Aurelius Victor vor augen gehabt, wüsste man nicht, dass ersterer unter Constantin, letzterer erst unter Constantius I. geschrieben hat'.

58 Enmann 1884's first chapter (340–356) is on Victor and Eutropius. His second, much more substantial chapter (356–396) is largely devoted to Victor and the *HA* (with some analysis of Eutropius). His third (396–407) looks at Victor and the *LB*, while his fourth (407–432) considers the *KG* and the work of Suetonius.

59 Summarised at Enmann 1884: 432 ff.

60 Enmann 1884: 443.

compilation of discourses subservient to his own special interest in the Christian community and its organisation, while St. Luke, who has much more frequently altered the wording of his source, has nevertheless kept so closely to it in essential points that its original character is more clearly perceived in his reproduction.[61]

Replace Q with the *KG* and St Matthew and St Luke with Victor and Eutropius, and this might well stand as a summary of Enmann's theory. It could still serve as a statement of the current *communis opinio* on the *KG*.

The importance of the *HA*, and of an *HA* written by six different authors under Diocletian and Constantine, to Enmann's original *KG* can scarcely be exaggerated. His essay's longest chapter, some forty pages, is devoted to unravelling the connections between the *HA*, Victor, and Eutropius, all on the assumption that Capitolinus *et al.* had priority. His delineation of the date and content of the *KG* took it for granted that the *scriptores* could be used to nail down a work written before the era of the Tetrarchs had finished.[62] So, it was naturally to the *HA* that Enmann compared the abilities and intentions of the hypothesised author of the *KG* (favourably).[63] None of this should be surprising, because (as we saw above) it was really the *HA* that structured the problem which Enmann set out to solve. That it antedated Victor and Eutropius, even as it seemed to know their work, was what made it necessary to posit the lost common source that Enmann believed he had discovered. This vital structural role of the *HA* in Enmann's theory can best be seen in the way that he treats the connections between the work of Victor and Eutropius. He starts by attempting to demonstrate that they share a common source for the third century.[64] He then moves back to their coverage of the second and admits that his method is much less revealing there.[65] It is at this point that he introduces the *HA*, which allows him, through its overlaps with both authors, to vindicate the idea of a common source. After an interlude on the links between *HAb* and *LB* and the role of Suetonius, Enmann summarises his view of the *KG*.[66] He then turns back to Victor and Eutropius, admitting that their relationship continues after the early fourth century and saying that we would understand it entirely differently if we analysed these two texts alone.[67] His solution was to posit, in addition to the *KG*, a separate continuation of the work, completed in roughly 357, which was the common source of Victor and Eutropius after the original ended.[68]

Throughout all this, the putative date of the *HA* plays an absolutely central role in Enmann's argument – as contemporary scholars recognised.[69] The connections between Victor and Eutropius are really explained around it, rather than for themselves. It was the *HA* that forced Enmann to resort to the awkward conclusion that two authors independently used one common source and then its separate continuation, one of them (Victor) relying on the latter for events only a few years before he himself set to work. That was partly a consequence of the methods of *Quellenforschung* that Enmann adopted, but it was mostly made necessary by his understanding of the *HA*. It should, however, have led him to question the viability of that method and that understanding. If the parallels between Victor and Eutropius had stopped

---

61 Harnack 1908: 251–252 (a translation of Harnack 1907).
62 Enmann 1884: 432.
63 Enmann 1884: 442–443.
64 Enmann 1884: 340–356.

65 Enmann 1884: 356.
66 Enmann 1884: 432–443.
67 Enmann 1884: 443–444.
68 Enmann 1884: 455–456.
69 *e.g.* Peter 1883.

with (say) the Emperor Carinus, that would have been a powerful piece of evidence for the existence of a lost common source and hence a vindication of the soundness of his methods. The fact they that they did not, and that he had to introduce an *ad hoc* hypothesis to save his overall idea, should have caused him to think again.

Even allowing for this flaw, Enmann's was a bold and elegant solution to the problem that he set out to treat – it was received with a good deal of enthusiasm.[70] It had three major virtues, which can be illuminated by comparing it to other near-contemporary works that treated similar problems. First, Enmann's theory explained a great deal: it seemed to hold the key to understanding the fourth-century historians in general. In contrast, Cohn treated much of the same material as Enmann with very similar methods, but could really only account for the first eleven chapters of the *HAb* and *LB*.[71] Second, Enmann's theory took seriously the texts themselves, working through what they said and trying to understand how they related to each other, but with a sceptical eye. Remarkably, for instance, he cut through much of the bibliographical pettifoggery in the *HA* itself. By way of contrast, compare the 1881 Halle dissertation of Paul Ebeling, entitled *Quaestiones Eutropianae*. Ebeling looks at many of the same passages as Enmann and considers many of the same questions, albeit starting from Eutropius instead of the *HA*. His conclusion is that, for most of the imperial section, Eutropius' source was none other than 'Junius Cordus', the cherished historical authority fabricated by the author of the *HA*.[72] Enmann avoided falling into traps like this. Third and finally, Enmann's work rendered much earlier scholarship superfluous: if he was right, then there was no real need to read Opitz, Wölfflin, Jeep, or Cohn. Indeed, Enmann refers to them rather less often than one might expect, certainly less than they refer to each other. These parallel efforts show just how much Enmann's theory was part of the general intellectual ferment of the time, but they also highlight the particular strengths of his approach, the things which made his conclusions so appealing – so easy to accept.

Hermann Dessau

Unfortunately for Enmann, the timing for this type of endeavour was not propitious. Just five years later, in an 1889 article in *Hermes*, Hermann Dessau would take up the question of the *Scriptores Historiae Augustae* and present the world with a radical solution, a solitary *scriptor Historiae Augustae*. Dessau was a prosopographer, and what bothered him at first were the names in the *HA*: many of these were attested nowhere else and were hardly appropriate to the epoch in which they were placed.[73] Other anachronisms emerged as he looked more closely at the text. Through a whole battery of lexical, textual, and historical arguments, Dessau then developed his radical solution: the *HA* was not, as it claimed to be, a collection of lives by six different authors writing under Diocletian and Constantine, but rather the work of a single

---

70 Peter 1883, though making some perceptive criticisms; Plew 1884.

71 On Cohn, see above.

72 Ebeling 1881: 42, 48 *e.g.*

73 Dessau 1889: 349 ff. Dessau would, of course, go on to play a very important role in the first edition of the *Prosopographia Imperii Romani* – on him, see the papers collected in Schmidt 2009. On names in the *HA*, see now Stover and Woudhuysen 2022a.

author writing towards the end of the fourth century. Looking at the passages on AD 238, the passages that had inspired Enmann to first hypothesise his *KG*, he concluded that the situation was exactly as it appeared on the surface: the author of the *HA* did in fact have Victor before his eyes as he was writing, because he was actually writing decades after Victor. Victor and Eutropius, not their hypothesised source, were the objects of the *HA*'s ire for their supposed errors on the year of the six emperors.[74] In fact, Dessau documented in remarkable detail quite how much the *HA* owed to Victor and Eutropius, how clearly it was using their works directly, at times verbatim, and how often it wove their narratives together.[75] His demonstration that the *HA* had simply plagiarised Victor's account of Septimius Severus long remained the single strongest argument that the work was written decades after it purports to have been and hence that the *scriptores* were a mirage.[76]

At one stroke, the pillar which carried so much of the weight of Enmann's *Kaisergeschichte* toppled over. If the *HA* was not itself a work of the Tetrarchic era, then one needed a completely different approach to the texts that the *Kaisergeschichte* purported to explain. Dessau himself, while far too polite to engage in overt polemic against Enmann, clearly saw this. He noted that the 'wörtlicher Uebereinstim-mungen' between the *HA*, Victor, and Eutropius had forced the hypothesis that they all shared a common source, since direct use of the latter two by the former had seemed impossible. His re-dating of the *HA* and his demonstration that depended directly on Victor and Eutropius simply removed the need for that hypothesis: 'dies ist indess nicht wahrscheinlich', as he put it, with some understatement.[77] In fact, Dessau was more generally sceptical about the whole concept of a common source for Victor and Eutropius. He rejected the idea that the *HAb* was an epitome and so could not advance the thesis adopted here. This meant that he had to admit some common lost source for Victor and Eutropius, but he was generally inclined to minimise what they owed to it.[78] He thought that Enmann's thesis entailed that Victor and Eutropius had followed their common source 'sclavisch'.[79] That was not so: they shared a common factual core for the second and third centuries derived from it, but they treated their materials very differently. As Dessau pointed out perceptively, where Victor's source was known (Suetonius early on in the *HAb*), he clearly did not reproduce it verbatim.[80] How likely, then, was he to have followed some lost source in the mechanical fashion Enmann had envisaged? All this called into question not only the specific conclusions of *Eine verlorene Geschichte*, but the methods by which they had been reached. Dessau's essay ought, besides its profound effect on study of the *HA*, to have cut down the *KG* in its prime. Subsequent work might have been expected to turn back to narrower theories of a lost source (*Suetonius auctus e.g.*), or to different conceptual frameworks (abbreviation of Victor, for instance).

Yet something like Enmann's theory stumbled on, apparently unaffected by what ought to have been a crushing blow. There were several reasons for this. Dessau's work was enormously controversial from the very start: it would be decades before his conclusions were widely accepted.[81] In some ways his

---

74 Dessau 1889: 372–373. Enmann is cited (361, n. 1) for the belief that the *HA* is attacking the sources of Victor and Eutropius.

75 Dessau 1889: 361–374.

76 Dessau 1889: 364–366.

77 Dessau 1889: 361.

78 Dessau 1889: 361, n.1. Barnes 1978: 91 is thus not quite right to say that Dessau 'reformulated the original dem-onstration' that the *KG* existed (*cf.* 1976a: 259–260).

79 Dessau 1889: 361.

80 Dessau 1889: 361–363.

81 See Chapter VII.

argument was simply too radical to command immediate assent, too fundamentally challenging to what was known and to the way that the history of antiquity was understood. A text that intentionally set out to deceive its readers about date, circumstance, and sources was a nightmare for *Quellenforschung*. As Arthur Stein put it in his admiring obituary: 'Dessau has wrested from us large portions of our supposed knowledge of the history of the Roman imperial age'.[82] Not everyone welcomed that.[83] In contrast, Enmann's work was much more in tune with contemporary intellectual fashion, much easier to digest. At the same time, though it had fundamentally undermined Enmann's ideas, Dessau's thesis also removed some more superficial obstacles to them. With the *HA* re-dated, there was no need for the awkward *ad hoc* hypothesis of a continuation to 357. It is for these and other reasons that Dessau's extraordinary insight did not end up consigning Enmann's *Kaisergeschichte* to an early retirement. As Syme put it: 'the postulate stands, since there is no other way of accounting for the literary phenomena'.[84]

The *KG* survived not because, as originally, it made sense of the *HA*'s relationship to Victor and Eutropius, but because of the idea Enmann had organised around that: his explanation of the relationship between Eutropius and Victor. For this new purpose, the *KG* worked admirably, elegantly even. At many points, it looks as though Eutropius is using the *HAb* as we have it, yet at almost every juncture he provides some small addition or alteration which could not have arisen from that text. Given the simplicity of his narrative, its restricted scope, and humble aims, it is difficult to imagine the author of a *breviarium* engaging in extensive research to provide supplemental titbits of information. That Victor and Eutropius shared a common source was what scholars after 1889 took more or less for granted, whether or not they gave that source the name of *Kaisergeschichte*. For Mommsen and Seeck, in their immediate responses to Dessau (both 1890), though the idea was hardly worth sustained comment, a common source was obvious.[85] In an 1897 book, Hermann Peter offered a more extended treatment, which took it for granted that Victor, Eutropius, and Festus shared a common source and that this was what Enmann (among others) had proved.[86] Peter's book was really a handbook of the Roman historians and its inclusion of the *KG* is a sign that Enmann's hypothesis was well on the way to acquiring that respectability that only reference works can bestow: it soon made its way into Georg Wissowa's revision of August Friedrich Pauly's *Realencylopädie*, volumes of which began to appear in the 1890s.[87] By the first decade of the twentieth century, it was as though Dessau had changed nothing: the *KG* had become the common source of Victor and Eutropius, to which it was possible that the *HA* had also had access. In 1904, Lécrivain devoted an entire chapter to Enmann's (and it was definitely his) *Chronique Impériale*.[88]

82 Stein 1932: 239: 'Dessau hat uns große Partien unseres vermeintlichen Wissens um die Geschichte der römischen Kaiserzeit entrissen'.

83 One element in the resistance to Dessau's theories in Germany perhaps lies in his being Jewish. It is noteworthy that the only two substantial obituaries of Dessau were both written by Austrian Jews working outside Germany: Stein, who was a professor at Prague (Pesditschek 2008) and Salomon Frankfurter (1933), another student of Mommsen who had written a doctoral thesis on the *HA*, before becoming chief librarian at the University of Vienna (Adunka 1956).

There is also a short obituary notice by Meyer 1932. German classics in the 1930s seems to have been keen to forget Dessau.

84 Syme 1980b: 268.

85 Mommsen 1890: 271 ff. (no mention of Enmann); Seeck 1890: 638 (perhaps explained by the fact that the author was, as he mentions, on holiday at the time).

86 Peter 1897: 2.137–138.

87 *e.g.* in *RE* 5.1 'L. Domitius (36) Aurelianus' (Groag) *passim* under the title 'Kaiserchronik'. The entry was published in 1903.

88 Lécrivain 1904: 423–436.

Lécrivain thought that the *HA* owed a great deal to the *KG*, but he also thought its existence proved by correspondences between Victor and Eutropius and was inclined to see them (along with Festus) as facile copyists of a common source.[89] In 1911, Ernst Hohl stated baldly that Enmann had proved that Aurelius Victor, Eutropius, and the *HA* shared a common source, which he then set about reconstructing.[90] In the 1920s, Baynes had recourse to it to deny that the *HA* used Eutropius, in service of his theory of a Julianic date for the former.[91] From thereon, the *KG* was to be a dominant feature of the study of fourth-century historiography. By the 1960s and 1970s, when Sir Ronald Syme began his intensive study of fourth-century historians, the *KG* was comfortably ensconced as the source of Victor and Eutropius.[92] Through the work of (especially) Barnes and his disciple R.W. Burgess, it has continued to be central to all discussion of the later Latin historians.[93] It now finds a home in works of reference, not just in entries for historians actually attested, but as an entity in its own right.[94] As Burgess himself put it in the *Oxford Dictionary of Late Antiquity*: the *KG*'s 'existence is now universally accepted by scholars'.[95]

Yet the post-Dessau *Kaisergeschichte* was flawed in its very conception. One could not simply remove the underlying structure of Enmann's argument and act as though nothing had happened: the question of the relationship between different fourth-century historical texts ought to have been rethought in its entirety. That, however, is what the scholarship has conspicuously failed to do. Throughout the twentieth century, it was simply taken for granted that – whatever might have happened to some aspects of Enmann's theory – the *KG* was a solid foundation for scholarly activity. As Ernst Hohl put it in 1937:

> Even if one leaves the *HA* entirely out of the game, the indispensable nature of Enmann's thesis is already evident from the links between Aurelius Victor, Eutropius, and the *Epitome*, which can be satisfactorily explained only through a common source, as Enmann deduced.[96]

Or as Timothy Barnes said, more than thirty years later, in an extended and influential treatment of the *KG*:

> Because Enmann's hypothesis is necessary to explain the resemblances between Victor and Eutropius, the controversy over the *HA* is irrelevant to its existence.[97]

Both these scholars, major figures in the intellectual history of the later Latin historians, treat the *HA* as though it were an incidental irritant in the theory of the *KG*, rather than fundamental to its conception. Not for the first or last time when it comes to Victor, the current scholarly consensus is really a series of accidents, in which conclusions have survived even as their premises have been refuted.

Moreover, unfortunately for the theory of the *KG*, scholarship has continued to progress over the century and a half since Enmann's essay was published. Through this, the *Kaisergeschichte* has furnished a spectacular example of scholarly mission-creep. Enmann's *KG* was used by Victor, Eutropius, and the *HA*,

89 Lécrivain 1904: 426–428, 434.
90 Hohl 1911: 187, 192 ff.
91 Baynes 1926: 48–50.
92 Syme 1968a: 105–106; Syme 1971a: 80 *e.g.*
93 See below, on the work of these two.
94 *HLL* 5.536 (Schmidt).
95 *ODLA* 'Kaisergeschichte' (Burgess).

96 Hohl 1937: 147: 'Selbst wenn man die HA ganz aus dem Spiele läßt, ergibt sich die Unentbehrlichkeit der These Enmanns schon aus den Berührungen zwischen Aurelius Victor, Eutrop und der Epitome, die sich befriedigend nur durch eine gemeinsame Quelle, wie Enmann sie erschlossen hat, erklären lassen'.
97 Barnes 1970a: 15.

though he talked rather more vaguely of its traces elsewhere. Over time, its influence has grown: to Festus, to Jerome and Ammianus, to the *Epitome*, and even to Orosius.[98] Enmann's *KG* author was 'ein höchst achtbarer historiker', but he wrote short summary biographies in the style of Suetonius.[99] Over time, he has grown in capacities and achievements. He imitated Tacitus; he made ever more extensive use of Greek sources.[100] He took a serious interest in *Verfassungsgeschichte*, or constitutional history.[101] Moreover, he went forth and multiplied. Further research using Enmann's method detected correspondences between Eutropius and other texts even after where the *HAb* breaks off in 360.[102] Still more disconcertingly, correspondences between Jerome and the *Epitome* continue even beyond the point where Eutropius concludes, which has led to the hypothesis of a so-called 'breviary of 378'.[103] This has put scholars into an impossible bind. As Burgess, the most forceful contemporary advocate of the *KG*, put it in 2005:

> If we apply the rules and procedures established for identifying the *KG* up to 358 to the material after 358, we are forced to posit three different known recensions of the *KG*: one concluding in 358, used by Victor in 361; one concluding in 364, used by Eutropius and Festus in 369/70; and one concluding in 378, used by Jerome, Ammianus, the *HA*, the *Epitome* . . . This is not a conclusion I adopt lightly. It is awkward, to say the least.[104]

This is the point at which someone needs to say that there is some fundamental problem with the 'rules and procedures' which have led to this position: the facts themselves have entailed a *reductio ad absurdum*.

The *KG* is nowadays treated as a sort of timeless verity, so fundamental to scholarship as to be barely worth thinking about. What we have tried to show here is that is actually a historical artefact: the product of a very particular time, place, and set of events. If Enmann had, by some happenstance, delayed the publication of his work until after Dessau, is it really likely that he would have essayed the *KG* in the form that he did? If Dessau had been somewhat less polite about Enmann, would the *KG* really have lumbered on without explicit modification? Yet, beyond the weaknesses that study of the *KG* in its context reveals, the extraordinary fluidity of its nature and the growth of its extent hint that something is wrong with the underlying theory as well. It is this to which we turn next.

Methods of *Quellenkritik*

We are not advocating here for the position of Den Boer, and others, who considers the whole notion of the *KG*, or something like it, to be absurd.[105] The problem identified by Enmann is a real problem, and it will not do to explain the intellectual and verbal similarities between our texts with some fund of orally transmitted details about Roman history, or by reference to the common mental framework of fourth-century education. Consider the parallels between the *HAb* and Eutropius set out in **TABLE 6.1**. Clearly, *something* is going on here. Indeed, even opponents of the *KG*, like Dufraigne, have been forced to posit

---

98 Orosius: Peachin 1988: 219–221; Sehlmeyer 2009: 203. More sceptical is Van Nuffelen 2012: 109.
99 Enmann 1884: 442–443.
100 Festy 1998: 156–159.

101 Nickbakht and Scardino 2021: 214–215.
102 Burgess 2005.
103 Schwartz 1980.
104 Burgess 2005: 190.
105 Den Boer 1972: 21–22, 28. Dufraigne 1975: xxvi–xxvii.

TABLE 6.1 – PARALLELS BETWEEN THE *HAb* AND EUTROPIUS

HAb	Eutropius
20.18: Britanniam . . . muro munivit per transversam insulam ducto utrimque ad finem Oceani.	8.19: Vallum per CXXXIII passuum milia a mari ad mare deduxit.★
21.3: Iuliam novercam . . . coniugem affectavit.	8.20: Novercam suam Iuliam uxorem duxerit.
24.5: Matrisque cultu, quae nomine Mammaea erat, plus quam pius.	8.23: In Mamaeam matrem suam unice pius.
25.1: Gaius Iulius Maximinus, praesidens Trebellicae, primus e militaribus . . . potentiam cepit.	9.1: Maximinus ex corpore militari primus ad imperium accessit.
39.13: Prima ad exercitum contione obtestaretur ignarum cladis Numeriani.	9.20: Prima militum contione iuravit Numerianum nullo suo dolo interfectum.
He fortified Britain with a wall across the island, reaching at both ends to the Ocean's edge.	He laid down a ditch through 133 miles from sea to sea.
He desired to have his stepmother Julia as a wife.	He married his stepmother, Julia.
He was more than pious in his devotion to his mother, whose name was Mammea.	He was especially pious towards Mammea, his mother.
Gaius Julius Maximinus, who was governing Trebellica, was the first from among the soldiers to seize power.	Maximinus was the first from the common soldiery to assume imperial power.
At his first address to the army he swore he was ignorant of the destruction of Numerian.	At his first address to the soldiers, he swore that Numerian had not been killed by his treachery.

★ On the text of this passage, cf. Chapter V.

their own lost sources to explain similarities between the texts, which is simply smuggling Enmann in through the back door.[106] The textual resonances between our surviving late-antique Latin histories are a genuine conundrum, one that ultimately requires a textual solution. The reason why applying Enmann's methods has led to the current absurd situation is that he failed to make one fundamental distinction: the *KG* is not a text, but a *minimal hypothesis*.[107] A formal analysis can reveal some fundamental weaknesses of Enmann's rules and procedures.

Let x be our lost source. Correspondences in our surviving sources a, b, c, and d in their various combinations (*ab*, *bc*, *abc*, *ad*, *cd* etc.) must *ex hypothesi* belong to x, provided we assume that these sources are independent of each other. On this basis, we can describe the minimal content of x as the set of these correspondences. That, however, does not mean that x could not contain other things. Logically speaking, it is very likely that some material from x would show up in only one of its descendants, *i.e.* in one of a, b, c, or d. It is also certain that x must have had material that was reproduced in no surviving source, since no single source is comprehensive of every element of x and our set of surviving sources is just a random sample. Statistical analysis, of the type we have discussed above (the product of the length of the two

---

106 *e.g.* Dufraigne 1975: xxxiii, with a lost history as the fundamental source of the *HAb* from Diocletian to Constantius II.

107 For this distinction between hypothesis and text, we are indebted to Farrer 1955. See also the amusing critique of the Q hypothesis by Goulder 1996.

sections divided by the length of their shared material), suggests that the population, *i.e. x*, is two orders of magnitude larger than the material shared in a pair of its descendants. For example, the eighth book of Eutropius (from Nerva to Alexander Severus) consists of 1,900 words. The corresponding portion of the *HAb* (*cc.* 12–24) consists of 2,800 words. The overlapping material between these two consists of about 425 words. This suggests that their shared source ought to have consisted of a minimum of 12,500 words (for just the period from 96 to 235) and was in all likelihood quite a bit longer, at *ca.* 20,000 words.

Fundamental to the reconstruction of *x* is the assumption that our extant sources are independent of each other, but Enmann's method of comparing parallel passages simply cannot demonstrate this. In the case of the *KG*, this is a particularly severe obstacle. Eutropius is, by general agreement, a core *KG* text, central to any reconstruction. Yet almost everyone now agrees that the *HA*, at least, used Eutropius, and there is absolutely no reason why other subsequent witnesses to the *KG* – Jerome, Festus, Ammianus – could not have used his work as well. In fact, *a priori*, when we see that they agree with Eutropius, that is the natural assumption – one that can be amply confirmed by further study.[108] As Farrer put it crisply in his critique of the Q theory for the Gospels:

> For if we find two documents containing much common material, some of it verbally identical, and if those two documents derive from the same literary region, our first supposition is not that both draw upon a lost document for which there is no independent evidence, but that one draws upon the other. It is only when the latter supposition has proved untenable that we have recourse to the postulation of a hypothetical source.[109]

No one has proved it untenable that the later texts used Eutropius' work. The periodic verbatim overlaps of several of these sources with it, far from demonstrating that this must have been the exact wording of the *KG*, could simply show nothing more than Eutropius' influence – in fact, in the case of Jerome, Festus, and Ammianus, there are excellent reasons to believe that they did indeed know and use his work.[110] Out of the texts supposedly indebted to the *KG*, that leaves only the *HAb* and Eutropius as suitable comparands, since the *HAb* precedes his *breviarium*.

This is why, strictly speaking, the *KG* is defined as the common source of Victor and Eutropius. Whatever the (often very compelling) parallels in ideas and arrangement between these two, their wording is never identical *in extenso*. This means that while we might be able to say (like Dessau) that some core of facts goes back to the common source, we have few sure means of reconstructing any of its features in detail. Confident pronouncements about the nature, style, and wording of the common source on the evidence adduced are unwarranted: it is, logically, a coin-toss between the moralising allusivity of Victor and the bare factual narration of Eutropius. Indeed, once we look closely at some of the overlaps between the two, it looks as though the *HAb* must be closer to the common source than Eutropius – at least according to the established rules of *KG-Forschung*. For example, in discussing how Diocletian convinced Maximian Herculius to step down, Eutropius says that 'his colleague reluctantly submitted to this' (10.27: *cui aegre collega obtemperavit*). This is patently parallel with the *HAb*, and so must reflect

---

108 On the *HA* and Eutropius, see Chapter VIII.
109 Farrer 1955: 56.

110 On Festus and Eutropius, see Chapter III. On Jerome and Eutropius, see Chapter VIII. On Ammianus and Eutropius, see Kelly 2008: esp. 240–253.

the common source: 'he brought Herculius most reluctantly to this view' (39.48: *in sententiam Herculium aegerrime traduxisset*). The key word is the adverb *aegre*. This is its only appearance in Eutropius, yet it was a favourite of Victor's, occurring some four times in the positive and another four in the superlative in the *HAb*.[111] In this instance, the common source of Eutropius and the *HAb* seems to be a text that sounds very much like Victor.

A hypothesis stands or falls on how well it works to explain phenomena – a lost text is something for the existence of which we have independent evidence. As soon as one starts considering Enmann's *KG* – a brief imperial chronicle arranged biographically – as a text that once existed, it becomes completely implausible. No one refers to the *KG* in antiquity.[112] No part of it has been transmitted in manuscripts. No scrap of it has been found on papyrus or parchment in Egypt's sands. Yet *everyone* is supposed to have read it. The *Historiae abbreviatae*, Ausonius, Eutropius, Festus, Ammianus, the *Historia Augusta*, the *Libellus breviatus*, Jerome, Orosius – *i.e.* every work of secular history from the period and some besides – are alleged to have used this phantom text as a source.[113] Compare an actual lost work that we can be sure was widely read in the period of the *Kaisergeschichte*'s supposed pomp: Sallust's *Histories*. Transmission is a mysterious process, and it is indeed strange that so important a text should not have survived.[114] Yet look what we do have: dozens upon dozens of quotations in the grammarians; careful allusions in later historians, like Victor and Sulpicius Severus; a possible epitome or imitation in Julius Exuperantius; several papyri; fragments of two late-antique manuscripts; excerpted letters and speeches with their own medieval transmission. Or take an example from Christian historiography, from *Kaisergeschichte* to *Kirchengeschichte*: the *Chronicon* of Eusebius. Completed early in the fourth century, Eusebius' slightly chimeric two-book compilation, with the first containing antiquarian material and the second a world chronicle, was enormously influential and widely read among later Christian authors.[115] Somehow the Greek text was lost, though what may be a bifolium from it has been found in a palimpsested manuscript in Vienna.[116] Yet we have such extensive evidence that we can reconstruct large parts of this lost work with something like certainty: translations and adaptations into three languages (Latin, Armenian, Syriac), as well as extensive quotations in Byzantine chroniclers.[117] This is what we should expect when a text that everyone read somehow failed to survive. Even if the *KG* was lost as a victim of its own success, rendered obsolete by its own utility – a popular, though curious, idea, and one that we are not quite sure actually happened in any existing cases, beyond perhaps Eusebius' – it would have left many traces of its existence: quotations, references, and so on, scattered along its path towards ubiquity and oblivion. As Burgess himself said in 1993, in relation to a different hypothesised lost source (Croke's *Stadtchronik*), had such a work existed:

111 For *aegre*: *HAb* 11.10, 13.2, 33.25, 42.20. For *aegerrime*: 9.9, 39.48, 40.23, 41.17.

112 One alleged reference is dealt with below.

113 The situation is the same in New Testament criticism, where the lack of any reference to Q is considered one of strongest objections to the theory. For a critique of Q, see Goodacre and Perrin 2004.

114 On Sallust's *Histories* in late antiquity, see Stover and Woudhuysen 2022b.

115 On the *Chronicon*, see Grafton and Williams 2006: 133–177, the first part of Burgess 1999, and Burgess

and Kulikowski 2013: 119–126. On its influence, see *e.g.* the second part of Burgess 1999, Crawford 2020, and Hollerich 2021.

116 Grusková 2013.

117 On the various sources for the text of Eusebius, see Mosshamer 1979: 37–83; there is also a good deal of interest to be found in Hollerich 2021. For the Armenian version: Karst 1911 (text); Burgess 1999: 25–26; Drost-Abgarjan 2006. Syriac: Burgess 1999: 26 and Witakowski 1987. Latin, by Jerome: Helm 1956, Burgess 1999: 23–25.

. . . surely every Latin historian of the empire would have used it, given the general dearth of written sources available from the third century. We could not help but have numerous comments about it, as historians referred to it, disputed it, contradicted it, failed to understand it.[118]

This is exactly what we do *not* have for the *KG*.

Enmann set out to characterise the text that he believed he had discovered on the basis of its minimal content: hence his idea that it was a series of short factual biographies. As we have shown, this is a simple logical and statistical error, but it is one universally made in scholarship on the *KG*. As Alan Cameron has stipulated: 'the *KG* cannot have been significantly more detailed than its various derivatives and continuations'.[119] The contradiction between the narrow text that Enmann delineated and the fecundity of his method – apt to discover ever more and ever wider uses of the *KG* – has led scholarship on late-antique Latin historiography into a dead end. Conceiving of the *KG* as a text – a finite thing rather than an unbounded hypothesis – inevitably leads to the invention of innumerable progeny for it, *ad hoc* explanations for all the material that the underlying method throws up. By 1929, it birthed for Fisher a new source, Z, to explain material in the later lives of the *Historia Augusta* which was dissimilar to the other Latin accounts, and its fecundity has not decreased.[120] Current scholarship on Roman imperial history juggles ten or so hypothetical or lost sources, 'fashionable phantoms', as Baldwin termed them: Burgess's three revisions of the *KG*, the *Leoquelle*, Marius Maximus, *Suetonius auctus*, Syme's Ignotus, the *Annales* of Nicomachus Flavianus, Eusebius of Nantes, and the *Historia Romana* of Symmachus the Younger.[121] This complexity stems from the need to account for what Enmann found within the outmoded framework that he established. We have rightly cast down from their perches the thirty-odd invented sources of the *HA*: Junius Cordus and his crew. Is it progress if we have merely set up other idols in their place? Literally thousands of pages have been devoted to discussing literally senseless questions: which of several hypothetical sources this or that section of the *HA* is using – is it the *KG* here or the *Annales* of Nicomachus Flavianus? Or is the *HA* itself the *Annales*? Did the *KG* use Marius Maximus or Ignotus? Is the *Origo Constantini* a combination of the *KG* and a lost biography of Constantine? Did the *Epitome* start out using *Suetonius auctus*, and then switch to the *KG*, before turning to the *Leoquelle*? One account has Jerome's *Chronicon* using Victor, Eutropius, and the *KG*; another uses four separate stemmata – all containing hypothesised works – to explain the *LB*; another identifies one Eusebius of Nantes as the author of the *KG* because Ausonius is *hypothesised* to have used the *KG* and a note in the margin of a thirteenth-century Latin manuscript says that he used this spectral Eusebius; another wonders whether a different version of the *KG* was translated into Greek.

Let us return to the real world and treat the *KG* as what it really is: an insight that the Latin historians of the fourth century share a good deal of material. Whence came that material? Two of the *KG* texts, the *HAb* and the *LB*, explicitly claim to be derived from Victor. Jerome asked Paul of Concordia for a copy of Victor's *Historia*. The only contemporary historian Ammianus mentions by name as a historian is Victor. The one fourth-century source that everyone can agree the *Historia Augusta* used was Victor.[122]

118 Burgess 1993b: 184.
119 Cameron 2011: 674.
120 Fisher 1929.

121 Baldwin 1993: 88.
122 That the *Historia Augusta* had used Victor was acknowledged even by Momigliano 1954: 31; see also Hohl 1955 and further Chapter VIII.

Victor, as we have shown, was the most famous and highly regarded Latin historian of his day. If there is one source that all the fourth-century Latin historians ought to have drawn from, then it is Victor. Only the assumption that the *HAb* is Victor's text, not a witness to it, and the belief that the *KG*, however much it has grown, was a short biographical collection, have obscured the obvious conclusion.

This is why it was so important to lay out the origins of the *KG* in scholarship of the later nineteenth century. We can see now that it, and precursor theories like Cohn's *Suetonius auctus*, are all attempts to solve problems that exist only when it is assumed that the *HAb* as it survives *is* Victor's work, no more and no less. Cohn's *Suetonius auctus* is the solution to an *HAb*–*LB* problem that simply vanishes if the *HAb* is an epitome – hence why he went to such lengths to dispute that thesis. Similarly, in its original formulation by Enmann, the *KG* solves an *HA*–Victor problem only if one accepts that the *HA* is earlier and that Victor's work survives in its entirety. Enmann's corollary continuation of the *KG* offers the answer to an *HAb*–Eutropius problem, but to arrive at it one has to assume that Eutropius was reading the *HAb*, not Victor's *Historia*. After Dessau, when the chronological problem that had given Enmann's work impetus was removed, the *KG* explained the relationships of the fourth-century Latin historians only on the assumption that the earliest witness to it, Victor, had made from it a simultaneously scrappy and bloviating summary. In all of its manifold formulations, the *KG* makes sense if, and only if, the *HAb* is the entirety of Victor's work. As Farrer said of Q: 'it hangs on a single thread; cut that, and it falls by its own weight'.[123] If the original text of Victor does not survive – as we have shown it does not – then Enmann's *KG* simply becomes an unnecessary postulate. He was fundamentally right that our surviving Latin texts reveal *eine verlorene Geschichte der römischen Kaiser*, even if he and his successors have been wrong about the nature, date, and authorship of that text – it was not a scrappy summary of imperial history covering precisely thirty-five Teubner pages (as H.W. Bird calculated with spurious precision).[124] Instead the common source that bequeathed ideas, facts, and phrasing to a host of later historians was a long, dense, and complicated work, whose original character can be best discerned not in Eutropius but in the *HAb*. In other words, Victor's *Historia* was the imperial history – the *Kaisergeschichte*, one might say, just not Enmann's *Kaisergeschichte* – that served as the source of the later tradition.

From the standpoint of the current scholarly consensus, what we propose is a radical position, and one that will require much of what we think we know about late-Roman historiography to be rethought. It is, however, radical only from the standpoint of contemporary scholarship, because that scholarship takes it for granted that the two Victorine texts are not what their titles say they are. Our interpretation provides a natural and plausible explanation for the evidence that we have, one that takes seriously what has been handed down in the manuscripts and fits the other data available to us. The currently accepted account of the nature of the *HAb* and the *LB*, and their place in late-antique historiography, is actually the extreme position. Enmann was forced to the 'interessante factum' that Aurelius Victor, even in writing the history of his own lifetime, was engaged merely in revising a historical narrative 'written almost simultaneously'.[125] Matthews suggests that, when they met in Rome in the late fourth century, Aurelius Victor lent to Ammianus a copy, not of his own work, but of the *KG*, from which

---

123 Farrer 1955: 62.
124 Bird 1989: 95, *cf.* Bird 1994: xiii. The calculation was cautiously endorsed by Burgess 1995a: 351, n. 13; Burgess 1995b: 113, n. 14 'perhaps a bit short'.

Sehlmeyer 2020: 333 more generously allows eighty pages.
125 Enmann 1884: 455: 'der überarbeitung einer fast gleichzeitig geschriebene geschichtserzählung'.

he had taken his material.[126] Discussing the manuscript title of the *LB*, Baldwin curtly dismisses it as a 'quadruple nonsense': not an abbreviation, and not derived from Victor, with a different terminal date, and sometimes fuller information.[127] Barnes and Schlumberger can account for the *LB*'s sources only by using four independent complex stemmata, each with multiple lines of influence.[128] Burgess's account of the sources of Jerome's *Chronicon* requires that Jerome did not in fact use the text he had obtained for imperial history, but an entirely different one with a similar set of facts.[129] Den Boer's analysis of Victor's Latin requires that he did not use particles in the way that every other Latin author did.[130] All of these positions and many more besides, widely accepted in contemporary scholarship, are radically incompatible with our evidence, unlike the theory defended here, which is grounded on the solid rock of what the texts and manuscripts actually say.

What we propose is, in short, a paradigm shift. In recent scholarship, there has been a penchant for extravagant metaphors to describe the work of source-critics: François Paschoud has compared them to astronomers, inferring the position of unseen planets mathematically, and even Alan Cameron has conceded that that might be a fitting description for so great an achievement as the discovery of the *KG*.[131] We would mischievously suggest an alternative formulation. Luminiferous aether offered a working solution to several observed problems in physics, and was widely accepted before Einstein, despite the fact that no experiment was able to prove its existence. With Einstein's special theory of relativity of 1905, however, luminiferous aether became an entirely superfluous hypothesis: a solution without a problem.[132] So too the *KG* seems to offer a plausible and elegant solution to several problems in our data, chief among them the relationship of Victor's *HAb* and Eutropius. If, however, the full text of Victor does not survive, then the problem of the chronology of our sources for Roman imperial history itself evaporates, and with it any need for the *KG* theory. In its place, we can offer something perhaps much more exciting: a long, lost, and Latin history written by a well-informed and scholarly pagan civil servant, who had definite stylistic and historiographical aims, and imperial connections running from Julian to Theodosius, first issued in the middle of the fourth century (around 360), and subsequently extended, possibly revised, or at least updated with additional material to 389.

We have tried to demonstrate that Enmann's *Kaisergeschichte* was flawed in its conception, reception, and logic. We have argued also that the core insight on which it was based is much better accounted for by the case we have presented here for treating the *HAb* and *LB* as epitomes of Victor's *History*. It is, however, unusual in the scholarly literature to find the *KG* discussed in these general and conceptual terms: much more often it is presented in a specific and rather rebarbative way. Let us, then, turn to the case that has been made for the existence of the *KG* through detailed discussion of individual passages and examine it.

126 Matthews 1989: 457.
127 Baldwin 1993: 82.
128 Barnes 1976a; Schlumberger 1974.
129 Burgess 2005; Burgess 1995a.

130 Den Boer 1975: 52.
131 Paschoud 1998a: 84–85; Paschoud 2002: 487; Cameron 2011: 628.
132 Darrigol 2005 provides an accessible overview of luminiferous aether and the impact of Einstein.

The case for the *Kaisergeschichte*

Since the 1960s, one scholar in particular has done more than any other to advance Enmann's *KG*: T.D. Barnes.[133] In a series of studies in the 1970s, he made a sustained case both for the existence of the *KG* and for locating its terminal point in AD 337, with its composition very soon after.[134] An impeccably logical scholar, Barnes was always careful to be clear that the *KG* was (strictly speaking) the common source of Eutropius and Aurelius Victor.[135] Other writers, he maintained, could be shown to have used it (and he assayed several demonstrations), but that was really an ancillary matter: the case rested on the *HAb* and Eutropius' *breviarium*.[136] Barnes took it for granted that the use of a common source by Victor and Eutropius for most of the third century had been established beyond doubt by Enmann, so did not devote sustained attention to proving that proposition.[137] He focused, rather, on the period from Diocletian to 337, keen to prove that Victor and Eutropius were remarkably parallel for those years, but not afterwards, and hence had used a common source.

Because of the way that Barnes defined the *KG* as the common source of the *HAb* and Eutropius, that the former is identical with the complete work of Victor is the foundational (if unacknowledged) assumption that underlies his demonstration of the *KG*'s existence. His proofs show this very plainly: he advanced four detailed ones. First, in describing the campaign of Galerius against the Persians in the 290s, the *HAb* (39.34–35) and Eutropius (9.25) give closely parallel accounts, but each has one detail about the emperor's army that is not in the other: the *HAb* says they were 'veterans and new recruits', Eutropius that they were from Illyricum and Moesia. Festus (25) offers something like both (that they were *limitanei* or border troops, from Dacia). Barnes held that, as a result, Eutropius cannot depend on the *HAb* and all three 'have independently used a lost source, namely the KG'.[138] Second, the *HAb* and Eutropius offer interestingly parallel accounts of key events in the history of the Tetrarchy (**TABLE 6.2**). Barnes says that the texts 'concur in gross error' here, by putting the appointment of the Caesars (293) after various events (the Persian war *etc.*) that occurred later.[139] Third, the *HAb* (40.5–8) and Eutropius (10.2.3–4, 4.1) share important details on the coup that brought Maxentius to power at Rome (as well as some phrasing *interim Romae = Romae interea* to introduce the story, *e.g.*). They also agree in apparent error on the fate of the hapless emperor Severus, sent by Galerius to suppress the usurper: both say he was killed at Ravenna (not Rome). Eutropius, however, supplies one important detail about the turbulent politics of this period not found in the *HAb*: that Licinius, the replacement (so to speak) for Severus in the imperial college, was from Dacia.[140] Fourth and finally, there are some rather vague verbal reminiscences in their accounts of

---

133 See esp. Barnes 1970a, 1976a, 1978, *cf.* 1970b (mainly devoted to the *HA*). This statement is not mere Anglophone bias: the general bibliography on the *KG* in *HLL* 5.536 (Schmidt) lists a first flurry of work in the late nineteenth and early twentieth centuries, a 1953 dissertation by Schön, and then only these three studies by Barnes.

134 Date: Barnes 1970a: 20; 1976a: 259; 1978: 94.

135 Barnes 1976a: 260.

136 *e.g.* Barnes 1978: 94: 'the KG has deliberately been defined as the common source of Victor and Eutropius. Its use by other writers requires specific proof'.

137 Barnes 1970a: 15; 1978: 92. He was particularly persuaded by 'errors' that Victor and Eutropius shared, especially (1970a: 16; 1978: 92) the 'battle of the Milvian Bridge' in the reign of Septimius Severus (on which see Chapter VIII).

138 Barnes 1970a: 18.

139 Barnes 1978: 93.

140 Barnes 1970a: 18–19.

TABLE 6.2 – THE *HAb* AND EUTROPIUS ON THE TETRARCHY

HAb 39.21–24	Eutropius 9.21–22.1
[*sc.* Carausius] Herculii metu, a quo se caedi iussum compererat, Britanniam hausto imperio capessivit. Eodem tempore Orientem Persae, Africam Iulianus ac nationes Quinquegentanae graviter quatiebant. Adhuc apud Aegypti Alexandriam Achilleus nomine dominationis insignia induerat. His de causis Iulium Constantium, Galerium Maximianum, cui cognomen Armentario erat, creatos Caesares in affinitatem vocant.★	. . . [*sc.* Carausius] a Maximiano iussus occidi purpuram sumpsit et Britannias occupavit. Ita cum per omnem orbem terrarum res turbatae essent, Carausius in Britanniis rebellaret, Achilleus in Aegypto, Africam Quinquegentiani infestarent, Narseus Orienti bellum inferret, Diocletianus Maximianum Herculium ex Caesare fecit Augustum, Constantium et Maximianum Caesares . . .
[Carausius] out of fear of Herculius, whom he had learnt had commanded his death, snatched Britain after he had taken up imperial power. At the same time the Persians were causing the East to tremble severely, while Julian and the Quinquegentan nations did the same to Africa. Meanwhile, at Alexandria in Egypt Achilleus (that was his name) had put on the insignia of tyranny. For these reasons, they called into kinship those who had been made Caesars, Julius Constantius and Galerius Maximianus, whose cognomen was Armentarius.	[Carausius], since Maximian had ordered that he be killed, assumed the purple and seized Britain. So, since things had been thrown into turmoil throughout the entire world – Carausius in rebellion in Britain, Achilleus in Egypt, the Quinquegentiani attacking Africa, Narses making war on the East – Diocletian promoted Maximianus Herculius from Caesar to Augustus and made Constantius and Maximianus Caesars.

★ The adjectival form *Quinquegentanae*, the transmitted text of both manuscripts of the *HAb*, is likely sound, despite occasional doubts: compare the forms in *ILS* 1194 (*Quinquegentaneis*), *CIL* 8.8294 = 20680 (*Quinquegentaneos*). *Quinquegentiani* is more common in the literary material (Eutropius 9.23; Orosius 7.25.4, 25.8; Jordanes, *Getica* 110, *Romana* 297, 300; *Passio S. Typasii veterani* 1 (*BHL* 8354 – likely derived from Eutropius: Woods 1993, *cf.* 1994); *cf.* John of Antioch fr. 247 Roberto: ε′ ἀνδρῶν Γεντιανῶν; Zonaras 12.31: πέντε τινῶν Γεντιανῶν), but that probably reflects the influence of Eutropius.

the death of Constantine (*HAb* 41.16 = Eutropius 10.8), but no other works mention the comet that was seen just beforehand.[141]

In each of these cases, Barnes's argument holds if and only if the *HAb* is the complete work of Victor. If it is an epitome, then his whole case for the *KG* collapses, because it is much more logical to assume that in each instance Eutropius was simply drawing on Victor's full *History*, to which the *HAb* is only a partial witness. In the third case, in particular, this can practically be demonstrated: the *LB* (40.3) tells us that Severus was killed near Rome, at a place called 'Tres Tabernae', which is probably what actually happened.[142] This thus looks very much like a point where Victor offered two parallel accounts of the obscure fate of this obscure monarch, only one of which has turned up in the *HAb* and Eutropius. It is worth noting also that, while it does not say that he was from Dacia, the *LB* offers us much the most detailed account of Licinius' background (41.9). In the second example, Barnes's proof actually helps to demonstrate that the case advanced in this book is correct. Logically, the subject of *vocant* in the *HAb* can

141 Barnes 1970a: 19–20, with the exception of the *Passio Artemii* 7 (from Philostorgius, *HE* 2.16a), plausibly derived from Eutropius in Greek translation.

142 On these events, *cf.* further Chapter X.

only be the various usurpers mentioned just before, but they certainly did not appoint Constantius and Galerius as Caesars: Diocletian has gone missing in the process of abbreviation. Moreover, the chronological confusion here (if such we term the causal connection between turmoil and the creation of the Tetrarchy) has arisen because the source of the *HAb* and Eutropius treated the usurpers from 284 to 305 *en bloc*, rather than distributing them at their proper chronological position. One author who showed a *penchant* for lumping together would-be Augusti was Victor. This is precisely what he did with the Gallic emperors of the mid-third century (from *ca.* 260 to the mid-270s), all included in an extended digression in the middle of the reign of Gallienus (who died in 268).[143] In other words, Barnes's supposed proof for the *KG* is really a vindication of Victor's *Historia*.

There is also an internal contradiction in Barnes' argument that points in the same direction. He envisaged the common source as a simple, factual text, basically followed faithfully by Eutropius, but also the main (perhaps the only) direct source of Victor.[144] Yet, even on the examples he gives, it would have needed to be substantially more detailed than either the *HAb* or Eutropius. In the case of Galerius' campaign, for example, it ought *ex hypothesi* to have said that his army comprised veterans and new recruits, as well as that it was drawn from the *limitanei* of Illyricum and Moesia. Eutropius also tells us that Galerius undertook scouting expeditions during the campaign. This is not in Victor, but ought to have been in their common source, which must also have contained every detail that they do share. If we extend that logic to every fact in both texts, that source would have been a remarkably detailed document. That sounds rather more like Victor's carefully researched *Historia* than the short and summary *Kaisergeschichte* of Enmann and Barnes.

After the 1970s, Barnes ceased to devote sustained attention to the *KG*, though he maintained his belief in its existence as a text finished soon after 337.[145] Since then, it is R.W. Burgess who has done most to keep the flame of *KG–Forschung* alive.[146] In a series of detailed and closely argued articles, Burgess has, besides offering the most cumulatively comprehensive case for the *KG* since Enmann, advanced a number of specific propositions. First, he argued that the fifth century's most enthusiastic list-maker, Polemius Silvius, used the *KG*, as did Ausonius, a medieval catalogue of whose works reveals that the lost text's author was one Eusebius of Nantes.[147] Next, he offered a detailed case that Jerome used the *KG* directly for his *Chronicon* and, against Barnes, defended a terminal date for it of 357.[148] Finally, Jerome's use of the *KG* was reaffirmed and extended to encompass Festus, Ammianus, and the *LB*, with the rather uncomfortable consequence that the *KG* stopped in 358, was continued to 364, and then again to 378.[149] To this was added the idea that Jerome (*Chron.* 77b^c) explicitly referred to the *KG* as a *Latina historia*.[150] This is a remarkable series of publications, clearly the product of sustained thought over an extended period of time: it would appear to put the existence of the *KG* beyond doubt.

143 *HAb* 33.7–14.
144 Faithful Eutropius: Barnes 1976a: 263; Barnes 1978: 92. Main direct source: Barnes 1970a: 20.
145 *e.g.* Barnes 1991: 347. Of other work at the time, it is worth noting Bird 1973, who put once again the case for a *KG* finishing in 357.
146 Burgess 1993a, 1995a, 1995b, 2005. Burgess collected several of these studies in 2011, with some additional notes.

147 Burgess 1993a. Partially recanted in Burgess 2011: 'Supplementary Notes', 4.
148 Burgess 1995a, 1995b.
149 Burgess 2005.
150 Burgess 2005: 166, n. 4; strictly the *Latina historia* is the collection of which the *KG* forms the imperial part (along with the *DVI* and something like the *OGR*).

To review every one of Burgess's hypotheses would require a substantial essay in its own right, so let us instead consider his argument at its strongest. In 1995, Burgess set out to demonstrate, with Rudolf Helm and against Theodor Mommsen, that Jerome's *Chronicle* made use not of Eutropius, but of the *KG* directly.[151] As he put it, this 'also provides final and irrefragable proof of the existence of the *KG*'.[152] He described the paper as 'the most complete and wide-ranging proof for the existence of the *KG* and for its use by Jerome ever assembled'.[153] At its close, he concluded that 'even the most hardened critic of the *KG*' would have to concede its existence.[154] How does this 'irrefragable' case stack up?

Burgess offers a 'meticulous empirical analysis', arguing on the basis of no fewer than forty-seven proof-texts that minute differences between Jerome and Eutropius prove: (1) that Jerome was using the *KG*, not Eutropius, and (2) that therefore the *KG* must have existed.[155] There is, however, a certain madness in his method. First, a heap of trivialities does not equate to a single piece of solid evidence: 'zero multiplied by ten thousand is still zero', as A.H.M. Jones said in a rather different context.[156] It is normal in Latin for the verb to be in either ultimate or penultimate position and one does not need a common source to explain why it is found that way in multiple texts.[157] In a three-item list – for example Parthicus, Arabicus, Adiabenicus, or Armenia, Mesopotamia, Assyria – there are in fact only six possible arrangements: so it is not exactly unlikely for two sources to independently come up with the same order.[158] Burgess makes no distinction between common and unusual language in assessing parallels between the sources. The participles *dictus*, *appellatus*, and *cognominatus* all mean roughly the same thing: that different sources use different combinations of them when referring to the victory titles that emperors won in late antiquity means nothing.[159] Or, take the language used for the death of the emperor Carus, struck by lightning. In antiquity a variety of expressions was used for lightning strikes: *ictu fulminis*, *fulmine ictus*, and *de caelo tactus* were probably the most common, but there were others.[160] That a number of sources do not use Eutropius' bizarre *vi divini fulminis periit* (9.18) reveals little.[161] Nor does Burgess always pay sufficient attention to textual criticism. Before he was struck by lightning, Carus captured Coche and Ctesiphon (the twin cities at the heart of Persian Mesopotamia). Burgess finds it significant that Jerome calls them *nobilissimas*, where Eutropius says *notissimas*: evidently Jerome's account come from reading the *KG*, not Eutropius.[162] One branch of Eutropius' manuscript tradition, however, the only one to transmit Valens' authentic victory title *Gothicus Maximus* and therefore almost certainly containing authentic ancient readings, does in fact read *nobilissimas* at this point.[163]

Even in its more substantive examples, however, Burgess' method does not actually produce results that support his thesis. If we are to believe in the *KG* theory, verbatim agreements between two or more

151 Burgess 1995a: 351–352.
152 Burgess 1995a: 352.
153 Burgess 1995a: 354.
154 Burgess 1995a: 369.
155 Burgess 1995a: 356.
156 Jones 1969: 321 (see Chapter VII).
157 Burgess 1995a: 357: 'Jerome parallels Eutropius in placing the verb in the penultimate position', *cf.* 358 (example no. 4).
158 Burgess 1995a: 361: 'the order of the names is different in Festus, which shows that Jerome is not copying him'; 358 (no. 5).

159 Burgess 1995a: 361.
160 *De caelo tactus* is Livy's favourite (twenty-four instances in the extant books). *Fulmine ictus*: Cicero, *De div.* 2.47; Livy 1.3.9; Valerius Maximus 9.12.1 *e.g.* *Ictu fulminis*: Cicero, *De off.* 3.25.94; Livy 42.20.5; Celsus, *De medicina* 3.26; Tacitus, *Ann.* 15.22.2; Suetonius, *Aug.* 97.2 *e.g.*
161 Burgess 1995a: 365. No ancient text other than Eutropius ever uses this form of words for being struck by lightning.
162 Burgess 1995a: 365.
163 Droysen 1879: 160.

KG sources must represent the reading of the common source. That source was (as for Barnes) 'by defini-tion, the common source of Victor and Eutropius', but a text most faithfully reproduced by the latter: 'a set of short imperial biographies'.[164] Yet in a significant number of cases, using this method produces two competing sets of agreement, both of which have an excellent claim to represent the text of the *KG*.[165] Consider this cluster of *testimonia* to the death of Verus:

> Jerome *Chron.* 205[k]: apoplexi extinctus est.
>
> Eutropius 8.10.3: subito sanguine ictus, casu morbi, quem Graeci apoplexin vocant . . .
>
> *LB* 16.5: ictu sanguinis, quem morbum Graeci apoplexin vocant . . . exstinctus est.
>
> *HA Marcus* 14.8: apoplexi arreptus perit.
>
> *HA Verus* 9.11: morbo, quem apoplexin vocant, correptus Lucius . . . detracto sanguine . . . perit.[166]

Burgess does not quote the *HAb* on the same events (16.9: *morbo consumptum*), and consequently errs in his conclusions. If we were to follow *KG* reasoning, we would be forced to conclude that the common source used the word *morbo,* as it features in the *HAb,* Eutropius, the *LB,* and the *HA* (*Verus* 9.11), and in the ablative in both Victor and the *HA*. We would further probably conclude that it must have forms of *ictus* and *sanguinis,* since they are found in both Eutropius and the *Epitome*. How is it then that Jerome (and the *HA Marcus* 14.8) has the ablative *apoplexi* as the cause of death and none of these other features of the common source? In this case, Burgess's logic would seem in fact to require that Jerome could not have been using the *KG*.

Alternatively, we might examine these various accounts of the building activities of Caracalla at Rome:

> Jerome *Chron.* 213[e]: Antoninus Romae thermas sui nominis aedificavit.
>
> Eutropius 8.20.1: Opus Romae egregium fecit lavacri, quae Antoninianae appellantur.
>
> *HA Sev.* 21.11: . . . et thermas magnificentissimas fecerit.
>
> *HA Carac.* 9.4: Opera Romae reliquit thermas nominis sui eximias.[167]

Once again, Burgess does not quote the relevant passage of Victor (*HAb* 21.4: *aucta urbs . . . ad lavandum opera pulchri cultus*). Comparing Victor and Eutropius, we would have to conclude that the common source had a form of the word *opus* and a derivative of *lavare*. How is it then that both Jerome and the *HA* omit this detail, but use the descriptor *thermas nominis sui*? We should note that the *HA* is the only other text in antiquity to use this formula for the names of baths.[168]

The same pattern can be seen in various accounts of the accession of Opellius Macrinus:

---

164 Burgess 1995a: 350.
165 We have selected these examples carefully to exclude instances where a *KG* advocate might (*ad hoc*) suggest that one of the two competing sets can be explained by an earlier extant text influencing a later one (the *HAb* and *LB* for the first eleven chapters; the *HA* with

Victor and Eutropius *e.g.*). We present these texts as given by Burgess, including ellipses.
166 Burgess 1995a: 369 and 359.
167 Burgess 1995a: 361.
168 *HA Alex.* 25.3; *Gord. Gordiani* 32.7.

Jerome 213[h]: Macrinus praefecturam praetorio gerens imperator factus.

Eutropius 8.21: Opilius Macrinus, qui praefectus praetorio erat, cum filio Diadumeno facti imperatores.

HAb 22.1: Opilius Macrinus, qui praefecturam praetorio gerebat, imperator eiusdemque filius Diadumenus nomine Caesar a legionibus appellantur.[169]

Burgess does not quote the *LB* here (22.1: *Macrinus cum Diadumeno filio ab exercitu imperatores creati*). Doing so would have disproved his conclusion. Both the *HAb* and Jerome have only Opilius as an *imperator*, whereas Eutropius has both Opilius and his son as *imperatores*: a 'compression error' as Burgess calls it. The *LB*, however, has the same idea as Eutropius in similar words. Further, the *HA* also calls both *imperatores* (6.2: *Macrini et Diadumeni imperatorum*). Which version was in the common source?

Precisely the same problem rears its head in discussion of various enemies of the first Tetrarchy:

Jerome *Chron.* 225[e-g]: Carausius . . . Narseus . . . Quinquegentiani . . . Achilleus.

Eutropius 9.22: Carausius . . . Achilleus . . . Quinquegentiani . . . Narseus.

HAb 39.20–23: Carausius . . . Persae . . . Quinquegentanae . . . Achilleus.[170]

Here, Burgess thinks it revealing that Jerome followed the ordering of the *HAb*, but otherwise paralleled Eutropius. Again, however, he does not quote the *LB*. It only has two of these events, but they are in the same order as Eutropius and in words closer to his than to those of any other text (39.3): *Charausio in Galliis, Achilleus apud Aegyptum* ~ 9.22 *Carausius in Britanniis rebellaret, Achilleus in Aegypto*. Hence, we ought to conclude that the common source had Carausius and then Achilleus, but how then to explain the different order found in Victor and Jerome? Moreover, why does Victor have the adjective (not noun) *Quinquegentanae*, paralleled in the epigraphic evidence, but none of the other sources? One more example that Burgess does not cite can perhaps drive the point home. The *HAb* (21.5), the *LB* (21.5), and Eutropius (8.20) all describe the location of Caracalla's death as *apud Edessam*. Jerome and the *HA* say *inter Edessam et Carras* (*Chron.* 217[d] ~ *Carac.* 17.1 with the elements reversed). So, which version did the common source give?

As these examples make painfully clear, there is no way one can lead back these texts to a unitary common source that was similar to Eutropius' *breviarium*. They can be explained if the common source was a lengthy and discursive text, one which gave complex accounts of events that might be summarised rather differently, but that is not Burgess' *KG*. In fact, the real reason that Jerome, the *LB*, Festus, and, at points, the *HA* have so much in common with Eutropius is that they have used Eutropius directly – their departures from his text, where they are not simply explained by late-antique authors being more than copying automata, are best explained by their using other sources to supplement his wildly popular work.[171] In making sport of Den Boer's attempt to attribute commonalities in the sources to shared school education, Burgess points out that *KG*-sceptics would take a different attitude to student essays that turned up with so many similarities as these sources.[172] His argument is equally vulnerable on this score. If two

---

169 Burgess 1995a: 362.
170 Burgess 1995a: 365.

171 On the popularity of Eutropius see below.
172 Burgess 1995a: 354, n. 25.

TABLE 6.3 – VICTOR AND EUTROPIUS: THE DEATH OF AURELIAN

HAb 35.8	Eutropius 9.15	LB 35.8
Qua causa ministri scelere, cui secretorum officium crediderat, circumventus apud Caenofrurium interiit, cum ille praedae conscientia delictique scripta callide composita tribunis quasi per gratiam prodidisset, quibus interfici iubebantur; illique eo metu accensi facinus patravere . . . 36.2: . . . auctores Aureliani necis maximeque Mucaporem ducem.	Occiditur **servi sui fraude, qui ad quosdam militares viros amicos ipsius nomina pertulit** adnotata, **falso manum eius imitatus, tamquam Aurelianus ipsos pararet occidere;** itaque ut praeveniretur, **ab isdem interfectus est in itineris medio, quod inter Constantinopolim et Heracleam est** stratae veteris; locus Caenophrurium appellatur.	Novissime **fraude servi sui,** qui ad quosdam militares viros amicos ipsius nomina pertulit annotata, **falso manum eius imitatus, tamquam Aurelianus ipsos pararet occidere, ab iisdem interfectus est in itineris medio, quod inter Constantinopolim et Heracleam est.**
For this reason, he perished at Caenofrurium, tricked by the wicked crime of a servant, to whom he had entrusted the position of secretary. That man, thinking of his loot and crime, handed over to the tribunes, as if he were doing them a favour, cunningly fabricated documents, in which their death was ordered. They, inflamed by that fear, perpetrated the crime . . . . . . the perpetrators of Aurelian's murder, especially the general Mucapor.	He [Aurelian] was killed by the treachery of his slave, who conveyed to certain military men (friends of the emperor) their names with annotations (he had deceitfully mimicked the emperor's hand) as though Aurelian was preparing to kill them; so, to anticipate this, he was killed by these same men in the middle of the route, which is the old road between Constantinople and Heraclea.	

or more student essays revealed as much verbal overlap as these two sources, we would not hypothesise that they were both drawing on a lost common essay: we would assume that one was copying the other.

An example – the various accounts of the death of Aurelian – illustrates this neatly (**TABLE 6.3**). According to Burgess' method the words in bold in Table 6.3, occurring as they do in both Eutropius and the *LB*, must represent the actual words of the common source.[173] Where then does the same story that Victor tells in the *HAb* (and on which the *HA* expatiates) come from, with its richer detail, identifying the traitorous *servus* as a secretary, evoking a plausible chain of command, and naming Aurelian's killer as the general Mucapor?[174] Whatever its source, it is obviously the story which is summarised and simplified in Eutropius and the *LB*. Following the logic of the *KG*, this would require us to believe that the *HAb* had access not to the *KG*, but to the *KG*'s source itself.

In fact, when one starts looking for it, this pattern can be seen over and over again: what must logically be the *KG*'s account of an event, or even its wording, looks as though it has been derived from Victor. If we were to believe Burgess' reconstruction, what must have been the *KG* story of the emperor

173 In fact, of course, the *LB* is dependent on Eutropius here, as we have shown elsewhere: Stover and Woudhuysen 2021.

174 *cf.* Chapter VIII.

TABLE 6.4 – EUTROPIUS AND JEROME: MAXIMIAN AND THE BAGAUDAE

Eutropius 9.20	Jerome, *Chron.* 287[d]
Ita rerum Romanarum potitus cum tumultum **rusticani** in Gallia concitassent et **factioni suae Bacaudarum nomen inponerent,** duces autem haberent Amandum et Aelianum, ad subigendos eos **Maximianum Herculium** Caesarem misit, qui levibus proeliis agrestes domuit et **pacem Galliae** reformavit.	Diocletianus in consortium regni **Herculium Maximianum** assumpsit, qui **rusticorum** multitudine oppressa, **quae factioni suae Bacaudarum nomen indiderat, pacem Galliis** reddidit.
So, when he [Diocletian] had obtained mastery over the Roman state, since the country-folk had stirred Gaul into rebellion (naming their party *Bacaudae*, with Amandus and Aelianus as their commanders), he sent Maximianus Herculius, the Caesar, to subjugate them; he tamed the rustics in some minor battles and restored peace to Gaul.	Diocletian took Herculius Maximianus as his partner in royal power; by crushing the great mob of country-folk (who had given the name of *Bacaudae* to their party), he restored peace to Gaul.

Maximian and the Bagaudae, the rustic rebels in Gaul whom he was sent to subdue, can be seen in **TABLE 6.4**. The structure and compass of Eutropius' and Jerome's brief narratives are nearly identical, and many of the words are the same. Every shared item must represent the actual words of the *KG*. Whence, then, came Victor's much more substantial account (*HAb* 39.17–19)?

> Namque ubi comperit Carini discessu Aelianum Amandumque per Galliam excita manu agrestium ac latronum, quos Bagaudas incolae vocant, populatis late agris plerasque urbium tentare, Maximianum statim fidum amicitia quamquam semiagrestem, militiae tamen atque ingenio bonum imperatorem iubet. Huic postea cultu numinis Herculio cognomentum accessit, uti Valerio Iovium; unde etiam militaribus auxiliis longe in exercitum praestantibus nomen impositum. Sed Herculius in Galliam profectus fusis hostibus aut acceptis quieta omnia brevi patraverat.

> For when, at the departure of Carinus, he [Diocletian] learnt that Aelianus and Amandus, having stirred up a band of rustics and brigands (whom the locals call Bagaudae) in Gaul and ravaged the countryside far and wide, were attacking most of the cities, he immediately commanded that Maximian be proclaimed emperor, a man trustworthy in friendship, although half-rustic, good in both his service and character. Later on, this man was given the name Herculius, in honour of that divinity, just as Jovius was given to Valerius; for this reason also the name was assigned to the auxiliary soldiers who were most outstanding in the army. But Herculius set out for Gaul and, after the enemy had been routed or surrendered, in a short time he brought everything to a peaceful conclusion.[175]

Once again, it looks like the *KG* is summarising and simplifying what is found in Victor. If we accept the *KG* theory, then, this must mean that Victor is – or was using – the *KG*'s source. If Victor had access to the *KG*'s source, then he was its twin, not its derivative. Yet, this is absurd, because, as Burgess makes clear, the *KG* is *by definition* the common source of Victor and Eutropius. The much simpler, much more logical explanation is that Victor's *Historia* is the common source of the tradition that Burgess has outlined, but that – for those short of time or attention, or both – Eutropius' simple and elegant narrative was irresistible.

---

175 For the meaning of *Carini discessu*, see Chapter X.

What of Burgess' identification of the *KG* with (part of) the *Latina historia* mentioned by Jerome?[176] The idea here (derived from Enmann and Rudolf Helm) is that Jerome had before him a work comprising something like the *Origo Gentis Romanae*, an epitome of Livy, and the *KG*, which was his basic source for supplementing Eusebius in his *Chronicon*. He referred to this collection as a *Latina historia*, hence proof of the existence of the *KG* (circuitously). This too is a phantom – a sort of *ersatz Corpus tripertitum*. In the *Chronicon*, a notice added to the material translated from Eusebius, Jerome does once refer to *Latina historia* (*Chron.* 77b[c]):

> In Latina historia ad verbum haec scripta reperimus: Agrippa apud Latinos regnante Homerus poeta in Graecia claruit, ut testantur Apollodorus grammaticus, et Euforbus historicus ante urbem Romanam conditam anni CXXIIII, et ut ait Cornelius Nepos, ante Olympiadem primam anni C.

> In Latin history, we find this written *ad verbum*: when Agrippa was ruling among the Latins, Homer the poet was famous in Greece, as Apollodorus the grammarian and Euforbus the historian bear witness, 124 years before the foundation of the city of Rome and (as Cornelius Nepos says) 100 years before the first Olympiad.

This is a rather elusive passage: how exactly it ought to be punctuated and understood is not obvious, so caution in interpretation is wise. With *Latina historia*, however, there are two basic possibilities: either Jerome is giving us the title of the work or a description of its nature. As a phrase, *Latina historia* is used almost exclusively by Jerome (ten attestations). The only other instances are in Augustine, Evanthius, and pseudo-Acro.[177] In all three of these cases, the signification is general, and the word *Latina* is used for an explicit or implicit contrast with texts written in Greek. The same is true of every other instance in Jerome.[178] Each of these contains an explicit comparison with Greek, Hebrew, or *barbara lingua*, save *Ep.* 60.5, which has a general meaning and an implicit contrast with Greek sources: 'Why should I mention the Roman generals, with whose mighty deeds, as if with some stars, Latin histories (*Latinae . . . historiae*) sparkle?' At first sight, there is no contrast with Greek in this passage of the *Chronicon*, so one might reasonably conclude that this, uniquely, is a concrete reference to a single work. That impression is, however, misleading. To see why, one needs to put this entry in the overall context of the *Chronicon*. The reason for its inclusion is to provide a date for Homer (in the late tenth century BC) and to correlate him with one of the Latin kings who ruled before the foundation of Rome. Crucially, this is not the only date for Homer that the work provides: he turns up twice elsewhere, once in the 1030s (69b[f]) and once in the 1010s (71b[b]), both times in entries original to Eusebius. Jerome, in putting him almost a full century later, was departing from his Greek original, on the basis of a Latin source: hence the reference to *Latina historia* here is, as in every other example, designed to draw a broad contrast with the Greek tradition. Consider also the content of the entry: it is obvious that its source was some sort of antiquarian compilation, one which cited many authors, like the text from which the extant *Origo gentis Romanae* was epitomised. That

---

176 Burgess 2005: 166, n. 4, 183, 190.
177 Augustine, *De civ.* 18.8: *nec Graeca nec Latina novit historia*; Evanthius 4.1: *praetextatas a dignitate personarum tragicarum ex Latina historia*; pseudo-Acro, *In Artem*

Poeticam 287 (355 Keller): *nostri Graecos imitari et historias Latinas scribere*.
178 *In Isaiam* 1.2.7 and 2.5.13; *In Dan.* 2.8; *In Amos* 3.8; *In Abdiam* l. 69; *In Jonam* l. 57; *In Mich.* 2.7; *In Soph.* l. 23; *adv. Iov.* 1.41; *Ep.* 60.5 and 72.2

seems to ill suit a compendium which relied on a scrappy *breviarium* like the *KG* for its imperial section. Finally, the assumption that there was, in fact, an *Ur-Epitome* of Livy, which underlay later brief texts of republican history (and which ought to have formed the first part of Burgess' underlying source for Jerome), has itself been challenged.[179]

As for Eusebius of Nantes, if he is not quite phantasmical, then there is a rather ghostly quality to him too. Our only sure attestation of the name is in a marginal note in an autograph manuscript of the *Historia imperialis* by the fourteenth-century Veronese scholar Giovanni de Matociis (BAV Chig. I. VII. 259, f. 119r).[180] This contains a list of works by Ausonius that includes the following item:

> Item ad eundem de imperatoribus res novas molitis a decio usque ad dioclecianum versu iambico trimetro iuxta libros eusebii nannetici ystorici.

> On the emperors who rebelled from Decius to Diocletian, in iambic trimeter, according to the books of the historian Eusebius of Nantes.

This work by Ausonius does not survive, so any discussion of its contents must remain speculative at best. That has not stopped Burgess from making some very specific suggestions about it.[181] He re-titles it the *Tyranni* and suggests that the work dealt with unsuccessful claimants to imperial power, rightly noting that the period between Decius and Diocletian was particularly rich in such figures. Because the supposed '*KG* texts' show an interest in usurpation, he then argues that Ausonius ought to have used the *KG* for his treatment of these usurpers. Given this and since de Matociis says that Ausonius used the works of Eusebius of Nantes, Eusebius of Nantes must be the author of the *Kaisergeschichte*. This argument has attracted both support and criticism.[182] Critics have pointed out that we actually have references to historians called Eusebius whose works covered roughly the correct period. One, mentioned by Evagrius (*HE* 5.24), wrote a history from Octavian to Carus. Two extracts on sieges from the second half of the third century are quoted in a Greek military compendium (Paris gr. 607) also ascribed to a Eusebius.[183] Both of these authors wrote in Greek. Obviously, if Ausonius' Eusebius is identified with either of these two – whether or not they are the same as one another – he cannot be the author of a Latin *breviarium* covering the emperors from Augustus to Constantius II.

The one thing that has not been sufficiently brought out in the oft-heated debate over the Eusebii (of Nantes and otherwise) is that the title quoted by de Matociis does not actually make any sense: there is a fundamental contradiction between the *imperatores* and those who *res novas moliti* (rebelled).[184] In the fourth century, *imperatores* were emperors – specifically Augusti – and not rulers in some vague sense,

179 Begbie 1967. In his supplementary notes published in 2011, Burgess claims that Rohrbacher 2009 successfully argues 'that the "Latina historia" was simply another later variant version of the *KG*, but with an epitome of Republican history prefixed' (2011: 4). Rohrbacher makes no such claim – not even mentioning the passage in Jerome – but rather argues that Jerome and Eutropius have a common source for the Republican section which is *not* identical with the *KG*.

180 On whom see Stover and Woudhuysen 2017.

181 Burgess 1993a: 495–499.

182 Usefully surveyed, with full bibliography, in Suski 2005.

183 Sivan 1992 argued that these Eusebii were both identical with Eusebius of Nantes. This has generally been rejected: Bleckmann and Groß 2016: 111–148; Suski 2005; and Burgess 1993a: 496–497.

184 We might also be a little uneasy about *nanneticus*. There is no sure evidence for the name of Condevincum having shifted to *civitas Namnetum* or *Namnetica* before the *Notitia Galliarum*, possibly to be associated

as Suski interprets the title.[185] The fact that two undoubted emperors are mentioned by name, Decius and Diocletian, cannot be coincidental here. For this reason, Green is right to conclude that Burgess' interpretation – which makes Decius and Diocletian mere chronological markers – is impossible. Just as impossible, however, is Green's own idea that Ausonius considered Decius and Diocletian to be illegitimate usurpers.[186] The project implied by Ausonius' transmitted title is about as coherent as a contemporary poet writing a catalogue entitled *Unsuccessful Presidential Candidates: From Ronald Reagan to Barack Obama.*[187] Any extrapolation from this title is fraught with extreme hazard, and the only safe course of action is to indeed assume that Eusebius of Nantes wrote *something* in multiple books which covered the period from Decius to Diocletian. That in itself rules out the possibility that this work is the *KG*. Eusebius' history had different termini from the *KG*, which no contemporary advocate would characterise as a complex multi-book work. We have seen already that H.W. Bird estimated that the *KG* was a mere thirty-five Teubner pages in length.[188] If we compare a putatively contemporary writer whose works are published in a Teubner edition – Firmicus Maternus – we find that his books range from 39 pages (I) to 141 (VI). The works of another putative contemporary, Hilary of Poitiers (also a Gallic author), have not been published by Teubner, but the books of his *De Trinitate* would range from roughly thirty to fifty pages in such an edition. The phrase *iuxta libros* is a recognisable formula for a condensed text, which suggests a work in at least three books (but likely more). In other words, at a minimum, the work of Eusebius of Nantes ought to have occupied at least ninety Teubner pages.[189] Even if one rejects these calculations, the fundamental point remains that the work of Eusebius of Nantes – judging by our one very slight *testimonium* – has no characteristics that match those of the *KG* as Burgess (or any of its other advocates) have envisaged it.

Burgess' case for the *KG* thus turns out to be more fragile than irrefragable. In fact, his own later work has been moving slowly towards recognising this. In his 2014 monograph on the regnal durations in the *Chronography of 354*, Burgess comprehensively surveys the information in the various '*KG* texts' on the lengths of emperors' reigns, and concludes that they cannot go back to a single unitary source in any straightforward way.[190] One of the places he ends up is not terribly distant from Den Boer: 'In fact, it may indeed have been the case that what we tend to think of as a specific text of the KG really developed into more of a tradition as the fourth century progressed'.[191] Whatever else one may say, this spells the end of Enmann's method. The problem demands a completely different solution.

---

with Magnus Maximus (Harries 1978), though note *CIL* 17.2.387 = 13.8999 (a dedication to the Gallic Emperor Victorinus) where the terminal *cN* has been expanded to *civitas Namnetum*.

185 Suski 2005: 64. Strictly, only Augusti had the title *imperator* and some well-informed contemporaries were precise about such things (Barnes 1982: 25–27). Not everyone observed this distinction strictly, however: Ammianus, for example, calls Julian an *imperator* at a time when he was still a Caesar (16.5.11).

186 Green 1999: 576–578.

187 A solution might perhaps lie in Eusebius having written about the Gallic Empire, which would match the *termini* given for his work rather neatly (Postumus perhaps having begun his career under Decius and Tetricus surviving into the reign of Diocletian, *cf.* Eutropius 9.13.2: *privatus diutissime vixit*).

188 See page 213 above. Calculation of length by Teubner pages is deficient in itself (see Stover and Woudhuysen 2022b: 13–14), but we use it here to illustrate a weakness in the *KG* argument.

189 The obvious counter-argument would be to point to the books of Eutropius, which are miniature. His work, however, is an outlier in every sense – no other work has these miniature books – and one gets the strong impression that the fact that there are *ten* is the important fact, as if Eutropius simply divided his work into ten sections. If so, this would give no parallel example. On condensed texts, see Chapter III.

190 Burgess 2014: 135–141.

191 Burgess 2014: 140.

Barnes and Burgess are both votaries of the *KG*, who self-consciously present their work as advocacy for it. A slightly different example can help to reinforce the conclusions reached from close examination of their case for the *KG*. Alan Cameron, among the most influential scholars of late antiquity in general and late-antique literature in particular, began his scholarly career as a *KG*-sceptic. In 1965, he referred to the text as 'a ghost of which little has been heard in recent years, the hypothetical anonymous *Kaiserchronik* of A. Enmann'.[192] This attitude well suited a scholar who (in Gavin Kelly's crisp formulation) was 'willing to cross the road to knock down a bad argument'.[193] By 1969, however, he had been won round: he accepted both that the *KG* existed and that it was 'almost certain' that Festus and Eutropius both used it.[194]

In his 2011 *magnum opus*, *The Last Pagans of Rome*, Cameron argued briefly that we have evidence from Greek sources for the Latin *KG*.[195] This was his only sustained treatment of Enmann's hypothesis and it is an atypical way to approach the subject: coming from a former sceptic, it might be expected to be more persuasive than other arguments, so it is worth probing a little. Cameron's argument runs as follows. The fragments of the Greek historian John of Antioch (sixth or seventh century: it is a controverted question) often read as a translation of Eutropius, but one very different from the extant fourth-century version of Paeanius.[196] Traditionally, John's source was identified as the translation made by the Lycian historian Capito (probably *ca.* 500), mentioned by the *Suda* in its entry on him (K.342). Yet another translation of Eutropius, however, was used by yet another historian, Theophanes the Confessor, in the eighth century and we have no explicit evidence to divine which of them (if either) might have used Capito. As a result, we would seem to need three Greek translations of Eutropius to explain the evidence. Cameron doubted that any 'so utilitarian work' would have been thrice translated and pointed out that at times John is very close to, but somewhat fuller than, Eutropius. The *ipsissima verba* of Eutropius, but with more material, is almost the definition of the *KG* as it is commonly envisaged. Hence, Cameron suggested, John did not use a translation of Eutropius at all, but rather a translation of Eutropius' source: the *KG*.[197] If true, this would be a significant breakthrough.

Unfortunately, there are serious problems with Cameron's argument, which can be easily seen by careful consideration of his proofs. His marquee example is that John includes an *à propos* quotation of Sallust in his account of Sulla (fr. 145.2 Roberto). While Cameron is surely right to think that this indicates that John had access (directly or indirectly) to a Latin source, it was hardly one like the *KG* as it is traditionally conceived, which was (if it needs restatement) a history of the emperors, not the Republic. Cameron does not spell this out, but one has to envisage that the hypothetical *KG* was included in a hypothetical compendium of all Roman history, which Eutropius hypothetically used, cutting out things like the quotation from Sallust. Even granting all this, if that compendium included substantial quotations from cited sources, was it really the kind of short summary of Roman history generally envisaged? Similarly, Cameron is right that John's claim that Constantius I acquired the nickname Παῦπερ (= Lat. *pauper*), from his frugality in using the silver dishes and couches of private individuals at feasts, implies a Latin source at some point in the tradition.[198] Unfortunately, no extant Latin text makes this claim about him.

192 Cameron 1965a: 249.

193 Kelly 2015: 232.

194 Cameron 1969a: 307.

195 Cameron 2011: 665–668.

196 On which, see below.

197 Cameron 2011: 666.

198 Cameron 2011: 667 for both of these examples.

TABLE 6.5 – THE DEATH OF GORDIAN III: PHILIP AS PRAETORIAN PREFECT

HAb 27.7–8	Festus 22	Jerome 241[a]	Eutropius 9.2.2–3	*LB* 27.2
Ibi gesto insigniter bello Marci Philippi **praefecti praetorio** insidiis periit sexennio imperii.	Isque de Perside rediens victor, fraude Philippi, **qui praefectus praetorii erat,** occisus est.	Cum victor reverteretur ad patriam, fraude Philippi **praefecti praetorio** haud longe a Romano solo interfectus est.	Rediens haud longe a Romanis finibus interfectus est fraude Philippi, qui post eum imperavit.	A Philippo **praefecto praetorio** accensis in seditionem militibus occiditur.

The closest analogue is a story in Eusebius of Caesarea's *Vita Constantini* (1.14.1–6) in which Constantius obtains vast wealth on demand from his willing subjects, in whose hands he generally preferred to leave gold and silver – an episode set off by an accusation of πενία, or poverty, against him. The same story is in Libanius (*Or.* 59.15, perhaps from Eusebius directly) and is clearly modelled on an episode in Xenophon's *Cyropaedia* (8.2.15–20). John may have had a Latin source, but this is a Greek tale. It is also very interesting that John's obituary of the emperor Julian (fr. 272 Roberto) seems to be derived from Eutropius (10.16.2–3), but is substantially longer.[199] That certainly proves that John had access to good material on Julian, but why he should have obtained that from the *KG* specifically (a short and summary work) is never made clear: the additional details in John do not turn up in any other *KG* text, which seems like it ought to be a mark against the idea. Cameron ends his case with the accounts given by Jerome (*Chron.* 227[m]), Eutropius (9.27.2), and Zonaras (12.32) of the triumph celebrated at Rome in 303 by Diocletian and Maximian.[200] The three texts are interestingly parallel (with Zonaras and Jerome sharing one significant detail), but Zonaras' sources are a famous problem (to which elsewhere Cameron argues the solution must be complex): to simply assert that this came from the *KG*, via John of Antioch, will not do.[201]

Besides these difficulties, it is easy to demonstrate beyond any doubt that John could not have been using what has been identified as the *KG*. For example, Burgess adduces a characteristic series of parallels on the death of Gordian III as evidence for the *KG* (**TABLE 6.5**). Festus and Jerome are very similar to Eutropius. Both of them, however, along with the two Victorine texts, specify that Philip was praetorian prefect. Hence, Burgess argues, the *KG* must have had *praefecti praetorii*: this is a necessary conclusion of Enmann's method.[202] Yet when we turn to the analogous passage in John of Antioch – which is obviously very close to Eutropius and by Cameron's approach ought to be a translation of the *KG* – no trace of the missing phrase is found.[203] Hence, if the *KG* is the source of the post-Eutropian texts that read like Eutropius but have additional details, John of Antioch provides no evidence for its existence. Instead, John offers a parallel case to our Latin sources, wherein Eutropius provides an overall framework into which material could be inserted.

199 The parallels are more extensive than Cameron 2011: 667 would suggest.

200 Cameron 2011: 667–668.

201 Cameron 2011: 688. On Zonaras, see Chapters IX and X.

202 Burgess 1995a: 363.

203 John of Antioch, fr. 225 Roberto: ἐκεῖθεν δὲ μετὰ τὸ πέρας ἐπανιών, ἕκτῳ τῆς ἡγεμονίας ἐνιαυτῷ, πρὸς αὐτοῖς ἤδη τοῖς ὅροις τῆς οἰκείας ἀρχῆς ὑπὸ Φιλίππου, τὴν βασιλείαν διαδεξαμένου, τοῦ κατ' ἐκεῖνο καιροῦ τὴν τῶν στρατιωτῶν νεολαίαν ἀσκοῦντος, ἐδολοφονήθη.

Three cases for the *KG*, two made by its greatest modern advocates, one advanced by a repentant sceptic, and no real proof. In each, the evidence assembled by Barnes, Burgess, and Cameron supports not Enmann's *KG*, but rather Victor's *Historia* as the lost common source. What we see in the complex connections between various historians cannot be explained by all of them mechanically using a single unitary source. Rather, it makes sense in an environment where Victor's work was the landmark study of Roman history and the principal source of Eutropius' imperial section, but where that convenient and condensed narrative also found many readers. More specifically, it was to Eutropius that later authors – Jerome or Paul the Deacon, for instance – often seem to have turned for a basic framework, into which information from Victor could be inserted, if need for it was felt. The *KG* can henceforth be consigned to the grand and growing museum of the history of classical scholarship. Insofar as Enmann's insights have validity, they need to be understood in the framework of Victor's *History*, not amidst the ruins of a nineteenth-century idea.

Victor and Eutropius

What then in the final analysis ought we to make of the central problem that the modern *KG* theory solves, the relationship between the *HAb* and Eutropius? We have shown that they must share some source, and the idea that it is Eutropius who most faithfully mirrors that source, rather than the *HAb*, is simple prejudice, at points demonstrably wrong. [204] Instead, their common source is Victor's *Historia* – that was where Eutropius turned both for the details of Roman imperial history and for the language in which to describe it. It would, however, be wrong to get the impression that Eutropius merely mined Victor for facts, quarried him for phrasing: we can see his debt on a much larger scale, in terms of the way that he structures his narrative of Rome under the emperors.

Victor had definite ideas about the shape of imperial history, most of which were connected with questions of constitutional arrangement. [205] His work (as we have seen) opened with a description of Octavian's position after Actium and a significant chronological calculation. [206] The family of Augustus (and it was important to Victor that it was a family) ruled down to the death of Nero (*HAb* 5.17), succeeded after an interval of chaos by another *gens*, the Flavians. [207] The first major moment of constitutional transformation came with the accession of Nerva, since this inaugurated a period of political experimentation: in particular, emperors from outside Italy (*HAb* 11.12–13). Significantly, this is also the point at which the *HAb* and *LB* begin to diverge markedly, suggesting that the narrative became more substantial. The next great transition occurred after the death of Alexander Severus with the accession of Maximinus (*HAb* 24.8–11). Surveying the course of Roman expansion from Romulus to Septimius Severus, Victor saw continuous growth, albeit in fits and starts (*certatim*). The succeeding emperors, especially Alexander,

204 *cf*. Burgess 1995: 349: 'Victor's own opinions and peculiar style and vocabulary have no reflection in Eutropius, as they could hardly help but have done if Eutropius had copied Victor'.

205 See further the Conclusion.

206 Chapter IV.

207 Victor specifically identified the Flavians as a *familia* (*HAb* 8.4). *cf*. *HAb* 9.1, where Vespasian is *hoc item ex genere*, referring back to Victor's discussion of the *Caesarum gens* (8.7) and their nature: the word perhaps has a double meaning.

managed to hold the line: 'the fact that it did not immediately slip was due to Alexander'. The accession of Maximinus was also a new constitutional development for Victor: just as non-Italians had come to the purple after Nerva, so after Alexander there was the first emperor from the common throng of soldiers, a man who came to power *suffragiis legionum*, 'with the support of the legions' (*HAb* 25.1). The death of Probus was another turning point (*HAb* 37.5–7, which we discuss further in Chapter VIII), leading to more constitutional experimentation (the Tetrarchy). Finally, a new period begins with the accession of Constantius I as co-Augustus with Galerius (*HAb* 40.1), followed by the swift rise of Constantine, which in constitutional terms meant ultimately the return of a single ruling *gens*.[208]

This way of thinking about Rome's past maps very closely on to Eutropius' history as well. The architecture of his work has never been properly studied, but it is clear that its structure was purposeful and carefully judged. In particular, Eutropius paid close attention to where his individual books had their starting points. For example, Book VI begins, in a sense, far too early: Book V has terminated after just over 1,000 words, half the length of all the other books. Yet the opening of the sixth book comes at a significant moment: the end of the era of Marius and Sulla and the terrible violence that their rivalry visited on the Roman people. The foreshortening of Book V is a sign that Eutropius had arranged this quite deliberately, one that can be confirmed when it is realised that his sixth book's opening, '*M. Aemilio Lepido Q. Catulo consulibus*, after Sulla had set the commonwealth in order, new wars were kindled' (6.1.1), echoes the famous incipit of Sallust's *Histories* (1.1R = 1.1M): 'the history of the Roman people, *M. Lepido Q. Catulo consulibus*, at home and on campaign, I have composed'. Eutropius was hardly alone in looking back to this part of Sallust. One of the few things we know about the mostly lost history of Granius Licinianus (for example) is that he stopped to draw attention to the beginning of the *Histories* when his own work reached that point.[209]

When we turn to Books VII–X of Eutropius – those which overlap in coverage with Victor and for which Victor was a major source – we find a fascinating structure. Book VII opens a little before the beginning of Victor's work, and yet the first words closely recall Victor's own opening (**TABLE 6.6**). The next book in Eutropius (VIII) begins with Nerva, as does the next phase in Victor's history. Eutropius baldly notes that this period was marked by prosperity and *boni principes*, but one needs to turn to Victor to find the reason why: because 'the city of Rome has in particular grown great by the bravery of foreigners and transplanted skills of outsiders' (*HAb* 11.13). The following book (IX) begins after the death of Alexander Severus, with the accession of Maximinus Thrax. The opening words recall both Victor's own language and his ideas (**TABLE 6.7**). What is interesting is that Eutropius' emphasis on Maximinus' background as a common soldier responds to Victor's conception of his reign as an important turning point, but is never explained in his *breviarium*. Finally, Book X of Eutropius begins with the accession of Constantius, once again in phrasing that closely recalls Victor's (**TABLE 6.8**). When Victor was writing, the short reign of Constantius I as Augustus was obviously significant, because his grandson (Constantius II) was on the throne. By *ca.* 370, as Eutropius penned his work, the house of Constantine had fallen and yet he retained Victor's arrangement.

---

208 Victor was very much aware of the Constantinian dynasty as a dynasty: *HAb* 34.7.

209 See Stover and Woudhuysen 2022b: 16–17.

TABLE 6.6 – VICTOR AND BOOK VII OF EUTROPIUS

HAb 1.1	Eutropius 7.1.1–2
Anno urbis septingentesimo fere vicesimoque, duobus etiam, mos Romae incessit **uni** prorsus **parendi.**	**Anno urbis septingentesimo fere ac nono** interfecto Caesare civilia bella reparata sunt. . . . Quare tres exercitus **uni** Caesari Augusto **paruerunt.**
In almost the seven hundredth and twenty-second year of the city, the custom arose at Rome of obeying one man absolutely.	In almost the seven hundredth and ninth year of the city, after Caesar had been killed, the civil wars were renewed . . . On this account, three armies obeyed one man, Caesar Augustus.

TABLE 6.7 – VICTOR AND BOOK IX OF EUTROPIUS

HAb 25.1	Eutropius 9.1
Gaius Julius Maximinus, who was governing Trebellica, was the first from among the soldiers (*primus e militaribus*) to seize power with the support of the legions, a man almost unacquainted with letters.	After him, Maximinus was the first from the ranks of the army (*ex corpore militari primus*) to come to imperial power by the will of the soldiers alone.

TABLE 6.8 – VICTOR AND BOOK X OF EUTROPIUS

HAb 40.1	Eutropius 10.1
Igitur Constantio atque Armentario **his** succedentibus Severus Maximinusque Illyricorum indigenae Caesares, prior Italiam posteriorque in quae Iovius **obtinuerat,** destinantur.	**His igitur** abeuntibus administratione rei publicae Constantius et Galerius Augusti creati sunt divisusque inter eos ita Romanus orbis, ut Galliam, Italiam, Africam Constantius, Illyricum, Asiam, Orientem Galerius **obtineret,** sumptis duobus Caesaribus.
Thereupon, when Constantius and Armentarius succeeded them, Severus and Maximinus, natives of Illyricum, were dispatched as Caesars, the first to Italy, the second to what Jovius had occupied	After they had retired from administering the state, Constantius and Galerius were made Augusti and the Roman world was divided between them, so that Constantius held Gaul, Italy, and Africa, Galerius Illyricum, Asia, and the East – two Caesars were also chosen

It is very suggestive that three of Victor's four divisions of imperial history – divisions which, we must stress, arise solely from an analysis of Victor's text – correspond with book divisions in Eutropius. The fact that the beginning of Victor's *Historia*, which must obviously represent the commencement of a book, also corresponds with a book division in Eutropius, strongly suggests that the others do as well. Of course, confronted by these parallels, one could always have recourse to the *KG*, and claim that this structuring of imperial history was already present in the source of Eutropius and the *HAb*. Indeed, some of these parallels were picked up by Nickbakht and Scardino, who attributed sophisticated constitutional history to the *KG*.[210] The periodisation in both texts, however, cannot be divorced from the intellectual apparatus which underpins the *HAb*. This means that the source of Eutropius and the *HAb* was much more similar to the latter than the former: not just a scrappy chronicle but an intellectually rich and reflective treatment of imperial history. In other words, it was Victor's *Historia*.

Though it has escaped attention, Eutropius in fact almost tells us this. At the end of his history, he includes an elegant *envoi* (10.18.3):

> For what remains ought to be described in a grander style (*stilo maiore dicenda sunt*), which we do not now so much pass over as keep back for grander craftsmanship in writing (*ad maiorem scribendi diligentiam*).

Eutropius' statement has generally been interpreted as meaning that contemporary emperors should be treated in panegyric, rather than history: it has been compared fruitfully with the ending of Ammianus.[211] While *stilo maiore dicenda* on its own could certainly refer to panegyric, the last sentence – especially *ad maiorem scribendi diligentiam* – cannot, since strictly panegyric is *spoken* not *written*.[212] Instead, Eutropius must be saying that treatment of the period after 364 awaits the more thorough treatment (*maior scribendi diligentia*) of a historian. After all, the very nature of a *breviarium* as a secondary text presupposes the existence of a *primary* text: where no primary text was available, Eutropius had no material on which to practise his craft. From the perspective of *ca.* 370, there was of course only one historian who might embark on the noble but demanding endeavour of writing contemporary history.

The realisation that Eutropius was heavily indebted to Victor's history might shed new light on what he was trying to achieve. Eutropius' work was an astonishing success. As we have seen, it was translated into Greek by Paeanius in 380, only a decade after its composition, and then again by Capito a century and a half later. It formed the basis of Paul's *Historia Romana*, and from there went on to provide the framework for the study of Roman history for the next 500 years, becoming in Michael Kulikowski's words 'the most influential textbook of Roman history ever produced'.[213] It was the model against which Festus reacted, was certainly read and exploited by Ammianus, the *Historia Augusta*, and Jerome as well. It even influenced the text of *Libellus breviatus*, due to Paul's deep familiarity with it.[214] Why was Eutropius so influential? Contemporary scholarship has no very good answer to this question. It is generally dismissive of both Eutropius and his work: 'little more than an epitome of the *KG*' (Burgess) by an author who mechanically reproduced his source 'largely unchanged' (Barnes).[215] On the standard account of the *KG*, where Eutropius was simply summarising a text already very like his own in style and scope, but *slightly*

210 Nickbakht and Scardino 2021: 'Vielmehr war der verfassungsgeschichtliche Einschnitt von 235 bereits in der EKG angelegt, die auch andere erstmalige oder einzigartige Erscheinungen in römischen Staatswesen systematisch erfasst zu haben scheint'.

211 Omissi 2018: 31; Den Boeft *et al.* 2018: 302; Ross 2016b: 295; Cameron 2011: 373; Paschoud 2001: 289; MacCormack 1976: 40.

212 See for example, Quintilian, *Inst.* 3.8.7; Augustine, *Contra Iulianum* 5.3.8; Julius Victor, *Rhet.* p. 103

Giomini/Celentano 1980, *HA Pesc.* 11.5 and *Alex.* 35.1. Only Jerome refers to writing panegyric, *e.g. Ep.* 108.21 or *In Gal.* 3.5.6, but *cf. Ep.* 65.11.

213 Kulikowski 2018: 150. Briefly, *T&T* 'Eutropius' (Reynolds). On the Greek translations, Malcovati 1943–1944; Fisher 1982: 189–193 (on Paeanius).

214 Stover and Woudhuysen 2021.

215 Burgess 2005: 167; Barnes 1978: 92.

fuller in detail, there is simply no reason for his popularity.[216] Nor is there anything to explain why his work enjoyed such rapid dissemination and sustained influence when the *KG* was buried in silence. The idea of the *KG* has blinded us to Eutropius' actual achievement.

The very fact that we assume that the *Ur*-source of Roman imperial historiography was essentially a slightly longer version of Eutropius is a testament to the success of his project. What if Eutropius' talent lay precisely in cutting through complex accounts, eliminating unusual vocabulary, and pruning away what he saw as extraneous to the historical facts? It is no accident that the short historical texts which come after him – Festus, Jerome's *Chronicon*, the *Libellus breviatus* – sound very much like him, such was his influence. Once we look at the issue in the correct perspective and consider his actual primary source for the imperial period, Victor, Eutropius' virtues become much clearer. He decocted a complex and obscurely written work into a readable and easy-to-remember format, with a keen eye for the elimination of digression and moralising, matched with a fine sense for how to organise a narrative. This was a rare accomplishment for an epitomator.[217] It is no surprise that Eutropius' work became *the epitome* for use in place of and alongside the much more difficult and obscure *Historia* of Victor. An astonishing success, then, but astonishing only to us.

The ideas advanced here will be controversial. So complete has been Enmann's triumph that in 2002 François Paschoud could write:

> The battle for Enmann's *Kaisergeschichte* is practically won. Even if controversies remain about the exact nature and extent of this work, I do not see today any serious doubt about the existence of a historical work treating in abridged form the imperial period of Roman history, which was used by Aurelius Victor, Eutropius, Rufius Festus, Jerome for his *Chronicle*, the *Historia Augusta* and the *Epitome de Caesaribus*.[218]

This is no different from what Burgess would write in 2018, significantly in a standard reference work, the *Oxford Dictionary of Late Antiquity*, a passage we have quoted in part already:

> Although its existence was controversial for almost a century following the first proof by Enmann, its existence is now universally accepted by scholars.[219]

We have argued that Enmann's theory is ultimately a product of its time, one that should have been jettisoned or refashioned root and branch after Dessau, but was instead merely shuffled around to play a

---

216 He cannot even have been much good as an epitomiser, since the imperial portion of the *breviarium* is some 8,000 words long: only twenty per cent shorter than Bird's calculation of the length of the *KG* (Bird 1989: 95).

217 Brunt 1980: 493; *cf.* Chapter III.

218 Paschoud 2002: xii–xiii: 'La bataille pour la *Kaisergeschichte* d'Enmann est pratiquement gagnée. Même si des controverses subsistent sur la nature et l'extension exacte de cette oeuvre, je ne vois pas que soit aujourd'hui mise sérieusement en doute l'existence d'un ouvrage historique traitant sous forme d'abrégé la période impériale de l'histoire romain, que a été utilisé par Aurélius Victor, Eutrope, Rufius Festus, Jérôme pour sa *Chronique*, l'*Histoire Auguste* et l'*Epitome de Caesaribus*'.

219 *ODLA* 'Kaisergeschichte' (Burgess).

slightly different role. The textual correspondences between Eutropius and the *HAb* are real, but far from implying the existence of a historical *breviarium* produced in 357, upon which both texts depend, they are due simply to the fact that the *HAb* is what its name implies: an abbreviated version of Victor's *History*, which history was Eutropius' source. Given the way that scholarship had been moving before 1883, towards a more refined understanding of the fashion in which the two Victorine works were transmitted and of their relationship to each other, this theory would have been reached rather sooner without Enmann. Indeed, at least in embryonic form, it was.

In 1900, the Kiel professor Alfred Schöne published a study of the *Chronicon* of Eusebius and Jerome's continuation, with the most important and penetrating discussion of Victor since the 1870s. Despite the monograph's date, its intellectual affinities really belong to the previous decades, to the world before Enmann. Schöne himself was just two years from retirement. He had been a professor at Leipzig until 1869 – his career partially overlapping with Opitz's time there – before moving on to positions at Erlangen, Königsberg, and Kiel.[220] What sparked Schöne's interest in Victor was the strong parallelism between Jerome and Ammianus on the character of Valentinian I and, in particular, the comparison of him to Aurelian that both make. Since it is *prima facie* unlikely that Ammianus was reading Jerome, this necessitates some common source. What, Schöne asked, is the middle term between Jerome and Ammianus? None other than Sex. Aurelius Victor. With brief reference back to the work of Opitz and Wölfflin, he then goes through the whole argument. The *HAb* and the *LB* are both epitomes. Both share some of the same characteristics throughout, and not just in the first eleven chapters, notably comparison of emperors to earlier historical figures. He makes note of the title *Historia* that our *testimonia* give to Victor's work. He pays closer attention to the transmission of the texts than his predecessors had and even raises the possibility that Paul the Deacon had access not to the *LB* but to Victor's original work.[221] He considers the different end-dates of the two works and suggests that there is no need to assume that Victor published his *Historia* all at once.[222] He even suggests that Eutropius could be largely derived from Victor.[223]

The one thing that he was lacking was evidence: the passage in Paul's *Historia Romana* that he discusses, which is simply a stitching together of Eutropius with lines found also in the *LB*, cannot actually be used to show that Paul had access to Victor's full *Historia*. What he needed – the *Scholia Vallicelliana* – would not be published until fourteen years later, and not ascribed to Paul for another sixty years after that. Schöne knew that he was offering no more than a tantalising hypothesis and in the conclusion of this section sets a challenge for future scholars:

> It is neither necessary for my task, nor is it possible given the present state of the text of the Victorine epitome, to pursue this investigation any further for now. But it will have to be done one day, taking into consideration the points I have set out above.[224]

220 See the *Catalogus Professorum Lipsiensium* (https://research.uni-leipzig.de/catalogus-professorum-lipsiensium/leipzig/Schoene_1194).
221 Schöne 1900: 213–217.
222 Schöne 1900: 218: 'Aber näher liegt noch eine andere Annahme, dass nämlich Aurelius Victor sein Werk nicht auf Ein Mal und als ein geschlossenes Ganzes herausgegeben habe'.
223 Schöne 1900: 215.

224 Schöne 1900: 218–219: 'Es ist für meine Aufgabe weder nothwendig, noch bei dem gegenwärtigen Zustande des Textes der Victorischen Epitome möglich, diese Untersuchung für jetzt noch weiter zu verfolgen. Aber es wird einmal geschehen müssen, unter Berücksichtigung der im Vorstehenden dargelegten Gesichtspunkte'.

No one answered this call. This was a retrograde scholarly project, built on the apparently obsolete assumptions of a quarter century earlier. Enmann is cited for a single point only, and one laden with irony: that the future student of the relationship of the works of Roman imperial history to each other must take special care to respect the particularities of each of the authors.[225] This cutting remark suggests that Schöne suspected that the future already belonged to Enmann and his *KG*. More worryingly, 'die scharfsinnige Hypothese von H. Dessau' is curtly dismissed with an avowal that the discussion will focus only on Ammianus and Jerome, but Schöne tips his hand when he gives a list of 'älteren Quellen', consisting of Livy, Suetonius, and the *Scriptores Historiae Augustae*.[226]

This brushing over of Dessau is the principal weakness of Schöne's case: it was also a missed opportunity. Far from being an obstacle, Dessau's work opened up new vistas for those who might follow the idea of Victor's *Historia*: he had made it possible, for the first time, to argue that Victor and Eutropius were *sources* of the *HA*, not debtors. The *HA* actually provides, as we shall see, one of the premier points of access to Victor's lost *Historia*. It would be remiss of us, then, not to broach that most forbidding of topics: the *Quellenforschung* of the *HA*, walled round by generations of scholarship, often seemingly impenetrable, or, to use Barnes' image, 'a battlefield long cumbered with the corpses of moribund theories'.[227] Best, then, to approach it indirectly. Let us start by considering a work of much smaller compass, a little jingle on the Roman emperors, written by one of the premier Latin poets of the last decades of the fourth century: the *Caesares* of Ausonius.

225 Schöne 1900: 219 (citing Enmann 1884: 398 ff.): 'Auch werden, wie schon bisher geschehen ist, im Zusammenhange hiermit Zosimus, Zonaras und die verwandten griechischen Quellen gebührend zu berücksichtigen sein, und vor Allem wird, worin ich der Mahnung von A. Enmann durchaus beistimme, man sich nicht mehr darauf beschränken dürfen, Übereinstimmung oder Widerspruch der einzelnen Schriftwerke unter einander bezüglich ihrer Überlieferung des

Thatsächlichen zu prüfen und zu konstatiren, sondern es soll zugleich auch der schriftstellerische Charakter der einzelnen Quellen, ihr litterarischer Zweck, ihr historisch-politischer Standpunkt und ihr persönliches Verhältniss gegenüber einzelnen Kaisern, mehr erwogen und besser berücksichtigt werden als gewöhnlich zu geschehen pflegt'.

226 Schöne 1900: 206 (quotation); 215 (other sources).
227 Barnes 1975: 373.

CHAPTER VII

AUSONIUS AND MARIUS MAXIMUS

We have argued so far that Victor wrote a long history, the first version of which was published in *ca.* 360 and which would become the foundational and most influential work of Roman historiography of the later fourth century (and beyond). An excellent place to test this hypothesis is Ausonius' *Caesares*, a summary treatment in verse of imperial history made by the leading Latin poet of the age. We show that Victor was Ausonius' main source for the emperors after Domitian. This modest conclusion has considerably weightier implications than might appear at first sight. Ausonius has often been thought to have used an earlier historical account of the emperors from Nerva to Elagabalus, the work of the so-called 'consular biographer' Marius Maximus. Marius Maximus is the keystone of most attempts to reconstruct the sources of the *Historia Augusta*. In consequence of this, he plays a very important role in the study of ancient historiography more generally, one quite out of proportion to the slender evidence for his existence. After surveying the development of scholarship on the sources of the *HA*, with particular attention to the work of Sir Ronald Syme, we show that Maximus is largely a phantasm. Far from being an important source for imperial history of the second and early third century, he is no more than yet another 'bogus author' cooked up by the *Historia Augusta*. The removal of Marius Maximus from serious scholarly consideration opens up once again the question of the *HA*'s true sources, one that we pursue in greater detail in Chapter VIII.

The *Caesares* is a *jeu d'esprit*, a series of short poems about the Roman emperors. The first part is based, as its author says, on Suetonius (*Caes.* 4), treating the lives of the emperors from Julius Caesar to Domitian in monostichs and tetrastichs.[1] These are followed by tetrastichs on the emperors who reigned after the terminus of Suetonius' biographies, concluding in the middle of some lines about Elagabalus – for these, no source is named. Ausonius was no historian, though a man of culture and wide reading, so it is probably reasonable to assume that his *Caesares* after Domitian are based substantially on a single source. A glance at the text shows that that work cannot be Eutropius', which was already developing into the

---

1 Text and commentary in Green 1991: 161–168, 557–569. The date of the *Caesares* is uncertain (see Green 1991: 558), though there is no particular reason to think that the favourable references to adoptive emperors points to a date after the death of Gratian. Eutropius (8.1.1) liked the adoptive emperors and dedicated his work to Valens, surely the fourth century's greatest beneficiary of nepotism. The *Caesares* perhaps ought to be associated with the verse epitome of Suetonius, *De Regibus* by Paulinus of Nola (Chapter III), but the date of that is also uncertain (Trout 1999: 56 puts it tentatively in the mid-380s).

standard summary of imperial history in the 380s. If we are right about Victor and his importance, then Ausonius' source ought to be none other than his *Historia*.[2]

For whatever reason, the consensus is that Ausonius did not draw on Victor's work. 'Nothing of significance links him closely with the recent histories of Aurelius Victor or Eutropius' declares his editor, R.P.H. Green.[3] This could hardly be further from the truth. Even if we have only the scanty remains of Victor's *Historia* in the *HAb* and the *LB*, virtually every line of the *Caesares* betrays its debt to Victor.

The *Caesares* and Victor

Let us begin with the imperfect conclusion on Elagabalus (*Caes.* 139–140):

> Tune etiam Augustae sedis penetralia foedas,
>   Antoninorum nomina falsa gerens?

> Do you not defile the inner sanctuary of the emperors' residence, falsely bearing the name of the Antonines?

The first line refers to the erection of a statue of the Syrian god after whom the emperor was named inside the imperial palace itself, early on in his reign. It is close to a paraphrase of a line in Victor (*HAb* 23.1): 'after the image of the god had been conveyed to Rome, he established altars to it in the innermost chambers of the palace (*in palatii penetralibus*)'.[4] The second line refers to the idea of the *nomen Antoninorum*, which is a Victorine theme, mentioned in the life immediately preceding Elagabalus in the *HAb* (22.2). In other words, the two things Ausonius tells us in this brief account are taken from Victor.[5] Armed with this key to Ausonius' method, it is not hard to spot signs of his influence elsewhere in the *Caesares*. The first life after the Suetonian section, Nerva, stresses that although he was called *princeps* he acted as a *parens*: 'aged Nerva, an emperor (*princeps*) in name, but a father (*parens*) in his disposition' (*Caes.* 95). This idea is something of a *Leitmotiv* in Victor. Consider *HAb* 39.8 on Diocletian: 'although he allowed himself to be called "master" (*dominum*), he played the part of a father (*parentem*)' (*cf.* 39.29) or *LB* 15.3, on Antoninus: 'so that they thought him a father (*parentem*) or a protector rather than a master (*dominum*) or an emperor (*imperatoremve*)'.

The same relationship between the *Caesares* and Victor holds for almost all the lives in between. The lines on Trajan (*Caes.* 100–101) say that he adopted Hadrian as his successor:

---

2 Enmann 1884: 443 suggested that Ausonius' source was the *Kaisergeschichte*; he has not found many followers in this, but insofar as Victor's *Historia* is the common source of the *HAb*, Eutropius, the *LB*, and the *HA*, his was a prescient instinct.

3 Green 1991: 591.

4 That the palace of the emperors had *penetralia* was itself an extremely rare idea, otherwise seemingly present only in Prosper, *Chron.* p. 483 Mommsen 1892, in a description of the death of Aetius. Calpurnius Siculus, *Ecl.* 4.159 speaks of the *penetralia* of Palatine Apollo while *Pan. Lat.* 6.16.1 mentions the *Palatini sacrarii . . . penetralibus*.

5 In addition, we have the probable beginning of the third line of the hemistich quoted without attribution in Pompeius Maurus (*GLK* 5.308): *Elio nam gabalus* (*cf.* Holtz 2005: 210). Green rejects the attribution on the grounds of the line's 'frivolous tone' (1981: 234), a curious standard to apply to the author of the *Cupido cruciatus*. Given the second line on the emperor's 'false name', Antoninus, a reference to his true name is exactly what we might expect. Victor gives particular emphasis to the name: see Chapter VIII.

hic quoque prole carens sociat sibi sorte legendi
    quem . . .

He also, lacking offspring, joins to himself by chance selection a man . . .

This is a remarkably firm stance on a famously murky issue, but one endorsed by Victor, who says that he died 'not before he had adopted Hadrian, his fellow citizen and relative (*civi propinquoque*), into imperial power' (*HAb* 13.11).[6] This line of Victor's is important, for it helps to explain what Ausonius goes on to say about Antoninus Pius (108–109):

Filius huic fato nullus, sed lege suorum
    A patria sumpsit qui regeret patriam.

This man was fated to have no son, but by his family's law he took from his native city a man who would rule the fatherland.[7]

The first hemistich seems to versify a line in Victor (*HAb* 15.6: *maribus frustratus*, 'disappointed in male heirs'). This is Victor's characteristically subtle way of saying not that Antoninus had no sons – he in fact had two – but that they died before he became emperor.[8] Ausonius' reworking obscures this subtlety and gives the erroneous impression that Antoninus fathered no son. The rest of the couplet details how Antoninus followed the custom of his 'family' (*lege suorum*), *i.e.* his predecessors among the adoptive emperors, in himself adopting a successor from his own *patria*. As we have seen, Victor thought it important that Hadrian was not only the relative but the fellow-citizen of Trajan, echoing Cassius Dio on this point.[9] Further, Victor, and Victor alone, holds that Marcus Aurelius was from the same town as Antoninus (*HAb* 16.1: *eodem oppido*).[10] Hence, *Caes.* 109 seems to refer to a unique fact in Victor, for he was the only historian to have the idea that the adoptive emperors generally chose their successors from their fellow-citizens and specifically that Antoninus and Marcus Aurelius shared a *patria*. There are other, smaller signs that Ausonius' account of the second-century emperors is indebted to Victor. Antoninus Pius is introduced (*Caes.* 106) with the words *Antoninus abhinc regimen capit* ('Next Antoninus took over guiding the state'). Victor was very fond of using the word *abhinc* to designate future time (from a particular point in the narrative): this is the only occasion on which Ausonius uses the word.[11] On Marcus Aurelius, Ausonius mentions Plato's famous dictum about philosopher-kings and says that he was better even than Antoninus Pius (*Caes.* 110–111). Victor quotes the same dictum in his treatment of Pius (*HAb* 15.3).

    The parallels continue through Ausonius' coverage of the emperors after Marcus Aurelius. Commodus was killed by a crushed neck (*Caes.* 116: *eliso . . . gutture*); this mirrors Victor's *faucibus pressis*

6 On the accession of Hadrian, see Syme 1958: 1.232–235, 240–241. Dio 69.1 says expressly that he had not been adopted by Trajan, and also (famously) offers the 'real story' of his accession. Eutropius (8.6.1) says that Hadrian became emperor without Trajan having willed it.

7 It is difficult to render in English the double sense of *patria*.

8 *PIR*[2] A.1513.

9 Chapter IV.

10 Victor says (*HAb* 15.2) that Antoninus Pius was from Lanuvium. Marcus Aurelius' paternal line seems have come from Spain, his maternal from southern Italy (*PIR*[2] A.694–695; C.350), but he had a sister and a daughter both with the name Cornificia, which was associated with a senatorial family from Lanuvium: it may represent an attempt to claim the town as a *patria* (Syme 1982–1983: 260–261.

11 *HAb* 12.12, 24.9, 37.5, 41.15 (*cf.* Green 1991: 567).

(*HAb* 17.9; *cf. LB* 17.6 *compressis faucibus*), and contrasts with the bloodless *strangulatus* of Eutropius (8.15) and the *HA* (*Commod.* 17.2). This death, the poet held, was a testimony to his mother Faustina's adultery (117), discussed also by Victor (*HAb* 16.2). The theme of Ausonius' treatment of Pertinax is the question of whether the Senate or the army ought to choose emperors (120–121), and that is a Victorine theme (*cf. HAb* 37.5). Ausonius' tetrastich on Didius Julianus emphasises how quickly the empire he sought was snatched from him (123): 'And swiftly the prize was stolen away from the lying old man' (*Et cito periuro praemia adempta seni*). Compare Victor, *HAb* 19.4: 'still, having seized what he had long desired he did not hold it for long'. His successor, Septimius Severus, receives the most substantial and laudatory treatment in the whole of what survives of the *Caesares*. Ausonius draws from Severus' career the lesson that low birth is no impediment to good character (128–129):

> Punica origo illi, sed qui virtute probaret
>   Non obstare locum, cui valet ingenium.

> His origin was Africa, but he would prove by his excellence that position offers no obstacle to a man whose nature is strong.

'Ausonius' notice of Severus is uniquely favourable', Green notes, and displays 'remarkable enthusiasm'.[12] There is no discernible reason within Ausonius' own work for Severus' prominence. Nor is it a particular feature of other Roman histories: not Eutropius, nor the *Historia Augusta*, nor, as far as we can judge, Ammianus' *Res gestae*. Hence, this idiosyncratic view probably reflects that of Ausonius' source. Severus also receives the most substantial treatment, as we have seen, in what survives of Victor in the *HAb*.[13] Victor was interested in the emperor, partly because of what he showed about the abilities of North Africans (20.5–6):

> All good men should have confidence in this, and especially I myself, who though born on a farm to a poor and uneducated father, have in these times achieved a more honourable mode of life, thanks to liberal studies such as these. This I consider characteristic of our race, that even though it is not particularly fecund of good men, nonetheless it does have some lofty individuals whom it has brought all the way to the pinnacle, such as Severus himself, than whom no one in the commonwealth was more distinguished.[14]

Who but Victor could have given Ausonius the notion that Severus represented a crucial turning point, and indeed one of the highs, of Roman imperial history? Further confirmation is found in the title of the tetrastich in Ausonius: *Severus Pertinax*. This is indeed a form of Severus' name, so it beggars belief to hold with Green that this is actually a scribal error derived from Helvius Pertinax eight lines above.[15] Instead, it is probably a reference to the idea in Victor that Severus gained the name Pertinax by dint of the fact that he killed those responsible for Pertinax's death (*HAb* 20.10). The following tetrastich, on Severus' successor, is entirely devoted to his names: Antoninus and Caracalla. Names were one of Victor's characteristic obsessions and both of these are discussed in his treatment of the emperor (*cf. HAb* 20.3 and

---

12 Green 1981: 235. Green 1991 *ad. loc.*
13 Chapter II.
14 On this passage, see the Appendix, no. V.

15 Green 1981: 233. On the name Pertinax, see *PIR*[2] S.487.

21.1).[16] On Caracalla's successor, Macrinus, and his son, Ausonius mentions how as praetorian prefect he turned on the one he was supposed to protect (135: *Principis hinc custos*), his inactivity (136: *Macrinus iners*), and his fitting death at the hands of the soldiers (138: *quae patitur meruit*). These are all particular themes of Victor's brief treatment: 'Caracalla was killed by a soldier, who had followed him as though to guard him' (LB 21.6: *quasi ad **custodiam** sequebatur*), 'I have discovered nothing about them [*sc.* the Macrini], except that they had savage and uncivil spirits' (*HAb* 22.2), and 'they were killed by those who had made them' (22.4).

All of this makes it clear that no source besides Victor is needed for Ausonius' *Caesares* after Suetonius. While a number of these facts are found in other authors, Ausonius shows particular agreement with Victor in emphasis, on the importance of Severus for instance, in 'error', on the origin of Marcus Aurelius, and in phrasing, most obviously in the treatment of Elagabalus. Indeed, Victor's influence on Ausonius is so marked that it can even be discerned in the Suetonian section. On Nero, Ausonius relates (68–69):

> Nomina quot pietas, tot habet quoque crimina vitae.
>   Disce ex Tranquillo: sed meminisse piget.

> As many names as family duty holds, so numerous also were his sins in life: learn from Tranquillus' account, though it is disgusting to mention them.[17]

Suetonius does indeed discuss Nero's crimes, but it is Victor who is ashamed to mention them (*HAb* 5.4): 'For he conducted the rest of his life (*vitae*) in such disgrace that I am disgusted (*pigeat*) and ashamed to mention (*memorare*) . . .'.[18] This conclusion should come as no surprise, if indeed Victor was the premier historian of Ausonius' day.

Ausonius and Marius Maximus

What about Marius Maximus? In some modern scholarship, Ausonius' *Caesares* are interlinked with a putative series of imperial biographies, from Nerva to Elagabalus, written by this individual, a source frequently invoked by the *Historia Augusta*. Unlike the many other writers dubiously cited by the *HA* – the grand parade of largely fictitious individuals solemnly invoked as attesting this fact or transmitting that document – two factors have lent Maximus some enduring solidity. First, the writings of a Marius Maximus are memorably condemned in the second of Ammianus Marcellinus' two highly entertaining digressions on the city of Rome (28.4.14): there was evidently a real author of this name, whose work found readers in late antiquity. Second, the *HA*'s source has been identified with the prominent general, senator, and prefect of the city of Rome L. Marius Maximus Perpetuus Aurelianus, cos. II 223 – a marshal

---

16 On Victor and names, see Chapter IV.
17 The sense is that in his different roles within the imperial family – as son, father, uncle, husband *etc.* – Nero committed a corresponding crime, *cf. HAb* 5.10–11.

18 This parallel was raised but summarily dismissed by Burgess 1998: 84.

of Septimius Severus, a man who had done well out of the civil wars, and who supposedly turned his hand to biography when Severus Alexander was on the throne.[19] On these points, weighty propositions have been rested. Grave authorities have maintained that Marius Maximus was the major source for Ausonius' imperial verses, that we can even deduce things about the nature of his biographical project from the poet.[20] That belief has limped on after a convincing and sceptical treatment of it by Green.[21] As we have shown, the source of Ausonius' verses is, besides Suetonius, the work of Victor: there is, then, simply no need for Marius Maximus, who is, incidentally, never named by Ausonius. It is worth pointing out, however, that the whole idea that the *Caesares* owe anything to his work was always a phantom. The origins of the error go back to an accident that befell a book at least 1,200 years ago.[22]

As printed, the *Caesares* offers tetrastichs on twenty-four emperors. Twelve of these are taken from Suetonius, so it was very tempting to suppose that the subsequent poems came from a work that also offered, it was assumed, lives of twelve Caesars: Marius Maximus. That idea, however, rests on the assumption that Ausonius's work, as we have it, is complete – this is vanishingly unlikely. The *Caesares* terminates imperfectly after only two lines on Elagabalus: this strongly suggests physical damage to a manuscript before the archetype. We have no idea how much material was lost at the end, but given that the most common reason for tail-less texts is the loss of a folio (or folios), it is much more likely to be a substantial number of lines (say sixty) than just the distich needed to complete the account of Elagabalus. We have no direct evidence for how far the *Caesares* originally stretched, but Ausonius promised to treat 'all the emperors (*cunctos*) of whom I have knowledge (*novi*)', so it seems reasonable to assume that it stretched down to the fourth century.[23] In other words, there are no grounds whatsoever to think that Ausonius owed anything to a work on the emperors from Nerva to Elagabalus, let alone to Marius Maximus: the accidents of manuscript transmission are a poor basis for literary reconstruction.

The true nature of the *Caesares* points to a deeper problem with modern approaches to Marius Maximus. Maximus is, to be sure, a rarity: the only named Latin authority used as a source by the *HA* to still command credibility, the lone survivor of the general reassessment of that work's nature begun by Dessau. No wonder: without him much of what we think we know about the sources of the *HA* for the period up to Elagabalus would simply fall away. Yet, as we have just seen with his supposed relationship to Ausonius, almost nothing written today about the Severan biographer withstands close scrutiny. To understand what has gone wrong, we must venture into murky waters indeed.

---

19 On Maximus' life and times, see Birley 1997b: 2694–2703, *PIR*[2] M.308. Syme 1971a: 135–145 is a lucid treatment, more reminiscent of the author's earlier prosopographical work than his discursive later studies of the *HA*.

20 The connection between the *Caesares* and Marius Maximus was crucial to Syme's arguments about the latter, though never properly substantiated: Syme 1968a: 90 and n. 1; 1968b: 496; 1971a: 57, 79, 83, 94; 1972a: 125, 1971b: 93; 1972b: *passim*. See also Barnes 1967: 66, n. 11; Chastagnol 1994: liv. There was a distinct Italian tradition that held the same: it is well surveyed by

Green 1981: 226. Della Corte 1975 is probably the most important piece on the pro-Maximus side.

21 Green 1981. Key points reiterated in Green 1991: 558–559. The case was accepted by Birley 1997b: 2713–2714, but the idea has survived – Callu *et al.* 1992: xv, Bird 1999: 851 – even among those who essentially accept Green's case: Meckler 1996: 365–366, Thomson 2012: 66–68 *e.g.*

22 On the transmission of Ausonius, see in general *T&T* 'Ausonius' (Reeve).

23 Ausonius, *Caes.* 44–45; *cf.* Green 1991: 557–558.

Like the crocodile, Marius Maximus is the relic of a distant era, surviving because he happens to fill a niche that suits him perfectly. Maximus is cited – along with thirty-six other authors – as an authority in the *HA*, chiefly for the earlier lives, from Hadrian to Elagabalus (138–222). Long consensus holds that the lives of the reigning emperors in this period (often called 'primary') have a more secure factual foundation than the accounts of usurpers and junior emperors interspersed among them ('secondary') and those who follow them (referred to as 'intermediate' and 'later').[24] Remarkably, this attribution is still taken seriously: over a century after Dessau's demolition of the structure he inhabited, the towering figure of Maximus still stalks the literature on later Roman historiography. His colleagues in the *HA* have all been discarded: almost no one now bothers to delineate the style and predilections of Junius Cordus or speculate on the career of Turdulus Gallicanus.[25] With Maximus, however, it is as though nothing, or at any rate very little, has changed since 1889. Whether because of his identification with a known historical figure, or because of the mention of a Marius Maximus by Ammianus, his existence is taken so for granted that it is rarely even discussed.[26] Yet while these factors might explain why Maximus has survived, they do not really account for his pre-eminent position. Counter-intuitive as it might seem, he owes his prominence to Sir Ronald Syme – counter-intuitive, because Syme is generally regarded as the prime adversary of Marius Maximus in the study of the *HA*. Syme's contribution to our understanding of that text is usually thought to reside in his resolute assertion of single authorship in the late fourth century (at a time when that was still not generally accepted) and his portrait of the author as a 'rogue *grammaticus*', revelling in the sheer literary artistry that fraud made possible.[27] In fact, however, he has been most influential in shaping, or rather misshaping, the way that the sources of the *HA* are understood. Unravelling the problem of Marius Maximus thus requires a digression on intellectual history.

Sir Ronald Syme and the *Historia Augusta*

It is perhaps too easy to underestimate the impact of Syme's turn to the *Historia Augusta* and to what was not quite yet late antiquity more generally. In the 1960s, he was probably both the most prominent Roman historian and the most important student of Latin historiography, his status receiving the official sanction of a knighthood in 1959.[28] Unusually, his influence permeated both the Anglophone world and European scholarship: it was Marcel Durry, after all, who described Syme (in his presence) as 'the emperor

24 On this distinction, very widespread in the *HA* litera-
    ture, see the summary in Stover and Kestemont 2016:
    143. It derives ultimately from Mommsen 1890 and was
    modified by Syme (esp. 1970a), who used it through-
    out his work though he never set out a comprehensive
    taxonomy of the lives in the *HA*.
25 In general on the *HA*'s authorities, see Syme 1976a.
    There were believers in the authenticity of Cordus down

to the 1960s: Syme 1968a: 96 and n. 6 collects them.
Defenders of Turdulus have been somewhat fewer.
26 Burgersdijk 2016: 250 is unusual in spelling out that
    'there is no reason to doubt Marius Maximus' historicity,
    if only because he is mentioned by Ammianus Marcel-
    linus'.
27 Syme 1968a: 207 for this formulation.
28 Bowersock 1994 provides an overview of Syme's life and
    work (*cf.* Bowersock 1980).

of Roman history'.[29] Moreover, when he began to work on the field, the later Latin historians were largely *terra incognita* to English-speaking classicists.[30] For Syme to devote his energies to the subject was (as Peter Brown said of A.H.M. Jones' *Later Roman Empire*) 'like the arrival of a steel-plant in a region that has, of late, been given over to light industries'.[31] The four books and numerous articles that he devoted to the topic represent a very substantial portion of his (enormous) output and are probably still unparalleled as a sustained treatment of the issue by a single scholar.[32]

It would, however, be a bold critic who held that Syme's work on the *HA* was his best.[33] By the time he turned to the subject, his prose was turning into a parody of the acute brevity of his earlier work.[34] He advanced his ideas in an often deeply obscure and highly repetitious way: slightly different versions of the same argument turning up in different places, never expressed pellucidly.[35] Much is left for readers to work out for themselves, or rests on a confusing mass of cross-citations to other things written by Syme: the abbreviation *op. cit.* peppers his footnotes. He tends to pile up long lists of proofs for his positions (rarely explained in any detail), lists that mash together a few good with many weak arguments. As Momigliano put it in a highly perceptive review of Syme's first monograph on the *HA*, 'bad evidence . . . does not become good simply because it is put together with other bad evidence', or, as Jones said, 'zero multiplied by ten thousand is still zero'.[36] The 'conservatism' of Momigliano and Jones on the *HA* – their refusal to do justice to the strength of Dessau's case – was not (perhaps) the most glorious moment in the careers of these distinguished scholars.[37] On Syme's methods, however, they had a point. Such caustic judgements by established scholars show that there were critics of Syme's work at the time, but his prominence, the vehemence with which he made his case, and his fearsome abilities as a controversialist hardly encouraged close scrutiny.[38] Momigliano's review drew forth an entire monograph to assail its conclusions, while Syme responded to Jones in a short note rigid with fury.[39] All this has helped to obscure the sheer strangeness of Syme's treatment of the *HA* and with it the very shaky foundations of much of what we think we know about the sources of that work.

---

29 See Syme 1965a: 249 (the discussion annexed to Syme's paper). Durry's qualification, 'et l'on devient empereur de l'histoire romaine à **Oxford**', is sometimes passed over.

30 Thompson 1947 was an important exception.

31 Brown 1967: 329.

32 Syme 1968a, 1971a (which reprints some of his papers relevant to the *HA*), 1971b, 1983 (which collects most of the rest; perhaps only Syme 1968b and 1968d should also be noted). Syme 1976a: 321 offers a sort of valediction to the *HA*, though his interest in the text never quite ceased.

33 *cf.* Momigliano 1973: 115 on the low quality of Syme's *HA* work set against his earlier achievements.

34 Syme's later work evinces a particular grudge against verbs. Crook 1959: 40 commented perceptively on Syme 1958 (not so hard-going as some later material) 'Syme's style is a reincarnation of the pointed, cynical, eclectic style of his hero [*sc.* Tacitus], ignoring the plain fact that English is not Latin'. Crook is also right that replacing the verb 'divine' in Syme's prose with 'guess'

often gives a more accurate impression of what is really going on.

35 A sense of how repetitive the argumentation is can be gleaned from study of Syme's treatment of the life of Verus in the *HA*: 1968a: 176–177; 1968b: 494, 498; 1970: 287–288; 1971a: 31–33. The same points recur (Mommsen wrong to include the *Verus* among the 'secondary lives'; the quality of information in the text; that it cannot come from Marius Maximus, because the *HA* says he wrote a life of Marcus in two books). This is all the more remarkable because his central points had already been made by Barnes 1967, which Syme routinely cites.

36 Momigliano 1969: 568; Jones 1969: 321.

37 In Jones' case, it led to *PLRE* taking an inconsistent and rather incoherent approach to the evidence of the *HA*, something pointed out by Barnes 1972b soon after the work's publication (a criticism he often reiterated, with characteristic vigour).

38 Besides Momigliano 1969 (devastating, beneath a genial cloak) and Jones 1969, see Cameron 1971.

39 Momigliano: Syme 1971b. Jones: Syme 1971c.

How did Syme come to the *Historia Augusta*? He had been using its evidence episodically from his very first publications, in the late 1920s and early 1930s, but nothing in these hinted that it would become the focus of his work.[40] Personal friendship with András Alföldi, who in the early 1960s was organising what would become the influential Bonn Historia-Augusta-Colloquia, was clearly one factor (Syme's fondness for conviviality perhaps helped here).[41] Syme was a regular participant in these conferences, which did much to make the idea of the *HA* as the late-fourth-century work of a single author the scholarly consensus.[42] The intellectual roots of his interest in the *HA*, however, are probably to be sought in the monumental study of Tacitus he published in 1958. It is in a short chapter there, 'Tacitus and Hadrian', that Marius Maximus first makes an important appearance in Syme's work.[43] These twelve pages form part of a general argument that the *Annales* were composed almost entirely under Hadrian, something that he suggested could be detected through a series of minute correspondences between that text and the history of the period in which Tacitus was writing.[44] It also contains, however, a curious, suggestive, and oblique account of the shape of later Latin literature.[45] For Syme, Hadrian's reign represented a disastrous turn in the literary history of Latin. True, it was the epoch (Syme argued) of Juvenal and Tacitus, but they were 'the last great names in the literature of the Romans'.[46] The future belonged to Suetonius. For Syme, the *De vita Caesarum* represented all that was bad in the writing of history. It was little more than a compilation of gossip, best where Suetonius was most distant from the events he described and less able to distort them, maliciously silent about its sources: 'a chronicle of ancient folly and depravity, compiled by a government official', which 'carried no political danger'.[47] It was the antithesis of Tacitus' bold and brilliant project, perhaps even written in conscious opposition to it – to Syme, true history and biography were incompatible.[48] Suetonius came at the start of an age of archaism in literature, a barren and feeble period, when 'there was nothing worth doing and nothing worth writing about'.[49] While Tacitus had no heirs among the later Latin historians (until Ammianus, at any rate), there was

---

40 Syme 1928: 47; 1930: 63 and n. 8, 65 and n. 2. These are his first two published articles on Roman history (see the bibliography in Syme 1979–1991: 2.855). By Syme 1938, he was making greater use of the text, but still not discussing it in any sustained fashion.

41 Alföldi: signalled by Bowersock 1994: 558, who also gives some insight into Syme's delight in good dinners in good company.

42 That this was still an open question in the mid-twentieth century is shown most clearly by Momigliano 1954. Chastagnol 1964 provides a useful overview of the debate into the 1960s.

43 Syme 1958: 2.492–503, at 503.

44 Syme 1958: 2.492–498 *e.g.* The case for the date is set out at greater length in 'Appendix H': 2.768–782. On Syme's dating, it is difficult to answer the criticisms of Crook 1959. Subsequent scholarship, though somewhat in Syme's shadow, has tended to move the *Annales* mostly into the reign of Trajan. Goodyear 1981: 387–393 showed (1) that references at *Ann.* 2.56.1, 60.4, and 4.5.2 to the power of the Parthians as rival to Rome are compatible only with a date of composition before Trajan's campaigns in 115–116 and (2) that Syme misinterpreted a key passage (*Ann.* 2.61.2), which refers not

to those campaigns extending the Roman Empire to the Persian Gulf, but instead to the new Arabian province (created in 106), which incorporated a significant slice of Red Sea coast (a conclusion affirmed from different, but equally convincing, premises by Bowersock 1975). With such a starting date, Goodyear suggested that composition might easily have been completed by 118. Potter 1991 adduced new evidence that lessened the awkwardness of Syme's arguments about the key passages of Tacitus but did not controvert the core of Goodyear's reasoning (his discussion of Tacitus' process of composition does, however, suggest that the writing of the *Annales* might easily have stretched into the reign of Hadrian). Woodman 2018: 85–87 argues that *Ann.* 4.5.2 must have been written between 114 and 116 (when Armenia was a Roman province).

45 Syme 1958: 2.498–503.

46 Syme 1958: 2.500.

47 Syme 1958: 2.502.

48 Syme 1958: 2.781–782. Syme's hostility to biography has deeper roots, *cf.* 1939: 7: 'At its worst, biography is flat and schematic; at the best, it is often baffled by the hidden discourse of human nature'.

49 Syme 1958: 2.502.

plenty of 'cheap and easy' biography: 'the type and model of Suetonius Tranquillus prevailed for centuries in the literature of the Latins', the *Historia Augusta* being merely a late example of all this.[50] Marius Maximus, a man of affairs in an era of civil war, had a particularly dishonourable role in this sorry tale of decline, for he was peculiarly equipped by circumstance to be a second Tacitus. 'Contemporary events ought to have pulled a man back to the theme and manner of the consular historian', but instead Marius 'evaded the true subject and confined himself to the biographies of emperors, continuing Suetonius'.[51] Greatness had beckoned to him, but he chose poorly.[52]

Syme never set out, in print at least, what led him from *Tacitus* to the *HA*, but the seeds of his later work probably lie in the complex of ideas in this short chapter. There are elements of cliché in what he says here: he was far from alone in having a low estimate of Suetonius and a high opinion of Tacitus. Yet his overall argument is very far from conventional. There are few who consider Suetonius not merely a symptom but the cause of the enormous declination in the quality of Roman history-writing. Fewer still would assign Marius Maximus a central role in that sorry tale. Moreover, what sets Syme apart is not that he took a dim view of later Latin literature, but that he took that view and then devoted decades of his life to studying Latin authors of the fourth century. Two factors perhaps drew him on in particular. The first was a consequence of his attempt to fix a Hadrianic date for the *Annales*. Cassius Dio's account of the period (Book LXIX) survives only in fragments, so any attempt to tease out the subtle connections between events in the *Annales* and the history of Hadrian required Syme to grapple with the emperor's life in the *HA*, for that work provided much of the evidence that he needed.[53] The second was tied up with his conception of the history of Latin historiography. Any attempt to sustain his view of the decline of Latin historiography and the triumph of Suetonius would require closer examination of the later Latin historians and of the biographical tradition in particular, *i.e.* the *HA*. Syme's later work on that text, in other words, grew out of – was perhaps even presupposed by – the ideas that he had advanced about Tacitus. He set his course for the *HA*, not because of any intrinsic interest in the text (which is not to say that such interest did not emerge later on), but because his treatment of Tacitus almost required it. From the early 1960s onwards, his publications show a deepening interest in the *Historia Augusta*, especially (though not exclusively) the lives of the second-century emperors.[54]

In 1968, the first of Syme's monographs on the *Historia Augusta* appeared. The book's ostensible object was to prove that the *HA* had taken inspiration from the *Res gestae* of Ammianus Marcellinus and that it was written in about 395: this was the subject it tackled first.[55] As contemporary critics noted, these arguments were neither original to Syme, nor especially convincing.[56] As an adjunct to this main case, Syme also offered a portrait of the roguish *scriptor* of the *HA*, engaged in literary fraud for fun and profit.[57] This closed the book and, as a highly original treatment of the literary aspects of the *HA*, attracted greater, if qualified, praise.[58] Sandwiched in between these sections and supplemented by two papers published

50 Syme 1958: 2.503 and n. 8.
51 Syme 1958: 2.503.
52 Some of these themes are reprised in Syme 1964a: 300–301 and in Barnes 1971: 191–192.
53 Syme 1958 already found it necessary to cite the *HA* extensively.
54 Besides his various contributions to the *HA* Colloquia, see also Syme 1960, 1962, 1964b, 1964c, 1965a, 1965b,

1968c, all of which use the *HA* (mostly the *Hadrian*) for problems of (primarily) early-second-century history (*cf.* Syme 1967 for another Hadrianic piece).
55 Syme 1968a: esp. 25–71 (Ammianus and the *HA*), 72–79 (the date of the *HA*).
56 Cameron 1971: 255 *e.g.*
57 Syme 1968a: 176–210.
58 Momigliano 1969; Jones 1969.

in the same year, there was a treatment of the subject that had really drawn Syme from the *Annales* to the *HA*: the quality of the text's information about the emperors of the second and third centuries and the question of its sources, the historical literature of the third century.[59] This was the unobtrusive motor of the work, the place where Syme essayed his most controversial ideas.

Syme's Marius Maximus

In the 1960s, the consensus was that the good material in the *HA* was all drawn from the work of Marius Maximus: that was, for instance, generally assumed when interested scholars began to meet at Bonn for the Colloquia.[60] That belief had, however, emerged more by default than anything else.[61] The Severan biographer had survived Dessau's paper on the *HA*, probably on the strength of the references to him in Ammianus Marcellinus and a Juvenal scholion.[62] Dessau himself seems to have accepted that Maximus was a genuine source of the *HA*, though (significantly) he did not identify him as the origin of its excellent information on some emperors.[63] In his highly influential treatment of the *HA* and its sources, which expressed deep scepticism about Junius Cordus (for instance), Mommsen also took it more or less for granted that Maximus lay behind much of the text.[64] In 1899, Giacomo Tropea would make the first serious modern effort to assemble the supposed fragments of his work and in 1906 Hermann Peter would include him in his long-standard collection of the fragmentary Roman historians, where he was clear that Maximus was the *HA*'s major source.[65]

Maximus had, however, subsequently fallen out of favour as the main source of the good information in the *HA*. For a season, he was replaced by a supposed annalistic historian of Severan date, who was thought to have furnished the bulk of the good material in the *HA*.[66] The annalist was regarded by Schulz as 'the best literary source for the history of the Roman Empire in general' and by Kornemann as superior to Tacitus.[67] While Norman Baynes dissented from such 'exaggerated laudation', he essentially accepted

59 Syme 1968a: 89–102; 1968b; 1968e. Besides those cited above, the paper by Syme's student Barnes 1967, is perhaps the most detailed demonstration of the quality of the *HA*'s information (for the *Verus*).

60 Chastagnol 1964: 70; Nesselhauf 1964: 92–93; Schwartz 1964: esp. 145, 160–162 (with some important reservations); Nesselhauf 1966: 132–135; Pflaum 1966: 144, 152; Seston 1966b; Stroheker 1966: 250–251, 255. See also Cameron 1964b: 372–373; Birley 1966a: 20, 313, 1966b: 250, n. 1; Seston 1966a: 880–881.

61 Birley 1997b: 2708–2714 offers a useful survey of Maximus *Forschung*, going back to the 1870s.

62 Since no one seems to have challenged the idea that Maximus wrote history at the time, it is often difficult to determine what actually underlies that judgement.

63 Dessau 1889: 348, 'Verhältnissmässig frei von Fälschungen sind die Stücke, für die den Autoren neben ihren sonstigen Quellen die inhaltsreichen und für sie bequem zu benutzenden Schriften des Marius Maximus vorlagen'. *cf.* 1892: 576, 589. Dessau 1892: 604 shies

away from identifying the 'older biographer of the emperors', who furnished much of the material for the better lives, by name.

64 Mommsen 1890: 269–270 (Maximus), and 271–272 (Cordus).

65 Tropea 1899. Peter 1906: clxxx–clxxxviii, 121–129, esp. clxxxviii.

66 Kornemann 1905; Schulz 1907. See also a series of commentaries on individual *vitae* – Heer 1904; Hasebroek 1921 (implicitly); Schwendemann 1923 – written by students of Domaszewski, who himself believed in the annalistic source (1900: 232–233). Acceptance of the annalistic source was not incompatible with the idea that the *HA* also used Maximus (or some other biographical source): he was just not the origin of its valuable information.

67 Schulz 1907: 213: 'die beste literarische Überlieferung . . . für die Geschichte der römischen Kaiserzeit überhaupt'; Kornemann 1905: 119 esp.

the case.[68] That even the careful and sceptical Baynes was persuaded gives some sense of how widespread belief in a major early Severan historian had become.[69] It was not until a forceful 1934 paper by Guido Barbieri that the annalist definitively met his end.[70] In his absence, Maximus had, really by default more than through any intrinsic merit, emerged as the *HA*'s major source, particularly under the impetus of Ernst Hohl, who frequently affirmed that conclusion without ever making a sustained case for it.[71] These rather convoluted and contingent developments lay behind the consensus of the 1960s.

Syme could hardly accept any of this, for it threatened to overturn the conclusions that he had reached in 1958. Obviously, the idea of a great annalistic historian was unacceptable to him and he devoted considerable energy to refuting a figure in whom few still believed: Tacitus could have no rivals.[72] Marius Maximus was, however, in some ways even worse. If Maximus was the sober, conscientious, and careful historian on whom much of the evidence for the second and early third centuries rested, then he was spectacularly ill-suited to the villainous part in which Syme had cast him. A consular historian in an age of civil war, he might well stand comparison to Tacitus. Moreover, the existence of a diligent and accurate biographer suggested that Syme was simply wrong about the shape of Latin literary history and about the division between history and biography. If the early third century had seen the production of a first-rate work of imperial history by a major political figure, then there was no sharp separation between worthless biography and serious history, no great decline after Tacitus, no barren wasteland of Suetonianism. If Marius Maximus was the *HA*'s major source, then the edifice that Syme had so carefully erected in 1958 would crumble.

Syme found an escape from this conundrum in another paper by Barbieri, published in 1954. In this, Barbieri examined in detail what the *HA* said about Marius Maximus and reached a startling conclusion: he was 'not the only source and not even the main source of the first part of the *H.A.*, but, so to speak, a supplementary or auxiliary source'.[73] This suited Syme perfectly, for from it he could argue that Maximus was always cited for additional information or inserted into what was clearly a pre-existing framework taken from elsewhere.[74] What he had provided for the author of the *HA* was clearly gossip and scandal, anecdote and colour. On that basis, Syme could maintain his original position that Marius Maximus was like Suetonius, but even worse: that he had written 'cheap and easy' biographies.[75] He was a mere 'scandalmonger', to use Syme's favourite characterisation.[76] That was, after all, what the *HA* said (or at any rate suggested) about the *homo omnium verbosissimus, qui et mythistoricis se voluminibus implicavit* (*Quadr.* 1.2), 'the wordiest of all men, who tangled himself up in volumes of mythical history'. Syme

68 Baynes 1926: 68–70, at 70. Baynes also rejected the methods used by Schulz to reconstruct the annalist.

69 *cf.* Lambrechts 1934: 177, who also took this position as standard.

70 Barbieri 1934. The paper also helped to collapse the distinction between 'historical' and 'biographical' sources for the *HA*.

71 Hohl 1934: 156; 1950: 289–293. Technically, Hohl believed that the *HA* had used the *Kaisergeschichte*, which had used Maximus.

72 Syme 1968b: 495–496; 1968e 135–137 *e.g.* Note that Syme was also very keen to minimise the achievement

and exaggerate the biographical nature of Cassius Dio's work: 1968a: 100; 1968e: 137 *e.g.*

73 Barbieri 1954: 43–66, 262–265, at 265.

74 Syme 1964b: 148, n. 51; 1968a: 92; 1968b: 497 ff. *cf.* Barbieri 1954: 44. In what follows, we do not pretend to cite every iteration of Syme's argument, but offer some support for each point. Birley 1997b: 2710–2711 usefully summarises the key propositions. The origins of this idea go back to Lécrivain 1904: 193–198, whose influence Syme acknowledged.

75 Syme 1968a: 84, 91, 170.

76 Syme 1968a: 91; 1968b: 500.

diligently collected the text's every unfavourable reference to the biographer and his proclivities.[77] The *HA* itself, he argued, was born of a desire to surpass Maximus in scandalous anecdote and comprehensive treatment of the emperors.[78] With Maximus firmly established as a tabloid author, the man who might have emulated Tacitus but chose not to, the author who had inspired the *HA*, Syme could maintain his view of later Latin literature: the triumph of biography over true history and the cessation of *magna ingenia*.[79]

Syme's Ignotus

Without Maximus, or rather with his Maximus, Syme needed some plausible explanation of the good material in the *HA*. His solution was disarmingly simple. Strip away the 'supplementary' portions of the primary *HA* lives, all *ex hypothesi* taken from Maximus, and you were left with a residue of solid information, the basic framework of the *vitae*. Syme did much to demonstrate that a lot of this was of excellent factual quality.[80] Given his views on Maximus, plain logic seemed to dictate that this must be attributed to another source, whom Syme termed Ignotus: a sober (favoured adjective), anonymous, careful biographer of limited fame.[81] He was perhaps active in imperial administration and wrote at Rome in the early third century (the reign of Severus Alexander). He took his inspiration from Suetonius, but was much duller and more factual than him.[82] Although Syme never put it so plainly, this meant that in reading the better *vitae* in the *HA*, one could (more or less) simply chalk up what was good to Ignotus and what was bad to Marius Maximus. While it is natural to think of Marius Maximus and Ignotus as, in some sense, opposed to each other, it is crucial to understand that in Syme's thought they are in fact inextricably interlinked. Ignotus emerged as a logical consequence of Syme's view of Maximus, for, granting his premises, you could not have one without the other: 'the dismissal of Maximus entails and enforces another biographer. That is, Ignotus'.[83] This hypothetical author was characterised almost entirely in relation to Maximus. Not dissimilar in date, circumstance, and literary project, they were utterly different in the way they went about their historical work. Marius Maximus and Ignotus were, in fact, two sides of the same coin: the different faces of biography in the age of the Severans.

As we have seen, Syme's work did not command universal assent when it first appeared and this was true also of his theory of the sources. Syme's student T.D. Barnes would build on his work and, in turn, Barnes' followers and students have kept the flame of Ignotus alive – but it is a minority position.[84] Paradoxically, however, Syme's arguments – the almost tidal force of his prominence – exerted quite as

---

77 *e.g.* Syme 1968a: 90–92; 1971a: 113–121.
78 Syme 1968a: 93.
79 Syme 1968a: 89–90 and ch. 17 'Biography against History', esp. 100–102; 1971a: 132–134.
80 *e.g.* in the *Antoninus Pius*: Syme 1968e: 137–139, or the *Verus*, Barnes 1967.
81 Syme 1968a: 92; 1968e: 142–145. His argument was partially foreshadowed by Lécrivain 1904: 191–192. Syme had conjured such a figure before: the earlier

Ignotus (there italicised) was the common source of Tacitus and Plutarch (1958: 2.647–676).
82 Syme 1968a: 92; 1968e: 145, 148.
83 Syme 1968b: 500.
84 Barnes 1967; 1972a: 73; 1978: 98–107 *e.g.*; Rubin: 1974: 233; 1980: 167–171 (not a student of Syme's, but note the effusive thanks to him at 7); Burgess 2000: 259, n. 2; Kulikowski 2007; *ODLA* 'Historia Augusta' (Burgess). See also Bauman 1977: 43 ff.; Champlin 1980: 56 and n. 64; Leaning 1989: 550 ff.; Benario 1997.

strong an influence on those who were unconvinced. Syme so entangled Marius Maximus and Ignotus that, as a contemporary critic put it, 'Ignotus is Maximus' exact double'. [85] They were both figures of the late second and early third centuries, both active in politics and administration, both spent much of their careers in Rome, both were inspired by Suetonius to write a set of biographies of roughly the same emperors, which were both then used by the author of the *HA*. Syme even went so far as to suggest that the work of Ignotus might have served as the inspiration for Marius Maximus, that it 'furnished help and a useful framework'.[86] Because of this, those who rejected Ignotus generally just allowed Maximus to expand to fill the gap: why posit two closely connected but subtly different sources, when only Maximus was needed? Opponents of Syme's thesis tended to direct their attentions to the weaknesses (and they were not few) of Ignotus, while treating the other Severan biographer as a straightforward matter. This can be seen in the earliest critiques of Syme's ideas. In a searching (in parts unanswerable) treatment, Alan Cameron asked, 'Why not Marius Maximus?', as though nothing really stood in his way.[87] Maximus has thus, essentially by default, emerged once again as the major source for the early *vitae* in the *HA*, just as he did when the great annalist faded away.[88]

Marius Maximus and the *Historia Augusta*

We have set these developments out at some length because it is only when the intellectual genealogy is traced that it becomes clear quite how arbitrary and contingent the current competing theories of the *HA*'s principal source are. Ignotus is not merely the neutral product of a careful and disinterested investigation of the *HA*'s sources: it has its origin partly as a saving hypothesis for a particular and idiosyncratic approach to the architecture of Latin literary history, which has pressed the *HA* into service. That history and biography, Tacitus and Suetonius, were incompatible and that the latter triumphed, ushering in a barren epoch in Latin literature, this was what really animated Ignotus: he was merely a convenient conceptual repository for good material in the *HA*. Yet, not only is Syme's theory strange, it is also wrong. Leave to one side the almost circularity of the case for Ignotus, an author who is both a hypothesis and the proof of that hypothesis. Syme's whole treatment of the *HA* required a conscious opposition between history and biography. As Momigliano showed, however, in a single lucid paragraph, nothing suggests that the author of the *HA* – putatively the heir to whole Suetonian tradition – clearly distinguished between these two modes of historical writing, let alone located himself firmly in one rather than the other: he seems to have thought (not unreasonably), that they were more or less the same thing, or at any rate different expressions of the same basic genre.[89] This generic blurriness was not merely an idiosyncrasy of

85 Cameron 1971: 262.
86 Syme 1968e: 148. *cf.* Syme 1971: 125.
87 Cameron, 1971: 263. *cf.* Birley 1971: 322: 'The arguments against Marius Maximus . . . are therefore far from compelling'.
88 Marius Maximus as the major source of the *HA* (by no means a comprehensive list): Alföldy 1972: 51 and n. 80; Schlumberger 1974: 124–133; Schlumberger 1976: 210–211; Chastagnol 1994: lii–lix; Birley 1995;

Birley 1997b; Bird 1999; Rohrbacher 2006: 107–108; Molinier Arbo 2009; Cameron 2011: 759, 778; Kemezis 2012: 408–409; Thomson 2012: 8, 19; Rohrbacher 2013; *FRH* 101 (Levick and Cornell 1.608–609); Rohrbacher 2016: 11–12; Schulz 2019: 177 and n. 37.
89 Momigliano 1969: 568. Momigliano 1984 (a review of Syme 1983) slightly nuances this view. Note also the satirical structuring of the review in numbered paragraphs – a favoured technique of Syme in his later

the *HA*'s author. Jerome, a much more serious and infinitely more learned figure, could say that Tacitus had written *vitae Caesarum*.[90] Victor himself, in the long fragment preserved in the *Scholia Vallicelliana*, speaks of 'examining the lives of the emperors (*vitas principum*)' in the course of what was very definitely a work of history.[91] Marius Maximus is, however, little better than Ignotus. His current position as the consensus answer to the question of the *HA*'s major source for the second and early third centuries is accidental. Other theories have been advanced with far greater passion and in much greater detail. When they have fallen away – often for good reason – Maximus has been left as 'the one identifiable candidate', the default answer.[92] It has to be someone and it might as well be him.

In fact, this entire debate – and with it most discussion of the *HA*'s sources, at least for the early lives – is misconceived. A simple error lies at its root: that we can, in some sense, trust what the *HA* says about Marius Maximus. For Syme and Ignotus, this was a proposition of central importance: Maximus' nature and project as a historian emerged entirely from what the *HA* said about him. Syme accepted that Maximus produced biographies of legitimate emperors only (*i.e.* no pretenders, *Quadr.* 1.1), that he wrote a life of Marcus Aurelius in two books (*Avid. Cass.* 6.7, 9.5), that he quoted letters and speeches (*Pert.* 15.8; *Marc.* 25.10), because the *HA* said that.[93] That Maximus was cited by the *HA* for 'the trivial, the anecdotic, or the scandalous' revealed the true nature of his history.[94] It was points like this that confirmed to Syme that Maximus could not be the source of the good information in the *HA*. Those who rejected Ignotus were not slow to point out a contradiction in Syme's approach: 'it is surprising to see one so sympathetic to the methods of the SHA succumb to such familiar devices [*sc.* the citations of Maximus] of the fraudulent researcher', as Cameron tartly put it.[95] Yet the more sympathetic case for Maximus as source equally rests on the *HA*. It is solely because the text cites him so frequently that he is assumed to lie behind it: 'the only possible source to be regularly acknowledged by name in the relevant portions of the *HA*'.[96] Reject as it might the details of the *HA*'s citations from Maximus, it accepts their basically factual nature.

None of this really withstands scrutiny. As we have seen, Momigliano was one of the few influential scholars of the *HA* to resist the mid-century move to regard the work as a forgery of Theodosian date. Yet it was he who put into words most lucidly the basic rule of evidence for the text: 'to be trustworthy any

writings. It is true that at *Prob.* 2.7 the *HA* contrasts Suetonius (and other, largely invented, figures) to Sallust, Livy, Tacitus, and Trogus and that elsewhere it condemns the same *quadriga* (*Aurel.* 2.1) and praises Suetonius more (*Quadr.* 1.1), but the basis for the comparison is what the author elsewhere calls *fidelitas historica* (*Tyr.* 11.6) and invariably contrasts with *eloquentia*, never anything to do with genre. As far as the *scriptor* was concerned, Marius Maximus wrote *historia* (*Avid. Cass.* 9.5). While he characterises the (surely invented) Acholius as a *scriptor vitae* at *Alex.* 48.7, by 64.5 he is simply *historicus*.

90 Jerome, *In Zach.* 3.14. In *Apologeticum* 5.3–4, Tertullian touches on the Neronian persecution and advises his audience *consulite commentarios vestros* if they wish to verify what he says, without specifying where they ought to look. In *Scorpiace* 15.3, he returns to the same theme and says (more helpfully) that he is thinking of the *vitae Caesarum*. As Barnes 1971: 201–202 pointed out, though generally interpreted as a reference to Suetonius, Tertullian is more probably thinking of Tacitus, *Ann.* 15.44.

The case was developed and expanded by Birley 2005: 259–260, 272–277. Jerome's reference all but guarantees that it must be correct. We are grateful to Benjamin Kolbeck of King's College London for pointing this out to us and providing considerable help on bibliography.

91 See Chapter V. It is noteworthy also that the compiler of the *CT* calls the biographical *DVI* a *historia Liviana* (Chapter II).

92 The phrase is from *FRH* 101 (Levick and Cornell 1.608), a penetrating contribution, which accepts Maximus, but casts a sceptical eye over the evidence for him and thus crystallises what is often left vague in the literature.

93 These examples taken from Syme 1968a: 90, but almost any page of what he wrote about Maximus could furnish additional proofs.

94 Syme 1968a: 91.

95 Cameron 1971: 264.

96 *FRH* 101 (Levick and Cornell 1.608).

statement of the *Historia Augusta* ultimately needs corroboration'.[97] For some reason, Maximus has been exempted from this stipulation. Quite how a body of scholarship that now takes for granted the slippery nature of the *HA* has managed to rest the analysis of its sources primarily on the claims made by the text itself is baffling. The convoluted nature of debate, with a now forbidding weight of bibliography, the too-good-to-check way that Ammianus mentions him, the fact that he can be identified with a known historical figure active in the early third century: these have perhaps combined to lend him a certain plausibility – created the niche into which the *HA*'s Maximus fits so very snugly. To escape this morass, it is necessary to rethink the problem from its foundations. Almost alone among modern scholars, François Paschoud has asked the right question: what would we think of Marius Maximus, 'si l'*Histoire Auguste* n'existait pas'?[98]

Considering the mountain of scholarship that the idea of the 'consular biographer' has generated, it is easy to forget that our evidence for Marius Maximus and his work, outside the *HA*, consists of only two short passages, one from the *Scholia in Iuvenalem* and another from the second of Ammianus' Roman digressions:

(1) *Scholia in Iuvenalem* 4.53 (57–58 Wessner): *si quid Palfurio, si credimus Armillato*

[1] Palfurius Sura consularis filius sub Nerone luctatus est. Post inde a Vespasiano senatu motus transivit ad Stoicam sectam in qua cum praevaleret et eloquentia et artis poeticae gloria, abusus familiaritate Domitiani acerbissime partes delationis exercuit. Quo interfecto senatu accusante damnatus est cum fuisset inter delatores. [2] Potentes apud Domitianum hi: Armillatus, Demosthenes et Latinus archimimus, ut Marius Maximus scribit.[99]

[1] Palfurius Sura, the son of a consul, wrestled under Nero.[100] Afterwards, for this reason, he was removed from the Senate by Vespasian and passed over to the Stoic school, in which, although he was preeminent by his eloquence and the fame of his poetic skill, he misused his friendship with Domitian to play the most bitter part of an informer. When Domitian was killed, Sura was condemned at the Senate's indictment, since he had been among the informers. [2] Those who had influence with Domitian were Armillatus, Demosthenes, and Latinus the archmime, as Marius Maximus writes.

(2) Ammianus 28.4.14–15

Quidam detestantes ut venena doctrinas, Iuvenalem et Marium Maximum curatiore studio legunt, nulla volumina praeter haec in profundo otio contrectantes, quam ob causam non iudicioli est nostri,

97 Momigliano 1973: 114–115.

98 Paschoud 1999b: 243 (*cf.* Paschoud 2009, reiterating some key points). Paschoud's penetrating study has only received one extended response, Schlumberger 2010, which demonstrates in great detail that there must be a source behind the *HA* and the *LB*. This is true and useful, but it in no way proves that that source was Marius Maximus. *cf.* more briefly Birley 2006: 21, whose points simply presuppose that Maximus was a historian, and Bertrand-Dagenbach 2004, who (after airing some scepticism) reiterates the current consensus. *cf.* also the intelligent and sceptical summary by Zinsli 2014: 78–83.

99 Montpellier H 125, f. 25v. *cf.* as well, St Gall 870, p. 94, which seems to put the break between the two scholia before *hi* (a clear one, signalled by two interpuncts: ⸬). Probus ends the first gloss after *damnatus*.

100 The 'Probus' scholion to this line in Juvenal (see below) offers considerable help in understanding the fabulous career of Palfurius Sura: from wrestling a Spartan girl,

cum multa et varia pro amplitudine gloriarum et generum lectitare deberent, audientes destina-
tum poenae Socratem, coniectumque in carcerem, rogasse quendam scite lyrici carmen Stesichori
modulantem, ut doceretur id agere, dum liceret: interroganteque musico quid ei poterit hoc prodesse
morituro postridie, respondisse 'ut aliquid sciens amplius e vita discedam'.

Some of them, hating learning as though it were poison, read Juvenal and Marius Maximus with
earnest care, pawing over no books beside these in their boundless leisure. The reason for this is
not a matter for my lowly judgement, since they ought (in view of the greatness of their fame and
their families) to be in the habit of reading many and varied things: they have heard how Socrates –
condemned to punishment and thrown into prison – asked some man skilfully playing a song by
Steisichorus the lyric poet, to teach him how to do the same, while he was permitted so to do. When
the musician asked him what good this could do him (since he was to die on the following day), he
answered 'that I might depart this life knowing one thing more'.

We shall deal with these in turn.[101]

Scholia to Juvenal

The so-called *Scholia vetustiora* to Juvenal are a heterogenous collection that seems to have arrived at roughly
its present form in the fifth century, though it has multiple textual layers of various dates: Townend has
even suggested a second-century core of factual material.[102] On the basis of the *scholia*, it is an article of
faith in discussions of Maximus that his work dealt with Palfurius Sura.[103] Looking at the text, however,
it is obvious that there are two *separate scholia* referring to two *different* phrases in the line.[104] The longer
first part explains the lemma *Palfurio*, since there was evidently a good deal to say about him. The shorter
second portion just glosses *Armillato*. That they are distinct is confirmed by the fact that a version of only
the first part (down to *damnatus*) is found in the 'Probus' glosses preserved by Giorgio Valla: this suggests
that a separate ancient commentary contained the first gloss alone.[105] There is no justification whatsoever

---

to excelling as an orator and a Stoic, to a prolific stint as
an *Auskunftsperson*, to exile.

101 Besides these two *testimona*, the *Geoponica* (9.14.2) cites
one Florentinus, who apparently relayed the information that he had seen and eaten the fruit of a vine
grafted onto an olive tree *chez* Marius Maximus. There
is nothing in the passage that suggests this Maximus was
an author, let alone a historian.

102 On the variegated nature of the *Scholia vetustiora*, see
in general Cameron 2010; Townend 1972. While
Cameron 2010: 571 rightly rejects Townend's theory
of a full-fledged second-century commentary on
Juvenal, he accepts the idea that there is a slight residue
of material which dates back that far. Our best general
guide to the fluidity of ancient exegetical material is
Zetzel 2005.

103 On both sides of the debate: Syme 1966: 260; Syme
1968a: 89; Birley 1995: 265; Meckler 1996: 367; Birley
1997b: 2684, 2725; Bird 1999: 852. It has also made its

way into the Juvenal scholarship: Townend 1972: 376.
Peter 1906: 121 rightly only printed the latter part of
the *scholion*.

104 Birley 1997b: 2684 obscures this by printing a modified
text, with no indication that it has been emended . . .
cum fuissent inter delatores potentes . . .

105 For the 'Probus text': Wessner 1931: 57. As we have
said, the *Scholia vetustiora* is a work of many different
strata, of different dates: one strand of commentaries is
associated with the name of Probus, because Giorgio
Valla printed indubitably ancient *scholia* which he attributed to an otherwise unspecified 'Probus' in his
1486 edition of Juvenal (the name is somewhat suspicious given the fame of Valerius Probus). On 'Probus',
see Zetzel 2018: 129; Anderson 1965. Michael Reeve's
demonstration (1984) that the 'Probus' *scholia* are in
cursus mixtus, and thus indubitably ancient and probably
written in the period between Apuleius and Augustine,
has attracted perhaps less attention than it ought.

for linking the first *scholion* to Marius Maximus. Hence, all we can say with certainty is that Maximus' work mentioned Armillatus, as did Juvenal (*cf. PIR*² A.1062), Demosthenes, who is otherwise unknown, and the archmime Latinus, who also features in Martial (9.29.7) and Suetonius (*Domitian* 15.3; *PIR*² L.129). This is not much evidence on which to base any conclusion, but it would tend to suggest that Maximus wrote about the same sort of things as Juvenal: hence why they both appear to have mentioned one of the same characters and why the work of the former was helpful in understanding the *Satires* of the latter. The reference also allows us to make a plausible deduction about date: the *Scholia* to Juvenal cite no dateable author later than the middle of the second century AD.[106]

Ammianus Marcellinus

Our second *testimonium* is in some ways even more informative. Clearly, Ammianus did not approve of Marius Maximus: not only did his work itself contain no 'learning' (*doctrina*), but it appealed to those who actively despised it. In this, Maximus was in the same class as Juvenal: a poet who did not teach anything useful and who did not offer an acceptable model for Latin style. Further, Ammianus says that Roman aristocrats ought to be reading 'many and varied things' and prods at them with an *exemplum* featuring Socrates. The obvious implication is that Juvenal and Marius Maximus were not very different in what they wrote. This would seem to rule out Maximus being a historian or biographer: like Juvenal, he ought to be a satirist. In fact, the idea that Maximus wrote satire is embedded at a deeper level in what Ammianus writes. Several scholars have noted that the Roman digressions draw their inspiration from the tradition of the Latin satirists.[107] Alan Ross has argued that the reference to Juvenal is meant to tip the reader off to this debt and he notes perceptively that it acts almost as a punchline for the second Roman digression.[108] That ought to inflect what we think about Marius Maximus' appearance here.

Whatever literary role we can assign to Ammianus' reference to Juvenal and Maximus, the fact remains that the literary fashion he invokes is a real historical phenomenon. The last decades of the fourth

---

106 Authorities are listed by Wessner 1931: 289–291. The one unknown, besides Marius Maximus, is the mysterious Q. Serenus, about whom we know exceptionally little for certain, save for the fact that, according to Terentianus Maurus, he wrote after Alfius Avitus. Unfortunately, we also do not know the date of Avitus, nor that of Terentianus. A third-century chronology has been advanced (Cameron 1980: 143, 145; Courtney 1993: 403, 406–407), but it rests on associating the poet Alfius Avitus with epigraphically attested figures of the third century who share that name (*CIL* 2.4110; 3.10436; *EAOR* 1.43; see in general Christol and Loriot 2001). This is perhaps less secure than is generally realised and we ought to keep in mind Cameron's caution (1980: 143) that Terentianus 'quotes no datable writer later than the mid-second century'. This is a situation that closely parallels that of the *Scholia* to Juvenal, which might make us sceptical about

dating the undatable after the dated. On Terentianus, see Keeline 2022.

107 Rees 1999; Kelly 2008: 166–167, 175; Sogno 2012: 372–377. In general, see Shanzer 2006. It is possible that a sharper distinction should be drawn between satire as we recognise it and satire as a Latin genre (written in hexameter, using *sermo quotidianus*, self-consciously in the tradition of Lucilius). As Wilamowitz-Moellendorff 1921: 42, n.1 puts it: 'there is not really Latin satire, there is only Lucilius, Horace, Persius, Juvenal'.

108 Ross 2015: 362–363, with n. 33 esp. (the fact that, *pace* Ross, the reference to Juvenal comes partway through the digression, rather than at its end, perhaps weakens this point, but it could still be understood as a wink at the reader). There is no contradiction between using and abusing Juvenal as Ammianus does: one can read and allude to things without thinking that they are improving, especially if they sharpen a comic point. *cf.* Den Boeft *et al.* 2011: 194.

century and the first of the fifth were a golden age for Latin verse invective. Claudian flung his barbs at Stilicho's enemies and the *In Eutropium* (in particular) might reasonably be thought satire.[109] Rutilius Namatianus tells us about his friend Decius, whose father, the suspiciously named Lucillus (the founder of Roman satire being Lucilius), rivalled Juvenal in his gift for invective (*De red.* 603–606):

> Than his playful satire (*satira*), with its wound-dealing Muses, neither Turnus nor Juvenal will be found more potent. His censorious file has restored that old-time decency and while it harries the bad, it instructs them to be good.

Turnus was an acquaintance of Martial (*Epig.* 11.9, 11.10, and 7.97) and a satirist who had enjoyed imperial favour under Titus and Domitian. Two lines of his are quoted in the 'Probus' *scholia* to Juvenal and he is later mentioned by John the Lydian alongside Juvenal and Petronius as transgressors of the 'law of satire' due to the vehemence of their invectives.[110] While it is rather unlikely that Namatianus' Lucillus wrote satire even 'more potent' than that of Turnus and Juvenal, the fact that he was writing formal satire at all – which is what the explicit mention of *satira* must mean – is noteworthy.[111] Given the date of the *De reditu* (417 or shortly thereafter), we can plausibly put the poetic career of Lucillus sometime in the last three decades of the fourth century, or perhaps even a little later.[112] No fewer than four extant Christian verse invectives from the same period (studied in detail by Alan Cameron) also testify to the general popularity of the genre: Prudentius' *Contra Symmachum*, and three anonymous productions, the *Carmen contra paganos*, the *Carmen ad Antonium*, and the *Carmen ad quendam senatorem*.[113]

Alongside these new satiric compositions, we can also detect a surge of interest in specifically Domitianic satire at this time. Not only do we owe the *Scholia* on Juvenal to roughly this period, but through them and Namatianus we have our only references to Turnus between Martial and Lydus. Even in fifth-century Egypt, Juvenal found readers, as an annotated papyrus of his works proves.[114] Sometime after 374, Ausonius wrote in the epilogue to his *Cento nuptialis* to Axius Paulus a little catalogue of satiric and erotic authors, including Juvenal, Martial, Apuleius, the *Fescennines* of the Hadrianic Annianus, and the Domitianic Sulpicia.[115] Sulpicia is also discussed by Martial, has two lines quoted by the *Scholia*, and as a result is usually characterised as a satirist.[116] This is important, because in the fourth- or fifth-century poetic collection known as the *Epigrammata Bobiensia* (which includes satirical epigrams by, among others,

---

109 On this question, see Birt 1888; Long 1996: 19–24.

110 *Scholia in Iuvenalem* 1.71; John the Lydian, *De mag.* 1.41.

111 Of course, the fourth and fifth centuries were a period of generic experimentation, which meant in the case of satire that authors experimented with different modes (Marolla 2021). This phenomenon can be seen in other genres as well: bucolic, for example is a hexameter genre, but the work of Endelechius (*ca.* 400) is not in that metre (Stover 2015). The simple fact, however, of generic experimentation does not remove generic expectation.

112 For the date, see the forceful arguments of Cameron 1967 for a journey in 417, a position dramatically confirmed by the discovery in 1973 of fragments of

the poem containing a reference to the second consulship of Constantius (the future emperor, *cos.* II in 417 – *CLRE* 368–369) – see briefly Wolff 2007: xix–xx (opting, xii, for composition in 418, given the elaborate nature of the poem).

113 Cameron 2011: 272–352. He notes as well that a good deal more which have not survived were written (320): 'If as many as four such compositions have survived – each by a different route – the probability is that many more once existed'.

114 Macedo 2016.

115 Green 1991: 139.

116 Richlin 2014: 110–129, with references to earlier bibliography. The lines are quoted in the Probus Juvenal commentary *ad* 6.537.

Probinus, *cos.* 395) there is a hexameter poem ascribed to Sulpicia, on Domitian's expulsion of the philosophers.[117] Majority opinion has regarded this poem as a fourth- or fifth-century forgery, but too little attention has been paid to James Butrica's persuasive arguments in favour of its authenticity.[118] It hardly matters for our purposes here, however, since either the inclusion of an authentic Domitianic satire in a collection of otherwise contemporary poetry, or the fresh composition of a satire/invective under the name of a Domitianic author (and set in his reign), would provide compelling evidence for the cachet of the genre and period in the later fourth century. Thus, even if Ammianus is providing a knowing literary wink with his mention of Juvenal, he is also attesting to a genuine phenomenon.

There is even some contemporary resonance in our historian's concerns about the lack of *doctrina* in Juvenal and Marius Maximus. From the beginning, satire had an uneasy relationship with learning: 'those genres in which *doctrina* is at home', wrote Juvenal's foremost contemporary commentator, Courtney, 'do not usually include satire'.[119] Even in Namatianus' account, we can detect a slightly apologetic tone: 'the wound-dealing Muses' seems to have been controversial. Paulinus of Nola accused his old teacher Ausonius of being more a satirist than a *parens* (*Carm.* 10.262–264) – not a compliment.[120] Perhaps aware of similar objections, Namatianus defends satire as educative: while it goes after the bad, 'it instructs them to be good'. This reflects a shift in views of whether Juvenalian satire was suitable for education, something that can be witnessed most profoundly in the differences in the use of Juvenal between the Vergil commentaries of Donatus and Servius and the Horace commentaries of Porphyrio and pseudo-Acro.[121]

In this context – a satirical excursus in the text of Ammianus, signalled by a reference to Juvenal – Marius Maximus would not only be out of place, he would deflate the entire conceit, unless he too was a satirist (and one of the age of Domitian at that). This would also make sense of his vogue: the fashion for Domitianic satire towards the end of the fourth century offers an ideal context in which to understand the resurgence of his popularity and it would also neatly explain why he is quoted in the *Scholia* to Juvenal.

What then do we actually know about Marius Maximus as an author? Once we exclude the *HA*, three things only:

1. He wrote about figures active during the reign of Domitian (*scholion*).
2. He had some connection of subject matter and/or style with Juvenal (*scholion*/Ammianus).
3. He was thought to be for people who recoil from 'learning as though it were poison' (Ammianus).

In a remarkable display of scholarly perversity, the propositions generally agreed upon about Marius Maximus in the literature are:

1. He commenced his work with Nerva.[122]
2. He was the imitator and continuator of Suetonius.[123]

117 The *Epigrammata Bobiensia* were edited by Speyer 1963; Sulpicia's poem is no. 37.
118 Butrica 2006; see also Jędrzejczak 2009.
119 Courtney 1980: 44.
120 See Witke 1971: 58. In general on the poem, Trout 1999: 78–84.
121 Cameron 2011: 410–411.

122 *FRH* 101 (Levick and Cornell 1.604 *e.g.*). The idea is closely bound up with the assumption that he has some relationship to Ausonius (above).
123 Birley 1997b: 2683, 2700 *e.g.* These first two propositions are simply stated in *OCD*³ *s.v.* 'Maximus, Marius' (Pelling) and in Browning's essay on biography in the *Cambridge History of Latin Literature* (1982: 723–724),

To these, we can add a third, which commands broad, if not universal support:

3. Ammianus used Maximus as a source.[124]

It is a sign of how back to front the scholarship on Maximus has become that the only things that are generally believed about his work are in nearly direct contradiction with our (admittedly scanty) evidence. Working only from the material outside the *HA*, we might reasonably suppose that Marius Maximus was a writer of satire, active in the late first or early second century. That he happened to share his names (both very common) with a Severan general and consul we would regard as mere coincidence.[125] On the testimony of the *Scholia* and Ammianus, no one would ever have supposed that Maximus wrote biographies of emperors, let alone that they served as a source for the *Res gestae*.

Marius Maximus, 'bogus author'

With this in mind, we can now turn to what the *HA* says about Maximus and investigate its testimony with the scepticism it merits. The fact that Marius Maximus is known from other sources does not lend the *HA* quotations from him any credibility whatsoever. Several other supposed historians who feature in the *HA* are known from elsewhere as genuine authors.[126] Phlegon of Tralles, the freedman of Hadrian, turns up at several points: as the author under whose name the emperor's autobiography was published (*Hadr.* 16.1) and as the source of a letter sent by Hadrian (*Quadr.* 7.6). Phlegon was a genuine author, whose *Book of Marvels* is extant and who wrote a number of other works, none of them Hadrianic history as the *HA* would have it.[127] He is mentioned twice by Jerome, so he was not unknown to later Latin literature.[128] One Nicomachus is credited in the life of Aurelian with translating a letter of Zenobia from Syriac into Greek (*Aurel.* 27.6). The most famous Nicomachus across the Roman world, from the second century up to the sixth, was Nicomachus of Gerasa, an authority on music and maths. Although he lived at least a century too early to be Zenobia's stenographer, he was a Syrian who wrote in Greek.[129] An Onesimus is cited several times in the lives of the *Quadriga tyrannorum* and on Carus, Carinus, and

attesting to their status as 'common knowledge'. They are both explicit postulates in Birley (for example, 1997b) and Syme (for example, 1972a). Mention should be made of the bold and original suggestion of Hartke 1932: 20 that Marius Maximus began not with Nerva but with Augustus, and was thus the 'Suetonius auctus' of Cohn.

124 Birley 1997b: 2718; Kulikowski 2007; Rohrbacher 2013. Thomson 2012: 21 does not mention Ammianus specifically, but says 'many writers drew upon his work'.

125 Lőrincz 2000 lists 260 instances of Marius as a *nomen* (59) and 945 of Maximus as a cognomen (70–72). Mention should be made here of the (few) scholars who have queried the identity of the *HA* author and the consul of 223. Gruter identified him instead with the legate Q. Venidius Rufus Marius Maximus Calvinianus (*PIR*² V.369); Lécrivain simply denied the identity

without proposing an alternative candidate (1904: 193–194); and Burgess, in a private communication reported by Bird (1999: 858), tentatively suggested the homonymous son of the consul of 223.

126 See in general on the *HA*'s authorities Syme 1976a: esp. 313, from whom the appellation 'bogus author(s)' seems to have its origin. Syme rather passes over those genuine authors to whom works are falsely attributed.

127 *Marvels*: Hansen 1996 (useful more generally). Other works: Photius, *Bibliotheca* cod. 97; *Suda* Φ.527. See also Baldwin 1996; Morgan 1999.

128 Jerome, *Chron.* 174ᵈ; *Quaest. Hebr.* 2 (p. 10.4–5 Lagarde).

129 On Nicomachus, see D'Ooge *et al.* 1926; McDermott 1977; Albertson 2014: 50–59. We have no evidence for his date, beyond the fact that he quotes Thrasyllus and was translated by Apuleius – it is easy to see how the *HA* might have put him in the wrong chronological context.

Numerian. There was indeed a Greek writer named Onasimus, who lived under Constantine and who is mentioned by the *Suda* (O.327).[130] The text calls him a historian and sophist, then goes on to list a number of rhetorical works – clearly, if he was a genuine historian, that was not the thing for which he was chiefly famous and there is no indication that he wrote about the later third century. A Gargilius Martialis is cited for a life of Alexander Severus (d. 235). Again, this Martialis is in fact a known author, who plausibly lived at the right time, if an inscription fixing the death of an individual with that name in 260 relates to him.[131] However, from what we know of him, his interests lay in horticulture, not imperial biography. Martialis' work was discussed by authors roughly contemporary to the *HA*: he appears once in the agriculturalist Palladius (of uncertain date, but probably late fourth or early fifth century) and once in Servius, so his name was perhaps tempting to anyone looking to invent sources for the third century.[132] Similarly, a Vergilian scholar called Haterianus is cited five times in the Verona *scholia* to Vergil and is probably to be identified with the Aetherianus (so the manuscripts, though they are generally emended) who features once in Macrobius' *Saturnalia*.[133] He is probably the origin of the Julius Atherianus quoted in the life of the Gallic emperor Victorinus (*Tyr.* 6.5–7). The slight apparent variation in the name offers no bar since the manuscript reading in the *HA*, Atherianus, is the same as the authentic Haterianus – differences in aspiration do not amount to genuine orthographic variants.[134] There are also other, more difficult cases. A Suetonius Optatianus turns up as a biographer (*Tac.* 11.7): Optatian is a well-known poet of the reign of Constantine.[135] Aelius Maurus is invoked for a detail about Septimius Severus (*Sev.* 20.1) and his name was perhaps inspired by Aemilianus Maurus, mentioned as a grammarian by Athenaeus.[136] The only other extant instance of the name Eusthenius, cited as a biographer of the tetrarchs and called Diocletian's *ab epistulis* (*Car.* 18.5), is given to a (probably fictional) participant in the poetic symposium known as the *Carmina XII sapientum*, a text of plausibly Tetrarchic date.[137]

In other words, Maximus – also attested in one major late-fourth-century text and some *scholia*, also invoked as a source by the *HA* – is far from alone. No serious scholar would hold that a 'biography' of Hadrian really circulated under Phlegon's name, that the horticulturalist Gargilius Martialis actually wrote a life of Alexander Severus, that the Vergilian scholar Haterianus composed a tract on the Gallic emperors, or even that the sophist Onasimus wrote about the late third century, though they were all genuine authors. It is thus completely illogical to reject them, but to solemnly accept that Marius Maximus was genuinely a biographer of the emperors. In fact, consistency surely requires us to believe that whatever

---

130 *PLRE* 'Onesmius 2'. That the fictive biographer was inspired by the genuine sophist seems much more likely than the convoluted and speculative theory of Chastagnol 1970: 72–77 (*cf.* Chastagnol 1976: 88 and Syme 1976a: 318–319) that he was invented on the strength of a reference to Onesimus in a letter of Jerome (*Ep.* 3) as part of a peculiarly elaborate joke. *cf.* Cameron 2014: 163.

131 Zainaldin 2020: 1–4: even if this identification is not accepted, then Martialis worked after Galen (whom he mentions) and before Palladius, so is most likely third century in date anyway.

132 Palladius: 4.9.9; Servius, *In Georg.* 4.148. He also appears in Cassiodorus, *Inst.* 1.28.6, who confirms that he wrote *de hortis*.

133 *Scholia Veronensia: In Aen.* 7.337, 9.362, 9.397, 10.243. Macrobius: 3.8.2 (see Kaster 2011 *ad loc.*). He may also lie concealed beneath the 'Hadrianus' of Servius Danielis, *In Aen.* 8.682.

134 It is worth noting that Atherianus and Aetherianus are not found in inscriptions, unlike Haterianus (especially common in Lepcis Magna – see the indices to *IRT*).

135 *PLRE* 'Optatianus 3'.

136 See Baldwin 1977: 39–40 (*cf.* Hock 1982).

137 See Friedrich 2002 in general on the date and nature of the text, and 425–426 on Eusthenius in particular.

he actually wrote, it was not history. These other real authors falsely cited also defeat the only positive argument Birley – one of his most influential advocates – gives for not treating Marius Maximus like the other *HA* authorities:

> Given that Maximus was in vogue at the time, moreover, it is hazardous to argue that the author of the HA invented the material for which he cites Maximus as his source. To be sure, he invented freely, not least a host of spurious authorities. But in the case of Maximus such a procedure would have been self-defeating.[138]

While Palladius surely wrote for a more restricted audience and the *Scholia Veronensia* represent a narrow corner of Vergilian scholarship, Servius' commentary and Macrobius' *Saturnalia* were mainstream and influential texts of the early fifth century, and indeed have (rightly or wrongly) been held up as works representative of the milieu in which the *Historia Augusta* was composed, while Jerome was widely read.[139] Mention of Phlegon, or Gargilius Martialis, or Haterianus was no less 'self-defeating' than that of Maximus – falsely attributing works to them might also have tipped the reader off that something was not quite right. In fact, ascribing otherwise unknown (likely invented) works to known authors is something of a hallmark of the author of the *HA*, one which stretches beyond historiography. He alleges that the culinary writer Apicius wrote *Amores* (*Ael.* 5.9; the passage is usually emended to remove this), that a late-third-century poet with the suspicious name Olympius Nemesianus wrote a *Halieutica* and *Nautica* (*Car.* 11.2), and gives an extremely dubious catalogue of Cicero's poetic works (*Gord.* 3.2).[140] There is no reason to think that Maximus was some exception to this general tendency.

It is noteworthy that in several of these parallel cases, the *floruit* of the genuine author lines up very neatly with the period for which they are cited in the *HA*. Phlegon was a freedman of Hadrian and is cited for information on that emperor. Onesimus was writing in the early fourth century and is cited for the late third. Martialis might have been writing in the mid-third century and is cited for the 220s and early 230s. This is the key to understanding what the *HA* author was doing with Marius Maximus. He was clearly capable of considerable canniness in the invention of authorities: in each case he has attributed fictitious testimony, opinions, and writings to known authors of roughly the right date. Evidently, he wanted to conjure up a source for the lives of the emperors from Hadrian to Elagabalus. To turn Marius Maximus the (probably) Domitianic satirist into a major historian of just the right period, all the author of the *HA* would have needed was a consular list.[141] There, he would have seen the entry for 222, Imp. Caesar M. Aurelius Antoninus Augustus IV and M. Aurelius Severus Alexander Caesar, immediately followed by that for 223: L. Marius Maximus Perpetuus Aurelianus II and L. Roscius Aelianus Paculus Salvius Julianus. Marius Maximus could thus be safely cited up to the death of Elagabalus, at which point he was clearly still alive. Everything about the way that Maximus is used in the *HA* thus suggests that he is just another invented authority.

---

138 Birley 1997b: 2682.
139 *cf., e.g.* Savino 2017: 17–22. On Jerome, see Burgess 1998: 83–84.
140 Nemesianus: see Stover and Woudhuysen 2022a. Cicero: the text in Pal. lat. 899 reads 'demerio et arathum et balcyonas et uxorium et nilum'. The Aratus is obvious, and the *Alcyonae* known to the grammarians

is easy to recover. Emendation has been employed more speculatively to extract a *Marius* and even a *Limon*: Eubank 1933: 237.
141 Domaszewski argued that consular lists were one of the *HA*'s favoured onomastic quarries (1918: 1, with references).

Cross-references and fictitious documents in the *Historia Augusta*

Once we start looking at Marius Maximus as a feature of the *HA*, rather than its source, we can understand the real role that he plays in the text. In 1911, Karl Hönn concluded from his detailed study of the citations of Marius Maximus in the life of Alexander Severus that not only were they all fraudulent, they were actually used to cross-refer to earlier lives in the corpus.[142] His analysis can be extended, in one way or another, to explain many of the references to Marius Maximus in the *HA*. The creator of the *HA* tried to avoid suggesting that the biographers – at least those before 'Vopiscus', the supposed author of the final lives – knew of each other's work.[143] He did this probably because the supposed chronological order of the *scriptores* does not neatly match the arrangement of the lives in the work, so conventional cross-references within the collection would make it obvious that something was fundamentally wrong. The author could not simply cross-refer between lives that were supposedly by different *scriptores*, who were working independently, and at different times. Marius Maximus was his way out of this conundrum: fabricated references to his imperial biographies made it possible to cite earlier lives without giving the game away. The 'consular biographer' was a created by the author of the *HA* to fill a particular exigency in his project.

A survey of the alleged fragments of Maximus can demonstrate quite how easy it is to detect this technique, once it has been understood: it runs right through the early lives in the *HA*.[144] The reference to Marius Maximus at *Ael.* 3.9 (fr. 8 Birley, 9 Peter), describing Hadrian's astrological expertise, is simply a back reference to *Hadr.* 16.7, with almost verbatim phrasing (*ad horam mortis futuros actus ante perscripserit ~ ad illam horam, qua est mortuus, scripserit, quid acturus esset*). Marius Maximus' supposed discussion of the famous *tetrafarmacum*, mentioned at *Ael.* 5.4–5 and *Alex.* 30.6 (fr. 9 Birley, 8 Peter), is a reference back to *Hadr.* 21.4, where this dish of pheasant, sow's udder, ham, and pastry is introduced. The passage in the *Aelius* explicitly parallels the author's own cross-reference, and that in *Alexander* refers to multiple books (*de quo in libris suis Marius Maximus loquitur, cum Hadriani disserit vitam*), nodding to the fact that Hadrian has been discussed in multiple books, that is, in both the *Aelius* and the *Hadrianus*.[145]

The life of Avidius Cassius is particularly rich in these back references, which allow the author to work in much material he has already covered in his treatment of Marcus Aurelius. The mention at *Avid. Cass.* 6.7 of the *Bucolici milites* (fr. 13 Birley, 11 Peter), who had terrorised Egypt, is really there to bring in what has already been said at *Marc.* 21.2. Again, the wording is almost identical: *nam cum et Bucolici*

142 Hönn 1911: 197: 'allen Zitaten ist eins gemeinsam: In allen ist dem Biographen der Gewährsmann M. M. identisch mit dem Corpus der Viten'.

143 Vopiscus (see *PLRE* 'Vopiscus') is the most fleshed out of the *scriptores* and clearly located in the fourth century: 'he' refers to Trebellius Pollio (*Aurel.* 2.1; *Quadr.* 1.2), Julius Capitolinus, and Aelius Lampridius (*Prob.* 2.7), but not as a source. What Lampridius (*PLRE* 'Lampridius') says about 'his' work suggests a date after the defeat of Licinius, though somewhat murkily.

144 Throughout this section, we give citations by the standard *HA* abbreviations and provide the numbering

of the 'fragments' of Marius Maximus in the schemes of both Birley 1997b and Peter 1906. The mentions of Marius Maximus in the *Hadrianus* (2.10, 12.4, 20.3, 25.4) may indicate that there were originally lives before that (*i.e.* of Trajan and Nerva), to which these are cross-references. This idea gains some support from the fact that *Alex.* 65.4–5 references an incident in the life of Trajan discussed by Maximus (fr. 2 Birley, Peter), as does *Hadr.* 2.10 (fr. 3 Birley, Peter).

145 *cf.* also Hönn 1911: 141.

milites per Aegyptum gravia multa facerent, ab hoc [sc. Cassio] retunsi sunt ~ et cum per Aegyptum bucolici milites gravia multa fecissent per Avidium Cassium retunsi sunt. The various sections (*Avid. Cass.* 7.2, 9.5, and 9.6) on Faustina and Avidius (fr. 14 Birley, 12 Peter) all look back to the treatment of the same at *Marc.* 24.5–6. The Antiochenes' support for Avidius (*Avid. Cass.* 6.5–6; fr. 15 Birley, 13 Peter) refers back to *Marc.* 25.8. The same pattern can be detected in the life of Clodius Albinus: 3.5, on Severus' plan to have Albinus and Niger succeed him (fr. 24 Birley, 21 Peter), looks back to *Sev.* 6.9 and *Pesc.* 4.7, where it is attributed to Severus' autobiography. The prophecy about Albinus' death (*Clod. Alb.* 9.3–4; fr. 25 Birley, 22 Peter: *venturum quidem in potestatem eius [sc. Severi] Albinum, sed non vivum nec mortuum*) guides the reader to *Sev.* 10.7 and to *Pesc.* 9.5, which has almost exactly the same words (*neque vivus neque mortuus in potestatem Severi venturus*). The account of the number (and perhaps fate) of Albinus' sons (*Clod. Alb.* 9.5; fr. 26 Birley, 23 Peter) refers back to *Sev.* 11.9. Finally, *Clod. Alb.* 12.13, on Severus' severity towards Albinus' supporters (fr. 27 Birley, 25 Peter), brings us back to *Sev.* 12.1 and 12.7.

This technique is particular obvious in the so-called 'secondary lives' (those of the usurpers and most of the Caesars up to Alexander Severus), stitched together from the primary ones as they are, but it is not limited to them.[146] As Hönn showed in 1911, however, it continues right down to the life of Alexander Severus, the last point at which the testimony of Marius Maximus is invoked. The reference to Maximus in *Alex.* 5.3 (fr. 23 Birley, 20 Peter) for Septimius Severus' marriage to Julia Domna actually goes back to *Sev.* 3.9 and *Geta* 3.1.[147] More significantly, *Alex.* 21.4 refers to the emperor's alleged habit of granting to his praetorian prefects senatorial rank during their tenure of the office. Marius Maximus is invoked for the earlier practice of giving them the *latus clavus* at the end of their term, something he allegedly said 'in the lives of several emperors' (*ut in multorum vita Marius Maximus dicit*; fr. 27 Peter). This practice is referred to in two different *HA* lives: *Comm.* 4.7 (fr. 16 Birley) and *Hadr.* 8.7 (fr. 4 Birley).[148]

With the exception of the two references in the *Aelius* (one of which is paired with an authorial cross-reference), all of these 'fragments' of Maximus cover material found in lives attributed to different *scriptores Historiae Augustae*.[149] This contrasts with the author's practice when it comes to closely associated lives in the collection attributed to the same *scriptor*, where simple cross-references suffice.[150] Cameron (independently of Hönn) recognised this troubling feature in 1971, and to explain it he had to hypothesise that the lives in which Marius Maximus is cited for material found in earlier *vitae* in the *HA* must have been written first.[151] This is, of course, absurd: it would not only entail an early composition of the life

---

146 This observation on the nature of the secondary lives goes back to Mommsen 1890: 246 ff. It is particularly striking that Marius Maximus turns up so often in the lives of usurpers, when the *HA* claims explicitly that he did not write about them (*Quadr.* 1.1).

147 Hönn 1911: 46–47

148 *cf. Antonin.* 10.7, for the grant of *ornamenta consularia* to his praetorian prefects. The *HA* has been accused of considerable confusion in its analysis of these three passages (long analysis by Chastagnol 1970: 39–68; more briefly Cameron 1971: 266–267; Bertrand-Dagenbach 2014: 93), especially in confusing *ornamenta consularia* (honorary consular rank) with the grant of

the *latus clavus* (membership of the Senate). While we would hesitate to defend any claim made by the *HA*, if you abstract these passages from the difficult question of whether they are historically accurate, it is far from clear that the author is confused about these two different honours.

149 Vulcacius Gallicanus: *Avidius Cassius.* Julius Capitolinus: *Marcus Aurelius* and *Clodius Albinus.* Aelius Spartianus: *Septimius Severus* and *Pescennius Niger.*

150 *e.g. Verus* 2.2, referring to *Marc.*, both attributed to Capitolinus; *Carac.* 1.2, referring to *Sev.*, both attributed to Spartianus.

151 Cameron 1971: 266–267.

of Alexander Severus, but would also require the *Avidius Cassius* to have been written before the life of Marcus and the *Clodius Albinus* before the life of Severus. The last, at least, is demonstrably false.[152] Hönn's account of the Marius Maximus references, as extended more broadly here, also provides a far better explanation for their preponderance in the secondary lives.

This pattern explains nearly half the supposed 'fragments' of Marius Maximus assembled by Peter and Birley. Most of the rest are either vague (*e.g. Geta* 2.1) or refer to documents: the letters, speeches, poems, and so on that the *HA* regularly invokes. It was with these that Maximus could play a second, subsidiary role. The author of the *HA* was acutely aware of the historiographical problem of including documents and the difficulty of passing them off as real testimony to the events about which he was writing.[153] Most of the fictitious documents in the later lives are introduced either with reference to fictional authors or with some elaborate back story: jingles about the sanguinary activities of Aurelian from one 'Theoclius' *Caesareanorum temporum scriptor* (*Aurel.* 6.4–6), or a letter of Valerian from the *scrinia* of the urban prefecture (*Aurel.* 9.1), for instance.[154] At points, the author goes to absurd lengths to reassure readers of the provenance of his material, as in the famous passage of the *Tacitus* (8.1):

> Lest anyone think that I have too boldly put faith in some Greek or Latin author, the Ulpian library contains in its sixth *armarium* an ivory book, in which this *senatus consultum* is written out in full, subscribed by Tacitus with his own hand.

In the earlier lives, the ruse is much simpler: Marius Maximus is the guarantor of the authenticity of any documents cited, whether they be witticisms of Elagabalus (*Heliog.* 11.6; fr. 29 Birley, 26 Peter), a letter of Pertinax (*Pert.* 15.8; fr. 21 Birley, 18 Peter), poems by Commodus (*Comm.* 13.1–2; fr. 17 Birley, 14 Peter), or the senatorial acclamations at his death (*Comm.* 18.1–20.5; fr. 19 Birley, 16 Peter), to which we will return. In this connection it is worth noting that the author twice employs suspiciously specific references, like those he provided for the Ulpian library:

> *Avid. Cass.* 6.7 (fr. 13 Birley, 12 Peter): ut idem Marius Maximus refert in eo libro, quem secundum de vita Marci Antonini edidit.[155]

> As the same Marius Maximus reports in the second book he published on the life of Marcus Antoninus.

> *Geta* 2.1 (fr. 22 Birley, 19 Peter): de cuius vita et moribus in vita Severi Marius Maximus primo septenario satis copiose rettulit.

> Whose life and character Marius Maximus records at sufficient length in the *primus septenarius* of his life of Severus.

152 As discussed in Chapter VIII.
153 On the documents in general see the still valuable study of Homo 1926; also Den Hengst 1987 and Burgersdijk 2010: ch. 6.
154 Compare the way that a large number of poems, almost certainly the composition of the author, are said to be translations from the Greek, though clearly written originally in Latin (Baldwin 1978).
155 The construction here is bizarre and very likely requires emendation. Our translation is merely illustrative.

Attempts to explain what *primo septenario* actually means have been in vain.[156] This is because it does not actually mean anything that we can recover – it is about as valuable to argue about it as to wonder what exactly the 'sixth *armarium*' of the Ulpian library was. It is simply part of the author's legerdemain.

Marius Maximus, or the ectoplasm

Once we eliminate the cases of cross-references and the authentication of documents, Marius Maximus appears no different to the rest of the *HA*'s bogus authors. As scholarship has exhaustively demonstrated, the *HA* uses these fictitious authorities to conceal and occasionally manipulate material derived from other sources. Let us conclude by examining two such citations in greater detail.

At *Marc.* 1.6, the author of the *HA* cites Maximus' authority for the legendary ancestry of Marcus Aurelius:

> Cuius familia in **originem** recurrens a Numa probatur sanguinem trahere, ut Marius Maximus docet; item **a rege Sallentino** Malemnio, Dasummi filio, qui Lopias condidit.[157]

> His family is shown to derive its bloodline from Numa, going back in its beginnings to him, as Marius Maximus explains; likewise from the Sallentine king Malemnius, the son of Dasummus, who founded Lopia.

At first sight, this very recondite information in the mouth of Marius Maximus looks highly suspicious, but it is not solely invention or, at any rate, not solely the invention of the *HA*. Eutropius provides what is clearly a related account (8.9): 'his paternal ancestry (*origo*) descended from Numa Pompilius, his maternal from king Solentinus (*a Solentino rege*)'. Moreover, some of the additional details in the *HA* have a certain plausibility to them: there was probably a Dasumius in Marcus' family tree (rather closer to him than the deep mythical past), so the claimed descent might reflect a genuine tradition.[158] Yet neither Eutropius nor the *HA* can be derived from the other. Eutropius seems to make the adjective *Sallentinus* into a name *Solentinus* (something confirmed by Paeanius' paraphrase), but offers no real information about him. Unlike the *HA*, he also provides a distinction between the paternal and maternal lines. This parallel without derivation has caused some to wonder whether the *KG* in fact drew on Marius Maximus.[159] Since, however, neither existed, we ought to be looking for another common source for Eutropius and the *HA* here.

Even more intriguing are the acclamations of the Senate after Commodus' death (*Comm.* 18.1). On the one hand, as supposedly 'documentary' material, they are entirely of a piece with the way that the author of the *HA* uses Maximus elsewhere. On the other, close analysis of them gives us a clue as to

---

156 Tropea 1899: 48 f. suggests that *septenarius* means 'seven years', because the first part of the life of Severus covered that period. Peter 1906: clxxxii, Birt 1920, and Barbieri 1954: 272–275 prefer a book in seven sections. Birley 1971: 322 f. suggests that Maximus conceived of Severus' reign as falling into three units of seven years (rejected by Barnes 1978: 53, who advances no alternative; Birley 1997b: 2741 is more cautious).

157 On this passage, see Chausson 2002.

158 Syme 1958: 2.791–792.

159 *e.g.* Barbieri 1954: 53 and n. 2.

their ultimate origin. Among the many terrible cries raised by the Senate on this momentous occasion, we find the following (*HA Comm.* 18.4):

> Hostis deorum, carnifex senatus, hostis deorum, parricida senatus: hostis deorum, hostis senatus.

> The enemy of the gods, the butcher of the Senate, the enemy of the gods, the murderer of the Senate, the enemy of the gods, the enemy of the Senate!

Many have defended these acclamations as genuine, a dubious proposition, since similar things are found frequently in the *HA* and never otherwise accepted as authentic, but such has been the spell cast by Maximus.[160] Even so, the evidence is against them. Victor tells us about Commodus' *damnatio* (*HAb* 17.10):

> When they learnt of his death, the Senate . . . together with the people decreed that he was an enemy of the gods and of men (*hostem deorum atque hominum*) and that his name ought to be erased.

The fact that Commodus was declared a public enemy is certainly true (*cf.* Dio 74.2.1: πολέμιος), but *hostis deorum atque hominum* is hardly the usual phrase for this.[161] Before Victor, it occurs only in the pseudo-Senecan *Octavia*, where the eponymous character applies it to Nero: *hic hostis deum / hominumque* (240–241). With characteristic sophistication, Victor used this intertext to link Commodus to Nero and characteristically this subtlety was lost on the later tradition. Eutropius, doubtless drawing on Victor, simplified it to *hostis humani generis* (8.15: 'the enemy of the human race'). The *HA*'s acclamations are equally inspired by Victor, not least because *hostis deorum* is vanishingly rare otherwise.[162] Yet the *HA* has clearly missed the subtle intertext, even though it elsewhere shows knowledge of Commodus as a new Nero.[163] The unavoidable conclusion is that this supposedly authentic set of second-century senatorial acclamations was actually composed after Victor and inspired by him. This also explains the similarity of some of these acclamations to those included in the *LB* on the death of Pertinax, especially *Comm.* 19.8: 'for your sake, we have been in fear (*timuimus*). O how fortunate we are, since a man like you is emperor (*te viro imperante*)!' and *LB* 18.6 'With Pertinax as emperor (*Pertinace imperante*), we have lived safely, we have feared no one (*neminem timuimus*)!' The marked similarity of these acclamations with those recorded in the *Gesta Senatus Romani de Theodosiano publicando* of 438 is not an incredible testimony to the conservatism of senatorial practice over a 250-year interval. Rather, it is an anachronism, a reimagining of what senators might have proclaimed on the basis of late fourth-century practice, inspired by the earlier work of a more sober historian.[164]

Marius Maximus 'the consular biographer' thus vanishes in a puff of smoke, replaced by Marius Maximus 'purveyor of fine cross-references and dubious documents to indigent fraudsters'. As he appears in the *HA*, Maximus is a feature of the text and not a source, with nothing but the name in common with the (probably) Flavian author mentioned by Ammianus and the *Scholia* to Juvenal. The author of the *HA*

---

160 For those who have accepted the acclamations, see Chapter VIII.

161 In the fourth century, standard usage would have been *hostis publicus*: *CTh* 6.4.22.3, 7.8.7, 7.16.1, 10.8.4.

162 Besides Victor and the *Octavia*, see Hyginus 2.28.

163 *cf.* Fukuyama 2013. Commodus as Nero: Penella 1980a: 383–384.

164 On the *Gesta*, see Baldwin 1981; Matthews 2000: 31–54; Salway 2013. Baldwin was right to be very sceptical of the acclamations in the *HA* in general and those in the *Commodus* in particular.

practically gives the game away when he describes Maximus' work with the word he used for that of (the invented) Junius Cordus – *mythistoria*, a term he had coined and one that is uniquely appropriate to his own work.[165] The vaunted consistency of his supposed twenty-nine 'fragments' (in Birley's numeration) reveal nothing more than the characteristic preoccupations of the *HA* itself: astrology, genealogy, poetry, imperial literary production, scandal.[166] One could pick twenty-nine passages of the *HA* at random and find exactly the same range of interests. Schlumberger, in the only substantive reply to Paschoud's 1999 provocation, thought he had found independent evidence for Marius Maximus in the overlaps between the *LB* and the *HA* up to the death of Elagabalus.[167] Many of these are indeed striking, but his chronological limit is off.[168] They continue up to the reign of Aurelian, half a century beyond Marius Maximus' supposed date.[169] In other words, the relationship to the *LB* is a feature of the *HA* itself, not one of its putative source. As Paschoud says, Marius Maximus is nothing more than an ectoplasm of the author of the *HA* itself – a flimsy and fraudulent conjurer's trick to ensnare the credulous.[170]

Getting rid of Marius Maximus, however, reopens the problem he has been thought to resolve: that there is much good historical information in the *HA*, but that its quality seems to decline after Elagabalus. It is possible, however, that this has been a *question mal posée*. Momigliano was right that all statements in the *HA* really need external corroboration to be trusted, but this rule has important consequences for how we assess its reliability. Where we have other rich evidence against which to weigh its testimony, we will find much more reliable information in the *HA* than for those stretches of the work where we are without parallel accounts. The apparent decline in the quality of the *HA*'s information for the period after the 220s or 230s is, at least in part, a reflection of the chance survival of other materials for imperial history. Cassius Dio's narrative ended with the reign of Alexander Severus. From that point on, we are left in the shakier hands of Herodian for most of the history of Alexander, Maximinus, and the emperors of the year 238. After that, due to the loss of Dexippus, we have almost nothing: there is no coherent narrative against which we can measure the *HA*'s testimony, although the recovery of the Vienna palimpsest has begun to put our understanding of the *HA*'s life of Gallienus, at least, in a slightly different light.[171] This problem is compounded by the marked decline in the quantity of surviving epigraphy after the Severans, which makes the prosopographer's task so much more arduous.[172] The sense that something changes drastically in

165 Paschoud 1999b: 246–247.
166 For astrology, Syme 1976b, Straub 1970. For genealogy, see for example *Gord.* 2.2, where Gordian I is said to be descended from the Gracchi and Trajan; Chausson 2007: 190 and Béranger 1974. On poems, see Den Hengst 2004. Imperial literary production: Burgersdijk 2010: 214, n. 638.
167 Schlumberger 2010.
168 See Chapter VIII for a fuller discussion.
169 For example: *LB* 27.1 *nepos* **Gordiani** *ex filia* ~ *HA Gord.* 22.4 *Hic natus est, ut plures adserunt,* **ex filia Gordiani**; *LB* 28.4 *Philippus* **humillimo** *ortus loco fuit* ~

Gord. 29.1 *Philippus Arabs,* **humili** *genere natus*; *LB* 34.2 *exstinctoque* **a suis** *Aureolo* ~ *Claud.* 5.3 *iudicio* **suorum militum** *apud Mediolanium Aureolum dignum exitum vita ac moribus suis habuit*; *LB* 34.4: *ex auro statuam prope ipsum* **Iovis** *simulacrum* ~ *Claud.* 3.4 *ante* **Iovis** *Optimi Maximi templum* **statuam auream**; *LB* 35.9 *Fuit saevus et sanguinarius et trux* ~ *Aurel.* 36.4 *severus, truculentus,* *sanguinarius fuit*.
170 Paschoud 2009: 181, *cf.* Paschoud 2007: 364.
171 See Zecchini 2017.
172 See, canonically, MacMullen 1982.

the *HA*'s nature with Elagabalus is at least partly an artefact of the transmission of other works. So, when we embark on the hunt for the *HA*'s sources, we ought to do it without the assumption that because in one part of the work we can corroborate what it says, a distinct source must lie behind it, different to whatever material formed the basis for other sections. That would be to assume our conclusion.

How then ought we to approach the question of the *HA*'s sources? Syme, Barbieri, and (especially) Lécrivain did have an insight about the structure of the work's narrative and how Marius Maximus is deployed within it.[173] What is ascribed to him does tend to look like a series of additions, seemingly grafted on to an otherwise often sound narrative. *Pace* Syme, we might call that narrative the work of *ignotus*, rather than Ignotus. Can we say anything about the nature of that source? There is no reason to think that it was biographical. Without Marius Maximus and Ignotus, the whole idea of a 'Suetonian tradition' disappears. This is not to say that Suetonius was without heirs, but his principal descendant was the author of the *HA*, whose achievement lay in part in reviving the genre of imperial biography.[174] In fact, we can be almost certain that the *HA*'s 'good' source was not biographical. Consider the life of Verus, which Syme thought offered the best evidence of the existence of Ignotus *qua* biographer. The *HA* is clear that biographical treatment of secondary emperors and usurpers was an innovation of its own invented authors, particularly Junius Cordus, which is to say that they are the author's own contribution.[175] What would be covered in such a *Life*? The events of the reign of Verus all properly belonged to that of his senior co-emperor Marcus – they were so intertwined that it would be difficult to narrate them separately. All that was left for a biographer was to catalogue the emperor's character and behaviour. Yet it is precisely the parts of the *HA* life of Verus treating his *mores* that critics like Barnes reject as 'passages interpolated into the main narrative'.[176] Instead, the good historical information on Verus – his eastern campaign – was drawn from a treatment of Marcus and his fellow emperor together: in other words, from a history of events in the middle of the second century. It is worth noting in this connection that Verus must have played a substantial and integrated role in Victor's treatment of Marcus. The *HAb* (16.3–9) embeds an account of Verus in the middle of its history of the age of Marcus, something seen also in the *LB* (16.6) and Eutropius, who provides a précis of Verus and his deeds, once again in the middle of his treatment of Marcus (8.10).

The *Quellenkritik* of the *HA*, and of its earlier lives in particular, needs to be undertaken anew. In his influential (if not uncontroversial) 1978 monograph on *The Sources of the Historia Augusta*, Barnes identified six major sources used by the author of the *HA*: Herodian, Dexippus, Eunapius, Marius Maximus, Ignotus, and the *Kaisergeschichte*.[177] Three of these – the three Latin ones, we might note – have now been banished: Marius Maximus, the biographer Ignotus, and the *KG*. To rebuild, we need to start with what can be proven on solid textual grounds: that the author of the *HA* drew on Eutropius and the historical work of Aurelius Victor.

173 Lécrivain 1904: 194: 'Or, l'analyse des vies nous a montré qu'aucune de ces citations ne faisait corps avec le récit, qu'elles avaient toutes été insérées plus ou moins maladroitement par le second compilateur dans le noyau historique tiré de la première source et qu'elles se rapportaient presque toutes à des morceaux non pas chronologiques, mais biographiques, anecdotiques et de peu de valeur'.

174 *cf.* Paschoud 2009.

175 *Macr.* 1.3. *cf.* Thomson 2012: 22.

176 Barnes 1978: 47.

177 Barnes 1978: 125.

CHAPTER VIII

THE *HISTORIA AUGUSTA*

'The problem of the *Historia Augusta*', Fergus Millar warned in 1964, 'is one into which sane men refrain from entering'.[1] Duly admonished, it seems wisest to approach one aspect of the text that is no longer controversial. Nearly all scholars agree that the author of the *HA* knew and used the work of Aurelius Victor: this was one of the factors that tipped Dessau off that the collection might not be what it claims.[2] Nevertheless, the issue of the *HA*'s debt to Victor has generally been relegated to no more than a footnote in the voluminous literature of *Quellenforschung* – an example of the use of breviarists, *Kaisergeschichte* texts, and minor historians. Real attention has been focused elsewhere.[3] As a result, even though many of the parallels we discuss below have already been marked and discussed in the scholarly literature, no one has ever assembled them before. The same might be said for Eutropius – while many scholars are willing to accept that the *HA* did indeed use the text of Eutropius, most of the actual evidence for this has been relegated to discussions of the *KG*.[4]

What follows is a new analysis of the *HA*'s sources, one freed at last from the illusions of the *KG*, Marius Maximus, and Ignotus. Instead, we focus on authors whose works survive (at least in part) and who were certainly familiar to and used by the mischievous *scriptor* of the *HA*: Victor and Eutropius. For reasons that will become obvious, it is Victor who here commands the lion's share of attention. In fact, this chapter can be thought of as a continuous exposition of the *HA* read against Victor's work – an exposition that is necessarily selective, because the wealth of material is so great. Our emphasis throughout is on verbal overlaps, as the surest guarantee of influence, rather than on vaguer (though often still revealing) similarities of ideas and fact. For this reason, it is the *Historiae abbreviatae* – Victor's *ipsissima verba* – that dominates, though the *Libellus breviatus* also has much to teach us. Eutropius and his *breviarium* play more of a supporting part, though they still manage to steal a few scenes – again our attention is primarily devoted to language. What this analysis reveals is the deep and pervasive influence that Victor's *Historia* had on the *HA* and the collection's lesser, though considerable, dependence on Eutropius. We will see the *HA*'s author plunder Victor for ideas, read other sources (particularly Herodian) through him, spin up entire conceits from a half sentence, misunderstand (sometimes amusingly) what he had written, and

---

1 Millar 1964: 124.
2 Dessau 1889: 361–374. Victor and the *HA*: see (*e.g.*) Hohl 1955; Chastagnol 1967; Syme 1968a: 106–107; Syme 1978b; Barnes 1978: 95; Chastagnol 1994: lxvii–lxviii; Festy 1999b; Rohrbacher 2013: 150–151; Burgersdijk 2017. Even the sceptical Momigliano 1954: 31 ('what seems to me the strongest single argument for a post-Constantinian date') accepted it (with some cavilling), *cf. ibid*. 43. Noteworthy, however, is Paschoud 1998b, who retracts his earlier support for the *HA*'s direct use of Victor and Eutropius, in favour of the *KG*. A similar

manoeuvre was deployed (rather falteringly) by Lippold 1991: 143–147, as part of his general argument that the *HA* was a Constantinian product somewhat revised in the early fifth century. See further below.
3 The title of Burgersdijk 2017 is instructive: 'Aurelius Victor, Festus and the Others: Minor Historians and Anonymous Sources in the *Historia Augusta*'. One only has to compare the amount of attention devoted to Marius Maximus to see the imbalance (Chapter VII).
4 For the *HA*'s use of Eutropius, the *locus classicus* is Dessau 1889: 361–374; *cf.* Rohrbacher 2013: 151–152.

occasionally take over entire sections verbatim. We will observe also the way that Eutropius' text was constantly beside him as he worked, a convenient source of clear and simple narrative. At times, we will be able to detect the *HA* using both historians in parallel, hopping between and even combining their accounts. The inescapable conclusion of this expedition into the wastes of the *HA* is that the collection owes an overwhelming debt to Victor (in particular) and Eutropius. That fact casts the *HA*'s idiosyncratic project in a new and interesting light, but it also raises important questions about Victor's *Historia* and the extent to which more of it might be recovered from the most dubious of places.

★ ★ ★

As we have seen, the complementary theories of Marius Maximus and Ignotus emerged from the need to account for the good information in the earlier part of the *Historia Augusta*: the lives of the emperors from Hadrian to the Severans. Not coincidentally, perhaps, these lives are also where Victor's influence on the text has been thought strongest, particularly in a long passage from the life of Septimius Severus – but this is far from the sum of Victor's influence. In fact, tell-tale signs of the use of his work can be traced right from the beginning of the *Historia Augusta*.

If the average scholar of the *HA* were asked to identify its most characteristic features, then the text's enthusiasm for scandal – for the salacious and the improbable – would surely feature prominently in any answer. That makes episodes of imperial depravity and misconduct a good test case for the *HA*'s sources. If what seem at first sight to be the peculiar interests of the work's author derive in fact from elsewhere, then that ought to inflect our conclusions about his degree of indebtedness to this or that text. Such gossipy material is less prominent in the early lives in the collection, but it is by no means altogether absent. What is immediately striking is how much of it, on close examination, seems to be derived from the work of Victor.

The 'good' emperors

Let us begin in the *HA*'s life of Hadrian, which we have already seen has a number of remarkable parallels to the *LB* threaded through its whole extent.[5] Towards the end of the *vita*, the author unsurprisingly provides a brief reference to the scandal surrounding the demise of Hadrian's favourite, Antinous (*Hadr.* 14.5–6):

> While sailing along the Nile, he lost his dear Antinous, for whom he wept like a woman. There are various rumours (*varia fama*) about this: some alleging that he had devoted (*devotum*) himself for Hadrian's sake; others asserting what both his good looks and Hadrian's excessive passion reveal (*quod et forma eius ostentat et nimia voluptas Hadriani*).

5 Chapter V.

The death of Antinous is a curious episode, and not only because of the mysterious circumstances under which it occurred. Although it left a vast archaeological legacy in the massive artistic and architectural programme to commemorate him, it is not widely discussed in historical sources: besides the *HA*, it turns up only in Dio (69.11.2–4) and the *HAb*.[6] Even on the scanty evidence we have, however, the version in the *HA* does not quite make sense: taken literally, it seems to suggest that Antinous' death was somehow caused by his physical relationship with Hadrian, an 'unfortunately obscure' insinuation, as one recent discussion points out.[7] Fortunately, prurient speculation about the mechanics of Antinous' demise is unnecessary, for Victor's account supplies the missing piece (*HAb* 14.7–9):

> On this account wicked rumours (*rumores mali*) arose, that he had defiled young men, and had burned for Antinous, his infamous servant, and for no other reason founded a city in his name and set up statues for this young man. Some people, indeed, interpret these actions as pious and devoted, for they say that Hadrian had desired to prolong the natural term of his life and the *magi* had demanded a volunteer in his place. When all refused, Antinous offered himself, and for this reason the aforementioned homages were rendered to him.

The two rumours the *HA* recounts are not actually about how Antinous died at all. Rather they are part of an explanation for why Hadrian named a city after him (Antinoöpolis or Antinoë in the Thebaid) and why he set up statues in his honour, facts that the *HA* has omitted in its obviously abbreviated account.[8] These honours, and not Antinous' death, were the subject of the rumours to which the *HA* alludes: according to Victor, Hadrian either performed them as a pious memorial for Antinous' *devotio* (ritual suicide), or because of his lust for the dead youth.[9] While there is little to link the two accounts textually, there can be no doubt that Victor is the *HA*'s source: both explicitly situate themselves as addressing the rumours (*rumores ~ fama*) that circulated about the event, not seemingly a feature of the discussion in our only other source, Cassius Dio (69.11.3). The real intertextual link between the *HA* and Victor on Hadrian, however, comes slightly later. The *HAb* concludes its account of Antinous and Hadrian with a (Sallustian) recusal:

> We will set this matter aside undecided (*nos rem in medio relinquemus*), although we do think that in a dissolute character, companionship with someone not even close to the same age is suspicious.[10]

We find this same recusal in the *HA*, not with Hadrian, however, but three lives later, in its discussion of the death of Verus. This leads us neatly to the lives of the other second-century emperors, where, once again, the influence of Victor is pervasive.

The life of Marcus Aurelius in the *HAb* is, as we have noted already, particularly odd. A good portion of it is taken up with the shocking allegation that Marcus murdered his brother Verus (*HAb* 16.5–8):

---

6 In general on Antinous and his commemoration, see Vout 2005, with Vout 2007: 52–135. It is striking that Pausanias 8.9.7–8 avoids the fate of Antinous entirely. Note also an appearance in Julian, *Caes.* 311d.

7 Galimberti 2017: 105.

8 *cf.* Birley 1997a: 248: 'The *HA* can be seen to have condensed its source drastically'. Cassius Dio (in epitome), our only other source for the incident, also mentions both the city and the statues (69.11.3–4).

9 On *devotio*, see Chapter II.

10 Sallust, *Cat.* 19.4: *nos eam rem in medio relinquemus. cf.* Cicero, *Pro Caelio* 48; Velleius Paterculus 2.48.4.

> A few days later Lucius died and this offered an opportunity for concocting the story that he was betrayed by the deceit of his kinsman. They say that Marcus, since he was tormented by envy at Lucius' accomplishments, practised a wicked act of deceit at dinner. For he smeared one side of a knife with poison and cut off part of the womb of a sow (*lita veneno cultri parte vulvae frustum . . . praecidit*), which was carefully separated from the other. When he had eaten that part, as is the custom among family members, he offered the other, which the venom had touched, to his brother. Men are not able to believe this about such a great man unless their own minds are prone to wickedness. [11]

As we have seen, the details of this plot are absolutely Byzantine. A story like this was catnip to the *scriptor* of the *HA* (*Marc.* 15.5):

> There is no *princeps* who is not the subject of dark rumour (*fama*): even Marcus came into common chatter. They said that he killed Verus with poison (*veneno*) in this way: he smeared one side of a knife with poison, and cut off part of the womb of a sow (*parte cultri veneno lita vulvam inciderit*), offering the poisoned part to his brother, and keeping the harmless part for himself.

Much of the phrasing we can attribute to the author of the *HA*: note, for example, the use of the cognomen Verus instead of the *praenomen* Lucius. Crucially, however, when he comes to the poisoned knife – the hinge of the plot – Victor's words are reproduced precisely, even to the point of inelegantly repeating the word *veneno* in the space of eight words.[12] The author sticks to the same formula when he recounts this incident in the life of Verus (11.2–4):

> There is a famous story – which is not compatible with Marcus' life – that Marcus offered Verus a part of the womb of a sow smeared with poison (*partem vulvae veneno inlitam*), after he had cut it with a knife tainted with poison on one side.

As before, incredulity that anyone could believe such a story is then expressed (*Verus* 11.4):

> But it is terribly wicked to think this about Marcus – even if the thoughts and deeds of Verus deserved it. We will *not* set this matter aside undecided (*nos non in medio relinquemus*), but spew it out wholly purged and refuted.

The words here are the same as Victor's discussion of Hadrian's commemoration of Antinous, but emphatically negated. The *HA* even copies Victor's judgement as to why this incident could not have happened (*HAb* 16.8: *Haec **in tanto viro** credere nisi animi ad scelus proni non queunt*), in an oblique reference to this same story earlier in the life of Verus (10.2: *illa fabula, quae in Marci vita posita est, abhorrens **a talis viri vita** sit exorta*). There is, in other words, a substrate of material from Victor that runs right through the *HA*'s accounts of Hadrian and Marcus Aurelius and with which the *scriptor* engages forthrightly.

Further evidence that the *HA* was indeed using Victor's account directly and *in extenso* can be found in the story that immediately follows the poisoning episode in the *HAb*. This is the strange scene in which a crowd of philosophers tries to detain Marcus from setting out on his Marcomannic war, pleading

---

11 On the text here, quoted and discussed in Chapter IV, see the Appendix, no. IV.

12 *Apropos* of this, it is worth noting in general that the *HA* is an inelegant text and we have not always tried to disguise this in our translations.

for him to explain certain obscure points of doctrine before he leaves them.[13] This anecdote – not entirely flattering to the emperor – is found not in the *HA* life of Marcus, but that of Avidius Cassius.[14] We also have the *HA*'s scabrous story about Marcus' wife Faustina leering at sailors (*Marc.* 19.7): 'Faustina, it is well known, at Caieta selected (*elegisse*) lovers for herself, both sailors (*nauticas*) and gladiators'. This is clearly derived from Victor's rather more judgemental account of the empress's behaviour (*HAb* 16.2):

> She had burst further into such a height of wantonness that, while residing in Campania, she would sit on pleasant spots by the beach, in order to select sailors (*ad legendos ex nauticis*), since generally they work in the nude, who were more suitable for her shameful acts (*flagitiis aptiores*).

In further support of the idea that these episodes are indeed taken from Victor is material about the earlier emperors found later in the *HA*. In the life of Elagabalus, there is mention of the city of Orestia in Thrace, which Hadrian had renamed Hadrianopolis (Adrianople). This leads the author to an anecdote about Hadrian's madness (7.9–10):

> For they say that the madness, in which he had ordered many senators to be executed, was softened by this [*sc.* renaming the city]. Antoninus earned the name Pius by saving these men, because later on he brought into the Senate the very ones all believed had been killed at the emperor's command.

In all the *HA*'s discussions of the reason why Antoninus was called Pius (*cf. Hadr.* 24.4 and *Anton.* 2.3–7), the fact that Antoninus saved senators from execution at the hands of Hadrian is always mentioned, but the dramatic scene in which he led into the Senate the senators everyone thought dead is found only in Victor.[15] A little later still in the life of Elagabalus, we come upon a typically salacious anecdote about the emperor (8.7): 'He took careful pains to seek out from almost the whole city and from the sailors (*ex nauticis*), *onobeli*, as he called them, ['men hung like a donkey'] who seemed particularly virile (*viriliores*)'. Yet, not even in this most *HA* of *HA* anecdotes are we actually witnessing anything original, besides (perhaps) some lexical virtuosity.[16] A very similar situation is described in Victor's treatment of the same emperor (*HAb* 23.2), and the *HA*'s anecdote is actually a reimagining of the same story in Victor about Faustina: note particularly *ex nauticis* and the comparative adjectives attesting to the men's anatomical aptitude (*flagitiis aptiores ~ viriliores*). As if to allay any doubt as to origin of the story, the *HA* immediately transitions to a discussion of Marcus' Marcomannic wars (*Heliog.* 9.10).

Together, these examples show quite how close at hand the author of the *HA* kept Victor's account of Hadrian, Antoninus Pius, and Marcus Aurelius. It was not, however, only Victor that he used. A long passage in the life of Marcus (16.3–18.2) is identical to the corresponding material found in Eutropius (8.10–14). Much of that same content (some of it verbatim) is also found in the *Libellus breviatus* (16.1–12), but in a different order.[17] Once we are no longer blinded by the notion of a *Kaisergeschichte*, we can see

---

13 *HAb* 16.9: *is Marcomannos . . . petiturus philosophorum turba obtestantium circumfunderetur, ne expeditioni aut pugnae se prius committeret, quam sectarum ardua ac perocculta explanavisset.*

14 *HA Avid. Cass.* 3.6: *iturus ad bellum Marcomannicum, timentibus cunctis, ne quid fatale proveniret, rogatus sit non adulatione sed serio, ut praecepta philosophiae ederet.*

15 *HAb* 14.13–15.1. On this passage, see the Appendix, no. III.

16 *cf.* Adams 1982: 21.

17 Of course, the *LB* incorporated Eutropius directly here: Stover and Woudhuysen 2021: 180.

clearly the plain truth that the *HA* is simply reproducing Eutropius. So, in these anecdotes about Hadrian, Antoninus, and Marcus Aurelius, even if the lexical overlaps and intertextual echoes are sometimes subtle, it is nonetheless clear that many of the scandalous, sensational, and salacious stories – characteristic features of the *HA* – really derive from Victor. That has considerable implications for our understanding of the *HA*'s sources. If what appears characteristic is actually derivative, then *a fortiori* much of the (uncharacteristically) reliable and factual information ought to have come from Victor's *Historia* as well.

Septimius Severus

As we move beyond these 'good' three emperors, little resonances continue. For example, we know from the *Scholia Vallicelliana* that Victor had the fullest discussion of how Commodus renamed the months of the year outside the *HA*, which is clearly indebted to him.[18] We have seen also that the senatorial acclamations at Commodus' death (attributed to Marius Maximus) were actually derived from Victor.[19] When we get to the life of Septimius Severus, however, we find an entirely different and much more obvious use of Victor. A substantial portion of the text (some ten per cent of the whole) is almost verbatim identical with the *HAb* (**Table 8.1**). That these passages are related is beyond dispute. The consensus of scholarship since Dessau – including even Momigliano – has been that the *HA* is the debtor and, despite a recent attempt to defend the contrary, there is no possibility that Victor is using the *HA*.[20] Take just one example: leading up to Severus' death, Victor gives a characteristic discussion of his rise to power from humble origins, and the role liberal studies played in it, echoing his earlier remarks (not found in the *HA*) (*HAb* 20.5). Severus, after enduring hardship, 'labour, cares, fear, uncertainties of every kind, as if a witness to the life of mortals', declared that it was all for naught: 'I was all things; it availed me nothing'. The *HA* reproduces some of this, but not only does it botch the concluding aphorism (it is 'flabbier' in A.R. Birley's phrase) – the author entirely misses the pointed Sallustian reminiscence, *vitae mortalium* from *Jugurtha* 1.2, on the superiority of Virtue to Fortune.[21] In typical fashion, Victor is reversing Sallust's point: Severus had everything – virtue, education, and success – and yet in the end, it meant nothing to him. The *HA* misses this entirely: it must be derivative.[22]

18 Chapter V
19 Chapter VII.
20 On the consensus, see above – the last notable dissents were Stern 1953: 17–27. The recent challenge is by Baker 2014: 92–104, whose argumentation is not pellucid. He advances three alternative explanations, without stating which he ultimately favours: that Victor and the *HA* have a common source; that Victor depends on the *HA*; that the textual commonalities are explained by 'interpolation', either from Victor to the *HA*, or vice versa. These three explanations are unconvincing on their own terms. The idea of a common source (other than Victor) shared by the *HAb* and the *HA* fails to account for the fact that the verbatim overlaps appear *in extenso* only here. The notion that Victor used the

HA is justified on the grounds that elsewhere he took material word for word (some seven of them) from Suetonius (*HAb* 18.5 vs *Vitellius* 15.2). There is a basic qualitative difference – which Baker elides – between copying part of a sentence and taking over entire paragraphs; moreover, copying *one* source (which is hardly what Victor was doing) does not require that he copied *all* sources. The idea of interpolation seems rooted in a fundamental misunderstanding of the mechanics of manuscript circulation.
21 Birley 1994: 40.
22 Much the same might be said about the earlier aphorism in *HA Sev.* 17.7, where Severus never provides an answer to his interlocutor's question, where Victor clearly did (*HAb* 20.11).

Table 8.1 – The *HA* and *HAb* on Septimius Severus

	HA Severus 17.5–19.4	*HAb* 20.1–30 (rearranged)
(17.5) And since to go through lesser matters is a lengthy endeavour, these are his great deeds: that after Julianus was defeated and killed, he dissolved the praetorian cohorts, deified Pertinax against the soldiers' wishes, ordered the abolition of the decrees of Salvius Julianus – this did not take effect –	(17.5): Et quoniam longum est minora persequi, huius magnifica illa: quod victo et occiso Iuliano praetorianas cohortes exauctoravit, Pertinacem contra voluntatem militum in deos rettulit, Salvii Iuliani decreta iussit aboleri; quod non obtinuit.	(20.1) Igitur Septimius, Pertinacis nece, simul flagitiorum odio, dolore atque ira commotior cohortes praetorias statim militia exemit cunctisque partium caesis Helvium senatusconsulto inter Divos refert; Salvii nomen atque eius scripta factave aboleri iubet; quod unum effici nequivit.
(6) and finally took the name Pertinax, not so much it seems because he wanted to, as because of the similarity of their characters.	(6) Denique cognomentum Pertinacis non tam ex sua voluntate quam ex morum parsimonia videtur habuisse.	(20.10) Et cognomento Pertinax, quamquam ob vitae parsimoniam similem ipsum magis ascivisse plures putent: nobis mens ad credendum prona acerbitati impositum.
(7) For he was thought cruel on account of the boundless slaughter of many people, and when one of his enemies offered himself in submission and said to him, 'What would you have done?', he was not softened by so wise a question and ordered him to be killed.	(7) Nam et infinita multorum caede crudelior habitus et, cum quidam ex hostibus eidem se suppliciter obtulisset atque dixisset illi 'quid facturus esses?', non emollitus tam prudente dicto interfici eius iussit.	(20.10) Horum infinita caede crudelior habitus (20.11) Nam cum quidam hostium, quem tamen, uti bellis civilibus solet, condicio loci ad Albinum detulerat, causa exposita novissime conclusisset: 'Quid, quaeso, faceres, si tu esses?' ille respondit: 'Ea perferrem quae tu'.
(8) He was in addition zealous for rooting out factions. He left almost no engagement except as the victor.	(8) Fuit praeterea delendarum cupidus factionum. prope a nullo congressu digressus nisi victor.	
(18.1) He subdued Abgar the king of the Persians. He placed the Arabs under Roman authority. He made the Adiabeni pay tribute.	(18.1) Persarum regem Abgarum subegit. Arabas in dicionem accepit. Adiabenos in tributarios coegit.	(20.13) At iste delendarum cupidus factionum, quo deinceps mitius ageret, necessitudinem facti ulcisci maluit, ne paulatim spe veniae in labem publicam per coniurationes procederetur
(2) Because Britain was the greatest glory of his empire, he fortified it with a wall constructed across the island at a perpendicular, terminating at the Ocean on each side. For this reason he received the name Britannicus.	(2) Britanniam, quod maximum eius imperii decus est, muro per transversam insulam ducto utrimque ad finem Oceani munivit. unde etiam Britannici nomen accepit.	(20.14) Felix ac prudens, armis praecipue adeo ut nullo congressu nisi victor discesserit (20.14–16) auxeritque imperium subacto Persarum rege nomine Aggaro. Neque minus Arabas, simul adortus ut est, in dicionem redegit provinciae modo. Adiabena quoque, ni terrarum macies despectaretur, in tributarios concessisset.
(3) He made Tripoli, from whence he came, very secure by crushing the extremely aggressive tribes, and granted to the Roman people a daily ration of oil, free and very generous, in perpetuity.	(3) Tripolim, unde oriundus erat, contusis bellicosissimis gentibus securissimam reddidit, ac populo Romano diurnum oleum gratuitum et fecundissimum in aeternum donavit.	

Table continues over

Table 8.1 continued

(20.18) His maiora aggressus Britanniam, quoad ea utilis erat, pulsis hostibus muro munivit per transversam insulam ducto utrimque ad finem Oceani.

(20.19) Quin etiam Tripoli, cuius Lepti oppido oriebatur, bellicosae gentes submotae procul.

(4) He was both implacable to offences and of singular judgement in promoting anyone who was effective.	(4) Idem cum implacabilis delictis fuit, tum ad erigendos industrios quosque iudicii singularis.	(20.20) Quae factu ardua facilius eo patrabantur, quo implacabilis delictis strenuum quemque praemiis extollebat.
(5) He was sufficiently dedicated to philosophy and the study of rhetoric, and very eager indeed for learning.	(5) Philosophiae ac dicendi studiis satis deditus, doctrinae quoque nimis cupidus.	(20.22) Philosophiae, declamandi, cunctis postremo liberalium deditus studiis
(6) He was the enemy of outlaws everywhere. He composed his own biography – in an honest fashion, including both private and public matters, albeit excusing only his vice of cruelty.	(6) Latronum ubique hostis. Vitam suam privatam publicamque ipse composuit ad fidem, solum tamen vitium crudelitatis excusans.	(20.21) Denique ne parva latrocinia quidem impunita patiebatur, in suos animadvertens magis, quod vitio ducum aut etiam per factionem fieri vir experiens intellegeret.
(7) The Senate made a judgement on him: that it was not fitting either for him to have been born or to have died (because he seemed both exceedingly cruel and exceedingly useful to the commonwealth).	(7) De hoc senatus ita iudicavit, illum aut nasci non debuisse aut mori, quod et nimis crudelis et nimis utilis rei publicae videretur.	(20.22) idemque abs se texta ornatu et fide paribus composuit.
(8) Even so, he was less circumspect at home, since he retained his wife Julia, famous for her adulteries, guilty even of conspiracy.	(8) Domi tamen minus cautus, qui uxorem Iuliam famosam adulteriis tenuit, ream etiam coniurationis.	(20.6) Quem quamquam exacta aetate mortuum iustitio elogioque lugendum sanxere, struentes illum iustum nasci aut emori minime convenisse.
(9) When he was suffering in his feet and paused his campaign, the soldiers were troubled at the news and made his son Bassianus (who was with him) Augustus. He ordered that he be lifted up and carried to the tribunal, and that all the tribunes, centurions, generals, and cohorts	(9) Idem, cum pedibus aeger bellum moraretur, idque milites anxie ferrent eiusque filium Bassianum, qui una erat, Augustum fecissent, tolli se atque in tribunal ferri iussit, adesse deinde omnes tribunos centuriones duces et cohortes	(20.23) Huic tanto domi forisque uxoris probra summam gloriae dempsere, quam adeo famose complexus est, uti cognita libidine ac ream coniurationis retentaverit.

(10) responsible for what happened be present, then had his son, who had taken the name of Augustus, stand up. After he had ordered punishment for all of those responsible for the deed except his son, when all of them were lying flat on their faces on the ground before the tribunal, begging for pardon, he touched his head with his hand and said, 'At last you sense that it is the head that rules, not the feet'.

(11) The following was a saying of his, since Fortune had led him by very many steps indeed from humble origins through the duties of letters and government service to imperial power: 'I have been all things and it profited me nothing'.

(10) quibus auctoribus id acciderat, sisti deinde filium, qui Augusti nomen acceperat. Cumque animadverti in omnes auctores facti praeter filium iuberet rogareturque veniam omnibus ante tribunal prostratis humi, caput manu contingens ait: 'Tandem sentitis caput imperare, non pedes'.

(11) Huius dictum est, cum eum ex humili per litterarum et militiae officia ad imperium plurimis gradibus fortuna duxisset: 'Omnia', inquit, 'fui et nihil expedit'.

(20.25–26) Nam cum pedibus aeger bellum moraretur idque milites anxie ferrent eiusque filium Bassianum, qui Caesar una aderat, Augustum fecissent, in tribunal se ferri, adesse omnes, imperatoremque ac tribunos, centuriones et cohortes, quibus auctoribus acciderat, sisti reorum modo iussit. Quo metu cum stratus humi victor tantorum exercitus veniam precaretur: 'Sentitisne', inquit, pulsans manu, 'caput potius quam pedes imperare?'

(20.28–29) Ortus medie humili, primo litteris, dehinc imbutus foro; quo parum commodante, uti rebus artis solet, dum tentat aut exquirit varia melioraque, conscendit imperium. Ibi graviora expertus, laborem curas metum et incerta prorsus omnia, quasi testis vitae mortalium: 'Cuncta', inquit, 'fui; conducit nihil'.

(19.1) He died at York in Britain, after he had subdued the tribes in Britain which seemed to be hostile, in the eighteenth year of his reign, finished off by a very serious illness, already an old man.

(19.1) Periit Eboraci in Britannia, subactis gentibus quae Britanniae videbantur infestae, anno imperii XVIII, morbo gravissimo exstinctus iam senex.

(20.27) Neque multo post in Britanniae municipio, cui Eboraci nomen, annis regni duodeviginti morbo exstinctus est.

(2) He left behind two sons, Antoninus Bassianus and Geta, to whom he had given the name of Antoninus in honour of Marcus.

(2) Reliquit filios duos, Antoninum Bassianum et Getam, cui et ipsi in honorem Marci Antonini nomen imposuit.

(20.30) Funus, quod liberi Geta Bassianusque Romam detulerant, mire celebratum illatumque Marci sepulcro, <quem> adeo percoluerat, ut eius gratia Commodum inter Divos referri suaserit fratrem appellans, Bassianoque Antonini vocabulum addiderit,

(3) He was interred in the tomb of Marcus Antoninus – the only emperor out of all of them whom he respected, to such a degree that he had Commodus deified and considered whether the name Antoninus ought to given to all later emperors, like Augustus.

(3) Inlatus sepulchro Marci Antonini, quem ex omnibus imperatoribus tantum coluit, ut et Commodum in divos referret et Antonini nomen omnibus deinceps quasi Augusti adscribendum putaret.

(4) At the urging of his children, who gave him a spectacular funeral, he was deified by the Senate.

(4) Ipse a senatu agentibus liberis, qui ei funus amplissimum exhibuerant, inter divos est relatus.★

★ The text here adopts the emendations of Stover 2020: 198.

Even so, it is worth noting that these passages are also very different: the elements are in a different order, the *HA* ruthlessly banalises Victor's prose, and not all the facts are the same. Some of these differences undoubtedly arise from what the author of the *HA* did to Victor's text, but it is important to remember that the *scriptor* did not have the *HAb*, our text of Victor, before his eyes – he was working with the real thing. Three facts are included in the *HA* passage which are not in the *HAb*, all of them apparently rooted in some reality: that Severus was granted the title *Britannicus*, that he introduced an oil-dole at Rome, and that he was deified *post mortem*. The first is attested by coins and inscriptions; the second is at least mildly consistent with the archaeological evidence; and the third is certainly true.[23] Are we to believe that in the midst of this extensive exercise in plagiarism the author of the *HA* blithely and inconspicuously slipped in three little findings of his own? Moreover, one sentence makes rather more sense in the *HA* than in the *HAb*: *horum infinita caede crudelior habitus* (20.10). It is perfectly obvious to us, and clear in the *HA*, that this is referring to Severus' execution of numerous senators. In the *HAb*, however, the only possible referent for *horum* is Severus' rivals, Clodius Albinus and Pescennius Niger, both mentioned in the previous sentence – this makes much less sense. The awkwardness of the *HAb* here suggests that there was indeed some fuller discussion of the topic – Severus' elimination of rivals, real and merely prospective – in Victor's original *History*. Finally, there are passages elsewhere in the *HA*'s life of Severus which present material cognate to Victor, such as in its discussion of Severus' education and (correct) identification of Leptis as his hometown (*Sev.* 1.2 ~ *HAb* 20.19), or in the author's aside to Diocletian on the folly of having children, which looks back to Victor's discussion of Caligula (*Sev.* 20.4–5 ~ *HAb* 3.5–6).[24] The parallel passage is, in other words, just the tip of a Victorine iceberg.

The obvious question that arises is *why* the *HA* borrows so extensively from Victor, apparently in this life alone. As we have seen, and will see further, the *HA*'s debt to Victor is constant, extending throughout the whole collection of lives, and yet it is true that nowhere else can we detect this kind of borrowing *in extenso*. The likely explanation is that it is purely an accident. At around 4,000 words, the *Severus* is of middling length for an *HA* life, while at 900 words the account of Severus in the *HAb* is one of the longest, second only to Gallienus before the Tetrarchy, where the biographical structure breaks down. Compare that with the opposite extreme, the measly 75 words the *HAb* devotes to Elagabalus, against the *HA*'s 6,000. Proceeding logically from our findings, we would expect that where we have more of Victor's original text, we will see more of its influence, but where we have less, we will see less. That is precisely what has happened with the *Vita Severi*: because we have (comparatively) so much of Victor, his influence is more obvious.

Confirmation of this can be found in the fact that the *HA* draws on Victor's account of Severus in other lives in the collection. The biography of Clodius Albinus (to whom the *HAb* devotes a mere twenty-four words), also contains demonstrable use of it (*Clod. Alb.* 1.1):

---

23 *Britannicus*: *IRT* 962, *CIL* 8.23708, 9.4959; *RIB* 1202 *e.g.* Oil dole: Brockaert 2011. Deification: Herodian 4.1.5, 4.2.1–3.1, and Eutropius 8.19.2; *cf. PIR*² S.487, which, however, erroneously claims that the *HAb* mentions the deification.

24 *HA Sev.* 1.4 *in prima pueritia . . . Latinis Graecisque litteris imbueretur* ~ *HAb* 20.28 *primo litteris, dehinc imbutus foro*; *HA Sev.* 1.5 *declamavit. postea studiorum causa Romam venit* ~ *HAb* 20.22 *declamandi, cunctis postremo liberalium deditus studiis*.

At almost one and the same time, after Pertinax had been killed at the instigation of Albinus (*auctore Albino*), Septimius Severus was named emperor by the army in Syria, Pescennius Niger in the East, and Clodius Albinus in Gaul.

There are two details here in particular that betray the *HA*'s debt to Victor, one relatively simple and one much more complex. Simple first: the phrase *auctore Albino* goes back to Victor's *Historia*, which evidently distinguished between Albinus, the *auctor* of the death of Pertinax (*HAb* 20.9; *cf.* Eutropius 8.18), and Didius Julianus, the *impulsor* (*HAb* 18.2; *cf. LB* 18.2). The *HA* makes no such distinction. Second and more complex: the *HA*'s placement of Severus in Syria at the time of Pertinax's murder in 193. The *HAb* (19.4) says something like this as well: 'Septimius Severus, who by chance was then as legate in Syria waging war in faraway lands (*in extremis terris bellum gerebat*), was made emperor'. This is a difficult point, since the *HAb*'s claim is obviously not true: Severus was not in Syria, but in Pannonia, where he was *legatus pro praetore*, and Victor seems to have known that (*LB* 19.2: *in Pannoniae Sabaria*).[25] Still, some of the words of the *HAb* are undoubtedly original, because they contain an imitation of Sallust: *Cn. Pompeius in extremis terris bellum gerebat* (*Cat.* 16.4). The intertextual connection with Pompey is strengthened by an immediately following description in the *HAb* of a battle at the Milvian Bridge near Rome preceding Julianus' demise (19.4): '[Severus] defeated him with his army near the Milvian Bridge, and the soldiers sent to pursue him as he fled cut him down in the palace at Rome'. This engagement is generally considered fictitious, but it recalls one version of Pompey's defeat of Lepidus at the Milvian bridge in 77 BC.[26] It thus looks as though Victor's account of the rise of Severus contained a complex and sustained comparison to Pompey. This is rather important, for the battle at the Milvian bridge is generally regarded as a '*KG* error', but it is clearly a product of this idea, one original to Victor.[27] How and why the underlying error about Syria ended up in the *HAb* is an important and interesting question (albeit one that we will not speculate on here). What is crucial, however, is the entirely nonsensical nature of the *HA*'s version, with Niger and Severus usurping in the same region. This confusion is even worse in the life of Didius (5.2), where in one line the emperor is afraid of the Syrian legions, and so sends a *primipiliarius* to kill Niger (which makes sense), and in the next, Niger is acclaimed emperor in Illyricum and Severus in Syria (which makes no sense at all).[28] The origins of the *HA*'s errors here must lie in Victor.[29]

Victor thus clearly provided much of the factual framework for what the *HA* said about the age of Septimius Severus. The life of Albinus gives us a tantalising hint about other ways in which the *HA* used Victor. It concludes with a fictitious letter of Commodus to the praetorian prefects, criticising Albinus (*Clod. Alb.* 14.4–5). It then goes on to say that Pertinax discovered this letter and wanted to use it to discredit his rival. 'It was for this reason', it concludes, 'that Albinus set in motion for Julianus the murder of Pertinax'.[30] The last five words are an almost direct quotation from Victor's account of Severus: *quare*

---

25 *cf.* Birley 1971: 158 and n. 1 who suggests Syria arose from a misunderstanding of 'Savaria'.

26 Florus 2.11; we do not know what version(s) were in Livy and in Sallust's *Histories*. At any rate, this must confirm Dufraigne's suggestion (*ad loc.*) that this battle at the Milvian bridge originates in Victor's text.

27 *KG*: Syme 1968a: 106; Barnes 1970a: 16; Barnes 1978: 92.

28 On *primipilaris* vs *primipilarius* see Adams 2013: 539.

29 This also neatly explains why the *HA* says (*Sev.* 21.3) that Hadrian was the *municeps ac nepos* of Trajan (see Chapter IV).

30 For this awkward construction, *cf.* Tacitus, *Ann.* 3.19.1; *Digest* 24.1.32.*praef.* (Ulpian); *TLL* 2.1196.80–1197.36 (Bögl).

Albinus occidendi Pertinacis Iuliano auctor fuit (*Clod. Alb.* 14.6) ~ *Pertinacis auctor occidendi* (*HAb* 20.9).[31] The author of the *HA* used a bare and tantalising idea from Victor as a prompt for his own fantasies: it gave him imaginative space in which he could practise his peculiar craft.

Caracalla

We see further borrowings in the *HA* life of Severus' son, Caracalla. Towards the end, the author tells the story of the murder of Papinian, in terms clearly borrowed from Victor (**TABLE 8.2**). The linguistic clues in the *HA*'s account are subtle, due to the author's ruthless rewording – *facile/facilitate parricidium, quam fieri, constet* – but nonetheless decisive.[32] Another misunderstanding on the *HA*'s part also helps to show once again how indebted he is to his source. Victor's point is a typically technical, even pedantic one regarding the imperial bureaucracy: the story told by the *curiosi memoriae* hinged on Papinian having charge of the *scrinia*, in which office he would have been asked to compose an imperial address to the Senate (an *oratio*). Victor alleges instead that he was praetorian prefect, hence not in charge of the *scrinia*, hence not asked to compose the *oratio*.[33] The author of the *HA* has done his best to adapt Victor's point, but missed its precise bureaucratic logic and omitted the *scrinia* altogether.[34] By attempting to adapt Victor, rather than to copy him, he has wound up making his borrowing more obvious.

The *HA*'s author then gives a summary of Caracalla's life in terms closely parallel not just to Victor but to Eutropius as well (**TABLE 8.3**). There is much to be learned here. Caracalla's funeral seems to happen twice in the *HA* (9.2 and 9.12), the first occasion drawing on Eutropius' account, the second using Victor's. The *HA* then provides a description of Caracalla's character in comparison with his father's, which has no analogue in Victor, but is quite close to Eutropius. The remaining anecdotes follow Victor, sometimes very closely, and include some rare details, such as the construction of the Via Nova, which is found only in these two texts.[35] The victory over the Alamanni is particularly recondite: this campaign is found only in the two passages here and Dio 78.13.4–6.[36] It is the first time that that people are mentioned in ancient historiography and Caracalla's victory near the River Main is found only in Victor (as we have seen), but confirmed by an inscription.[37] The *HA* reports this fact only in passing, using the

31 No other ancient texts speak of an *auctor occidendi*.

32 Note also that both texts (*Carac.* 8.1; *HAb* 20.33) introduce the episode by discussing the fact that other people have opinions on it.

33 On the career of Papinian, see *PIR*[2] A.388, Kunkel 1967: 224–229. We know from the *Digest* (20.5.12. *praef.*) that Papinian was *a libellis* at some stage and he was certainly later praetorian prefect, so what Victor says about his offices here is rooted in *realia*. Herodian 4.5.3 ff. has Caracalla deliver a speech in the Senate, but Dio 78.3.3–4 (in epitome; with Peter the Patrician, *ES* 136) might suggest that he pled a sore throat and said little: perhaps that explains why Victor wrote the ambiguous *destinandam orationem*, which might be the root of some of the *HA*'s confusion.

34 While *dictare orationem* is clearly meant to sound technical it is a vanishingly rare collocation and certainly not bureaucratese: the only real parallel is Cicero, *De fin.* 4.22.62 (referring to a fictitious speech). If the *scriptor* meant to say that prefects did not deliver speeches (the logic of the passage is murky and much hinges on whether *Carac.* 8.6–7 is an expansion of 8.5, or a different tale altogether), then his claim was certainly false.

35 On the situation of the Via Nova, see DeLaine 1997: 20, 131.

36 It is possible also that Asinius Quadratus (Chapter IV) discussed it.

37 *CIL* 6.2086. *cf.* Drinkwater 2007: 43–44. Further Chapter IV.

TABLE 8.2 – THE *HAb* AND *HA* ON CARACALLA

HAb 20.33–34	*Carac.* 8.5–7
This victory was made more shameful by the demise of Papinian, as the *curiosi memoriae* think, for they relate that he had charge of the *scrinia* of Bassianus at that point in time, and after he had been directed, as is the custom, to fashion as quickly as possible an address for delivery [*sc.* before the Senate] (*destinandam orationem*), out of grief for Geta he said that parricide could not be veiled with the same ease as it was committed (*haudquaquam pari facilitate velari parricidium qua fieret*), and therefore he was executed. But these reports are flagrantly absurd, since it is very well known (*constet*) that he was praetorian prefect, and he would not have been capable of crudely directing such abuse against that man whom he loved and obeyed.★	Many say that Bassianus, after he had killed his brother, commanded him [*sc.* Papinian] to explain away the crime in the Senate and in front of the people, but that after he responded that a parricide was not as easily excused as committed (*non tam facile parricidium excusari posse quam fieri*) . . . but this cannot stand at all, for it is very well known (*constat*) that the prefect does not compose speeches (*dictare orationem*) and that he was killed as a partisan of Geta.

★ On this difficult passage, see the Appendix, no. VI.

same words as those in the *HAb*, but all in support of an anachronistic fiction: that Caracalla was granted the victory title *Alamannicus*.[38]

Let us continue to Caracalla's relationship with his mother, a rich topic in Victor, which we have already examined from other angles.[39] Here we can actually see in some detail how a complex of errors, usually attributed either to the *KG* or to Marius Maximus, have crept into the Latin tradition through misunderstanding of Victor's dense and allusive prose.[40] Victor does (wrongly) say that Julia Domna was Caracalla's stepmother.[41] Victor never says, however, that Caracalla married his stepmother: his wording, *coniugem affectavit*, instead must mean that he 'desired' his stepmother for a wife, perhaps with a shade of simulation thrown in. The phrasing was rare, but the only real parallel, in pseudo-Acro's commentary on Horace, makes its meaning clear: there, it is explained that a certain Villius, trying to have an affair with Sulla's daughter Fausta, was 'wretched' (*miser*), 'since he desired an aristocrat's daughter as his wife (*quoniam nobilis filiam affectavit uxorem*)'.[42] Eutropius, however, missed this subtlety and used instead the normal Latin expression for marriage, *uxorem ducere*. It was Eutropius' phrasing that percolated down in the rest of the Latin tradition, including the *HA*: hence the idea of a marriage of Caracalla and Julia Domna. At the same time, Eutropius might well contain a slightly fuller version of Victor's original

38 Not in fact attested before 331 (*MAMA* 7.305 – the Orcistus dossier), in spite of the frequent wars of the third and early fourth centuries. See in general *RE* 1.1280 (Seeck).
39 Chapter IV.
40 *KG*: Schlumberger 1974: 118–119; Bird 1984: 136 and n. 23. Marius Maximus: Dufraigne 1975: 133; Penella 1980a: 383. Marius Maximus via the *KG*: Syme 1971a: 123.

41 Julia Domna was, of course, the second wife of Septimius Severus (*PIR*² S.487) and it may that that explains the error here. It is also possible that Victor preferred to make her the stepmother, because that helped to exculpate Caracalla – his version does place as much of the blame as possible on the woman.
42 Pseudo-Acro, *In Serm.* 1.2.64. *cf.* Ammianus 28.1.14, Victor of Vita 1.31, both hardly describing actual marriage.

TABLE 8.3 – THE *HAb*, *HA*, EUTROPIUS, AND JEROME ON CARACALLA

HAb 21.1–6 (rearranged)	*HA Carac.* 9.1–10.6	Eutropius 8.20 and Jerome, *Chron.* 213
	(9.1) Bassianus vixit annis quadraginta tribus. Imperavit annis sex. (2) *Publico funere elatus est.*	anno imperii sexto, mense secundo, vix egressus quadragesimum tertium annum. *Funere publico elatus est.*
(4) ad lavandum absoluta **opera** pulchri cultus	(3) *Fuit male moratus et patre duro crudelior* . . . (4) **Opera** *Romae* reliquit thermas nominis sui eximias . . .	*morum fere paternorum fuit, paulo asperior et minax. Opus Romae* egregium fecit lavacri, quae thermae Antoninianae appellantur, nihil praeterea memorabile.
(1) Ceterum Antoninus in cognita munerum specie plebem Romanam adficiens, quod indumenta **in talos demissa** largiretur, Caracalla dictus, cum pari modo vesti **Antoninianas** nomen e suo daret.	(7) Ipse Caracalli nomen accepit a vestimento, quod populo dederat, **demisso usque ad talos**, quod ante non fuerat. (8) Unde hodieque **Antoninianae** dicuntur caracallae huiusmodi . . .	[*cf.* Jerome, *Chron.* 213[e]: Antoninus Romae thermas sui nominis aedificavit.]
(4) atque aucta urbs magno accessu **viae novae** (4) Aegypti sacra per eum **deportata Romam**	(9) Idem **viam novam** munivit . . .	[*cf.* Jerome, *Chron.* 213[d]: Antoninus Caracalla cognominatus propter genus vestis, quod Romae erogaverat, et e contrario Caracallae ex eius nomine Antoninianae dictae]
(6) **Corporis reliqua** luctu publico relata Romam atque **inter Antoninos** funerata sunt.	(10) Sacra Isidis **Romam deportavit** . . .	
(3) Namque **Iuliam novercam**, cuius facinora supra memoravi, forma captus coniugem affectavit . . .	(12) **Corpus** eius **Antoninorum sepulchro** inlatum est, ut ea sedes **reliquias** eius acciperet . . .	
	(10.1) Interest scire quemadmodum ***novercam*** *suam* **Iuliam** *uxorem duxisse* dicatur . . .	*Inpatientis libidinis, qui novercam suam Iuliam uxorem duxerit.* [*cf.* Jerome, *Chron.* 213[f]: Antoninus tam impatiens libidinis fuit, ut novercam suam Iuliam uxorem duxerit.]
(2) **Alamannos, gentem** populosam ex equo mirifice pugnantem, prope Moenum amnem **devicit.**	(6) Alamannici nomen adscriberet (nam **Alamannorum gentem devicerat**).★	

★ 'Bassianus lived for forty-three years; he reigned for six. He was given a public funeral'; 'He was endowed with a wicked character and was crueller than his harsh father . . . He bequeathed to Rome public works: extraordinary baths named after him'; 'He received the name of "Caracalla" from a garment stretching to the ankles, which he had given to the people and which had not existed before. For this reason, to this very day *caracallae* of this kind are called *Antoninianae* . . . He also paved a new road'; 'He conveyed to Rome the rites of Isis. . .'; 'His body was interred in the tomb of the Antonines, so that that burial-place should receive his remains . . . It is important to know the fashion in which it is said that he married his stepmother Julia . . .'; 'He took the title "Alamannicus" (for he had conquered the Alamannic people) . . .'. We use bold to indicate overlaps between the *HAb* and *HA* and italics for those between the *HA* and Eutropius.

TABLE 8.4 – THE *HAb* AND *HA* ON JULIA DOMNA

HAb 21.3	*HA Carac.* 10.2
For he desired to have his stepmother Julia, whose crimes I have mentioned above, as a wife, captivated by her beauty, after she, rather slyly, had presented herself with bared body to his youthful gaze, as if she were unaware of his presence, and when he said 'I would wish, if it were permitted, to have use of that', she replied much more naughtily (for she had taken off her modesty with her clothes) 'It is your pleasure? Obviously it is permitted'.	She was very beautiful. By carelessness she bared most of her body, and Antoninus said to her, 'I would like that, if it were permitted', and she reportedly responded, 'If it is your pleasure, then it is permitted. Or don't you know that an emperor hands down laws, and doesn't receive them?'★

★ Intertexts with Velleius and Herodotus: Chapter IV. Dullness of dialogue: *pace* Reekmans 1997: 189, n. 65, who was not aware of the intertexts which show that the *HA* is clearly indebted to Victor. Note the technical flavour of *leges dare, non accipere*: as a moment with the subscriptions to constitutions in the *Codex Theodosianus* shows, a law was indeed given (*data*) by the emperor and received (*accepta*) by a magistrate.

sentence than the *HAb*. His *impatientis libidinis* contains an echo of a later line in the *HAb* which has the same phrasing (39.11, of Carinus): *libidine impatiens militarium †mulctas affectabat*.[43] The author of the *HA* also clearly borrows from Victor's depiction of the subsequent seduction, but without the crucial intertexts with Herodotus and Velleius, and with notably duller dialogue (TABLE 8.4).

There may well be more of Victor's work concealed in the lives of Caracalla and Geta than we can now trace from the surviving text of the *HAb*. The evocative phrase at the end of the *Geta* (7.4) 'marked out for slaughter' (*ad necem destinabat*) is paralleled only in the *HAb* (33.20: *destinata ab eo ad necem*) in all of ancient literature. The account of Papinian's murder in the *Caracalla* is introduced with the phrase *aliis alia referentibus* (7.1: 'each man offering a different version'), a construction paralleled only by the *HAb* (39.48: *aliis alia aestimantibus*). Further, the same life uses the adverb *aegerrime* to describe the way that the soldiers took the news of Geta's murder (2.7). This is the word's only occurrence in the *HA*, but it occurs four times in the 10,000 words of the heavily abbreviated *HAb* (9.9, 39.48, 40.23, 41.17). Similarly, the author uses the rare adverb *tumultuarie* (*Carac.* 6.4); the earliest known use of this word is in the *HAb* (40.17). Finally, the *HA* and the *LB* are the only Latin sources for Caracalla's obsession with Alexander the Great, and they are also the only sources to note the way that the emperor altered his facial expression to look like his hero, something they do with similar wording: *truci fronte* (*LB* 21.4: 'a savage countenance') ~ *vultu etiam truculentior* (*Carac.* 2.1: 'also rather savage in his expression'). Logically enough, the *LB* connects this transfiguration with Caracalla's visit to Alexander's tomb at Alexandria, where the *HA* implausibly puts it at his entrance to adulthood, to draw a contrast with its (fantastical) account of his good-natured character as a child. Once again, even though this detail seems to ultimately derive from Victor, the *HA* has refashioned it for its own literary purposes.

43 See the Appendix, no. XIV for the text of this passage.

Diadumenianus and Macrinus

We have seen already that what are generally regarded as the idiosyncratic quirks and obsessions of the *HA* often have their roots in Victor's work. The *HAb*'s treatment of Diadumen(ian)us, the hapless son of Caracalla's successor, Opellius Macrinus, is highly suggestive in this regard. Describing the feelings of the legions, the *HAb* says (22.2): 'Because they had an enormous longing (*ingens . . . desiderium*) for their lost *princeps*, they called the young man Antoninus'.[44] Obsession with the *nomen Antoninorum* is one of the well-worn tropes of the middle lives of the *HA*: Burgersdijk has identified it as one of the text's most characteristic features, alongside forged documents and speeches.[45] Yet here is the germ of the idea in Victor.[46] Indeed, this very line is plagiarised three times in the *HA*, including once in the life of Caracalla and once in a fictitious speech.[47] In other words, the *HA* is not merely dependent on Victor for information and wording: many of the key features of its approach to history are in fact Victor's ideas.

The *HA*'s account of the younger Macrinus also confirms that its author had no qualms in re-purposing Victor not just for historical narrative, but for forged documents. The *HAb* concludes the brief life of Macrinus and Diadumenus with a passage we have already discussed (*HAb* 22.3–4):

> Horum nihil praeter saevos atque inciviles animos interim reperimus. Qua gratia mensibus ferme quattuor ac decem vix retento imperio, per quos creati fuerant, interfecti sunt.[48]

> I have discovered nothing about them, except that they had savage and uncivil spirits. Due to this, they kept their power for scarcely fourteen months and were slain by the very ones who had made them.

Eutropius takes over the results of Victor's research (8.21):

> Then Opilius Macrinus, who was praetorian prefect, and his son Diadumenus were made emperors, and did nothing worth mentioning (*nihil memorabile*) due to the brevity of their tenure.

The key word *nihil* is simply copied over, but the ideas are different: where Victor said he was able to uncover nothing about them, Eutropius says that they did nothing worth mentioning: a subtle, but important, distinction. The *HA*, perhaps, is less subtle (*Diad.* 8.2–3):

> In his fourteenth month of power (*imperii*), due to the uncivil (*incivilem*) and harsh reign of his father, he was killed (*interfectus est*) along with his father, not in his own name, although I have discovered (*repperiam*) that he also committed savageries (*saevisse*) beyond his years against a great number of people.

---

44 On his name, see Chapter IV.

45 Burgersdijk 2010: 118–210. See also Scholtemeijer 1976.

46 *cf.* Syme 1971a: 85–87; Langenfeld 2017: 147.

47 *HA Carac.* 8.9: *Qui* [*sc.* Macrinus] *cum filio factus in castris imperator filium suum, qui Diadumenus vocabatur, Antoninum vocavit, idcirco quod a praetorianis multum Antoninus desideratus est; HA Diad.* 1.5: *intellego praeterea desiderium ingens Antoniniani nominis apud vos manere;* 6.10: *cum esset ingens desiderium Bassiani Caracalli, Antoninum appellatum satis constat.*

48 On this passage, see Chapter IV.

It is hard not to see the influence of Victor here. This is the only occurrence of the adjective *incivilis* in the *HA*, and the author echoes Victor's first-person claim about research (*reperimus* ~ *repperiam*).[49] In both cases, what the research uncovered was Diadumenus' savagery (*saevos* ~ *saevisse*). This is, however, not even the most important debt that the *HA* owes to Victor at this point: that is the emperor's name itself. All of our epigraphic, numismatic, and Greek evidence gives him the name Diadumenianus – Victor is the first author to call him Diadumenus.[50] The reason for the alteration is almost certainly literary. Recall the one thing that Victor discovered about him was his *saevus animus* and compare Martial discussing a *puer delicatus* (*Epig.* 3.64.8): 'this is the scent of your kisses, Diadumenus, my savage (*saeve*) boy'. This is the only other person named Diadumenus in Latin literature, although the name is not all that rare in inscriptions.[51] The fact that both are called *saevus* can hardly be a coincidence. This suggests in turn that the form Diadumenus is Victor's own invention – he certainly draws attention to the odd nature of the name with the ablative *nomine*.[52] The fact that Victor's form is nearly universal in the subsequent Latin tradition – including in Eutropius and the *HA* – is a testament to his influence.[53]

With this in mind, we can now turn to the *HA*'s account of Diadumenianus' father, the emperor Opellius Macrinus.[54] This is an important life in the collection structurally, since its prologue introduces the fictional authority Junius Cordus, who will go on, as we have seen, to be the author's foil for the next several lives. Cordus was, we are informed, particularly devoted to research on the more obscure wearers of the purple, though without much success (*Macr.* 1.4): 'For he uncovered few things, and things not even worth mentioning (*nam et pauca repperit et indigna memoratu*)'. This is a straight amalgam of Victor and Eutropius' judgement of Macrinus and his son, *repperit* from Victor and *indigna memoratu* from Eutropius' *nihil memorabile*. This is a further indication of just how flimsy the author's personae are, since, as we have seen, he adopts the same verb in the first person for the same notion in the life of Diadumenus.[55]

Significantly, shortly after this, the *HA* quotes a historian named Aurelius Victor (*Macr.* 4.2–4), who is the mythical first Victor of early-modern scholarship:

> Indeed, these are the words of Aurelius Victor, called 'Pinius': Macrinus was a freedman, a male prostitute, engaged in servile duties in the imperial house: his honour was for sale, his life disgraceful (*vita sordida*) under Commodus. He was dismissed even from these most wretched duties by Severus and banished to Africa, where, so that he might veil the disgrace of his condemnation, he put his

---

49 The adverb *incivilius* is also found once in *HA Aurel.* 21.5. We discuss Victor's claims about his research in Chapter IV.

50 See Chapter IV.

51 *TLL Onomasticon* III.123.80–124.83 (Reisch); Solin 2003: 2.928–930.

52 On this technique, see Chapter IV. There are parallels for a historian calling an emperor by a (nick)name that seems to be their own invention: Cassius Dio routinely refers to Elagabalus as 'Sardanapalus', for example (the emperor's names are unusually complex: *PIR*[2] V.273, *cf.* Chapter IV).

53 Rohrbacher 2020 discusses the intertexts between the *HA* and Martial in the treatment of Diadumenus, with a particular focus on *saevitia*. He argues that the idea is

authentic to the *HA*, but fails to take adequate notice of Victor's text, which put his conclusions in something of a different light.

54 It is worth noting that while Victor (and, following him, Eutropius and the *HA*) calls the emperor Opilius, his *nomen* seems to have been Opellius, judging by the Greek tradition and the epigraphic evidence (*PIR*[2] O.108). Opilius was a genuine *gentilicium* and this may be merely an orthographic variant, but given Diadumenus, it seems possible that this is a Victorine feature (could it have something to do with *opilio*, 'shepherd'?).

55 Though the *HA* life of Diadumenus is generally printed after that of his father, Macrinus, in the principal manuscripts of the *HA* it comes before it. The most recent discussion of the manuscript order is Thomson 2012.

effort into reading, pleaded little cases, practised declamation, and finally taught in a school (*lectioni operam dedisse, egisse causulas, declamasse, in ludo postremo dixisse*). Moreover, through the patronage of his fellow freedman Festus, he was granted the golden ring and was made an *advocatus* of the fisc under Verus Antoninus.[56]

We do not need to assume that the author of the *HA* is transmitting genuine bits of Victor here.[57] Indeed, that assumption would contradict what we know about the way the *HA* uses surviving sources, such as Herodian (directly or indirectly).[58] Nonetheless, there is at least one corroborated piece of information here, that Macrinus practised law (*cf.* Dio 79.11.1). What is also significant is the style. The extended *oratio obliqua* is not at all typical of the *HA*, although it is found in Victor (*e.g. HAb* 29.5). This piling up of loosely related clauses looks like a parody of Victor's style, and one can perhaps detect some distant echoes, such as Macrinus' *vita sordida* (*cf. LB* 18.2: *origine ortus sordida*) and his activities in Africa (*lectioni . . . dixisse*), which one can compare with Severus' African education (*HAb* 20.22: *Philosophiae, declamandi, cunctis postremo liberalium deditus studiis*). The lives of the two Macrini, in short, show the *HA*'s author not only aping Victor, but doing so with a knowing wink.

Elagabalus

At the deaths of Macrinus and Diadumenianus, imperial power passed to Elagabalus, whose life in the *HA* again shows the heavy impress of Victor's *History*. First his name: Victor refers to this emperor as Heliogabalus, a transparent attempt to transform the Semitic name for the sun god Elagabal into a vaguely Greek appellation.[59] That is what the *HA* calls him throughout. The *HAb* suggests that Victor was fairly keen on the idea that he was in fact the illegitimate son of Caracalla, introducing him simply as *Bassiano genitus*, 'fathered by Bassianus' (*HAb* 23.1). The *LB* gives more detail: *Caracallae ex Soemea consobrina occulte stuprata filius*, 'the son of Caracalla, from his secret adultery with his cousin Soaemias' (23.1). The *HAb* (23.1) goes on to explain how, when his 'father', Caracalla, was killed, he fled (*confugerat*) and sought 'asylum, as it were' (*tamquam asylum*), in the temple of the sun god Elagabal, which is how he got his name. This stands in sharp contrast to our other sources, which convey the idea that Caracalla was his father only as a (dubious, and, for the Greeks, deliberate) rumour.[60] The *HA*, however, knew this story of Elagabalus' parentage and its account (*Heliog.* 2.1–3) leaves little doubt as to its derivation from Victor:

56 In the *HA*'s usage, Verus Antoninus ought to be Lucius Verus (*PIR*[2] C.606), an emperor about whose name it shows considerable confusion. This is absurd, since Macrinus was born in 164 or 166 (*PIR*[2] O.108), only a few years before Verus died. At any rate, Verus reigned long before Commodus and Severus. It perhaps gives the *HA* too much credit to read *verus* as an adjective (*i.e.* 'the true Antoninus', *cf. Heliog.* 8.4: *Pseudoantoninum*), in which case it might refer to any of the emperors who bore the name Antoninus.

57 On the 'first Victor', see Chapter VI. On this passage of the *HA*, *cf.* Chapter V.

58 See the classic study by Kolb 1972.

59 *HAb* 23.1 and *LB* 23.2 both explicitly identify the deity as a sun god. The *HA*, and indeed much of the later Latin tradition, uses Victor's name: *PIR*[2] V.273: 142, to which add Eutropius 8.22; the heading of the tetrastich in Ausonius' *Caesares*; AM 26.6.6; Servius, *In Aen.* 7.180; Pompeius Maurus, *In Don.* (*GLK* 5.309); Polemius Silvius 18; Jordanes, *Getica* 15.88. This case is not so clear cut as some of the others in Victor, since there is also an instance in the Liberian Catalogue (*Chron. 354* (p. 74, l. 33)).

60 Dio 78.31.3, 78.32.2–3; Herodian 5.3.10; Eutropius 8.22.

Table 8.5 – The *HAb* and *HA* on the naming of Alexander as Caesar

HAb 23.3	*Heliog.* 5.1
Magis magisque Alexandri, quem comperta Opilii nece Caesarem nobilitas nuncupaverat, amor cumularetur	In . . . Alexandrum, quem Caesarem senatus Macrino interempto appellaverat, inclinavere animos.★
More and more, love for Alexander, whom the nobility had named Caesar at the death of Opilius, was piled up.	They turned their minds to Alexander, whom the Senate had called Caesar after Macrinus had been killed.

★ *cf. Heliog.* 10.1: *in Alexandrum omnes inclinantes, qui iam Caesar erat a senatu eo tempore, consobrinus huius Antonini* and *Macr.* 4.1, on which see Turcan 1993: 122, 168, and 182–183. One interesting point is that while the *HA*'s use of *inclinare* at *Heliog.* 5.1 and 10.1 closely reflects Herodian 5.8.2 (ἐπιρρεπεστέρας τοίνυν τὰς γνώμας πρὸς τὸν Ἀλέξανδρον εἶχον), the idea that the Senate made him Caesar at the death of Macrinus is not in Herodian, but only in Victor.

> He was so dedicated to his mother Symiamira, that he did nothing in the commonwealth without her will, all the while as she committed every manner of outrage in the palace itself, living like a whore. She fornicated (*stupro*) with Antoninus Caracalla, resulting – it is commonly thought – in the conception of this Varius or Heliogabalus. It is said that he, after his supposed father Antoninus was killed by the faction of Macrinus, fled (*confugisse*) to the temple of the god Heliogabalus, as if to an asylum (*velut in asylum*), so as not to be killed by Macrinus.[61]

The *HA* includes information about Elagabalus' parentage which goes beyond what is in the *HAb* to include what the *LB* tells us, with a lexical resonance in the word *stuprum*. What we see here, then, behind the text of the *HA*, is what the original *Historia* of Victor narrated. Almost immediately thereafter we get another evocation of *HAb* 22.2: the people's *ingens desiderium* for an Antoninus (*Heliog.* 3.1). Victor and the *HA* also share the detail that the Senate had named Severus Alexander Caesar after Macrinus' death and before they recognised Elagabalus (**Table 8.5**). Virtually every word has been changed by the author of the *HA*, but the sentences are substantially identical in form.

Once again, it was not merely historical details that the *HA* took from Victor – scandal and anecdote were mined out too. The body of Elagabalus suffered various indignities after death, as the author of the *HA* narrates, his language ever so close to the *LB* (**Table 8.6**). The gruesome details the two texts share, as well as the parallelism of structure and vocabulary, makes the link between them certain.[62] Yet there are three important differences at the end of these two accounts. First, the *HA* calls the emperor *Tractatitius*, where the *LB* calls him *Tractitius*. Second, the *HA* adds the name *Impurus*. Finally, the texts give slightly different accounts of why he received these names: in the *LB*, they are explained simply from what happened to his corpse, whereas in the *HA* they denote the (terrible) things he did while alive. In

---

61 *cf. HA Carac.* 9.2; *Macr.* 15.2. In contrast, *Macr.* 9.4 and *Heliog.* 1.4 present his relationship to Caracalla as just something people said.

62 See Turcan 1993: 191–193.

TABLE 8.6 – THE *LB* AND *HA* ON ELAGABALUS' INDIGNITIES AFTER DEATH

LB 23.6–7	*Heliog.* 17.1–5
His body was dragged (*tractum est*) through the streets of the city by the soldiers like a dead dog (*more canini cadaveris*), calling him with military humour 'The Bitch Pup of an Unbowed and Rabid Lust'. At last, when the narrow opening of the sewer (*cloacae*) could not fit his body, it was brought to the Tiber and thrown into the river (*in fluvium proiectum est*), with a weight added so that it would never surface (*adiecto pondere ne umquam emergeret*). He lived for sixteen years, and was named Tiberinus and Tractitius (*Tiberinus Tractatitiusque appellatus est*) on account of what had happened to him.★	He was then dragged (*tractus*) in public. Injury was heaped on his corpse (*cadaveri*), such that the soldiers were going to shove it into the sewer (*in cloacam*). But since it happened that it could not fit into the sewer, it was thrown into the Tiber (*in Tiberim abiectum est*) at the Pons Aemilius with a weight tied on to it so it could not float (*adnexo pondere ne fluitaret*), such that it would never receive burial . . . After death, he was named Tiberinus and Tractatitius (*appellatus est . . . Tiberinus et Tractatitius*) and the Impure One (*Impurus*) and many other things besides, if the things which seemed to have been done under him were to be at some point designated.

★ The *LB*'s phrase for humour is *militari cavillo*, perhaps inspired by Tacitus, *Ann.* 1.23.3: *militaribus facetiis*, on which see below.

each of these instances, the *LB*'s version seems like it must be closer to the original. The emperor's body was 'dragged' (*tractus*), not 'handled' (*tractatus*). Tiberinus and Tractitius form a natural pair, whereas *Impurus* is intrusive. Elagabalus obviously received the nickname *Tiberinus* because of his final resting place, not because of any riverine pursuits while alive: Cassius Dio (who may well have witnessed these memorable events) is absolutely clear that the epithet arose from what was done *post mortem*.[63] The *HA*'s account is Victor's version, embellished.

Even these embellishments are not entirely original. Alföldy was surely right to see that the word *Tractatitius* had obscene sexual connotations, even if he went too far in thinking that it was an actual nickname used for Elagabalus.[64] Bruun's suggestion that the author of the *HA* was himself responsible for the transformation, prompted by the emperor's sexual habits, is surely closer to the truth.[65] Still, he was probably inspired by Victor. In the *HA*'s epic treatment of Elagabalus' sexual proclivities it never once uses the word *tractare* in its sexual sense.[66] In one obscure sentence, however, the *HAb* uses not only that word but also a form of *impurus* (23.2): 'not even naughty and lascivious women were something more impure (*impurius*) than this man: indeed, he sought out from the whole world the most obscene men, to ogle or to fondle (*tractandis*)' their bodies.[67]

63 Dio 80.1.1: καὶ γὰρ καὶ ταύτην τὴν προσηγορίαν, ἐπειδὴ τὸ σῶμα σφαγέντος αὐτοῦ ἐς τὸν Τίβεριν ἐνεβλήθη, ἔλαβεν, *cf.* Zonaras 12.14.
64 Alföldy 1976: 17–18.
65 Bruun 2003: 96. *cf.* Mahklaiuk 2020: 226.
66 It does use *adtrectatio* at 12.4. On the rich range of sexual meaning of *tractare*, see Adams 1982: 186–187.

67 The Latin is deeply corrupt: *Hoc impurius ne improbae quidem aut petulantes mulieres fuere: quippe orbe toto obscoenissimos perquirebat visendis tractandisve artibus libidinum ferendarum.* Alföldy 1976: 18 already adduced the parallel of this passage.

Alexander Severus

Victor's influence is even more evident in the rich and lengthy biography of Alexander Severus, often regarded as central to unravelling the *HA*'s date and purpose.[68] Let us start with one factual sign of this: the name of the emperor's birthplace. While the *HA* correctly calls the town *Arca* at *Alex.* 1.2 and 5.1, at 13.5 it calls it *Arca Caesarea*. This is a revealing mistake. In the Lebanon, there was a very ancient town known as Arce: its inhabitants are mentioned in the Bible and it appears under this name in numerous Greek and Latin sources down to the fourth century.[69] It was indeed the *patria* of Alexander Severus (Dio 79.30.3). At some stage, certainly by the reign of Antoninus Pius, Arce received the name Caesarea. The appellation 'Caesarea of Lebanon' (ΚΑΙCΑΡΕΙΑC ΛΙΒΑΝΟΥ) is amply attested by its coinage and by an inscription, but seemingly never occurs in a literary text.[70] The crucial point here is that the town was always either Arce or Caesarea, but never both combined. Whence, then, has the *HA* fashioned the chimerical *Arca Caesarea*? It arises from a misunderstanding of Victor, who says (in a characteristically elliptical fashion) that the town 'had the double name of Arce and Caesarea' (*HAb* 24.1: *cui duplex Caesarea et Arce nomen est*). This is an accurate description of the onomastics, but one can see how it might all too easily have led a rogue grammarian to think erroneously that the name was *Arca Caesarea*.

As we have seen before, Victor's influence extended far beyond the 'factual' in the *HA*. The text claims that Alexander considered banning male prostitution (*Alex.* 24.4):

> He had the idea of forbidding the *exoleti*, which Philip actually did afterwards, but was afraid that through prohibition he would turn public disgrace into private desires, since people in the grip of madness demand illicit things all the more when they are forbidden.[71]

The actual ban mentioned here is indeed found in Victor's account of Philip the Arab's reign. As is his wont, our historian goes on to explain why the prohibition was ineffective, with a general point about the difficulties of legislating in matters of morality (*HAb* 28.7): 'since mortals seek all the more eagerly perilous things which are forbidden them'. There can be little doubt here that Victor is the *HA*'s source – indeed, for Sir Ronald Syme, this represented one of the most compelling pieces of evidence for the *HA*'s dependence on Victor.[72] What is interesting is the fact that the author of the *HA* transplants Victor's idea into the mind of Alexander: 'we can observe', says Penella, 'the biographer shaping what he took from Aurelius Victor into a common form of statement (the unfulfilled intention) – more precisely,

---

68 Most notably, if not with generally accepted results, in the work of Baynes 1926. On the life in general, see Hönn 1911; Jardé 1925; Bertrand-Dagenbach 1990.

69 Genesis 1:17; Josephus, *Ant.* 1.139, 9.285; Pliny, *HN* 5.74; *Itinerarium Antonini* 148; Jerome, *Quaest. Hebr* 10.15–18 (p. 17 Lagarde); Stephanus of Byzantium, *Ethnica* 1.430 *e.g.* On the town, see *RE* 3.1117–1118 (Benzinger); the entry in Smith 1854–1857: 1.189 remains useful. It seems to have become a *colonia* under Elagabalus (Dąbrowa 2019: 272–273).

70 *RPC* 4.3, nos 3980, 6770, 6777–6779, 6780–6781, 6783–6790 (all issued under Antoninus Pius); *CIL* 3.183, which calls the inhabitants *Caesarenses ad Libanum*.

71 *cf. Heliog.* 32.6, with Turcan 1993: 228. Butrica has denied that the *exoleti* of this passage are male prostitutes (and indeed that that is what the word means), but he does not account for the fact that the parallel passage in Victor has *ephebi pro meritorio*, which makes the interpretation certain, even if it is possible that the *HA* does not use the right terminology (2005: 227–228).

72 Syme 1968a: 107. See also Chastagnol 1966: 54–56; Chastagnol 1967: 95–97.

into a version of the general form that especially contributes to the desired *Tendenz*'.[73] In other words, what we see here once again is Victor supplying the raw material for the *Historia Augusta*'s idiosyncratic historiographical project.

After the putative ban on male prostitution, the *HA* turns to relating some of Alexander's genuine measures (24.5–24.6), items that also appear in Victor, albeit without many lexical overlaps. For example, the *HA* notes Alexander's devotion to his mother, which is also a motif in Victor's treatment, though the former's wording (*Alex.* 26.9: *in matrem Mammaeam unice pius fuit*) betrays its debt to Eutropius (8.23: *In Mamaeam, matrem suam, unice pius*).[74] The *HA* goes on to note that some people claimed that Elagabalus made Ulpian and Paulus praetorian prefects, as opposed to the conventional opinion that it was Alexander himself who had done this (*Alex.* 26.5: *Paulum et Ulpianum . . . quos praefectos ab Heliogabalo alii dicunt factos, alii ab ipso*).[75] This is usually understood as a glancing reference to Victor, who does indeed credit Ulpian's appointment to Elagabalus (*HAb* 24.6):

> Adhuc Domitium Ulpianum quem Heliogabalus praetorianis praefecerat eodem honore retinens Pauloque inter exordia patriae reddito, iuris auctoribus, quantus erga optimos atque aequi studio esset edocuit.[76]

> He kept Domitius Ulpianus, whom Heliogabalus had made praetorian prefect, in that very position and sent Paullus back to his homeland at the start of his reign – both of these were authorities in the law. By these actions, he thoroughly demonstrated how much he favoured the best men and was inclined to zeal for fairness.

Victor's claim here is generally considered erroneous, but at least one Roman legal historian asserts that the idea 'may have to be taken seriously'.[77] Whatever the case may be, the author of the *HA* is guilty of gross misunderstanding: reading Victor too quickly, he accuses him of saying that Paulus was also a praetorian prefect, as if *eodem honore* could go with *Pauloque*.[78]

Long stretches of what follows in the life of Alexander are generally regarded as pure fiction.[79] Towards the end of this epic *vita*, however, we reach some seemingly genuine historical content: the story of Alexander's campaigns in the 230s and his ultimate demise (*Alex.* 55–59). The beginning of this section shows unmistakable borrowing from Victor (*Alex.* 55.1–3):

> Having set out from there against the Persians with a great war-machine (*magno igitur apparatu inde in Persas profectus*), he conquered Artaxerxes, a most mighty king (*regem potentissimum*), when he himself visited the wings of the army, urged the soldiers on, went about with his guardians, did a great deal with his own hand, and by his words led each individual soldier to praiseworthy deeds. When he had routed and put to flight such a great king (*fuso denique fugatoque tanto rege*) – who had come to war with 700 elephants, and 1,800 chariots with scythes, many thousands of cavalry – at once he returned to

---

73 Penella 1981: 187.

74 *cf. HAb* 24.5: *matrisque cultu, quae nomine Mammaea erat, plus quam pius*.

75 See Cleve 1998.

76 Schott's hypercorrection of the MS *Pauloque* to *Paulloque* is rightly reject by Nickbakht and Scardino 2021. The text here is very difficult and may require further surgery.

77 Bauman 1995: 385.

78 A point that Syme was fond of making: Syme 1970b: 313; 1971a: 148; 1978a: 229–230; *cf.* Chastagnol 1967: 90–91 and Bertrand-Dagenbach 2014: 110–112.

79 For example, the emperor's chapel (29.2) with statues of the better emperors, Apollonius, Christ, Abraham, and Orpheus.

Antioch. With the booty that he had plundered from the Persians, he enriched his army, since he had ordered that the tribunes, and the generals, and the soldiers themselves were to keep what they had plundered in the settlements. Then, for the first time, there were Persian slaves among the Romans, though they indeed he returned when a ransom for them had been received – for the kings of the Persians are indignant at the idea that any of their people should be enslaved elsewhere. He gave the ransom either to those who had captured the slave or paid it into the treasury.

Compare the *HAb* (24.2) on the same events:

Although a young man, he nevertheless had abilities beyond his years – at once he began a war against Xerxes, king of the Persians, with a great war-machine (*apparatu magno*). When he had been routed and put to flight (*quo fuso fugatoque*) . . .

What overlaps with Victor is nearly verbatim, while what is not in the *HAb* could represent either material derived from his *Historia* or the *HA*'s own invention (and the extravagant enumeration of the Sassanian army is certainly suspicious). The life of Alexander then moves, in characteristic fashion, to a speech the emperor delivered in the Senate, cited (we are to believe) precisely by date from the *acta senatus* (*Alex.* 56.2–9):

From the *Acta Senatus*, 25 September: 'The Persians, conscript fathers, we have conquered. There is no need for a long speech – all you ought to know is what weapons they possessed, what *apparatus* of war. First, there were 700 elephants, all outfitted with towers, archers, and a mass of arrows. Of these we captured thirty, 200 lie dead, and eighteen we led away. There were 1,800 scythed chariots. We could have taken 200 of them – their horses slain – but since they can be easily fashioned, we decided not to. We routed 120,000 of their horse, and killed in battle 10,000 cataphracts, which they call *clibanarii*. With their armour, we have armed our own soldiers. We captured and sold many of the Persians. We have retaken the land between the rivers – Mesopotamia I mean – which was abandoned by that foul beast [*sc.* Elagabalus]. We routed and set to flight (*fusum fugavimus*) Artaxerxes, mightiest of kings (*potentissimum regem*) in fact as well as in title, such that the whole land of the Persians saw him flee and where once our standards were taken, the king himself fled, leaving his own standards behind. This, conscript fathers, is what happened'.

Of course, this oration is pure fantasy – with an admixture of pedantry – but what we can see from it is how the *HA* echoes and re-elaborates the few facts it has already related using Victor, retaining traces of his language (*apparatus, fusum fugavimus*).[80]

What follows in the *HA* is a brief (fictitious) address to the people (*Alex.* 57.1–2), a genuine bit from Herodian giving a contrary account of Alexander's campaign, a description of the festivities to celebrate his victory (57.4–7), accounts of campaigns that seem never to have happened, along with titles never seemingly granted (58.1), and various benefactions (58.2–5).[81] Then comes the inevitable sequel,

---

80 Indeed, the *HA*'s author was so taken with Victor's notion of Alexander's *apparatus* that he mentions it twice elsewhere, later in the same life (61.8) and in the life of Maximinus (11.9).

81 *Alex.* 57.3: *nam et amisisse illum exercitum dicunt fame, frigore ac morbo, ut Herodianus auctor est contra multorum opinionem* ~ Herodian 6.6.3: καὶ τῶν τριῶν μοιρῶν τοῦ στρατοῦ ὧν ἔνειμε τὸ πλεῖστον ἀποβαλόντι διαφόροις συμφοραῖς, νόσῳ πολέμῳ κρύει.

TABLE 8.7 – THE *HA* AND VICTOR ON ALEXANDER'S GERMAN CAMPAIGN

Alex. 59.1–4	*HAb* 24.2–3
After this he lived with the huge affection of the people and Senate and set out on a German campaign (*ad Germanicum bellum profectus est*), everyone both wishing him victory and unwilling to let him go accompanied him for one hundred and fifty miles. It was a very grave situation both for the commonwealth and for himself (*rei publicae atque ipsi*): Gaul was being laid to waste by the predations of the Germans (*quod Germanorum vastationibus Gallia diripiebatur*). And it doubled his shame that even with the Parthians already defeated this nation – which always seemed to be subject to petty emperors – would threaten the commonwealth's neck. Over long distances, then, and with happy soldiers, he made his attack (*contendit*). But when he discovered the legions there in rebellion (*ibi . . . seditiosas legiones*), he ordered them to be disbanded (*abici*).	. . . in Galliam maturrime contendit, quae Germanorum direptionibus tentabatur. Ibi tumultuantes legionum plerasque constantissime abiecit.★ . . . he hurried to Gaul with great haste, since it was being assailed by the plundering of the Germans. There, he disbanded with great firmness the majority of the legions, which were in rebellion. *cf. LB* 24.1: hic bonus rei publicae fuit, aerumnosus sibi. He [Alexander Severus] was good for the commonwealth, but disastrous for himself.

★ The resemblance between this passage and the *HA* was first spotted by Chastagnol 1967: 91–92.

campaigns against the Germans, and with it, a return to the Victor (**TABLE 8.7**). Where the *HAb*'s account of these campaigns is very brief (thirty-two words), the *HA* is rather longer (nearly 800). Some of the additional material is clearly free composition, such as the *acta senatus*. As for the rest, we can but wonder.

These matters dispatched, we come at last to Alexander's final campaign (on the Rhine) and his death, a subject that has occasioned no end of discussion. The *HA* and the *HAb* offer an account of events that is clearly related, both by minor verbal similarities and by locating Alexander's murder in a place that was both Britannia and Sicilia (**TABLE 8.8**). It might be thought that this was some kind of gross error on Victor's part. There is no imaginable reason why Alexander, embarking on a German campaign, would end up in Britain (at an otherwise unattested place called Sicilia), and our other sources are clear enough that he met his end near Mainz.[82] It is now generally supposed that Alexander died at Bretzenheim, the *Vicus Britonnum*, a district of Mainz attested under that name since the Carolingian period – the origin of the place name probably lies in the long-standing presence of British soldiers serving there, the *numeri Brittonum*, revealed by inscriptions.[83] The long-standing consensus imagines that Victor must have had access to some rather detailed source which gave the precise locale, but that he then mangled the details

---

82 Herodian (our only contemporary source) 6.7.6, 8 is vague, but puts us in Germania, on the Rhine (*cf.* Zosimus 1.13.2). *Chron. 354* (p. 147) and Jerome, *Chron.* 216ᶜ (*cf.* Prosper *Chron.* p. 347 Mommsen 1892 and Cassiodorus, *Chron.* 931) confirm Mainz. Bertrand-Dagenbach 2014: 170 (following Böhme-Schönberger 2004: 15) erroneously states that Orosius (7.18.8; a passage clearly derived from Jerome) is the first to place the assassination at Mainz.

83 See, in general, Schumacher 2004. German toponyms ending in -*heim* do not guarantee a Germanic origin; nearby Pforzheim, for example, undoubtedly derives from the name of the Latin *vicus Portus*. The other etymology offered for Bretzenheim is that it was the seat of a chieftain Britto (*vel sim.*) – defended most recently by Böhme-Schönberger 2004, the idea is disposed of by Schumacher. *Numeri*: see Bertrand-Dagenbach 2014: 169–170 and Schumacher 2004. On the *numeri* of the Roman army in general, see Southern 1989.

TABLE 8.8 – THE *HAB* AND *HA* ON THE LOCATION OF ALEXANDER'S MURDER

HAb 24.4	*Alex.* 59.6–7
For when the soldiers quailed at the great force of his severity (*severitas*) – it was for this reason that he obtained the name Severus – as he was quartering by chance with a few men (*agentem casu cum paucis*), they cut him down at *Vicus Britanniae*, which is nicknamed Sicilia.	Finally, while he was quartering with a few men (*agentem eum cum paucis*) in Britannia, or Gaul (as other people think), in a *vicus* which has the name Sicilia, some soldiers, and especially those who did well from the largesse of Elagabalus, killed him, not with unanimous support, but like common cutthroats, since they were not able to stand a severe (*severum*) prince.

in his retelling.[84] The *HA* is, perhaps, to blame for this view, since it unquestionably places one possible location for the death of Alexander in Britain, and scholars have tended to read what they see in the text back into Victor.

Interpretations hitherto have, however, read around our evidence, rather than confronted what Victor actually says. The text is basically sound, for it occurs in both the *HAb* and the *HA*, so the core information here is a genuine fourth-century belief that the death of Severus Alexander occurred in a place called *Vicus Britanniae*. This is clearly the location to which Victor is referring: it is just that the significance of his typically recondite and precise wording has been missed. Strange as it might seem, there is no particular reason why *Vicus Britanniae* should mean *Vicus in Britannia* or even *Britanniae Vicus*, two normal ways of saying 'a village in Britain'.[85] Taken on its own, *vicus Tuscus* (for example) could mean a village in Tuscany, but only if one did not know that it was a notorious street in Rome.[86] Considerable antiquarian energy seems to have been directed towards unravelling how different *Vici* got their names. See for example this discussion in Varro (*De ling. lat.* 5.32.159):

> On the Esquiline is the Vicus Africus, so-called because hostages from Africa were said to be held there during the Punic War. The Vicus Ciprius gets its name from *ciprum*, because the Sabine citizens added to the city settled there, who named it from a good omen, since *ciprum* in the Sabine language means good. Nearby is the Vicus Sceleratus, so-called from Tullia the wife of Tarquinius Superbus, because she ordered the coachmen to drive the carriage over her father, who there was lying slain.

We also have evidence that the way these names worked – how they ought to be used – was becoming a topic of controversy in late antiquity. We can see this in the orthographic discussion in the *Appendix Probi* (134–137), which is making the general point that the name of a *Vicus* should be given in the genitive (or as an adjective), not a nominative in apposition:

> vico capitis Africae non vico caput Africae
> vico tabuli proconsolis non vico tabulu proconsolis
> vico castrorum non vico castrae
> vico strobili non vico strobilu

---

84 *e.g.* Hönn 1911: 81–82; Jardé 1925: 85; Dufraigne 1975: 139; Lippold 1991: 116–117; Groß-Albenhausen and Fuhrmann 2009: 234–235. The idea goes back at least to Schiller 1883: 783 and n. 3.

85 This is the mistake in Böhme-Schönberger 2004: 11–12.
86 Plautus, *Curc.* 482; Varro, *De ling. lat.* 5.84.6.

Indeed, there is some evidence that even in antiquity one and the same *vicus* could be named either with a genitive or an adjective.[87] As a student of grammar and antiquarian lore, not to say a world-class pedant, Victor would have been attuned to questions like this. In his prose there ought to be no substantial difference between *Vicus Britanniae*, *Vicus Britannicus*, and *Vicus Brittonum*: he may well, indeed, have come up with the formulation *Vicus Britanniae* as a learned touch. Severus Alexander was thus killed not merely near Mainz, but precisely at Bretzenheim: that was what readers of Victor's *Historia* ought to have learnt.

The next problem is *Sicilia*. No place near Mainz that we know bears such a name, which has caused considerable scholarly disquiet. Schumacher cleared away two centuries of unprofitable speculation by pointing out that in the life of Pertinax, the *HA* describes how the soldiers came to murder the emperor (*Pert.* 11.6): 'having entered the porticoes of the palace, they went as far as the place which is called "Sicilia" (*ad locum qui appellatur Sicilia*) and "Jupiter's Dining Room" (*Iovis cenatio*)'.[88] No one knows precisely what part of the palace this refers to, but it has been reasonably surmised that a dining hall is intended (*cf. Iovis cenatio*). The name *Sicilia* has been explained by the fact that Augustus gave his own private chambers the nickname *Syracusae*, or else because the association of Sicily with a lavish table was proverbial.[89] Hence, Schumacher concluded that the reference must be to a banqueting hall in the *vicus* at Mainz, where the actual assassination took place.

To Schumacher's evidence, one might add that Victor's phrase *cui vocabulum Sicilia* is Tacitean. Tacitus uses this formula to introduce a nickname, such as for the centurion Lucilius, who was called 'Give me another!' (*Ann.* 1.23.3: *et centurio Lucilius interficitur, cui militaribus facetiis vocabulum 'Cedo alteram' indiderant*).[90] He uses similar wording for the sobriquet 'pseudo-Philip' that Romans gave the last king of Macedonia, Andriscus: *cui ut degeneri Pseudophilippi vocabulum impositum* (*Ann.* 12.62.1). The formulation closest to Victor's, however, is used for a place, Tiberius' villa near Terracina: 'they were dining in his villa, which was nicknamed the Grotto . . . in a natural cave' (*Ann.* 4.59.1: *vescebantur in villa, cui vocabulum Speluncae . . . nativo in specu*). *Spelunca*, or 'the Grotto', is clearly a name derived from the actual rock formations in which the scene takes place. Hence, Victor's phrase ought to be translated as 'they cut him down at Vicus Britanniae, which is nicknamed Sicilia'.[91]

We can learn something significant about Victor's original account of Alexander's death from this episode in the *HAb*. His *Historia* evidently drew close connections between three emperors who attempted to restrain the army and who shared names and characteristics: Publius Helvius Pertinax, Septimius Severus Pertinax, and Severus Alexander. Septimius Severus took the name Pertinax to express that he was his legitimate successor, just as Alexander took the name Severus to stress his family connection with Septimius.[92] Victor was aware of this and he used these names to tie the three together: he

87 See for example, Cicero, *Pro Roscio*, where he refers to going *ad balneas Pallacinas* (18) in one passage but to the *vicus Pallacinae* in another (*apud schol. Gronov.* p. 314 Stangl).

88 See Schumacher 1982: 85–92 and 2004.

89 Schumacher 2004: 8.

90 Another military nickname he mentions is Caligula for Gaius Caesar: *quem militari vocabulo Caligulam appellabant* (*Ann.* 1.41.2).

91 It is worth pointing out that there is a second Bretzenheim (near Bad Kreuznach), less than twenty miles from Mainz. While the two toponyms could be heterogenous, their proximity is at least suspicious. Right outside this Bretzenheim is an extraordinarily luxurious Roman villa of the second or third century; in the 1960s an enormous mosaic depicting Oceanus and (if the reconstruction is to be trusted) precisely dated to AD 234 – the year before Alexander's murder – was found in the dining room. In general on the villa, see Hornung 2011.

92 On the names of Severus and Alexander, see *PIR*[2] S.487 and A.1610.

says that Severus was called Pertinax because of his cruelty as much as because of the restrained habits he shared with his namesake (*HAb* 20.10), and that Alexander was called Severus because of his severity in dealing with the soldiers (*HAb* 24.4) and may even have shared Pertinax' extreme thriftiness by serving half-eaten food (*LB* 24.5 and *HA Pert.* 12.2; *cf. HAb* 18.1: *immodice parcus*).[93] If Pertinax was killed in the 'Sicilia' in the palace, then having Severus Alexander murdered in a place near Mainz with the same name completed a complex web of associations between the three emperors. Many of the details of this elaborate triptych can be found in the *HA*, but *without any of the connections being made explicitly*. The text completely omits comparison with Pertinax's character in its paraphrase of Victor's account of the name of Severus; it portrays Alexander as a rather enthusiastic eater (*Alex.* 37.11); it makes Sicilia the name of a village in either Britain or Gaul. The ends met by Pertinax and Alexander are meant to be parallel, and that they happen in a place with the same name can hardly be coincidental. As noted above, the life of Pertinax has been reduced to mere scraps in the *HAb* and so it is hardly surprising that we do not have any of the circumstances around his murder in the text; nonetheless, tantalising glimpses may well emerge from careful collation of the *HA*, *HAb*, and *LB*.

With this in mind, the shortcomings of the *HA* become clear. Just as we saw above with Eutropius and Julia Domna, the *HA* is here the source of a definite error through its inattention to Victor's text. Eutropius had no problem understanding the original, with his crisp *periit in Gallia militari tumultu* (8.23: 'he died in Gaul in a riot of the soldiery') nor did Jerome, who added a more precise location to Eutropius' formulation: *Alexander occiditur Mogontiaci tumultu militari* (*Chron.* 216[c]: 'Alexander was killed at Mainz in a riot of the soldiery'). While we can hardly blame the *HA*'s author for not spotting the Tacitean allusion, his transformation of Victor's original into *in Britannia . . . in vico cui Sicilia nomen est* has blinded centuries of readers to what Victor was actually saying. Beyond this, it also reveals something about the *HA*'s sources and methods. The alternative location, *in Gallia*, must come from Eutropius. Confronted by this seeming difference in his two sources, the *HA* simply combined them, giving the absurd impression that the event definitely happened in a *vicus* named Sicilia, which was in either Britain or Gaul. This retreat into clumsy combination at the first sign of difficulty is a revealing insight into how the author of the *HA* operated.

From Hadrian to Alexander Severus, the *Historia Augusta* reveals varied and significant debts to the work of Aurelius Victor. His *Historia* was – perhaps unsurprisingly – mined for factual information, but it also provided the raw material for the *HA* author's fantasies and was the genesis for some of his mistakes. It is clear that Victor was not the *HA*'s sole source – we have already seen that Eutropius had an important role to play as well – but he has some claim to be its primary inspiration. It is particularly revealing that when the *HAb* swells into uncharacteristic fullness in its account of Septimius Severus, we suddenly discover that considerable portions of the *HA* are copied verbatim from Victor. This close connection has implications for our understanding of Victor's work as well – there are moments where the *HA* offers (or seems to) material that probably comes from his *Historia*. We have been able only to scratch the surface here – there is much more to be done. Still, the results are revealing.

---

93 Interestingly, the *HA* takes a rather defensive posture in its treatment of Alexander's entertainments, stressing multiple times the appropriate moderation of his banquets (*Alex.* 37.2–12). It nonetheless acknowledges his *parsimonia* in bestowing gifts (*Alex.* 37.1).

★ ★ ★

General consensus holds that there is a real and material shift in the *HA* around the life of Alexander Severus, as we move from the primary and secondary lives to the intermediate *vitae*: a decline in the quantity of factual information and an amping up of the fantastical and the invented. This notion, as we have seen, is partially due to the idea of Marius Maximus, and that, as we have shown, is hardly tenable.[94] Even so, it would be foolish to deny that *something* changes in the *HA* as it plunges deeper into the mists of the third century. Yet, as we will go on to demonstrate, one thing remains constant: the *HA*'s debt to Victor.

Six emperors

The death of Severus Alexander in AD 235 and the accession of Maximinus Thrax pitched the political order of the Roman Empire into an extended period of turmoil. Maximinus' rule seems not to have been all that popular with key parties in the Roman state and in 238 a series of revolts in Italy and North Africa produced a year with six emperors: Maximinus, three members of the same family, all (helpfully) called Gordian, and two elderly senators, Pupienus and Balbinus. Gordian I and II were proclaimed emperor at Thysdrus in North Africa – their usurpation was swiftly crushed by troops loyal to Maximinus. News of the death of the Gordians, whose proclamation had been greeted with enthusiasm in Italy, led in swift succession to an emergency *vigintivirate* and then the appointment of Pupienus and Balbinus, two aged senators, as emperors, with a mandate to resist the vengeful Maximinus. Gordian III (grandson of Gordian I) was then awkwardly wedged into this new regime by popular pressure. Maximinus was slain by his own troops during an invasion of Italy, as his siege of Aquileia faltered. Pupienus and Balbinus were tortured and then murdered by the Praetorian Guard in Rome relatively soon afterwards. Only the youthful Gordian III lived to see the autumn.[95] Given the notorious complexity of these events, it is no surprise that the narrative of the *Historiae abbreviatae* (25–27) becomes obscure and hard to follow, even leaving to one side its obvious compression. The situation is hardly better in the *HA*, but there the problem is really extension: the same events are treated across three different lives, the *Maximini duo*, the *Gordiani tres*, and the *Maximus et Balbinus*.[96] It is as hard for the reader as it was for the *scriptor* to keep track of things. Further muddying the waters, scholarly opinion generally holds that in its discursive narrative of the tumultuous reigns of these emperors, the *HA* drew extensively on Greek sources: Herodian in particular, but perhaps Dexippus as well.[97] In spite of this contrast and this consensus, here too Victor is at the heart of the *HA*'s account, with Eutropius following close behind.

94 *cf.* Chapter VII.

95 On events from 235 to 238 (though with an emphasis on the year of the six emperors itself), see the exhaustive treatment of Dietz 1980; Loriot 1975: 688–724 remains useful (see also Townsend 1955; Syme 1971a: 163–178). There is much of interest to be found in the commentaries on some of the relevant *HA* lives by Lippold 1991 and Brandt 1996. Not the least confusing aspect of the period is its uncertain chronology. In general, Peachin 1990 offers a clear, careful, and balanced overview of the terrain.

96 The lives can be conveniently consulted, with brief commentary, in Paschoud 2018, but *cf.* Stover 2022.

97 Mommsen 1890: 262–268; Barnes 1978: 60–64; Lippold 1991: 59–84; Paschoud 1991 (Dexippus used directly; Bleckmann 1995b argues characteristically for

The *HAb*'s treatment of Maximinus Thrax is extremely brief and largely focused on his rise to power. The text says (25.1) that he was 'the first from among the soldiers to seize power with the support of the legions' (*primus e militaribus . . . potentiam cepit suffragiis legionum*, *cf. LB* 25.1), and goes on to note that the senators ratified this selection. In spite of the palpable abbreviation, we can detect Victor's influence on Eutropius (9.1), who describes Maximinus as:

> The first from the body of soldiers (*e corpore militari primus*) to come to empire at the will of soldiers alone, since no senatorial decree forbade it (*cum nulla senatus intercessisset auctoritas*), even though he himself was not a senator (*neque ipse senator esset*).

Eutropius is using *intercedo* here in a technical sense, to mean 'veto' in the context of legislation.[98] His account differs a little in emphasis from that of Victor, who says that the *patres* 'approved' the appointment of Maximinus, though under menaces.[99] This is crucial, because it helps to prove that the *HA* took over Eutropius' narration wholesale. That is suggested by its claim that Maximinus was 'the first from the body of the soldiers and not yet a senator' to become emperor (*Maximin.* 8.1: *e corpore militari et nondum senator*), even though the author had made up a speech of Alexander Severus just three chapters earlier bestowing senatorial rank on him (*Maximin.* 5.4). It is confirmed when it says baldly that Maximinus became emperor 'without a decree of the Senate' (*sine decreto senatus*), which gives the impression that the Senate never approved election. Here, the *HA*'s author has simply misunderstood Eutropius' technical use of *intercedo* and read the word (more normally) as 'intervened', 'interceded', or 'happened'. As a result, he ends up giving a version that turns a potential (but misleading) implication of Eutropius' text into hard fact.[100]

In contrast, at the end of the Maximinus' reign we can see once again in the *HA* the tell-tale agglutination of Eutropius and Victor. The *HA* says – in a manoeuvre exactly parallel to the one it deployed in discussing the location of Alexander Severus' death – that Maximinus ruled for 'a three-year period as some people say, a two-year as others' (*Max. Balb.* 15.7: *ut quidam dicunt per triennium ut alii per biennium*). Victor, who generally conceived of regnal duration in terms of the number of complete years, is explicit that it was a *biennium*, or two full years, from the ratification of his rule by the Senate (by 25 March 235) to the acclamation of Gordian I (late winter or early spring of 238).[101] He goes on to specify that

a Latin intermediary, *cf.* Martin 2006: 64–66); Chastagnol 1994: lxiii, lxiv; Barnes 1995: 11–12; Rohrbacher 2013: 163–166 (*cf.* Rohrbacher 2016: 13 *e.g.*); Paschoud 2018: x–xix. Potter 1990: 365–369 offers a rare and perceptive dissent (*cf.* Homo 1919).

98 For *intercedo* as 'veto', see *e.g.* Cicero, *De leg.* 3.18. This is the only use of *intercedo* in Eutropius, which suggests that he is indeed using it in the narrow, technical sense. Note also that *auctoritas senatus* means specifically 'a decree of the Senate' (*cf. e.g.* Cicero, *De leg.* 2.37: *senatus vetus auctoritas de Bacchanalibus*).

99 *HAb* 25.2: *Quod tamen etiam patres . . . approbaverunt.*

100 *cf.* Jerome, *Chron.* 216[d]: *Maximinus primus ex corpore militari sine senatus auctoritate ab exercitu imperator electus est.*

101 *HAb* 26.1: *biennium summae potitis.* The rough date of the Senate's recognition of Maximinus can be inferred from his co-optation into the *sodales Antoniniani* on 25 March 235 (*CIL* 6.2001; Peachin 1990: 26). The date of the accession of Gordian I is a controversial matter, within relatively narrow bounds (Dietz 1980: 345–347 collects earlier opinions). Peachin 1989 (*cf. idem* 1990: 28) advanced the case for mid/late March 238, primarily on the basis of the papyrological evidence. Sartre 1984 (*cf.* Loriot 1974; 1975: 689, 720) argued for a slightly earlier chronology, with the events at Thysdrus in January 238 (or perhaps even December 237). Victor's statement – and his precision in such matters – ought to play a greater role in the debate: the acclamation of Gordian I took place before Maximinus had reigned for three full years.

TABLE 8.9 – THE *HAb* AND *HA* ON THE ACCESSION AND REIGN OF GORDIAN III

HAb 27.6–7	*HA*
Clodio Caelioque Romae intra Palatium caesis Gordianus **solus** regnum **obtinuit** . . .★	*Gord.* 22.9: Gordianus adulescens **solus teneret** imperium.
In Persas profectus est, cum prius Iani aedes quas Marcus clauserat patentes more veterum fecisset.†	*Gord.* 26.3: Gordianus aperto Iano gemino, quod signum erat indicti belli, **profectus est contra Persas**.
After Clodius and Caelius had been cut down at Rome inside the palace, Gordian alone won royal power . . .	The young man Gordian alone held imperial power.
He [*sc.* Gordian] set off against the Persians, after he had first opened in the manner of the ancients the doors of the temple of Janus, which Marcus had closed.	Gordian, after Janus Geminus had been opened (which was a sign of war being declared), set off against the Persians.

★ For the reading *Caelioque* see Chapter IV.

† This passage might incidentally prove that Orosius had not read Victor. At 7.19.4, he discusses the opening of the doors of Janus by Gordian, explicitly citing Eutropius (for information that was also in Victor) and claiming that he cannot remember whether anyone wrote about their having been closed after Vespasian and Titus, when Victor explicitly says Marcus Aurelius did that: *Gordianus admodum puer in orientem ad bellum Parthicum profecturus, sicut Eutropius scribit, Iani portas aperuit: quas utrum post Vespasianum et Titum aliquis clauserit, neminem scripsisse memini.*

Maximinus' reign stretched to a third year, if one takes his death as the end-point, which happened in late spring or early summer.[102] Eutropius, in contrast, says simply that Maximinus reigned for a *triennium* and a few days.[103] Having lifted the *biennium* from Victor, the *HA* ineptly combines it with the *triennium* taken straight from Eutropius.

As the *scriptor* continued to pick his way through the period after the death of Maximinus, however, we can see that he reverted to using Victor alone. This is clear in his account of the death of Pupienus and Balbinus and of the sole reign of Gordian III (TABLE 8.9). If we compare the corresponding passages in Eutropius, it becomes clear that the author of the *HA* must have been drawing on Victor directly.[104]

So at the end of the era of Maximinus, as at its beginning, the *HA* relies on Victor, Eutropius, or some combination of the two. In between, the situation is a little more complex.

Herodian and the *Historia Augusta*

One of the most striking things about the *HA*'s narrative of the year 238 is that it repeatedly cites the work of three Greek historians: Herodian, Dexippus, and Arrian.[105] As we have seen, the *HA*'s citations are not

102 *HAb* 27.5: *imperio ad biennium per huiuscemodi moras annus quaesitus.* Spring: Sartre 1984: esp. 58. Summer: Peachin 1989.

103 Eutropius 9.1: *triennio et paucis diebus.*

104 Eutropius 9.2: *Balbinus et Pupienus in Palatio interfecti sunt, soli Gordiano imperium reservatum . . . Ianum*

Geminum aperuit et ad Orientem profectus Parthis bellum intulit

105 For Herodian and the *HA*, see Kolb 1972; for Dexippus, see Paschoud 1991 and the essays in Mithoff *et al.* 2020. There are a few citations of Herodian (*Clod. Alb.* 1.2 and 12.14, in conjunction with Marius Maximus;

TABLE 8.10 – HERODIAN AND THE *HA* ON THE ACCESSION OF GORDIAN I

Herodian 7.5.3	*Gord.* 8.4–5
συνέβαινε δὲ ἐκείνης τῆς ἡμέρας, ἧς ταῦτα ἐπράττετο, οἴκοι τὸν Γορδιανὸν διατρίβειν ἡσυχάζοντα, δεδωκότα τοῖς καμάτοις ἀνάπαυλαν ἀργίαν τε ταῖς πράξεσιν. οἱ δὲ νεανίσκοι ξιφήρεις σὺν παντὶ τῷ πλήθει, βιασάμενοι τοὺς ταῖς αὐλείαις ἐφεστῶτας, εἰσπηδήσαντες **καταλαμβάνουσιν αὐτὸν ἐπί τινος σκιμποδίου ἀναπαυόμενον**, περιστάντες δὲ **χλαμύδι πορφυρᾷ περιβάλλουσι** σεβασμίαις τε τιμαῖς προσαγορεύουσιν.	Tunc adclamatum est: 'aequum est, iustum est. Gordiane Auguste, di te servent. Feliciter imperator es, cum filio imperes'. His actis propere ventum est ad oppidum Tysdrum, **inventusque** senex venerabilis post iuris dictionem **iacens in lectulo, qui circumfusus purpura** humi se abiecit ac retrectans elevatus est.
It happened that on the day when these things occurred, Gordian was resting at home, having been granted respite from his labours and leisure from his affairs. Armed with swords, the young men along with the whole crowd, having overpowered those standing before the outer doors, rushed in and found him reclining on a little couch. Surrounding him, they wrapped him in a purple cloak and saluted him with the title of Augustus.	Then came the acclamation: 'It is right, it is just. The gods keep you, Gordian Augustus! You are our emperor with good fortune, when you reign with your son'. This done, they swiftly came to the town of Thysdrus, and found the venerable old man lying in bed after administering justice. They draped him in purple, but he hurled himself to the ground and though resisting was lifted up.

to be trusted, something rather confirmed by the fact that the famous historian Arrian died a good half century before the events he is supposed to have recorded.[106] Herodian and Dexippus, however, were genuine historians of the third century AD, who certainly wrote about events of the 230s.[107] It is generally accepted that the *HA* has indeed drawn on their works for this year of six emperors.[108] Certainly, it is very close to Herodian in some passages. Compare, for example, the *HA*'s description of the accession of Gordian I (TABLE 8.10). Though they differ in details and emphases, at one point in this episode the *HA* could almost be a translation of the corresponding portion of Herodian.

At first glance, Victor's account of these events seems to have been very different. The *HAb* (26.1–2) says:

> Repente Antonius Gordianus Africae proconsul ab exercitu princeps apud Thysdri oppidum absens fit. Quo ut accitus pervenit, tamquam ea re creatus foret, seditione excipitur.[109]

> Suddenly, Antonius Gordianus, the proconsul of Africa, was made emperor by the army at the town of Thysdrus, though he was absent. When he came there after he had been summoned, he was caught up in the rebellion (*seditio*), as if he had been made emperor for this purpose.

Diad. 2.5; *Alex.* 52.2 and 57.3) and Dexippus (*Alex.* 49.3) before these lives. There is also one reference to Herodian in *Tyr.* 32.1, for a usurper active under Maximinus.

106 On Arrian's life and times, see Stadter 1980: 1–18. Besides the famous historian, it is worth noting that one L. Annius Arrianus was consul in 243 (*PIR*² A.635). This Arrian is mentioned explicitly in the *HA* (*Gord.* 29.1). The coincidence of author and consul is

intriguing in light of what we have found with Marius Maximus (Chapter VII).

107 On Herodian, see Chapter IV. On Dexippus, see Chapters IV and X.

108 Paschoud 2018: xiv–xix provides a convenient overview.

109 We read *Thysdri* for *Thydri* with D'Elia 1968. It is not obvious whether *ea re* (Schott's conjecture for **p** *care*, **o** *tare*) should be understood as an ablative of purpose, or of cause.

Here as elsewhere, Victor's account has been wrecked by abbreviation. As it stands, there is no explanation of what the *seditio* which precipitated the acclamation of Gordian I was. We can only understand it if we have something like Herodian's narrative in mind, where a gang of youths murdered an official and decided to try to cover up their crime by turning it into a revolt, with the proconsul Gordian at its head (7.4–5). Yet Victor's account differs from Herodian's in one key respect: the latter is clear that Gordian was present in Thysdrus when he was proclaimed, where the former has him absent in an unspecified location, summoned to the town, and then presented with a *fait accompli*.[110] The *HA* seems to follow Herodian very closely in its account of this whole episode. Yet we can still see traces of Victor's version, particularly with its repeated use of the word *seditio* in explaining the circumstances of the accession of Gordian I elsewhere.[111] More significantly, it makes the specific point that Gordian was not present when he was acclaimed. Instead it makes the acclamation – with the *HA*'s standard cry *di te servent!* – happen near Thysdrus and then has the band of rebels go to the town to find their emperor. So while in general the passage quoted just above follows Herodian's version of events, in one key detail it is much closer to Victor.[112] This raises the question: did the author of the *HA* subtly modify Herodian's narrative to make it conform to Victor's? Or was some of this material from Herodian already in Victor?

One key detail in the *HA*'s account of the siege of Aquileia in 238 might suggest an answer. After their defeat by the civilian inhabitants of the city, the *scriptor* makes Maximinus' soldiers 'blush that armed men were thus nearly defeated by unarmed' (*Maximin.* 22.1: *erubescebant armati sic paene ab inermibus victi*). This is a suspiciously subtle and sophisticated sentiment. If we look back to Victor's account of the accession of Maximinus, he gives a very specific reason why the senators accepted his acclamation by the army: 'since they considered it dangerous for those without arms to resist an armed man' (*HAb* 25.2: *dum periculosum existimant inermes armato resistere*). The siege of Aquileia, in the *HA*'s telling, proved just the opposite: that people without weapons could successfully resist armed men. That this idea must have come from Victor is proved by the fact that this whole section of the text follows Herodian so closely as to be almost a translation. Yet the corresponding line in the Greek historian does not make the explicit contrast between unarmed and armed, but simply states that the soldiers were ashamed to be defeated by a mob of civilians.[113]

What we see here in the *HA* is an idea of Victor's used to modulate the narrative of Herodian. Is the author of the *HA* responsible, or was this already in his source? As we have seen, there is good evidence that Victor had read Herodian.[114] It would, therefore, be unwise to ignore the possibility that the *HA* is

---

110 This is apparent both in 7.5.3 (see Table 8.10) and stated explicitly in 7.6.1.

111 *Maximin.* 13.6: *subita et ingenti seditione Gordianum senem, virum gravissimum, qui erat pro consule, imperatorem fecerunt* (*n.b.* this passage makes the soldiers responsible); *Gord.* 7.3: *quemadmodum seditio inter Maximinianos et rusticos vel Afros orta placaretur. cf.* Herodian 7.5.1: ἐς ἀπόστασιν

112 The apparent discrepancy between the *HA* and *HAb* concerning Gordian's location (near Thysdrus or elsewhere) might easily be explained if the abbreviator (characteristically) deleted the true referent of *quo*, since the passage could still just about be made to work

grammatically (*cf.* on particles Chapter IV). It is also possible that the *HAb*'s text means 'away at Thysdrus', implying that the acclamation happened elsewhere *cf.* Dacier 1681 *ad loc.*

113 Herodian 8.3.9: πολλάκις ἐν ἀέρι ὑπὲρ τῆς πόλεως μαχομένην. ὅπερ εἴτε ἀληθῶς ἐφαντάσθη τισίν, ἢ καὶ βουλομένοις μὴ ἀσχημονεῖν τοσοῦτον στρατὸν πρὸς ὄχλον δημοτῶν πολὺ ἐλάττονα μὴ ἀντισχόντα, δοκεῖν δὲ ὑπὸ θεῶν ἀλλὰ μὴ ὑπὸ ἀνθρώπων νενικῆσθαι, εἰπεῖν οὐχ ἔχω· τὸ δὲ παράδοξον τῆς ἀποβάσεως ποιεῖ πάντα πιστεῦσαι. *cf.* Paschoud 2018: 142–143.

114 Chapter IV.

sometimes reading Herodian *through* Victor.[115] In fact, the very oddity of the *HA* for once citing the real works of real historians might make us wonder whether the *scriptor* has simply lifted the references from his actual source (a not unusual practice in antiquity). It is suggestive also that in those passages where the *HA* does seem to have derived from Herodian (directly or otherwise), the authority cited is most often Arrian.[116] Even if much of the material in the *HA*'s narrative of 238 goes back to contemporary Greek historians, therefore, it clearly also relies extensively on Victor and Eutropius.

'*Scriptorum inperitia*'

The fact that the *HA* is using both Victor and Eutropius in the lives of 238 is important, because, in them, the *scriptor* makes several rather prickly assertions of his own accuracy, accusing unnamed Latin writers of some fundamental misunderstandings. His indictment of these erroneous predecessors runs as follows: they claimed wrongly that there were only two Gordians, and not three (*Gord.* 2.1), that the youngest Gordian (III) was a praetorian prefect (*Max. Balb* 15.6), that the emperor reigning with Balbinus was called Pupienus (rather than Maximus: *Maximin.* 33.3–4; *Max. Balb.* 15.5, 16.7), that Pupienus was to be credited with the victory over Maximinus (*Max. Balb.* 15.5), and that Pupienus was present himself at Aquileia for that victory (*Maximin.* 33.3; *Max. Balb.* 16.7). At first blush, all of these seem to be references to Victor, because the *HAb appears* to make these mistakes. That was what led Enmann, writing before Dessau and accepting the *HA*'s putative date, to note incredulously that it was almost as if Capitolinus, the *HA* 'author' of these lives, had had Victor's text before his eyes.[117] Scholars have generally followed his lead in assuming that Victor made these mistakes and is the primary target here.[118] This is, however, not quite true. Because the *HA* seems to hit upon the 'right' solution to these problems in the face of Victor's supposed errors, scholars have been inclined to treat its account of 238 a little too generously. In fact, close study of it confirms the *HA*'s basic dependence on Victor and Eutropius and suggests that, once again, its author was often far from competent in his handling of them, usually misled by idiosyncratic obsessions.

The problem in 238 to which the *HA* devotes the most attention is that of what it insists was the 'real' name of the Emperor Pupienus: Maximus (*Maximin.* 24.5, 33.3–4; *Gord.* 10.1, 19.9, 22.1; *Max. Balb.* 1.2, 15.1–18.2, almost twenty-five per cent of the life (!)). It is obvious that the *HA* had some source(s) which referred to the emperor as Maximus (as, we might note, Herodian does *passim*), others that referred to him as Pupienus (as most Latin sources do), and that its author was very uncomfortable with the idea that these were the same man.[119] Indeed, at times the *HA* insinuates darkly that there had been some attempt to erase Maximus from history, and put in his place the impostor Pupienus (*Max. Balb.* 15.4):

---

115 One other possible sign of this is the name of Maximinus' son. Inscriptions show that he was called C. Iulius Verus Maximus (*PIR*[2] I.619), but Victor gave his cognomen as Maximinus (*HAb* 25.2), which is what the *HA* calls him *passim*. Herodian never mentions his name.

116 Arrian: *Maxim.* 33.3; *Gord.* 2.1; *Max. Balb.* 1.2. In the lives of the emperors of 238, Herodian is cited only

at *Max. Balb.* 15.5 and 16.6 (both discussing the same point).

117 Chapter VI.

118 For example: Dessau 1889: 372–373; Schlumberger 1974: 138; Bird 1984: 124; Nickbahkt and Scardino 2021: 222 *e.g.*

119 On Pupienus' names, see Chapter IV.

> But many people say that Maximinus was defeated at Aquileia not by Maximus, but by the emperor Pupienus, and that he was killed together with Balbinus, with the result that they omit the name of Maximus.

There are two points at issue here: was it a mistake to call the emperor Pupienus instead of Maximus; and did Victor make that mistake? In each case, the answer is emphatically no. Pupienus and Maximus were both part of the emperor's full nomenclature and contemporaries referred to him by both. In general, it seems as though Pupienus was slightly favoured as his name, appearing often unaccompanied by Maximus in coins and inscriptions.[120] The *HA*'s criticism, in other words, is both nonsensical and erroneous – indeed, it betrays an anachronistic attitude to onomastics, assuming that an individual in the first half of the third century could only have a single diacritic.[121] Victor, unsurprisingly, had a much more sophisticated grasp of the emperor's nomenclature. The *HAb* refers to him in three different ways: Clodius Pupienus (26.7), Pupienus (27.4), and simply Clodius (27.6). It is possible that the *HA*'s confusion arose from reading Victor, though it is hardly certain that it did. In any case, Victor was not in error here.

That ought to make us look a little more sceptically at the other mistakes the *HA* attributes to the Latin writers. The question of the number of Gordians is more complex than it first appears. Of course, there were only two important Gordians: Gordian I, whose proclamation as emperor began the turmoil of 238, and Gordian III (his grandson), who was emperor from 238 to 244. The problem was the middle Gordian (II) – the son of the first, a shadowy figure caught up in the usurpation of his father and soon killed – and whether he was to be counted as one of the Gordians.[122] Ammianus, an astute reader and a careful historian, mentions in the extant text only a Gordian *senior* and a Gordian *iunior* (23.5.17; 26.6.20): Gordian I and Gordian III. Herodian is fairly elusive on the matter: there is brief mention (7.7.2) of Gordian II as co-emperor with his father and one instance (8.6.3) of the phrase 'two Gordians' (Gordian I and II), but otherwise he focuses on Gordian I and Gordian III.[123] The issue caused considerable confusion for later Greek historians.[124] It is not clear that thinking of two Gordians rather than three is a mistake, as opposed to the elision of a point of detail in the history of an unusually complex period. In any case, Victor certainly featured three Gordians in his account. While the *HAb* mentions only two, it interprets a prodigy of the eldest Gordian as meaning that 'he would birth empire for his *children*' in the plural (26.4: *liberis pariturum imperium*), a phrase that requires more than one other member of the dynasty. The *LB* (26–27) is usefully explicit that there were three Gordians, with the third the son of the daughter of the first, an account not at all inconsistent with the prodigy in the *HAb*. So once again, Victor did not make the mistake against which the *HA* railed. He did, however, provide crucial source material for it. The *HA* copies the interpretation of the prodigy from Victor, but transforms it (characteristically) into a horoscope (*Gord.* 20.1–3).[125] Moreover, the *scriptor* misunderstands his source, producing a version quite

---

120 Peachin 1990: 150–156.
121 On the 'diacritic system', see Woudhuysen 2019; Stover and Woudhuysen 2022a.
122 Dietz 1980: 74–77; Peachin 1990: 144–149.
123 At Herodian 7.9.5–7, the son of Gordian I is mentioned, without any suggestion that he was an emperor.

124 Zosimus 1.14–16 and Zonaras 12.17–18. Interestingly, the *Chronicon Paschale* mentions Γορδιανὸς Σενίωρ (p. 501, 502 Dindorf).
125 On the importance of astrology to the *HA*, see Straub 1970 and Syme 1976b.

different from that in Victor (*Gord.* 20.1): 'the response was that his son [*sc.* Gordian II] would be both son and father of an emperor, and that he also would be emperor'.[126]

It is a similar story with the question of whether Pupienus defeated Maximinus and did so personally at Aquileia.[127] While the *HA* does attribute these errors to Latin writers, it is really a point incidental to the author's obsession with the emperor's name. The *scriptor* is also inconsistent on the question of what the Greek tradition said about Pupienus' role in the victory: he asserts that Herodian and Dexippus claimed he was not even present for the battle (*Max. Balb.* 16.7), when just a few lines earlier he had explicitly attributed to Dexippus the idea that 'Maximinus was conquered by Maximus' (15.5). Victor is clear that Pupienus deserved credit for the victory (*HAb* 27.4): 'Pupienus defeated (*confecit*) them at Aquileia; afterwards the remaining soldiers abandoned those conquered in battle little by little'.[128] In any case, while the text in the *HAb* might be thought to imply that Pupienus was present at Aquileia, it does not say so explicitly. Victor's account of these events is in fact entirely consistent with one of the versions of the story that the *HA* attributed to Dexippus. The *scriptor* made much of the *scriptorum inperitia* (*Max. Balb.* 15.6) in accounts of AD 238 – Victor, however, was very far from ignorant.

In fact, in all these cases of alleged error but one, the *HA* is certainly not talking about Victor. Instead, Eutropius is the target of its ire. It is his *breviarium* that refers to the emperor only as Pupienus, that says definitively that he defeated, indeed killed, Maximinus at Aquileia (using a passive construction like that found in the *HA*), and that definitely has only two Gordians (9.1.2–2.1):

> . . . [*sc.* Maximinus] a Pupieno Aquileiae occisus est deserentibus eum militibus suis cum filio adhuc puero . . . Postea tres simul Augusti fuerunt, Pupienus, Balbinus, Gordianus, duo superiores obscurissimo genere, Gordianus nobilis, quippe cuius pater, senior Gordianus, consensu militum, cum proconsulatum Africae gereret, Maximino imperante princeps fuisset electus.

> Maximinus was killed at Aquileia by Pupienus together with his son who was still a boy – his soldiers deserted him . . . After this, there were three Augusti at the same time: Pupienus, Balbinus, and Gordian. The first two were of very low birth, but Gordian was an aristocrat, since his father (the elder Gordian), when he was proconsul of Africa, was made emperor by the agreement of the soldiers during the reign of Maximinus.[129]

Only one 'error' that the *HA* attacks is not to be found in Eutropius (*Max. Balb.* 15.6): 'that the child Gordian was praetorian prefect, as many are unaware that he was often carried on people's shoulders to be shown to the soldiers'. This is a deeply confused and confusing accusation – the logical connection between the idea that Gordian III was praetorian prefect and the fact that he was carried on people's

---

126 Paschoud 2018: 247 fails to note the *HA*'s dependence on Victor here, calling the horoscope 'entièrement inventé'.

127 Pupienus seems still to have been at Ravenna, mustering forces, when Maximinus was killed and the siege ended: Herodian 8.6.5.

128 The place name is, in fact, Schott's plausible restoration. Scholars of Victor have persisted in seeing in this passage a claim that Pupienus was responsible for the death of Maximinus (as *conficere* would normally mean – *TLL* 4.203.54–204.46 (Hoppe)). In fact,

here as elsewhere, Victor uses *conficere* in the rare but attested sense of 'defeat': *TLL* 4.204.66–75 (Hoppe); *HAb* 40.18: *Denique eum . . . Rufius Volusianus praefectus praetorio ac militares duces levi certamine confecere*; see Chapter IV for a different rare sense in which Victor used the same verb. The context makes this clear, for Maximinus and his son could hardly be abandoned by their troops if they were already dead.

129 Of course, Eutropius also confuses the relationship between Gordian III and Gordian I.

shoulders is completely mysterious.[130] The praetorian prefecture is generally believed to have come from Victor, who is assumed to have been in error here, on the basis of a very difficult passage in the *HAb* (27.1):[131]

> Iisdemque per Africam diebus milites Gordianum, Gordiani <. . .> filium, qui forte contubernio patris Praetextati – is <. . .> ac deinceps praefectus praetorio – intererat, Augustum creavere.

> In those same days in Africa, the soldiers made Augustus Gordian, the <grand>son of Gordian, who was by chance in the service of his father Praetextatus (he was <. . .> and then praetorian prefect).[132]

The text is manifestly corrupt at this point and abbreviation has no doubt done little to help its clarity. Scholarship has vainly struggled with the question of whether the Gordian made emperor here is Gordian II, Gordian III, or some confused amalgam of the two. The issue is further complicated by the fact the manuscripts of the *HAb* have not the *praetextatus* of the editions, but rather *praetextatiis*. As we have argued elsewhere, correctly understood, Victor is here saying not that any Gordian was made praetorian prefect, but rather that Praetextatus – the father of Gordian III – held that office.[133] So, while the *HA* may be reliant on Victor here – because nowhere else is the praetorian prefecture associated with the family of the Gordians – it is not clear that he had made the mistake the *scriptor* attacks.

The fact that the *HA* happens to alight upon some of what are generally agreed to be the facts of the year 238 should not blind us to its author's severe deficiencies: his reliance on Eutropius, who himself was prone to occasional mistakes, and his shoddy reading of Victor's often complex prose.

Valerian and Gallienus

At the end of the *HA*'s life of Maximus and Balbinus, there is the great lacuna – the hole in the text that has swallowed up the lives of Philip the Arab and Decius. We emerge from it in the very different environment of the 250s and the 260s, with the (appropriately) mutilated account of the emperor Valerian (r. 253–260) and his son Gallienus (r. 253–268).[134] The lacuna conceals a significant discontinuity in the text – indeed in Roman history – yet after it, as before, Victor is a crucial source of and inspiration for the *HA*.

This is true even in the short and patchily preserved life of Valerian, where the *HA* has created a nonsensical amalgam of Victor and Eutropius, a pattern we have seen before. In his account of the catastrophic end of Valerian's reign, Victor was quite clear that the emperor died soon after being captured by the Persians (*HAb* 32.5):

---

130 The shoulders have never been satisfactorily explained and are not commented on by Brandt 1996: 231 or Paschoud 2018: 336–337. In Herodian 7.10.8 the boy is displayed to the mob (not the soldiers) before he is made emperor and in *HA Max. Balb.* 9.4 he is shown to them after he has become Caesar, but how these episodes might have been linked to the praetorian prefecture is very far from clear.

131 Brandt 1996: 231, with reference to earlier literature – the point was already in Dessau 1889: 372.

132 On the text, see the Appendix, no. VII.

133 Stover and Woudhuysen forthcoming b.

134 On the lacuna, see Stover 2020.

Persarum regis, cui nomen Sapor erat, dolo circumventus foede laniatus interiit imperii sexto anno, senecta robustiore.

Caught in a trap by a stratagem of the king of the Persians, who was named Shapur, and foully mutilated, he perished in the sixth year of his reign, still rather hearty in his old age.

Eutropius (9.7) misread this reference to Valerian's age at the time of his capture – he was over sixty – to stretch out the duration of his captivity, as if he reached old age during it: 'once captured he grew old in disgraceful servitude among the Parthians' (*captus apud Parthos ignobili servitute consenuit*).[135] Confronted by this contradiction in his sources, the author of the *HA* tries to combine them, to absurd effect (*Tyr.* 12.1): 'the old man grew old among the Persians' (*senex apud Persas consenuit*). The author needed Eutropius' version for his depiction of Gallienus: the idea of Valerian still living in servitude and his wastrel son making no effort to secure his release is a major theme of both the *Two Gallieni* and the *Thirty Tyrants*.[136] Yet he was also clearly reading Victor in parallel and using him as a source for key ideas.

The same is true of the *HA*'s better-preserved life of Valerian's son and heir. The reign of Gallienus was an era of turmoil, when numerous usurpers rose up, hydra-like in their multiplicity. In the *HAb* (33.6–7), Victor attributes the constant usurpations to Gallienus' general dissolution and specifically to his *amours*:

Inter haec ipse popinas ganeasque obiens lenonum ac vinariorum amicitiis haerebat, expositus Saloninae coniugi atque amori flagitioso filiae Attali Germanorum regis Pipae nomine; qua causa etiam civiles motus longe atrociores orti.

Amidst these events, he frequented taverns and dives; he clung fast to the friendship of pimps and wine-dealers; he abandoned himself to his wife Salonina and his disgraceful passion for the daughter of Attalus, King of the Germans, called Pipa. For this reason, civil rebellions by far more savage broke out.

We have already looked at this colourful passage for its allusion to Sallust on Lepidus.[137] Unsurprisingly, it was taken up by the author of the *HA* in the life of Gallienus, although as a throwaway comment at the end, in a discussion of the length of his reign (*Gall.* 21.6): 'for he is said to have always made nocturnal visits to taverns (*popinas*), and to have lived with pimps (*lenonibus*), mimes, and other lowlifes'. The derivation from Victor is clear: the conjunction of *popinae* and *lenones* is found only in Victor and the *HA*, but the latter's rewording has obscured the Sallustian intertext.[138] It is a similar story with Gallienus' barbarian consort, Pipa. She is mentioned by the *HA* as an aside in a discussion of the name of Saloninus, the son of Gallienus, in terms obviously derived from Victor: 'he had a destructive passion for the barbarian princess called Pipa'.[139] In the life of Gallienus, however, while it has borrowed much from Victor, the *HA* has not taken his core idea: that the emperor's habits and affairs *caused* the usurpations.

---

135 One can compare the very hostile account of Lactantius (*DMP* 5.2–4, discussed already in Chapter IV) which puts some unspecified period of time between when Valerian was captured and his death, but does not actually say it was lengthy. For his age, *PIR*² L.258.

136 *e.g. Gall.* 1.1, 10.5 (*cf.* 5.6); *Tyr.* 12.1.

137 Chapter IV.

138 *cf.* the incident reported in AM 14.1.9.

139 *Gall.* 21.3: *quamvis perdite dilexit, Piparam nomine, barbaram regis filiam.* 'Pipara' is almost certainly simply an error for 'Pipa' caused by anticipation of *barbaram*.

When, however, we come to the *Tyranni Triginta* – the *HA*'s collection of miniature lives of those numerous usurpers – this notion assumes a prominence that it does not have in the life of Gallienus. It is repeatedly invoked as an explanation for usurpations: six separate instances, all in very similar language that mirrors Victor.[140] Each of these is based on that germ of an idea from Victor: that it was Gallienus' visits to dives and brothels, his cosiness with pimps and wine-dealers, and his destructive passion for his barbarian concubine Pipa which caused the endless rebellions that scarred his reign. In fact, two of these sentences are actually closer to Victor (*Tyr.* 3.4 and 9.1) than they are to what the *HA* itself says in its account of Gallienus. What looks like an obsession of the *HA*'s author thus turns out to be an idea entirely derived from Victor.

One instance of this is particularly revealing. At *Tyr.* 5.6, the *HA* provides a similar, but more general, version of this origin story for the troubles of the 260s:

> I believe all of these were sent from the gods (*quos omnes datos divinitus credo*), so that the power of possessing Roman soil would not be given to the Germans, while that plague [*sc.* Gallienus] was ensnared in the evils of unheard-of luxury (*inauditae luxuriae*).

At first sight, this might seem to combine Victor's explanation for usurpation under Gallienus with an idiosyncratic religious conviction of the *HA*'s author. In fact, however, none of this is original. The belief in heaven's intervention is a lightly retouched version of one of Victor's moral ruminations transmitted in the *LB* (16.4):

> I believe it should be credited to the divine (*credo divinitus attributum*) that, when the law of the universe or Nature brings forth something unknown to mortals (*hominibus incognitum*), it is ameliorated by the counsels of rulers as if by the remedies of medicine.[141]

Victor's idea is that when unprecedented events (*incognitum*) occur, Nature, the gods, or the cosmos provide rulers fit to mitigate them.[142] The *HA*'s point is that when a ruler himself gets involved in unprecedented evils, the divine will raise up (provincial) Romans to ensure that the Germans do not make inroads into Roman territory. Perhaps this is meant as a joke at the morally serious Victor's expense; perhaps the author of the *HA* really did feel that strongly about the integrity of the Roman Empire. In either case, this shows him rather bad at formulating general maxims and rather mendacious in copying a first-person statement (*credo*) from his source.

The *HA* author's willingness to simply take over Victor's ideas is on display elsewhere in these biographies. One of the most sustained threats to Gallienus' rule came from the general Postumus, a

---

140 *Tyr.* 3.4: *ab omni exercitu et ab omnibus Gallis Postumus gratanter acceptus talem se praebuit per annos septem, ut Gallias instauraverit, cum Gallienus luxuriae et popinis vacaret et amore barbarae mulieris consenesceret*; 8.9: *non vino, non floribus, non mulierculis, non popinis, ut facit Gallienus*; 9.1: *Tusco et Basso conss. cum Gallienus vino et popinis vacaret cumque se lenonibus, mimis et meretricibus dederet ac bona naturae luxuriae continuatione deperderet*; 23.1: *cum dissolutionem Gallieni, pernoctantis in publico, ferre non posset*; 26.1: *Pudet iam persequi, quanti sub Gallieno fuerint tyranni vitio pestis illius, si quidem erat in eo ea luxuria, ut*

rebelles plurimos mereretur; 29.1: *dum Gallienus popinatur et balneis ac lenonibus deputat vitam . . .* (the *hapax popinatur* has not been sufficiently queried: perhaps read *popin<as frequent>atur, vel sim.*).

141 On the text here, see the Appendix, no. XVI. *cf. LB* 13.10: *Quae omnia eo maiora visebantur, quo per multos atque atroces tyrannos perdito atque prostrato statu Romano in remedium tantorum malorum divinitus credebatur opportune datus.*

142 See also Chapter IV.

military commander who usurped in AD 260, killing Gallienus' son Saloninus at Cologne.[143] Postumus' revolt established what historians calls the 'Gallic Empire', a *de facto* independent statelet north of the Alps.[144] The *HAb* (33.8–14) provides the most extensive treatment of the Gallic Empire outside the *HA* – this makes it obvious that the latter is extensively indebted to Victor. For example, the *HA*'s author explains the murder of Postumus by his own troops as due to the fact that 'the Gauls are always desirous of revolution' (*Tyr.* 3.7: *Galli novarum rerum semper sunt cupidi*), a sentiment he repeats elsewhere (*Alex.* 49.5, *Quadr.* 7.1).[145] Victor had precisely the same opinion, though it appears in a different context (*HAb* 42.17): 'For this reason, to avoid a revolution among the Gauls, who are reckless by nature' (*Qua causa ne quid apud Gallos natura praecipites novaretur. . .*). Once again, we see a Victorine idea being spun by the *HA* into a sustained theme.

Often, however, the *HA*'s use of Victor is clumsier. It is in the miniature biography of Postumus' short-lived successor Marius that we get one of the most spectacular examples of this.[146] Both Eutropius and the *HA* give Marius a suspiciously short tenure of the imperial office: the former (9.9) says that he was killed 'on the second day' (*secundo die*) of his reign, while the latter (*Tyr.* 8.1) says that he reigned 'for three days' (*triduo*). Two or three days might make scant difference, but here it means that the *HA* is not simply copying Eutropius. More worryingly, neither statement can possibly be true, since we have coins of Marius minted at Cologne, with multiple (competently executed) die series.[147] Even granting extreme haste, this could not have been done in a mere two or three days. As Chastagnol discerned decades ago, a glance at Victor solves the problem (*HAb* 33.12): *Hoc* [sc. Marius] *iugulato post biduum Victorinus deligitur*.[148] This means that Victorinus was acclaimed after two days' deliberation, not that Marius was assassinated after two days. The placement of *post biduum* outside of the absolute makes this clear.[149] Further, *post biduum* can be plausibly interpreted in two ways: 'after two days' or 'two days afterward' (although strictly, the latter should translate *biduo post*), giving a duration of two or three days in total. This line of Victor gave rise to the errors found in the *HA* and Eutropius *independently*.[150]

It is important to note that we can see here yet again how a '*KG* error' arises from the misreading of Victor.[151] It is also instructive to observe what the *HA* does with that misreading, bringing in Cicero's mocking reference to the hours-long suffect consulship of C. Caninius Rebilus on the last day of December 45 BC (*Ep. fam.* 7.30.1).[152] This is not as learned as it might seem, since Rebilus' gloriously short consulship was mentioned by Tacitus (*Hist.* 3.37.2), Pliny the Elder (*HN* 7.53.54), Plutarch (*Caesar* 58.2), and Suetonius (*Nero* 15.2; cf. *Iul.* 76.2), and was later discussed by Cassius Dio (43.46.3) and Macrobius at some length (*Sat.* 2.2.13 and 2.3.6). Here we get a rare glimpse from the inside, as it were,

143 On Postumus, see also Chapter IV; key details are provided by Zosimus 1.38.2. The chronology is difficult, but 260 seems most likely: Peachin 1990: 38–39; Drinkwater 1987: 95–102.

144 Though seemingly not separatist in either intention or ideology – on the Gallic Empire, see Drinkwater 1987.

145 See Bertrand-Dagenbach 2014: 169.

146 On Marius, see *PIR*[2] A.1555; Drinkwater 1987: 35.

147 *RIC* 5.2: 377–378.

148 Chastagnol 1974: 53–54.

149 Compare *HAb* 26.1: *quis biennium summae potitis*, and 41.1: *Maximinus ad Orientem post biennii augustum imperium fusus fugatusque*.

150 As Gavin Kelly has pointed out to us, *iugulato post biduum* is rhythmical (a *tardus*), which might explain why both Eutropius and the *HA* made this mistake.

151 This is a 'foundational' *KG* error, in that it is listed by Enmann 1884: 379.

152 See Rohrbacher 2016: 37–38.

of the *HA*'s limitations. We can grant that its author had all sorts of ludic and literary conceits which informed his method of working, but the underlying truth here is that he has simply misunderstood his source – fantasy is rooted in error.

Error is, of course, usefully diagnostic – where we can show that the *HA*'s text arose from misunderstanding Victor, there can be little doubt that he was its source. The *HA* can, however, perhaps also help us to gain a fuller picture of Victor's original work. Again, Marius provides an example. This ephemeral emperor was allegedly a blacksmith and this occupation apparently gave rise to much amusement. In a very difficult passage (and one made more obscure by textual corruption), Victor tells us about one of the witticisms that circulated (*HAb* 33.11):

> For this reason, it was said in jest that it was no wonder if Marius was attempting to restore the Roman state, which Marius the *auctor* of that same art, stock, and name had forged.[153]

The meaning of this joke is by no means easy to divine. It is tempting to assume that this has something to do with Gaius Marius, an important figure for Victor and one who from humble origins scaled the heights of power.[154] Unfortunately, there is no evidence whatsoever that the more famous Marius was a blacksmith: all Plutarch tells us is that his father was a labourer, but he makes no suggestion that Marius himself practised a trade before his military service.[155] If we look at the *HA*, however, the point becomes clearer (*Tyr.* 8.3):

> He was a vigorous man, to be sure, and climbed the ranks all the way to imperial command; many people named him Mamurius, and others Veturius, given that he was a blacksmith.

The reference here is to Mamurius Veturius, the legendary smith from the days of Numa: when the *ancile*, a bronze buckler, fell from heaven as a pledge of Rome's empire, the king had Mamurius make eleven identical shields to prevent the real one from being stolen.[156] This was how Mamurius strengthened the Roman state – so he was an outstanding exemplar (*auctor*) of the blacksmith's art. His name was thought to derive from 'Mars' and so too was the name Marius – there was indeed a story that the Marii descended from Mars.[157] To a pedant like Victor, it might seem reasonable to say that Marius and Mamurius were the same name. This is an instance where neither the *HAb* nor the *HA* gives the complete story: it is only by combining them that the joke makes sense, leading us one step closer to Victor's lost original and giving us some sense of its depth and complexity.

There are other points in the story of the Gallic Empire, however, where the *HA* is recycling rather simpler material. Marius' successor, Victorinus, was undone by concupiscence. The usurper raped the wife of a quartermaster, named Attitianus, who stirred up a rebellion in retaliation, in which Victorinus was killed. Victor narrates this in some detail (*HAb* 33.12–13), at least partly because he had an obvious

153 This translates the manuscript reading, which is likely corrupt. On the text here, see Shackleton Bailey 1981: 179 and the Appendix, no. IX.

154 Stover and Woudhuysen 2020 [2015].

155 Plutarch, *Marius* 3.1: γενόμενος δὲ γονέων παντάπασιν ἀδόξων, αὐτουργῶν δὲ καὶ πενήτων. The comparison is assumed by Drinkwater 1987: 52.

156 Servius, *In Aen.* 8.664; Plutarch, *Numa* 13.1–7.

157 Mamurius: via the Oscan form Mamers, *cf.* Varro, *De ling. lat.* 5.10.73. For the connection, see also Ovid, *Fasti* 3.259–260 and Servius *In Aen.* 8.664. Marius: Plutarch, *Marius* 46.8: ἐν ἀρχῇ παῖς Ἄρεως ὠνομάζετο.

axe to grind against quartermasters (*actuarii*), a bureaucratic class in which graft and corruption were allegedly endemic. The story gave him an opportunity for a moralising digression that also touched on rivalries within the bureaucracy – it is hard to think of a more Victorine set of themes. Eutropius crunched this narrative down to a bare summary, but his debt is obvious in the fact that, while he omitted the bulk of the story, including the aggrieved husband's name, he included his office, referring to him as *actuario quodam*.[158] In the grand scheme of things, this was an unimportant detail, but anyone reading Victor's history might well have got the opposite impression. What is interesting is that the *HA* has clearly drawn some of its account of Victorinus – including this detail – directly from Eutropius.[159]

The era of Valerian and Gallienus (who died in 268) makes plain something we have seen throughout: that the relationship of the *HA* to Victor is constant in its existence, but variable in its particulars.[160] Sometimes he provided the *HA* with some structuring idea, to which it then returned repeatedly. At others, his difficult text led the biographer into error. Throughout, it is obvious that the *HA*'s author was using both Victor and Eutropius, perhaps even on occasion reading the former's complex work through the latter's influential epitome. What emerges most tantalisingly, however, is the way that the *HA* can perhaps help us to recover aspects of Victor's account lost in abbreviation.

Tetricus

The last Gallic emperor was Tetricus (r. 270–273), who formed, so to speak, a bridge between the age of the usurpers and the emperors of the later third century. Victor's account of his accession has clearly been copied by the *HA* (**Table 8.11**). All of the *HA*'s additions, which give the impression that it is a fuller and more detailed account, are probably fictitious. The existence of Victorinus' son is nowhere else attested.[161] No other source gives Victoria the additional name Vitruvia and it is deeply suspicious: as a *gentilicium*, it is not really an alternative (*sive*) to her given name, nor is there any evidence that it was used by her family (her son was M. Piavonius Victorinus).[162] It also seems unlikely (though not impossible) that Victoria was related to Tetricus, whose full name, C. Pius Esuvius Tetricus, shares no elements with those of her family.[163] It is possible that these are *recherché* details that happen to survive in the *HA*, but it seems more likely that they are just fictional padding for an account taken from Victor.

---

158 Eutropius 9.9: *Victorinus postea Galliarum accepit imperium, vir strenuissimus, sed cum nimiae libidinis esset et* **matrimonia** *aliena* **corrumperet**, *Agrippinae occisus est* **actuario quodam** *dolum machinante, imperii sui anno secundo.*

159 *Tyr.* 6.3: *Victorinus in imperio remansit, qui et ipse, quod* **matrimoniis** *militum et militarium* **corrumpendis** *operam daret,* **a quodam actuario**, *cuius uxorem stupraverat, composita factione Agrippinae percussus.*

160 On the death of Gallienus, see Chapter X.

161 *PLRE* 'Victorinus 1a'; *PIR*[2] P.402. Drinkwater 1987: 65.

162 *PLRE* 'Victorinus 12'; *PIR*[2] P.401. Vitruvius was itself a very rare *nomen*: Lőrincz 2002: 178 lists only two examples.

163 *PLRE* 'Tetricus 1'; *PIR*[2] E.99; the possibility of a connection is not ruled out by Drinkwater 1987: 39, 66. Esuvius is a very rare name, but it may be significant that it crops up most often in Africa: *AE* 1996, 1748; *CIL* 8.24338, 8.16591; *ILS* 470; *BCTH* 1930–1931, 140 (otherwise found in Britain: *RIB* 3.3079, and Rome: *ICUR* 2.5711). Drinkwater 1987: 126 favours a Celtic origin on the basis of the tribe mentioned by Caesar (*BG* 2.34.1, 3.7.4, 5.24.2) and the god Esus (Lucan, *BC* 1.445; *CIL* 13.3206), but if so, it is somewhat surprising that it is so poorly attested in the region. Further, the tribe were the Essuvii and one ought to be careful with geminate consonants (*n.b.* M. Essuvius Empivius: *BCTH* 1900, 15, *CAG* 13.02, p. 407, both inscriptions from Gallia Narbonensis).

TABLE 8.11 – THE *HAb* AND *HA* ON THE ACCESSION OF TETRICUS

HAb 33.14	*Tyr.* 24.1
Interim **Victoria** amisso **Victorino** filio, legionibus grandi pecunia comprobantibus **Tetricum imperatorem facit**, qui familia nobili **praesidatu** Aquitanos tuebatur, **filioque eius** Tetrico **Caesarea** insignia impartiuntur.	Interfecto **Victorino** et eius filio mater eius **Victoria** sive Vitruvia **Tetricum** senatorem p. R. **praesidatum** in Gallia regentem **ad imperium** hortata, quod eius erat ut plerique loquuntur adfinis, Augustum appellari **fecit filiumque eius Caesarem** nuncupavit.
In the meantime, Victoria, after she lost her son Victorinus, having bought the legions' approval for a great deal of money, made Tetricus emperor – from a noble family, he oversaw the Aquitani as governor. The honours of a Caesar were also granted to his son Tetricus.	After Victorinus had been killed along with his son, his mother Victoria or Vitruvia summoned Tetricus, a Roman senator, and governor in Gaul, to empire, since according to many people she was his relation. She had him named Augustus and proclaimed his son Caesar.

This attempt to bulk out Victor is in fact characteristic of the whole of the *HA*'s account of Tetricus. His reign, and with it the Gallic Empire, was brought to an end (not without some double-dealing) by the emperor Aurelian (r. 270–275), the man who perhaps more than any other dragged the Roman Empire out of the crisis of the third century.[164] Eutropius gives us an engaging account of what happened (9.13):

> Superavit in Gallia Tetricum apud Catalaunos ipso Tetrico prodente exercitum suum, cuius adsiduas seditiones ferre non poterat. Quin etiam per litteras occultas Aurelianum ita fuerat deprecatus, ut inter alia versu Vergiliano uteretur: 'Eripe me his, invicte, malis' [*Aen.* 6.365].

> [Aurelian] defeated Tetricus in Gaul at Châlons, Tetricus himself betraying his army, whose continual rebellions he could not endure. Hence, he had even begged Aurelian in a secret communication to do this, using the line of Vergil, among other things, 'Save me, unconquered one, from these evils'.

The *HA* clearly derives its version of this story at *Aurelian* 32.3 from Eutropius (almost verbatim at points: *ipso Tetrico exercitum suum prodente*) and the same can be said of *Tyr.* 24.2–4: they both quote the line of Vergil and use the phrase *ferre non posset*. Nonetheless, even if the *HA* has taken its basic framework and some of its wording from Eutropius, the factual material must originally come from Victor. He alone (*HAb* 35.3–4) gives details about the military revolt that Tetricus faced in Gaul, even naming his rival as Faustinus, a *praeses*:

> Simul Germanis Gallia demotis, Tetrici, de quo supra memoravimus, caesae legiones, proditore ipso duce. Namque Tetricus, cum Faustini praesidis dolo, corruptis militum, plerisque peteretur, Aureliani per litteras praesidium imploraverat . . .[165]

---

164 *PLRE* 'Aurelianus 6'; *PIR*[2] D.135.

165 Faustinus' existence is confirmed by Polemius Silvius (20), who adds the detail that this rebellion took place at Trier. *cf. PLRE* 'Faustinus 1'; Drinkwater 1987: 77–78. On the text here, see the Appendix, no. XI.

TABLE 8.12 – THE *HAb*, EUTROPIUS, AND THE *HA* ON THE DEPOSITION OF TETRICUS

HAb 35.5	Eutropius 9.13	Tyr. 24.4–5
Ipse post celsum biennii imperium in triumphum ductus, Lucaniae correcturam, filioque veniam atque honorem senatorium cooptavit. (*cf. LB* 35.7: . . . correctorem Lucaniae provexit . . .).	Ingressusque Romam nobilem triumphum quasi receptor Orientis Occidentisque egit praecedentibus currum Tetrico et Zenobia. Qui quidem Tetricus corrector Lucaniae postea fuit.	Quare cum Aurelianus nihil simplex neque mite aut tranquillum facile cogitaret, senatorem p. R. eundemque consularem, qui iure praesidali omnes Gallias rexerat, per triumphum duxit, eodem tempore quo et Zenobiam Odenati uxorem cum filiis minoribus Odenati, Herenniano et Timolao. Pudore tamen victus vir nimium severus eum quem triumphaverat conrectorem totius Italiae fecit, id est Campaniae, Samni, Lucaniae Brittiorum, Apuliae, Calabriae, Etruriae atque Umbriae, Piceni et Flaminiae omnisque annonariae regionis, ac Tetricum non solum vivere, sed etiam in summa dignitate manere passus est, cum illum saepe collegam, nonnumquam commilitonem, aliquando etiam imperatorem appellaret.
He, after lofty imperial power of two years' duration, was led in triumph; . . . \<Aurelian\> \<granted him\> the correctorship of Lucania, offered his son pardon, and admitted him to senatorial rank (*cf. LB*: he promoted him to *corrector* of Lucania . . .).	Having entered Rome, he celebrated a famous triumph, as if he were the re-conqueror of east and west – Tetricus and Zenobia went before his chariot. Tetricus, indeed, was afterwards *corrector* of Lucania.	Therefore, since Aurelian did not often devise anything simple or mild or calm, he led in his triumph a senator of the Roman people, who was also a consular and who had ruled all of Gaul with the power of a *praeses*, at the same time as Zenobia, the wife of Odaenathus, with her young sons Odaenathus, Herennianus, and Timolaus. Nevertheless, in spite of being an excessively strict man, he was overmastered by shame and made the man over whom he had triumphed *corrector* of the whole of Italy: that is Campania, Samnium, Lucania, the Bruttii, Apulia, Calabria, Etruria and Umbria, Picenum and Flaminia and all the annonarian regions. He suffered Tetricus not only to live, but to remain in the highest dignity, as he often called him 'colleague', sometimes 'fellow soldier', and once even 'emperor'.★

★ *Italia annonaria* was the civil diocese containing northern and some of central Italy (Chastagnol 1963 *passim*).

At the same time, after the Germans had been driven out of Gaul, the legions of Tetricus (whom I have mentioned above) were slaughtered: their own general their betrayer. For Tetricus, since he was under attack after the majority of the soldiers had been corrupted by the treachery of Faustinus the *praeses*, had begged in letters for the protection of Aurelian.

Eutropius (and the *HA*) attach great explanatory importance to these *seditiones*, but do not actually explain them: only Victor did that. Note also the ablative absolute, *proditore ipso*, and his seeking help *per litteras*.

This is important because Victor, Eutropius, and the *HA* diverge when it comes to the precise detail of what happened after Aurelian had deposed Tetricus (TABLE 8.12). All three agree that Tetricus was led in triumph, then returned to favour by Aurelian, and granted office. There is, however, a divergence over what that office was. Victor's account here is wrecked by abbreviation, obvious in the severe anacolouthon, but the basic elements are clear: Tetricus was made *corrector Lucaniae*, he and his son were pardoned, and one or both of them was co-opted into the Senate.[166] Eutropius simplified this into merely the grant of the correctorship. The *HA*, however, spins an elaborate tale that Tetricus was made *corrector totius Italiae* and then dilates on the regard in which Aurelian held him. Scholars, while not universally persuaded, have been much taken with the idea that Tetricus was indeed the last in a line of *correctores totius Italiae*, perhaps with special reference to Lucania, but not solely for that region.[167] It suits a pattern in which 'extraordinary' *correctores* for the whole, or large parts, of Italy were gradually replaced by ordinary provincial governors with that title, so the *HA*'s testimony has been more attractive than one might expect. This is, however, not the only mention of Tetricus' fate in the *HA*. When we come to its summary of Aurelian's achievements, we get a different account, one much closer to Victor and Eutropius (*Aurel.* 39.1): 'after the triumph, he made Tetricus *corrector* of Lucania, and his son remained in the Senate' (*Tetricum triumphatum correctorem Lucaniae fecit, filio eius in senatu manente*). Curiously enough, scholars have been more willing to give credence to the extravagance of the *Vita Tetrici* in the *Tyranni Triginta* than to this simple and sober notice. Doublets such as this in the *HA* often represent the use of both Victor and Eutropius, but in this case they are in agreement. So, from what source did *corrector totius Italiae* spring? Rather than demonstrating sophisticated knowledge of third-century administrative arrangements, we would suggest that it came from no source at all, save the fecund imagination of the *scriptor*. If one looks at the whole context of the passage it is a tissue of extravagant fabrications. Tetricus was of noble birth, per Victor, but nothing suggests he was a *consularis*. He did not rule *omnes Gallias* but was rather just governor of Aquitaine. *Ius praesidalis* does not actually seem to have existed.[168] Samnium was not a separate province until the middle of the fourth century.[169] We can be morally certain that Aurelian never called Tetricus colleague, fellow soldier, or emperor. It is disingenuous to pluck one fact out of this farrago and call it historical evidence. The reason for *totius Italiae* is simple one-upmanship: just as the *HA*'s author was not content with Tetricus merely *praesidatu Aquitanos tuebatur* and so asserted that he *iure praesidali omnes Gallias rexerat*, so too he could not have a simple *correctura Lucaniae*, and thus turned it into a *correctura totius Italiae*. No external source is necessary: this is just (as Drinkwater has put it) evidence of his 'inability to leave well alone'.[170] So here, as we have seen in many places, the *HA* had recourse to the familiar combination of Eutropius, Victor, and fantasy.

Aurelian

The same pattern of relationships between the *HA* and Victor that we have seen throughout so far holds for the rest of the *HA*'s account of the emperor Aurelian, one of its more substantial lives. Here too we find a combination of Victor, Eutropius, and misunderstanding in the text's account of a revolt of

---

166 On the text see the Appendix, no. XII.

167 Chastagnol 1955: 173–174, with reference to earlier literature (*cf.* Chastagnol 1963: 375 ff.); Giardina 1986: 12–13; Christol 1986: 58–60; Porena 2003: 61. *PLRE* 'Tetricus 1' and *PIR*² E.99 are more sceptical.

168 *cf. TLL* 10.2.876.43–877.42 (Pade).

169 Chastagnol 1963: 366.

170 Drinkwater 1987: 66.

TABLE 8.13 – THE *HAb* AND EUTROPIUS ON THE MINT-WORKERS

HAb 35.6	Eutropius 9.14
Neque secus intra urbem monetae opifices deleti qui, cum auctore Felicissimo rationali nummariam notam corrosissent, poenae metu bellum fecerant usque eo grave uti per Caelium montem congressi septem fere bellatorum milia confecerint.	Hoc imperante etiam in urbe monetarii rebellaverunt vitiatis pecuniis et Felicissimo rationali interfecto. Quos Aurelianus victos ultima crudelitate conpescuit.
In the same fashion, the workmen of the mint were destroyed inside the city. They, at the instigation of the *rationalis* Felicissimus, had shaved the legend on the money. So out of fear of punishment they started a war so serious that having met in battle on the Caelian hill they defeated almost 7,000 fighters.	During his reign the mint-workers also revolted in the city, since the coinage had been corrupted and Felicissimus the *rationalis* killed. Aurelian repressed them with the utmost cruelty after they had been defeated.★

★ The meaning of *vitiatis pecuniis* is not completely clear: our translation is based on the suggestion of Haklai-Rotenberg 2011: 13, n. 68.

mint-workers at Rome, an unusual and severe outbreak of disorder. Victor provides our most detailed narrative of this rebellion, which Eutropius adapted and simplified (TABLE 8.13). In the *HA* (*Aurel.* 38.2–4), this event merits only a brief notice, and that only to introduce a document, an (invented) letter of Aurelian to his (invented) adoptive father, Ulpius Crinitus:

> There was under Aurelian also a war with the mint-workers, at the instigation of Felicissimus the *rationalis* (*Felicissimo rationali auctore*). He repressed (*conpescuit*) this most sharply and strictly, though 7,000 of his own soldiers were killed (*septem tamen milibus suorum militum interemptis*), as the letter sent to Ulpius Crinitus – the man thrice consul who had earlier adopted him – shows: 'Aurelian Augustus to his father Ulpius. As though it were fated that every war I wage, every disturbance, grow worse, so also a revolt within the city walls has created a most serious war for me (*bellum mihi gravissimum peperit*). At the instigation of Felicissimus (*auctore Felicissimo*), lowest of slaves, to whom I had entrusted the procuratorship of the fisc, the mint-workers have raised their insurgent spirits. They have been crushed, though 7,000 of the Lembarii, Riparenses, Castriani, and Dacisci have been killed (*septem milibus . . . interemptis*). From this it is evident that no victory without difficulty has been granted to me by the immortal gods'.

This represents an almost perfect conflation of Eutropius and Victor. Eutropius guides the overall structure and much of the vocabulary. His work is, however, ambiguous as to the role of the *rationalis* Felicissimus, noting only that he was killed. The *HA* turned instead to Victor, and to avoid misunderstanding copied his exact phrase *auctore Felicissimo* (twice), to indicate the man's role as the instigator of the rebellion. Further, unlike Victor, Eutropius did not classify this as a war (*bellum*), nor did he indicate the scale of the conflict, with at least 7,000 soldiers involved. Of course, the author of the *HA* could not resist so large and so precise a number, so he took it over, while misconstruing it. Victor tells us that the mint-workers defeated 7,000 combatants (*bellatores*), using *conficere* in the specific sense we saw above in the account of the events of 238. The *HA*, however, missed this nuance and gives us the totally implausible idea that 7,000 of Aurelian's soldiers were killed (along with, presumably, a much higher number of rioters), a shocking, and certainly false, figure. The letter that follows adds nothing but mystification: it is simply confected from Eutropius and Victor, as its language suggests, with some flights of fancy added, like the invented regiments.[171]

In the *HAb*, the revolt of the *monetarii* is swiftly followed by mention of two building projects at Rome, the Temple of the Sun and the Aurelian walls, and the establishment of a pork-dole for the city's inhabitants (35.7; *LB* 35.6):

> His tot tantisque prospere gestis fanum Romae Soli magnificum constituit donariis ornans opulentis, ac ne unquam quae per Gallienum evenerant acciderent, muris urbem quam validissimis laxiore ambitu circumsaepsit. Simulque usus porcinae carnis quo plebi Romanae affatim cederet prudenter munificeque prospectavit.

> After such manifold and great success, he established a splendid shrine to the Sun at Rome, adorning it with rich offerings, and to avoid what had happened because of Gallienus ever coming to pass again, he fenced round the city with a broader circuit of the strongest possible walls. At the same time, he prudently and munificently provided for the supply of pork, so that he might grant it abundantly to the Roman people.

Every feature of this swift survey of Aurelian's domestic measures can be found in the *HA*, which is obviously indebted to Victor. The pork crops up at *Aurelian* 35.2: 'For the same Aurelian apportioned pork to the Roman people, which even today is distributed' (*Nam idem Aurelianus et porcinam carnem p. R. distribuit, quae hodieque dividitur*). Not only is the wording (especially the rare periphrasis *porcina caro*) obviously indebted to Victor, but the pork-dole itself (certainly historical) is found only in these three texts, and Victor, who alone mentions the infrastructure put in place to support it, was clearly the source of such information as existed.[172] The walls are mentioned twice in the *HA* life of Aurelian, once at 39.2 in conjunction with the Temple of the Sun, but also before that, at 21.9:

> His actis cum videret posse fieri, ut aliquid tale iterum quale sub Gallieno evenerat, proveniret adhibito consilio senatus muros urbis Romae dilatavit.

> These things done, since it seemed that the sort of the thing which took place under Gallienus could happen again, having taken the advice of the Senate, he extended the walls of the city of Rome.

The reason given here for this expansion of Rome's circuit is lifted straight from Victor (*HAb* 35.7): *ne unquam quae per Gallienum evenerant acciderent*.[173] We have already discussed this passage as evidence for abbreviation in the *HAb*: though unspecified, the event referred to must be barbarian incursions into Italy that reached far enough to threaten Rome.[174] The author of the *HA* knew this, since he plagiarised this

171 No other source mentions *Lembarii, Riparensii, Castriani,* or *Dacisci. Riparii milites* were a recognised category (*CTh* 7.1.18 of AD 400: note also *castricianis*). *Dacisciani* also crop up at *HA Claud.* 17.3. Perhaps significantly, Lactantius, *DMP* 27.8 claimed that Galerius wished to rename the Roman Empire the *imperium Daciscum*: the word is no doubt meant to sound ridiculous.

172 Terminology: there is only one secure use of *porcina caro* before Victor (Lactantius, *DI* 4.17.20). Evidence for the pork-dole: Dey 2011: 188; Durliat 1990: 49.
173 Noted by Syme 1978a: 222–223.
174 Chapter IV.

same line earlier on in the life of Aurelian, in a context that makes it clear. Discussing the invasion of Italy by the Marcomanni (in historical reality, probably the Juthungi), he says (*Aurel.* 18.4):

> In the midst of that fear, as the Marcomanni were pillaging everything, huge rebellions were put into motion at Rome, since all were afraid that the very thing which took place under Gallienus would happen again (*ne eadem quae sub Gallieno fuerant provenirent*).

Despite its double invocation, however, this invasion of Italy is never even mentioned in the *Two Gallieni*. A reader solely dependent on the *HA* for third-century history would literally have no idea what the text is talking about here. The idea makes sense only in its original context, in Victor. In both of these cases, as if to wink at his source, the author immediately follows up with another fact drawn from elsewhere in Victor. At *Aurelian* 18.5, he has an invocation of the Sibylline books, probably inspired by Victor's mention of them in the life of Claudius (*HAb* 34.3; *cf. LB* 34.3). At *Aurelian* 21.11, he brings in Nero's annexation of the Cottian Alps and Pontus Polemoniacus (*addidit Nero, sub quo Pontus Polemoniacus et Alpes Cottiae Romano nomini sunt tributae* ~ *HAb* 5.2, *LB* 5.2; *cf.* Eutropius 7.14.5).[175] This latter passage, dealing with the expansion of the *pomerium*, is itself marked by profound misunderstanding of Victor's account of the reign of Nero.[176] There can be few clearer illustrations of the way that the *HA* has used Victor, or of its author's often doubtful competence in so doing.

The other reference to the Aurelian walls in the *HA* is found in a long summary of Aurelian's achievements, which also brings in the Temple of the Sun. Again, this follows Victor ever so closely (*Aurel.* 39.1–2):

> Templum Solis magnificentissimum constituit. Muros urbis Romae sic ampliavit, ut quinquaginta prope milia murorum eius ambitus teneant.[177]

> He established a most splendid temple of the Sun. He so enlarged the walls of the city of Rome, that its circuit included almost fifty miles of wall.

Subtle lexical cues (*magnificentissimum* ~ *magnificum*, *ambitus* ~ *ambitu*) indicate derivation from Victor. The passage also shows the *HA*'s tendency to exaggerate: the circuit of the Aurelian walls is actually a little under twelve miles, not nearly fifty.[178]

After buildings and cheap meat, both *HA* and *HAb* move on to some of Aurelian's reforms (**TABLE 8.14**). The *HA* is clearly close to Victor here, but there are some revealing differences. Victor's account of these reforms is insistently fiscal. He emphasises fines paid to the treasury (*calumniae fiscales*), *quadruplatores* (a very rare Ciceronian word), informers who received a quarter of the property of those they denounced, and the way that the records of both were publicly burnt.[179] There is some evidence in Ammianus that the reign of Aurelian did represent a kind of watershed for tax records.[180] It is possible that in the

175 *cf.* Syme 1978a: 229.
176 *cf.* Syme 1978a: 229–230.
177 *cf.* Chastagnol 1967: 92–94.
178 Lanciani 1892: 88. Dey 2011: 18 states that Lanciani's calculations yield a total a little over twelves miles, but his figure of 18,837.5 metres ('ciffra esatta e definitiva') yields 11 miles, 1,240 yards, 2 feet, and 10 inches.

179 For this meaning, pseudo-Asconius, *In II Verr.* 2.21 (*enarratio*), who also offers the less plausible explanation that they denounced crimes under a quadruple penalty.
180 AM 26.6.7: Petronius, the father-in-law of Valens, sought out debts going back as far as Aurelian, though *n.b.* the reference to *quadrupli nexibus* (Victor's influence?).

TABLE 8.14 – THE *HAb* AND *HA* ON AURELIAN'S REFORMS

HAb 35.7	*Aurel.* 39.3–5
Deletaeque fiscales et quadruplatorum quae urbem miserabiliter affecerant calumniae consumptis igni tabulis monumentisque huiuscemodi negotiorum atque ad Graeciae morem decreta abolitione, inter quae avaritiam peculatum provinciarumque praedatores contra morem militarium quorum e numero erat immane quantum sectabatur.	Idem quadruplatores ac delatores ingenti severitate persecutus est. Tabulas publicas ad privatorum securitatem exuri in foro Traiani semel iussit. Amnestia etiam sub eo delictorum publicorum decreta est exemplo Atheniensium, cuius rei etiam Tullius in Philippicis meminit. Fures provinciales repetundarum ac peculatus reos ultra militarem modum est persecutus, ut eos ingentibus suppliciis cruciatibusque puniret.
Denunciations to the fisc and those of the informers – which had wretchedly afflicted the city – were expunged: the documents and records of this sort of transaction were destroyed by fire and, in the Greek fashion, an amnesty was decreed. In the course of this – against the normal practice of military men, from whose number he had come – he ruthlessly pursued greed, embezzlement, and the plunderers of the provincials, as far as he could.	He went after informers and denouncers with enormous strictness. On one occasion he ordered that the public documents be burnt in the Forum of Trajan to free private individuals from danger. Under him an amnesty for public crimes was decreed, after the example of the Athenians – a topic mentioned also by Tullius in the *Philippics*. He pursued provincials guilty of extortion and embezzlement as thieves, beyond the usual military practice, to punish them with terrible tortures and cruelties.

original, Victor made some causal connection between the revolt of the *monetarii* and these measures. The *HA* ignores this quite specific and technical angle, preferring a more colourless and general attack on informers, *delatores*, as yet another illustration of Aurelian's *severitas*.[181]

This move by the *HA* away from Victor's quite specific context for these measures also leads its author to make an interesting mistake. Victor allusively connects this *abolitio* of various fiscal instruments with Greek practice. In context, this probably refers to Solon's cancellation of debts in Athens, a rather fitting parallel.[182] The author of the *HA* has picked up on the reference to the Greeks, but wrongly connects it to the amnesty offered to supporters of the Thirty Tyrants after 403 BC, mentioned by Cicero at *Philippics* 1.1 (discussing the aftermath of Caesar's murder), to whom the *HA* also makes specific reference.[183] This, of course, makes no sense: neither of those circumstances were about the cancellation of fines or confiscations; rather, they were concerned with amnesty for crimes committed. Misled by Victor's allusive reference, the *HA*'s author here attempted an unnecessary and suspect show of erudition, which really reveals only that he has not understood the thrust of his source. Moreover, this is not even all that erudite, as *amnestia*, a revealing word, shows. In his speech, Cicero refers to, but does not use the Greek word ἀμνηστία, while also avoiding its Latin derivative, *amnestia*. This suggests that the author of the *HA* was using another source for this episode. That source was possibly Valerius Maximus, the first Latin author to use *amnestia*, in his account of the events at Athens in 403 (4.1.ext.4). Alternatively, the source might have been the one used by Orosius 7.6.5, which mentions both Cicero and the Athenians:

181 *cf. HA Antonin.* 7.2.
182 Aristotle, *Const. Ath.* 6; Plutarch, *Solon* 15.3–7.
183 Ramsey 2003: 86.

> So, that splendid and renowned amnesty (*amnestiam*) of the Athenians, which indeed the Senate – at the instigation of Cicero – had attempted to introduce at Rome, after Julius Caesar had been killed . . .

Valerius Maximus was hardly a primary source for events at Athens in the late fifth century BC, nor is it likely that whatever Orosius used was more than tralaticious.

The account of Aurelian's legal and fiscal reforms concludes in both texts with his vigorous prosecution of peculation in provincial administration. The *HA* also seems to miss the precise thrust of Victor's *provinciarum praedatores*, who are surely those set over provinces who plundered them – the *HA* instead speaks of provincials who had engaged in extortion and embezzlement, as if *provinciarum* were a descriptive rather than an objective genitive. Further, in one phrase the *HA* parallels Victor closely, *ultra militarem modum* ~ *contra morem militarium*, and in so doing mangles his point. Victor is emphasising not that Aurelian prosecuted those guilty with punishments that went beyond usual military justice, as the *HA* has it, but rather that he prosecuted such offences at all, 'against the usual practice of military men' – after all, he was one of them. Paschoud tries to rescue the *HA* here by recourse to the *KG*, arguing that it is not possible that the *scriptor* misread Victor, since he is 'parfaitement clair', and so instead must have been reading a more ambiguous discussion in the *KG*. On the contrary, the *HA* really is just that bad.[184]

After the fiscal measures, the *HAb* goes on to narrate Aurelian's death (of which more anon). The *HA*, however, has not yet finished with his achievements. This time it echoes not Victor, but Eutropius, almost verbatim (**TABLE 8.15**). A moment of carelessness here has let the mask slip. *Aurelian* 39.1 (*templum Solis magnificentissimum constituit*) and 39.6 (*in templo Solis multum auri gemmarumque constituit*) are an obvious doublet, but the word *magnificentissimum* links the first to Victor, while the *auri gemmarumque* links the second to Eutropius. What we can see here is the author of *HA* at work, as we have already seen him earlier in the *Aurelian* and in other lives, switching between his sources: copying, adapting, banalising, and often misconstruing.[185] It is noteworthy that while Eutropius leaves Aurelian's intentions with regard to Dacia vague, attributing what happened to neglect, the *HA* converts this into a definite plan for withdrawal.[186]

In the *HAb*, we next come to Aurelian's death, which happened as he set off for a campaign against the Persians. Victor tells us that (*HAb* 35.8):

> . . . ministri scelere, cui secretorum officium crediderat, circumventus apud Caenofrurium interiit.

> He perished at Caenofrurium in an ambush, instigated by the wickedness of the servant to whom he had entrusted responsibility for his correspondence.

Eutropius does not give us the office of this individual, merely saying that Aurelian 'was killed by the deceit of his slave' (9.15.2: *occiditur servi sui fraude*). It seems unlikely that by this date an actual *servus* held

---

184 Paschoud 1996: 188.
185 It is worth pointing out that this passage has been held up by Paschoud 1998b: 270 (*cf.* Paschoud 1996: 178–192) as a 'mathematiquement démontrable' proof of the *HA*'s use of the *KG*. The doublet shows the exact opposite: there is no mythical *KG* that lies behind the *HA*, but instead Victor and Eutropius.

186 *TLL* 7.1.2228.35–46 (Reichmann-Ehlers) notes a sense of *intermitto* as *praevalente vi deserendi, omittendi*, but the examples it provides are mostly compatible with the sense 'neglect'; Eutropius is included in them, but only by being glossed from the *HA*.

TABLE 8.15 – EUTROPIUS AND THE *HA* ON AURELIAN'S ACHIEVEMENTS

Eutropius 9.15.1	*Aurel.* 39.6–7
Templum Soli aedificavit in quo infinitum auri gemmarumque constituit. Provinciam Daciam quam Traianus ultra Danubium fecerat intermisit, vastato omni Illyrico et Moesia, desperans eam posse retinere, abductosque Romanos ex urbis et agris Daciae in media Moesia collocavit appellavitque eam Daciam, quae nunc duas Moesias dividit.	In templo Solis multum auri gemmarumque constituit. Cum vastatum Illyricum ac Moesiam deperditam videret, provinciam Transdanuvinam Daciam a Traiano constitutam sublato exercitu et provincialibus reliquit, desperans eam posse retineri, abductosque ex ea populos in Moesia conlocavit appellavitque suam Daciam, quae nunc duas Moesias dividit.
He built a Temple of the Sun, in which he deposited an infinite quantity of gold and gems. He neglected the province of Dacia, which Trajan had created beyond the Danube: since all of Illyricum and Moesia had been ravaged, he gave up as hopeless the possibility of keeping it. He gathered the Romans withdrawn from the cities and countryside of Dacia in the middle of Moesia and called that region Dacia, which now separates the two Moesias.	He deposited a great deal of gold and gems in the Temple of the Sun. Since he saw that Illyricum and Moesia had been ravaged and destroyed, he abandoned the Transdanubian province of Dacia established by Trajan, withdrawing the army and the provincials, giving up as hopeless the possibility of keeping it. He gathered the people from it in Moesia and called that region his own Dacia, which now separates the two Moesias.

so lofty a position of trust: instead *servi sui fraude* looks like an infelicitous paraphrase of *ministri scelere*. The *HA* seems to give more details, attributing the crime to 'one Mnesteus, whom he had as *notarius secretorum*'.[187] All, however, is not as it seems here. Zosimus gives the name of the conspirator as Eros, with a description that looks like a calque of one in Latin similar to the *HAb*'s.[188] Mnest(ha)eus is not a widely attested Latin or Greek name (unlike Mnester), but it has a suspiciously similar shape and sound to Victor's *minister*.[189] Even more suspicious is that Mnestheus is a character in Vergil (*Aen.* 4.288; 9.171 and 781) and that the one thing the poet tells us about him is that he was the founder of the *gens Memmia*, Memmius being a name of several important Roman aristocrats from the later fourth to the early sixth centuries.[190] Likewise, *notarius secretorum* looks like a real bureaucratic title, but is attested nowhere else: even if it is an official designation, it could hardly date from before the fourth century.[191] Not for the first time, the *HA* can be caught here making up some specific and pseudo-technical details to pad out what it found in Victor.

After introducing the subject thus, the three texts give virtually the same anecdote: that Aurelian's secretary forged in the emperor's hand a dossier of those slated for execution and showed it to the

187 *Aurel.* 36.4: *Mnesteum quendam, quem pro notario secretorum habuerat.*

188 Zosimus 1.62.1: ἦν τις ἐν τοῖς βασιλείοις Ἔρως ὄνομα, τῶν ἔξωθεν φερομένων ἀποκρίσεων μηνυτὴς τεταγμένος. One of the *glossaria* defines *apocrisarius* as *minister secretorum*: *TLL* 8.1004.44–45 (Bulhart).

189 Olivarius simply conjectured *Mnestei* at *HAb* 35.8, a clever suggestion further supported by the fact that the conventional medieval abbreviation for *minister* began

with *mn*; but Eutropius's *servi* looks too close to Victor's *ministri* to suggest corruption. It is more likely that the *HA* derived the name *Mnesteus* from Victor's *minister*.

190 *PLRE* 'Orfitus 3', 'Placidus 2'; *PLRE* II: 'Symmachus 9–10'.

191 The closest analogue is found in a constitution dated to 367, *CTh* 6.35.7: *Omnes, qui intra consistorii secreta veneranda notariorum funguntur officio . . .*

officers whose names he had inserted to foment a conspiracy. There are no decisive verbal links between them, until the end where Victor says (*HAb* 35.8): 'and these men, set aflame by fear, committed the crime' (*illique eo metu accensi facinus patravere*). We have already discussed the resonances of this passage with Velleius' description of Caesar's assassination, which also uses the words *facinus patravere*.[192] The *HA* has exactly the same idea as Victor, with considerable elaboration but (crucially) without the intertext: 'since they burned with fear . . . they suddenly fell upon the emperor and killed him' (*Aurel.* 36.6: *cum exarsissent timore . . . principem subito adorti interemerunt*). To be 'inflamed with fear' is a bizarre, unnatural, and evocative expression: Victor gleaned it from Tacitus, who uses in connection with an ambush that happened during a campaign against the Parthians (*Ann.* 15.4.2: *circumventi ira magis quam metu ceteros accenderant*). It is worth noting that Victor's phrase only really makes sense in the context of the intertext with Tacitus, who joins *ira* (what one normally burns with) to *metus*. The very rarity of the notion guarantees a connection between Victor and the *HA*, but the latter has destroyed the allusion by rephrasing.

Even the death of Aurelian does not bring an end to the *HA*'s use of what Victor had said about him. Victor summarises Aurelian's character with a single word, *severitas* (*HAb* 35.12). This, as we have seen, was the dominant theme of the whole *HA* life of the emperor, evoked some fifteen times over its course. Eutropius takes a harsher line, terming it *crudelitas* (9.13.1 and 9.14). At two points the *HA* seems to acknowledge this difference of opinion: *Aurelianus* 31.4: 'Indeed, the cruelty (*crudelitas*) of Aurelian or, as some say, his strictness (*severitas*) was so obvious . . .' and 49.3: 'as the majority say, in order to preserve strictness (*severitatis*), but as some others claim, out of enthusiasm for cruelty (*crudelitatis*)'. This opposition between *severitas* and *crudelitas*, however, might itself not be original to the *HA*'s author, but instead come from another part of Victor's history, his account of Valentinian I. The case is slightly complex, but worth unravelling.

Jerome mentions the similarity between Aurelian and Valentinian in his *Chronicon* (244ᵃ):

> Valentinianus egregius alias imperator et Aureliano moribus similis, nisi quod severitatem eius nimiam et parcitatem quidam crudelitatem et avaritiam interpretabantur.

> Valentinian was in some respects an outstanding emperor and similar in his character to Aurelian, except that his excessive strictness and parsimony were construed by some as cruelty and greed.[193]

This is interesting, because it is very close to the *LB*'s summary (45.5) of Valentinian's character: 'parsimonious, strict, vigorous, but corrupted by vices, especially greed' (*parcus, severus, vehemens, infectus vitiis maximeque avaritiae*). A comparison between Valentinian and Aurelian is also found in Ammianus (30.8.8), who (as we have seen) also makes oblique reference to the latter's bonfire of records (26.6.7). All this suggests that a version of Victor's *History* contained a discussion of Valentinian's character that compared him to Aurelian and brought out the way that his good qualities could appear as bad ones (and did to some). The author of the *HA* has taken this and run with it, but applied the 'eye of the beholder' quality

---

192 Chapter IV. It is also suggestive that *LB* 35.2 contains an explicit comparison of Aurelius to Julius Caesar.

193 Burgess 2005: 177 suggests that the long clause after *nisi* relates not to Valentinian, but Aurelian. This makes little sense syntactically (for what contrastive idea is there to explain *nisi*, unless it is *egregius*?) and it would also be odd to include this assessment of Aurelian's character only when chronicling the 360s (the sentiment is also rather too generous for an emperor Jerome deprecated, *cf. Chron.* 223ᶜ).

to Aurelian, rather than Valentinian. In this connection, the *HA*'s invention of an adoptive father for Aurelian is intriguing. This fictive figure was supposedly called Ulpius Crinitus, a name meant to denote his claimed ancestry from Trajan, M. Ulpius Traianus by birth (*Aurel.* 10.2):

> Ulpius Crinitus, who used to claim that he was of the family of Trajan (*de Traiani genere*), and who was in truth a most brave man and very similar (*simillimi*) to Trajan, who was depicted with the same Aurelian in the Temple of the Sun . . .[194]

In Victor, we do find a man who was supposedly descended from Trajan and 'most similar' to him: Theodosius. In the *Scholia Vallicelliana*, Victor uses just the same key word that we find in the *HA*:

> It is well established that sometimes the power which lies hidden in seeds bursts forth after a long period of time, just as happened with the emperor Theodosius, of the line of Trajan (*de Traiani imperatoris stirpe*), who, though born many years after, was extremely similar (*simillimus*) to him.[195]

It seems that the author of the *HA* has taken Victor's description of Theodosius and invented a character in the life of Aurelian in order to recycle it. This is perhaps confirmed by a minute detail in the *HA*, which asserts that there was a painting of Ulpius with Aurelian in the Temple of the Sun. The *LB* explains that the similarity of Theodosius and Trajan could be examined via writings about the latter and *paintings* of him (48.8: *Traiano similis, quantum scripta veterum et picturae docent*).

The extensive use of Victor in the *Aurelian*, as in the *Thirty Tyrants* before it, is no happenstance – instead it confirms exactly what we have already found with the life of Septimius Severus. The *HAb*'s chapter on Gallienus and the usurpers (33) is the longest in the text, at nearly 800 words, while the chapter on Aurelian (35) is itself a (relatively) substantial 350 words. That we can here document the *HA*'s borrowing so extensively arises merely from the accident that Victor's abbreviator chose to be less severe in his condensation for these emperors – the more that is preserved, the more we find.

The kings of Rome and the emperors after Aurelian

Victor's influence continues through to the very end of the *HA*. The biography of the emperor Tacitus opens with a description of the interregnum that followed Aurelian's death, including an antiquarian discussion of the interregnum that had followed the death of Romulus (*Tac.* 1–2). As is widely acknowledged, this whole complex of ideas almost certainly derives from what Victor says about Aurelian (*HAb* 35.12): 'and also for him alone – as if he were Romulus – the appearance of an interregnum (*interregni species*) occurred, but much more glorious'.[196] Indeed, as Den Hengst has aptly put it, the whole *Vita Taciti* is little more than 'a series of variations on themes by Victor'.[197] What is less well understood – and

---

194 The idea that Trajan had the cognomen Crinitus is found in Eutropius 8.2.1 and John the Lydian, *De Mens.* 4.23 – it is very tempting to suppose that it had its origin in Victor (since John's account is probably not derived from that of Eutropius).

195 Whatmough 1925: 140.
196 *cf.* Syme 1971a: 237–242; Syme 1978b: 177, 179; Callu 1996; Rohrbacher 2013: 151.
197 Den Hengst 1994: 104.

worth examining in greater detail – is the extent to which, through this borrowing, the *HA* imports and mutilates one of Victor's structuring ideas in the history of the late third century.

For Victor, Aurelian – a new Romulus – was the first in a sequence of emperors who formed a second age of the Roman kings, something he conveyed through a series of subtle links to the 'history' of the regal period. Such comparisons were in vogue in the middle of the fourth century, when there was an enthusiasm for Rome's archaic past.[198] So, Victor says, there was the 'appearance of an interregnum' – *species*, one of his favourite words, always denotes appearance versus reality in the *HAb* – not an actual interregnum, the particular constitutional arrangement of appointing an *interrex* in abeyance since 52 BC.[199] The *HA* has failed to understand this, and not only turns the interregnum into constitutional reality, but makes Tacitus and his ephemeral successor Florianus the quasi-*interreges* between Aurelian and Probus (*Tac.* 14.5). This shows no awareness of Victor's historical cycle, for to him Tacitus was obviously a second Numa: chosen by the Senate, which had taken back the right of selecting the emperor from the *militaris ferocia*, the savagery of the soldiers.[200] This was the same quality that Livy said Numa had attempted to soften by his founding of the Temple of Janus (1.19.2):

> Since he saw that it was not possible for men to grow accustomed to these [*sc.* new laws], indeed that their spirits had been made savage (*efferari*) by military service (*militia*), he deemed it sensible that his savage (*ferocem*) people be soothed by giving up the business of arms.

The one thing the *HAb* says about Florianus is that he took power, without the authorisation of either the Senate or the soldiers (36.2: *nullo senatus seu militum consulto imperium invaserat*). This is reminiscent of Servius Tullius, Rome's sixth king, whom Livy emphasises was the first to rule without popular appointment (1.41.6 and 1.46.1: *iniussu populi*) – Victor's phrase also comes very close to Dionysius of Halicarnassus' description of that situation.[201] There is simply no trace of these ideas in the *HA*.

Victor saw Probus, the slightly more durable emperor of the 280s, as like Ancus Marcius, Rome's fourth king. There were multiple overlapping elements to this comparison. Both were soldiers, both were builders, and both played a significant role in training their successors – their deaths also marked major moment of transition in the structure of the Roman state. In Livy, Ancus was a warlike king, who set out to fight the Latins with a newly conscripted Roman army (1.33.1: *exercitu novo conscriptu*). Victor characterises Probus as possessing both 'a vast knowledge of war' (*ingenti belli scientia*) and skill 'in training (*exercitandis*) soldiers in various ways' (*HAb* 37.2).[202] He further claims that the emperors of the first Tetrarchy had received their schooling in *militia* from Aurelian and Probus (*HAb* 39.28: *Aureliani Probique instituto*). This emphasis on education is interestingly reminiscent of Tarquinius Priscus' claim in Livy that: 'both at home and on campaign, under a teacher (*magistro*) not be regretted – Ancus, the king

---

198 Doignon 1966; Brugisser 1989.
199 On the last *interreges* see Broughton 1951–1960: 2.236–237.
200 *HAb* 36.1: *militari ferocia legendi ius principis proceres recepissent*. Syme 1980b: 277–278 might be right to suspect textual corruption in this passage.

201 Dionysius of Halicarnassus 4.8.2: μήτε βουλῆς ψηφισαμένης μήτε τῶν ἄλλων τῶν κατὰ νόμον ἐπιτελεσθέντων. The broader discussion in Dionysius (4.8–12) is equally instructive. *cf. DVI* 7.5: *quasi precario regnare coepit* and Cicero, *De rep.* 2.37.
202 In the first of these, there may be an echo of Sallust's description of Marius, *Iug.* 63.2: *militiae magna scientia, animus belli ingens domi modicus*.

himself – he had learnt Roman laws and Roman rituals' (1.35.5). Yet for Victor, in spite of his military prowess, Probus' ultimate goal was peace: 'when all had been recovered and pacified, he is reported to have said that soldiers would soon be superfluous' (*HAb* 37.3: *receptis omnibus pacatisque dixisse proditur brevi milites frustra fore*). To illustrate the point, Victor emphasises the way that, after his victories, Probus set his troops to construction projects: 'they were forced to drain his native city with reservoirs and a ditch; for it was being damaged by the soil, swampy with the deluge of winter' (*HAb* 37.4: *ad siccandam lacunis ac fossa urbem ipsi patriam adigerentur, quae palustri solo hiemalibus aquis corrumpitur*). One of Ancus' signal achievements was also in ditch-digging: he oversaw the excavation of the *fossa* of the Quirites, one among several major construction projects (Livy 1.33.7–9). Finally, for Victor, Probus' death represented a major constitutional turning-point: the moment when the power of the soldiery began to wax and the Senate lost its right to choose emperors (*HAb* 37.5). In Livy's telling, the demise of Ancus was also a moment of political transition, for Tarquinius Priscus was the first to aggressively canvass support and cultivate popular favour in his quest for royal power (1.35.2).

The *HA* takes over the key ideas in Victor's account of Probus, but without the faintest awareness of the underlying comparison to Ancus Marcius that is so important to them. It attributes expertise in military science, *rei militaris scientia*, to Probus, albeit in a certainly fictitious speech by the probably fictitious Manlius Statianus (*Prob.* 12.2).[203] Famously, it also identifies Probus' 'school of generals', in Syme's phrase (*Prob.* 22.3):

> He did many feats with his own hand, and trained (*instituit*) the most distinguished generals. For from his teaching (*disciplina*) came Carus, Diocletian, Constantius, Asclepiodotus, Hannibalianus, Leonides, Cecropius, Pisonianus, Herennianus, Gaudiosus, Ursinianus, as well as the others at whom our fathers marvelled and among whom are counted several good emperors.[204]

Opinion has been divided as to the historicity of this claim, even though it is in the main plausible: Barnes, for example, has noted that this idea 'could well be true even if the author of the *Historia Augusta* invented it out of his own imagination'.[205] In any case, the *scriptor* did not invent this out of whole cloth: whatever the status of the last six individuals mentioned – all otherwise unattested, but some of them onomastically plausible – the underlying idea here is taken from Victor.[206] The *HA* also relates Probus' dictum on the superfluity of soldiers no fewer than three times: *brevi milites necessarios non futuros* (*Prob.* 20.3, 20.5, and 22.4). Its phrasing is, however, clearly derived Eutropius (9.17), who in turn had taken it from Victor: *pace parata dixit brevi milites necessarios non futuros*.[207] In contrast, the *HA*'s account of the emperor's construction activities leaves no doubt as to its origin in Victor (*Prob.* 21.2):

> Nam cum Sirmium venisset ac solum patrium effecundari cuperet et dilatari, ad siccandam quandam paludem multa simul milia militum posuit ingentem parans fossam.

---

203 *PLRE* 'Statianus'.
204 Syme 1968a: 171. For a detailed discussion, see Sancho Gómez 2019.
205 Barnes 2011: 28. See also Porena 2003: 107–108.

206 The first five are all well-known and important figures of the late third and early fourth century: *PLRE* 'Carus', 'Diocletianus 2', 'Constantius 12', 'Asclepiodotus 3', 'Hannibalianus 3'.
207 With *pace parata*, *cf. HAb* 37.3: *pacatis*.

TABLE 8.16 – LIVY AND THE *HAb*: DEATH BY LIGHTNING

Livy 1.31.8	HAb 38.3
Tullus, struck by lightning (*fulmine*), burned (*conflagrasse*) to death with his household. He reigned with great military glory (*gloria*) for thirty-two years.★	When, his enemies defeated, unwisely overly eager for glory (*gloriae inconsulte avidior*), Carus went beyond Ctesiphon, the famous city of Parthia, he burned to death, struck by lightning (*fulminis tactu conflagravit*).

★ *cf.* Valerius Maximus 9.12.1: *Tullus Hostilius fulmine ictus cum tota domo conflagravit*; *DVI* 4.4: *fulmine ictus cum regia conflagravit.*

For when he had come to Sirmium and wished to make his ancestral soil more fruitful and to extend it, in order to drain some large swamp, he set many thousands of soldiers together preparing a huge ditch.

The *HA* has, characteristically, both shifted and flattened what Victor says, turning the region around Sirmium's swampy soil into a single giant swamp and missing the seasonality of the problem – in the process, it has lost an intertext with Sallust.[208] As we will see, the *HA* also nods to Victor's idea of Probus' death as a moment of transition.

Victor's sequence of kings continues into the reign of Carus and his two sons, Carinus and Numerian. The death of Carus by lightning harks back to the fate of Tullus Hostilius, Rome's third king (**TABLE 8.16**). The *HA* copies the content of Victor's sentence, but in paraphrasing loses the intertextual framing of Carus as Tullus (*Car.* 8.2):

> But when Carus, eager for glory (*avidus gloriae*), at the strong urging of his prefect, who wanted death for him and his sons in his desire to reign, continued his march forward, he was killed by sickness according to some, by lightning (*fulmine*) according to most.

After the death of Carus, his son Numerian was nominally in charge of the legions on their march home. He died in suspicious circumstances, something that was concealed from the army. The alleged architect of this scheme was his praetorian prefect and father-in-law Aper, who is said to have employed the pretext that the emperor was suffering from a malady of the eyes to justify his travel in a closed litter. Behind its curtains this actually contained his corpse. Victor used this event to link Numerian to his first-century predecessor Claudius, and through him to Tarquinius Priscus, Rome's fifth king, with a sophisticated intratextual nod. What he says of Numerian's corpse recalls his account of the death of Claudius (**TABLE 8.17**). The *HA* once again misses the connection here and its language betrays the influence of Eutropius, although one phrase comes from Victor (*a vento ac sole subtrahere*).[209]

---

208 *Iug.* 37.4: *hiemalibus aquis paludem fecerat.*

209 *Car.* 12.1–2: *quo mortuo, cum oculos dolere coepisset, quod illud aegritudinis genus nimia utpote vigilia confecto familiarissimum fuit, ac lectica portaretur, factione Apri soceri sui, qui invadere conabatur imperium, occisus est. Sed cum per plurimos dies de imperatoris salute quaereretur a milite, contionareturque Aper idcirco illum videri non posse, quod oculos*

invalidos a vento ac sole subtraheret, foetore tamen cadaveris res esset prodita. ~ Eutropius 9.18.2: *cum oculorum dolore in lecticula veheretur, inpulsore Apro qui socer eius erat, per insidias occisus est. Et cum dolo occultaretur ipsius mors, quousque Aper invadere posset imperium, foetore cadaveris prodita est.*

TABLE 8.17 – THE *HAb* ON THE DEATHS OF CLAUDIUS AND NUMERIAN

HAb 4.15	*HAb* 38.8
Ceterum funus uti quondam in Prisco Tarquinio **diu occultatum**, dum arte mulieris corrupti custodes aegrum simulant atque ab eo mandatam interim privigno quem paulo ante in liberes asciverat curam reipublicae.	Denique **diu** facinus **occultatum**, dum clausum lectica cadaver specie aegri, ne vento obtunderetur acies, gestabatur.
But his corpse, as once had happened with Priscus Tarquinius, was concealed for a long time, while the guards, suborned by feminine wiles, pretended that he was sick and that care of the state had been entrusted by him in the meantime to his stepson, whom a little before he had adopted among his children.	In fact, the crime was concealed for a long time, while the corpse was carried along – it was shut up in a litter under the pretence of an illness, lest the wind harm his eyesight.

The final emperor in the sequence of kings was the debauched Carinus, Numerian's brother, who in Victor clearly evokes the age of Tarquinius Superbus, the last king of Rome. As that king's son, Sextus Tarquinius, raped Collatinus' wife Lucretia when the Romans were besieging Ardea, so Carinus, 'unable to control his lust, pursued the [wives?] of his soldiers' (*HAb* 39.11: *libidine impatiens militarium †mulctas affectabat*).[210] The soldiers nursed their rage and sorrow, waiting until after his victory against Diocletian to strike him down (*infestiores viri iram tamen doloremque in eventum belli distulerant*).[211] The terminology here reflects Livy's preferred adjective for Tarquinius, *infestus* (1.42.1, 2.19.6, 2.20.1, and 9.34.5), and his description of how Brutus turned the people's sorrow for the fate of Lucretia into rage (1.59.2: *totique ab luctu versi in iram*). All of this is missing in the *HA,* which instead expatiates in a general way on Carinus' decadent habits (*Car.* 16–17).

The state of the extant *HAb* does not permit us to grasp in full the richness and sophistication of Victor's attempt to cast the emperors before Diocletian as a recapitulation of the kings of Rome. We can, however, at least see a sequence of seven emperors – Aurelian, Tacitus, Florianus, Probus, Carus, Numerian, and Carinus – who reproduce features of the seven kings, though not in the precise order in which they reigned. Tempting as it might be to think of this as merely a literary game of some sort, Victor is explicit in his discussion of the apparent interregnum that he actually believed in what he was saying (*HAb* 35.13):

> Quod factum praecipue edocuit cuncta in se orbis modo verti nihilque accidere quod rursum naturae vis ferre nequeat aevi spatio.

> This fact in particular teaches us that all things cycle back like a circle, and that nothing happens which the power of nature is not able to bring back after the interval of an age.

Unsurprisingly there is no hint of this broader philosophy of history in the *HA*, which instead takes (for example) the interregnum after Aurelian, or the fates of Carus and Numerian, as discrete events. It

---

210 On this passage, see the Appendix, no. XIV. 211 On the death of Carinus, see further Chapter X.

has plundered Victor (and Eutropius) for its account of the emperors after Aurelian, but it has failed to understand that his portrait of the age reflects a deeper underlying idea.

This does not mean, however, that the *HA*'s author was entirely unaware of Victor's conception of history, or unresponsive to it. The most historiographically significant passage in the whole collection comes at the beginning of the lives of Carus, Carinus, and Numerian, prompted by the death of Probus. Meditating on this calamity, the author avers that (*Car.* 1.1):

> The death of Probus shows clearly enough that the commonwealth is ruled by Fate, and that it is sometimes brought to the heights (*ad summum evehi*), only to be dragged back down to the depths.

Not only does this echo a Victorine notion (*cf. LB* 18.3: *ad summos provectus*), but its placement betrays awareness of Victor's idea that the death of Probus was a structurally significant moment in Roman history. The *HA* goes on provide a brief recapitulation starting from Romulus (*ut a Romulo incipiam*), pointing out Rome's alternating highs and lows, and in the period after Marcus Aurelius highlighting only Septimius Severus and Severus Alexander as bright spots in the general gloom (*Car.* 3.4): '[Rome] knew no good after this period up to Alexander Mammaeae, besides the diligence of Severus'. These two emperors are also singled out in a historiographically significant passage earlier in Victor, which begins in an identical fashion (*HAb* 24.8–9):

> A Romulo ad Septimium certatim evolans Bassiani consiliis tamquam in summo constitit. Quo ne confestim laberetur, Alexandri fuit.

> From Romulus to Septimius, soaring by fits and starts, by the *consilia* of Bassianus, it stood, so to speak, at a pinnacle. The fact that it did not immediately slip is due to Alexander.

Not only does Victor betray a more progressive or teleological view – despite the vicissitudes expressed by *certatim*, the Roman state continually expanded from Romulus to Severus – but he also believed that there were discernible patterns repeating themselves throughout history. The *HA*, however, goes on to make precisely the opposite point: there is no lesson to be learned from surveying all of Roman history, except for the fact of mutability (*Car.* 3.7):

> Nihil tam gratum esse fortunae, quam ut ea, quae sunt in publicis actibus, eventuum varietate mutentur.

> Nothing pleases Fortune so much as for those things that pertain to affairs of state being altered by the *varietas* of events.[212]

Both the context and specific allusions suggest that the author of the *HA* had Victor in mind in this digression, but what we get is a moral entirely opposite to the one that Victor drew from studying Roman history. There is no meaning, no repeating pattern, no teleological progress, no terminal decline: there is only *varietas*.[213]

---

212 Little can be said in favour of the *HA*'s Latin here – Magie's translation is helpful in suggesting a direction for any would-be translator.

213 On this passage, see also Molinier Arbo 2021.

★ ★ ★

With Carus and his sons we come to the end of the *Historia Augusta*. The work's chronological conceit forbids the author from following Victor and Eutropius any further and treating the reign of Diocletian and his coevals and successors (including Constantine), with whom the *scriptores* were supposed to be contemporary. The conclusion of the penultimate life, the fantastical *Quadriga tyrannorum*, explains the rationale (15.10):

> There remain for me Carus, Carinus, and Numerian, for Diocletian and those who followed him ought to be described in a grander style (*stilo maiore dicendi sunt*).

This line recalls the ending of Eutropius, with its gracious nod to Victor's *Historia* as the masterwork of Roman history (10.18.3):

> For what remains ought to be described in a grander style (*stilo maiore dicenda*), which we do not now so much pass over as keep back for grander craftsmanship in writing (*ad maiorem scribendi diligentiam*).

In the context of the *Historia Augusta* this allusion to Eutropius, himself alluding to Victor, raises an obvious question. Why, at the height of the chronological conceit, would the *scriptor* of the *HA* copy a line from an author writing decades after the supposed date of composition? Perhaps the imitation is more than simply verbal. Instead, by alluding to this passage of Eutropius nodding to Victor, the *HA* is tacitly acknowledging the importance of both of these authors to his historiographical project.

The debt to Victor

As we have seen, the influence of Victor is one of the constants of the *HA*. It is spread throughout, from the life of Hadrian to that of Carus and his sons, detectable in both sober and factual biographies, like that of Marcus, and fanciful and novelistic ones, like that of Aurelian, obvious in primary, secondary, intermediate, and later lives (to use a classification rooted in Syme's work).[214] Victor provides the foundation of some of the *HA*'s most distinctive features: the speeches sometimes repurpose Victor's own words, some of the letters are fabricated to fill in the back-story to Victor's account, and some of the *HA*'s characteristic obsessions – the theme of the *nomen Antoninorum* for instance – arise from a throwaway remark in Victor.[215] Moreover, all of this can be documented almost entirely on the basis of what survives of Victor's own words in the *HAb*. How much of Victor's work might lie undetected in the *HA*? If the extensive borrowing, indeed copying, in the *Vita Severi* arises merely from the accident that the abbreviator who fashioned the *HAb* left a fairly substantial life of Severus, then the *HA*'s actual debt to Victor could well be an order of magnitude greater than we can now detect. This has profound ramifications for

---

214 See Chapter VII.

215 It is worth noting that the *nomen Antoninorum* plays a considerable role in Syme's ruminations on the *HA*: see, *e.g.*, 1971a: 78–88.

the *Quellenforschung* of the text. If we do not, in fact, have the full text of Victor, and not even the full text of his treatment of Severus, how many other sources do we need to posit for the *HA*? This is a real and not a rhetorical question. It would be incautious to suggest (or even imply) that Victor and Eutropius were the *HA*'s only sources – so eclectic and chaotic a text clearly drew on a broader range of material. At the same time, many of the standard answers to the old question of the *HA*'s sources have now been rendered obsolete. The *KG* and Marius Maximus have been disposed of, and with them must go Syme's Ignotus. The author may have drawn directly on Herodian and Dexippus (given that he knows that Greek authors called Pupienus Maximus, for example), but he may also have found some of the Herodianic narrative already digested by Victor. It is a similar story with some of the factual material in the early lives: it is thought, for example, that what the *HA* says about the Commodian months must derive from a good source, since our only real analogue for it heretofore has been Cassius Dio. Now we know, thanks to the *Scholia Vallicelliana*, that it was in Victor before the *HA*. How much of the rest of the text might also have come from his *Historia*?

In the 1977–1978 Bonn *Historia-Augusta-Colloquium*, Syme published an influential paper, entitled 'Fiction in the Epitomators'.[216] Despite its title, this is really a paper about Victor – with only a few glancing references to Eutropius and a stray footnote that happens to mention Festus.[217] Syme employs a definition of 'fiction' which does not correspond to the ordinary sense of the word, bringing together scandal, anecdote, invented characters, rituals, poetry, heroic deaths, and other things into one jumble, with no particular regard for the historicity of any of the individual facts he cites. For example, when we have an undoubted first-century instance of consultation of the Sibylline books from Tacitus (*Ann.* 15.44) and several from the fourth century, including one mentioned by Ammianus (23.1.7), why ought we consider the third-century examples fictitious?[218] What Syme really means by 'fiction' is 'characteristic features of the *HA*', and what he points to is the troubling fact that almost every disturbing component of the *scriptor*'s approach to historiography is found in more muted form in the *HAb* and *LB*: 'the epitomators by sporadic items anticipate the plethora pervading the HA'.[219] We have documented this tendency yet further – scabrous insinuations, puns on imperial names, recondite antiquarian details, inventive genealogies, a fascination with minor usurpations, dubious ethnic stereotyping, prodigies, prophecies and omens, human sacrifice, the *nomen Antoninorum* – all of these, and more, are already found even in our mutilated remains of Victor's work. What this means is that even where the *HA* is at its most bizarre, that need not entail any deep originality on its part.

And yet – unlike in the *HA* – very few of these features in the Victorine works can safely be dismissed as simply fictional. Syme thought he had caught the *LB* in the invention of a historical personage, when it describes how Gallonius Basilius brought the imperial robes to Claudius II at the command of the dying Gallienus (*LB* 34.2).[220] Syme never deigned to explain in detail why he found Gallonius such a suspect character (a far from unusual circumstance in the 1970s). It seems to have been a combination of unhappiness about the name Basilius (not a standard cognomen), the presence of probably fictitious Gallonius Avitus in the *HA* (*Quadr.* 15.6), and a scepticism about the story of the accession of Claudius II as it is

---

216 Syme 1980b. See also Birley 1996.
217 Eutropius crops up intermittently in Syme 1980b, but is never the main focus. Festus: Syme 1980b 268, n. 7.

218 Syme 1980b: 270, 275.
219 Syme 1980b: 275.
220 Syme 1980b: 273.

told in the two Victorine texts – Constantinian 'propaganda'.[221] Yet, none of these reasons is particularly compelling. Basilius is not a standard cognomen, but it is a real diacritic, if rare in the Latin world.[222] Perhaps more plausibly in the case of Gallonius, it is also an attested *signum*, or nickname.[223] Gallonius Avitus may be a suspicious individual, but there were certainly second-century senators and equestrians with the *nomen* and probably third-century ones as well.[224] There is nothing inherently implausible about a prominent actor in the politics of the 260s called Gallonius – the idea that it represents a corruption of Gallienus (occasionally canvassed) is the triumph of irrational suspicion over basic textual criticism.[225] Even if the story of Claudius' designation by Gallienus is entirely fictitious (a subject on which we take no position here), that is no particular reason to assume that those featured in it were also invented. In fact, we might expect a half-competent propagandist to have used a real person to embellish a false story – the *devotio* of Claudius II, for instance, features Pomponius Bassus (as we have seen), undoubtedly a genuine mover and shaker in the era of Gallienus and his successors.[226] The 2004 publication of an inscription from Sardinia which appears to contain the woman's name Cornelia Gallonia in close proximity to that of the emperor Valerian is also intriguing, though caution is warranted, since no photographs have been published.[227] If this were a court of Scots law, then the verdict we would return in the case of HM Advocate (Syme) vs the *Libellus breviatus* 1980 would at its most damning be 'not proven'.

At the same time, we have shown just how often the *HA* misreads Victor, sometimes to absurd effect: putting the *Vicus Britanniae* in Britain, making Paulus and Gordian III praetorian prefects, giving the usurper Marius a three-day reign, mangling Aurelian's fiscal measures, making Nero expand the *pomerium*, and understanding the interregnum after Aurelian as a literal historical fact. So we are caught on the horns of a dilemma: we cannot safely assume that even the most bizarre claims in the *HA* do not come from Victor, but we can never be sure that the author has actually understood his source. Closer attention to the borrowings from Victor can show how the *scriptor* practised his craft. Sometimes, he took two or three words and spun them into a whole speech, letter, or acclamation. At others, he reproduced extended sections almost verbatim. At still others, he replaced every word but kept Victor's structure. Finally, at times he condensed lengthy and complex discussions into bare and crude summaries. All of this conspires together to indicate just how much of Victor's *Historia* might be in the *HA*: in fact, the extended overlaps that we have discussed above warrant us to count even very minute correspondences between the two texts as showing derivation.

---

221 Syme 1980b 270, and Syme 1980a: 261: 'The name *Basilius* speaks for itself'. On the accession of Claudius, see Chapter X.

222 Lőrincz 2005: 140; *LGPN* lists seventeen instances of the name Βασιλεύς.

223 *PLRE* 'Maximus 48', an urban prefect under Constantine.

224 Second century: II: *PIR*² G.50, 51, T.344. Third century: G.52.

225 Birley 1996: 73–74: Gallonius Basilius somehow derived from a gross misinterpretation of the Greek *Gallienos basileus* (based on a made-up sentence from a hypothetical Greek source).

226 Chapter IV.

227 Girotti 2004; *AE* 2004, 673. Eck and Heil 2021 raise some serious objections to accepting the published text of this inscription, but they can do little to impugn Gallonia beyond suggesting it is a misread Salonina (the wife of Gallienus) – until the inscription is published more fully, it seems unwise to either categorically reject or accept it. They are also explicit (215 and n. 18) that they start from Syme's premise that Gallonius Basilius is invented, which might be thought to pre-judge the issue.

One reason that this fundamental insight has escaped attention is the incommensurate nature of the *HA* and the *HAb*. One is a sprawling and chaotic collection and the other an epitome that is simultaneously discursive and exiguous – the former is always likely to swamp the latter. This suggests that a shift in methodology might be in order. So far in this chapter, we have taken the fairly conventional approach (if from radical premises) of looking for connections between the *HA* and *HAb*, demonstrating Victor's priority, and trying to parse the significance of that debt. That is entirely sufficient to show that the *HA*'s author owed an enormous amount to Victor, but it leaves us in some doubt as to the provenance of the material in the *HA* that has no apparent connection to his work. It might be more profitable to instead start with the *HAb* and see how much of it can be found in the *HA*. If an overwhelming proportion of this drastically abbreviated work occurs in the collection, then it is reasonable to suppose (in fact, statistically demonstrable) that a very considerable part of the *HA*'s extant text was derived from Victor, including sections where there are no connections to the *HAb*.[228] The precise proportion will depend on what we think the original length of Victor's work was – but it will never be small.[229] With this in mind, let us take a second look at the first and last lives of the *HA*.

Carinus

Last first. The *Historiae abbreviatae* treats the reign of the last-surviving scion of the house of Carus, Carinus, in a highly compressed account (39.1–13), most of which is taken up by a character sketch of Diocletian. Yet nearly every element of this account is mirrored in the *HA*, starting right from the moment when Diocletian first assumed imperial office, after the death of Carinus' brother Numerian (**TABLE 8.18**). Gavin Kelly has called Victor's description here 'a case of anachronistic titulature', because the rank of *comes domesticorum* did not yet exist in the 280s.[230] It is worth noting, however, that Victor does not in fact give Diocletian this title, as Zonaras, for example, does when describing the same events – as R.I. Frank pointed out, 'though the title might not have existed then the corps and office did'.[231] Anachronism or not, the care with which the author of the *HA* has reproduced Victor's exact (and unparalleled) description of Diocletian's role before his accession is noteworthy.

The *HAb* next offers us Victor's nuanced account of Diocletian and a comparison of him with Marius (*HAb* 39.2–8).[232] This ambiguous comparison clearly fitted ill with the *HA*'s need to offer something close to panegyric of an emperor under whose rule this biography was meant to have been written. Consequently, it is the only part of the *HAb*'s account largely omitted. Its mention of Diocletian's jewelled sandals, however, was evidently too good to pass up, so the *HA* author switches them to his adversary, Carinus: *HAb* 39.2 'He lusted after the might of gems (*gemmarum*) for his feet' ~ *HA Car.* 17.1 'He had gems (*gemmas*) on his shoes'. Victor's ambivalent portrait of Diocletian's character likewise invited

---

228 On the methodology here (which treats the overlaps between the *HA* and *HAb* as independent samples derived from Victor's work) see Chapters III and VI.

229 For some thoughts on this question, see the Conclusion.

230 Kelly 2008: 120.

231 Zonaras 12.31: ἄλλοι δὲ κόμητα δομεστίκων αὐτὸν γενέσθαι φασί; Frank 1969: 43.

232 See Stover and Woudhuysen 2020 [2015].

TABLE 8.18 – THE *HAb* AND *HA* ON THE DEATH OF NUMERIAN

HAb 39.1	*HA Car.* 13.1
By the agreement of the generals and tribunes Valerius Diocletianus, then in command of the *domestici* (*domesticos regens*), was selected as emperor on account of his wisdom (*ob sapientiam*). He was a great man (*magnus vir*), albeit with the following quirks . . .	All proclaimed Diocletian – to whom already many omens of imperial power were said to have been given – with divinely inspired agreement. At the time, he was in command of the *domestici*, a distinguished man, crafty . . . always of deep deliberation (*domesticos tunc regentem, virum insignem, callidum . . . consilii semper alti*), though sometimes of steely countenance, but suppressing the agitation of a restless heart by self-control (*prudentia*) and excessive obstinacy.

TABLE 8.19 – THE *HAb* AND *HA* ON DIOCLETIAN

HAb 39.8	*HA Car.* 15.6
And the fact that he willed this, it is generally agreed, teaches the prudent man that savagery (*atrocitatem*) in reality is more damaging than savagery in words.	Necessity dragged that man to the savagery (*atrocitatem*) of this killing [*sc.* of Aper].

TABLE 8.20 – THE *HAb* AND *HA* ON THE BATTLE BETWEEN DIOCLETIAN AND CARINUS

HAb 39.11	*HA Car.* 18.1
Carinus ubi Moesiam contigit, illico **Margum iuxta Diocletiano congressus**, dum **victos** avide premeret suorum ictu interiit.	Nam contra **Diocletianum** multis proeliis conflixit, sed ultima pugna **apud Margum commissa victus** occubuit.
Carinus, when he reached Moesia, in that very spot on the banks of the Margus met Diocletian in battle; while he was over-eagerly harrying those he had defeated, he was killed by a blow from one of his own men.	For he fought against Diocletian in many battles, but when the final battle was joined at Margus, he died after being defeated.

engagement (**TABLE 8.19**). This is the only occurrence of the word *atrocitas* in the *HA*, and the author uses it to expand Victor's point: that *atrocitas* of deeds matters more than *atrocitas* of words. Confronted by an undoubtedly brutal action – the sudden and public slaughter of the praetorian prefect Aper – the author of the *HA* excuses it by blaming brutal *anankē*.

When it comes to the battle between Diocletian and Carinus, which settled the destiny of the empire, almost every word in the parallel accounts is different, but the structure of their sentences is similar (**TABLE 8.20**). Interestingly, the author of the *HA* has either misunderstood or deliberately misconstrued Victor's account by making Carinus the defeated party, rather than Diocletian.

TABLE 8.21 – THE *HAb* AND *HA* ON DIOCLETIAN'S ADDRESS TO THE TROOPS

HAb 39.13	*HA Car.* 12.2–3
Thereupon, Valerius in his first public address (*contione*) to the army . . .	Then a huge public address (*contio*) was held . . . my grandfather recalled that he had been present at that public address (*contioni*), when Diocletian had killed Aper with his own hand.

TABLE 8.22 – PARALLELS BETWEEN THE *HAb* AND *HA* IN DIOCLETIAN'S ADDRESS

HAb 39.13	*HA Car.* 13.2
He swore, gazing upon the sun with drawn sword (*educto gladio*), that he was not party to the murder of Numerian and that he was himself not desirous of becoming emperor – with this he stabbed Aper who was standing next to him.	. . . with drawn sword (*educto gladio*), pointing at Aper, the praetorian prefect, he pierced him through.

The death of Carinus at the end of this battle produces another memorable connection: *HAb* 39.12 *is finis Caro liberisque* ~ *Car.* 18.3 *hic trium principum fuit finis, Cari, Numeriani et Carini.* The two texts share a single common word – *finis* – but the structure, the placement, and the thought are wholly derived from Victor. This last point has some important ramifications, for this is a characteristic phrase of the *HA*, occurring on three earlier occasions where the *HAb* offers no parallel.[233] Of these, significantly, the one in the *Maximini duo* 24.1 – *hic finis Maximinorum fuit* – translates Herodian 8.5.2 τοιούτῳ μὲν δὴ τέλει Μαξιμῖνος καὶ ὁ παῖς αὐτοῦ. This provides another indication that the *HA* read Herodian (at least partly) mediated through Victor.[234]

Because of the chaotic and confused condition of the *HAb*, the death of Carinus is followed by Diocletian's address to the troops on his accession, which (as we have shown) almost certainly belongs before that event: an example of clumsy abbreviation.[235] The *HA* has taken this event over as well (**TABLE 8.21**). What is particularly notable here is that the *HA*'s source for Diocletian's address to the troops is ostensibly his own grandfather, yet his account of the event is actually drawn from Victor, as the parallels make clear (**TABLE 8.22**). The absolute *educto gladio* is found only five times in antiquity: in these two passages, once in Dictys, and twice in Vergil commentaries.[236] This makes one wonder if the Vergil quotation (*Aen.* 10.830) that follows this dramatic moment in the *HA* was also originally in Victor. The *HAb* then reminds its readers that Aper's crime was to have killed Numerian, and briefly characterises

233 *Heliog.* 33.8: *hic finis Antoninorum nomini in re p. fuit; Maximin.* 24.1; *Aurel.* 37.1: *hic finis Aureliano fuit. cf.* Paschoud 2002: 393, who adds *Max. Balb.* 15.1 (*hunc finem habuerunt boni imperatores*), which is not quite as parallel.

234 It is also worth pointing out the parallelism between *Caro liberisque* and Μαξιμῖνος καὶ ὁ παῖς αὐτοῦ, which is obscured in the *HA*'s rephrasing of both works.

235 Chapter IV.

236 Dictys 2.40; Ti. Claudius Donatus, *In Aen.* 9.424 (*cf.* 7.526 and 12.287); and Filagrius, *In Buc.* 9.6. It attained some popularity in the sixth century: Cassiodorus, *Variae* 4.27, 28; Gregory the Great, *Dialogi* 4.23, 24, *Moralia in Iob* 9.25; *Lex Gundobada, Capitula* 27.

TABLE 8.23 – THE *HAb* AND *HA* ON NUMERIAN'S ELOQUENCE

HAb 39.13	*HA Car.* 7.1 and 11.1
. . . cuius dolo, uti supra docuimus, **adolescens bonus facundusque** et gener occiderat.	7.1. Numerianum, **adulescentem cum lectissimum tum etiam disertissimum** . . . 11.1. Numerianus, Cari filius **moratus egregie** et vere dignus imperio, **eloquentia** etiam praepollens
By his treachery, as we explained above, a good and eloquent young man – indeed his son-in-law – had been slain.	7.1. Numerian, a young man both most excellent and most eloquent . . . 11.1. Numerian, the son of Carus had an excellent character and was truly worthy of empire, he was also exceptionally powerful in eloquence.

the boy emperor (**TABLE 8.23**). Three of the four words that the *HAb* uses to characterise Numerian – *adolescens*, *bonus*, and *facundus* – are the sum total of the *HA*'s knowledge of him *ante mortem*: indeed, its whole account of Numerian simply consists in giving examples of eloquence (*Car.* 11.1–3).[237] Virtually every word in the *HAb*'s exiguous treatment of Carinus thus finds a counterpart in the text of the *HA*.

Hadrian, once more

Exactly the same pattern can be observed in the first life in the *HA*. We have already discussed the clear use of Victor in the *HA*'s discussion of the fate of Antinous. While the rest of the borrowings are subtler than this marquee example, they are by this point no less compelling. In the *Historiae abbreviatae*, Hadrian's story begins with his adoption by Trajan and his accession, which Victor tells us some people believe was 'due to the favour (*favore*) of Plotina, Trajan's wife' (*HAb* 13.13). Plotina is mentioned six times in the *HA*'s life of Hadrian: the first three occurrences are in conjunction with a form of *favor* (*Hadr.* 1.10: *favente Plotina*; 4.1: *Plotinae quoque favore*; and 4.4: *favore Plotinae*), and the fourth is also clearly derived from Victor (4.10):

> Nor is there a lack of people who assert that Hadrian was only adopted through the support of Plotina (*factione Plotinae*) when Trajan was already dead.

The *HAb* then tells us that Hadrian established peace in the east and returned to Rome (14.1: *pace ad orientem composita Romam regreditur*). This is a transparent sign of abbreviation, since the text has so far given no indication of Hadrian's locale. The *HA* also tells us that Hadrian endeavoured to establish peace, and not just in the east but in the whole world (*Hadr.* 5.1: *tenendae per orbem terrarum paci operam intendit*). We then get a whole paragraph showing how Hadrian did in fact set eastern affairs in order (*Hadr.* 5.2–9),

237 *cf.* Penella 1983b, who notes that this may be part of a broader contrast in the sources between the good and eloquent Numerian and the bad and rhetorically unskilled Carinus (*cf.* Chapter X). On this passage see further Stover and Woudhuysen 2022a.

concluding with his return to Rome with the same words as Victor, *Romam . . . regressus* (5.10). Here the six words of *HAb* 14.1 quoted above make sense only as a summary of a paragraph very much like *HA Hadr.* 5.1–10.

The *HAb* (14.2) then discusses Hadrian's introduction of rites and laws, in the manner of the Greeks and Numa Pompilius. Numa is not mentioned in the *HA* life of Hadrian, but it does have him conduct *sortes Vergilianae*, which yield a passage of Vergil talking about Numa and his introduction of law to Rome (*Hadr.* 2.8; *cf. Aen.* 6.809–811). These same Vergilian verses were alluded to by Victor elsewhere, as we have shown.[238] The *HAb* speaks next of the Eleusinian mysteries (14.4), which appear at *Hadr.* 13.1, and then the Antinous affair (*HAb* 14.7–9), where we have already shown that Victor is the *HA*'s source (*Hadr.* 14.5–6). After this in the *HAb* (14.10) comes the death of Aelius, Hadrian's subsequent descent into madness and summoning of the Senate:

> In the meantime, with Aelius Caesar dead (*Aelio Caesare mortuo*) and Hadrian himself not of sound mind (*animo parum valeret*) and consequently held in contempt, he called a meeting of the Senate to appoint a Caesar.

The *HA* mentions Aelius twice in the life of Hadrian. One of these instances has the same ablative absolute and idea as found here (*Hadr.* 24.1: *Et **mortuo Aelio Vero Caesare** Hadrianus ingruente tristissima **valetudine***; *cf. Antonin.* 2.4: *per malam valetudinem*). The absolute crops up again at *Antonin.* 4.1, followed by Hadrian summoning the Senate (*mortuo Aelio Vero . . . dies senatus habebatur*). On that occasion, according to Victor, Hadrian saw Antoninus supporting his aged father-in-law and decided to adopt him (*HAb* 14.11):

> As they hastened there, he happened to catch a glance of Antoninus easing (*levantem*) the trembling steps of his father-in-law (*soceri*) or father with his hand (*manu*). Extremely delighted by this, Hadrian order him to be legally adopted (*adoptatum*) as Caesar.

This whole passage is taken over at *HA Antonin.* 4.2: 'Arrius Antoninus came there easing (*levans*) the steps of his father-in-law (*soceri*), and for this reason is said to have been adopted (*adoptatus*) by Hadrian'.[239] There follows in the *HAb* Hadrian's execution of senators (14.11 ~ *Hadr.* 24.4; *Antonin.* 2.4, 2.6), and his death at Baiae (14.12 ~ *Hadr.* 14.6–10). The text's account of Hadrian closes with the Senate's refusal to deify him (*HAb* 14.13 ~ *Hadr.* 27.2), which softened when Antoninus brought forth the senators thought killed and so was granted the title Pius (14.13–15.1). While this story is hinted at in *HA Antonin.* 2.4 and 2.6, it is actually (as we have already seen) only told at *Heliog.* 7.9–10.

So, just as we saw with Numerian and Carinus, virtually every piece of the *HAb*'s treatment of Hadrian is incorporated into the *HA*, albeit piecemeal and with frequent and ruthless rephrasing. In the ordinary understanding, the first *HA* life – sober, factual, dull – could hardly be more different from the last – extravagant, fictional, madcap. What they share – along with every life in between them – is the use of Victor. The fact that both of these lives manage to incorporate nearly every word of the *HAb*'s scrappy treatment is the most noteworthy finding of all. As we have said, the interesting question is not how much

238 Chapter IV.

239 The first part is used also at *Antonin.* 2.3: *soceri fessi iam aetatem **manu** praesente senatu **levare***.

of the *HA* is reflected in the *HAb* – it cannot help but be a very small amount in proportion – but how much of the *HAb*, the scanty remains of Victor's *Historia*, we have reflected in the *HA*. The answer – in itself revealing – has enormous implications for understanding the nature of the *Vitae diversorum principum et tyrannorum a Divo Hadriano usque ad Numerianum a diversis conpositae.*

★ ★ ★

This chapter is no more than a first attempt to treat the *HA*'s sources, freed from the grip of the various phantasms that have haunted that curious and rambling structure for so long. While many of the individual intertexts have been noted in the past, the combination is, in large part, *de novo*. The results of this investigation could hardly be clearer: the *HA* is overwhelmingly indebted to Victor and, to a lesser extent, to Eutropius. From Victor, its author took historical material of course, but also ideas, wording, jokes, notions, obsessions, sometimes even whole chunks of text. His work seems to be in constant dialogue with the *Historia*, almost an epic of plagiarism. He gives every impression of having attempted to exploit his source to the hilt. Particularly notable is how often he paraphrases the same phrase or passage from Victor at multiple points in his composition: our incomplete account has documented twenty passages from Victor alluded to a total of fifty-eight times in the *HA*, and there are undoubtedly more.[240] From Eutropius, the *scriptor* quite often borrowed structure: when Victor was too unwieldy, too complex, or too difficult, he turned to the brisk pages of that *breviarium* for guidance. From the two, he sought to concoct something new: he was not always, or even mostly, good at this. Throughout, we have shown the *scriptor* ineptly handling the material that he had at his disposal: mangling allusions, missing ideas, attempting displays of erudition that reveal only the shallowness of his culture. We ought not to underrate the difficulty of the task that he set himself, odd as it was. But we ought also not to assume that there is deep significance to his every idiosyncrasy. Whatever his votaries might claim, he was not always very good at his job.

Impostures

This portrait of the *HA*'s author and his sources may also tell us something about the nature of the work itself. The use of Victor (and Eutropius) has to this point been considered no more than a minor and subsidiary feature of the text's composition. As Alan Cameron put it:

---

240 Listed here for convenience: *HAb* 13.13 ~ *Hadr.* 1.10, 4.1, 4.4, 4.10; *HAb* 14.10 ~ *Hadr.* 24.1, *Antonin.* 4.1; *HAb* 14.11 ~ *Antonin.* 2.3, 4.2; *HAb* 14.13–15.1 ~ *Hadr.* 27.2, *Antonin.* 2.4, 2.6, *Heliog.* 7.9–10; *HAb* 16.5–8 ~ *Marc.* 15.5–6, *Verus* 10.2, 11.2–4; *HAb* 16.2. ~ *Marc.* 19.7, *Heliog.* 8.7; *HAb* 20.22 ~ *Sev.* 1.5, 18.5; *HAb* 19.4 ~ *Clod. Alb.* 1.1, *Did.* 5.2; *HAb* 20.9 ~ *Clod. Alb.* 1.1, 14.6; *HAb* 22.2 ~ *Carac.* 8.9, *Diad.* 1.5, 6.10, *Heliog.* 3.1; *HAb* 22.3–4 ~ *Diad.* 8.2; *Macr.* 1.4; *HAb* 23.3 ~ *Heliog.* 5.1, 10.1; *HAb* 24.2 ~ *Alex.* 55.1–2, 56.2–9, 61.8, *Maximin.* 11.9; *HAb* 26.2 ~ *Maximin.* 13.6, *Gord.* 7.3; *HAb* 33.6 ~ *Gall.* 21.2, 21.6, *Tyr.* 3.4, 8.9, 9.1, 23.1, 26.1, 29.1; *HAb* 35.5 ~ *Tyr.* 24.4–5, *Aurel.* 39.1; *HAb* 35.6 ~ *Aurel.* 38.2, 38.3; *HAb* 35.7 ~ *Aurel.* 18.4, 21.9, 39.1–2; *HAb* 37.3 ~ *Prob.* 20.3, 20.5, 22.4; *HAb* 39.13 ~ *Car.* 7.1, 11.1.

The fact is that there is only one unmistakable reference in the *HA* to a book written after the death of Constantine, and that is the one to Victor spotted by Dessau, an entirely different case. Not an allusion, but one of countless interpolations into the main narrative from a subsidiary historical source. I am sure it never occurred to the *HA* author that Victor's account of Severus might be idiosyncratic enough to give him away, and it is most unlikely that contemporary readers noticed.[241]

This is, of course, absurd. Victor was made urban prefect in 389 by the pious Theodosius; the pagan Julian had put up a statue of him; figures as diverse as Ammianus and Ausonius, Jerome and probably Symmachus knew and respected his work.[242] No historian was as well known as Victor in the second half of the fourth century, everything about his historical work was idiosyncratic, and the true number of borrowings from his work in the *HA* is an order of magnitude greater than previously acknowledged. The problem of the *HA*'s copying of Victor is not one that can be merely dismissed as something that it was 'most unlikely that contemporary readers noticed'. N.H. Baynes' comment in 1926 was perceptive, and truer than he knew:

> I agree with Dessau that the S.H.A. directly consulted the *Caesares* of Aurelius Victor . . . I would even go further: I think it probable that Victor's work may have suggested to the S.H.A. the composition of the Historia Augusta.[243]

In other words, the use of Victor is not incidental to the *HA*, but fundamental to its project: it is the premier anachronism in the text. Compared to it, geographical solecisms, incorrect offices and titles, dubious onomastics, and any of the dozens of other suspicious features that can be winnowed from it are insignificant. Making progress on figuring out why the author of the *HA* plagiarised extensively the most widely admired Latin history of the fourth century – and how he thought that he could get away with it – may in turn shed new light on the nature of the collection itself.

There are several other pseudonymous texts from antiquity that pretend a much earlier date than that at which they were truly composed: Dares the Phrygian's account of the Trojan War, the treatises of Dionysius the Areopagite, and the Cynic epistles of Socrates and Heraclitus, to give but a few examples. Many of these works adopt this imposture for a relatively simple reason: they aim to make their sources look like their debtors.[244] So, 'Dares' predates Homer; 'Dionysius' predates Proclus; 'Socrates' and 'Heraclitus' show that Cynic philosophy was the original, while the Academy, the Peripatos, and the Stoa were secondary and derivative.[245] Pythagoreans were particularly prone to this imposture, attributing Platonic and Aristotelian commonplaces to earlier Pythagorean philosophers, making the former look second-hand.[246] Apuleius did the same thing for Plato, attributing Stoic paradoxes to Plato's dialogues, thereby making the Stoa just another tent in the vast caravanserai of Platonism.[247] Parabiblical and apocryphal

241 Cameron 2014: 159.
242 Chapter V.
243 Baynes 1926: 72.
244 The standard treatment of pseudonymous works in antiquity is Speyer 1971, who, however, gives only brief coverage of these sorts of chronological imposters, mentioning Dictys, Dares, and the *HA*.

245 The Cynic epistles: Malherbe 1977. Dares: Clark 2020, Merkle 1999. Pseudo-Dionysius: Wear and Dillon 2007.
246 Bonazzi 2013.
247 Stover 2016: 85–88.

Christian texts are likewise rife with this device. The *Virtutes Simonis et Iudae*, 'The Miracles of Simon and Jude', for example, pretend to go back to a Hebrew account written by their disciple Abdias, translated into Greek by one Craton or Eutropius, and finally rendered into Latin and arranged into ten books by the famous Julius Africanus, before being excerpted in the text we have now.[248] The Latin version of the 'Life of Adam and Eve', the *Vita Adae et Evae*, derives its account of the protoparents from stone tablets on which Eve had her story incised, which (naturally) survived the Flood and were finally read again by Solomon, long after the books of Moses and the account in Genesis were composed.[249]

Dares is a particularly interesting example here, because he offers a compound chronological fraud. In the letter introducing the translation, readers are invited to judge:

> . . . what they think offers more truth: what Dares Phrygius, who himself lived and fought in the same war in which the Greeks besieged the Trojans, recorded for posterity, or whether Homer, who was born many years after this war was waged, should be trusted. On this matter, the judgement at Athens was that Homer should be held as a madman, since he wrote that gods waged war alongside men.[250]

Homer was, of course, Dares' ultimate source, but one more proximate was Dictys of Crete's *Ephemeris*, a Latin translation of a Greek account of the Trojan war, likewise ascribed to a combatant, which was produced probably a century before Dares.[251] Like Dares, Dictys' account begins with an introductory letter. The writer, one L. Septimius describes to his addressee, Q. Aradius Rufinus, the incredible sequence of events that led to the rediscovery of Dictys's work: an earthquake in Crete during the thirteenth year of Nero's reign broke open the ancient tomb of the Cretan warrior, revealing a manuscript written in Phoenician script. Dares' letter, in contrast, provides no such specific chronological indication, but it does not need to. The identity of the writer and the addressee are enough on their own, for they are none other than Cornelius Nepos and Sallustius Crispus, respectively. Hence, not only does Dares precede Homer, but the supposed discovery of his work also precedes the supposed discovery of Dictys' by more than 100 years. The imposture of the author of our text of Dares was so complete in its success that his Dares would be called the first writer of history *apud gentiles*, before Herodotus, by Isidore of Seville (*Etym.* 1.42.1), writing probably within a century of the fraud.[252] These examples of chronological imposture to conceal true sources cast an interesting light on the *HA*. Horsfall has already drawn attention to the close similarities in method and focus between Dictys and the *HA*: 'fictitious learned controversies', 'an acutely developed interest in names', 'a perverse fascination with names of authors, titles of works, book numbers, and the like'.[253] Perhaps the similarities run deeper still.

If use of Victor and Eutropius is fundamental to the *HA scriptor*'s writing of history, then it is entirely plausible that the whole Diocletianic and Constantinian charade is designed to make the biographies

---

248 See Rose 2013.

249 *Vita Adae et Evae* (recens. lat. *V*) 50.1–52.2 (ed. Pettorelli and Kaestli 2012: 426–428).

250 Dares Phyrgius, *praef.*: *utrum verum magis esse existiment, quod Dares Phrygius memoriae commendavit, qui per id ipsum tempus vixit et militavit, cum Graeci Troianos obpugnarent, anne Homero credendum, qui post multos annos natus est, quam bellum hoc gestum est. De qua re Athenis iudicium fuit, cum pro insano haberetur, quod deos cum hominibus belligerasse scripserit.*

251 On Dictys, see Merkle 1989, 1999; Gainsford 2012; Clark 2020: 55.

252 *cf.* Clark 2020.

253 Horsfall 2008–2009: 60.

appear to be their sources. Consider once again the death of Commodus, with its vivid senatorial acclamations: a reader, and not a critic, juxtaposing Victor with the *Vita Commodi* would have the definite impression that the *HA* has recorded the *ipsissima verba* of that dramatic episode, where Victor has simply copied and summarised.[254] In that light, it is not strange at all for the author to foreground Eutropius' concluding line in his penultimate life: it makes Eutropius and Victor follow in his footsteps. Besides the sheer joy in fraudulence that Syme, no doubt rightly, highlighted as a key feature of the *scriptor*, the imposture has a historiographical purpose. In 1969, Arnaldo Momigliano wrote in a review of Syme's *Ammianus and the* Historia Augusta:

> I am, however, still waiting for an interpretation of the H.A. that tells me in simple words why a writer of about A.D. 395, if there was one, decided to split himself into six authors allegedly writing between c. 293 and 330.[255]

In more than a half century, Momigliano's challenge has yet to receive an adequate answer. This is because of a misunderstanding of the text's sources. If the sources of the *HA* – Marius Maximus or Ignotus – were already a century or so old in the era of Diocletian and Constantine, then it is very hard to see why it should matter whether the text was written at the end of the fourth century or the beginning. If, however, the principal sources of the text date from the second half of the fourth century, then pretending dates between 293 and 330 makes all the difference. Moreover, if the point is to make Victor and Eutropius the debtors, then having six authors is indeed much better than having one, and it is better still for those six authors to rely in turn on some three dozen second- and third-century sources. Between the six authors and their sources, a whole tradition of imperial historiography is spun from nothing. 'A false picture of literary productivity obtains', noted Syme, with an insight even keener than he knew:

> The bleak and barren years of the third century are endowed with an efflorescence of authorship. Another unpropitious epoch, that of Diocletian and Constantine, engenders a school of biographers . . . that is, when the 'traditional date' of the *HA* is accepted and commended.[256]

The *coup de grâce* is to make those sources, like Marius Maximus and Junius Cordus, reproduce the words and ideas of Victor and Eutropius. Suddenly the latter two become simply late and derivative authorities, while the *HA*'s reader gains access to their earlier and more original sources.

A sly, if slightly silly, ruse is thus perpetrated. Could any reader have been hoodwinked if the *Historia* of Victor was still popular and in wide circulation, as the external evidence demonstrates? This question is no different to asking whether anyone actually believed Dictys or Dares over Homer – and the answer to that question must be yes, even in the Byzantine world, where Homer's *Iliad* was widely read.[257]

---

254 No shortage of modern scholars have taken the *HA* acclamations as basically accurate: Hopkins 1983: 15; Aja Sanchez 1993; Aldrete 1999: 131–132; Molinier Arbo 2010; Tacoma 2020: 127.
255 Momigliano 1969: 569.
256 Syme 1971a: 280.

257 On Dictys, Gainsford 2012: 60; Merkle 1989. On Dares, Clark 2020. See also Kim 2010, esp. 18, where he briefly discusses both Dictys and Dares, in the context of the larger ancient debate about Homer's trustworthiness.

The same is true of pseudo-Dionysius.[258] A remark recorded in the *Suda* indicates that some were fully willing to believe that Proclus had plagiarised St Paul's disciple (Δ.1170):

> One should know that some of the pagan philosophers, and Proclus especially, often used the insights of the blessed Dionysius, and indeed his exact words, and from this one can hazard the theory that the older philosophers in Athens, appropriating his works for themselves . . . concealed them, so that they would seem the originators of his divine discourses.

It was not until 1895 that scholars could finally prove that it was the other way around.[259] The author of the *HA* has kept his ruse going even longer. We have a substantial body of contemporary scholarship built on the idea that the *HA* gives us access to Victor's sources, and that Victor – *despite everyone acknowledging that he predates the* HA – offers little more than a crude supplement to what the text tells us in lavish detail.[260] It is hard to argue with such success.

The *HA* survives; Victor's *Historia* does not. But we should not be ungrateful to such vicissitudes of transmission. In the mountain of misunderstanding, obfuscation, and fantasy that is the *HA*, a deal, perhaps a great deal, of Victor's *Historia* survives, still waiting to be quarried.

258 As with the *HA*, there have been rather wild and implausible theories to explain the plagiarism. Saffrey's basic story (2000: 236) essentially makes it pseudo-Dionysius' project to render Christianity palatable to pagan philosophers, while Lankila (2011) sees it as a deliberately crypto-pagan text dressed in Christian garb to keep it alive. The parallels with some modes of interpretation of the *HA* (particularly in Ratti, for example) are rather obvious. No one seems to have considered the simpler possibility that the point is to demonstrate Christian theology's priority over Proclean philosophy, particularly since the early *scholia* to the text make explicit reference to the idea that Plato had stolen his philosophy from Moses (see Saffrey 1990: 240), and the author himself says that 'it is the Greeks who make

unholy use of godly things to attack God' (*Ep.* 7.1080a, translation from Wear and Dillon 2007: 131). The point is perhaps most lucidly demonstrated by the way that the *Book of Hierotheus*, a sixth-century Syriac work heavily dependent on the pseudo-Dionysian corpus, claims that its author was Dionysius' teacher (Perczel 2009: 33–34).

259 Koch 1895 and Stiglmayr 1895.

260 To give just one example, see Paschoud 1996: 176 on the death of Aurelian: 'le present développement [*sc.* in the *HA*] correspond à ce qu'on lit chez Aurélius Victor (35.8) et Eutrope (9.15.2). 'Vopiscus' est plus explicite que les deux abréviateurs, dont le récit est concentré à l'extrême'.

CHAPTER IX

AMMIANUS MARCELLINUS AND NICOMACHUS FLAVIANUS

Victor played an enormously important role in both the imagination of the *Historia Augusta*'s author and in his work: the collection is a sort of twisted *hommage* to his influence, right down to its core conceit of six authors writing under Diocletian and Constantine. That ought to encourage us to think carefully about two other works that have often been seen as central to the *HA*'s project: the *Res gestae* of Ammianus Marcellinus and the *Annales* of Nicomachus Flavianus.[1] The authors of these two Roman histories, both written in Latin at the end of the fourth century, could scarcely be more different. Ammianus is *the* historian of the later Roman Empire, the man whose writings structure so much of what we think about the period and the way that we think it. Nicomachus Flavianus is a much more ghostly figure, but (perhaps in part because of that) the tendrils of his influence have been detected everywhere in the historiography of late antiquity. The current consensus holds that Victor has little to do with either of them and little to tell us about their projects. This chapter tests that standard view, by analysing what influence his *Historia* might have had on them, but also by examining Ammianus and Flavianus in the light of a proper understanding of what Victor had achieved.

The Lonely Historian

Famously, Arnaldo Momigliano's Ammianus is a lonely individual.[2] And no wonder: pre-eminent by quality and quantity among the extant historians of late antiquity, Ammianus has long been treated by scholars in splendid isolation, as a historian without contemporary rivals or comrades – an impression that, as we have seen, he did little to discourage.[3] There is a single exception to Ammianus' image of his own bleak seclusion: Aurelius Victor, the one contemporary historian that he mentions as a historian in his *Res gestae*. Yet Ammianus appears to evince no stylistic tics, no shared ideas, no obvious intellectual sympathy with Victor's work. That creates a paradox, one of which Momigliano himself was well aware:

> In mentioning Aurelius Victor, Ammianus qualifies him as an historian. There is, however, no sign that he used or even appreciated Aurelius Victor's summary of imperial history. Victor's booklet was less jejune than other fashionable histories (such as those by Eutropius and Rufius Festus), but still belonged to that type of 'official' and superficial history against which Ammianus was reacting.[4]

---

1 Syme argued that Ammianus was the main target of the *HA*'s imposture (Chapter VII). Nicomachus Flavianus has been held to be either the major source or the author of the *HA* (Bleckmann 2015 offers an overview, *cf.* Paschoud 2018: xxxii–xxxviii).

2 Momigliano 1974.

3 Chapter I.

4 Momigliano 1974: 1400. Momigliano was far from alone in worrying at this point. Compare Syme 1980b: 274: 'Trivial anecdotes crowd out essential facts in many of these potted biographies. Thus Aurelius Victor, praised by Ammianus for his *sobrietas*, devotes inordinate space to three omens, to the verdicts of the *haruspices* – and to his own reflections thereon'; see also Ross 2018: 319.

To escape the obvious implication that Ammianus saw Victor as a true historian, an intellectual *confrère*, Momigliano was forced to a provocative conclusion, however drily expressed – one that demands a response. It is simply impossible that Ammianus would have accepted his qualification of Victor's *History* as 'superficial', since the one thing he says explicitly about the *scriptor historicus* in intellectual terms is that he was a man worthy of emulation *sobrietatis gratia*. Momigliano (and virtually every other modern historian) might have thought of Victor as superficial – Ammianus did not. The fact that he seems to have hardly used Victor's historical work is much more troubling, especially given that we know for certain that he engaged with both Eutropius' and Festus' *breviaria*, without ever acknowledging them as historians.[5] We have considered already the general conundrum of Ammianus' attitude to Victor, but what he says also raises questions specific to the *Res gestae*, questions in particular of Victor's influence on it. It is to these that we must turn next.

An informant?

It is not fair to say that historians have entirely dismissed Victor as a source for Ammianus. Rather, they have maintained that it was just the man, not his historical work, that was of interest to the author of the *Res gestae*: Victor was a personal informant. John Matthews has put the point with characteristic crispness:

> Ammianus' real interest in Aurelius Victor was surely that, being at Sirmium when Julian advanced upon it in 361, he was able to furnish information about the advance, and especially the attack upon nearby Bononia, which found the general defending it in an embarrassing state of unpreparedness (21.10.6). Aurelius Victor belongs to that class of participants, 'versati in medio' . . . [6]

Let us test this proposition. If there is one place in the extant *Res gestae* that Ammianus ought to have had recourse to Victor's personal experience, it would be his account of Anatolius' administration in the Balkans, since Victor had served on the prefect's staff.[7] Ammianus remarks on how, when Anatolius was in charge of Illyricum (*Anatolio regente tunc per Illyricum praefecturam*), his careful stewardship supported an effective mustering of supplies for Constantius' Sarmatian campaign in 357 (19.11.2–3). He singles out the prefect's care for the *res vehicularis*, or postal service, remarking that in the past it had 'emptied countless homes' (*clausere domos innumeras*), but that Anatolius' reforms (*correctione*) had brought it into good order. This was one factor that led the provinces to flourish, as they never had under any other prefect up to the present day (*ad praesens*). Ammianus presents this unusually happy situation as common knowledge (*inter omnes constat*), which may have been true, at least among seasoned observers of provincial bureaucracy in the middle of the fourth century. By sheer good fortune, however, we happen to have Victor's thoughts on Anatolius' reforms, in a digression in his treatment of the reign of Trajan (*HAb* 13.5–6):

> . . . simul noscendis ocius, quae ubique e republica gerebantur, admota remedia publici cursus. Quod equidem munus satis utile in pestem orbis Romani vertit posteriorum avaritia insolentiaque, nisi quod his annis suffectae vires Illyrico sunt praefecto medente Anatolio.[8]

5 Chapter I.
6 Matthews 1989: 457–458. *cf.* Kelly 2008: 147

7 Chapter I.
8 Victor's phrase, *pestis orbis Romani*, is rare and almost

. . . in order to gain swift intelligence of everything happening anywhere in the commonwealth at once, he applied the remedy of the public post. But in fact the greed and extravagance of those who came after turned this fairly useful public service into a plague on the Roman world, except that in these years the resources have been sufficient in Illyricum, thanks to Anatolius the prefect healing it.

Victor is here making precisely the same point as Ammianus: before Anatolius, the *cursus publicus* was a mere conduit of misery, but his reforms had put a stop to that.

This, however, is not merely an instance of shared information or even shared ideas: there seems to be the ghost of a textual relationship here as well. The absolute constructions *Anatolio tunc regente per Illyricum* and *praefecto medente Anatolio* are precisely parallel. The different verb is due to Victor's medical metaphor, introduced in the previous sentence (*admota remedia*) and then continued through his evocation of the plague, but the similarity of sound and shape between the two is striking.[9] They also both provide an indication of time: Victor tells us that it is only 'in these years' (*his annis*) that Anatolius has healed the problems afflicting the *cursus*, while Ammianus tells us that no prefecture 'up to the present' (*ad praesens*) has been as well administered as Illyricum under Anatolius. Hence in the one passage that ought above all to provide evidence for Victor acting as Ammianus' personal informant rather than his historical source, there seems instead to be an intertextual relationship. This is significant. Ammianus would himself have passed through Illyricum during the prefecture of Anatolius, as his commander, Ursicinus, criss-crossed the Empire – he would have been able to see the improvement in the postal service.[10] Yet still, he seems to have used Victor's *Historia* as his source.

Ammianus and Victor, 353–360

Pro captu lectoris habent sua fata libelli, and the respective fates of the *Res gestae* and the *HAb* have left us with the barest whisper of an overlap in coverage between the two – the seven years from 353 to 360. This is not, at first sight, rich territory for those inclined to hunt for allusion. Momigliano, and Gavin Kelly after him, are right that the evidence for Ammianus' use of Victor is rather elusive.[11] Perhaps, however, that is because the wrong question has been asked.

Looking for Victor in the ample pages of Ammianus is a difficult and disappointing endeavour. An alternative method is needed and comparison to the *Historia Augusta* can help here. As we have seen in the detailed treatment of the lives of Hadrian and Carinus, the correct approach is not to tot up how much of the *HA* is derived from the *HAb* and then assess Victor's degree of influence, for the results will be necessarily exiguous and disappointing (respectively).[12] Even if one reckons up all the resonances discussed in the previous chapter, the quantity is a negligible percentage of the *HA* as a whole, outside the life of

---

certainly an allusion to Sallust, *Hist.* 4.60.17R = 4.69.17M, where Mithridates characterises the Romans as a plague on the world. The richness of this comparison – empire transforming the Romans from disease into patient – is striking. On the text here, see further the Appendix, no. II.

9 Compare the same metaphor in Claudian, *De cons. Stil.* 2.204–205.
10 See especially AM 16.10.21; in general *PLRE* 'Marcellinus 15'.
11 Kelly 2008: 241.
12 Chapter VIII.

Severus (fortuitously). Instead, the question to ask is, how much of what we now have of Victor's *Historia*, in its fragmentary state, can be found in the *HA*? The answer to that is a huge amount, in excess of fifty per cent. That is the figure that matters, for if more than half of a very selective treatment of Victor turns up in another text, then we can be confident that his influence on it was enormous. In the same way, for Ammianus and Victor the thing that we need to work out is what proportion of the *HAb*'s final 300 or so words, which only actually cover the period from 353 to 357 (*HAb* 42.12–25), is found in the vastly more detailed coverage of Ammianus' first extant eight books (XIV–XXI), which contain a detailed narrative of the years from the death of Magnentius to Julian's proclamation as Augustus. This yields a very different estimate of their relationship.

Both historians cover Constantius' promotion of his cousin Gallus to the position of Caesar and *de facto* heir, with particular emphasis on his change of name (AM 14.1.4 *Constantii nominis efferebatur* ~ *HAb* 42.9 *Constantius Gallo, cuius nomen suo mutaverat*). They both also discuss Gallus' cruelty in much the same language, focusing on his savagery and 'violent character', with Victor's *saevitia* and *animum trucem* corresponding to Ammianus' *saeva* and *suopte ingenio trucem*.[13] As E.A. Thompson stressed long ago, Ammianus' estimation of Gallus was no commonplace, yet we find its essence already present in Victor.[14] Both historians also include almost the same phrase, 'by the emperor's command' (*HAb* 42.12 *iussu Augusti* ~ AM 14.11.21 *iussu imperatoris*), to describe the circumstances of Gallus' death. In treating a different victim of the cut and thrust of politics, both specify that the usurper Silvanus was 'compelled' to take up the purple and that what compelled him was *metus*, fear.[15] The *HAb*'s implicit account of Silvanus' usurpation as a series of misunderstandings and missed opportunities, which it never quite spells out, is consistent with Ammianus' much more extended narrative of events.[16] Both texts use parallel phrases to describe Julian's barbarian adversaries at the battle of Strasbourg, *nationes feras*, 'savage tribes' in Victor (*HAb* 42.17), characterised by *barbara feritate*, 'barbarous savagery' in Ammianus (16.12.2). Both also speak of the *decor* (grace) with which Constantius gave the Sarmatians a king.[17]

This brings us to Ammianus' obituary of Constantius II and Victor's summary of his character, which terminates the *HAb* and has much the same character. Here, there are parallels in both wording and structure (**TABLE 9.1**). The structural parallels are strong and compelling, even if the actual lexical resonances are rather slight. The exception is the praise of Constantius' handiness with a bow, where our two histories are so close as to guarantee a textual relationship.[18] This makes it look very much as though Ammianus' obituary for the emperor he loathed drew inspiration from Victor's contemporary character sketch.

13 *HAb* 42.12 *ob saevitiam atque animum trucem Gallus Augusti iussu interiit* ~ AM 14.11.3 *Gallum suopte ingenio trucem per suppositos quosdam ad saeva facinora ideo animatum*.

14 Thompson 1943. It is striking that his wide-ranging survey of attitudes towards Gallus, which emphasises how idiosyncratic Ammianus' views were, does not mention Victor.

15 *HAb* 42.14 *Silvano in imperium coacto* ~ AM 15.5.16 *in consilia cogebatur extrema*; *HAb* 42.16 *per metum* ~ AM 15.5.32 *metu calumniarum*.

16 The usurpation of Silvanus has attracted a voluminous bibliography, largely focused on how it is represented by

Ammianus. Perhaps the most perceptive guide is Hunt 1999. The fact that Ammianus' account is already found *in nucleo* in the *HAb* is a fatal objection to Drinkwater's theory (1994) that the contours of the Silvanus affair were Ammianus' invention.

17 *HAb* 42.21 *magno decore* ~ AM 17.13.30 *hoc decore augente sollemnitatem* (Constantius' speech).

18 To *dirigere* or *destinare* arrows is a rare locution, and Victor is the first to use it. The other instances (significantly clustered after his work) are Julius Valerius, *Res gestae Alexandri* 1.23; Ambrose, *De Patriarchis* 11.49; Jerome, *Liber tertius adversus libros Rufini* 20; *Chronicles*

TABLE 9.1 – VICTOR AND AMMIANUS ON CONSTANTIUS II

Victor	*HAb* 42.23–24★	Ammianus	21.16
Literary culture	litterarum ad elegantiam prudens atque orandi genere leni iocundoque	Imperial dignity	(1) Imperatoriae auctoritatis cothurnum ubique **custodiens**
Hardiness	laboris patiens	Appointments	(2–4)
Archery skills	**destinandi sagittas** mire promptus	Literary culture	(4) Doctrinarum diligens adfectator
Food	cibi	Food	(5) edendi potandique moderatione
Sleep	somni	Hardiness	(5) valetudinem ita retinuit firmam
Sex	libidinis atque omnium cupidinum victor	Sleep	(6) Somno contentus exiguo
Imperial dignity	cultu genitoris satis pius suique nimis **custos** . . .	Sex	(6) castus
Appointments	Haec tanta tamque inclita tenue studium probandis provinciarum ac militiae rectoribus, simul ministrorum parte maxima absurdi mores adhuc neglectus boni cuiusque foedavere.	Archery skills	(7) maximeque perite **dirigendi sagittas**

★ '. . . well educated in rhetoric and with a smooth and charming style of oratory, enduring of hardship and marvellously skilled at directing arrows, a victor over food, sleep, lust, and all the passions, dutiful enough in his reverence for his father, but too much the warden of his own veneration . . . These qualities, so great and so illustrious, have been sullied by his feeble effort in selecting the rulers of provinces and military commanders, the uncouth customs of the majority of his servants, and his neglect hitherto of every good man'. *cf. LB* 42.18.

In one essential aspect, however, scholarship has sharply distinguished these two accounts. Victor's description – probably written while Constantius was still alive – has been regarded as panegyrical, or 'quasi-panegyrical'.[19] Ammianus', in contrast, is patently subversive, making even an ostensibly straightforward list of Constantius' good features an opportunity for criticism.[20] This distinction has arisen partially because of a lack of attention to Victor's allusive methods. Immediately before this, as we have seen, he makes an explicit comparison of Constantius to Pompey the Great.[21] H.W. Bird has characterised this as 'flattery', but the effect might be a touch less favourable if one considers that, as he wrote, civil war

I, 12:2 (Vulgate); Origen (Rufinus), *In Psalmos homiliae* psalm 36, homily 3.3; Claudian, *De IV cons. Hon.* 530; Ti. Claudius Donatus, *In Aen.* 5.519–521, 12.392–397; Servius, *In Buc.* 5.11; 'Lactantius Placidus', *Enarrationes* 12.6; Vegetius 2.15.6; Quodvultdeus, *De tempore barbarico* 2.4; Filagrius, *In Buc.* 5.11; Cassiodorus, *Exp. Psalm.* 44, l. 172.

19 *e.g.* Omissi 2018: 31–32; Kaldellis 2017: 44–45; Ross 2016b: 297; Kelly 2007: 229; Nixon 1991: 122–125.
20 On the obituary in general, see den Boeft *et al.* 1991: 239–242.
21 Chapter IV.

loomed between Constantius and an opponent who was fresh from victory in Gaul, introduced earlier as *Iulianus Caesar* (*HAb* 42.17).[22] One did not need Victor's knowledge of Roman history to know how that had ended. The *Scholia Vallicelliana* further complicate this picture: Victor observed, *à propos* of Domitian, that he had rarely found that an emperor with a penchant for archery was useful to the Roman state.[23] Here, much later on, he mentions Constantius' skill in shooting arrows – an alert reader ought to be able to connect the dots. There is thus no real difference of attitude between the two historians, appearances being what they may. If Ammianus – as seems very likely – had Victor's obituary in mind here, his praise gains a layer of irony: not even Constantius' skill at arms was actually laudable.

That Ammianus did indeed have Victor in mind in composing his obituary of Constantius is confirmed by a significant allusion that comes at its end. In his more explicitly critical remarks, the historian's final target is Constantius' Christianity, which he memorably characterises as a *religio absoluta et simplex*, 'a plain and simple faith', that the emperor had mixed up with *anilis superstitio*, 'old-womanish superstition'. He illustrates this judgement by describing how Constantius' desire for doctrinal uniformity in the Church had damaged the imperial postal service. Bishops were constantly travelling through the Empire, using the public post, to attend endless synods summoned by the emperor (21.16.18), with consequences that Ammianus expresses using the vivid metaphor of hamstringing a horse (*succidere nervos*).[24] The phrase used here to describe the animals of the *cursus publicus*, *iumenta publica*, is hardly the normal expression.[25] Elsewhere in Latin literature, it is found only in Victor, in his description of how (allegedly) the youthful Constantine fled from the court of Galerius, killing the post-horses as he went to stymie his pursuers (*HAb* 40.3; *LB* 41.2).[26] As another fourth-century historian said of Constantius, the apple did not fall far from the tree.[27] In Victor's telling, the career of the first Christian emperor began with an abuse of the public post and the slaughter of its horses. In Ammianus' account, his son metaphorically hocked the entire system in his efforts to force the bishops to agreement. It is worth noting that this damage to the *cursus publicus* was a genuine contemporary criticism of Constantius, though never elsewhere so vividly expressed, which perhaps strengthens the intertext.[28]

The lost books of the *Res gestae*

So, where we can actually compare the extant narratives, we find that a substantial portion of the exiguous remnants of Victor has some relationship to Ammianus. What then of the account of earlier periods? Of course, we do not possess Ammianus' history from Nerva to Magnentius, but cross-references to that period in the extant books do allow us to gain some sense of what he had said.[29]

22 Bird 1994: 205.
23 Chapter V.
24 *cf. e.g.* Livy 44.28.15
25 The official term would appear to have been *veredus* (used over fifty times in the *CTh*); *equus publicus* crops up a few times (Lactantius, *DMP* 24.6, 7 *e.g.*). *cf.* AM 14.11.19 (*iumenta* with no adjective) and 14.6.16 (*equos . . . publicos*).

26 See further Chapter X.
27 *cf.* Eunapius, *ES* 3 = Blockley fr. 13: 'but, as the proverb says, "the ear appears on the stalk"; and at that time Constantius showed that he was his father's son'. The original context is not preserved.
28 Hilary of Poitiers, *Collectanea antiariana Parisiana* A.IV.25 (Feder p. 64).
29 On the cross-references, see Frakes 1995.

TABLE 9.2 – AMMIANUS AND VICTOR ON THE JOINT EMPIRE OF MARCUS AND VERUS

AM 27.6.16	Victor
In hoc tamen negotio Valentinianus morem institutum antiquitus supergressus non Caesares sed Augustos germanum nuncupavit et filium **benivole** satis. Nec enim quisquam antehac **adscivit** sibi pari potestate collegam praeter principem Marcum qui Verum adoptivum fratrem absque diminutione aliqua **maiestatis imperatoriae socium** fecit.	*LB* 16.5: Is propinquum suum Lucium Annium Verum ad imperii partem novo **benivolentiae** genere **ascivit**. *HAb* 16.3: fratrem Lucium Verum in **societatem potentiae** accepit.
In this matter, however, Valentinian went beyond the custom the ancients established and named his brother and son not Caesars but Augusti, benevolently enough. For no one before this had assumed a colleague equal in power, save the *princeps* Marcus, who made his adoptive brother Verus, his partner without any diminishing of his own imperial majesty.	He assumed his relation Lucius Annius Verus unto a share of empire, with a new kind of benevolence. He took his brother Lucius Verus as a partner in power.

We have already mentioned the *devotio* of Claudius II as a prime example of Ammianus' debt to Victor.[30] Another could be his offhand reference to Antinoë as the city 'which Hadrian founded in honour of his *ephebus* Antinous' (22.16.2: *Antinou, quam Hadrianus in honorem Antinoi ephebi condidit sui*). The only other Latin author who refers to the founding of Antinoë and the only other one to call its namesake an *ephebus* is Victor.[31] Ammianus' brief reference to the joint empire of Marcus and Verus in his discussion of Valentinian's promotion of Valens to joint Augustus parallels both the *HAb* and *LB* (27.6.16) (TABLE 9.2). As we have seen, Victor *societas potentiae* is a direct reflection of Dio's characterisation of the novel political arrangement, which in turn suggests that Ammianus' *socius* (*imperatoriae maiestatis*) is a reflection of Victor's phrasing.[32] In his treatment of Caracalla's reign, Victor introduced the Alamanni to history as a *gens populosa*, a learned gloss of their name, derived from Greek authorities.[33] When Ammianus describes the Alamanni before the battle of Strasbourg (16.12.6), the same phase crops up. Another example is the death of the emperor Decius and his son in battle against the Goths in the dark days of the middle of the third century. For obvious reasons, Ammianus mentions them twice in the final book, as he contemplated another Gothic war that was so damaging to the Empire (31.5.16, 13.13):

The emperors Decii, father and son, fell (*ceciderunt*) fighting the barbarians.

We have learned that Decius fighting fiercely with the barbarians was laid low by a fall from his horse . . . and thrown into a swamp, he could not emerge and could not be found (*abiectumque in paludem nec emergere potuisse nec inveniri*).

---

30 Chapter IV.
31 *HAb* 14.7: *urbem conditam eius nomine aut locasse ephebo statuas*. See also Chapter VIII.

32 See Chapter IV.
33 Chapter IV.

The first of these uses the same verb as that found twice in the *HAb* on the emperors' fates (29.4: *cecidere*; 5: *cecidisse in acie*). More significantly, the second is extremely close to the tale of the same events in the *LB* (29.3): 'In barbarian territory, in the midst of the chaotic mêlée, he sank in the swirls of a swamp (*gurgite paludis submersus*), so that not even his corpse could be found (*potuerit inveniri*)'. It is true that a very similar account is found in two later Greek historians – Zosimus and Zonaras – but Ammianus is linked closely to the *LB* by vocabulary (*paludis ~ paludem*, *submersus ~ emergere*, *nec inveniri*).[34] More significantly, his account agrees specifically with Victor's in having two Decii (unlike Zosimus) and making only one of them sink into the mire (unlike Zonaras). This is an impressive list given the small number and limited extent of the cross-references.

Still more telling is something that Ammianus says about the emperor Diocletian. In a discussion of the court ceremony of *adoratio*, he remarks that (15.5.18):

> Diocletianus enim Augustus omnium primus extero ritu et regio more instituit adorari, cum semper antea ad similitudinem iudicum salutatos principes legerimus.

> Diocletian Augustus was the first of all to command that he be adored, using a foreign custom and as if he were a king, since I have read that all the emperors before were always greeted like magistrates.

Precisely the same idea is found also in Jerome's *Chronicon* (296ᶜ), though he combines it with Diocletian's sartorial innovations:

> Primus Diocletianus adorari se ut deum iussit, et gemmas vestibus calceamentisque inseri, cum ante eum omnes imperatores in modum iudicum salutarentur.

> Diocletian was the first to order that he be adored like a god and that gems be fixed to his clothing and shoes, when all the emperors before him were saluted after the fashion of magistrates.

There is no question that these passages must have some textual relationship (*primus, adorari, antea ~ ante eum*; *ad similitudinem iudicum ~ in modum iudicum*), and Ammianus is explicit (*legerimus*) that he was drawing on a written source. They are both very close to Eutropius' description of the same subject.[35] His *breviarium*, however, lacks the crucial detail that emperors were greeted *like magistrates*. For this reason, these passages have been thought to offer one of the strongest proofs for Jerome's and Ammianus' use of a Eutropius-like *Kaisergeschichte*.[36]

Of course, as we have shown, this is the result of an unsound method – instead, the source of all three is Victor. Compare *HAb* 39.4:

> Namque se primus omnium Caligulam post Domitianumque dominum palam dici passus et adorari se appellarique uti deum.

> For he was the first of all the emperors after Caligula and Domitian who allowed himself to be publicly called 'master', and to be worshipped and acclaimed as a god.

---

34 Zosimus 1.23.3; Zonaras 12.20.

35 Eutropius 9.26: *primus regiae consuetudinis formam magis quam Romanae libertatis invexerit adorarique se iussit, cum ante eum cuncti salutarentur.*

36 Burgess 1995a: 366 *e.g.*

Ammianus and Jerome have different verbatim overlaps with the *HAb* (*primus omnium* in the former, *ut[i] deum* in the latter). More importantly, the underlying idea in both is original to Victor – a point he made in dialogue with Pliny's *Panegyricus*, as we have seen.[37] Confirmation that Victor is the original here can be found in what Jerome goes on to say about imperial clothing: that earlier emperors had merely exceeded common clothing, *privatus habitus*, by a purple mantle (*et chlamydem tantum purpuream a privato habitu plus haberent*). While related to Eutropius, the key idea there comes from the same passage of Victor (*HAb* 39.6: *communem habitum supergressi*), who in turn had taken it from Sallust's description of Marius.[38] All of this points towards the conclusion that Ammianus' discussion of Diocletian – both the extant brief mention at 15.5.18 and by extension the treatment in the lost books – made use of Victor's work. There is a small but telling confirmation of this in the fact that Ammianus (19.11.4) and Victor (*HAb* 40.10) provide the information that the province of Valeria was named for Diocletian's daughter, the wife of Galerius – they are the only two sources to make this explicit.

The example of Diocletian's ceremonial inclinations is particularly revealing because it is not often that we can triangulate between so many different sources to see Victor's role so clearly. When, elsewhere, we have thinner material, it would be wise to keep this in mind. It also helps to illustrate that Ammianus seems to have made use of Victor throughout the lost portion of his work: from Hadrian, close to its beginning, right down to Diocletian, whose reign had opened the century in which Ammianus lived and which he described in such great detail.

Julian to Valentinian

So far, we have focused on the connections between Ammianus and the *HAb* – the results are impressive, given how little material there is on which to base them. The *HAb*, however, is not our only witness to Victor's *Historia*. We have already seen how one of the *Scholia Vallicelliana* sheds new light on Ammianus' view of Constantius. Another is equally revealing. Ammianus describes Julian as 'most similar to Trajan (*Traiani simillimus*) in the glorious progress of his campaigns' (16.1.4). The superlative is striking: it is the only one used in this section, a list of comparisons to *boni principes*. The only other place in all of ancient literature where someone is described as *simillimus* to Trajan is in the *HA*, as we have seen, and the *Scholia*.[39] In the latter, it is Theodosius who is compared to the Spanish emperor, and Victor used a sophisticated intertext with Cicero to describe how in certain stocks (*stirpibus*) there is a hidden power of seeds to blossom after a long period of dormancy.[40] Ammianus also follows up his comparison of Julian to Trajan with a reference to a Ciceronian metaphor about trees: 'as the authority of Cicero teaches us, "the full height of all arts delights, just as with trees, but not the roots and stock (*stirpes*) in the same way"'.[41] Ammianus' allusion here may well be subversive. Given the widespread (and, indeed, officially

---

37 Chapter IV.
38 Eutropius 9.26: *Nam prius imperii insigne in chlamyde purpurea tantum erat, reliqua communia.* Stover and Woudhuysen 2020 [2015].
39 Chapters VIII and V.
40 See Chapter V, p. 174.
41 AM 16.1.5. The reference is to *Orator* 147.

encouraged) comparison between Trajan and the reigning Emperor Theodosius, suggesting that another emperor was in fact the 'most similar' to Trajan may have been a deliberate provocation.[42]

There are also significant and sustained overlaps between Ammianus and the *LB*, which (ending as it does in 395) has a much greater degree of chronological continuity with the extant *Res gestae* (finishing in 378) than the *HAb*.[43] They share a string of rather striking parallels on the era of the joint reign of Constantius II and Julian, where the *HAb* and Ammianus (as we have seen) are closely linked. Both speak of *acervi* (heaps) of Alamannic dead after the battle of Strasbourg in 357, a surprisingly rare usage in antiquity.[44] They tell us also that Constantius II was sleepless in the days before his death and locate Mopsucrene (the *statio* where he died) 'at the foot of Mt Taurus'.[45] They also both critique the way that the dead emperor was under the thumb of his wives, eunuchs, and courtiers, a tricolon other Latin sources omit.[46] They both say Julian saw fire in the heavens the day before his death and also both tell us, with one significant verbal overlap, that he entered his final combat defended only by a shield (AM 25.3.3 *scuto inter tumultum* **arrepto** ~ *LB* 43.2 **arrepto** *tantum clipeo*).[47] They both have Julian worry on his deathbed that by nominating a successor he might expose him to danger (*LB* 43.4; AM 25.3.20). They also both conclude by specifying that he died *medio noctis*, 'in the middle of the night' (*LB* 43.4; AM 25.3.23). In reflecting on his reign, they describe him as *superstitiosus*.[48] Ammianus does this with a comparison to Hadrian, using a phrase describing his inclination towards divination very much like Victor's (preserved in the *HAb*).[49]

The parallels extend beyond the death of Julian. Ammianus and the *LB* both report that Varronianus, the father of the short-lived emperor Jovian, had a dream in which the future of his family was revealed to him: the details are different, but it looks very much as though they go back to the same common source.[50] The *Res gestae* and the *LB* are the only two texts to describe how Gratian the elder (father of Valentinian and Valens) was nicknamed *funarius* ('rope-man') because of a famous incident in which he repelled some soldiers who were trying to take a rope from him (*LB* 45.2; AM 30.7.2).

The obituary of Valentinian I is, however, a still more significant, though not uncomplicated, example of the way that Ammianus used Victor. Both Jerome and Ammianus compare the Pannonian emperor to Aurelian – we have already discussed how this idea is likely to go back to Victor.[51] Unlike Jerome, however, Ammianus also links Valentinian to Hadrian (30.8.10):

---

42 The evidence for contemporary comparisons between Theodosius and Trajan is conveniently assembled in Hebblewhite 2020: 25, n. 2.

43 Schlumberger 1974: 208–232 offered a systematic survey of these connections from Constantius II to Theodosius, though denying any direct link between the two.

44 *LB* 42.14; AM 16.12.53, 63. Livy speaks twice of *acervi caesorum* (22.48.3, 23.15.8), as does Ammianus thrice (19.1.9, 11.14, 31.13.6) and *cf.* Firmicus Maternus, *De errore* 20.7. Nazarius (*Pan. Lat.* 4.30.1) has *acervi corporum*.

45 *LB* 42.17; AM 21.14.1. *LB* 42.17: *in radicibus Tauri montis apud Mopsocrenen*; AM 21.15.2: *Mobsucrenas . . . sub Tauri montis radicibus*. No other Latin source (Eutropius 10.15.2 or Jerome, *Chron.* 242[b] e.g.) gives this detail.

46 *LB* 42.19: *Spadonum aulicorumque amori deditus et uxorum*; AM 21.16.16: *uxoribus et spadonum gracilentis uocibus et palatinis quibusdam nimium quantum addictus. . . cf.*

47 Fire in heaven: *LB* 43.8.

48 *LB* 43.7; AM 25.4.17. A criticism noticeably not in Eutropius 10.16.3.

49 AM 25.4.17 *praesagiorum sciscitationi nimiae deditus, ut aequiperare videretur in hac parte principem Hadrianum* ~ *HAb* 14.8 *Hadriano cupiente fatum producere. cf. HAb* 26.4 (on Gordian I and divination): *huius scientiae usu immodice prudens erat*; and 39.48 (on Diocletian): *imminentium scrutator.*

50 *LB* 44.2; AM 25.10.16. In the former Varronianus is told to call his unborn son Jovian, and in the latter he is promised the consulship – is there a connection to the cult of Zeus Hypatos/Jupiter Consul (suspiciously, *HA Quadr.* 3.4 features a *Iovem consulem vel consulentem*)?

51 Chapter VIII.

Eutropius 1.15.12: *nimium amicis et familiaribus credens, mox etiam uxoribus deditior.*

> Besides this, the aforementioned emperor seethed inwardly with envy, and knowing that the majority of vices often assume the appearance of virtues, he was always quick to mention that *livor* against severity is the inseparable companion of the correct exercise of power. As those of the highest rank always think everything is permitted to them and are quite prone to suspect their opponents and to overthrow their betters, so he hated the well-dressed, the learned, the wealthy, the noble; and he carped at the brave, that he alone might seem to be distinguished in the gentle arts. It was with this vice, I have read (*legimus*), that Hadrian burned (*exarsisse*).

The core of this comparison is dissimulation: like Hadrian, Valentinian masked his own inadequacies and exaggerated his virtues through detraction of the brave, the learned, and those who possessed other good qualities (including the well dressed). This matches the, at best ambiguous, characterisation of Hadrian in Victor. The *LB*'s Hadrian is talented to be sure, in music, singing, geometry, painting, and sculpture, but these talents exist alongside a darker strain in his nature (14.6):

> He was various, manifold, many-formed . . . checking the impulse of his mind by a certain device, he artfully concealed his baleful, envying, and desirous nature, his insolence in his manner of self-presentation, simulating self-control, easygoing-ness, and clemency, and concealing the passion for glory with which he burned (*flagrabat*).

This is precisely the quality in Hadrian to which Ammianus is referring in the comparison of Valentinian to him – note also that in both texts the emperors 'burn' with this particular vice (*exarsisse* ~ *flagrabat*).[52] Once again, Ammianus is explicit that he was using a written source here (*legimus*).

It is not only the characterisation of Hadrian that Ammianus owed to Victor, but the very idea of comparing Valentinian to him. The *LB* notes that Valentinian (45.6):

> Et in his, quae memoraturus sum, Hadriano proximus: pingere venustissime, meminisse, nova arma meditari, fingere cera seu limo simulacra.

> And in those matters, which I will mention, he was very similar to Hadrian: he painted most charmingly, had a good memory, devised new armaments, and sculpted in wax and clay.

Ammianus provides this same list in his enumeration of Valentinian's virtues (30.9.4):

> Venusteque pingens et fingens et novorum inventor armorum: memoria . . . incitato.

> He painted charmingly, and sculpted and was an inventor of new armaments, with a good memory.[53]

There is one superficial difference between Victor and Ammianus on this point. Victor is outwardly positive – he is comparing their skill in craftsmanship. Ammianus is explicitly negative – Valentinian shares a vice with Hadrian. Was the use of this comparison to Hadrian to criticise Valentinian also Victor's, or was that an innovation by Ammianus? Given the menacing and dark portrayal of Hadrian in Victor, it seems at least possible that he meant it critically, even if he did not say that in so many words. Perhaps Ammianus could read between the lines.

---

52 Compare also the treatment of Hadrian's character in the *HA* (see Chapter V).

53 It is worth noting that the qualities in these characterisations are hardly standard tropes of panegyric.

What remains of Victor's history does not afford us his complete picture of either Hadrian or Valentinian's reign, or of its relationship to Ammianus, so while we can be certain that there is an important connection here, it is hard to be precise about its nature and extent. There is one other point that perhaps helps us to round out the picture. Michael Kulikowski has drawn attention to a fascinating and subtle link between Ammianus' depiction of the events immediately following Valentinian's accession (26.4.5) and those immediately following Hadrian's in the *HA* (*Hadr.* 5.1–4). Ammianus, Kulikowski argues:

> when he came to describe the disaster that descended upon the world with the death of Julian, borrowed a motif and a method of casting aspersion from a suggestive parallel . . . which is today extant in the *Vita Hadriani*. A great conquering emperor had died after invading the East. His successor had relinquished Roman territory ignominiously in the aftermath of the hero's death, and upon that followed barbarian devastation.[54]

This is plausible and persuasive, even if the point is not fully worked out. What has been omitted in the ellipses are the three words 'in Marius Maximus', Ammianus' putative source. Besides the general objections to the Marius Maximus thesis that one might raise, we have argued that, on the contrary, this paragraph of the *HA* in particular bears tell-tale signs of having been copied from Victor.[55] That in turn suggests, along with all of our other evidence, that Victor's *Historia* inspired the way in which Ammianus compared Valentinian's reign to Hadrian's, a comparison as subtle and multifaceted as the emperors in question themselves.

As we have already seen with the *HAb*, the *LB* shows that Ammianus turned to Victor not only for points of detail, but also for structuring ideas.

Ammianus' style

All of this demonstrates that Ammianus really did think of Victor as a true *historicus*, that is, as a worthy source for his history, one to be drawn to the reader's attention, not half-concealed in allusion. It is worth inquiring, then, whether he used him also as a *scriptor*: a model of style and composition. Bruno Bleckmann has insightfully observed that Ammianus' method as a historian, especially his interweaving of historiographic and philosophical observations into his narrative, is redolent of Victor's:

> The honorific *scriptor historicus* is granted to Aurelius Victor (but not to Eutropius or Festus) by Ammianus presumably not only for stylistic reasons, but also because his work has a complex structure in which reflective excursuses and passages drawn from his sources are artfully woven together, and the *breviator* is thus committed to the same historiographical method that Ammianus employed with the greatest virtuosity.[56]

This licenses us to ask a further question: how much did Victor's peculiar Latinity influence Ammianus?

54 Kulikowski 2007: 250.
55 Chapter VIII.
56 Bleckmann 1997: 21: 'Den Ehrentitel scriptor historicus billigt Ammian dem Aurelius Victor (nicht aber Eutrop oder Festus) wohl nicht nur aus stilistischen Gründen, sondern weil sein Werk eine komplexe Struktur hat, in der reflektierende Excurse und aus den Quellen geschöpfte Passagen kunstvoll verwoben sind, und der Breviator damit dem gleichen historiographischen Verfahren verpflichtet ist, das von Ammian in größter Virtuosität betreiben wurde'.

One could never mistake a line of the *Historiae abbreviatae* for a line of Eutropius, or Festus, or Orosius: Victor writes in a way that is both distinctive and self-consciously literary. We have elsewhere discussed the richness of Victor's style and the range of literary reference that he deployed.[57] Sallust may have been the principal influence on him, but his prose is not that of Julius Exuperantius, who strove to present a tolerable facsimile of the Sallustian style: Victor's goal was more ambitious. The same, of course, can be said, and has been said, of Ammianus.[58] There is no contemporary author, historian or otherwise, who sounds as much like Victor as the author of the *Res gestae*: Huysmans was ahead of his time in linking the two on stylistic grounds.[59] What gives rise to this is not large-scale borrowing, after the clumsy pattern of the *Historia Augusta*. Instead, Ammianus' debt is revealed in a large number of little phrases, which are found with significant frequency in Ammianus and for which Victor had already shown a strong predilection, as revealed by the *HAb*.[60] While these kinds of resonances, what one might call *flosculi Victorini*, prove little individually, their cumulative effect is to give Ammianus' prose a Victorine tinge:

> *accitus venit*, 'comes/came summoned' (*HAb* 26.2, 32.4 ~ AM 15.8.4, 26.1.7, 26.8.13)
>
> *ad munimentum*, 'for safeguarding' (*HAb* 13.9, 38.2, 40.8 ~ AM 24.2.2)
>
> *annonae specie*, 'under the guise of distributing the grain dole' (*HAb* 1.9, 9.12 ~ AM 20.4.6)
>
> *atrocitas rerum*, 'savagery of deeds', *cf.* Cicero, *Phil.* 11.6 (*HAb* 39.8 ~ AM 14.11.32)
>
> *augusto habitu*, 'in imperial garb' (*HAb* 38.1 ~ AM 20.4.22)
>
> *caeli facies*, 'the face of heaven' (*HAb* 41.14 ~ AM 24.2.17)
>
> *castra castellaque*, 'camps and fortifications' (*HAb* 41.18 ~ AM 23.6.4)
>
> *castra (in) opportunis locis*, 'camps in suitable locations' (*HAb* 13.4 ~ AM 24.1.13)
>
> *cogitatum scelus*, 'a thought-out crime' (*HAb* 10.3, *LB* 10.10 ~ AM 29.1.34)
>
> *comperto interitu*, 'when the demise was discovered' (*HAb* 26.5 ~ AM 22.11.3, 30.2.1)
>
> *confestimque*, 'and straightaway' (*HAb* 17.10 ~ AM 15.5.6, 19.2.6, 24.4.30, 25.10.9, 28.1.22, 28.6.18)
>
> *consumpti anni* (*consumpti biennii, etc.*), 'years consumed' (*HAb* 3.9, 41.15 ~ AM 27.3.4)
>
> *contractus undique*, 'gathered from everywhere' (*HAb* 2.4, 32.1 ~ AM 14.2.20, 27.10.6)
>
> *cuius nutu*, 'at whose nod' (*HAb* 39.36 ~ AM 15.1.2)
>
> *cunctis annitentibus*, 'with everyone's support' (*HAb* 40.4 ~ AM 30.8.4)
>
> *eique adventanti*, 'and to the one approaching' (*HAb* 35.4 ~ AM 16.2.12, 30.5.1)
>
> *facinus patrare*, 'to commit a crime' (*HAb* 5.15, 35.8 ~ AM 16.11.8)
>
> *fato quodam*, 'by a certain fate' (*HAb* 20.6, *LB* 9.16 ~ AM 19.12) (*cf. HA Diad.* 9.5)
>
> *gens populosa*, 'a numerous race' (*HAb* 21.2 ~ AM 16.12.6, 31.2.16)
>
> *haud multo* (outside the set phrase *haud multo post*), 'not much' (*HAb* 7.1, 40.27 ~ AM 22.7.5, 25.7.2)

---

57 Chapter IV.

58 For an overview of changing interpretations of Ammianus' literary project, see Blockley 1996. The most insightful characterisation of him as an author and stylist is Kelly 2008.

59 Huysmans 1884: 45–46.

60 We confine ourselves here to phrases that occur disproportionately often in Victor relative to the surviving body of Latin literary texts: *i.e.* a phrase that is not used or is used only a handful of times before the middle of the fourth century, but that then appears in the 10,000 words of the *HAb*, or one that is otherwise significantly overrepresented in that text relative to what we might expect given earlier usage.

iisdem diebus, 'in those same days' (*HAb* 40.3, *LB* 41.2, 41.4 ~ AM 22.4.9)

immane quantum, 'terrifying how much' (*HAb* 23.6 ~ AM 23.6.50, 23.6.78, 24.4.2)

immaturo interitu, 'untimely demise' (*HAb* 3.3 ~ AM 14.11.27)

incertum quo, 'it is uncertain what' (*HAb* 39.36, 41.11, 41.22 ~ AM 14.1.10, 14.7.7, 14.7.20, 31.12.3, 31.15.4)

incredibile quantum, 'unbelievable how much' (*HAb* 10.1, 40.24, *LB* 10.3 ~ AM 17.12.17)

ingenium acrius, 'sharper mind' (*HAb* 2.1, *cf. LB* 20.5 ~ AM 27.8.10)

insidiarum metu, 'in fear of plots' (*HAb* 23.1 ~ AM 16.11.14, 31.16.4)

insontes (pariter et) noxii/nocentes, 'innocent and guilty alike' (*HAb* 40.4, *LB* 2.9, 25.2 ~ AM 26.6.7)

inter exordia, 'at the beginning' (*HAb* 2.3, 24.6 ~ AM 17.4.3, 21.1.4, 21.7.1, 24.5.4, 25.9.3, 28.1.6, 29.1.28, 30.6.3)

intestinae clades, 'internecine slaughter' (*HAb* 39.48 ~ AM 21.5.1)

invitamentum ad, 'invitation to' (*HAb* 41.21 ~ AM 29.2.6)

ira dolorque, 'rage and sorrow' (*HAb* 39.11 ~ AM 29.5.46)

leges aequissimae, 'most equitable laws' (*HAb* 9.5, 39.44, *LB* 9.6 ~ AM 16.10.12)

longo intervallo, 'after a long interval' (*HAb* 34.2, 42.13 ~ AM 16.12.18, 19.9.7, 20.6.9, 22.8.41, 23.6.12)

luctu publico, 'with public mourning' (*HAb* 21.6, *LB* 16.13 ~ AM 22.14.7)

morbo consumptus, 'consumed by sickness' (*HAb* 1.2, 16.9, *LB* 16.12, 41.15 ~ AM 16.12.66)

more veterum, 'in the custom of the ancients' (*HAb* 9.9, 27.7 ~ AM 18.5.8, 26.8.12)

multiplici clade, 'multiple killing' (*HAb* 3.9 ~ AM 31.13.18)

neque minore studio, 'and with no less zeal', *cf.* Suetonius, *Iul.* 28.1 (*HAb* 39.44 ~ AM 20.9.1)

neque secus, 'not otherwise' (*HAb* 3.11, 4.4, 35.6 ~ AM 26.9.4)

nequiens tolerare, 'unable to bear' (*HAb* 40.2 ~ AM 27.3.6)

orbis Romanus, 'the Roman world' (*HAb* 13.6, 41.2, *LB* 35.2, 39.1, 41.19, 43.1 ~ AM 16.1.1, 17.5.13, 19.2.4, 19.11.6, 21.13.13, 22.9.1, 23.5.19, 24.3.9, 25.9.7, 26.2.5, 26.4.5, 26.5.13, 27.11.1, 31.4.5)

pace composita, 'with peace restored' (*HAb* 14.1, 40.16 ~ AM 19.11.7)

pari fortuna, 'with the same fortune' (*HAb* 21.2 ~ AM 24.4.18)

pari modo, 'in the same way' (*HAb* 21.1, 29.5, 39.39, *LB* 32.4 ~ AM 17.12.16, 22.9.5, 24.5.9, 26.5.2, 28.5.6, 31.15.13)[61]

pedibus aeger, 'with a malady of the foot' (*HAb* 20.25 ~ AM 28.6.14)

per opportunos locos, 'through convenient places' (*HAb* 3.16 ~ AM 28.2.1)

pergere protinus, 'proceed straightway' (*HAb* 38.2 ~ AM 15.4.1, 19.8.6, 24.5.1)

praemiorum illecebris, 'by the enticements of rewards' (*HAb* 40.7 ~ AM 31.16.3)

profluvio sanguinis, 'with a flow of blood' (*HAb* 33.28 ~ AM 23.1.5, 25.3.9)

quibus confectis, 'these things completed' (*HAb* 21.5 ~ AM 19.5.7)

---

61 Ammianus does not have the vastly more common
eodem modo and Victor has it only once (*HAb* 37.3)

quo cognito, 'when this was discovered' (*HAb* 17.10 ~ AM 14.2.20, 14.11.13, 16.8.7, 16.12.45, 17.10.8, 21.13.7, 24.7.7, 31.8.5)

ratione quadam, 'by a certain process', used to describe the workings of fate, *cf.* Gellius, *NA* 7.2.7 (*HAb* 34.6 ~ AM 29.1.34)

rem divinam . . . repente, 'suddenly during the sacrifice', *cf.* Suetonius, *Aug.* 1.1 (*HAb* 26.3 ~ AM 22.14.4)

rupta pace, 'the peace broken' (*HAb* 41.8 ~ AM 15.8.6)

satisque constat, 'it is quite well known that', *cf.* Suetonius, *Dom.* 1.1, 10.5 (*HAb* 39.8 ~ AM 23.6.7)

spe praemiorum or *praemii*, 'in hope of reward' (*HAb* 31.2, 34.7 ~ AM 20.11.12, 26.6.13, 29.5.28)

spe veniae, 'in hope of pardon' (*HAb* 20.13 ~ AM 21.4.6)

sidus crinitum, 'a long–haired star' (*HAb* 41.16, *LB* 9.18 ~ AM 30.5.16)

tantus tamque, 'so great and so . . .' (*HAb* 42.24 ~ AM 16.10.19, 31.13.5)

tranquillis rebus, 'in a peaceful situation' (*HAb* 14.5 ~ AM 14.4.3, 14.8.6, 18.7.6)

trepidus ac repentinus, 'fearful and sudden' (*HAb* 33.21 ~ AM 26.7.13)

unde cognomentum, 'whence the nickname' (*HAb* 3.4, 24.4 ~ AM 14.5.8)

(uti) supra docuimus, 'as we have explained above' (*HAb* 4.9, 39.13 ~ AM 17.14.1, 24.2.18, 25.10.4, 28.1.51, 29.5.16, 30.5.16)

votis omnium, 'by the prayers of all' (*HAb* 40.14 ~ AM 15.8.14, 23.5.18)

Unfortunately, the *LB* is not so reliable a guide to Victor's language as the *HAb*, due to its reworking by Paul the Deacon.[62] Even so, there is a not insignificant residue of phrasing which is also found in Ammianus:

caeli temperie, 'with fair weather' (*LB* 41.24 ~ AM 21.6.7, 27.12.18)

causante eo, 'at his pleading' (*LB* 4.8 ~ AM 25.5.3, 27.2.1)

cuius post obitum, 'after whose death' (*LB* 16.7 ~ AM 14.11.6, 31.3.3)

flens obtestor, 'appeal with tears' (*LB* 10.11 ~ AM 18.3.2)

incredibile dictu est (quo) quanto, 'it is unbelievable to say how much' (*LB* 42.21 ~ AM 25.3.10, 31.10.18)

incuria vetustatis, 'long–standing neglect' (*LB* 1.5 ~ AM 20.11.6)

indumentum regium, 'royal garment' (*LB* 34.2, 41.7 ~ AM 14.11.20, 25.10.14)

labor militum, 'the soldiers' graft' (*LB* 1.5 ~ AM 16.4.4, 26.8.9)

magnis sumptibus, 'with great expense' (*LB* 12.8 ~ AM 21.16.15)

matrimonii species, 'the appearance of marriage' (*LB* 33.1 ~ AM 14.4.4)

omnibus absumptis, 'all dead' (*LB* 41.1 ~ AM 25.7.4)

transfuga quidam + ducere/ductare, 'led by a certain deserter' (*LB* 43.2 ~ AM 19.5.5)

vasti corporis, 'of vast body' (*LB* 42.6 ~ AM 15.7.4)

vinctis a/post tergo manibus, 'hands tied behind back' (*LB* 8.3 ~ AM 15.7.4, 19.9.2)

vitam laqueo finire, 'end one's life with the noose' (*LB* 42.8 ~ AM 26.6.20, 28.6.30)

---

62 Chapters IV and V.

Besides these, there are also relatively uncommon individual words of which Ammianus was evidently fond and which had already appeared in Victor:

> *aegerrime* (*HAb* 9.9, 39.48, 40.23, 41.17, *LB* 9.11 ~ AM 18.6.18, 25.6.13, 26.10.6)
>
> *affectans* (*HAb* 5.10 ~ AM 14.1.10, 15.12.4, 25.4.18, 26.3.5, 31.14.5)
>
> *anxie* (*HAb* 14.6, 20.25, 30.2, 39.45, 41.2 ~ AM 16.12.6, 17.1.3)
>
> *imperitandi* (*HAb* 40.2 ~ AM 23.6.36, 27.7.4, 27.12.1)
>
> *incondite* (*HAb* 19.2, 20.34 ~ AM 16.12.37, 22.6.2, 26.6.18, 27.2.6, 31.13.7)
>
> *inconsulte* (*HAb* 38.3, 40.21 ~ AM 16.12.31, 16.12.40, 21.3.3, 23.5.3, 24.6.13, 26.7.4)
>
> *lenitudo* (*HAb* 16.9 ~ AM 15.2.6, 16.5.13, 18.10.4, 22.9.16, 24.1.8, 25.4.9, 29.2.22, 30.8.6)
>
> *stipatores* (*HAb* 33.21, *LB* 24.4 ~ AM 16.10.2, 17.13.6, 19.1.7, 19.7.8, 19.11.12, 20.8.14, 24.4.4, 27.10.10)
>
> *suopte* (*HAb* 35.9 ~ AM 14.11.3, 15.5.7, 16.12.68, 18.6.18, 22.11.3, 25.8.14, 27.11.5, 29.3.2, 29.5.52)
>
> *tumidior* (*HAb* 9.11, 41.23 ~ AM 30.6.3)
>
> *tumultuarie* (*HAb* 40.17 ~ AM 24.2.18)

While these words and phrases represent the barest fraction of the sum total of Ammianus' surviving work, cumulatively they make up more than one per cent of what survives of Victor in the *Historia abbreviata*. Logically, if we had Victor's work entire, then this list could easily increase tenfold. That Victor influenced Ammianus' style should come as no surprise, since he was (on the basis of contemporary *testimonia*) the premier Latin writer of history in the decades that Ammianus was first contemplating and then composing his history. After all, Ammianus called Victor (21.10.6) 'a man worth imitating (*aemulandum*) on account of his seriousness'. *Aemulatio* is an important theme in Ammianus's history: the challenge for every emperor, for example, was to *aemulare* the good princes of the past (15.1.3, 16.1.4, 22.9.11, 25.2.3, 31.10.18). *Aemulatio* was, however, not merely for princes: it was important for historians as well, to imitate the best in their predecessors and surpass their shortcomings.[63] There is only one historian Ammianus singles out by name as worthy of *aemulatio*: Aurelius Victor. The reference in the *Res gestae* to Victor as *the historian* was, it turns out, an elegant acknowledgement of the debt that Ammianus owed him. Pre-eminent he may now appear, but the lonely historian knew that he had a predecessor in the difficult and demanding task of writing Roman history in the fourth century.

Ammianus in the light of Victor

Positing a major history of the Roman Empire completed in its final edition in the years just before Ammianus published his *Res gestae* might at first sight seem to diminish the originality and importance of that work. That is the case, however, only if one is determined to see Ammianus as essentially isolated.

---

63 On Ammianus and *aemulatio*, see the excellent overview
   by Ross 2018.

Looked at another way, a proper understanding of Victor's *Historia* actually helps to better contextualise the *Res gestae*, while casting more light on those areas where its author was truly innovative. Consider style: Ammianus' Latin is highly idiosyncratic, and it is not made any less so by its debt to Victor. Even if, however, elements of his formidable vocabulary are deployed to imitate his predecessor, his decision to write in prose rhythm, unlike Victor, is what gives his Latin its unmistakable feel.[64] Or take the asymmetry of his work: we only have a little over half of Ammianus' history, the last eighteen out of the original thirty-one books. These cover the period from 353 to 378, a rate of less than two years per book. Yet Ammianus tells us that he began with Nerva, which means that he whipped through the preceding quarter millennium in just thirteen books, the coverage more compressed by a factor of ten. If indeed there was a recent landmark history of the whole period, then much less space would have been needed to cover the earlier material, particularly if Ammianus took a different approached or focused primarily on points of disagreement. What might that have looked like in practice? We have no particular reason to believe, from the surviving texts, that Victor paid detailed attention to the mechanics of military campaigns (as opposed to their objectives or consequences). Insofar as he did cover them, he depicted them through the 'eye of command'. In contrast, military history was one area in which Ammianus excelled, particularly with his narration from the soldier's point of view, 'the face of battle'.[65] If we look at Ammianus' cross-references to his earlier books, many of them are to campaign narratives.[66] They would have been an ideal complement to a standard narrative structured instead by close attention to constitutional change and the machinery of government – like Victor's history.

This perhaps suggests a broader point of comparison and contrast. Both authors are relatively forth-coming about themselves. Victor offers a digression in his treatment of Septimius Severus, on how he came from a humble background in Africa, with an uneducated father, and gentled his condition through study of the liberal arts.[67] Ammianus has (*inter alia*) his famous conclusion, where he calls himself 'a soldier once, and Greek' (31.16.9: *miles quondam et Graecus*). In these, both historians cast themselves as (in some sense) outsiders who had made it in the Roman imperial system. Yet the routes by which they had entered were very different: Victor through education and civil service, Ammianus through the military. It looks as though this had ramifications in their histories. Victor's villains are, more often than not, the *milites*: the soldiers for whom not even the whole world was enough (*HAb* 18.2). His heroes are generally the competent and the well educated, among both emperors and civil servants. Ammianus, by contrast, tends to look at things from the perspective of soldiers, and often the rank and file at that. Some of what he says about the troops has a slightly apologetic flavour to it, as (for example) in his account of the battle of Adrianople, where considerable emphasis is placed on the bravery and endurance of the infantry, sabotaged by incompetent commanders (31.13.1–11). In this respect, Ammianus' *Res gestae* might offer a sort of riposte to Victor's view of Roman history. This would mean that Victor's work had some impact on the *nature* of Ammianus' historical project – that what he set out to do in the *Res gestae* was shaped by

---

64 On prose rhythm in Ammianus, see Kelly 2013.
65 The terminology here, and the contrast, is taken over from Kagan 2006 (partly derived, of course, from Keegan's famous 1976 book).
66 Frakes 1995: 243–245.
67 Chapters I and IV.

what Victor had already done. It is possible that this impact stretched even to the work's scope. Ammianus began his history with Nerva, a starting point that was traditionally understood as marking an intention to continue Tacitus, who broke off with Domitian. Given the coincidence of the close of the *Histories* and opening of the *Res gestae*, this is a reasonable enough hypothesis, though the extent of Tacitus' influence on Ammianus has been (convincingly) disputed.[68] It is, however, at least curious that Victor seems to have regarded the reign of Nerva as a particular turning point in Roman constitutional history. With Nerva, and his adoption of Trajan, non-Italians were for the first time at the centre of Roman politics, and this in turn gave new life to Rome's institutions, 'through the virtue of outsiders and their engrafted talents' (*HAb* 11.13).[69] To Ammianus, the self-proclaimed *Graecus*, this would have been an eminently appropriate place to begin.

These are mere soundings. The relationship between the two premier Latin historians of the second half of the fourth century is worthy of considerably deeper study in its own right. All we have done here is enough to show that Ammianus was not nearly so lonely after all.

The *Libellus breviatus* and Greek historiography

One reason that the full extent of Ammianus' debt to Victor has not been more generally realised is the confounding factor of Greek sources for Roman history. It is a natural and plausible supposition that the *Graecus* Ammianus would have had access to Greek sources.[70] As we have already seen, in some of the passages in which Ammianus overlaps with Victor there are indeed Greek analogues. For this reason, very little attention has been given to any direct relationship between Ammianus and the Victorine texts, as opposed to a baffling web of indirect links, often routed through Greek.[71] Questions about any connection between Ammianus and the *LB* (in particular) have thus been drained of urgency, subsumed into a larger, more famous, and fiendishly complex puzzle: the relationship of late-antique Latin and later Greek historiography, one of those things sent to vex would-be Roman historians. Any deep consideration of this vast problem would take us far beyond the scope of the present study. Since, however, Victor's historical work is intimately bound up with it, it is perhaps worth sketching its lineaments – no easy task.

68 The view that Ammianus was Tacitus' self-conscious heir was long standard: *e.g.* Thompson 1947: 17; Syme 1968a: 7. Matthews 1989: 31–32 and n. 45 is sometimes presented as being the definitive challenge (Bowersock 1990: 246; Kelly 2008: 2, n. 6), but in fact scepticism had been building for some time (Flach 1972; Blockley 1973; Wilshire 1973; Borszák 1976) and Matthews' own position was more nuanced than is sometimes allowed (little stylistic influence, but Ammianus imagined as opening his work by looking back to Tacitus: 456). Barnes 1998: esp. 192–195 offered (characteristically) a reaction that was both judicious and insightful. Though the most comprehensive overview of Ammianus' relationship to Tacitus was offered by Neumann 1987, the entire subject was put on a new footing by Kelly 2008: 13–30 and 175–185. The succinct and convincing statement of the case for scepticism in Kelly 2009: 350–353 also raises important methodological points. The question of the relationship between Ammianus and Tacitus is partly textual, but also partly historiographical: deeply ingrained within the study of the Latin historians is the idea that there was no serious history-writing between them. As we have seen, this was a motivating idea for Syme (see Chapter VII) but attracts broader support in, *e.g.*, even the highly sophisticated Marincola 1997. See further the Conclusion.

69 On this passage, see Chapter IV.

70 On the Greek background to Ammianus' work, see Barnes 1998: 65–78.

71 Opitz 1874 is a notable exception to this general tendency.

Perhaps we can start by observing that the problem is at two levels, the specific and the general, though of course they can easily blend into one. The specific normally involves the *in-extenso* consideration of a single text (passage by passage) against others, or of multiple texts on a single event. Such cases are innumerable and tend to attract *ad hoc* solutions, ones that, however convincing individually, produce in the aggregate a very contradictory picture of the relationship between Greek and Latin.[72] The general is more concerned with higher-order questions: were Latin and Greek separate historical traditions in late antiquity, largely closed off from each other?[73] If not (as seems certain), when and how did they interact? In particular, in which direction did material tend to travel, from Latin into Greek, or vice versa? It sometimes seems as though the debate is really about which language had primacy in the history-writing of late antiquity. Part of the problem is that good general points can be made for the pre-eminence of either Latin or Greek. Though it has been somewhat passed over in debate, it is worth remembering that our best-documented case is of a Latin work influencing Greek historians. Eutropius' *breviarium* clearly had an enormous impact on Greek historiography: translated by Paeanius and Capito, used by John of Antioch, Theophanes, and others.[74] On the other hand, there are some sound reasons to put Greek first. We can trace a succession of secular Greek historians in the grand style from Cassius Dio in the third century right down to Agathias in the sixth, or even later. Though most of their works are not fully extant, the remnants have a monumental feeling to them – late-antique Latin historiography can look rather puny in comparison. At the same time, in field after field of late-ancient literary endeavour, we can document the enormous impact that Greek had on Latin: philosophy, theology, medicine. Why should history be any different?

These are questions far too broad and demanding for the present work. For our purposes, mention need only be made (for now) of Zosimus, whose *New History* dates from the fifth or sixth century, and Zonaras, who wrote an *Epitome historiarum* in the twelfth.[75] Though frustrating and often incoherent – a 'poor superstitious creature' as Bentley called him – Zosimus is a vital source for Roman history, especially in the fourth and early fifth centuries.[76] Zonaras is equally important: his coverage up to the time of Alexander Severus is a principal witness to the work of Cassius Dio, while he offers an exceptionally rich and detailed narrative of the rest of the third and the fourth century. These two – and many other works besides – present two major problems: they seem to show some relationship to each other that cannot be explained by their use of any extant source (this is part of the problem of the so-called *Leoquelle*), and they seem at points to have some connection to the extant Latin histories of the fourth century.[77]

72 *e.g.* Barnes 1978 on the *HA* or the now voluminous commentary on that work in the Budé series. Bruun 1995 is a good example of a study of a very specific point that must range wide and deep to reach its solution.

73 This is clearly one of the major issues that underlies the later chapters of Cameron 2011, though his interests are much more extensive than mere historiography.

74 Chapter VI. Paeanius' translation found readers down into at least the fourteenth century: Nicephorus Gregoras, *Vita Constantini* 33 (*e.g.*) vs Paeanius (p. 173 Droysen = Eutropius 10.5).

75 The date of Zosimus is not obvious: he mentions Olympiodorus of Thebes (5.27.1), whose history went down to 425 (Photius, *Bibliotheca* cod. 80 (56b)), and Evagrius

Scholasticus (5.24) might imply that his work was used by Eustathius of Epiphania, whose work went down to 503 (as Evagrius tells us). Cameron 1969b argued for the very last years of the fifth or (more likely) the first few of the sixth century. His case has been widely accepted, but is actually rather weak: see Ridley 1972: 278–280; Damsholt 1977; Schmidt-Hofner 2020: 217, n. 1. It is better to leave the dates vague, though the fifth century has much to recommend it (*cf.* Liebeschuetz 2003: 215). On Zonaras, see Banchich and Lane 2009: 1–19.

76 Bentley 1713: 21.

77 On the *Leoquelle* (a misnomer) the classic treatment is Bleckmann 1992.

This is where Victor comes in, for the *LB* (in particular) has numerous links with later Greek sources, especially Zosimus and Zonaras, as is well known and well documented.[78] Such connections both grow more frequent and become stronger as we approach the end of the third century and proceed through the fourth. Here we present a selection of instances where the *LB* is closely parallel to the Greek tradition, offering details or ideas found only otherwise in the Greek sources:

29.2   The death of Decius; *cf.* Zosimus 1.23.3 and Zonaras 12.20.

29.2   The obituary of Decius; *cf.* Zosimus 1.21.1 and 1.21.3.

29.3   What happened to Decius' corpse; *cf.* Zonaras 12.20 and Ammianus 31.13.13.

31.2   The origin of Aemilianus (from North Africa); *cf.* Zonaras 12.21.

33.1   Gallienus' peace with a German king; *cf.* Zosimus 1.30.3.

35.2   Aurelian's battles in Italy in 270–271; *cf.* Dexippus (*BNJ* 100 fr. 6 (McInerney)), Zosimus 1.49.1, and Peter the Patrician, *ES* 175.[79]

35.3   The existence of the usurper Septimius; *cf.* Zosimus 1.49.2.

38.6   The existence/name of the usurper Sabinus Julianus; *cf.* John of Antioch fr. 246 Roberto (= Zosimus 1.73.1).[80]

38.8   The circumstances of the death of Carinus; *cf.* John of Antioch fr. 246 Roberto (= Zosimus 1.73.3).[81]

39.7   The circumstances of the death of Diocletian; *cf.* Socrates, *HE* 1.2.10.

40.1   Galerius was the uncle of Maximinus; *cf.* Zosimus 2.8.1.[82]

41.4   Details about Constantine II and Licinius the Younger when made Caesars; *cf.* Zosimus 2.20.1.

41.13   Constantine's *bon mot* about Trajan; *cf.* Peter the Patrician, *ES* 191.

41.16   Constantine's nickname 'Trachala'; *cf.* Cedrenus 1.472–473 (ed. Bekker).

41.22   Details of the proclamation of Magnentius; *cf.* Zosimus 2.42.2–3 and Zonaras 13.6.

41.25   Details of the proclamation of Vetranio, *cf.* Zosimus 2.43.1.

42.7   Magnentius' origins; *cf.* Zosimus 2.54.1

45.4   Gratian's age at his accession, *necdum plene puberum* = Zosimus 4.12.2, οὔπω πρὸς ἥβην.

Interpretation of this phenomenon has been sharply split, for logically it could mean one of two things. First, the overlap might be explained by the hypothesis that material derived from a Latin tradition that

---

78 This was established by Graebner 1905, attacked by Hohl 1911, and rehabilitated by Schlumberger 1976: 134–232. Parallels between the Greek tradition and the *HAb* are dealt with in more detail in Chapter X.

79 We accept the identity of Peter the Patrician and the so-called *Anonymus post Dionem*; on which vexed question see below.

80 The only extant manuscript of Zosimus fails just as Carus, the father of Carinus, is made emperor. Fortune made partial amends by ensuring that it overlaps verbatim with a fragment of John of Antioch in the *EI* (70). It is

thus a reasonable, though not certain, supposition that what John says next about Carinus is also from Zosimus.

81 See Chapter X.

82 Lactantius *DMP* 18.4 makes him an *affinis*. In strict or technical usage, an *adfinis* was a relation by marriage (Modestinus in the *Digest* 38.10.4.3) and that is how the word has been generally understood (*TLL* 1.1217.45–1219.47 (Vollmer)), but Lactantius may be evidence that it had a broader frame of reference (if he did not simply make a mistake).

appears in the *LB* was later used independently by Greek sources – this is the current opinion in much continental European scholarship, Schlumberger, Bleckmann, and Paschoud the names most prominent.[83] Second and alternatively, it could be posited that the *LB* had access to (now lost) Greek materials which were also used (again independently) by later Greek authors – this is the solution favoured by a majority of Anglophone scholars, Barnes and Cameron in the lead.[84] Obviously, recognising the *LB* for what it is – an epitome of Victor – has important implications for this question, since its immediate source is indeed Latin: Victor's *Historia*. A single example, involving Ammianus, both demonstrates that the Greek tradition does indeed owe something to the Latin and begins to illustrate those implications.

The *LB* reports in its account of Constantine that emperor's *bon mot* about Trajan (*LB* 41.13): 'He had the habit of calling Trajan a wall-plant (*herbam parietariam*) because his name was inscribed on many buildings'. Precisely the same saying of Constantine, though without the explanation, is found in a fragment from Peter the Patrician preserved (if that is not a misnomer for a maltreated palimpsest) in the *Excerpta de sententiis*: 'he called Trajan a wall-plant (βοτάνην τοίχου)'.[85] Significantly, Ammianus also has the quip but suppresses the reference to Constantine with a generic *dicitur* (27.3.7): 'the emperor Trajan is said to have suffered from this vice, and for this reason they jestingly called him a wall-plant (*herbam parietinam*)'.

Where does the story originate? The image of Trajan's name covering buildings like so much ivy is a memorable one and we might be tempted to chalk it up to the general fund of good stories about great emperors, available to Greek as to Latin authors without one needing to derive it from the other. That temptation should be resisted. At first sight, this might look like a general reference to climbing plants, on the strength of the obvious parallelism of *herba parietaria* and βοτάνη τοίχου. In fact, however, Latin *herba parietaria* is the name of a specific plant that was commonly used for medicinal purposes, our pellitory-of-the-wall (*parietaria judaica*).[86] Cassius Felix (2.11: *herbam perdicion id est parietariam*) and the pseudo-Apuleian *Herbarius* (82.1: *herba perdicalis . . . alii muralem dicunt, alii parietariam*) both mention it and suggest that its proper Greek name was περδίκιον. Dioscurides (4.85) preferred ἑλξίνη, but importantly no Greek source ever calls it plain 'wall plant'.[87] Moreover, while the Greeks did very occasionally speak of βοτάναι on τείχη, the words were collocated extremely rarely and never to identify any specific plant.[88] This means that Peter's βοτάνη τοίχου is a Greek calque, something made more obvious by the

83 Schlumberger 1974: 223–224, 235, 239 ff.; Bleckmann 1992: esp. 400–403; Paschoud 1994 *e.g.*

84 Barnes 1976a: 265–267; Barnes 1978: 119–120; Cameron 2011: esp. 669–670.

85 Peter the Patrician, *ES* 191: Ὀκταβιανὸν Αὔγουστον κόσμον τύχης ἐκάλει, τὸν δὲ Τραιανὸν βοτάνην τοίχου. The attribution of these fragments is a famous problem: are they simply from Peter the Patrician or do they belong to the anonymous continuator of Dio, first conjured under that name by Müller? Opinions differ and the issue is rather opaque to outsiders. Potter 1990: 395–397 is a very useful introduction; see also Cataudella 2003: 437–440 and Cameron 2011: 678–679. Banchich 2015: 3–9 offers a very clear overview and a persuasive case for accepting Peter as the author. Stylometric analysis points in the same direction.

86 *e.g.* Vegetius, *Mul.* 2.129.11. See in general *TLL* 10.1.394.10–36 (Gatti).

87 Interestingly, the *Hippiatrica Berolinensia* 22.34 transliterates it: φύλλα βοτάνης σιδηρίτιδος, ἣν Ῥωμαῖοι παριταρίαν καλοῦσι. *LSJ s.v.* περδίκιον identifies the plant as *polygonum maritimum* (a variety of knotweed), but nothing in Theophrastus, *Historia Plantarum* 1.6.11 (the reference provided) would seem to require that.

88 The only other Greek example known to us is in the *Hippiatrica Berolinensia* (Apsyrtus) 66.4: Βοτάνη τίς ἐστιν ἐν τοῖς τείχεσι καὶ ταῖς πέτραις γενομένη, ἣν ἰατρῶν μὲν παῖδες πολύγονον ὀνομάζουσιν, ἰδιῶται δὲ σύμφυτον, καὶ Μακεδόνες ὀστεοκόλλον, προφῆται δὲ παλλάντιον <αὐτὴν καλοῦσιν>. Here, however, it is clearly a description of a specific herb, rather than a name – the point of the whole passage is to describe a plant that has many names.

fact that the glossators list βοτάνη as a translation of *herba*.[89] Constantine's saying was thus transmitted in the language in which he would have uttered it, if in fact he ever did: Latin.[90] So at least in this particular case it is certain that the source of the *LB*, Ammianus, and the Greek tradition represented by Peter the Patrician was Latin.

Was that source definitely Victor's *Historia*? That the *LB* preserves the fullest version of the anecdote, offering both the attribution and the explanation, strongly suggests so, but it can perhaps be demonstrated. Immediately following the quip in the *LB*, without any explicit connection, we find a reference to Constantine's construction of a bridge over the Danube (41.13: *hic pontem in Danubio construxit*). In the *Res gestae*, too, the saying comes up suspiciously close to bridge construction. Ammianus invokes it in his account of the urban prefecture of Lampadius, given to that most senatorial of vices: putting his name on things other people had built. That account is book-ended by reference to two bridges. Before it, we are reminded that the elder Symmachus had dedicated the *pons Valentiniani* (27.3.3), not an entirely new construction, but rather the existing *pons Aurelius* restored or replaced (though Ammianus does not say this).[91] Afterwards, we are told that at the end of his prefecture Lampadius was forced by popular anger in Rome to flee to the Milvian Bridge, which the historian acidly notes was built by Scaurus (27.7.9).[92] This is a rather suggestive context for an anecdote that seems in Victor to have been linked to a bridge over the Danube.

In any case, the connection between Constantine's quip and Trajan appears to be original to Victor, who had a more extended series of links between the two emperors. Constantine's construction of a bridge over the Danube is a rather recondite fact. The only other place it is mentioned in antiquity is the *HAb* (41.18):

Pons per Danubium ductus; castra castellaque pluribus locis commode posita.

A bridge was constructed over the Danube, and camps and fortifications were appropriately placed in many locations.[93]

This is significant, since in this passage, Victor echoes an earlier part of his history, describing the construction of a bridge over the Danube, built by none other than Trajan (13.4):

Castra suspectioribus aut opportunis locis exstructa, ponsque Danubio impositus.

Camps were built in the more critical or appropriate places, and a bridge was put up on the Danube.

89 *TLL* 6.3.2614.36 (Kornhardt); *Glossa Graeco-Latina* (Goetz and Gundermann 1888: 258); *Hermeneumata Amploniana, Hermeneumata Monacensia, Hermeneumata Stephani* (Goetz 1892: 73, 200, 360).

90 It is important to note that *herba parietaria* is not the sort of Latin phrase which would have been bandied about in official circles, and so is not subject to the criticisms of Cameron 2011: 661 that 'whatever traces of Latin we find in Peter surely derive from Peter himself rather than any hypothetical fourth-century Latin source'. In any

case, Cameron does not himself subscribe to the identity of the continuator of Dio with Peter.

91 Den Boeft *et al.* 2009: 45.

92 *cf. DVI* 72.8.

93 Otherwise, it is attested by coins and the *Chronicon paschale* (p. 527 Dindorf), which was then copied by Theophanes AM 5820; hence Bleckmann 1997: 22 is incorrect to list this as a parallel between Theophanes and Victor.

Clearly, it is in the context of a shared construction project that Constantine's remarks about his predecessor belong, and that context is only in Victor. Moreover, there is no reason to think that he recorded the saying as a criticism of Trajan, rather than a vivid evocation of quite how much he had built. The negative gloss appears to be Ammianus' alone: proof in itself of derivation.[94] Hence the *herba parietaria* gives us good reason to think that the common source of Ammianus and the later Greek tradition was indeed Victor's *Historia*.

The idea advanced so far in this chapter is, in one sense at least, not new, as we have already hinted. For more than four decades significant figures in continental classical scholarship – Schlumberger, Bleckmann, Paschoud, Festy, Zecchini, Baldini, and others – have asserted that there was an extensive lost Latin history, written by a pagan author who was a Roman senator, which was used by Ammianus and the *LB*, not to mention the *HA*, while also influencing the later Greek tradition.[95] This Latin source, they argue, was the origin of the material shared between the Latin and Greek tradition, such as the anecdote about the *herba parietaria*.[96] Where we differ sharply from them is on the identity of its author. For them, it was Virius Nicomachus Flavianus: aristocrat, bureaucrat, friend of Symmachus, supporter of the usurper Eugenius, and long canvassed as the paladin of the pagan cause as it lay dying.[97] A romantic figure, if seen from a sufficient distance.

The *Annales*

Everything that touches Nicomachus Flavianus is the subject of considerable controversy, from the true nature of his cultural and religious convictions to the chronology of his career.[98] Argument rages with especial ferocity about a work of history that he wrote, under the title (so it is generally assumed) of *Annales*. Broadly speaking, the divide is (once again) between scholars in France, Germany, and Italy, who see Flavianus as the *fons et origo* of much in late-antique historiography, and Anglophone scholars, who see him as a non-entity (at least *qua* historian).[99] The continental contingent would emphasise Flavianus' centrality to understanding the *HA*'s date, context, and *Tendenz*, as well as his role as the source of material

94 A point well made by Stuart 1908, an incisive article that, though now rather dated in its assumptions, makes clear that Ammianus' accusation – if it was meant to be taken seriously – was completely unfair.

95 A comprehensive bibliography would run to many pages, but some of the key works are: Schlumberger 1974, 1985; Bleckmann 1992, 1995a; Paschoud 1994; Festy 1999a: xii–xxxviii *passim*; Zecchini 1993: 51–62; Baldini 2000: esp. 97–177. On this debate, especially as it touches on the *LB*, see also Stover and Woudhuysen 2021.

96 *e.g.* Schlumberger 1974: 199 with 205–207 (the 'annalistic source' is Flavianus); Bleckmann 1995a: 97; Bruun 1995: 471–472; Festy 1999a: 190–191.

97 *PLRE* 'Flavianus 15'.

98 The indispensable guide is Cameron 2011: 627–690 (*cf.* Cameron 2012), with extensive citation of those who take a less sceptical approach. See also the judicious treatment by Van Hoof and Van Nuffelen 2020a: 36–58.

99 The divide is not quite so linguistic as that might imply, something noted by Birley 2004: 47–48, who (2003: 129–132) himself takes a sympathetic view of the Flavianus thesis; *cf* Cecconi 2013, an Italian sceptic.

found in the later Greek tradition. The *anglosassoni* generally regard the first of these as a proposition that can be refuted without evidence – since (almost) no evidence for it has been provided – and the second as possible in principle, but erroneous in fact. The struggle has been ongoing in its current form at least since Jörg Schlumberger's 1974 monograph brought Flavianus and the *Annales* back into view and T.D. Barnes' peppery review article set out some of the major objections two years later.[100] Since then, publications have come thick and fast (particularly in the pages of the *Historia Augusta Colloquia*) and it seems likely that one reason the debate has generated rather more heat than light is that it is now difficult for anyone not already invested in the controversy to approach the key questions, so laden with bibliography have they become. The strength of feeling that the issue clearly evokes has much to do at the general level with the attitude (on both sides) that the key points have been made sufficiently often and sufficiently clearly that further discussion is pointless.

The vigour of polemic and the elephantine weight of scholarship can obscure quite how limited our evidence is for the mousey *Annales*. They are directly attested by only a single and perplexing honorific inscription, erected some thirty-five years after Flavianus had committed suicide in the aftermath of Eugenius' defeat. This was the work of his grandson, one Nicomachus Dexter, and was the capstone of a vigorous lobbying effort designed to rehabilitate his grandfather.[101] This inscription includes a copy of a typically verbose imperial epistle addressed to the Roman Senate, one that is at times hard to construe, perhaps because the verbal haze helped in its general object of saying that the emperor had not meant for Flavianus to kill himself at all (whatever people might have thought). It is this letter, and this letter alone, that mentions the *Annales*. In truth, it does not actually tell us all that much about Flavianus as a historian:

> . . . so that whatever wrong was done him by blind and deceitful accusations, you [*i.e.* the senators] may judge to have been far removed from what the emperor [*i.e.* Theodosius] wished, for his enormous goodwill towards that man [*i.e.* Flavianus] – carried so far as the annals that he wished to be dedicated to himself by his quaestor and prefect – stirred the spiteful envy of wicked men.[102]

That is all we know about the *Annales*, awkwardly wedged into an already overstuffed sentence as a concrete illustration of imperial favour. We are in almost total ignorance of the work's nature, scope, ambition, and contents. We do not know for certain whether it covered the Republic or the Empire, whether it was history in the grand style or a *breviarium* of some sort.[103] We have no explicit evidence for its circulation (a sharp contrast with Victor, we might note). We cannot even be certain that *Annales* is truly its title, rather than (say) a description of its contents or structure.[104] All we know is that it existed and that his family were rather proud of it. As Alan Cameron memorably put it:

---

100 Schlumberger 1974; Barnes 1976a.
101 *CIL* 6.1783 of AD 431, studied in great detail in Hedrick 2000 (esp. Ch. 1). *CIL* 6.1782 calls Flavianus *historicus disertissimus*. *cf.* Girotti 2015.
102 *CIL* 6.1783: . . . *ut quidquid in istum caeca insimulatione commissum est, procul ab eius / principis voto fuisse iudicetis, cuius* [*sc.* Theodosius] *in eum* [*sc.* Nicomachus] *effusa benivolentia et usq(ue) ad an/nalium quos consecrari sibi a quaestore et praefecto suo voluit provecta / excitavit livorem inproborum*. It is hard not to shake the feeling that something has dropped out between *annalium* and *quos*

– more may well have gone wrong than this. *Insimulatio* is a rare word, with an 'official' flavour (*CTh* 6.4.22.3, 9.16.10, 9.41.1, 16.7.7; Symmachus, *Relationes* 21), but note Cicero, *Pro Fonteio* 39.42: [*sc.* Piso] *tamen in falsam atque iniquam* **probrorum insimulationem** *vocabatur*. Piso Frugi also wrote *Annales*: tantalising.
103 Schlumberger 1985 is an effort to prove that it must have been an imperial history: it is not terribly convincing.
104 We continue to use it as a title of convenience.

> What do we actually know about Flavian's *Annales*? Let us be frank. Not a single word survives. Not a single reference in any literary text of any sort or date. . . . [T]he entirety of our knowledge of the very existence of Flavian's *Annales* is confined to members of his own family![105]

On the basis of the letter, it seems reasonable to suppose that Flavianus was commissioned by Theodosius while in his service to write some sort of historical work, which he completed in 390 or shortly thereafter, at a time when he must have been rather busy with his official duties.[106] That is about as much as we can say with anything even resembling the ghost of certainty. Yet none of this has seriously impeded Flavianus' rise to premier position among the Latin historians of late antiquity, at least in some circles.

In this respect, the case of Flavianus looks rather like the case of the *Kaisergeschichte*. Both are entirely lost texts, with no evidence for their circulation, which have nonetheless been strenuously asserted to have exercised a profound influence on our surviving tradition. If anything, the comparison is too kind to the *KG*. Flavianus is, at least, a well-attested individual, whose *Annales* can be dated and said with certainty to have existed, and who can himself be fixed in a reasonably well-known social and cultural environment. The comparison has been made explicitly both by Flavianus' votaries and by his opponents. Paschoud, with characteristic elegance, has pointed out that 'tout ce qu'il dit des *Annales* de Nicomaque Flavien s'applique aussi à la lettre à l'EKG'.[107] In riposte, Cameron has contrasted the methods used to reconstruct and identify the two works, with a trademark twist of the knife at the end:

> Paschoud has recently compared himself to an astronomer, using mathematical calculations to discover unknown planets. This grandiose image might be applied to the identification of the so-called Kaisergeschichte (*KG*) or Imperial History, whose existence was inferred from the remarkable degree of coincidence in content, structure, and verbal formulation (notably shared errors) in the surviving works of Aurelius Victor, Eutropius, the *Historia Augusta*, and *Epitome de Caesaribus*. But for the method used to 'recover' Flavian's *Annales*, astrology would be a more appropriate analogy.[108]

The sharpness of this response perhaps reveals that, whatever the general merits of his case, here Paschoud has hit something of a nerve. It is rather unfortunate for Cameron, Burgess, and others that in attacking the Flavian thesis they have (not without reason) targeted their fire at the exiguity of the evidence for his work and its importance. As we have seen, this is the principal weakness of Enmann's theory and not merely an objection that can be swatted aside.[109] Whatever 'degree of coincidence in content, structure, and verbal formulation' the supposed witnesses to the *KG* share cannot be explained by Enmann's solution: it is seeking to account for a genuine pattern in our evidence, but the approach is flawed. The same is true of the *Annales*. Putative connections to the *Historia Augusta* can now be dismissed, in the light of what we have demonstrated about the sources of that work. When it comes to the connections between fourth-century Latin historiography and later Byzantine historians, however, the matter is slightly more complicated. These links are real, but they cannot be explained by Flavianus.

---

105 Cameron 2011: 629.
106 Cameron 2011: 629–633.
107 Paschoud 2006b: 339. *cf.* Paschoud 1998a: 82 ff. for an earlier comparison.

108 Cameron 2011: 628; Burgess 1998 had made much the same criticism more than a decade earlier.
109 Chapter VI.

Flavianus and Servius

Let us take just two exemplary cases, from outside the *HA*, where Flavianus has long been hypothesised as a source, and analyse what is really happening. First, a commentary. In his notes on Vergil's description of the Shield of Aeneas' depiction of Actium, Servius invokes Suetonius as the source for an anecdote about Augustus (*In Aen.* 8.680):

> Naturaliter enim Augustus igneos oculos habuisse dicitur, adeo ut quidam eques Romanus, interrogatus ab eo, cur se viso verteret faciem, dixerit 'quia fulmen oculorum tuorum ferre non possum', sicut ait Suetonius.

> For Augustus is said to have had naturally fiery eyes such that a certain Roman knight, asked by him why he was averting his face, answered, 'Because I cannot bear the lightning of your eyes', as Suetonius says.

Obviously, something has gone wrong here.[110] The general idea reported by Servius is clearly in Suetonius, but not the anecdote and saying that accompany it.[111] We can probably rule out the possibility that something has dropped out of Suetonius in transmission: the lines are too clean and coherent to allow for the possibility that material has been accidentally omitted from the manuscripts due to a mechanical error, only to be quoted elsewhere. Instead, it is much more likely that Servius made a mistake in attributing the line to Suetonius. He was, unfortunately, a rather clumsy excerptor, quite capable of misattributing or misunderstanding his sources.[112]

How did this error arise? Thanks to Servius Danielis, the version of the Vergil commentary produced in the early Middle Ages with extensive supplementation from Servius' major source (probably the work of Aelius Donatus, active in the middle of the fourth century), we can get a sense of what has happened.[113] Servius Danielis has an additional line in the commentary, something Servius excised when putting his entry together. Significantly, that additional line – clumsily placed between *adeo ut* and *eques* – has the same sentiment as the saying attributed to Augustus: *obtutum eius nemo contra aspectare posset ~ fulmen oculorum tuorum ferre non possumus*. This suggests that Servius' source said something like:

> Naturaliter enim Augustus igneos oculos habuisse dicitur, adeo ut obtutum eius nemo contra aspectare posset, sicut ait Suetonius.

110 This episode is the subject of a thorough study by Prchlík 2015 (with reference to earlier literature), from the conclusions of which we dissent.

111 *cf.* Suetonius, *Aug.* 79.2: *oculos habuit claros ac nitidos, quibus etiam existimari volebat inesse quiddam divini vigoris, gaudebatque, si qui sibi acrius contuenti quasi ad fulgorem solis vultum summitteret.*

112 There appears to be no systematic study of the accuracy of Servius' citations, but it was certainly patchy: see, *e.g.*, Haynes 2015, focused on Ovid. There are other examples where Servius explicitly attributes a quotation

to an author in whose works it cannot be found. At *In Buc.* 2.11, he writes: *nam, ut etiam Plinius dicit in naturali historia, omnis medicina aut a contrario aut a simili quaritur.* These words are not found in our text of the *Natural History*, but are close to the Latin translation of Oribasius' *Commentarium in Aphorismos* 5.22: *omnis curatio duobus praecipue modis fit aut a contrario aut a simili.*

113 For Donatus as the source of Servius Danielis (a controversial question), see Lloyd 1961; Goold 1970; Keeline 2013. There are alternative solutions (*e.g.* Daintree 1990), but they are less convincing.

This would be an entirely defensible paraphrase of what the biographer of the Caesars tells us. When Servius went to revise his source (early in the fifth century), he replaced the generic Suetonian characterisation with a much more vivid anecdote drawn from a different work. In doing so, however, he failed to remove the reference to Suetonius, an author to whom he only occasionally referred, much less often than we might expect, given the nature of his subject and the premier position of the *Vitae Caesarum* for the history of Caesar and Augustus.[114] This, in other words, looks like a cut-and-paste job where the scissors and glue have been handled rather clumsily. That the reference to Suetonius goes back to Servius' source, not Servius himself, is confirmed by the unobtrusive phrase *sicut ait*. This is only elsewhere used twice in all of Servius to introduce an authority (*In Aen.* 6.760 and 11.700). In contrast, in Servius Danielis, that is to say, in just the material that is not found in Servius, it is deployed seven times when invoking a source.[115]

From where, then, did Servius get this story? If the major source of Servius Danielis is indeed Aelius Donatus' commentary on Vergil, then we might have some weak indication that it is from something published after *ca.* 360, when Donatus is thought to have written.[116] At any rate, we hardly need to speculate. The only other source for the anecdote is none other than the *LB* (1.20):

> When a certain soldier averted his eyes from Augustus' face, and was asked why he did this, he responded, 'Because I cannot bear the lightning of your eyes' (*quia fulmen oculorum tuorum ferre non possum*).

Servius' source was thus the same as the source of the *LB*: that is to say it was Victor's *Historia*, a work produced after AD 360 which offered a great store of information to any would-be commentator. That Victor was the source of all this material is confirmed by our final witness to Augustus' gaze: Julian's *Caesares*, a text which (as we have seen) owed significant debts to him.[117]

With a proper understanding of Victor, there is simply no need to involve Nicomachus Flavianus, as Schlumberger and Prchlík have done (or the *KG*, as Festy has): any role for his *Annales* is simply an unnecessary postulate.[118] Their argument runs something like this: Servius and the *LB* share a common source, which derived much of its information for this period of imperial history from Suetonius, but was not the same as the *Vitae Caesarum*. The *LB* is chiefly indebted to the work of Nicomachus Flavianus and Servius too moved in the right circles to have used the *Annales*. Therefore, the common source is Flavianus – Servius refrained from naming him because it was politically dangerous, and used Suetonius as a shorthand because that was the major source of the *Annales* at this point. From here, they extend the analysis to John the Lydian, who shares with the *LB* that significant remark about it being better for

---

114 Servius, *In Georg.* 3.8, 3.105; *In Aen.* 1.292, 5.602, 6.6, 7.612, 7.627, 12.185. Compare the hundreds of citations of Sallust.

115 *In Aen.* 1.149, 1.535, 2.761, 8.51, 8.291, 9.603, and *In Buc.* 8.12. Servius, in contrast, generally reserved the phrase for Vergilian cross references, using it six times (*In Aen.* 6.423 and 8.625; *In Georg.* 2.109, 2.389, 2.427, and 3.244). Servius Danielis only has this usage three times (*In Aen.* 8.291 and 10.545; *In Buc.* 9.7). It is

worth noting that the two Servian uses for an authority are most probably simply calques from Donatus: the lack of intervention by Servius Danielis makes it difficult to prove one way or the other.

116 On Donatus, see Kaster 1988: 275–278.

117 *Caesares* 309b. See Chapter V.

118 Prchlík 2015; Schlumberger 1974: 25–26, 61–62 with n. 211 (Flavianus is unnamed, but he is the source here), 244, n. 52, and 246, n. 56. Festy 1999a: 64.

Augustus neither to have been born nor to die. Clearly, he too had access to the *Annales*, with its *Suetonius auctus* approach to the reign of Rome's first emperor.[119] To the advocates of Flavianus, he thus offers something like an explanation for a set of rather awkward facts.

Yet, at every step, Victor is a more economical and convincing solution, better supported by the evidence. He is the named source of the *LB*, he is mentioned by name as a source in John the Lydian, the epigrammatic judgement about Augustus makes sense only in the context of the *HAb*, and he (but not Flavianus) was writing early enough and in the right circles for the story to have reached the emperor Julian. Servius – always a little shaky in his attributions, especially when splicing new information into Donatus – has simply made a mistake. If he was using Flavianus in the way that his advocates envisage – as a recent and wide-ranging work of history – it is curious that elsewhere he explicitly defined the word *Annales* as the history of the distant past.[120] The idea that he suppressed the name of Flavianus for political reasons might politely be described as unconvincing. Servius was writing at the very earliest in the 410s, if not somewhat later still.[121] If Flavianus was ever in such serious official disfavour as is sometimes envisaged, then it is hard to believe that it lasted beyond 398, by which point his son was being invited to court: in 399–400 he held the urban prefecture.[122] With a touch of whimsy, Macrobius would even make Servius and Flavianus dining companions in his *Saturnalia*, set in 384 but written after 431.[123] Late ancient Rome was no stranger to official viciousness and vicious officiousness, but it was not the Soviet Union: systematic censorship of literary culture by the imperial regime simply did not exist. On the other hand, Servius did not generally cite recent authors – as Murgia observed: 'Servius himself wanted his work to be timeless' – hence no reference to Victor.[124] In the contest between incompetence and conspiracy, there is generally only one winner.

Flavianus and Zosimus

Our second test case is the historian Zosimus. Besides the general controversy over Zosimus' sources, explored further in Chapter X, there is a specific problem regarding his extremely compressed treatment of the first two dozen emperors – from Augustus to Elagabalus – in a paltry six chapters of his first

---

119 Schlumberger 1974: 62 and n. 211.
120 Servius, *In Aen.* 1.373: *ANNALES inter historiam et annales hoc interest: historia est eorum temporum quae vel vidimus vel videre potuimus, dicta ἀπὸ τοῦ ἱστορεῖν, id est videre; annales vero sunt eorum temporum, quae aetas nostra non novit: unde Livius ex annalibus et historia constat.*
121 Kaster 1988: 356–359 collects the key evidence, which is ambiguous in specifics, but clear in general direction (*i.e.* the fifth century). Cameron 1966 remains foundational on these questions; see also Cameron 2011: 231–272. In general, it seems as though Macrobius' decision to include Servius in the *Saturnalia* (an anachronism he acknowledges) continues to exert a pull on his dating that is quite unjustified, even among those who were early to see through it. Murgia 2003 argues

(somewhat opaquely) for composition before the sack of Rome in 410 (debate over which ought to have influenced Servius' commentary). As he himself says (64): 'These are not very strong arguments, since references to contemporary events in Servius are close to nonexistent'.
122 *PLRE* 'Flavianus 14'.
123 See Cameron 1966, whose arguments are not seriously undermined by Murgia 2003.
124 Murgia 2003: 68. If Servius had referred to Victor by name, then the problem of his date would be considerably simpler than it is. Donatus, his major source and whipping boy, was the great exception among contemporaries to Servius' aversion to citation by name; another was Avienius, also mid-fourth century, *cf.* Woudhuysen 2019.

book (1.6–11). Festy noticed that despite its brevity Zosimus' treatment of Tiberius to Domitian has a large number of overlaps with the *HAb*: Tiberius' self-imposed exile in Capri, Caligula's assassination by Chaerea, Claudius' domination by eunuchs and freedmen, *etc*.[125] Not every one of them is especially impressive, although Burgess goes too far when he says they all 'turn out to be illusory'.[126] Consider the case of Caligula's killer Chaerea:

> *HAb* 3.14: For this reason, at the instigation of Chaerea those in whom Roman virtue was present were moved to free the commonwealth from such a great disaster (*tanta pernicie rempublicam levare*) by running him [*i.e.* Caligula] through; and the noble deed (*excellens facinus*) of Brutus, when Tarquin was driven out, would have been brought back . . .

> Zosimus 1.6.2: Chaerea freed the state from bitter tyranny (ἐλευθερώσαντος πικρᾶς τὸ πολίτευμα τυραννίδος) by this act of daring (τολμήματος).

Not only are there some close correspondences of vocabulary between Zosimus and the *HAb*, there is also a parallelism of ideas.[127] Against the general characterisation of imperial assassins, they make Chaerea out to be motivated by a desire to restore the Republic, a characterisation found otherwise only in Josephus.[128] This means that Victor and Zosimus share a very peculiar and recondite historiographical tradition, against the common view that attributes Chaerea's assassination of Caligula to private animosity.

Alternatively, we might consider Zosimus' treatment of Claudius, Nero, and the emperors of AD 69. His brief comment on Claudius' dependence on his freedmen (1.6.3) – 'Claudius handed over what pertained to him to eunuch freedmen' (Κλαυδίου δὲ τὰ καθ᾿ ἑαυτὸν εὐνούχοις ἀπελευθέροις ἐκδόντος) – is exactly parallel to Victor's 'freedmen, to whom he had handed himself over' (*HAb* 4.3: *libertorum . . . quibus semet dediderat*). Zosimus' refusal to discuss the crimes of Nero and his ephemeral successors points in the same direction (1.6.3): 'Of them I have decided to not say anything at all, so that not even the memory of their outrageous and unnatural deeds might endure'.[129] This first-person recusal mirrors a similar statement by Victor (*HAb* 5.4): 'he conducted the rest of his life in such disgrace, that I am embarrassed and ashamed to mention anyone of this sort, much less a ruler of nations'.[130] It does not matter, as Burgess contends, that Victor is actually deploying *praeteritio*, and does indeed go on to describe Nero's crimes in lurid detail – the point is simply that he declared that emperor's deeds ought not be mentioned, and this declaration was memorable enough that it was picked up on by his readers, such as Ausonius.[131]

These are hardly trivial parallels, if not of themselves decisive – further proof can be had by extending one's view slightly. One of the few things that Zosimus says about Augustus is that he ruled with moderation after being taught by Athenodorus.[132] We have already seen how this was a theme of

---

125 Festy 1998: 160–162. See also Paschoud 2000: xlvi and 134–136.

126 Burgess 1998: 86.

127 Note in particular how (*excellens*) *facinus* and τόλμημα both usually have implications of villainy, but are used positively in this context.

128 See Chapter IV.

129 Zosimus 1.6.3: Νέρων τε καὶ οἱ μετ᾿ αὐτὸν εἰς μοναρχίαν παρῆεσαν, περὶ ὧν ἔκρινα μηδὲν παντάπασιν διελθεῖν

ὡς ἂν μηδὲ ἐπ᾿ ἐκμελέσι καὶ ἀλλοκότοις πράξεσιν αὐτῶν καταλείποιτο μνήμη.

130 *HAb* 5.4: *eo dedecore reliquum vitae egit, uti pigeat pudeatque memorare huiuscemodi quempiam, nedum rectorem gentium, fuisse.*

131 Burgess 1998: 86, who mentions this, without quite realising its import. See also Chapters V and VII.

132 Zosimus 1.6.2: Ὀκταβιανοῦ δὲ ὅμως δόξαντος μετρίως μεταχειρίζεσθαι τὴν ἀρχήν, ἐξ οὗ μάλιστα ταῖς Ἀθηνοδώρου τοῦ Στωικοῦ συμβουλαῖς ἐπείσθη.

Victor's *Historia* and was picked up from there by Julian.[133] He also calls Severus 'inexorable towards small faults' (1.8.2: περὶ τοὺς ἁμαρτάνοντας ἀπαραίτητος). This uses the same word as Julian to describe Severus' implacable quality (*Caes.* 312d: ἀπηνὲς καὶ ἀπαραίτητον). Yet the stronger parallel is with Victor, who had called Severus *implacabilis delictis* (*HAb* 20.20). Zosimus' wording is about as literal as possible a translation of Victor's phrase. The fact that Zosimus agrees with Julian, and yet provides a more extended parallel with the *HAb*, which pre-dates the *Caesares*, means that Zosimus or his source was not drawing on Julian, but on Victor.[134]

What this means is that there is a real connection between the first part of Zosimus' first book and Victor, which cannot merely be swatted away. For Festy, however, this use of Victor is mediated to Zosimus through Nicomachus Flavianus via Eunapius.[135] Why do we need Flavianus at all? One reason Festy gives is that there are details in Zosimus that are not found in the *HAb*, even in the highly compressed narrative of Tiberius to Domitian: to wit, the name of Domitian's killer Stephanus. If, however, the *HAb* is not the entirety of Victor's work, the objection simply evaporates. Combine that with the fact that Stephanus is mentioned in the *LB* (11.11), which Paschoud considers confirmation of the Flavianus thesis, and it becomes perfectly obvious that the origin is Victor.[136] Whether or not there was a Greek intermediary between Victor and Zosimus, Flavianus is simply superfluous.[137]

The *Annales* and the *Historia*

These are but two building blocks in the impressive Flavianic façade, but their example can stand for many others. Insofar as the outriders of Flavianus have identified genuine problems in the relationship between our extant sources, they are much more likely to be solved by reference to Victor. This holds true even for the two main pillars of the construct: the relationship between Latin and Greek historiography, the subject of the next chapter, and the sources of the *Historia Augusta*, the subject of the previous one. The proponents of Flavianus are right to look for a major and basically reliable historical source underpinning much of the *HA*, albeit in distorted form, but as we have seen, that source seems to be Victor's *Historia*. The only real 'proof' of the importance of Flavianus to the *HA* that his advocates have advanced is the fact that the *scriptor* quotes a Nicomachus as a source in the *Aurelian*, just as it cites an Aurelius Victor in the *Opilius Macrinus*. Might this be another sly footnote, as Paschoud has argued?[138] In context, however, this identification is far from compelling. Nicomachus is explicitly cited as a translator from Syriac into Greek

133 Chapter V.
134 Paschoud does not comment on this phrase in 1.8.2, but elsewhere, *e.g.* on the death of Commodus (2000: 136), he considers the similarities between Julian and Zosimus as evidence for Eunapius being the latter's source. Be that as it may, at least in this instance, it is not possible that Julian is Zosimus' ultimate source *pace* Mendelssohn 1887 *passim* (*cf.* Scavone 1970: 57).
135 Festy 1998. His inclusion of Eunapius rests on the arguments of Baldini 1984: 179–230; briefly, the idea is that Eunapius included a précis of events up to the reign of Aurelian (which overlapped with Dexippus), before beginning his narrative proper after Dexippus concluded.
136 Paschoud 2000: xlvi and 135. There are, perhaps, even hints of an intellectual debt to Victor in Zosimus. His emphatic statement that the rise of Augustus marked a transition to rule by one man at Rome (1.5.2) recalls the opening lines of the *HAb* (Chapter IV).
137 We consider the relationship between Victor and Zosimus in greater detail in Chapter X.
138 Paschoud 1996: 147–149.

of a letter written by the Palmyrene Zenobia (*Aurel.* 27.6). Probably the most famous Nicomachus across the Roman world, from the second century up to the sixth, was Nicomachus of Gerasa, an authority on music and maths – he was a Syrian who wrote in Greek.[139] There is nothing in context which would make a reader think of an aristocrat from an old Roman family.[140] This is much more likely a case of the *scriptor* of the *HA* repurposing the name of an existing author who wrote in an entirely different genre.[141]

In its way, scholarship on Flavianus has in recent years implicitly acknowledged this. It has moved towards assigning to the *LB* a particularly prominent role as a witness to the *Annales* and at the same time has suggested that Flavianus used the work of Victor.[142] These points are defensible insofar as they show that the possible Latin history which was used by Ammianus and which influenced the later Greek tradition had something to do with Victor, but they do not tell us anything about Flavianus. Instead, they tell us about Victor's *Historia*. Everything that the *Annales* are supposed to do, his *Historia* does better. The fact that Victor was demonstrably the most well-known secular Latin historian of late antiquity, a scholar whose work does not survive entire but has still left a formidable legacy, forestalls the fatal objections to the Flavianus theory.

What then is left for Flavianus and his *Annales*? Not, it must be said, very much beyond the bare fact of their existence. We maintain agnosticism on their coverage: there is simply no decisive evidence to show whether they covered the Republic, the Empire, both, or indeed some other carefully delineated period. The one thing of which we can be fairly certain is that they were commissioned by Theodosius – 'the wishes of a Roman emperor were commands', as Cameron succinctly puts it – and released sometime soon after 390.[143] The final edition of Victor's *History* was issued at the earliest in 388 and he must have been in favour at the court of Theodosius to have been made urban prefect at roughly the same time. All this seems a little too close for coincidence. It would not be the first time that a Roman emperor had commissioned a short history not so long after Victor had produced a large-scale work. The same situation obtained under Valens around 370, when Eutropius and Festus were commissioned to write their *breviaria* just a few years after Victor had published the first edition of his *Historia*. Valens' interest seems to have been twofold: to supplement what was available with a brief treatment of Republican history and to boil down Victor's difficult history of the Empire into a more easily digestible and usable form. This suggests the possibility – and we stress that this is *only* a possibility – that Flavianus' composition might have played a similar role. Perhaps it was a Republican history, to give a prequel to Victor; perhaps it was yet another epitome of the *Historia*.[144]

139 On Nicomachus, see D'Ooge *et al.* 1926; McDermott 1977; Albertson 2014: 50–59.

140 This is thus an entirely different case to the appearance of an Aurelius Victor in the *Macrinus*, where everything about the 'quotation' from him (its African details, its style, its vocabulary) is indeed redolent of his work.

141 Bleckmann and Groß 2016: 69 also reject an association with Flavianus, instead preferring to associate the *HA*'s Nicomachus with Nicostratus of Trebizond, who is known to have written about the Palmyrene empire.

142 For scholarship on the *LB* and Flavianus, see Stover and Woudhuysen 2021: 150–151. Flavianus and Victor: Festy 1998 *e.g.*

143 Cameron 2011: 630.

144 One could object that the title *Annales* precludes such a work, but we do not actually know whether that was the title of the work or a (slightly grandiose) description in the rather defensive inscription. Further, Eutropius probably did not entitle his work *breviarium* (Chapter III), but rather *Historia Romana*, a title more suited to a larger-scale work. One possibility would be that Flavianus arranged material from Victor (whose work was obviously not strictly chronological) year by year for easier consultation. Far from making a third epitome of Victor implausible, the fact that two separate ones survive by two different routes suggests there may

This chapter has examined two works that have loomed over Latin history-writing at the end of the fourth century: the spectral *Annales* of Nicomachus Flavianus and the very real *Res gestae* of Ammianus Marcellinus. In each case, Victor helps us both to understand and to contextualise these very different authors. Ammianus emerges from this examination as no longer the stylite of some historiographic desert, but rather an author constantly in dialogue with Victor's work – influenced by his language, his approach to history, and what he had said about Rome's past and its present. This is in no way to deny the originality or achievement of the *Res gestae* – if anything, it helps us to see them more clearly. With Flavianus, Victor helps to cut the *Annales* down to size. Part of the reason that they have bulked so large in debate is that a very real problem that needs to be explained. Yet Flavianus is not the right character to play the major role that he has been assigned as the point of contact between the earlier Latin and later Greek histories. This is not to deny that some such point of contact must exist, if only because of the relationship between the *Libellus breviatus* and material transmitted in the Greek tradition. The arc of the argument constructed so far suggests Victor as the obvious candidate, not least because we know that he was actually being read by at least one Greek in sixth-century Constantinople. The only way to consider the question is to examine what the later Greek historians share with Victor. It is to this that we turn next.

well have been still more in antiquity. At any rate, Ammianus' failure to mention Flavianus' work suggests, unavoidably in our opinion, either that it appeared too late for him to use it, which is entirely possible, or else that it was of a similar scope and ambition to the other works by characters in his history whom he fails to mention as authors, the *breviaria* of Eutropius and Festus.

CHAPTER X

GREEKS AND LATINS

Nicomachus Flavianus is the last of a series of phantoms that Part 2 this book has sought to dispel. As with the elimination of the *Kaisergeschichte* and Marius Maximus, removing the haze that he has cast over the study of late antique history-writing allows us to see things more clearly, but it also raises some acute questions. Of these, the deepest and most important is whether the *Historia* of Victor influenced Greek historiography in late antiquity and thereafter. It is obvious that the material in the *Libellus breviatus* that we have already discussed points in this direction, but to confirm that historians from Zosimus to Zonaras were indebted (directly or otherwise) to Victor we ought also to find connections between their works and the *Historia abbreviata*. For whatever reason, little work has been done (outside the context of Flavianus) on connections between the *HAb* and the Greek tradition and almost nothing on the possibility of the former influencing the latter. The *HAb*'s moralising and sententious character has perhaps discouraged effort, where the plainer and more factual nature of the *LB* has made it easier to spot points of contact.

This chapter therefore starts by examining the relationship between the *HAb* and the Greek tradition. The logical hunting ground for any links between them is the period from the middle of the third century onwards. Down to that time, the narratives of Dio, Herodian, and (possibly) Asinius Quadratus present a powerful confounding factor, since they were used by Victor, but were also available to later Greek historians. When they give out, the problem can suddenly come into sharper focus. We show that there are sustained commonalities of facts, language, and ideas between the *HAb* and a revolving cast of Greek historians, most prominently Zosimus and Zonaras, though Peter the Patrician and John of Antioch also have a role to play. Throughout, we demonstrate that where these links between Victor and the Greeks exist, there are invariably compelling reasons to believe that his *Historia* was the original source to which they were indebted. It is, of course, impossible to survey here the whole history of the century from Gallienus to Julian, picking out the common threads of Latin and Greek historiography, but by selective treatment of particularly important episodes, we show that there is a continuing debt to Victor in the Greek tradition's account of the period. We then turn to the difficult question of how Victor's work became known in the Greek world. Though excessive certainty would be foolish and we ought to envision multiple points of dissemination for it, we show that Eunapius of Sardis perhaps played an important role here. A better understanding of Victor's influence on the Greek tradition leads us to the *Origo Constantini imperatoris* and the *Laterculus* of Polemius Silvius – two Latin works that have tended to sit somewhat outside the historiographical mainstream, at least compared to the *Kaisergeschichte*, the *Historia Augusta*, or Nicomachus Flavianus. Both, we argue, owe considerable debts to Victor and the *Origo* may even be a major witness to his *Historia*.

This final chapter surveys a variety of topics, loose ends (so to speak) from the unravelling that has preceded it. In many cases, what we say here is little more than exploratory – it might nevertheless give some sense of where the study of late-antique historiography can profitably turn, armed with a more accurate picture of Victor's work.

★ ★ ★

The age of Gallienus

In hunting for connections between Victor and the Greeks, the place to start is the death of Gallienus.[1] Victor provides a detailed and unique account of this important event, one that combines material known elsewhere only in Latin or only in Greek into a seamless and coherent narrative. It is a rather complex example, with many moving parts, but it is worth detailed study.

The story begins with the usurpation of Postumus in Gaul, at the very beginning of Gallienus' sole reign, in AD 260.[2] Only the *HAb* and Zosimus tell us that Postumus was a military commander there before his usurpation. Moreover, they do so in closely parallel phrases (**TABLE 10.1**). The loss of authority over Gaul cast a shadow over Gallienus' whole reign and left the historian of his epoch without much to say that was cheering to a Roman audience. One of the few bright spots was the success of the general Aureolus, dispatched to northern Italy in the late 260s to ward off invasion by Postumus.[3] Zosimus (1.40.1) gives the most detailed account of Aureolus' career, but Victor alone (*HAb* 33.17) reveals that he was in command of the legions in Raetia.[4] Alas, Aureolus turned against his rather feckless imperial master and made a bid for supreme power. This stirred Gallienus to action and he defeated Aureolus at the place that came to be known as *pons Aureoli*, now Pontirolo – an authentic detail unique to the two Victorine texts (*HAb* 33.18; *LB* 33.2). From there, the rebel general fled to Milan, where he was soon trapped. Zonaras offers a description of what must be the same battle (without the name of the bridge) and its aftermath, one that is closely parallel to Victor (**TABLE 10.2**). Through all this, the Greek tradition is closely linked to the *HAb*, but the latter (besides being much the earliest extant source) preserves crucial details that strongly suggest its priority.

That impression only grows stronger as the story continues. With the usurper now trapped in Milan, Gallienus settled in for a siege. During this, a conspiracy against him was formed – it would prove fatal. Victor gives a unique account of how Aureolus forged a document, purportedly from Gallienus, sentencing several of his commanders to death, and covertly dropped it over the city's walls (*HAb* 33.20, cf. *LB* 33.2). Upon its discovery, those named in it formed a conspiracy to protect themselves. Zonaras has the conspiracy already in existence before the siege, but put on hold for its duration, until the conspirators discovered that they had been unmasked (12.25). These accounts are entirely complementary, since Zonaras does not detail how or why the conspirators thought they had been found out.[5] In any case, the

---

1 Bleckmann 1997: 24–26 has already signalled this as an important point in the tradition, albeit in the hunt for traces of Flavianus. *cf.* Ratti 1999, who wants to make the accounts of both Victor and Zosimus derive from the *KG*. On the events surrounding Gallienus' death and the texts that relate them, see Migliorati 2016, Christol 2014 (who highlights in particular the importance of Victor's contribution), Hartmann 2006, Ratti 1999, and Saunders 1992. All of these, while presenting valuable insights and analyses, are ultimately concerned with the kind of *Quellenforschung* – the conjuring of lost sources such as the *KG* and the *Leoquelle* – that we criticise here.

2 On Postumus, see Chapter VIII.

3 *PLRE* 'Aureolus'.

4 The text here is problematic, for as transmitted it names not Aureolus (though he reappears at 1.40.3), but Aurelian (Αὐρηλιανὸν vs Αὐρίολον, see Paschoud's *apparatus ad loc.*), whom it says was stationed at Milan. It is tempting to assume a scribal error here, as editors since Syllburg have done, and correct the text, but it is quite possible that Zosimus simply could not keep the names straight.

5 Saunders 1992: 90–91 admits this possibility, although he prefers to think of them as separate.

TABLE 10.1 – THE *HAb* AND ZOSIMUS ON POSTUMUS

HAb 33.8	Zosimus 1.38.2
Postumus, qui forte barbaris per Galliam praesidebat, imperium ereptum ierat.	Πόστουμος ἀρχὴν ἐν Κελτοῖς στρατιωτῶν ἐμπεπιστευμένος ἐς τὸ νεωτερίσαι προήχθη.
Postumus, who was by chance in charge of the barbarians throughout Gaul, had proceeded to seize imperial power.	Postumus, who had been sent to govern the troops among the Gauls, proceeded to usurpation.

TABLE 10.2 – THE *HAb* AND ZONARAS ON HOSTILITIES AT MILAN

HAb 33.18	Zonaras 12.25
[Aureolum] fusum acie Mediolanum coegit.	ὁ Αὐρίολος ἐτρώθη καὶ εἰς Μεδιόλανα κατεκλείσθη
He confined Aureolus to Milan, after he had been routed in battle.	Aureolus was wounded and hemmed in at Milan.

important detail is that only Victor and Zonaras assign the principal role in this conspiracy to the future emperor Aurelian (*HAb* 33.19, Zonaras 12.25).[6]

The plot was successfully put into action: a false report was given to Gallienus that the enemy were upon them, he set off at once without his bodyguards, and was killed by a spear. The parallels between the *HAb* and the Greek sources are sustained and striking (**TABLE 10.3**).[7] The account in the *HAb* is extremely close to that of Zonaras: both provide the generic message that enemies were attacking, both emphasise the sudden nature of Gallienus' response, both specify that it is uncertain who killed him but that the weapon that was used was a spear, and both explicitly attribute his death to blood-loss with identical phrasing. Indeed, resonances with Zonaras continue beyond the emperor's assassination, as he and Victor are the only ones to mention the Senate's execution of Gallienus' relations after his death was announced at Rome (*HAb* 33.31 ~ Zonaras 12.26). That in itself is significant, for (as we have seen) in Victor that episode is part of an extended series of links between Gallienus and Tiberius – not an historiographical agenda known to Zonaras.[8] At the same time, one phrase in Victor – on Gallienus' lack of bodyguards – is identical with Zosimus. Seen in the round, this is a quite extraordinary series of connections between the *HAb* and the Greek tradition.

This was by no means the only version of Gallienus' demise that circulated in late antiquity (and later still). After the first part of the quote in Table 10.3, Zonaras immediately provides a second account. In this, Heraclianus (the praetorian prefect) burst into Gallienus' tent at night as the emperor lay sleeping, told him that the enemy were upon him, and proceeded to vindicate his warning by killing him (12.25).[9]

6 Does the confused text of Zosimus 1.40.1 (above) offer a distant echo of this point?

7 *cf.* Bleckmann 1997: 25.

8 Chapter IV.

9 *PLRE* 'Heraclianus 6'.

TABLE 10.3 – THE *HAb*, ZONARAS, AND ZOSIMUS ON THE DEATH OF GALLIENUS

HAb 33.21–31	Zonaras 12.25–26	Zosimus 1.40.2–3
Qua causa, Aureliani consilio, cuius gratia in exercitus atque honos praestabant, simulata **proruptione hostium** *nullis*, uti **re trepida ac repentina** solet, *tectum stipatoribus* tabernaculo educunt nocte intempesta, **teloque traicitur**, cuiusnam per tenebras incertum . . . Nam cum **profluvio sanguinis vulnere tam gravi mortem sibi adesse intellegeret**, insignia imperii ad Claudium destinaverat honore tribunatus Ticini retinentem praesidiariam manum . . . At **senatus** comperto tali **exitio** . . .	Στέλλουσί τινας, **πολεμίους ἐπιέναι** τῷ Γαλιήνῳ ἀγγέλλοντας· ὁ δὲ **αὐτίκα** ἐξώρμησε κατ' αὐτῶν, ὥρας ἤδη ἐφεστώσης ἀρίστου, καὶ ὀλίγων συνεφεπομένων αὐτῷ . . . **καί τις** κατ' αὐτοῦ τὸ δόρυ ἠκόντισεν. ὁ δὲ **πληγεὶς** τοῦ ἵππου κατήνεκτο, καὶ ἐπὶ μικρὸν διαρκέσας **ἐκ τῆς τοῦ αἵματος** ἐτελεύτησε **ῥύσεως** . . . Ἐν Ῥώμῃ δέ γε **ἡ σύγκλητος** μαθοῦσα **τὴν** τοῦ Γαλιήνου **ἀναίρεσιν** . . .	ἄνδρα δὲ εὑρὼν εἰς τὰ τοιαῦτα προχειρότατον ὃς τῆς τῶν Δαλματῶν ἦρχεν ἴλης, ἐγχειρίζει τούτῳ τὴν πρᾶξιν. ὁ δὲ ἐπιστὰς τῷ Γαλλιηνῷ δειπνοποιουμένῳ, καὶ φήσας ἀγγεῖλαί τινα τῶν κατασκόπων ὡς Αὐρίολος ἅμα τῇ σὺν αὐτῷ δυνάμει προσάγει, τοῖς τοιούτοις ἐπτόησεν λόγοις. ὅπλα τε οὖν ᾔτει καὶ ἀναθορὼν ἐς τὸν ἵππον σύνθημα τοῖς στρατιώταις ἐδίδου μετὰ τῶν ὅπλων ἀκολουθεῖν, καὶ **οὐδὲ τοὺς δορυφοροῦντας ἐκδεξάμενος** ἤλαυνεν. γυμνὸν οὖν ὁ ἰλάρχης θεασάμενος ἀποσφάττει.
For this reason, on the advice of Aurelian, whose influence and honour in the army were outstanding, during a pretended sally of the enemy, they led him [*sc.* Gallienus] from his tent at the dead of night, protected by no bodyguards (as is usual when the event is doubtful and arises suddenly); he was transfixed by a missile, at whose hand is uncertain due to the darkness . . . For when he recognised that his death was at hand from a wound so serious due to the loss of blood, he had sent the insignia of the empire to Claudius, who was in command of the garrison company at Pavia with the rank of tribune . . . But the Senate, having learned of his demise . . .	They dispatched messengers to announce to Gallienus that the enemy was advancing. He immediately proceeded against them, since the time for a meal had already arrived, and only a few accompanied him . . . One [of the horseman chasing him] cast his spear at him. Struck, he fell from his horse and after hanging on for a little while, he died from loss of blood . . . At Rome when the Senate learned of Gallienus' demise . . .★	Having found a man best prepared to do this, who was in command of the troop of Dalmatian cavalry, he [Heraclianus] entrusted the deed to him. He [the cavalry officer] was stationed by Gallienus as he supped and said that one of the scouts had sent word that Aureolus was advancing with his forces. This news startled him, and he called for his armour. Having mounted his horse, and given a signal to his soldiers to follow as soon as they were armed, he set off supported by no retainers. And so the cavalry commander [*praefectus alae*] saw that he was unprotected and killed him.

In the table, bold type in the *HAb* and Zonaras indicates agreements in wording, while the italics in the *HAb* indicates material found only in Zosimus, which is there bolded.

★ ἄριστον (*LSJ* s.v.) originally meant breakfast, and later the midday meal. In still later Greek, it seems to have come to mean a meal in general: see *e.g.* the homily attributed to Eusebius of Alexandria (*PG* 86.1.357bc), on whom there is a helpful article by MacCoull 1999 (arguing for composition in the eighth century).

The *HA* (*Gall.* 14.1–9) offers a very similar story, in which Heraclianus and one Marcianus are identified as the key conspirators, along with a cavalry commander called Cecropius (or Ceronius), a *dux Dalmatarum*.[10] Marcianus and Cecropius sent word to Gallienus of the attack, Gallienus mustered his troops, and was then killed by Cecropius. Zosimus betrays traces of this version, in ascribing a leading role in the conspiracy to Heraclianus and making a commander of Dalmatian cavalry play an important part. Despite a general scholarly preference for this version of events, it is somewhat nonsensical.[11] Why would Heraclianus bother with the ruse of an impending attack if he was just going to kill Gallienus in his tent anyway? Why would Marcianus and Cecropius give Gallienus a chance to muster his troops and, if he did, how did they then manage to kill him? The key thing in the assassination of an emperor was getting him alone. Examples are legion: Commodus was killed by his wrestling partner recruited into the conspiracy; Caracalla was assassinated when he went to ease his bladder (*levandae vesicae gratia* as the *HA Carac.* 7.1 says). At first sight, little in this alternative tradition appears to make sense.

That Zonaras provides two separate versions of the death of Gallienus should indicate that he had two separate sources, nor would we wish to deny that there were multiple accounts of that event in circulation, in antiquity and thereafter. This does not mean, however, that Zonaras' two accounts represent two separate and integral ancient traditions. We have seen already with the *Historia Augusta* that the compiler sometimes offers multiple treatments of the same material derived separately from Victor directly and mediated through Eutropius.[12] In fact, every narrative of the death of Gallienus outside Zonaras mixes together points from both of his versions. Zonaras' second account and that in the *HAb* are clear that the attack happened at night (*intempesta nocte* ~ νυκτός). Zosimus (1.40.2) has Heraclianus as the principal conspirator and the commander of some Dalmatian cavalry as the man who dealt the fatal blow. The *HA* has a version closer to Zonaras' second – with Heraclianus as the main actor – but includes the fatal false message, and like Zosimus has the commander of the Dalmatian cavalry as the assassin.[13] This looks like a classic case where a complex original account of events in the darkest days of the third century – to which all extant ones are ultimately indebted – has generated considerable confusion in later sources, producing results that look wildly divergent, but are in fact explained by shared derivation with a sprinkling of contamination. Given the starring role the *HAb* plays in any attempt at reconstruction, that complex original ought logically to be Victor's – can we prove this?

Zonaras' first version and Victor's in the *HAb* provide a coherent and compelling account of how the conspiracy against Gallienus actually functioned. Crucially, it hinged on a particular point about Gallienus' psychology. The plot makes sense only if the conspirators surmised that Gallienus would rashly charge off without waiting to marshal his bodyguards, when danger suddenly presented itself. This is a key component of Victor's portrait of the emperor's character. While the dominant theme of his depiction is Gallienus' indolence – *socordia* (*HAb* 33.17) – he makes it clear that the emperor was capable of surprisingly strenuous and hasty action, when he had exhausted all other options, particularly in the face of

---

10 The *HA* also mentions Claudius, but is clear that he was not part of the plot. It is hard not to think that its description of Claudius' standing was just copied from Victor (on Aurelian): *HAb* 33.21 *Aureliani consilio, cuius gratia in exercitu atque honos praestabant* ~ *HA Gall.* 14.2 *Claudius quidem, ut suo dicemus loco, vir omnium optimum,*

electus est, qui consilio non adfuerat, eaque apud cunctos reverentia.

11 In general, Saunders 1992.

12 The summary of Aurelian's achievements (Chapter VIII) is instructive.

13 *cf.* Ratti 1999: 262–263.

peril.[14] This is what had brought him to Milan in the first place: 'after peril began to approach, at last he left the city [*sc.* of Rome]' (*HAb* 33.16: *postquam periculum propinquabat, tandem urbe egreditur*). This same characteristic – of energy only in desperate circumstances – is crisply put in the *HA*: 'more than ready for every vice, if he were secure' (*Gall.* 5.9: *si esset securus, ad omne dedecus paratissimi*). It is only Victor, however, who specifically identifies this aspect of his character and explains its significance. Before Gallienus' appointment as Caesar, Victor notes that the Tiber ominously flooded: this betokened how the changeable nature (*fluxum ingenium*) of the young man would wreak destruction on the state (*HAb* 32.4). In other words, the shared account of the *HAb* and Zonaras represents an integral development of a historical idea that is authentic to Victor, one not reproduced in its entirety by any other source.[15]

The same might be said for the theme of simulation, which plays such an important role in the plot against the emperor. Victor has Gallienus celebrate triumphs to commemorate pretended victories: 'that what he had simulated might be more readily confirmed' (*HAb* 33.15: *quo promptius simulata confirmarentur*). It was this in particular that led to the revolt of Aureolus, provoked by the 'indolence of such an idle commander' (*HAb* 33.17: *socordia tam ignavi ducis*). After initial success against the usurper, Gallienus was at length undone by the forgery of Aureolus, which ignited the fatal conspiracy. In fitting fashion, after ignoring for most of his reign (in Victor's telling) real assaults on Roman soil, it was a 'simulated attack of his enemies' (**simulata hostium proruptione**) which led to his final downfall. As so often, there is considerable artistry in the way that Victor has arranged his ideas and historical events: the fall of Gallienus is the fruit of everything that was flawed in his character, flaws present right from his accession as emperor. Needless to say, there is no trace of this pattern in any of the other source (besides some faint echoes in the *HA*), and yet the simulated attack is the key part in every account of the emperor's demise.

Claudius and Aurelian

This still leave the question of the identity of the conspirators. As Saunders has already noted, this is the key difference between the two versions of Gallienus' death.[16] In Zonaras' first account and Victor, the future emperor Aurelian is the only conspirator named. In Zonaras' second account it is Heraclianus. All of our other sources, whomever they include in the fluctuating list of the conspirators, omit Aurelian and include Heraclianus. Whatever else might be said, Aurelian's involvement is not inherently implausible: to argue, as Saunders does, that there is 'no evidence to show that Aurelian was in contention for the principate at that time' is to ignore the explicit statement of Victor that his 'influence and honour in the army were outstanding (*HAb* 33.21: *gratia in exercitu atque honos praestabant*).[17] More importantly, however, Aurelian's ultimate responsibility for Gallienus' death is once again an idea integral to Victor's *History*. The spark that lit the fuse, in Victor's telling, was the forged letter of Aureolus (*HAb* 33.20):

---

14 *HAb* 33.1: *cum a Gallia Germanos strenue arceret, in Illyricum properans descendit*, and *HAb* 33.3.

15 *cf.* Christol 2014: 163, who speaks of the 'grande cohérence dans sa construction' of Victor's version.

16 Saunders 1992: 82–93.

17 Saunders 1992: 91. See also Christol 2014: 181–182.

> Ducum Gallieni tribunorumque nomina quasi destinata ab eo ad necem astu composuit.

> With guile he put together a list of the names of the generals and tribunes of Gallienus, as though he had marked them out for slaughter.

Exactly the same sequence of events would lead to Aurelian's own death seven years later, when (as we have seen) a disgruntled minister forged a document purporting to sentence some of the army's officers to death, who then pre-emptively assassinated the emperor.[18] Victor's description of the latter episode provides ever-so-close a parallel of language (*HAb* 35.8):

> Cum ille . . . scripta callide composita tribunis quasi per gratiam prodidisset, quibus interfici iube-bantur.

> When he had handed over to the tribunes, as if he were doing them a favour, cunningly fabricated documents in which their deaths were ordered.

This lends a sense of *contrapasso* to Aurelian's demise: that he was undone by the same stratagem which led to Gallienus' death, for which he was himself responsible. In other words, an elaborate thread runs through Victor's account of the 260s and the 270s, linking closely the deaths of the man under whom the Empire nearly fell apart and of his fierce successor, who stitched the pieces back together.[19]

In the case of Aurelian, however, the accidental death through fraudulent paperwork is found in *all* of our major sources: Eutropius (9.15), the *HA* (*Aurel.* 36.5), Zosimus (1.62.2), and Zonaras (12.27). So why does Victor (and Victor alone) have the same account of Gallienus' death?[20] Here the fact that he puts Aurelian at the centre of the plot against Gallienus is very significant: whether or not (as Dufraigne and others believe) the forged dossier of Aureolus is a retrojected doublet, it seems an integral part of an account that makes Aurelian party to the assassination of Gallienus.[21] This means that not only does the version of events common to Zonaras and Victor go back to a common Latin source (as Saunders has already argued), but also that Victor must be that source. Confirmation comes in Julian's *Caesares*, which has Helios (to whom Aurelian dedicated a temple, *HAb* 35.7) pronounce that justice had been done since Aurelian suffered what he committed.[22] This cannot be merely a general observation. Many emperors were (or were believed to have been) party to conspiracies against their predecessors and were themselves killed in turn: Pertinax, Didius Julianus, Macrinus, and Philip to name but a few. For Aurelian, then, Julian ought to mean something more specific. That is precisely what we find in Victor: Aurelian was murdered in a sequence of events exactly mirroring his own conspiracy against Gallienus.

One final significant feature of Victor's account and Zonaras' first version is that Gallienus did not die immediately, but only somewhat later, due to loss of blood. This was crucial because it meant that there was time for him to appoint a successor and Victor tells us – the story is preserved in both the *HAb* (33.28) and the *LB* (34.2) – that he appointed Claudius. This is usually regarded as an invention,

---

18 Chapter VIII.
19 This alone disposes (were disproof needed) of *PLRE*'s suggestion ('Heraclianus 6') that Victor names Aurelian in error for Heraclianus.
20 A point emphasised in Migliorati 2016: 247.

21 Dufraigne 1975: 163; Bird 1971; *cf.* Ratti 1999: 265.
22 Julian, *Caes.* 314a: Ἀλλ᾽ ἀπέτισε τὴν δίκην, ἣ λέληθεν ἡ δοθεῖσα ἐν Δελφοῖς μαντεία· Αἴκε πάθοι τά κ᾽ ἔρεξε, δίκη δ᾽ ἰθεῖα γένοιτο;

partly because of doubts about whether the person mentioned in the *LB* as conveying the *indumenta regia*, Gallonius Basilius, existed, doubts that (as we have seen) are not entirely warranted.[23] The point, however, is not whether this is true or false, but simply whether it is integral to the account of Gallienus' death or not. The answer to this question must be 'yes', for including it gives us a coherent picture of the conspiracy against the emperor. Aurelian was the favourite of the army and well positioned to seize imperial power. Unfortunately, his plot went awry in one crucial aspect: Gallienus did not die swiftly enough, nor alone. Instead, he was found by his retainers mortally wounded, but with sufficient life left in him to thwart his assassins and name a successor. It is only, however, Victor (in the *HAb*) who supplies the crucial information that Aurelian was the army's favourite. Here, as throughout the history of Gallienus, it is his account – discernible even in its current fragmentary state – which lies behind the messy, largely Greek, tradition that we find elsewhere.

This is not merely a phenomenon of the history of Gallienus and Aurelian, but can be confirmed by close attention to the treatment in the sources of the intervening emperor, Claudius II, victor over the Goths and putative ancestor of Constantine. Victor's account of Claudius is dominated (as we have seen) by his supposed *devotio*.[24] Facing a serious barbarian threat, the Romans turned to the Sibylline books, which decreed that the first man of the Senate must devote his life for Rome to be victorious. Pomponius Bassus who had the *ius primae sententiae dicendae* volunteered, but Claudius, 'a man . . . devoted to the commonwealth' (*dediti rei publicae*) (*HAb* 34.1), overruled him, declaring that he was the *princeps* of all, and thus *a fortiori* the *princeps senatus* (*HAb* 34.1–6 and *LB* 34.1–3). Here, Victor interrupts the tale with a moral discussion (*HAb* 34.5–6):

> Afterwards the emperor gave his life as a gift to the commonwealth. Therefore to good men the safety of the citizens, and their own long-lasting remembrance are dearer; these things profit not only their glory, but also by some inner process (*quaedam ratio*) the good fortune of their descendants.

Zonaras, too, sets a scene in the Senate, where there is deliberation as to whether there ought to be a campaign against a usurper, or against the barbarians who were ravaging Illyricum. Claudius opts for the latter, declaring: 'war on the usurper is in my interest, but war on the barbarians is in the interest of the commonwealth and a war for the commonwealth must be preferred'.[25] This cannot but be the same event as that described in Victor: both are set in the context of a discussion in the Senate, both focus on Claudius' concern for the good of the *res publica*, both result in his campaign against the Goths. Victor is our earliest extant source for this episode: despite the popularity of Claudius as the (mythical) progenitor of the house of Constantine, no Constantinian source before him actually alludes to this particular instance of his *virtus*.[26] It has indeed been suggested Victor was himself the originator of this story.[27] Yet, its echo is in Zonaras.

23 Chapter VIII.
24 Chapter IV.
25 Zonaras 12.26: ὁ Κλαύδιος ἔφη ὡς "ὁ πρὸς τὸν τύραννον πόλεμος ἐμοὶ διαφέρει, ὁ δὲ πρὸς τοὺς βαρβάρους τῇ πολιτείᾳ, καὶ χρὴ τὸν τῆς πολιτείας προτιμηθῆναι". For πολιτεία as *res publica*, see Mason 1974: 77 (*s.v.* 2).

26 Syme 1980b: 270–271 implies that it goes back to Constantinian propaganda, though the argumentation is not pellucid.
27 Baldini 2002 *e.g.*

The *HAb* thus shows a series of close connections to Greek sources in its narrative of the reigns of Gallienus, Claudius, and Aurelian. Moreover, in each case of overlap, it is clear that the underlying ideas are original to Victor. The explanation for this is surely that Victor's *Historia* was used – through one route or another – by later Greek authors.

After Dexippus

For Roman history of the third century, there is one potentially awkward issue that might reduce our confidence in the conclusions drawn so far, or at least somewhat limit their scope. We know that this period was treated in considerable detail by the lost historical work of the Athenian *littérateur* Dexippus, who as a contemporary of high rank was well placed to offer a richly detailed account.[28] The Athenian was certainly an important source for Byzantine historians and (as already suggested) it is possible that Victor himself had used his work.[29] There is then the possibility that some of what we are seeing here is not actually use of Victor by the Greeks, but use by both Victor and the Greeks of Dexippus's *Chronicle* or *Scythica*, or both. There are limits to how much of what we find in the sources this would explain: as we have seen, there is every reason to think that the *devotio* of Claudius is Victor's own work. Moreover, the very negative portrait of Gallienus that underlies all we have discussed above is alien to the Greek tradition in the third century: Dexippus appears to have admired Gallienus, Porphyry certainly thought of him warmly, and Christians had every reason to approve of an emperor who had ended his father's persecution.[30] Such consensus is extraordinary: Victor's hostility to the emperor was authentically his own. Still, Dexippus might cloud our picture of a Greek tradition indebted to a work in Latin that appeared in 360.

To control for this possibility – to provide proof that the Greek tradition is indeed indebted directly to Victor and *in extenso* – we need to look at events after the reign of Aurelian, where Dexippus concluded his historical work.[31] There was no historian writing in Greek whose work both covered this period and could have been read by Victor before 360, so there is no possibility that a common source can explain connections between his *Historia* and the Greek tradition.[32] If, therefore, we can show the same pattern of connections between Victor and the Greeks for the period after 275 as we find before it, then we can confidently conclude that Victor's *Historia* was a significant influence on the later Greek tradition – particularly for the period after the narratives of Dio and Herodian had given out.

---

28 In general, see *BNJ* 100 (McInerney). Millar 1969 remains a deeply rewarding treatment of the man, his work, and his world.

29 Chapter IV.

30 Dexippus: Armstrong 1984. Porphyry: *Vita Plotini* 12. Christians: Eusebius, *HE* 7.13 (quoting a rescript of Gallienus to Dionysius, the bishop of Alexandria, *i.a.*).

31 The *Chronicle* seems to have ended with events in 269/270 (*BNJ* 100 fr. 2 (McInerney)) or slightly earlier (fr. 1 = Eunapius). The *Scythica* included Aurelian (fr. 6), but its terminal point is unclear – certainly nothing would license us to extend it much beyond 275. Eunapius (t. 2) seems to have thought that Dexippus was still alive under Probus (d. 282), but no later.

32 This is not, of course, to claim that there were no Greek historians active in the period – the evidence for the lively tradition of history-writing in Greek is assembled by Janiszewski 2006. While, however, there was plenty of local history (see his second chapter) and some biographies of individual emperors (his fourth, though Onasimus ought to be ejected from this: see Chapter VII), there were no universal histories in the tradition of Dexippus. Eunapius certainly covered the period in his history, but he was writing after Victor and we might wonder about how detailed his account was (see below).

The rise of Diocletian

In the year 284, Diocletian was proclaimed emperor in the east, probably at Nicomedia, by a Roman army that had recently returned from a victorious campaign in Persia.[33] The circumstances leading up to this pivotal event, as well as its immediate aftermath, are notoriously murky, involving as they do the deaths (possibly murders) of two emperors: Carus (r. 282–283) and his son Numerian. At first sight, our sources do much to make this tangled episode still more obscure than we might expect. Yet examined closely, they reveal a complex set of parallels and complementarities between the Greek and Latin historical traditions. In the discussion of Diocletian's origins and rise to power, Zonaras provides an account extremely similar to that found in Eutropius and the *LB*. All three texts say that he was from Dalmatia, born in lowly circumstances, and that some people alleged he was the freedman of a senator called Anullinus.[34] At the same time there are significant links between these three and the *HAb*, the *HA*, and Peter the Patrician (Zosimus' account having vanished into the lacuna that mars the end of Book I and beginning of Book II) (**TABLE 10.4**). The shifting constellation of relationships in this network of texts is striking. Zonaras agrees with the linked accounts of the *HAb* and *HA* that Diocletian was in command of the *domestici* (interestingly using a Latin calque: κόμητα δομεστίκων) immediately before his accession. Zonaras, the *HAb*, the *HA*, and Eutropius recount how, at the very moment he first addressed the army as emperor, Diocletian disposed of his major rival, the praetorian prefect Aper (father-in-law to Numerian), in a dramatic and public fashion: executing him with a sword in front of the troops. We have already discussed how the accounts in the *HAb*, Eutropius, and the *HA* of Diocletian's acclamation are closely parallel, with tell-tale signs of derivation from Victor (such as the Vergilian phrase *educto gladio*).[35] Now, Victor (*HAb* 39.13) makes Diocletian affirm two things immediately before running Aper through: *obtestaretur ignarum cladis Numeriani neque imperii cupientem se fuisse*. Only the first of these is reprised by Eutropius (*iuravit Numerianum nullo suo dolo interfectum*), and the *HA* has neither in its account (*Car.* 13.1–3). The first one, however, is also found in Zonaras and in terms so close to Victor that they could almost be a translation: διεβεβαίου μὴ κοινωνῆσαι τῷ φόνῳ τοῦ Νουμεριανοῦ. He adds that Diocletian turned toward Aper, who was standing next to him, and declared: 'This is his [Numerian's] murderer!' (οὗτος . . . ὁ ἐκείνου φονεύς). Exactly the same *dictum* is adduced in the *HA* (*'hic est auctor necis Numeriani'*). The second is found in the very different account of Peter the Patrician, in what is once again close to a translation: μὴ διὰ τὸ τῆς βασιλείας ἐφίεσθαι. This is a striking shared detail about an emperor who, as Victor well knew, was greedy for power and its trappings (*HAb* 39.2–6).[36] Peter and Victor also share the inconspicuous detail that Diocletian solemnised this statement with an appeal to the gods: Victor has him 'gazing at the sun' (*solem intuens*), while Peter more generally has him swear by the divine (τὰ τότε σεβόμενα θεῖα μαρτυρόμενος). For Peter, this event occurs in the context of Diocletian's killing of

33 The location hangs by a rather slender thread: only John of Antioch (fr. 246 Roberto, probably from Zosimus) explicitly attests it. Barnes 1981: 4 and n. 18 and 1982: 49 with 62 and n. 73 attempts to find the same information in Lactantius, *DMP* 19.2, but that works only if one deletes *Maximianus* (as a gloss) and then assumes Lactantius wrote an ambiguous *ipse* to mean Diocletian (who has not been mentioned for several sentences).

34 It is worth noting that C. Annius Anullinus (*cos.* 295, proconsul of Africa during the persecution) was a much-favoured servant of the Tetrarchy, whose consulship appears (unusually) to have preceded much of his career – a high honour.

35 Chapter VIII.

36 On this passage, see also Stover and Woudhuysen 2020 [2015].

Carinus. This is not where Victor puts the story, but Peter's wording is, we might note, very close to that found earlier in the *HA*.[37] Through all this haze of detail, the Greek tradition has repeated connections to the Latin and specific debts to Victor.

While Diocletian was being proclaimed Augustus by the army in the east, the surviving scion of the house of Carus, Carinus, was still alive and reigning in the west. His rule was, however, not unchallenged, for the praetorian prefect Sabinus Julianus had usurped power in Pannonia when news of Carus' death trickled out. A three-sided civil war thus loomed. Carinus made for the Balkans along the Danube (the same route Julian would take nearly eighty years later), presumably intent on subduing or co-opting Julianus before Diocletian and his army could advance. Julianus had other ideas, however, and launched an invasion of Italy. Carinus deviated from his route, caught Julianus' army at Verona, and defeated it. From there, he marched into Illyricum and met Diocletian in battle at a *municipium* called Margus. Once again he was victorious, but caught up in a conspiracy, he was assassinated by his own men at the moment of his triumph – leaving Diocletian in sole control of the Roman world.

This succinct version of the turmoil of 284 – slightly speculative but eminently plausible – cannot be found in any survey of these complex events.[38] That is because it emerges only from the Victorine texts, correctly read. Yet, throughout his fragmentary narrative of the same material, John of Antioch (and probably Zosimus before him) shows some remarkable coincidences of detail with the *HAb* and *LB*.[39] At the time of his brother's death, Carinus was in Gaul, as Victor alone tells us.[40] Only Victor gives his route, 'skirting Italy', to the Balkans.[41] Our only evidence for Julianus' existence – besides a handful of coins – is in the *HAb* (39.10), the *LB* (38.6), and John of Antioch (fr. 246 Roberto = Zosimus 1.73.1).[42] It is only the *HAb* that provides the crucial detail that, having seized power, Julianus headed into Italy:

37 Peter the Patrician, *ES* 181 Καρῖνον ἀνελεῖν . . . διὰ τὸ ἐλεεῖν τὴν πολιτείαν ~ *HA Car.* 10.2 *Carino, quem vir rei publicae necessarius Augustus Diocletianus habitis conflictibus interemit.*

38 There is a crisp overview in Barnes 1981: 4–5 and a much more discursive one in Altmayer 2014: 142–183.

39 On the question of John of Antioch's relationship with Zosimus, see Chapter IX.

40 The *HAb* (38.2) says that Carus sent Carinus *ad munimentum Galliae*, then (39.17) that Aelianus and Amandus (leaders of the *Bagaudae*) revolted *Carini discessu*. This is often understood (Dufraigne 1975, Bird 1994 *ad loc.*) as 'at the death of Carinus', but that is not what *discessus* means generally (it can have that sense, but it is surprisingly rare: *TLL* 5.1.1311.27–1313.10 (Graeber) – see sense 2). Barnes 1981: 4 (with n. 16) states that Carinus was in Rome in January 284, but the evidence cited (*ILS* 608, the restoration of a bridge at Ostia; *CJ* 8.53.5, a law posted at Rome in January 284) in no way requires it – Victor's explicit evidence deserves greater credit and makes it easier to understand how Carinus could have obtained the title Britannicus (presumably by a campaign over the Channel), *cf.* Nemesianus, *Cynegetica* 63–71 for his northern campaigns. That Eutropius (9.19.1) mentions how Carinus *matrimonia nobilia corripuit* need not imply he was in Rome (if these

were senatorial marriages), since it is not clear when the affairs in question took place.

41 *HAb* 39.9: *Interim Carinus, eorum quae acciderant certior spe facilius erumpentis motus sedatum iri, Illyricum propere Italiae circuitu petit.*

42 Julianus has caused considerable confusion, even giving rise to two separate entries in *PLRE* ('Iulianus 24', 'Iulianus 38'), as though the *HAb* were telling us about a different Julianus to the one mentioned by the *LB* and Zosimus. This is all because Schott made a bold but misguided attempt to fix the text of the *HAb*, which transplanted Julianus to Italy (see the Appendix, no. XIII). There is in fact no contradiction between the *HAb*, the *LB*, and John of Antioch: they are all describing a praetorian prefect who seized power in the Balkans (his coins call him *Pannoniae Aug.*), then crossed into Italy, where he was defeated by Carinus – the fact that his coins (*RIC* 5.2: 593–594, *cf.* Estiot 2010) call him M. Aurelius Julianus and the *LB* and John Sabinus Julianus is simply no obstacle to identifying them. Estiot's dismissal of John of Antioch's explicit statement of Julianus' office is unnecessary (2010: 402–403): presumably after Julianus usurped, Carinus would have appointed a new praetorian prefect, *i.e.* Aristobulus, who was in office during the battles against Diocletian.

TABLE 10.4 – ZONARAS, THE *LB*, THE *HAb*, EUTROPIUS, THE *HA*, AND PETER THE PATRICIAN ON DIOCLETIAN'S ORIGINS AND RISE TO POWER

Zonaras 12.31	*LB* 39.1	*HAb* 39.1, 13
Διοκλητιανὸς δὲ τὴν ἡγεμονίαν λαχών, ὃς Δαλμάτης μὲν ἦν τὸ γένος, πατέρων δ᾽ ἀσήμων, τινὲς δὲ καὶ ἀπελεύθερον αὐτόν φασιν Ἀνουλίνου συγκλητικοῦ, ἐξ εὐτελῶν στρατιωτῶν δοὺξ Μυσίας ἐγένετο. ἄλλοι δὲ κόμητα δομεστίκων αὐτὸν γενέσθαι φασί· δομεστίκους δέ τινες τοὺς ἱππέας νομίζουσι. διαλεγόμενος δὲ τοῖς στρατιώταις διεβεβαίου μὴ κοινωνῆσαι τῷ φόνῳ τοῦ Νουμεριανοῦ· καὶ ἐν τῷ ταῦτα λέγειν στραφεὶς πρὸς τὸν Ἄπρον ἔπαρχον ὄντα τοῦ στρατεύματος 'οὗτος' ἔφη 'ὁ ἐκείνου φονεύς', καὶ αὐτίκα τῷ μετὰ χεῖρας ξίφει αὐτὸν ἀνεῖλεν.	Diocletianus Dalmata, Anulini senatoris libertinus, matre pariter atque oppido nomine Dioclea, quorum vocabulis donec imperium sumeret Diocles appellatus.	Valerius Diocletianus domesticos regens ob sapientiam deligitur, magnus vir . . . Igitur Valerius prima ad exercitum contione cum educto gladio solem intuens obtestaretur ignarum cladis Numeriani neque imperii cupientem se fuisse, Aprum proxime astantem ictu transegit.★
Diocletian took up imperial power. He was Dalmatian by birth, of low-born parents, and (according to some) a freedman of the senator Anullinus; he went from being a common soldier to the *dux* of Mysia. Others say that he became *comes domesticorum*; some think the *domestici* were cavalry. While addressing the soldiers, he maintained that he had no part in the murder of Numerian and as he was saying this, he turned towards Aper, who was the praetorian prefect. 'This is his murderer!', he said, and immediately killed him with the sword in his hand.	Diocletian was a Dalmatian, a freedman of a senator named Anullinus, his mother and hometown sharing the name Dioclea, from which he was called Diocles, until he took up imperial power.	Valerius Diocletian, then in command of the *domestici*, was selected as emperor on account of his wisdom. He was a great man . . . Therefore, Valerius, in his first address to the army, swore, gazing at the sun with drawn sword, that he was not party to the murder of Numerian and that he was himself not desirous of becoming emperor – with this he stabbed Aper, who was standing next to him.

★ *Cupiens* is here an adjective, a Tacitean usage (*e.g. Ann.* 16.6.1, 15.46.1).

For when he was undertaking to plunder the Veneti, eager to seize imperial power upon learning of the death of Carus, he marched to block the enemy's advance.[43]

Carinus met Julianus in battle near Verona: we know the precise location only from the *LB* (38.6), but it can be plausibly deduced from a guarded reference to civil strife in a panegyric delivered only thirty-odd years after the battle (*Pan. Lat.* 12.8.1). Only the two Victorine texts tell us that Carinus was victorious, and the *HAb* (39.11) goes on to say that he next went to meet Diocletian in Moesia. The battle of the Margus was a famous event, but only the *HAb* tell us that Carinus won it: as he pressed his advantage, he was slain by his own soldiers (39.11: *dum victos avide premeret, suorum ictu interiit*).[44] John of

43 On the text here, see the Appendix, no. XIII. The date of Julianus' usurpation has been the subject of some uncertainty. General scholarly consensus has doubted Victor's connection of it with the death of Carus, on the grounds that a whole year would then have intervened between the usurpation and Carinus' reaction to

it. That, however, assumes that Carinus was at leisure in Rome, rather than on campaign in Gaul, or even Britain. An overlooked fact is that Polemius Silvius agrees with Victor's date (see below).
44 If the intriguing arguments of Rose 2021 are accepted (and they are persuasive), then this will have been a

Eutropius 9.19.2–20.1	HA Car. 13.1–2	Peter the Patrician (ES 181)
Diocletianum imperatorem creavit, Dalmatia oriundum, virum obscurissime natum, adeo ut a plerisque scribae filius, a nonnullis Anullini senatoris libertinus fuisse credatur. Is prima militum contione iuravit Numerianum nullo suo dolo interfectum, et cum iuxta eum Aper, qui Numeriano insidias fecerat, constitisset, in conspectu exercitus manu Diocletiani percussus est.	Diocletianum . . . Augustum appellaverunt, domesticos tunc regentem, virum insignem, callidum . . . Hic cum tribunal conscendisset atque Augustus esset appellatus et quaereretur quem ad modum Numerianus esset occisus, educto gladio Aprum praefectum praetori ostentans percussit, addens verbis suis: 'hic est auctor necis Numeriani'.	Ὅτι ἐν αὐτῇ τῇ οἰκείᾳ ἀναγορεύσει ὁ Διοκλητιανὸς τὰ τότε σεβόμενα θεῖα μαρτυρόμενος ἔλεγεν μὴ διὰ τὸ τῆς βασιλείας ἐφίεσθαι Καρῖνον ἀνελεῖν, ἀλλὰ διὰ τὸ ἐλεεῖν τὴν πολιτείαν.
[The army] made Diocletian emperor. A native of Dalmatia, a man of so very obscure a birth that he is considered by some people to have been a freedman of a senator named Anullinus. In his first address to the soldiers, he swore that Numerian had been killed by no stratagem of his, and standing next to Aper – who had devised the conspiracy against Numerian – Diocletian struck him down with his own hand in full view of the army.	They selected as Augustus Diocletian, who was then in charge of the *domestici*, a remarkable man and clever . . . When he mounted the rostrum, he was acclaimed Augustus and asked how Numerian had been slain, with a drawn sword he pointed at Aper the praetorian prefect and struck him, adding his own declaration, 'This is the author of Numerian's murder!'	At his own proclamation, Diocletian, swearing by the divinities then worshipped, said that he did not kill Carinus out of desire for imperial power, but as a mercy to the state.

Antioch, however, tells a very similar story in rather similar words, though he seems to locate it during the campaign against Julianus (fr. 246 Roberto: τρέψας ἐν τῇ μάχῃ τούτους, τῶν σὺν αὐτῷ τινῶν ἐπελθόντων . . .).[45] By all accounts, Carinus' downfall came from his lack of self-control. According to the *HAb*, *LB*, and John of Antioch, he had pursued the wives of some of the officers, and they nursed their grievance until the battle was over. In the *HAb*, this is explicitly stated (39.11):

> Because he was unable to resist his lust, he pursued the [wives] of his soldiers, whose outraged husbands nevertheless nursed their rage and sorrow until after the outcome of the battle.[46]

pre-Diocletianic tradition, for the emperor appears to have commemorated a victory at Margus on friezes that were later recycled for the Arch of Constantine (195). On the date of the battle, see Stefan 2016.

45 So the transmitted text, but in dealing with an excerpt from a fragmentary work itself seemingly based on Zosimus, who was not always given to precision, we ought to be cautious.
46 See the Appendix, no. XIV.

TABLE 10.5 – THE *LB* AND JOHN OF ANTIOCH ON THE KILLING OF CARINUS

LB 38.8	John of Antioch, fr. 246 Roberto
Ad extremum trucidatur eius praecipue tribuni dextera cuius dicebatur coniugem polluisse.	τῶν χιλιάρχων ἑνός, οὗ τὴν γυναῖκα διαφθείρας ἔτυχεν, ἀνελόντος αὐτόν.
At the end he was cut down at the hand of one tribune in particular, whose wife he is said to have violated.	One of the tribunes, whose wife he happened to have violated, killed him.

In the *LB* and John of Antioch it is only implicit, but both texts use identical phrases to tell us that the actual deed was done by one of the tribunes whose wife Carinus had seduced (**TABLE 10.5**). Throughout these fast-moving and confusing events, John (and probably Zosimus before him) is very close to the two Victorine texts in his phrasing and ideas.

Diocletian's rise to power occurred in one of the most obscure periods of Roman history, and even in our few sources contradiction and confusion abound. What is nevertheless remarkable is just how many links there are between the various Latin texts with connections to Victor – the *HAb*, the *LB*, Eutropius, and the *HA* – and a shifting constellation of Greek sources: Peter the Patrician, John of Antioch and Zonaras, with Zosimus lurking in the background. This suggests a basically unitary tradition underlying both Latin and Greek. That tradition presented these events in deeply moralising fashion, it was allusive and literary, and also endowed with a keen eye for anecdote. The earliest extant witness to that tradition is the Latin *HAb* and features of it can be traced back to ideas or facts that were distinctively Victor's. There was no history in Greek that might have served as the common source of both Victor and the Greek tradition. In other words, the economical assumption is that in the 280s, as in the 260s and 270s, Victor's *Historia* underlay much of the later Greek tradition about Roman history.

The rise of Constantine

It would be wrong to think, however, that Victor's influence over the Greek tradition was confined to the late third century: it is just the case that in that era, when the tidal pull of Dio's massive work had long since faded, it is perhaps easier to detect. In fact, we see exactly the same pattern of dependency in the much more brightly illuminated age of Constantine. Here there are specific and compelling parallels between the Latin tradition in general – and Victor's account in particular – and Zosimus' *New History*.

In AD 305, Constantine left the court of Galerius in the east and journeyed to Gaul, where he met his father Constantius – when the latter expired at York in 306, he was thus on hand to slip into his jewelled sandals.[47] Fairly soon after this, an elaborate and dramatic story about Constantine's ride west was spun, first detectable in Lactantius' *On the Deaths of the Persecutors* (24.5–8), a work written *ca.* 315. Galerius, Lactantius said, had been deeply reluctant to let him go. When he could refuse no longer, he

---

47 The episode is crisply surveyed in Barnes 2011: 61–63.

TABLE 10.6 – THE *LB* AND ZOSIMUS ON CONSTANTINE'S FLIGHT

LB 41.2–3	Zosimus 2.8.2–9.1
Hic dum iuvenculus a Galerio in urbe Roma religionis specie vice obsidis teneretur, **fugam arripiens** atque **ad frustrandos insequentes** publica iumenta **quaqua iter egerat** interfecit et ad patrem in Britannia situm pervenit; et **forte isdem diebus** ibidem Constantium parentem fata ultima perurgebant. Quo mortuo cunctis qui aderant annitentibus, sed praecipue Croco Alamannorum rege, auxilii gratia Constantium comitato imperium capit.	Κωνσταντῖνος . . . ἤδη μὲν ἔχων ἔννοιαν ἐν ἑαυτῷ βασιλείας, εἰς μείζονα δὲ καταστὰς ἐπιθυμίαν ἀφ' οὗ Σεβῆρος καὶ Μαξιμῖνος τῆς τοῦ Καίσαρος τιμῆς ἔτυχον, ἔγνω . . . ἐξορμῆσαι δὲ πρὸς τὸν πατέρα Κωνστάντιον ἐν τοῖς ὑπὲρ τὰς Ἄλπεις ἔθνεσιν ὄντα καὶ τῇ Βρεττανίᾳ συνεχέστερον ἐνδημοῦντα. Δεδιὼς δὲ μή ποτε **φεύγων** καταληφθείη (περιφανὴς γὰρ ἦν ἤδη πολλοῖς ὁ κατέχων αὐτὸν ἔρως τῆς βασιλείας) τοὺς ἐν τοῖς σταθμοῖς ἵππους, οὓς τὸ δημόσιον ἔτρεφεν, ἅμα τῷ φθάσαι τὸν σταθμὸν κολούων καὶ ἀχρείους ἐῶν τοῖς ἑξῆς ἑστῶσιν ἐχρῆτο· **καὶ ἑξῆς τοῦτο ποιῶν τοῖς μὲν διώκουσιν ἀπέκλεισε τὴν ἐπὶ τὸ πρόσω πορείαν,** αὐτὸς δὲ προσήγγιζεν τοῖς ἔθνεσιν ἐν οἷς ἦν ὁ πατήρ. **συμβὰν** δὲ τὸν αὐτοκράτορα Κωνστάντιον **ἐν αὐτῷ** τελευτῆσαι **τῷ χρόνῳ** . . . ὁρῶντες δὲ Κωνσταντῖνον εὖ ἔχοντα σώματος οἱ περὶ τὴν αὐλὴν στρατιῶται . . . τὴν τοῦ Καίσαρος ἀξίαν αὐτῷ περιέθεσαν.
While still very young, he was held in the city of Rome by Galerius under pretence of religion, as a sort of hostage; he took flight and killed the public beasts wherever his journey took him to stymie his pursuers. He made it to his father who was located in Britain, and it so happened there that in those very days final fate overtook his parent Constantius. After his death, with the assent of everyone present, especially Crocus king of the Alamanni, who had accompanied Constantius as an ally, Constantine seized the empire.	Constantine . . . who already had designs on imperial power, increased his lust for it from the moment that Severus and Maximinus had obtained the rank of Caesar. He determined . . . to go to his father Constantius, who was in the provinces on the other side of the Alps, usually stationed in Britain. Concerned that he not be caught as he fled – for his desire for empire was already quite clear to many people – at each station he hocked the horses, which the public authorities maintained, just as he arrived there, and leaving them behind now unfit he used those stabled next in line. By doing this continuously, he prevented his pursuers from their onward journey and proceeded to the provinces where his father was. It so happened that the Emperor Constantius died at this very time . . . Perceiving that Constantine was a handsome figure, the praetorian guard . . . granted him the rank of Caesar.

had hoped to delay him through various schemes. The wily Constantine, however, had sped off and – no slight trick – removed the imperial post-horses stabled at the various stopping points en route, thwarting any possibility of pursuit (*sublatisque per mansiones multas omnibus equis publicis evolavit*).[48] Galerius nearly wept when he learnt of the escape (tears of rage, one presumes). The story of the flight is probably a fable, designed it seems to distance Constantine from Galerius, an emperor to whom he owed rather more than he might have liked to admit. It seems to have been the 'official version' for much of his reign: something like it turns up in Eusebius' *Vita Constantini* (1.20–21) and in Photius' summary of the history of Praxagoras of Athens (*Bibliotheca* cod. 62), though neither mentions the horses.

Zosimus reproduces the tale of Constantine's flight from the east and his version of it is clearly closely related to the one found in the *LB* (**TABLE 10.6**). These two accounts are textually linked, such

---

48 *cf. DMP* 24.7: *nudatus . . . cursus publicus*. The mention of the *cursus publicus* in *Pan. Lat.* 6.7.5 (*ca.* 310) might hint that the story was already in existence then.

that at points one could almost be a translation of the other. In fact, the connection here is so close that Blockley actually included the passage from the *LB* in his edition of Eunapius as a possible fragment (fr. 17.2): an entirely logical deduction, on a certain view of Zosimus' sources.[49] We know now, of course, that that cannot be so, because the *LB* derives from Victor. What it says here is in fact very closely parallel to Victor's own words, as preserved in the *HAb* (40.2–3):

> Quod tolerare nequiens Constantinus, cuius iam tum a puero ingens potensque animus ardore imperitandi agitabatur, fugae commento cum ad frustrandos insequentes publica iumenta quaqua iter egerat interficeret, in Britanniam pervenit; nam is a Galerio religionis specie ad vicem obsidis tenebatur. Et forte iisdem diebus ibidem Constantius patrem [vel parentem] vitae ultima urgebant. Quo mortuo cunctis qui aderant annitentibus imperium capit.

> Unable to endure this [*i.e.* the appointment of Severus as Caesar], Constantine, whose huge and powerful spirit was driven as early as his boyhood by a burning desire to rule, took to flight, killed the public beasts wherever his journey took him to stymie his pursuers, and made it to Britain. For he was being held by Galerius like a hostage under the guise of religion. And so it happened there in those very same days that the end of life overtook his father Constantius. When he was dead, with the assent of everyone present, Constantine seized the empire.

While the links in phrasing between the two Victorine texts are extensive, they differ in details, and at points Zosimus is even closer to the *HAb* than to the *LB*. For example, both specify that Constantine's flight was precipitated by the appointment of Severus and Maximinus as Caesars and their description of his ambition are exactly parallel (*iam tum* ~ ἤδη; *animus* ~ ἔχων ἔννοιαν ἐν ἑαυτῷ; *ardore imperitandi* ~ ἔρως τῆς βασιλείας).

Here, once again, we have a story that a Greek text shares with Victor and, once again, that story seems to be original to his *Historia*. In Lactantius, the post-horses are said colourlessly to have been 'removed' (*sublatis*). Victor will have none of that: Constantine killed them. There is a ludicrous edge to this version: if one can just about imagine the imperial princeling freeing horses to impede pursuers, then it stretches credulity to its breaking point to have him stopping regularly to hock dozens or even hundreds of mounts – grisly and time-consuming work. It does, however, both neatly subvert what is meant to be a favourable story and make Constantine from the first an ambiguous and menacing figure (a Victorine theme, *cf. HAb* 40.14–15). Victor was a bureaucrat with very definite ideas about the management of the *cursus publicus* (*cf. HAb* 13.5–6, with Chapter IX), which places Constantine's abuse of the system under an even deeper pall of shame. Note also the rare phrase *vice obsidis*, 'like a hostage' – as though to hint that Constantine was not simply a prisoner of Galerius at all.[50]

Zosimus' account is thus clearly derivative. Even so, it actually helps to clarify some aspects of the story found in the *HAb* and *LB*. Both Victorine texts seemingly put Constantius in Britain at the time of Constantine's flight. This is generally regarded as a mistake, for a near-contemporary panegyric (*Pan. Lat.* 6.7.5) states that Constantine arrived as his father's fleet began to cross the Channel and a fourth source

---

49 For the relationship between Eunapius and Zosimus, see below.

50 Otherwise only at Gellius, *NA* 16.10.11, AM 29.5.16, 31.5.7. For *vice* in a generally comparative sense, *cf.* Lewis and Short II.β.

(discussed below) puts Constantius in Boulogne, about to make the crossing.[51] Zosimus provides the missing link: he states that Constantius was 'often spending time in Britain' (τῇ Βρεττανίᾳ συνεχέστερον ἐνδημοῦντα). This was indeed true and could easily give rise to the misconception that he was actually present in Britain at the time in question.[52] Such precision could easily have been lost in abbreviation and, looked at carefully, neither *HAb* nor *LB* is perhaps so categorical as has been thought. Constantine's journey did indeed end in Britain and *ibidem* is exactly the kind of word the compiler of the *HAb* struggled with. The *LB*'s awkwardly pleonastic *situm* also hints at something more.[53] It is striking that Zosimus here might help us to clarify what Victor originally wrote.

The literary efflorescence – in both Greek and Latin – that marked the reign of Constantine made writing its history a very different endeavour to working out what had happened in the reign of Gallienus or during the rise of Diocletian, especially for any budding Greek historian: there were alternatives to a difficult, allusive, and complex Latin masterwork. Yet, here once again we find that a Greek historian is clearly derivative of ideas expressed in the *HAb* and *LB*. There is, in other words, a thread of continuity in the rather battered garment that forms the Greek historical tradition from Gallienus to Constantine: it can be found in Victor. In fact, the parallels stretch almost to the terminal point of his *Historia*.

The misrule of Constans

As AD 350 approached, ten years after the defeat and death of his brother Constantine II in civil war, the gout-wracked emperor Constans spent his time in extravagant dissipation (or so our sources tell us).[54] Among his many vices, his barbarian retinue was of particular concern to Victor (*HAb* 41.23–24):

> Externarum sane gentium compressis motibus, quarum obsides pretio quaesitos pueros venustiores quod cultius habuerat, libidine huiuscemodi arsisse pro certo habetur.

> For he quelled the rebellions of the foreign peoples, and kept their more attractive boys in style as hostages obtained for a price. Hence it is thought certain he burned with a desire of this sort.

Something is going on here, since hostages are not generally purchased by their captors. Indeed, the conjunction of *pretium* and *obsides* would conventionally signify precisely the opposite (as in Livy 45.42.7, *e.g.*): that is, not the buying of hostages, but rather the ransom by which they are redeemed. This suggests a typically Victorine reversal: these are 'hostages' bought and paid for by their captor. What exactly he intended by this is not clear. Victor could mean '"hostages" – actually attractive boys bought for a price',

51 Barnes 1976b: 191; 1981: 27; 2011: 61–62; It is worth noting that Lactantius was not interested in his specific location (*DMP* 24.8).

52 Barnes 1982: 60–61. Two attested visits in thirteen years is a lot by the low standards of most emperors, but our evidence for Constantius' movements is thin and there may well have been more. On Britain's place in the politics of the fourth-century empire, see Woudhuysen 2021b.

53 Editors generally delete *situm*, but the MSS are unanimous and Festy 1999a was right to print it, particularly given Zosimus' ἐνδημοῦντα in the parallel passage.

54 On the tradition of the dissolute Constans and its contemporary political implications, see Woudhuysen 2018a.

if a particle (say *quippe* inserted between *obsides* and *pretio*) was omitted in the process of abbreviation, implying that Constans pretended that his acquisitions were hostages when in fact they were not. Or the *pretium* itself could be metaphorical, that is, the warfare Constans waged to obtain them, with attendant cost of blood and treasure. Even if we cannot be certain what he meant, we have seen enough to know that there is here a sly Victorine twisting of a particular knife.

Whatever exactly is going on, it is striking that identical behaviour by Constans is described in Zosimus (2.42.1):

> βαρβάρους γὰρ εὐπροσώπους ὠνούμενος καὶ ἔχων ἐν ὁμήρων τάξει παρ' ἑαυτῷ . . .

> While purchasing good-looking barbarians and keeping them with him in the ranks of hostages . . .

This is precisely parallel to Victor. In fact, virtually every word of Victor's Latin is paralleled in Zosimus' Greek, which could almost be a translation at this point.[55] The *HAb* and Zosimus, in other words, simply cannot be independent of one another, on this point at least. As Paschoud has already noted, Zosimus' claim is absurd, since hostages are not bought, and no other sources, Latin or Greek, offer anything remotely similar that might help us to grasp the point.[56] Paschoud thinks this evidence for a common source, which is no doubt true. It is worth pointing out, however, that that source ought to be Latin, and not Greek, for some of the particular incongruities in Zosimus make sense only in the former language. Zosimus' ἐν ὁμήρων τάξει is particularly odd. Paschoud translates it as 'en tant qu'otages' ('as hostages'), which is defensible but not exactly the normal sense of ἐν τάξει: no other extant Greek work ever speaks of 'ranks of hostages' or 'the position of hostages'.[57] All this suggests some deeper confusion is at work. Significantly, perhaps, the phrase ἐν τάξει, in the idiomatic adverbial sense of 'in good order' (*cf.* Plato, *Laws* 1, 637e), would on its own be a defensible translation of Victor's *cultius*, a rare adverb that would have presented a challenge to any ancient translator.[58] Still more tellingly, Zosimus uses the fairly bland εὐπροσώπους, literally 'pretty-faced', to describe Constans' hostages. The word εὐπρόσωπος is in general a fine rendering of *venustus* (ἐπαφρόδιτος would perhaps be a more direct equivalent), since it normally means 'pretty' or 'charming'. In this passage, however, Victor is using the word in its rare but attested etymological sense of 'sexy' (from *Venus*).[59] While Zosimus' εὐπρόσωπος could have been derived from a Latin source with the word *venustus*, Victor's *venustus* is not likely to have come from a Greek source with εὐπρόσωπος. Moreover, not only do these two passages draw ultimately on a common Latin source: we also have every reason to believe that that source was Victor's *Historia* – the text in which the complex of ideas was created. Sexual misconduct with hostages was a particular bugbear of Victor's.[60] He also

---

55 βαρβάρους (= quarum) εὐπροσώπους (= venustiores pueros) ὠνούμενος (= pretio quaesitos) ἔχων (= habuerat) ἐν . . . τάξει (= cultius), ὁμήρων (= obsides).

56 Paschoud 2000: 267–268.

57 Paschoud 2000: 113. Zosimus uses the collocation on two other occasions (3.7.7 and 6.12.3), neither of which provides much illumination (both may be derivative of this usage).

58 *TLL* 3.1693.7–25 (Sigwart), the comparative very early usurped the positive adverb. It is also possible that ἐν ὁμήρων τάξει translates a phrase like Victor's *ad vicem obsidis, cf. HAb* 40.2.

59 *cf.* Apuleius, *Met.* 9.27: *tam venustum tamque pulchellum puellum*; Catullus 97.9: *hic futuit multas et se facit venustum.*

60 Compare *HAb* 39.46 on the misbehaviour of the emperor Maximian: *Quippe Herculius libidine tanta agebatur, ut ne ab obsidum corporibus quidem animi labem comprimeret.*

had a strongly stated aversion to male prostitution (the unavoidable implication of *pretio quaesitos*). This occasioned an extended outburst in his account of Philip the Arab (*HAb* 28.4–9), involving a (somewhat opaque) description of a prodigy, Philip's son, and a ban on male prostitutes.

This is not the only connection Victor makes between the reigns of Constans and Philip. Immediately preceding the prodigy is a reference to the Secular Games held by Philip in 248, to commemorate the thousandth anniversary of the founding of Rome. This prompts Victor to yet another reflection (*HAb* 28.2):

> And, since the name Philip brings it to mind, in my own day the 1,100th anniversary of the city passed, celebrated with no ceremony, in the consulship of one Philippus, so little is the care of the city of Rome in these days.

This is a reference to the year 348 – the consulship of Fl. Philippus and Fl. Salia – in the reign of Constans himself.[61] Whatever deeper connections Victor is trying to draw – and in the current state of the text it is really not clear – it can hardly be coincidental that the *HAb*'s only reference to the reign of Constans outside of its forty-first chapter is in close proximity to a discussion of male prostitution. Philip the Arab, who both celebrated the anniversary games and tried to ban male prostitution, is made to stand in sharp contrast to Constans, who neglected the Secular Games and turned suspiciously good-looking barbarian boys into prostitutes. The Secular Games, linked as they were with the *saeculum* (the maximum span of a human life), were often associated with moral renewal: Augustus' *ludi saeculares* coincided with his marriage legislation and Claudius was *censor* during his games.[62] In that context, the comparison that Victor draws is apt indeed. All of this makes clear that the ideas behind the passage shared in Zosimus and in Victor are original to Victor, and thus that his *Historia* is Zosimus' ultimate source.

There is one final connection that can be drawn out from Victor's account of Constans. One of the most important passages in Zosimus that Paschoud has long argued must originally have come from a Latin source is the lengthy discussion of the Secular Games found at 2.1–7, which includes a substantial quotation from a Sibylline oracle.[63] This is far from an unreasonable position, for the *ludi saeculares* were an authentically Italic religious institution, featured often in Latin literature, but vanishingly rare in Greek.[64] Zosimus (2.7.1–2) blames the decline of Rome on the neglect of the games that should have taken place in the third consulship of Constantine (AD 313). There are important differences between Zosimus and Victor, foremost among them the fact that the former is concerned with the Augustan cycle of games (followed by Domitian and Severus in AD 88 and 204 respectively), whereas the latter hews to the tradition inaugurated by Claudius in 47, and followed by Antoninus Pius in 148 and Philip in 248.[65] The congruences, however, are more important: no author besides these two ever specifies that the abeyance of the games was an index of decline. Whatever divergences of detail between the two exist, there is a continuity of theme between Zosimus and Victor here – that theme was Victor's.

---

61 *CLRE* 230–231. This is a sign of abbreviation, for the reference works only if one knows also that the emperor Philip was consul in 248.

62 Malloch 2013: 183–184.

63 Paschoud 2000: 192–205 (*cf.* Paschoud 1975: 131, 151, 168).

64 Outside Zosimus, the only references appear to be Phlegon, *De longaevis* 6.3, Cassius Dio 54.18.2, and Herodian 3.8.10.

65 On the games, the best introduction is the lucid discussion of Malloch 2013: 181–185.

This conclusion is of a piece with everything else that we have seen in examining a range of events over a period of roughly 100 years. The Greek tradition is repeatedly cognate in what it says about the emperors from Gallienus to Constans with material found in the *HAb* and in every instance there are signs of Victor's priority.[66] His *Historia* is one of the springs from which the later Greek tradition flows.

★ ★ ★

We have seen that a string of Greek historians, especially Zosimus and Zonaras, are closely linked with Victor's *Historia* in their accounts of Roman history from the era of Gallienus onwards, links that cannot be explained by the use of a common Greek source, not least because no Greek historian writing before Victor covered the entire period. We have shown that, throughout, the facts, ideas, and interpretations that they share are original to Victor and have demonstrated that in several cases details in the Greek suggest direct derivation (at some stage) from his work. In aggregate, it seems inarguable that Greek historiography in late antiquity and thereafter used material from Victor. That follows logically from the long-acknowledged connections between the *LB* and the Greeks (once one realises what the *LB* is), but it can also be shown from the *HAb*, incontestably fragments of Victor's own work, in his own words.[67] In questions of transmission, however, the aggregate gets us only so far: to explain the patterns that we see, specific people had to read Victor and use his work. That brings us to a question that we have so far skirted. The Greek tradition is deeply indebted to Victor – how?

Eunapius and Zosimus

It would be rash to suppose that material from Victor entered the Greek tradition only once. We have seen that John the Lydian had access to his work in sixth-century Constantinople and exploited it.[68] Though we have only fragments of Peter the Patrician's history, it would be unsurprising if he – a civil servant with excellent Latin – had also used it directly.[69] Scholars have also perhaps been too quick to dismiss the idea (if they have entertained it at all) that Zosimus – a bureaucrat, after all – might have had enough Latin to consult some sources in the language directly: they should perhaps be more cautious about assuming that the confused state of his work reflects a lack of ability, rather than the difficulty or unfinished nature of his project. We ought also to keep in mind that influence need not always be an indication of direct use: Julian's *Caesares* reproduces many of Victor's ideas, but that does not necessarily mean that the emperor had pored over the work himself.[70] Similarly, we should remember that – inconvenient as it is for tidy-minded moderns – ancient historians were far from averse to reading one source through (or alongside)

66 Links between Zosimus and the *HAb* for the emperors before Gallienus are discussed in Chapter IX.
67 For the *LB* and the Greek tradition, see Chapter IX.
68 Chapter V.
69 Banchich 2015: 17–22 conveniently collects the *testimonia* to Peter. Cameron 2011: 640 is sceptical that Peter's

Latin was good enough to tackle long literary works in the language, but all sources praise his learning and it is hard to believe that Cassiodorus would have called him eloquent repeatedly (*Variae* 10.19.4 e.g.) unless he really was capable in it.
70 Chapter V.

a later work derived in whole or in part from it.[71] One reason that debate over the sources of the Greek tradition has been so contentious is perhaps that scholars have tended to pursue unitary solutions: multiplicity is likely to be closer to the truth.[72] True as they may be, however, generalities will carry us only so far. If material from Victor entered the Greek tradition, then it did so because individual authors read his work and used it in their own. We need, in other words, to consider specifics.

Of the Greek sources that we have examined so far in this chapter, the first to survive more or less intact and probably the most important is the *New History* of Zosimus, whose narrative of the third and fourth centuries shows repeated and significant connections to Victor.[73] Zosimus is also the only one of those Greek historians about whose sources we have explicit evidence from an informed reader. In his *Bibliotheca*, the ninth-century scholar and churchman Photius tells us that Zosimus' work was little more than an abbreviated version of Eunapius' lost history: 'one might say that he did not write history himself, but transcribed the work of Eunapius, differing only by his concision'.[74] Given that he could read both works in full (and we cannot), Photius' opinion ought to carry considerable weight: it would be unwise to doubt that Eunapius was a major source for Zosimus' work.[75]

The question, however, of the precise relationship between the two is slippery and much disputed: there are sharply divergent estimates of the exact nature and extent of Zosimus' debt to Eunapius. On one side is the idea, most associated with Antonio Baldini and François Paschoud, that Zosimus was more or less a mechanical copyist of Eunapius – that he was 'dumm' in Paul Speck's acid characterisation of a view he did not share.[76] On the other is the position that Zosimus – while hardly antiquity's most original or careful historian – was perfectly capable of drawing on more than one source, supplementing Eunapius with material he found elsewhere, and inserting his own ideas, predilections, and obsessions.[77]

In general terms, the idea that Zosimus was far from totally dependent on Eunapius has much to commend it. The *New History* opens long before the reign of Claudius II, the starting point, Photius says, of Eunapius' work (which began after the end of Dexippus' *Chronicle*). In the period before the 270s, Zosimus implies that he was looking at more than one source.[78] Whether we believe him or not is another question, but his disordered and often confusing narrative is entirely compatible (indeed, might partly be explained by) use of multiple sources. Even in the *New History*'s account of the period from Constantine onwards – which must (taking Photius at his word) have been derived from Eunapius – it is possible to assemble an impressive list of divergences (in both fact and emphasis) between Zosimus and his supposed source.[79] Though incomplete, the *New History* also terminates in 410, where Eunapius' finished in 404.

---

71 See Chapter VIII on the *HA*'s use of Victor and Eutropius *e.g.*

72 *cf.* Cameron 2011: 689, an observation he largely honoured in the breach.

73 On Zosimus' date, see Chapter IX: though uncertain, it seems very likely that he was writing earlier than Peter the Patrician and certainly earlier than John of Antioch.

74 Photius, *Bibliotheca* cod. 98 (84b).

75 Photius, *Bibliotheca* cod. 77 for his remarks on Eunapius.

76 Baldini 1984: 19–74, 119–178; Paschoud 2000 *e.g.* (esp. lxix–lxxi) – their views have evolved over the years, but are usefully summarised in Baldini and Paschoud 2015. Speck 1991.

77 *e.g.* Petre 1965; Scavone 1970; Ridley 1969–1970; Ridley 1972; Blockley 1980; Liebeschuetz 2003: esp. 213; Cameron 2011: 644–654; Van Nuffelen 2015: x–xi; Schmidt-Hofner 2020. This tendency has perhaps not always clearly distinguished between whether Zosimus was mechanically derivative of his sources' texts or of their ideas, a distinction with a very considerable difference.

78 As, *e.g.*, on the fate of Ulpian (1.11.3), where he says that he is uncertain because historians differ.

79 Ridley 1969–1970: 585–590.

From that point on, Zosimus used the history of Olympiodorus of Thebes as his major source – one sign of this being the transformation in his attitude to the *generalissimo* Stilicho, which veers suddenly from savage indictment to sympathy.[80] It is suspicious too that while Zosimus is careful to attribute an error to Olympiodorus in a section that must largely derive from his work (5.27.1) – the classicising historian's equivalent of a footnote – he never breathes a word about Eunapius. Photius, we might note, had read Olympiodorus (*Bibliotheca* cod. 80), but never hints that his history played any role in Zosimus' work. That makes it not unreasonable to wonder quite how attentively or at what length he had read an author whom he characterised as 'an impious man in religious matters'. We ought perhaps to be cautious about taking his statement of the relationship between Eunapius and Zosimus too literally.

There are also good specific reasons to doubt that Zosimus can merely have transcribed Eunapius with concision. The *New History*'s extant narrative of the period from Aurelian to AD 355 in Books I and II occupies some 15,000 words. In estimating the original length, we must also make some allowance for a substantial lacuna that has swallowed the account of Diocletian and the Tetrarchy, which elsewhere Zosimus implies he had covered in some detail (*e.g.* 2.34.1) and which Photius says marked the point at which his narrative expanded (*Bibliotheca* cod. 98). We know that Eunapius wrote his history in fourteen books and a marginal note in one of the Byzantine compilations that preserve most of our fragments from it tells us that the second opened with the emperor Julian's appearance on the public stage in 355.[81] It is very difficult to believe that Eunapius' first book was so long that 15,000 words or more could represent a concise version of it, not least because the author explains that he has treated the period it covered with some dispatch.[82]

Set against these spurs to scepticism is the fact that it is difficult to argue that any specific episode or passage in Zosimus could not have been derived from Eunapius. Take the Secular Games. The conventional understanding of Zosimus' long digression on the subject (above) makes it come ultimately from the Hadrianic author Phlegon of Tralles, who is known to have written a work on Roman festivals and who quotes the same Sibylline oracle as Zosimus in the context of the *saeculum* in another work, the *De longaevis* (6.3).[83] That Eunapius was the direct source for this material has been denied, both by Ludwig Mendelssohn (Zosimus' most important editor before Paschoud) and more recently by Alan Cameron, who prefer (respectively) derivation directly from Phlegon (with some supplementation), or

80 Zosimus' debt to Olympiodorus was acknowledged as far back as Reitemeier 1784 (the starting point for modern study of the historian) and already canonical by the time of Martin 1866. On Olympiodorus, see the classic essay by Matthews 1970 (esp. 81–82, on Zosimus' use of him).

81 Photius, *Bibliotheca* cod. 77; Boissevain 1906: 76.

82 Eunapius, *ES* 5 = Blockley fr. 15: Τὰ μὲν οὖν ἀπὸ τῆς Δεξίππου συγγραφῆς ἐς τοὺς Ἰουλιανοῦ καθήκοντα <καιροὺς> ὡς ἐνῆν μάλιστα διὰ τῶν ἀναγκαίων ἐπιτρέχουσιν ἱκανῶς ἐν τοῖς ἔμπροσθεν δεδήλωται. This calculation has rather negative implications for the theory that Eunapius' Book I also contained a summary of events from Augustus to Aurelian (Chapter IX). Eunapius'

Lives of the Sophists (*VS*) is *ca.* 21,500 words long, which (given its monographic nature) might give us the upper limit for his book lengths.

83 On Phlegon, see Chapter VII. For his work on festivals, *Suda* Φ.527: Περὶ τῶν παρὰ Ῥωμαίοις ἑορτῶν. We might be a little cautious about this attribution. Sibylline oracles were not such exclusive texts that we can rule out two writers using the same one independently, nor is it immediately obvious that the *ludi saeculares* qualified as an ἑορτή. Did Phlegon really include a large chunk of material from Valerius Maximus 2.4.5 (closely parallel to Zosimus 2.1)? In any case, the mention of Severus in Zosimus 2.7.2 shows that his source cannot have been Phlegon solely (who died long before 204).

through a fifth-century (Greek) intermediary.[84] The major reason Mendelssohn and Cameron give is that the discussion in Zosimus involves a good deal of chronology (including precise consular dates) and that Eunapius was famously averse to precision in such matters (as his preface, *ES* 1 = Blockley fr. 1, makes clear).[85] Superficially, this looks rather persuasive. On closer inspection, however, it falls apart. The whole point of the digression in Zosimus is to illustrate the way that Constantine's neglect of Roman institutions brought ruin on the Empire – that was very definitely an *echt* Eunapian theme.[86] Any discussion of the Secular Games had to include chronological references, because it was only by pointing out that a particular year had come and gone that one could see that they had not been held. Even Eunapius might have stooped to including a few temporal specifics to illustrate such a juicy topic so close to his heart – he provided a remarkably precise set of chronological indicators for the moment when he met the philosopher Prohaeresius, for instance.[87] It is also perhaps worth viewing Eunapius' attack on chronology with a little more scepticism than it has generally attracted. He certainly bashed Dexippus for being obsessed with chronology, especially Athenian *archons* and Roman consuls, yet not a single consular date survives in the fragments of the latter's work. Such notices were clearly vulnerable in transmission and Eunapius' own history could well have included rather more chronology than either his thundering preface or the extant fragments suggest. There is, in other words, no good reason to deny that the account of the Secular Games in Zosimus came from Eunapius.

Taken together, these two points help to show that the problem of the precise relationship between Eunapius and Zosimus is a serious and difficult one, far too weighty for us to even properly review here, let alone begin to solve it. We bring it forward, however, because it might seem to present a significant obstacle to the idea that Victor was an important source of information for the Greek tradition in general and Zosimus in particular. If Eunapius was the dominant influence on Zosimus (as is generally acknowledged) and Eunapius was defiantly Greek in his culture (as is generally thought), then surely it is impossible for him to have been a conduit for material from Victor into the Greek tradition?

84 Mendelssohn 1887: xxxvii and notes on 54–55; Cameron 2011: 650–651. They arrive at this view partly through a contradictory attitude to the digression and Eunapius: for Mendelssohn, the digression is too serious for the frivolous Eunapius; for Cameron, it is too disjointed and disproportionate for a historian who was certainly more accomplished than Zosimus. *cf.* Liebeschuetz 2003: 208, 'a quite disproportionate excursus on the Secular Games at Rome, which reads as if it had been taken straight out of a book on Roman antiquities'.

85 Cameron 2011: 651 alleges two other grounds: (1) that the length of the oracle is disproportionate and would have been avoided by Eunapius (whose other quotations from such texts are shorter and who generally disliked excessive detail); and (2) that Zosimus' description of the 'collapse and barbarisation of the empire' is too dark for the era of Eunapius. On the first, the deduction seems very risky given that we have Eunapius only in fragments and long oracles would have been a prime candidate for excision by the compilers of Constantine Porphyrogenitus' encyclopaedias (which preserve most of our fragments of Eunapius). Moreover, Eunapius was perfectly comfortable with the accumulation of

pointless detail when it suited some polemical purpose (*e.g.* the lengthy story of the actor whose performance of Euripides' *Andromeda* in the reign of Nero produced lethal diarrhoea in the audience: *ES* 52 = Blockley fr. 48.1). On the second, Eunapius was certainly capable of an exaggeratedly gloomy view of his own day: *e.g. ES* 48 = Blockley fr. 46.1, where Theodosius drives the Empire to ruin or *ES* 53 = Blockley fr. 48.2 where 'unnumbered tribes' of barbarians enter the Empire.

86 To judge by Zosimus 2.32–34 (*e.g.*) and Photius, *Bibliotheca* cod. 77. Cameron 2011: 650–651 denies that Zosimus does blame Constantine alone for neglect of the Secular Games, instead saying that he makes Constantine and Licinius jointly responsible (*cf.* his translation – 'they ought to have held the festival . . . Since they did not . . .'). This is true only up to a point. Zosimus names both emperors as consuls in the year when the games ought to have occurred, but he very much does not attribute the neglect to both of them explicitly: the verbs are impersonal.

87 Eunapius *VS* 10.1.1–5: his own age, Prohaeresius' age, the time of year, time of day, and astrological season.

Two sophistic historians

At first sight, Eunapius is a rather unlikely reader of Victor. A passionate Hellene, whose intellectual world was centred on Athens and its schools, he located his history in the tradition of Dexippus.[88] He was not, seemingly, much interested by Latin things or Latin culture. Alan Cameron has, quite reasonably, denied that he had any knowledge of the Latin language and (less defensibly) extended this to the idea that he was totally uninfluenced by Latin sources.[89] What interest in, or connections with, an African scholar-turned-senator of impeccable Latinity could he have had? Even if students of late-ancient historiography had been inclined to hunt for connections between the two, there is little overlap in their historical coverage. Our epitomes of Victor's work say relatively little about the period after 350, but that is the era from which almost all our fragments of Eunapius happen to come.[90]

Yet, Victor and Eunapius are rather closer than they first appear. It was certainly chronologically possible for Eunapius to have read Victor's work. Though the dates of Eunapius' history have been the subject of intense controversy, on any chronology he was at work long after Victor's *Historia* was available and had become the premier Latin history of its day.[91] Moreover, Victor and Eunapius moved in overlapping social and intellectual spheres. Victor's patron, Anatolius, was, as we have seen, passionately devoted to Greek sophistic culture, particularly in its Athenian form – the recipient of a panegyric from Himerius (*Or.* 32), our primary example of the rhetorical tradition at Athens in the fourth century.[92] Anatolius was a correspondent and sparring partner of Libanius, from whose circle he drew many of his staff. Victor would have served alongside a number of the sophist's friends and protégés, men who had obtained their preferments at his recommendation, products of the Greek rhetorical schools of Antioch and Athens. There is something of a Greek colour to this period of Victor's career. This was Eunapius' world.[93] A native of

---

88 *ES* 1 = Blockley fr. 1.
89 Cameron 2011: 637–644.
90 Examination of Blockley's maximalist edition of Eunapius can offer only the material on Carinus (fr. 5.1–2, discussed below) as a (more or less) explicitly ascribed fragment from before the reign of Constantius.
91 Liebeschuetz 2003: 179–187 offers a masterful introduction to this difficult and disputed topic. To sum up very briefly, in his *Lives of the Sophists*, written after Alaric's invasion of Greece in 395 (*VS* 7.3.1 and 8.3.4), Eunapius both mentions a historical work already published (covering no events certainly later than Valens) and suggests he intends to write another (*VS* 7.3.4, 8.1.10–2.3), which will (*inter alia*) include Alaric's activities. The extant fragments of his work (which the *Excerpta de Sententiis* says are taken from the 'new edition': Boissevain 1906: 71) go up at least to the Isaurian attacks on Pamphylia in 404 (*ES* 78 = Blockley fr. 71.4). Photius, *Bibliotheca* cod. 77 (54a) says that he had read two versions of Eunapius' history (πραγματείας, he later calls them ἐκδόσεις), both of which terminated in 404. There are thus two closely linked questions: when the two editions of Eunapius' work appeared and what the two editions read by Photius represented. Developing the insights of Chalmers 1953, Barnes 1978: 114–123

argued that its first edition terminated in 378 (not 395, as was then the consensus) and was written by *ca.* 380. This was strongly challenged by Paschoud 2006a [1980]: 93–106, who reasserted 395 as the terminal date of the first edition (*cf.* Goulet 1980; Blockley 1981–1983: 1.24–25; Barnes 1981: 273, n. 5 accepted that he might need to move the terminal date down to 383 as a result). The earlier chronology is perhaps preferable (*cf.* Liebeschuetz 2003), though this is not a question that rewards confident certainty. As for Photius, he has traditionally been understood as providing evidence for two authorial editions of Eunapius' history. Given, however, that Photius says that (1) the two versions covered the same period (which *prima facie* contradicts what Eunapius himself implies) and (2) that the second had been purged of hostile references to Christianity in such a way that its text became nonsensical at points (πολλὰ τῶν χωρίων διὰ τὰς γεγενημένας τῶν ῥητῶν περικοπὰς ἀσαφῶς ἐκκεῖσθαι), we might wonder if instead he had the second edition of Eunapius' history and an epitome thereof (with Eunapius' name attached to it, *cf.* Chapter III; though Baker 1988 does not mention epitomes, he arrives at a not dissimilar conclusion).
92 Chapter I.

TABLE 10.7 – VICTOR AND EUNAPIUS ON THE NATURE OF HISTORY

HAb 35.13	Eunapius, *ES* 14 = Blockley fr. 21.3
Quod factum praecipue edocuit cuncta in se orbis modo verti nihilque accidere quod rursum naturae vis ferre nequeat aevi spatio.	Ἔοικε μὲν οὖν καὶ ἄλλως ὁ χρόνος ἐν ταῖς μακραῖς περιόδοις καὶ κινήσεσι πολλάκις ἐπὶ τὰ αὐτὰ καταφέρεσθαι συμπτώματα.
This fact in particular teaches us that all things cycle back like a circle, and that nothing happens which the power of nature is not able to bring back after the interval of an age.	Thus it seems in other respects that time is often brought back round in its long circuits and cycles to the same occurrences.

Sardis, he was one of the last students of Prohaeresius, the philosopher who was (at least according to Eunapius) the great adornment of Athens. It was the interests fired in those days that prompted Eunapius to write *The Lives of the Sophists*, our principal source for the intellectual world of the city in the fourth century. Eunapius is the one who provides the memorable description of Anatolius' descent on Athens, like a new Persian invasion, driven by a 'golden madness' (*VS* 10.6.3) to see the venerable city.[94] Prohaeresius himself had an unnamed friend on Anatolius' staff, the man who tipped him off on the correct formula to win the impossible rhetorical competition that the prefect held on that occasion (*VS* 10.6.10.). It is not merely the case, however, that Eunapius and Victor were linked only by Anatolius and Athens. Victor was, of course, favoured by the emperor Julian and a major influence on his *Caesares*. While Eunapius was still a youth during Julian's reign, the last pagan emperor looms large as the near-divine centrepiece of his history (*ES* 5 = Blockley fr. 15). Eunapius is explicit that he knew people who had been close to Julian (a point to which we will return). In the abstract, then, it makes perfect sense for Eunapius to have had recourse to Victor's *Historia*. At the very least, they would have had mutual acquaintances.

More than milieux, however, Victor and Eunapius shared ideas about how history worked: they display a similar philosophical timbre in their explanation of events. Both believed that history repeats itself, not simply in a general sense but in a highly specific way (**TABLE 10.7**). Both looked to (once again highly specific) 'laws of nature', which to them explained causal links (**TABLE 10.8**). Both were given to moralising digressions – in which they reflected on the general state and behaviour of mankind – that intruded into their narratives.[95] Both sometimes ended these with notes of doubt.[96] Both believed passionately in the value of education, especially for those engaged in an active political life.[97] Both were interested in the effect that growing up in poverty had on the characters of men who rose to greatness.[98] Both grappled with the balance between mercy and severity that an emperor needed to show and both saw clemency as a sign of confidence.[99] Both were firmly committed to the idea that the character of

93 Basic details of life and times in *PLRE* 'Eunapius 2'. See also Penella 1990 (esp. 1–38), an elegant and perceptive study of his life and works.

94 Chapter I.

95 For Eunapius, *e.g. ES* 35 = Blockley fr. 34.9.

96 *e.g. HAb* 14.9 *nos rem in medio relinquemus* ~ Eunapius, *ES* 35 = Blockley fr. 34.9 ἀλλὰ ταῦτα μέν, ὅπῃ γνώμης ἔχει τις καὶ κρίνει, οὕτως ἐχέτω.

97 Eunapius, *ES* 45 = Blockley fr. 44.1 on the importance of education, especially in the past, to warfare: a sentence Victor could have written.

98 Eunapius, *ES* 39 = Blockley fr. 41.1; for Victor, see Stover and Woudhuysen 2020 [2015].

99 Eunapius, *ES* 25 = Blockley fr. 34.9 vs *HAb* 9.3.

TABLE 10.8 – VICTOR AND EUNAPIUS ON LAWS OF NATURE

HAb 3.5	Eunapius, *ES* 10 = Blockley fr.18.4
. . . quasi naturae lege, quae crebro tamquam ex industria malos e bonis, agrestes ex doctioribus et ceteros huiuscemodi seu contra gignit.	καὶ καθάπερ οἱ Πυθαγόρειοί φασι, μονάδος ἐπὶ δυάδα κινηθείσης οὐκέτι τὴν τῶν ἀριθμῶν ἠρεμεῖν φύσιν ἀλλὰ διαχεῖσθαι καὶ ῥεῖν ἐς πολύ . . .
. . . as if by a law of nature, which frequently produces seemingly on purpose bad children from good people, ignoramuses from the learned, and others of this sort or vice versa.	But just as the Pythagoreans say, as a monad is moved toward a dyad, the nature of the numbers remains no longer fixed, but is dissolved and flows into multitude . . .★

★ See also Eunapius, *ES* 34 = Blockley fr. 34.4: Ὥσπερ οὖν οἱ φυσικοί φασι πάσης κινήσεως εἶναι τέλος ἀκινησίαν.

the emperor determined the well-being of the state.[100] Both were keen on the use of medical similes and metaphors.[101] Both were, in their own ways, what one might call 'sophistic historians': eager to draw connections between contingent historical events and constant philosophical truths, and equally committed to relating both in highly wrought and intricate prose (which sometimes loses in clarity what it makes up for in ambition). Eunapius himself coyly suggests that he had predecessors when he says that the period his history covers had yet to find a 'well-known' (ἐμφανής) historian – that is to say, for his audience, one who wrote in the right kind of Greek. The fact that he was happy to compress his narrative of 270–355 into a single book points in the same direction.

'So what?', might come the reasonable riposte. Linked as they are in various ways, the argument would go, it is simply impossible that Eunapius used Victor, for the general cultural factors adduced above and for the specific reason that his Latin was probably not up to the task. This is a rather narrow perspective: successful as his ferociously Hellenic self-presentation has been, it would be wrong to think of the historian from Sardis as entirely closed off from alien wisdom. One fragment of his work, for instance, runs '*they say* that the love of money is the source of all evil', a clear allusion to the Bible.[102] Moreover, the yes/no question of whether Eunapius could have read a long Latin history ignores crucial facts about his working method. Eunapius is clear that his work was not his alone: it was a κοινὸν ἔργον, as he describes it – a common endeavour. He had been urged to it by conversation with other cultured individuals who were devotees of the emperor Julian: 'those who in our lifetime were markedly superior in their learning', 'remarkable men, famous for their learning'.[103] Not only did they encourage Eunapius, they even offered to help him in his work. Of their number, the most important (or at any rate the one singled out in an extant fragment) was Julian's physician, Oribasius, who told Eunapius it would be an act

100 *e.g.* Eunapius, *ES* 48 = Blockley fr. 46.1 on Theodosius, or *ES* 24 = Blockley fr. 28.1 on Julian. For Victor, see *e.g.* the discussion of Gallienus, above.
101 For Victor, see Chapter IX on Anatolius. Eunapius, *ES* 24 = Blockley fr. 28.1, *ES* 69 = Blockley fr. 67.9 *e.g.*
102 Eunapius, *ES* 38 = Blockley fr. 39.9: φιλοχρηματίαν φασὶ πηγήν τινα πάσης κακίας τυγχάνειν . . . Compare

1 Timothy 6:10: ῥίζα γὰρ πάντων τῶν κακῶν ἐστιν ἡ φιλαργυρία. The language is entirely Christian and the closest parallel is Isidore of Pelusium, *Ep.* 3.217 (*PG*): τὸν τῆς φιλοχρηματίας ὄχλον, ἅτε πάσης κακίας πηγήν . . .
103 Eunapius, *ES* 1 = Blockley fr. 1, *ES* 5 = Blockley fr. 15.

of sacrilege for him not to write history.[104] The good doctor even produced a memorandum of Julian's deeds for the historian.[105] Oribasius had been with Julian in Gaul. In one of his letters from that time, the emperor exaggeratedly said that it would be a miracle if he kept his Greek up in such surroundings: it was clearly a Latin world.[106] Oribasius' extant medical works include a number of Latin glosses, generally taken over from his sources (in particular Dioscorides), but interesting all the same in this most Greek of genres – his early translation into Latin also hints at a western context for some of his activity.[107] It seems reasonable to suppose that he had picked up not a little Latin. In other words, even if Eunapius was himself quite incapable of reading even elementary Latin (not an assumption we ought to make lightly), that need hardly have mattered. He had considerable help and it stretches credulity to imagine that none of the learned men on whose labours he relied had recourse to the work of the only historian that Julian himself had honoured.

Indeed, we might even know the identity of Eunapius' informant: Tuscianus. A rhetor of this name, student of the famous sophist Julian of Cappadocia, was active at Athens in the middle of the fourth century. He was an important source for the *Lives of the Sophists* and Eunapius generously credits his recollections on more than one occasion – like the historian, he was from Lydia, but a little older, since his anecdotes clustered in the period before Eunapius arrived in Athens.[108] An individual with the same name was a connexion of Libanius and served on the staff of Anatolius (as an *assessor*), the praetorian prefect and Victor's patron.[109] Attempts have been made to deny that these were one and the same individual, but their identity seems almost certain.[110] For one thing, Τουσκιανός was a very rare name in the Greek world and it multiplies entities to create two of them active in the same region at the same time.[111] For another, Libanius credits his Tuscianus (in a letter to Anatolius) as (*Ep.* 345.3) a 'practitioner of eloquence and skilled in judging it' (λόγων δημιουργός τε καὶ κριτὴς ἀγαθός) – clearly a man with serious rhetorical interests, like the Tuscianus known to Eunapius. Finally, Eunapius says that he did not provide a biography of Tuscianus in his *Lives of the Sophists* because he had already discussed him in the account of Julian in his *History*.[112] Why did he do this, given that he was quite willing to offer lives of Prohaeresius and Libanius, even though they too had featured in his history? As R.J. Penella has pointed out, the reason must be that Tuscianus was – unlike Libanius and Prohaeresius – notable principally for his actions in the political sphere, the world that Eunapius' history covered, as he explain to his readers (*VS* 8.2.3).[113] The theme of Eunapius' references to Tuscianus is of possibilities unrealised – 'he would have been Prohaeresius, if Prohaeresius had not been' (*VS* 10.4.2) – and that perfectly suits someone who had shown promise at Athens, but left that world with it yet unfulfilled. He probably held some government job: that was one of the things that Libanius lobbied Anatolius to obtain for him and serving as an *assessor* was a well-trodden

104 *PLRE* 'Oribasius'.
105 Eunapius, *ES* 5 = Blockley fr. 15.
106 Julian, *ELF* 8.
107 Oribasius, *Collectiones medicae* 2.52.2, 5.6.33 (a definition found in Galen, *De rebus boni malive suci* vol. 6 p. 805 Kühn), 11.η.1, 11.ι.3, 11.ι.5, 11.ι.6, 11.κ.1, 11.λ.9, 12.ξ.2, 15.1:10.40, 44.2.1 (from Galen *De methodo medendi* vol. 10 p. 340 Kühn?). Translation: Gitner forthcoming.
108 *VS* 9.2.15; 10.4.2. See *PLRE* 'Tuscianus 1'.

109 *PLRE* 'Tuscianus 2'.
110 As in *PLRE*, which splits Tuscianus into two separate entries. Penella 1990: 138 is quite right to resist this.
111 *LGPN* reveals only a second-century L. Aburnius Tuscianus, from Heraclea Salbace. In this respect, the case of Tuscianus is quite unlike that of the Anatolii in Libanius and Eunapius (Chapter I), where more proof is needed to identify the two.
112 *VS* 9.1.3.
113 Penella 1990: 138.

route to higher office. Given that he had been mentioned in the treatment of Julian, he presumably held that position in the later 350s or the 360s. Tuscianus was certainly acquainted with Julian, for he disapproved of the emperor's opinion that Libanius was superior to Prohaeresius.[114] All this would suit what we know of Libanius' Tuscianus – active in the bureaucracy in the 350s – very neatly indeed. They must be one and the same person.

We might thus reconstruct the career of Tuscianus: after studying under Julian of Cappadocia before 350, Tuscianus failed to obtain a permanent position in the Athenian schools. Chucking in the academic life, he entered the bureaucracy and eventually made it on to the staff of Anatolius in Illyricum; from there he went on to some higher office, probably under Julian. His dual background in Athens and politics, with their attendant connections, would have made him an unusually valuable informant for Eunapius years later: it is no wonder that Blockley (and others) assumed that he was an important source for Eunapius' *History* as well as his *Lives*.[115] Whatever department Victor belonged to on the prefect's staff, it is hard to believe that he would not have come across Tuscianus. Despite his Greek rhetorical background, Tuscianus must have had a reasonable competence in Latin to do his duties. Take these facts together – Tuscianus worked with Victor, knew Latin, and was an informant of Eunapius – and the hypothesis that he served as the conduit by which Victorine materials might have ended up in Eunapius becomes rather attractive.

The links between these two fourth-century historians – at times tantalisingly close – make the idea that Eunapius derived some of his material from Victor possible, perhaps even plausible. Indeed, scholarship has moved falteringly in this direction. It is widely acknowledged that Eunapius is essential to solving the conundrum of the relationship between the *Libellus breviatus* and Zosimus, indeed passages from the former are even printed in the standard edition of Eunapius' fragments.[116] At the same time, it has increasingly been recognised that there is cognate material in Zosimus and the *Historia abbreviata*.[117] At any rate, what we have shown here is that the issue of Zosimus' debt to Eunapius (wherever we settle on that question) is no obstacle to the notion that much of what we read in the *New History* had its origins in Victor's work. None of this is to deny that Eunapius was a self-confident and able historian in his own right, to paint him as an author likely to have been simply derivative – quite the opposite in fact. On the Secular Games, for example, Victor's and Zosimus' underlying ideas are clearly related, but the material has been totally reworked in the latter to apply to a different cycle of games and supplied with a detailed antiquarian excursus. While both could have been features of Victor's original, it is equally possible that Zosimus' account is a garbled version of some scholarly elaboration of a passing comment in his *Historia*, more than appropriate to what we know of Eunapius' work. Changing the cycle of games, for example, makes Constantine rather than Constans the guilty party, which is entirely of a piece with Eunapius' characterisation of the two. His portrayal of Constantine was unrelentingly negative, while what little evidence we have for his views on Constans (*VS* 10.7.1–8) indicates a tepid appreciation for his patronage

---

114 *Suda* A.784, Λ.486: it is true that the *Suda* makes him Phrygian (not Lydian), but that could be a simple mistake (Eunapius is hardly likely to have misidentified a fellow countryman), or a misunderstanding: Libanius' Tuscianus had spent time in Phrygia (*Ep.* 348.2).

115 Blockley 1981–1983: 1.23.

116 Blockley frs 7.1, 7.2, 8, 11.2, and 12. *cf.* Barnes 1976a: 266–267.

117 Festy 1998; Paschoud 2000: 267 *e.g.* albeit with Nicomachus Flavianus as an unnecessary intermediary.

of Prohaeresius. Victor was, in contrast, no fan of Constans and while his characterisation of Constantine could never be mistaken for panegyric, there were positive aspects to it. One can only imagine Eunapius' lip curling if he had read Victor's very favourable description of Theodosius, an emperor for whom he certainly did not have a high regard. If Eunapius did indeed use Victor, then that use ought to be seen through the lens of engagement, rather than any straightforward debt.

Eunapius and Victor

In fact, it is almost certain that Eunapius did use Victor, at least to a limited extent, and this conclusion can be shown *without recourse to Zosimus*. Very little survives from what was originally Eunapius' first book, but the *Suda* preserves a long fragment describing the tyrannical behaviour of Carinus, the short-lived son, co-emperor, and successor of Carus (*Suda* K.391 = Blockley fr. 5).[118] In Eunapius' telling, as soon as Carinus' father died he became a tyrant, nay, worse than a tyrant: 'his outrages of well-born children were not thought outrageous, so common were they' (παίδων μὲν γὰρ <εὖ> γεγονότων ὕβρεις διὰ τὸ σύνηθες οὐδὲ ὕβρεις ἐνομίσθησαν).[119] He invented trumped-up charges against people and then judged them himself (ὁ δὲ ἐγκλήματά τε ἀνέπλαττε καὶ ἐδίκαζε τοῖς ἀδικουμένοις). He butchered wealthy citizens for his own amusement and as they were cut down explained that it was because they had not complimented him enough on his appearance, or because they had not shown sufficient appreciation when he was giving declamations as a school-boy (τῶν δέ, ὅτι λέγοντα, ὅτε ἦν μειράκιον, οὐκ ἐθαύμασαν ὡς ἐβούλετο), or even because they had been guilty of simply laughing in his presence. In a few bold brush strokes, we get here a portrait of an emperor out of control, raging against his own subjects.

Much of this indictment is precisely parallel to Eutropius' account of Carinus (9.19.1):

> Omnibus se sceleribus inquinavit. Plurimos innoxios fictis criminibus occidit, matrimonia nobilia corrupit, condiscipulis quoque, qui eum in auditorio vel levi fatigatione taxaverant, perniciosus fuit. Ob quae omnibus hominibus invisus non multo post poenas dedit.

> He debased himself with every kind of iniquity. He killed a vast number of innocent men on trumped-up charges, he defiled well-born brides, he was even destructive to his fellow students who had niggled him in the lecture hall with gentle teasing. For these reasons, not long afterwards he paid the penalty, hateful as he was to all men.

In both texts, we find three distinct and specific allegations against Carinus, presented in a similar order. They both begin with sexual misconduct, both specifying that its victims were aristocratic, then turn to the prosecution of innocents on trumped-up charges, all standard items in the repertoire of criticism of tyrants.[120] They conclude, however, with the much more unusual (if not otherwise unparalleled) slaughter of people who had insulted Carinus' academic performance as a child. Correspondences such

---

118 The *Suda* fragment is not explicitly attributed to Eunapius, but portions of it reappear at Δ.1205, E.133, M.83, and Y.15, each ascribed to him by name. The rather complex style of the passage would hint at its origins even were the attribution not preserved.

119 The supplement is Casaubon's, accepted by Blockley.

120 Though Eutropius places *matrimonia nobilia corrupit* second, the sexual implication of *sceleribus inquinavit* is obvious.

as these cannot be happenstance: they require some textual relationship between the two accounts. That relationship can, however, hardly be direct. It is impossible on chronological grounds that Eutropius used Eunapius, while the account in Eunapius provides more information than Eutropius and varies considerably at the level of detail. Instead, Eunapius must have had access to Eutropius' source.[121] The arc of the argument presented so far, of course, suggests that source ought to be none other than Victor.[122]

In this case, however, there is specific evidence supporting that assumption. As we have already seen, Victor makes the claim that Carinus' sexual incontinence led to his downfall, which finds a distant echo in the Greek tradition represented by John of Antioch (probably based on Zosimus).[123] While this extract from Eunapius breaks off before we learn what happened to Carinus, it seems very likely that this was the prelude to a description of his downfall, as indeed it is in Eutropius. Even more intriguingly, though the *HAb* says nothing specifically about Carinus' (lack of) rhetorical abilities, one of the only things it does mention about his brother Numerian is his eloquence – he is described as *bonus facundusque* (*HAb* 39.13). This is an odd detail to include, especially in a severely abbreviated account, and it must have formed a key part of Victor's discussion of Numerian – as we have seen in Chapter VIII, this characterisation forms the basis of the *HA*'s treatment of that emperor. The obvious reason for the emphasis on Numerian's eloquence, as Penella discerned, is to contrast with the lack-lustre oratorical abilities of his brother Carinus:

> Exaggerating Numerian's eloquence – and, by implication, pointing to Carinus' lack thereof – would have been in keeping with the general black-and-white contrast between the two brothers.[124]

The *HAb*'s description of Numerian's eloquence presupposes an account of the faltering rhetorical style of his brother – the antitype of the virtuous boy-prince, cut down in his youth. In other words, what we have in the *HAb* and the *HA*, on one side, and Eutropius and Eunapius, on the other, are two halves of a single coherent account. We have every reason to believe that that account was Victor's: this means that Eunapius reproduced at least one idea from his *Historia* – by whatever route or through whatever intermediaries it may have reached him.

This is the only substantial fragment of Eunapius from the first book of his history, which treated events from the end of Dexippus' work to Julian's appearance on the imperial stage. As we have seen, the first book's treatment of events from *ca.* 270 to 355 must have been rather cursory. Although few fragments of its account of Constantine have survived, our *testimonia* indicate that Eunapius had a good deal to say about that emperor (little of it complimentary).[125] Given that, it is difficult to believe that Eunapius tackled the emperors after Aurelian at anything other than a rapid clip. It is striking, then, that his account of Carinus shows Eunapius intellectually indebted to the Latin tradition and to Victor in particular. In a way, this is unsurprising, for Victor's *History* may well have offered the fullest and most detailed account of the period between Aurelian and Constantine. For the years from 275 to 306, there was no obvious Greek source, in contrast (for instance) to the reign of Constantine, where Eunapius

---

121 *cf.* Blockley 1981–1983: 2.130, n. 12.
122 For the relationship between Victor and Eutropius, see Chapter VI.
123 See above.

124 Penella 1983b: 276.
125 Besides Photius (above), see *Suda* K.2285 = Blockley fr. 9.1.

would have been able to use the works of Eusebius (if he could stomach them), or the more palatably pagan (if still regrettably laudatory) history of Praxagoras of Athens.[126] For the history of this most obscure period, perhaps using Victor was a necessity?

If Eunapius did use Victor – through whatever means – in his first book, then we are licensed to wonder how much he may have used him elsewhere and to what degree the influence of Victor's *Historia* on the Greek historians was filtered through him. As we have said, it is likely that Victor's work entered the Greek historical tradition at several different times and in several different ways, but we might wonder if Eunapius played a particular role in the process – his early date and considerable reputation provide a plausible explanation for how materials cognate to Latin fourth-century historiography lurk scattered across the Byzantine tradition.

This analysis of the relationship between Victor and the Greek tradition has necessarily involved some slightly speculative reconstructions. That ought not to obscure the fact that a host of Greek historians reveal considerable debts to the two Victorine works, debts that go far beyond the connections long acknowledged between Zosimus and the *LB* in their narratives of the third and fourth centuries. As we saw in Chapter IX, comparison of the *New History* and the *HAb* reveals that this relationship begins as early as the reign of Augustus. As we have shown above, it continues down almost to the terminal point of the first edition of Victor's history, in AD 360, and may well continue beyond that. It is by no means limited to Zosimus, but takes in Eunapius, Peter the Patrician, John of Antioch, and Zonaras as well. It is worth emphasising the conservative and minimalist nature of the survey undertaken here, confined as it has been largely to the periods where no earlier common source in Greek might confound any analysis. It is entirely possible that careful triangulation between the accounts of the first, second, and early third centuries in the later Greek tradition, the Victorine texts, and the contemporary narratives of Josephus, Cassius Dio, and Herodian would reveal still more the Latin impress in Zonaras κτλ.

In a way, it is hardly surprising that Victor had such an influence on later Greek historians interested in Rome's past, for he moved in a cultural milieu that was partly Hellenic, he used Greek sources to write his *Historia*, and he clearly had a good knowledge of Greek literature and erudition more generally.[127] It is easy to imagine that his work found readers in the Greek-speaking regions of the Roman Empire. We began our overview of the way in which his work entered the bloodstream of Greek historiography by emphasising that it probably did so on several occasions. While we have seen that Zosimus is particularly indebted to Victor, that Eunapius must have been an important source of his, and that Eunapius was both closer to Latin circles than has been realised and certainly drew some of his material from Victor, it would be wrong to conclude that what we see is anything so simple as a chain linking Victor to Eunapius and Eunapius to Zosimus. Instead, we ought probably to envisage Victor's *Historia* being read by several Greek historians, who both drew on it directly and used the work of predecessors who had done the same. There can be few greater testimonies to Victor's influence than his ability to cross the divide between Greek and Latin, few better compliments for a man who emphasised the virtues of cosmopolitan empire than this.

---

126 On whom see Barnes 2011: 195–197.   127 Chapters I and IV.

★ ★ ★

Some loose ends need to be tied up. We have argued that the tales of the flight of Constantine, as found in *HAb* 40.2–3, *LB* 41.2–3, and Zosimus 2.8.2–9.1, came originally from Victor's *Historia*. That same story is, however, found in a fourth text, the *Origo Constantini imperatoris*, or *OCI* (2.4):

> Tunc eum Galerius patri remisit. Qui ut Severum per Italiam transiens vitaret, summa festinatione veredis post se truncatis Alpes transgressus ad patrem Constantium venit apud Bononiam quam Galli prius Gesoriacum vocabant. Post victoriam autem Pictorum Constantius pater Eboraci mortuus est, et Constantinus omnium militum consensu Caesar creatus.

> Then Galerius sent him back to his father. In order to dodge Severus while he was crossing Italy, with the utmost haste he killed the post-horses behind him, crossed the Alps, and came to his father Constantius at Boulogne, which the Gauls previously used to call Gesoriacum. His father Constantius, after his victory over the Picts, died at York and Constantine was made Caesar with the consent of the whole army.

Despite the differences in wording, this is precisely the account that we have found in the two Victorine texts:

> ad frustrandos insequentes (*HAb, LB*) ~ ut . . . vitaret; publica iumenta . . . interficeret (*HAb*), publica iumenta . . . interfecit (*LB*) ~ veredis . . . truncatis; pervenit (*HAb*), ad patrem . . . pervenit (*LB*) ~ ad patrem . . . venit; quo mortuo (*HAb, LB*) ~ mortuus est; cunctis qui aderant annitentibus (*HAb, LB*) ~ omnium militum consensu.

At the same time, there is material shared only with Zosimus, such as the mention of the Alps (*Alpes transgressus* ~ ὑπὲρ τὰς Ἄλπεις): the latter's κολούων could well be a translation of the *OCI*'s *truncatis*. On the surface then, the four accounts we have of Constantine's flight – in the *HAb*, the *LB*, Zosimus, and the *Origo* – look very much like four derivatives of a single source, and that source ought to be Victor's *Historia*. What does that mean for the nature and origin of the *Origo*? To answer that we need to explore this mysterious little text in greater detail.

The *Origo Constantini imperatoris*: nature and date

The *Origo Constantini Imperatoris* (the manuscript title), or 'History of the emperor Constantine', is a very short account (*ca.* 1,600 words) of Roman imperial politics from roughly the end of the first Tetrarchy to AD 337, dominated (naturally enough) by the emperor from Naissus.[128] It has an importance entirely out of proportion to its size, because it offers a clear, factual, and remarkably detailed narrative of the period, often providing us with our only evidence for crucial episodes.[129] This is curious, because the

---

128 Text in Moreau 1968: 1–10; Cessi 1913a (with extensive introduction); and König 1987 (with an exhaustive commentary).

129 For example, no other text gives us any insight into the manoeuvrings that led to the first war between Constantine and Licinius (*OCI* 5.14–15), or even names Bassianus and Senecio, the key figures in it.

OCI is a Latin text and our understanding of the course of events in the age of Constantine is generally dominated by Greek sources: Eusebius of Caesarea, most importantly, but also Zosimus.[130] Moreover, it has long been recognised that, while the *OCI* has much unique material on the early fourth century, it also contains sections that have been taken verbatim from Orosius.[131] Orosius has been used for details about Constantine *qua* Christian emperor, which tends to suggest that the work's main source was pagan, or at least secular, and that some later reader wanted a more rounded picture.

As a result of all this, it is hardly surprising that the *OCI* has attracted a good deal of scholarly attention, largely focused on two broad subjects. First, there is the question of date: both of the core material and of the later Christian redaction (as it is generally supposed). Various solutions have been proposed. Elimar Klebs, whose work really marks the start of modern research on the *OCI*, put the original soon after the death of Constantine, a position also influentially advocated by Barnes.[132] Others have argued for composition later in the fourth century, under Valentinian, or even Theodosius.[133] Primarily because of the presence of Orosian material, the redactor has generally been located rather vaguely in the early fifth century.[134] Second and related, there has been the issue of where the non-Orosian material came from and, in particular, of the *OCI*'s relationship to the *Kaisergeschichte*, against which background most discussion of the text has occurred. Barnes opined firmly in various places that the *OCI* had nothing to do with the *KG*, representing a different strand of the historical tradition.[135] In contrast, R.W. Burgess has suggested that the *OCI* did indeed use Enmann's imperial history and Giuseppe Zecchini went so far as to posit that the *OCI* is in fact an extract from the *KG* itself.[136] Views on these two issues are often interlinked, though the same ideas lead to completely contradictory conclusions. For Barnes, it is the *Origo*'s independence of the *KG* that is the single strongest argument for a date soon after 337.[137] In contrast, for Zecchini, it is the fact that the *Origo* dates to 337/340 that makes it most plausible that it is in fact the *KG*.[138] The degree of disagreement that the *OCI* has attracted on fundamental issues would by itself license another investigation, but it is the removal of the *KG* – the lodestar of *OCI* scholarship – that makes it an urgent task, one that must be conducted from the ground up.[139]

What do we actually know about the *OCI*? The text survives in a single manuscript (Berlin Phillipps 1885), written probably in the early ninth century at Verona.[140] That manuscript was once part of a larger historical compilation, now split into multiple volumes, which offered a sort of universal

---

130 Lactantius' *DMP* is an obvious exception, but Constantine reigned for a nearly a quarter of a century after his narrative ceases.

131 In Moreau 1968, these passages are in italics.

132 Klebs 1889; Barnes 1970a: 27; 1989. This date has some claim to be the modern consensus: Zecchini 1993: 35; Aussenac 2001; Barnes 2011: 27.

133 Valentinian: Neri 1992: 279–282 (this is a summary of Neri's views, which are complex; strictly, he argues for composition under Valentinian, but based on earlier Constantinian materials). Theodosius: König 1987: 19–28.

134 König 1982: 19; Neri 1992: 237–238; Zecchini 1993: 21–23 (specifically under Constantius III). Only Den

Boer 1972: 106, 167 ff. seems to have put the whole work after Orosius.

135 Barnes 1970a: esp. 27; Barnes 1989.

136 Burgess 1993a: 491 and n. 1, *cf.* Burgess 1995a: 367 n. 38; Zecchini 1993: 37–38. König 1982 has a much more complex picture of the text's sources (summarised by the diagram on 26). Neri 1992: 238–243 also posits a convoluted genesis for the text, including use of a biographical source and the *KG*.

137 Barnes 1989: 161 *e.g.*

138 Zecchini 1993: 35 ff.

139 *KG*: Chapter VI.

140 The fullest and most up-to-date account of the MS is in Tondini 2011: 213–239; see further below.

history assembled out of condensed texts (for convenience designated B in what follows).[141] Some of these are presented as excerpts (Phill. 1885 f. 47v: *ex libro Dialogorum S(an)c(t)i Gregorii Papae*), others as epitomes (St Petersburg Lat. Q.v.IV no. 5 f. 1r: *incipit epitoma ex libris Pompei Trogi*), and still others are introduced more laconically, like the *OCI* itself (Phill. 1885 f. 30v), or without any title at all. As a general presumption, it is reasonable to suppose that texts for which the compilation is our only source are excerpted or epitomised.[142]

In the case of the *OCI*, this presumption can be confirmed. It is hinted at generally by the rather disjointed character of the narrative. The short and sorry story of the tetrarch Severus (r. 305–307), for instance, is split over several different sections, with a good deal of repetition, as though it is the derivative of some longer and more complex history which needed to introduce him at several different points.[143] It is also suggested specifically by the way that the text generally marks the end of an emperor's reign with a notice *imperavit/regnavit annos . . .* which is very similar to its opening words (1.1), *Diocletianus cum Herculio Maximiano imperavit annos XX*, as though the history of those two emperors came before in the original.[144] Abbreviation can, however, also be demonstrated from the text itself. In 307, the emperor Galerius invaded Italy to deal with his upstart son-in-law Maxentius, proclaimed emperor at Rome in 306. The campaign was a failure – Maxentius persuaded enough of the invading regiments to desert to wreck it – and Galerius had to retreat in ignominy, turning over parts of Italy to his soldiers for plunder, to keep their loyalty.[145] Here is how the *OCI* recounts these events (Phill. 1885, f. 31v):

> Qui contemptus agnovit promissis   virorum [146]
> maxenti partes suas deseruiss& quibus
> perturbatus r&tro versus est & ut mili
> te suo praeda(m) quamcumque conferr&
> flamminiam iussit auferri ille ad constan
> tinum refugit ·

Editors have consistently obscured this by putting a full stop (and sometimes a paragraph break) after *auferri*, but, as written, the *OCI* says clearly that Galerius fled from Italy to Constantine.[147] This is hopelessly wrong: Galerius and Constantine were hardly bosom friends and, in any case, the former retreated from Italy to the Balkans, while the latter seems to have been on the Rhine at the time.[148] The one who

---

141 The scope of the original can be most easily grasped from Mommsen 1892: 3–5, though the details of his reconstruction have been challenged (Cessi 1913b: 72–74; *cf.* Tondini 2011: 218–226). The other MSS are Berlin Phillipps 1896 and St Petersburg, National Library of Russia Lat. Q.v.iv no. 5 and Lat. Q.v.9. Troncarelli 2014 makes a compelling case that the original compilation also included extracts from a lost life of Boethius later used by Giovanni de Matociis (on whom see Stover and Woudhuysen 2017). A date in the early ninth century is suggested both by the palaeography (see below) and by the list of Byzantine emperors in Phillipps 1896 ff. 84v-85r, which terminates with Leo V (d. 820): plenty of empty space for Michael II who died in 829.

142 Which is not to say that they necessarily are. For instance, Adams 1976: 15 and n. 5 was sceptical that *Anonymus Valesianus* II was a series of excerpts from some larger work, though it is tempting to think it a single continuous one.

143 *OCI* 3.5–6, 4.9–10; note that we are twice told (3.5, 9.9) which part of the empire he ruled.

144 *imperavit annos*: 3.8, 4.12, 5.29, 6.35.

145 Lactantius, *DMP* 27 narrates all this as only he can.

146 The MS leaves space for four or five letters after *promissis*.

147 Moreau 1968: 3; Mommsen 1892: 8; Cessi 1913a: 6.

148 Barnes 1982: 64, 70.

fled to Constantine in the aftermath of Galerius' invasion was Maximian (Diocletian's *quondam* colleague), who had fallen out spectacularly with his son Maxentius. Comparison with the account of Lactantius makes this very clear: he puts Galerius' failed invasion, Maximian's blow-up with Maxentius, and his flight to Gaul in quick succession.[149] In a process of abbreviation, all this has dropped out: an easy mistake to make given the exceptionally complex political manoeuvrings that marked the period after 305.

Besides being a condensed text, the *OCI* has also incorporated material from several other works. Generally, scholars have limited this process to Orosius and referred to it as 'interpolation', but neither point bears scrutiny.[150] Interpolation is in general an unhelpful term when thinking about a condensed text, let alone one that forms part of a compilation with other condensed texts. It is also a clumsy description of what has happened here. It is certainly true that the *OCI* uses Orosius' text, but material from it has been carefully woven through, rather than simply inserted – it is clearly integral to the work as we have it.[151] Moreover, the *OCI* has not drawn on Orosius alone, but also shares some verbatim wording with Jerome's *Chronicon*, even where there are significant differences of fact (such as whether Theodora was the daughter or stepdaughter of Maximian).[152] When a text has taken some material verbatim from one source, as the *OCI* does with Orosius, the logical conclusion is that word-for-word overlaps with other sources also reflect borrowing. That is much more plausible, than, for instance, supposing that Jerome happened to have read and used the *OCI* (assuming it even existed in some form close to its present one at the time he was writing) for two points only.[153] Economically, we might suppose that the person who created the epitome and the person who incorporated Orosius/Jerome were one and the same; indeed, it is hard to imagine another scenario, given how well integrated the material from the *Historiae adversus paganos* is.

The *OCI* is thus an abbreviated Roman history, drawing in part on Orosius and Jerome, and surviving in a single medieval manuscript: that is what we *know* about it. With that in mind, let us now turn back to those two questions that have preoccupied students of the *OCI*: date and sources. On the date, it is striking how certainly scholarly opinion has fixed the text in late antiquity, given that we have almost no real evidence. Clearly, the *OCI* dates to after the 410s AD and before the early ninth century, the *termini* supplied by the use of Orosius and the writing of the manuscript itself. Beyond that, we have no precise indications of date. There are, however, some signs that it belongs later, rather than earlier in that range: that, in other words, the *OCI* is not a late-antique text.[154] For example, it never describes

---

149 Lactantius, *DMP* 27–29.1.

150 *e.g.* Barnes 1989: 161 and n. 13.

151 *OCI* 5.29 on the fates of Licinius and Martinianus is a good example. Note also the way that extracts from Orosius have not been inserted in their original order (*OCI* 5.29 = Orosius 7.28.20–21; *OCI* 6.33 = Orosius 7.28.1 *e.g.*).

152 *OCI* 1.1 *relicta enim Helena priore uxore, filiam Maximiani Theodoram duxit uxorem, ex qua postea sex liberos Constantini fratres habuit* ~ Jerome, *Chron.* 225ᵍ *Constantius privignam Herculi Theodoram accepit, ex qua postea sex liberos Constantini fratres habuit.* The wording of Eutropius 9.22.1 is identical to Jerome here and he might equally be the source, but a further correspondence suggests that it is the *Chronicon* that has been used:

OCI 6.35 *item Constaninus cum bellum pararet in Persas in suburbano Constantinopolitano villa publica iuxta Nicomediam dispositam bene rem publicam filiis tradens <. . .>* ~ Jerome, *Chron.* 234ᵇ *Constantinus cum bellum pararet in Persas in Acyrone villa publica iuxta Nicomediam moritur anno aetatis LXVI.* In this case, Orosius is more distant (7.28.30): *cum bellum in Persas moliretur, in villa publica iuxta Nicomediam, dispositam bene rem publicam filiis tradens, diem obiit.*

153 As argued by Barnes 1989: 161, n. 13.

154 It seems possible that an understanding of the early Middle Ages as an era that saw 'the triumph of barbarism and religion' made scholars disinclined to consider the possibility that a detailed work of Roman history like the *OCI* might have been produced during

any emperor as an Augustus (the correct title for a senior emperor). Throughout, it refers to emperors as *Caesares* and *imperatores*. Strictly, an *imperator* was an Augustus, so one might wonder if this was an idiosyncratic way of drawing distinctions within the imperial college.[155] The *OCI*, however, uses *imperator* and *Caesar* interchangeably (*e.g.* 3.8 and 5.13 of Licinius on his appointment) – it also uses *Caesar* of several emperors who were (or claimed to be) Augusti.[156] The only supportable interpretation of these data is that the *OCI* does not distinguish between Augusti and Caesares. This is almost unimaginable in a fourth-century text (let alone a detailed fourth-century history), but it is perfectly understandable in one of a later vintage. The compiler also seems to have been tripped up by confusingly similar late-Roman names: as we shall see, he applies an anecdote on the drinking habits of (Galerius) Maximinus Daia to Galerius (Maximianus).

An early-medieval date would, moreover, suit the extremely paratactic style of the text and make sense of its grammar. Editors have treated the *OCI* as self-evidently late antique, so they have put a good deal of effort into cleaning up a text that offers rich opportunities for ingenuity – Moreau's apparatus often runs to a third of the page. Readers thus generally encounter an *OCI* that in many ways looks classical. A glance at the manuscript, however, shows that the situation is rather more complex. Whether because of a difficult archetype, inexperience, or incompetence, the scribe of Phillipps 1885 clearly found the task of copying the *OCI* a struggle, hence writing *scripsum* where *Crispum* (Constantine's son) must be meant (*OCI* 5.23), for instance. Editors are right to correct this kind of slip, but they have also gone further and removed a host of post-classical features from the text: accusative absolutes, the alternating use of *in* with the ablative or accusative and verbs of motion, or, indeed, its general flexibility with the case system.[157] We might note also the way that the *OCI* likes its verbs with a stated subject and uses *ille* pronominally, without any particular emphasis.[158] Any one of these points or examples might be explained individually by scribal error or idiosyncrasy, but cumulatively they make sense only in a post-classical text, especially a work of history. With all this in mind, our working assumption ought probably to be that the *OCI* is an early-medieval work, in the form that we have it. None of this is to deny (as if it could be denied) that the *OCI* had access to excellent source material on the age of Constantine, but that in no way means it is a text roughly contemporary with him. It merely makes more pressing the question of what that source was and (in particular) whether it was Victor's *Historia*.

---

it. Gibbon's famous phrase is perhaps more quoted than understood and his view of the early Middle Ages was much more sympathetic than it might seem to imply (see Woudhuysen 2018b).

155 Barnes 1982: 25–26.

156 *OCI* 3.6: Constantine and Maxentius on their accession. See Barnes 1982: 5, 13 (Constantine first took the title Augustus; Maxentius avoided it for a little while, but was never Caesar). At *OCI* 4.9, the manuscript reads *quo caesar Maxentius factus est imperator*, generally corrected to *quo casu*, though it is possible that this is a reference to his later decision to take the title Augustus.

157 In the following examples, the text of the *OCI* is as in the MS. Accusative absolute: *Licinium ad Illyricum reversum* (5.13), *Bizantium Constantinus invasit, victoria maritinam Crispum convenientem* (5.27). *In* with ablative and verb of motion: *in urbe perduxit* (4.10), *equo pricipitatus in fluvio* (4.12), *in campo mardiense* (5.17). Flexibility in case system: *minatus civitatis interitum* (3.6), *apud Verona* (4.12), *Bassianus Italia medius obtineret* (5.14), *Licinius et Valens credentes Constantino* (5.18), *trachiam, moessia, minorem syctiam possideret* (5.19), *et vastata tracia et moessiam* (5.21), *filio et uxore superstitem* (5.29), *Dalmatium filium fratri sui* (6.35).

158 As, *e.g.*, 4.10: *ille iugulatus est*.

Victor and the *Origo*

At first sight, the *OCI* appears to have little to do with either the *HAb* or the *LB*: there is a reason, after all, that Barnes denied any commonalities with the *KG* tradition. That appearance, however, is deceptive, largely a consequence of length and of focus. The *OCI* is a very short text, but at *ca.* 1,600 words it covers the era of Constantine in considerably more detail than either the *HAb* (40.14–41.21 = *ca.* 1,000 words) or the *LB* (39.5–41.17 = *ca.* 900 words). Moreover, the *OCI* is much more interested in the nuts and bolts of imperial history – who went where, when, and what battles they fought – than either of the Victorine epitomes, which give considerable space to more general characterisation of the emperors and less chronologically fixed reflection on their actions. To give a concrete example, the *HAb* (41.6–9) and *LB* (41.5–7) both dispatch the two civil wars of Constantine and Licinius in around sixty words: the *OCI* (5.16–29), in contrast, uses about 600, slightly over a third of its entire length. Eyeballing the three texts and noting that they are different is rather like looking at Florus and Julius Obsequens and concluding that they have little in common: true, so far as it goes, but it does not go very far.

When one reads the three texts with this in mind, it becomes obvious that they have some very significant commonalities, which link the *OCI* to the *HAb* and the *LB*, separately and together. The *HAb* starts its account of the second civil war between Constantine and Licinius (AD 324): *Itaque sexennio post, rupta pace* . . . The ablative absolute *rupta pace* is very rare: before Victor, it is found once in Seneca (*Hercules furens* 416) and once in Cyprian (*Ad Donatum* 10).[159] After, it was used by Eutropius (6.6.2) and Ammianus (15.8.6), who both probably drew it from Victor. The other place in which it turns up is at the start of the *OCI*'s account of the conflict of AD 324 (5.23): *rupta iam pace utriusque consensu.*[160] A rare phrase, used not only to describe the same events but at precisely the same point in the narrative: it is hard to think of a stronger intertext. The wording of Eutropius (10.6.1) on the same events – *pax reconciliata ruptaque est* – makes it almost certain that Victor is its origin. The quality of these connections between the *HAb* and the *OCI* licenses us to conclude that a string of weaker (though still revealing) commonalities also reflects Victor's influence (**TABLE 10.9**). In each case, both texts share some significant wording when describing events during the chaotic period of the second Tetrarchy. In the first example in Table 4.9, it is worth noting that the idea of someone *desertus a(b) suis* is surprisingly rare in Latin literature before Victor: it is not quite so revealing as *rupta pace*, but it is a strong link.[161] In the third, beyond the shared wording (itself an unusual formula for 'territorial control'), it is interesting that the *OCI* refers to Maximian the elder as plain *Herculius*, probably Victor's innovation.[162] For two texts that at first sight are very different, the *HAb* and *OCI* turn out to have a lot in common.

It is a similar story with the *LB*. Here, because of the nature of the text, there are fewer verbal overlaps, but what we do have is suggestive. One of the *OCI*'s rare character sketches describes Licinius as 'raging with greed, cruelty, and lust' (5.22: *avaritia crudelitate libidine saeviebat*). A conventional trio, to be sure, but the only other place it occurs with the verb *saevire* is in Eutropius describing Caligula (7.12.4:

---

159 *cf. pax rupta*: Lactantius, *DMP* 3.5.
160 The MS (f. 34v) reads *uxoribus eorum · Corrup/ta enim pace* – as Valesius saw already, the solution is something like *corruptis. Rupta enim* . . .

161 Cicero, *Ep. Att.* 4.3.2; Livy 35.30.2; Suetonius, *Galba* 19.2 (*n.b.* also Justin 39.2.6).
162 Chapter IV.

TABLE 10.9 – COMMONALITIES IN THE *HAb* AND THE *OCI*

HAb	OCI
40.7: When Severus was going around the walls, deserted by his own troops (*desertus a suis*), whom Maxentius had bribed with the promise of rewards, he fled (*fugiens*) and, besieged at Ravenna (*Ravennae*), perished.	3.6: Severus was suddenly deserted by all his own troops (*desertus ab omnibus suis*) and fled to Ravenna (*Ravennam fugit*). (*cf.* 4.9)
40.8: Galerius, in recognition of their long-standing friendship, made Licinius Augustus, and, leaving him behind (*eoque . . . relicto*) to guard Illyricum and Thrace, made for Rome.	3.8: At that time Galerius made Licinius Caesar in Illyricum. Then, leaving him behind (*illo relicto*) in Pannonia, he returned to Serdica . . .
40.1: Severus and Maximinus both Caesars and native sons of Illyricum were despatched, the former to Italy, the latter to the regions where Jovius had held sway (*in quae Iovius obtinuerat*).	3.5: Meanwhile two Caesars were appointed, Severus and Maximinus. To Maximinus was given command of the East . . . Severus took Italy and whatever Herculius used to hold sway over (*quicquid Herculius obtinebat*).

TABLE 10.10 – THE *LB* AND THE *OCI* ON THE FATE OF SEVERUS

LB 40.3	OCI 4.10
Severus Caesar was snuffed out by Herculius Maximian at Rome at *Tres Tabernae*, and his body was interred in the tomb of Gallienus, nine miles outside of the city on the *Via Appia*.	Summoned there on behalf of his son Maxentius, Herculius came and having tricked Severus with a false promise, took him into custody, led him into the city dressed as a captive, and put him under guard in public house on the Appian Way, thirty miles outside the city. Afterwards, when Galerius was making an assault on Italy, Severus' throat was slit, and he was brought back to within eight miles of the city, and interred in the tomb of Gallienus.

avaritia, libidine, crudelitate saeviret). We do not need to guess where Eutropius got it from, since we have the *LB*'s description of Commodus (17.3): 'more enraged than everyone else with lust, greed, and cruelty' (*saevior omnibus libidine atque avaritia, crudelitate*).[163] There is also one very significant factual commonality, on the fate of the tetrarch Severus (**TABLE 10.10**). No other texts give us this level of detail about these events, which were of considerable obscurity: most sources erroneously locate his death at Ravenna.[164] The *OCI* and *LB* are linked not only by general factual points, but also by the specific location of

163 *cf. LB* 41.8: *avaritiae cupidine omnium pessumus neque alienus a luxu venerio . . .*

164 See the helpful commentary of König 1987: 102–103, *cf.* Hanson 1974. The account is different from, but perfectly compatible with, what Lactantius says, *DMP* 26.9–11. *HAb* 40.7 (above) has normally been read as saying Severus died at Ravenna, but that is partly a question of punctuation (do we put a comma before *obiit*?) and partly of abbreviation.

TABLE 10.11 – THE *LB* AND THE *OCI* ON MAXIMINUS DAIA

LB 40.9	*OCI* 4.11
When he was drunk (*ebrius*) he would issue certain commands (*iubebat*) not in his right mind. Since he would regret them after they were performed, he instructed (*statuit*) that whatever he had enjoined be delayed until the sober time of morning.	Therefore Galerius was so given to drink (*ebriosus*) that since in his cups he would issue commands (*iuberet*) which should not be carried out, at the advice of his prefect he gave instructions (*constituerit*) that no one should fulfil his commands after luncheon (*ne iussa eius aliquis post prandium faceret*).

Gallienus' tomb on the *Via Appia*, a monument that appears in Latin literature only here.[165] There is indeed a (sadly dilapidated) mausoleum of the right date at roughly that spot, one where a fragment of porphyry, the imperial stone, has been found.[166] Significantly, the text that comes closest to the version of the *LB/OCI* is Zosimus (2.10.2). Characteristically, he is rather confused about what is going on, but he does situate the death of Severus at τι χωρίον . . . ᾧ τρία καπηλεῖα προσηγορία, a literal translation of *Tres Tabernae* into Greek.[167]

Another very significant overlap occurs in the description of the crapulence of Maximinus Daia (TABLE 10.11). The two passages share significant overlaps in both content and wording (*ebrius* ~ *ebriosus*; *iubebat* ~ *iuberet*), even though, as mentioned above, the *OCI* appears to be talking about the wrong Galerius. The *LB* helps to explain this confusion. While Galerius was indeed one of Maximinus' names, he is rarely called by it in literary texts. One exception is the preceding sentence in the *LB* (40.18): *Galerius Maximinus . . . Daia dictus*. Equally interesting is the comparison of these two versions of the tale with an earlier story in Eusebius:

> And he was carried to such a degree of madness and drunkenness that he would go mad while in his cups and give commands drunk which he repented of later on, when he was sober.[168]

This is meant to be a damning tale, coming in the midst of a whole litany of the emperor's enormities. Eusebius' Maximinus might get raging drunk, but all that he feels the next morning is regret. The Maximinus in the *LB* and the *OCI* also might get raging drunk, but he takes precautions, leaving instructions (while sober) for his drunken commands to be disregarded. Given the undoubted priority of Eusebius, this looks very much like an attempted exculpation. That very same manoeuvre is deployed by Victor in the *HAb* (13.10) to downplay the *vinolentia* of Trajan:

---

165 The *Chronography of 354* (p. 148) has Severus kill himself on the *Via Latina* at the third milestone.

166 Johnson 2009: 42–47. The mausoleum is apparently now largely used for prostitution: Victor would regard that as a vindication of his view of Gallienus, that frequenter of *popinae* and associate of *lenones* (*HAb* 33.6).

167 Zosimus puts the death of Severus on the way from Ravenna to Rome, which cannot be true unless he took a rather scenic route.

168 *HE* 8.14.11: παροινίας γε μὴν καὶ μέθης ἐς τοσαύτην ἠνέχθη φοράν, ὡς ἐν τοῖς πότοις παρακόπτειν καὶ τῶν φρενῶν παρεξίστασθαι τοιαῦτά τε μεθύοντα προστάττειν, οἷα ἀνανήψαντα αὐτὸν τῇ ὑστεραίᾳ εἰς μετάμελον ἄγειν.

He softened the effects of his proclivity to drink – a vice that afflicted Nerva as well – by prudence, forbidding that anything he commanded after lengthy banquets (*iussa post longiores epulas*) be carried out.

The language here closely recalls what we are told of Maximinus in the *OCI* (*iussa post longiores epulas* ~ *iussa . . . post prandium*). This intertextual or intratextual relationship produces a doubly exculpatory explanation for an unflattering charge hurled at Maximinus by his contemporaries: he had the good sense to mitigate the effects of his carousals on his governance and, in so doing, he was like Trajan.

The *OCI* thus shares some very significant verbal overlaps with the *HAb*, two major factual ones with the *LB*, and in a couple of instances seems to be connected to both at the same time. This suggests that it is – in spite of appearances and whatever its origin – a text linked very closely indeed with the *Historia* of Victor. Given the current state of our evidence, it is difficult to be any more precise about this relationship – it is possible, for instance, that the *OCI* is derived from a lost late-antique text that made extensive use of Victor. Given the data that we have, however, the economical assumption is that it is (like the *LB*) a descendant of Victor's *Historia*, probably originating in Italy, where Paul the Deacon still had access to the full text in the middle of the eighth century.

The transmission of the *Origo*

That is precisely the direction in which the evidence of transmission points. The compilation of which the *OCI* forms a part (B) was almost certainly assembled at Verona. Though nothing in the manuscript explicitly ties it to that city, a cluster of arguments securely locates it there. First, and most importantly, it has a remarkable overlap with another (twelfth-century) historical compendium, preserved in Pal. lat. 927 (often referred to as P). This was certainly compiled at Verona, as its *annales* for the city (f. 214v–216r) and a short poem about a fire there in 1172 demonstrate (f. 219v), at the monastery of Santissima Trinità (see the touching poem by the scribe on f. 3v).[169] Opinion diverges on the precise relation of these two compilations: it has been suggested that P is derived from B (perhaps through an intermediate stage) and, alternatively, that they are both independent witnesses to an earlier compilation.[170] The issue has perhaps been clouded by a tendency to reconstruct the relationship by looking at textual details, rather than each compilation as a collection of material. If we examine the excerpts that P and B have taken from Eutropius, for instance, we can see that they share a great deal, but that B has some material not in P and, crucially, P has some material not in B.[171] The only explanation for this pattern is that they both draw independently on an earlier compilation, one which must (given their overlaps) already have been a collection of excerpts. Given P's provenance, this stage of scholarly activity must have taken place at Verona. Second, the script and decoration of B both suit Verona well and can easily be paralleled in manuscripts

169 f. 219v is the end folio and so probably provides a *terminus ante quem* for the MS.
170 Mommsen 1892: 260 suggested that P might have been copied from B, perhaps via an intermediary (Adams 1976: 17–20 was sympathetic). Cessi 1913a: ix argued in contrast that P and B were both derived

independently from a common source (followed by Moreau 1968: x). P cannot be a direct copy of B, since the latter was almost certainly in Metz by the time the former was made: Tondini 2011: 230–231.
171 Conveniently accessible in Droysen 1879: xiv–xx.

certainly produced there.[172] Third, the annotating hands in B can be traced in other manuscripts that were certainly produced at Verona.[173]

When thinking about the transmission of the *OCI*, then, we need to focus on northern Italy. That is significant, because the region played an important part in the dissemination of Paul the Deacon's works. The earliest extant manuscripts of the *Historia Langobardorum* (from the very end of the eighth century or the early ninth) seem to have been produced there, possibly at Verona itself.[174] The *Scholia Vallicelliana*, which of course preserve Paul's annotations and excerpts from texts that he had read, survive in a copy derived from one made for Grausus, bishop of Ceneda (modern Vittorio Veneto), in the same region.[175] Sure enough, the Verona compilation itself contains extracts from Paul's *History* (Phill. 1885 f. 50r ff.): this puts the *OCI* tantalisingly close to the milieu of Paul the Deacon. As we know, Paul produced an epitome of Victor's work, one which worked in material from other later authors (Jordanes and Eutropius) to create an integrated whole. It is thus very tempting to think that the *OCI* was a parallel effort.

The *Origo Constantini Imperatoris* thus stands revealed as potentially another early-medieval witness to the *History* of Sextus Aurelius Victor, possibly produced in the circle of Paul the Deacon by someone familiar with his writings. Future work on the text ought to proceed within the framework of Victor, and the *OCI* can perhaps usefully expand our sense of both the coverage and the character of his *Historia*.

Polemius Silvius

The final loose end is, strange as it may sound, a calendar. In the year 448, a Gallic *érudit* named Polemius Silvius sat down to write a comprehensive Roman and Christian calendar, interspersed with various bits of trivial erudition – a summary of regal and imperial couture, for example, or a list of the Latin verbs for animal sounds.[176] This *laterculus*, as it was titled, is a very curious project and perhaps it is no surprise that Silvius' major entry in the historical record is a jejune reference in the *Gallic Chronicle of 452* for the year 438, noting that one Silvius, after a career in government service, lost his mind and started writing on religion.[177] In this curious farrago, wedged between January and February, one item is a list of emperors and usurpers called the *Nomina principum Romanorum*.[178] For centuries, this list – which occasionally includes figures of considerable obscurity – floated around unmoored, an isolated curiosity in the Latin historiographical tradition.[179]

172 Cessi 1913b: 74–76. The capital letters in B, with the chambers coloured red, green, and yellow, are characteristically Veronese (Polloni 2007: 191, *e.g.*, with numerous plates in the article).

173 Most easily grasped from Venturini 1929: 124–125 and plate III (though she disavowed certainty on the Berlin MSS). One does not have to accept that Pacificus of Verona lies behind all this (see La Rocca 2004 for a sceptical overview) to see the similarity.

174 The palimpsested Assisi, Biblioteca Comunale S. Franceso, Fondo Antico presso la Biblioteca del Sacro Convento 585 (f. 155r ff., late s. VIII, *CLA* 3.279); St Gall 635 (s. VIII/IX, *CLA* 7.945, from Verona itself); Cividale di Friuli, Museo Archeologico

Nazionale XXVIII, Bischoff 1994: 45 and n. 128, 54; McKitterick 1999: 335–336.

175 Chapter V.

176 Now available in a splendid edition by Paniagua 2018, from which we cite the text.

177 *Chron. 452* 121 (Mommsen 1892: 660).

178 Paniagua 2018: 238–243.

179 Only two MSS of this section survived: Brussels, Bibliothèque Royale 10615–10729, which contains the whole of the *Laterculus*, and Rome, Biblioteca Vallicelliana E.26, which transmits the list, along with several other excerpts from the *laterculus*, none labelled as such. See Paniagua 2018: 29–31.

One of Burgess' major achievements was to take a significant step towards solving the riddle of Silvius' list.[180] He showed that it had certain *textual* relationships with representatives of the Latin historical tradition of the fourth century: the *HA*, Jerome, Eutropius and, of course, Victor. For Burgess, this obviously meant that Silvius had access to their source, that is, to the *KG*. Although we have already dispensed with the *KG*, that does not mean that we are cutting Silvius adrift once more.[181] Burgess has already shown that there is at least one particular link between Silvius and Victor, on Tetricus and his son's surrender to Aurelian: *Laterculus* 20 'The two Tetrici, father and son, who handed themselves over to the same [Aurelian] (*se eidem dederunt*)' ~ *HAb* 35.12 'and [Tetricus] handed himself over to him (*eique . . . se dedit*).[182] Strengthening this link is the fact that immediately following in Silvius we have a reference to Faustinus, who rebelled against Tetricus, a usurper of whose existence we otherwise know only from the *HAb*.[183] This seems significant. In fact, this is just one of several places in which only the *HAb* and the *Laterculus* mention a particular usurper.[184] Silvius' conscientious inclusion of usurpers – far more than we have any right to expect in such a short text – is curious and really ought to be, as Burgess avers, a reflection of the proclivities of his source. Lavish attention to usurpers was absolutely a feature of Victor's *Historia*.

Such are far from the only agreements between the Victorine texts and Silvius. They agree in 'error', for only the *LB* and Silvius give Alexander Severus the name Marcellus before his accession and both do it in the context of Elagabalus' appointment of him as Caesar: *Laterculus* 18 'under [Elagabalus] Marcellus was Caesar' ~ *LB* 23.4 'Elagabalus made his cousin Marcellus, who was afterwards called Alexander, Caesar'.[185] They also agree in truth. For example, the *Laterculus* notes that 'Valerian, captured by the Persians, died in their hands' (19). As we have already seen, Eutropius was misled by Victor's mention of Valerian's old age when he became a captive and described him as growing old in captivity (not the same thing).[186] There is no trace of this idea in Silvius. Both the *Laterculus* (20) and the *HAb* (39.10) put the usurpation of Sabinus Julianus in 283, after the death of Carus but during the reign of Numerian. We could also point to the (sparing) editorial comments in the *Laterculus*: Burgess has already noted how Silvius (15) used the same words, *dedecus* and *scelus*, to describe Nero's crimes as Victor (*HAb* 5.4 and 11).[187] More significantly, the only other emperor on whose morals Silvius comments is not Elagabalus or Gallienus, but Constans: 'Constans, brother of the aforementioned emperor and of life most infamous, was killed' (22). As we have seen, Victor made much of Constans' character.

Taken together, all this textual evidence suggests what might naturally be concluded from the identity of Victor's *Historia* with what remains of the idea of a *KG*: Victor was Silvius' source. Indeed, Victor's *Historia* works even better as Silvius' source than the supposed *KG*, since the *Laterculus*' two departures from the *KG* tradition identified by Burgess – the inclusion of Aemilianus as a legitimate emperor and his enumeration of three Gordians – were undoubtedly found in Victor (*cf. HAb* 31.3 and *LB* 26.1, respectively).

---

180 Burgess 1993a: 492–494.
181 Chapter VI.
182 Burgess 1993a: 493.
183 *PIR*[2] F.131.

184 A list can be found in the appendix to Burgess 1993:
       499–500.
185 On his names, see *PIR*[2] A.1610 and Chapter IV.
186 Chapter VIII.
187 Burgess 1993a: 493.

TABLE 10.12 – POLEMIUS SILVIUS AND THE *OCI* ON HANNIBALIANUS' TITLE

Laterculus 21	*OCI* 6.35
Dalmatius, frater illius de matre alia (de quo nati sunt Gallus et Iulianus qui imperavit) <. . .> factus est rex regum gentium Ponticarum.	Dalmatium filium fratris sui Dalmati Caesarem fecit. Eius fratrem Annibalianum data ei Constantina filia sua regem regum et Ponticarum regionum constituit.
Dalmatius, his brother from another mother, who was the father of Gallus and Julian who was later emperor <. . .> was made King of Kings of the Pontic peoples.	Constantine made his brother Dalmatius' son Dalmatius Caesar. He appointed his brother Hannibalianus King of Kings and of the Pontic regions, having given his daughter Constantina to him in marriage.

One final point of connection is worth separate and slightly more detailed treatment. Late in Constantine's reign, as he geared up for war with Persia, his nephew Hannibalianus was given the extravagant and suggestive title of *Rex regum et Ponticarum gentium*, 'King of kings, and King of the Pontic peoples'. Only two texts record this, Polemius Silvius and the *OCI* (**TABLE 10.12**). There is undoubted confusion in Silvius, partly authorial, perhaps, such as the possible conflation of Dalmatius *père* and Dalmatius *fils*, but partly textual as well, with a likely lacuna in which the name of Hannibalianus dropped out.[188] The fact of that title, however, is undoubtedly authentic, since he is called *rex* by Ammianus (14.1.2: *Hanniballiano regi fratris filio*) and coins also attest that he was a king.[189] No other sources give him this precise honorific, too specific, too grandiose, and too strange to be anything but authentic, even though we know it was never more than aspirational. This means that Silvius and the *OCI* share a source and that source we have independently identified as Victor's *Historia*. We do not, however, have to rely here on hypothesis alone. Only one text gives us actual information about the scope of Hannibalianus' intended role. That text is the *LB* (41.20):

> Hi singuli has partes regendas habuerunt . . . Hannibalianus, Delmatii Caesaris consanguineus, Armeniam nationesque circum socias.[190]

> Each of them had a region to rule . . . Hannibalianus, the brother of Dalmatius Caesar, Armenia and the allied peoples all around.

The relationship between Polemius Silvius, the *OCI*, and the *LB* is no mere abstraction, but a reflection of their shared dependency on Victor's *Historia*.

---

188 Mommsen 1892: 522 supplied <*factus est Caesar Hanniballianus frater praedicti*>, suggesting a *saut du même au même*.

189 See in general Mosig-Walburg 2005.

190 Editors usually print *circumsocias*, but there is no evidence this is a word and some manuscripts divide the two.

★ ★ ★

This chapter has surveyed much ground, albeit from a high vantage point, mapping only the contours of a *terra* still very largely *incognita*. It is only a starting point: a series of suggestions for how we might begin the work of rethinking late Roman historiography, beyond the core texts of Eutropius, Ammianus, and the *HA*. We have suggested that some of Victor's *Historia* trickled down to the later Greek tradition, probably in part via Eunapius' *History*. We have then shown that a hitherto unmoored and unexplained bit of historiogaphical flotsam – the *Origo Constantini* – is probably yet another early-medieval version of part of Victor's *Historia*, produced in the same milieu as Paul's *Libellus breviatus*, and that the fifth-century list of emperors by Polemius Silvius is likewise indebted to the same source. Every one of these topics would be a fruitful avenue for future research: some of them, done properly, could well occasion a book in their own right. We have pointed them out here since they are the necessary consequence of taking Victor's singular reputation in antiquity seriously – that work we must, for now, leave unfinished. To draw this study to a close, we would like to offer some first thoughts on what we should think of Victor not as a source for other texts, but as a historian in his own right.

Conclusion

Victor the Historian

'A large book on a poet little read even in universities might seem to require justification, if not apology. I offer neither' was Alan Cameron's defiant introduction to his 500–page study of the poet Claudian.[1] This book is even longer and its subject is even less read than Claudian was in 1970 – the court poet of Honorius might be evaded by undergraduates, but Victor is avoided even by scholars. Still, we offer no apology. As justification for this study of the best attested but least understood of the historians of the later Roman Empire we might invoke the radical nature of its conclusions and their far-reaching consequences. We have shown that Victor wrote not the shabby epitome that is generally identified as his work today, but rather a monumental *Historia*. The first effort to write Roman imperial history in Latin since the days of Tacitus and Suetonius, Victor's work was the wellspring of a revival in the study of Rome's past that would stretch into the fifth century and beyond – that entire tradition was in his debt. He provided both the fundamental narrative and a way of thinking about it that was profoundly influential, so much so that what often seems at first sight to be merely the basic scaffolding of Roman history turns out on closer inspection to be Victor's own construction. When his *Historia* assumes its proper place in the study of late-antique historiography, it both answers some very old questions and asks some new and disconcerting ones.

The route that we have taken in this book has been long, perhaps even circuitous at times, so a summary is in order. In Chapter I, we offered a survey of Victor's life and some remarks about the reception of his work in antiquity and the present day. The major point to emerge was the disconnect between the high opinion of contemporaries and the sorry state of the history attributed to him. In Chapter II, we took a closer look at the two works – the *Historiae abbreviatae* and *Libellus breviatus*, to give them their correct titles – that are preserved under Victor's name in manuscripts. We showed that both texts are presented as epitomes of a larger *Historia* and that there are good reasons to take that claim at face value. Chapter III offered a broader study of the genre of epitome in Latin, demonstrating that both the *HAb* and the *LB* are entirely consistent with what we know of it. Chapter IV studied in detail the sources, literary culture, and ideas of the *HAb*, showing that it is witness to a remarkable sophistication, range of reference, and artistry in prose, but also that it bears clear signs of abbreviation. The chapter then demonstrated that – though they are well disguised – the *LB* shares many of these features with the *HAb*. It closed by showing that the two works make most sense as witnesses to a single longer lost historical work. Chapter V examined the reception of Victor's *History*, and demonstrated the enormously high regard in which it was held and the number of readers that it found. It then presented new evidence that Paul the Deacon had access to the complete text of Victor's work in southern Italy in the later eighth century and that he compiled the *Libellus breviatus*.

---

1 Cameron 1970: v.

411

Part 2 of the book turned to the implications of this new Victor for the study of Roman historiography in late antiquity. Chapter VI surveyed the reception of Victor in modern scholarship down to the later nineteenth century, before turning to Enmann's *Kaisergeschichte*. It demonstrated that this idea arose in a specific intellectual context from a key misapprehension about later Latin historical texts. It then further showed that it is conceptually flawed and offers an inadequate explanation of our evidence. A key consequence of this realisation is that – for the first time – we can explain what Eutropius was trying to do in his *Historia Romana* and account for the extraordinary popularity of that work. Eutropius distilled Victor's complex and idiosyncratic (not to mention lengthy) philosophical history into a brief digest – easy to read, easy to remember. Chapter VII turned to Marius Maximus, the 'consular biographer', tracing the intellectual history of this slippery figure, before showing that the idea that he was a historian is a crucial part of the fiction of the *Historia Augusta*. That opened afresh the *Quellenforschung* of the *HA*, the subject of Chapter VIII. Close study shows that Victor and (to a lesser extent) Eutropius are major, if not *the* major, sources of the text – in fact, the explanation for the conceit that it is a multi-author compilation of the late third and early fourth century lies in its peculiar author's desire to obscure that fact. Chapter IX opened by examining Ammianus Marcellinus, and shows that he was indebted to Victor, certainly for facts and language, but perhaps also for structuring ideas. It then entered the treacherous waters of the study of Nicomachus Flavianus, arguing that, insofar as his adherents have identified a real problem in the relation between Latin and Greek history-writing in late antiquity, Victor provides a much simpler explanation for it. Chapter X turned to that problem in its own right and demonstrated that Greek historians – from Zosimus to Zonaras – drew on Victor. One conduit through which his influence flowed may have been the work of Eunapius of Sardis. The Greeks led us back at the end to the *Origo Constantini Imperatoris* and the *Laterculus* of Polemius Silvius, two final witnesses to Victor's achievement. The *OCI*, in particular, deserves close attention – there are serious reasons to think that it is an epitome of part of Victor's work, or of another late-antique history that lent very heavily on it.

Along the way, we have presented a great deal of new (or newly interpreted) material, along with a host of novel arguments, ideas, and suggestions. We have advanced the latter with varying degrees of certainty and by no means anticipate that all of them will be adopted forthwith – in some cases, our purpose is as much to inspire fresh debate about ideas that have petrified in the last century of scholarship, as to suggest that we have arrived at a definitive solution. The *KG* has long been due for a post-Burgess rethink; Marius Maximus has sat untroubled by anyone except Paschoud for far too long; the stylistic and lexical resonances between Victor and Ammianus would deserve close attention, even if the *HAb* were the sum total of Victor's work; the obvious post-classical features of the *OCI* have been studiously avoided. At the same time, we might reasonably draw a distinction between some new *facts* that we have presented – facts that have been glossed over or misunderstood in scholarship – and some of the *hypotheses* we have suggested. It would be too simple to say that this is merely the difference between the first and second halves of this book, but there is an element of that in the distinction. These new facts include:

1. The manuscripts of both texts attributed to Victor present them as condensed works, epitomes of his books of Roman history. Commentators have provided independent and *ad hoc* dismissals of the manuscript titles, but they require a systematic explanation, one that takes seriously the

fact that the only two works transmitted under the name of Victor are called 'abbreviated' in the title.

2. There is a fundamental incompatibility between the ambitious style and register of the *Historiae abbreviatae* and its scope and contents. If the *HAb* is the totality of Victor's work, why did he fail so miserably in his endeavour to write history? One can obviously treat Victor as just an isolated deviant (and many have), but that still begs the question of why so much and such very sophisticated reading – Sallust, Tacitus, Suetonius, Velleius, Livy, Cicero, Cassius Dio, Josephus, Herodotus – was employed to so little effect. In no other ancient Latin work has such writerly craftsmanship wrought so shoddy a product. At the same time, no one has unblinkingly confronted how often the *HAb* actually fails to make sense, whether through intrusive particles, bizarre collocations, or inexplicable omissions.

3. Victor was the most highly regarded secular Latin historian of the second half of the fourth century. *Ad hoc* explanations have been provided for why the emperor Julian honoured Victor with a statue, why Jerome sought out his *Historia*, why Theodosius made him urban prefect, and why Ammianus praised him and his historical work. None of these carries conviction on its own, and no one has attempted to explain the pattern.

4. The *Libellus breviatus* is not itself an ancient text. Despite its terminal date of 395, its relationship to Jordanes and Isidore guarantees that it was written no earlier than the seventh century. That makes urgent the question of how such a late text knows so much about Roman history. Moreover, the *LB* has a textual relationship to the work of Paul the Deacon, who was the first person to use it and who says that he had consulted the *Historia* of Victor. That textual relationship means that Paul either compiled the *LB* or that it was produced so close to him as to yield effectively the same conclusion.

5. One of the *Scholia Vallicelliana*, evidence for the reading of Paul the Deacon, ascribes material to Victor found in neither the *HAb* nor the *LB*, but written in a style very close to that of the former, while including a line found in the latter. These *Scholia* have been in print for more than a century, and yet no one has explained where this material could have come from, why it has Victor's name attached to it, and how Victorine material not from the *HAb* could have been available in early-medieval Italy.

6. One of the few indubitable textual anachronisms of the *Historia Augusta* is the use of Victor, whose account of Septimius Severus was plagiarised *in extenso* and verbatim. Given Victor's fame, this cannot be dismissed as mere accident or oversight. Any attempt to explain the bizarre task that the *scriptor* of the *HA* set himself must explain this flagrant anachronism.

Every existing theory of Victor and of the Roman historiography of late antiquity fails to account for these facts and should be considered untenable, absent radical modification. Our explanation of them is economical, even simple: both the *HAb* and the *LB* are just what they purport to be, abbreviations of Victor's historical work. *Pluralitas non est ponenda sine necessitate*, as they say. Any rival account must face them squarely.

The shape and structure of Victor's *History*

'Only when demolition is complete can reconstruction commence', as Tim Barnes put it at the opening of his fittingly pugnacious study of Tertullian, published in 1971.[2] Much of this book has been concerned with the *pars destruens*, for there is much that needs to be reconsidered. The work of reconstruction – the *pars construens* – will be broader and longer. It might begin with a little thought about the definite formal characteristics of Victor's *Historia*, in the first instance in the version that appeared in AD 360. What we say here is in part speculative – an attempt to think through the problems, rather than necessarily solve them. Still, it helps to illuminate the work and some of the key questions about it.

First, length. On the slight evidence of epitomised works whose originals survive, we might guess that Victor's history was roughly 120,000 words long, ten times longer than the *HAb* or the *LB*. It could have been shorter: 80,000 words (the length of Valerius Maximus), perhaps even 70,000 words (Suetonius). It could equally have been longer, although it is unlikely that it exceeded 150,000 words. In assessing the question of length, two factors might nudge us towards the upper end of the range. First, the *Scholia Vallicelliana* include an extensive moralising reflection on Domitian and archery, which is not found in the *HAb*. Despite the intense interest that text's compiler took in digressions, he evidently did not include all of them. Second, if the *OCI* does indeed reflect Victor's narrative of the civil wars between Constantine and Licinius, there may have been a good deal more 'kings and battles' than survives in either the *HAb* or the *LB* (neither of which betrays much interest in the subject). Caution is sensible, but it would be wrong to minimise either the scale or the scope of Victor's *Historia*, given the bewildering variety of its progeny.

Second, structure. We know from the title of the *LB* that Victor's history consisted of multiple books (*ex libris*). Can we discern the lineaments of these books in our surviving epitomes? Victor was given to pausing for historical reflections, exploring the deeper meaning of the events and figures he had been discussing. He also had definite views about the key moments of transformation in Roman history. The coincidence of these reflective digressions with important transitions allows us to get some sense of the way that Victor understood the structure of imperial history. One model might result in five distinct movements:

I. From Augustus to Domitian (*HAb* 1.1–11.11, *LB* 1.1–11.15)
II. From Nerva to Alexander Severus (*HAb* 11.12–24.6, *LB* 12.1–24.5)
III. From Maximinus to Probus (*HAb* 24.7–37.4, *LB* 25.1–37.1)
IV. Carus and the rise of the Tetrarchy (*HAb* 37.5–39.48, *LB* 38.1–39.7)
V. The house of Constantius I and Constantine (*HAb* 40.1–42.25, *LB* 40.1–42.12)

For Victor, these periods were marked by moments of historical and constitutional transformation: regardless of whether these were the formal divisions of his work, they correspond to real phenomena in his thought. Imperial history began half a millennium after the expulsion of the kings with a return to the rule of one man, Augustus, and the succeeding dynasties of two *gentes*, the Caesars and the Flavians.

---

2 Barnes 1971: 2.

With Nerva and his adoption of Trajan came an opening-up of the imperial office, the first emperors from outside Italy and an era of constitutional experimentation. In this period, the Empire continued its expansion, particularly under Trajan and Septimius Severus. Its growth faltered thereafter, but it continued to be held together (however shakily) until Alexander Severus was cut down at Bretzenheim. Maximinus, his successor, was in Victor's view a barbarian, perhaps by his origin but certainly in his lack of literary culture. Literary culture was the one thing that had kept the Empire going under the Caesars when virtue failed. The opening up of imperial office after Nerva might easily have been presented as a process of degeneration. To Victor, however, it was one of rejuvenation, at least in part because the emperors who succeeded Nerva were imbued with a liberal education. This is what distinguished the third from the second centuries. Maximinus was the first true outsider, the first emperor to lack the training in letters that might make even barbarians Roman. The result was that the great mass of soldiers – from whose ranks Maximinus was the first emperor – became the dominant force in the Empire, a change hastened by Gallienus' policy of banning senators from military offices. After Aurelian – with the (purported) interregnum, the Senate's appointment of Tacitus, and Probus' dream of a world without soldiers – the Senate and civil institutions of the Roman Empire seemed to have a real chance of obtaining primacy once more. These hopes were, however, dashed by the murder of Probus, and the soldiers achieved an unfettered power of making emperors. What followed was a period of civil war and further constitutional experimentation, with the pseudo-college of Carus and his two sons, the rise of Diocletian, and the establishment of the Tetrarchy, which for Victor once again brought outsiders into the heart of the Roman state. With Constantius I and Constantine, there was at last a return to the rule of one family, as history turned back in its cycles (something in which Victor believed almost literally). These movements correspond to sources that we know Victor had read. From Augustus to Domitian, Suetonius' and Tacitus' works were at hand. Up to Alexander Severus, the massive history of Cassius Dio was available, with Herodian covering events to Gordian III. For much of the rest of the third century, there were the works of Dexippus. For the era of the Tetrarchy, it seems that there was no single history available, but we have seen that Victor went to considerable lengths to unearth what had happened, reading Nemesianus and Lactantius. With Constantine at last, Victor entered the period of his own *memoria*.

Given this striking conjunction, we might wonder whether Victor's five phases of imperial history were the structural units of his *Historia*. There are hints of this in both Victor's debtors and his sources. Eutropius was the first and perhaps most important of Victor's successors. Three of Victor's phases correspond with individual books of Eutropius' *Historia Romana*: the first with Book VII, the second with Book VIII, and the fifth with Book X (the third and fourth correspond to Book IX). As we have pointed out, the accession of Nerva in particular has no special significance to Eutropius, which makes his decision to open a book with it look a little like a calque.[3] Sallust was the single most important influence on Victor's style, ideas, and project. Sallust had written *Histories* in five books. We have demonstrated elsewhere that these books were very long indeed (like the single-book *Jugurtha* that preceded them) – 20,000 words or more.[4] The Sallustian practice of mammoth books in historical works found later imitators in Velleius (also an important influence on Victor), and in the historian known as Hegesippus, who adapted Josephus' seven-book *Jewish War* into a five-book Latin history at some stage in the fourth century.

3 Chapter VI.   4 Stover and Woudhuysen 2022b.

TABLE C.1 – THE OPENING OF VICTOR'S *HISTORIA* AND CHAPTER 43 OF THE *LB*

Victor's *Historia*	*LB* 43.1
HAb 1.1: Anno urbis septingentesimo fere vicesimoque, duobus etiam, mos Romae incessit **uni** prorsus parendi.	Igitur Iulianus, redacta ad **unum** se orbis Romani curatione, gloriae nimis cupidus in Persas proficiscitur.
LB 1.1: Anno urbis conditae septingentesimo vicesimo secundo, ab exactis vero regibus quadringentesimo octogesimoque, mos Romae repetitus **uni** prorsus parendi.	
In almost the seven hundredth and twenty-second year of the city, the custom arose at Rome of obeying one man absolutely.	Julian therefore, since charge of the Roman world had been returned to him alone; excessively greedy for glory, he set off on campaign against the Persians.
In the seven hundredth and twenty-second year from the founding of the city, the four hundredth and eightieth after the expulsion of the kings, the custom was revived at Rome of obeying one man absolutely.	

One attractive thing about this theory is how neatly it lines up with what we have deduced independently about Victor's original and know of Latin epitomes more generally in late antiquity. We have shown that the period for which the *HAb* and *LB* have consistent verbal overlaps – what we now identify as the first book of Victor's work – was covered in around 20,000 words. On the basis of a comparison of the *HAb* and Eutropius, we can conclude that the second book – from Nerva to Alexander Severus – was roughly the same length.[5] If Victor's *History* was originally a five-book collection in the Sallustian mode, with a total length of somewhere in the range of 100,000 to 125,000 words, then the *HAb*, with its 11,000 words, would be an epitome of nine to eleven per cent coverage: very much within the usual range for the genre. The *LB* with its 8,000 words for chapters 1–42 would be somewhat less extended and the same would be true of the four corresponding books of Eutropius (which come to about the same total), but neither would be unusual. These five books would also have the consequence of slicing the *HAb* up to into relatively even-sized chunks, with Book I taking up *ca.* 2,700 words, II 2,500, III 2,400, IV 1,300, and V 1,700. This would be consistent, we might note, with the pattern of the epitomator's initial enthusiasm for their project diminishing in the middle before reviving at the end. All this suggests that the five periods of imperial history might represent individual books: that what Victor published in 360 was a work entitled *Historia* in five very long *libri* of approximately 20,000 words each.

Of course, as we have demonstrated, Victor's work appeared in more than one edition. Can we deduce anything about the structure and scope of the later version(s) from which the *LB* was derived? Given that the first edition of Victor's *Historia* concluded in 360, we can be fairly certain that the material that follows in the *LB* (*i.e.* from chapter 43 onwards) represents the beginning of a new book, a normal pattern in the serial publication of historical works. That might be confirmed by the way that the first line of *LB* 43 recalls the beginning of the *Historia* (**TABLE C.1**). When did this later version finish? We

---

5 For these calculations, which both independently gave a minimum of 11,260 words (suggesting a total of 20,000 each), see Chapters III (p. 69) and VI (pp. 209–210).

TABLE C.2 – CONSTANTIUS AND GRATIAN COMPARED

HAb 42.23–25	LB 47.4–5
Mild and merciful in his affairs, well educated in rhetoric (*litterarum ad elegantiam prudens*) and with a smooth and charming style of oratory, enduring of hardship and marvellously skilled at directing (*destinandi*) arrows, a victor over food, sleep, lust, and all the passions (*cibi somni libidinis atque omnium cupidinum victor*), dutiful enough in his reverence for his father, but too much the warden of his own veneration. These qualities, so great and so illustrious, have been sullied by his feeble effort in selecting the rulers of provinces and military commanders, the uncouth customs of the majority of his servants, and his neglect hitherto of every good man. And to sum up the truth briefly: just as nothing is more outstanding than the emperor himself, so there is nothing more savage than most of his civil servants.	Gratian was moreover not a little educated in letters (*litteris haud mediocriter institutus*), in writing poetry, speaking elegantly (*ornate*), and solving *controversiae* as rhetors do. By day and night he did nothing beyond thinking about archery and believed that hitting the target (*destinata*) was the greatest pleasure and a skill divine. He was sparing of food and sleep and a victor over wine and lust (*parcus cibi somnique et vini ac libidinis victor*); he would have been endowed with every good quality, if he had exerted his mind to grasping the science of ruling the commonwealth, to which he was almost a stranger, not merely in his desires but also in practice.

know of course that it went up to the civil war between Magnus Maximus and Theodosius, since that was the point at which the Paul the Deacon found it necessary to add material from Jordanes to bring the narrative down to 395. So, it seems likely that this later version terminated in *ca.* 388. That was not a logical point at which to pause, unless one happened to be writing very soon afterwards – such is what we might imagine happened with this extended version of Victor's work. That Victor's urban prefecture fell in 389 also seems significant.[6] A second edition with an additional book covering the period from 361 to 388 seems to lie behind the *Libellus breviatus*.

Things may, however, have been a little more complex than this. There is evidence in Jerome's *Chronicon*, written before 388, that there was already a Victorine account of events after 360 in circulation somewhat earlier.[7] Ammianus also seems to have made much heavier use of Victor for events from 360 to 380 than seems reasonable if the later edition appeared only just before his own work was completed. Furthermore, if we look closely at the text of the *LB*, we find very little evidence for any historical information that postdates 379, save the usurpation of Maximus. There is moreover a close correspondence between the description of Gratian's character in the *LB* and that of Constantius, with which the first edition of the *Historia* had concluded (**TABLE C.2**). Not only are the two *ethopoeiae* shown in Table C.2 parallel in content and arrangement with close verbal resonances – covering, in order, education, literary production, archery, moderation in food, sleep, and sex – they also each conclude with a fatal flaw. As Constantius would have been an excellent, even outstanding, emperor were it not for his ministers, so Gratian would have been an ideal ruler if he had actually attempted to learn how to rule and put that

---

6 See the Conclusion to Part 1, *cf.* Stover and Woudhuysen 2021: 173–174.

7 If Eunapius' history predated 390 (a controversial question – see Chapter X), it too would be relevant here.

learning into practice. They also come at structurally similar points in their respective narratives: in each case, the emperor had relatively recently assumed a colleague – Constantius the Caesar Julian, Gratian the Augustus Theodosius.

We have seen how the additional material in the later edition of Victor's *Historia* began with a reference to the opening of the earlier version. What we have here looks like a clear echo of its ending, which may well suggest the termination of a book. On this hypothesis, the sixth book of Victor's history originally concluded with the description of Gratian's character after the accession of Theodosius as co-Augustus. For Victor, this would have been a momentous event – a new chapter in the ongoing history of how the Roman Empire grew in power 'through the virtue of outsiders and engrafted talents' in the person of a very descendant of Trajan himself. What then of the remaining material in the *LB* – the usurpation of Magnus Maximus, the death of Gratian, and the character of Theodosius? We do not need to assume that there was yet another book, and, indeed, the historical coverage of the 380s in the *LB* is rather sketchy. Instead, it seems more likely that Victor appended to his book a *coda* on Theodosius, which drew together some of his previous themes and made a specific comparison to Augustus (*LB* 48.14–15). Whether his designation as urban prefect was a goad or a reward is not clear. It was this version of Victor's *Historia* – six books, from Augustus to Gratian, with an elegant supplement on Theodosius – that survived in southern Italy until the eighth century, where it was found by Paul the Deacon, who put it once again at the centre of Roman imperial history.

From historiography to history

'A book must be its own justification and must stand or fall on its own merits', was Fergus Millar's judicious introduction to his study of Cassius Dio.[8] This book is a treatment of Victor's work and its influence – those are the topics that it has set out to examine, that are its justification. What actually happened in the Roman world from Augustus to Theodosius has generally been a secondary concern, but a proper understanding of Victor will have a profound effect on that subject. We cannot possibly outline its consequences in any detail, but we can point to some of the avenues down which future research might profitably proceed.

Victor has usually been treated as an idiosyncratic, late, and derivative historian. He has heretofore dwelt generally in the footnotes, and often only in lists of *fontes* for various historical events. Taking him seriously means moving him from the footnotes to the text, giving much more careful consideration to his narrative of events, particularly for facts and anecdotes for which he is the sole surviving source. These are found everywhere – even in the coverage of the twelve Caesars, where we are fortunate enough to have (for various portions) Suetonius, Tacitus, Dio, Velleius, and Josephus, there is a considerable residue of material only in Victor. In the life of Nero, for example, the much-discussed *Quinquennium Neronis*, which in Trajan's estimation outstripped the reigns of other princes, is found only in Victor – it deserves new attention. If Victor can contribute to our understanding of the Julio-Claudians, how much more important might he be to the history of his own day? In our narrative of the age of Constantius II, the

8 Millar 1964: vii.

HAb has generally played only a bit part. Any future account will have to take it seriously as *the* contemporary account, the work that set the tone for later sources. In cases like these Victor is likely to nuance and complexify our understanding of events, but in other areas he may simplify things. The history of the Gallic Empire, for example, is written from snippets in Greek (Zosimus and Zonaras) and Latin (the *HAb*, the *LB*, the *HA*, and Eutropius), supplemented by the evidence of the coinage and a few inscriptions. The subject is famously problematic and fraught with controversy, with even basic details of chronology much disputed. The realisation that all extant accounts are in the shadow of, if not directly indebted to, Victor might bring considerable clarity. The *HAb* shows that Victor dealt with the Gallic Empire in a monographic digression in the midst of his treatment of Gallienus. That both explains the chronological confusions that bedevil the sources and also suggests that they might be resolved by closer attention to what precisely Victor claimed. As for the fact that Victor's arrangement turned a run-of-the-mill sequence of usurpers into something like a coherent political phenomenon – that remains to be considered.

More broadly, identifying a basically reliable – albeit difficult and sometimes tendentious – history at the core of the whole *HA* has obvious and urgent ramifications. Although the author of the *HA* continually twists and misconstrues that source, no bit of historical information from the text can be blithely discarded, even from the later lives. Anything in them *could* be fantasy and pure invention, but they could also be distorted reflections of a reliable historical narrative. This does not make the *HA* problem any easier. Indeed, in some ways, it makes it even more difficult. At the very least, however, it opens up the possibility of mounting a coherent defence of the historicity of *some* of the material in the later lives, albeit one fenced round by caution. The earlier assumption that there simply was no extended Latin narrative covering the third century from before the *HA* – that is to say, the *KG* hypothesis – has been shown to be not quite true. Working out the ramifications of that conclusion for understanding the history of the period is a task yet to be begun.

A withering critic might suggest that all we have done is rearrange the furniture in the drawing room of later-Roman history-writing. That there is a lost history behind Eutropius, the *HA*, the *HAb*, the *LB*, and Jerome is not actually controversial. Our innovation lies in showing that the name of Victor should be associated with that source, and not merely with the *HAb*. Yet that one small revision makes all the difference. It means we know something about the scope, style, and historiographic method of the text, that we have a generous, if occasionally incoherent, selection of its *ipsissima verba*. It allows us to see that the commonalities between the historians of the later Roman Empire betray an idiosyncratic approach to the shape and development of Rome's history. Above all, it suggests the lineaments of a new history of Roman attempts at writing history in Latin. There was a long abeyance (of two centuries) after the age of Hadrian, in which the writing of history in the grand style was exclusively the province of the Greek language. This was shattered by the appearance of Victor's *Historia* in 361, a long and literarily ambitious history from Augustus to Constantius and Julian, in constant engagement and dialogue with Sallust and Tacitus, offering not only facts but also theories and arguments about the deeper meaning and patterns of the historical events. This book inspired a movement, with the appearance of the imperially sponsored histories of Eutropius and Festus within a decade, the equally ambitious and complex history of Ammianus within three, as well as the virtual parody of the *Historia Augusta*. Even more broadly, we start finding history everywhere in Latin, from Jerome's *Chronicle*, Rufinus' translation of Euserbius, Hegesippus' Sallustian reworking of Josephus, Augustine's polemical historiography, Sulpicius Severus, Orosius' universal history, and the lost works of Nicomachus Flavianus, Sulpicius Alexander, and Renatus Profuturus Frigeridus. As a matter of chronology, this movement began with Victor – as a matter of intellectual history, he provided the impetus for this renaissance of historical writing in Latin.

Ammianus may have had scant regard for the history being written in his own day – but he was living at a time when more history was being written in Latin than at any point in the previous quarter millennium. Given that, it is no wonder that the one contemporary historian he saw fit to acknowledge is the one who started it all, the farm boy from North Africa, the *scriptor historicus* Sextus Aurelius Victor.

THE TEXT OF VICTOR

One factor that has in particular hampered appreciation of Victor and his work is the state of the text of the *Historiae abbreviatae*. Relying as it does on the very exiguous thread represented by **o** and **p**, the text is transmitted in a very corrupt condition. This situation is hardly unique to Victor: other related historical texts, for example the *Historia Augusta* and Ammianus Marcellinus' *Res gestae*, are transmitted in a similarly appalling state. Those two works have, however, the advantage of centuries of conscientious editorial activity, which has transformed the corrupt manuscript text into mostly readable prose, free from obvious errors. For whatever reason, Victor has not been the beneficiary of similar treatment: editors have been content to leave trivial scribal slips in the text, often attributing them to Victor's supposed incompetence as a historian. Before considering individual passages that we have quoted in the course of this study, let us look at two egregious examples of editorial neglect and malfeasance.[1]

The transmitted text of the *HAb* (17.10) calls Commodus' successor Aulus Helvius Pertinax. This has been diagnosed as an error, 'a mistake not shared with any other writer'.[2] That the *praenomen* of the emperor Pertinax was actually Publius is amply demonstrated by inscriptions, coins, and papyri.[3] The name is not, however, well attested in Latin texts: only the *HA Pert.* 1.1 records it, where the principal manuscript gives the nonsense *Publicus*. Editors rightly delete the intrusive *c* in the *HA*. Why do they not adopt the same approach for Victor? *Aulus* is a standard Latin *praenomen*, abbreviated *A*, as is *Publius*, abbreviated *P*. The archetype, or pre-archetype, of our two Victor manuscripts probably read *A. Helvio Pertinaci*, which, one will note, is just one letter, and even (in some scripts) just one stroke, removed from the correct reading, *P. Helvio Pertinaci*. There is absolutely no reason to think this anything other than a quotidian scribal slip. Or take the name of a usurper under Gallienus: Ingenuus. At *HAb* 33.2, the manuscripts read *Ingebum*, which is what Pichlmayr chose to print.[4] This does not mean that Victor thought his name was 'Ingebus'. In many periods of Latin from late antiquity onwards, there was rampant confusion between b and v – indeed we have a fifth- or sixth-century grammatical treatise by one Martyrius dedicated to just this problem.[5] This means that *Ingebum* and *Ingeuum* are nothing more than trivial orthographic variants – the archetype merely missed a stroke over the *e* to spell *Ingenuum*. A sensible

---

1 Discussions of individual textual points are cited when relevant, but some of the principal studies on Victor's text include Maehly 1855, D'Elia 1968, Shackleton Bailey 1981, Soverini 1984–1985, Bird 1985, and Rudoni 2010.
2 Bird 1984: 18.
3 *PIR*[2] H.73.
4 Pichlmayr 1970: 109.

5 The *De b muta et v vocali* (*GLK* 7.165–199), written before the middle of s. VI, for Cassiodorus uses it extensively in the *De Orthographia*. *pace* Zetzel 2018: 304 and Kaster 1988: 310, it is easy to imagine that he was both the son of Adamantius and that his name was Adamantius Martyrius. Rather than assuming that Cassiodorus has confusedly mixed the names of father and son, this is precisely what his usage suggests (*GLK* 7.147: calling him once Adamantius Martyrius and once Martyrius).

editor would print *Ingenuum*, as Dufraigne and Nickbahkt and Scardino have indeed done.[6] Every derisive '*sic!*' (*vel sim.*) appended to this line of Victor ought more justly to be targeted at Pichlmayr and his predecessors. Even marquee examples of Victorine error are almost certainly textual. This is the case with *Nerva Cretensi* at *HAb* 12.1, which should obviously read *Nerva Cocceio*, with a Tacitean reversal of the names, also attested at Dio 68.1.1.[7] D'Elia and others have defended the manuscript reading on the basis of the preceding line, *HAb* 11.12: *Hactenus Romae seu per Italiam orti imperium rexere, hinc advenae quoque.*[8] This ignores the fact that nothing makes sense about the treatment of Nerva in the *HAb*, an obvious sign of abbreviation. Only an understanding of Victor that makes him essentially incompetent would assume that he made such a gross error about an emperor whose origins were well documented. At any rate, we know he did not say Nerva was from Crete (*cf. LB* 12.1). The point of the previous line is not that Nerva himself was from outside of Italy, but that he chose a non-Italian – Trajan – as his successor.

These are just a few examples where corrupt text has been confidently pointed to as evidence of Victor's incompetence. They are easy pickings, but they show just how poorly Victor has been edited. Ammianus offers a thought-provoking comparand: his work too is transmitted independently in just two manuscripts, one of them in mere fragments, both of them fairly corrupt.[9] What would we think of his work if editors had treated his text as conservatively as they have treated Victor's?

Much more of this sort could be offered and, indeed, in many such cases, the responsible remedy is the dagger. In his review of Dufraigne's text, Tarrant quoted Housman's injunction (as regards the *Appendix Vergiliana*) on how the sensible editor 'will be slow to emend the text and slow to defend it, and his page will bristle with the obelus'.[10] This may well take things a bit too far, especially considering how much our knowledge of fourth-century Latinity has improved: scholarly opinion, for example, is starting to recognise that the text of Ammianus requires a much more activist approach than that in favour early in the twentieth century.[11] Even so, it remains remarkable that editors have wielded the dagger so sparingly: Pichlmayr obelises only *nequaquam* at 5.10, *Sardonius* and *satisque* at 13.3, *perduci* at 33.31, and *simulata* at 35.12; Nickbahkt and Scardino *externis societati humanius* at 5.10, *Sardonius* and *satisque* at 13.3, and *celebrio* at 24.5; while Dufraigne does not dagger a single passage.

For these (and other) reasons, what Tarrant wrote in 1978 remains as true today as it was then: 'a new edition of Aurelius Victor is much needed'.[12] What we offer here is just the first tentative step towards that goal, with discussion of the passages particularly relevant to this book. In each passage, our emendations are marked with italics.

---

6 Dufraigne 1975: 39, although he goes too far in not even providing an apparatus entry to point out the trivial mistake in the manuscripts; Nickbahkt and Scardino 2021: 102 record this correctly.

7 Schott proposed *Narniensi*, on the basis of *LB* 12.1. This has its attractions, but judging by the *HAb* Victor did not usually introduce someone with a bare geographic epithet (*cf.* 28.1: *Marcus Iulius Philippus Arabs Thraconites*).

8 D'Elia 1968: 142–143. Dufraigne 1975: 99 also defends it.

9 See Kelly and Stover 2016.

10 Tarrant 1978: 360, quoting Housman 1902: 339.

11 As argued by Kelly 2022. The Dutch commentators on Ammianus propose dozens of departures from Seyfarth's very conservative text in each book of the *Res gestae*. See also Colombo 2017.

12 Tarrant 1978: 355. On Nickbahkt and Scardino's recent edition, see Stover 2021b.

I

HAb 5.1: Eo modo L. Domitius (nam id *certe nomen* Neroni, patre Domitio, erat) imperator factus est.

op read *certi lucius domicius nero nomen*. Schott was right to delete *lucius domicius nero* and Pichlmayr and Nickbakht and Scardino were equally right to follow him. This is almost certainly an incorporated gloss – there is another in **p** just a few lines later, where *narrantur scelera neronis* intrudes between 5.6 *eo levius*. This solution might help explain the error *certi*: the gloss might have read *i.* [*sc. id est*] *lucius domitius nero*, which then displaced the original terminal vowel of *certe*.

II

HAb 13.5: Simul noscendis ocius, quae ubique e re publica gerebantur, admota *remedia* publici cursus

op transmit *media*, which is perhaps just able to be construed as 'means', but it is an odd usage, included by the *TLL* amid a grab-bag of not-quite-parallel passages, all of which are in the singular and none of which have a verb like *admovere*.[13] Read instead *remedia*, on the basis of the broader medical metaphor Victor uses in the passage (*cf.* 13.6 *pestem, Anatolio medente*), which is appropriate with the given verb, in the sense of to apply a remedy; *cf.* Seneca, *De ben.* 6.16.4: *remedia . . . admovit*, *De ira* 3.39.4: *remedio palam admoto*, and *Ep.* 64.8: *remedia . . . admoveantur*.

III

HAb 14.13–15.1: At patres ne principis oratu quidem ad Divi honorem eidem deferendum flectebantur; tantum amissos sui ordinis tot viros maerebant. Sed postquam subito prodiere quorum exitium dolori erat, quique suos complexi censent quod abnuerant [15.1] *ac T. Aelio* Antonino cognomentum Pii.

This is essentially what **op** read, with a minor corruption of *at helio* (**o**) or *atthelio* (**p**), and it also makes good sense: 'but after the ones whose demise was the source of their sorrow were suddenly brought forth, each one embraced his own, and they granted what they had refused and bestowed the cognomen *Pius* on T. Aelius Antoninus'. The problem is that Schott tried to make the text of the *HAb* align in its chapter divisions with the already printed text of the *LB*, and so inserted a chapter break *into the middle of a sentence*. Shockingly, every editor since has followed suit without so much as a thought. Further, with Victor's careful sensitivity to nomenclature it is very clear that the manuscript reading *T. <A>elio* is correct: after adoption, Antoninus would have borne Hadrian's name in addition to his own, and the correction to Aurelius is both unnecessary and wrong.[14]

---

13 *TLL* 8.591.41–47 (Bulhart).

14 As in Pichlmayr 1970: 94. Dufraigne 1975: 110 is more sensible, as are Nickbahkt and Scardino 2021: 74, although both omit the *praenomen*.

IV

HAb 16.7: Namque lita veneno cultri parte vulvae frustum, quod de industria *solverat*, eo praecidit consumptoque uno, uti mos est inter familiares, alterum, qua virus contigerat, germano porrexit.

op read *solum erat*. This is impossible. Not only is the sense itself dubious, the idiom *de industria*, 'deliberately' or 'carefully', requires the subject to be Marcus, and the tense of *praecidit* suggests we should have a pluperfect in the relative clause. Ultimately the manuscripts present what is simply a minute scribal error: a stray suspension mark above the *u* of *soluerat*, turning it into *solu[m] erat*.

V

HAb 20.6: Quod equidem gentis nostrae reor, quae fato quodam bonorum *parce* fecunda, quos eduxerit tamen *usque ad summa celsos* habet velut Severum ipsum . . .

For *parce*, **op** read *parte*; Schott conjectured *partu*, which is clever but banalising. Wölfflin's *parce* is probably the best solution yet offered (though Dacier's *parum* deserves consideration), and has been printed by Pichlmayr, Dufraigne, and Nickbahkt and Scardino. The second phrase, transmitted as *quemque ad celsa suos* in **p** and *quemque ad sua celsos* in **o**, has defied understanding. Dufraigne's translation (which follows **o**, with Pichlmayr) does not really mean anything (1975: 26): 'Et c'est assurément à mon avis le propre de notre nation, qui, par une sorte de destin, est peu féconde en hommes de mérite, d'élever pourtant tous ceux qu'elle a fait naître, chacun à la place qui lui est propre'. Bird presents what is as much a paraphrase of Dufraigne's French as a translation of Victor's Latin: 'This, in my opinion, is really characteristic of our race which, by some quirk of fate, is sparingly productive of good men, yet those whom it has raised it extols, each according to his own merits'.[15] The same might be said of Nickbahkt and Scardino: 'Folgendes erachte ich nämlich als ein Charakteristikum unseres Volkes, welches durch eine Schicksalsfügung wenig ertragreich an Rechtschaffenen ist: Diejenigen, die es dennoch hervorgebracht hat, sind, jeder auf seinem Gebiet, überragend'.[16] The failure of these translations indicates that the underlying textual problems cannot be simply papered over. The passage seemingly imitates Tacitus, *Ann.* 6.27.4: *quippe Aemilium **genus fecundum bonorum** civium, et **qui** eadem familia corruptis moribus, inlustri **tamen** fortuna egere*. Hence, the sense ought to be that even though Victor's *gens* does not produce many great talents, it does produce some particularly outstanding individuals. Casaubon, working before **o** was discovered, attempted to fix *quemque* to *cumque*, understanding *quoscumque eduxerit tamen* with the first element in tmesis. But **o** points the way forward: the fact that it has the difference of word order from **p** could suggest something in the archetype was misconstrued by the scribe of **p** as a transposition mark, and indeed one mark is all we need to turn the problematic *ad sua* to the sensible *ad summa*; *cf. e.g.* Seneca, *Ep.* 95.37: *educit ad summa*. That in turn suggests the real problem with *quemque*, since one word that would naturally be expected before

---

15 Bird 1994: 22. Compare the pre-Dufraigne translation of Nixon 1971: 72, which is equally wrong, but in different ways: 'This I believe is characteristic of our race, which by a certain quirk of fate is ungenerous in its

production of good men. Those whom it has produced, however, it keeps as its own, each of them, after they have attained eminence'.

16 Nickbahkt and Scardino 2021: 83.

ad summa is *usque*; *cf.* Lactantius, *DI* 7.1.1: *usque ad summa perduximus*; Marius Victorinus, *Comm. Gal.* 2: *usque ad summa surgentibus*; Augustine, *Contra Faustum* 21.13: *ab imis usque ad summa*; and especially *HA Tyr.* 22.1: *usque ad summa rei p. pericula . . . usque ad summum rei p. periculum*.

Finally, in a case of inexplicable textual conservatism, editors up to Nickbakht and Scardino have printed a full stop before *velut* (it goes back at least as far as Arntzen's 1733 Amsterdam edition, on the basis of a note by Dacier; Schott had used a colon). This banished, we at last arrive at a text capable of easy understanding and in productive dialogue with the subversive comment by Tacitus: 'This I consider characteristic of our race, that even though it is not particularly fecund of good men, nonetheless it does have some lofty individuals whom it has brought all the way to the pinnacle, such as Severus himself . . .'.[17]

VI

> *HAb* 20.33: Quippe quem ferunt illo temporis <*momento*> Bassiani scrinia monitumque, uti mos est, *destinandam orationem* quam celerrime componeret . . .

The first problem is **op**'s *illo temporis*. It is easy enough to construe and understand – which is probably why it is printed in every modern edition of the text, but nonetheless quite impossible as a Latin phrase without a referent for *illo*; *cf. e.g.* Tacitus, *Hist.* 4.82.2: *illo temporis momento*; Suetonius, *Aug.* 78.1: *in illo temporis spatio*; and Augustine, *De bapt.* 1.12.19: *in illo temporis puncto*. The early editors, from Schott onwards, understood this and silently corrected it to the colourless *illo tempore*, which is paralleled by *HAb* 28.3: *ferunt illo tempore*. Better, however, to follow Tacitus as a guide: Victor is speaking of a specific point in time – *i.e.* the murder of Geta – so *momento* should be supplied after *temporis*.

The more serious problem occurs later in the same line. **op** transmit *destinando Romam*, which is obviously impossible. Most attention has focused on *destinando*: in his notes to the *editio princeps*, Schott says that some people have proposed *destinanda* as if it were a substantive object of *componeret*. This conjecture has found general favour, even though a substantive use of *destinandum* is unparalleled. Modern editors have been untroubled by *Romam*, even though the murder of Geta certainly took place when he and his brother were both already in Rome. Why would Papinian have been ordered to send something *to Rome*? The only discussion of this point we are aware of is by Casaubon, who valiantly argued that Victor must be relying on a tradition that placed the murder of Geta immediately after Severus' death, while the brothers were still in Britain. Such ingenuity does not convince: Victor himself is explicit that both Caracalla and Geta returned to Rome with their father's body (*HAb* 20.30: *funus, quod liberi Geta Bassianusque Romam detulerant*).

Instead, the way forward was marked out by Schott, who proposed emending to *dictando orationem* guided by the parallel account in the *HA Carac.* 8.6: *dictare . . . orationem*. *Orationem* for *Romam* is

---

17 Incidentally, this passage might shed light on a curious error in Eutropius (8.18.1) concerning Severus: *Solus omni memoria et ante et postea ex Africa imperator fuit.* This is patently false: the emperor who came to power just six years after Severus' death, Opellius Macrinus, was from Caesarea in Mauretania. Inattentive reading, however, of Victor's nuanced claim in this passage could well have given the impression that Severus was the only African emperor.

exceptionally clever, given the that the former was often abbreviated $\overline{orom}$ in minuscule, but a form of *destinare* surely ought to stand, given that it is one of Victor's favourite words (seven other instances in the *HAb*). There is a simple explanation for how this might have happened which explains the termination of the gerund as well. If the archetype, or a manuscript at a pre-archetypal stage, had omitted the termination of *destinandam* and supplied it interlinearly, it may have appeared as follows:

> am
> destinand$\overline{orom}$

Written like this, these two words were almost destined to be read *destinando romam*.

VII

> *HAb* 27.1: Iisdemque per Africam diebus milites Gordianum, Gordiani <. . .> filium, qui forte con-
> tubernio patris *Praetextati – is* <. . .> ac deinceps praefectus praetorio – intererat, Augustum creavere.

We have discussed this passage elsewhere.[18] Suffice it here to say that where every editor has printed *praetextatus*, **op** actually read *praetextatiis*, which suggests a deeper corruption in the whole passage.

VIII

> *HAb* 29.4: Decii barbaros trans Danubium persectantes *Abruti* fraude cecidere.

op read *bruti* (Dufraigne erroneously credits them with the reading *a bruti*). This might be acceptable in terms of Latinity, 'by the trickery of Brutus', but it is not acceptable historically, since there is no known Brutus to whom we might attribute the *fraus*.[19] Gruter instead saw that this was a very simple error: the place where Decius died was called Abritus, spelled variously (Ἄβρυτος in Dexippus, *BNJ* 100 fr. 22 (McInerney)). Hence the locative *Abruti*.

IX

> *HAb* 33.11: Hinc denique ioculariter dictam nequaquam mirum videri, si rem Romanam Marius
> reficere contenderet, quam *Mamurius* eiusdem artis auctor stirpisque ac nominis solidavisset.[20]

The manuscripts read *Marius* for *Mamurius*. Editors have been content to follow them, presuming this is a reference to C. Marius (also mentioned at *HAb* 39.6). There is, however, no evidence that can connect C. Marius to ironworking of any kind. Instead the *auctor* of the art of metalworking was the legendary smith Veturius Mamurius. Given the frequency of Victor's references to the regal period, and

---

18 See Stover and Woudhuysen forthcoming b.

19 Nickbahkt and Scardino 2021: 100 opt for 'Brutus', without much justification (see Stover 2021b).

20 On the text here, see Shackleton Bailey 1981: 179.

the reign of Numa in particular (*HAb*: 1.3, 14.2, 35.12), and the fact that the *HA* makes direct reference to Mamurius in the corresponding passage (*Tyr.* 8.3), it is very likely that an iterated *Marius* replaced an original *Mamurius*. Hence, it should mean, 'it would seem not at all surprising if Marius tried to reforge the Roman state, which Mamurius, the author of the same craft, and of the same line and name, had strengthened'.

X

> *HAb* 34.2: Quippe ut longo intervallo Deciorum *memoriam* renovaverit.

op read *morem*. The singular is unusual: dying is not an action one can make habitual, and one would expect the plural for the moral sense. The intertext with Cicero (*Phil.* 13.27), however, makes the sense and referents clear: *Deciorum quidem multo intervallo per hunc praeclarum virum memoria renovata est.* Given how close these passages are, and the ease with which an original *memoriam* could be corrupted to *morem*, *memoriam* should be printed.

XI

> *HAb* 34.2: Namque Tetricus, cum Faustini praesidis dolo corruptis *militum plerisque* peteretur, Aureliani per litteras praesidium imploraverat.

op read *militibus plerumque*. For the transmitted text to stand, *plerumque peteretur* must mean that Tetricus was 'subject to frequent attacks', but the other occurrences of *plerumque* in the *HAb* carry the sense of 'generally' (16.2, 33.23), and that is hardly appropriate to the context. Read instead *plerisque* with *corruptis* and *militum* as a partitive – 'since the majority of the soldiers were corrupted by the schemes of Faustinus the *praeses*'.

XII

> *HAb* 35.5: Ipse post celsum biennii imperium in triumphum ductus . . . Lucaniae correcturam . . . filioque veniam atque . . . honorem senatorium cooptavit.

There is no way this incoherent passage can stand, but it is not clear that this is a manuscript problem. In brief, the nominative *ductus* must be modifying Tetricus, but the subject of *cooptavit* must be Aurelian. The *TLL* valiantly tries to save the text by positing a virtually otherwise unattested sense of *cooptare* as *valde optare*, adducing a passage in pseudo-Hilary (*Libellus apologeticus contra Arianos* 11) which is not really parallel because in that instance there is an explicit contrast with a preceding *optare*.[21] Bird and Nixon translate it as 'obtained', which is unsupportable.[22] Instead, the appearance of *senatorium honorem* means

---

21 *TLL* 4.895.9–62 (Gudemann).

22 Nixon 1971: 90; Bird 1994: 37.

this must be the idiom of *cooptare in*, meaning 'to grant membership'. Further, logic demands that *venia* was granted not only to the son, but Tetricus as well. All of this implies that we are dealing with a series of incomplete fragments:

> *in triumphum ductus*: Tetricus was led in triumph
>
> *Lucaniae correcturam*: Aurelian granted him the correctorship of Lucania
>
> *filioque veniam atque*: Aurelian gave <him> and his son pardon and . . .
>
> *honorem senatorium cooptavit*: Aurelian bestowed on one or both of them membership in the Senate

What an editor should print is perhaps too philosophical a question to address here, since it is not clear whether the confusion goes back to the abbreviator who produced the *HAb* or if the passage was mangled in its transmission.

XIII

> *HAb* 39.10: Namque is cum Venetos *correpturus* ageret, Cari morte cognita imperium avens eripere, adventanti hosti obviam processerat.

op read *correptura*, which is obviously corrupt. Schott, noting the occurrence of the rare noun *correctura* in passage XII, corrected it accordingly. The problem is that this is historically unlikely – the office of *corrector Venetiae et Histriae* is not attested in this period, while Julianus is elsewhere called a praetorian prefect – and still syntactically dubious in the phrase *Venetos correctura ageret* (Bird and Nixon use paraphrase to avoid confronting it).[23] Instead, it is a simple case of a corrupt termination. The normal meaning of *corripere*, which makes perfect sense in context, is 'plunder', and the person with his mind set on plunder was surely Julianus. Hence, this means that the usurper Julianus was making moves to plunder the inhabitants of Venetia, and the future participle is used here in a precisely analogous way to *HAb* 6.3: *cum lorica tectus Galba tumultum leniturus contenderet* . . . Clearing up the fact that Victor did not in fact call Julianus a *corrector Venetiae* removes the need to posit two different Juliani who rebelled at the same time (as in *PLRE* 'Iulianus 24' and '38'), and the incongruity of the *HAb* and the *LB* (38.6) referring to two different figures in otherwise parallel accounts.

---

23 Nixon 1971: 95; Bird 1994: 42.

XIV

HAb 39.11: At Carinus ubi Moesiam contigit, illico Marcum iuxta Diocletiano congressus, dum victos avide premeret, suorum ictu interiit, quod libidine impatiens militarium †*mulctas* affectabat, quarum infestiores viri iram tamen doloremque in eventum belli distulerant.

o reads *ml'tas*, **p** *mulctas*. Pichlmayer and Dufraigne simply print *multas*, which cannot be right; Schott was on firmer ground when he conjectured *nuptias*.[24] The problem is that the confusion in **op** is very unlikely to have arisen from an extremely common word. Cicero uses *mulierculae* for camp-followers (*Cat.* 2.23), which is a possibility. Another would be *militunia*, the technical term for the wife of a soldier, though that is an extremely rare word and not attested until Aldhelm.[25] An *obelus* is safest course of action, but we are in no doubt as to the general significance given the parallel in the *LB* (38.8): *Ad extremum trucidatur eius praecipue tribuni dextera, cuius dicebatur coniugem polluisse.*

XV

HAb 39.48: Et quamquam aliis alia aestimantibus *Valeri* gratia corrupta sit, nobis tamen excellenti natura videtur ad communem vitam spreto ambitu descendisse.

The manuscripts read *veri gratia*, a puzzling phrase which has nonetheless escaped critical attention: the *TLL* entry for *gratia* feels the need for an explanatory gloss, adding parenthetically *i. veritas sincera*.[26] The issue at stake is whether Diocletian's abdication was compelled or not (*LB* 39.5: *sponte*; Lactantius *DMP* 18.1: *ut eum cogeret*; *cf. Pan. Lat.* 6.15.4). A simple solution is at hand: Victor seems to have almost exclusively referred to Diocletian with the *gentilicium Valerius*. Hence one might conjecture a missing syllable *-al-* in *veri*: *Valeri gratia*, 'the good deed of Valerius'.

XVI

The *LB*, with its more robust transmission and conventional style, does not pose nearly as many problems. One passage, however, which Pichlmayr daggered is worth discussing.

LB 16.4: Credo divinitus attributum ut, dum mundi lex seu natura *aliquid* hominibus incognitum gignit, rectorum consiliis tamquam medicinae remediis *leniatur*.

The manuscript readings for the two doubtful points are: *aliudve quid* and *leniantur*. Pichlmayr daggers the first, while Festy prints it with no alteration. The former is on firmer ground – *aliudve quid* being not exactly Latin – although his despair is unwarranted. The *ve* is a tip-off that we are dealing with

---

24 Nickbakht and Scardino 2021 also print *multas*, but they do propose the supplement *<mulieres>* in their apparatus.

25 *TLL* 8.971.8–14 (Bulhart).

26 *TLL* 6.2.2216.27 (Häfner).

an intrusive gloss. The obvious word we need is *aliquid*, as in 'when the law of the universe or nature produces *something* unknown to people'. What happened is that the (erroneous) archetypal reading *aliud* was corrected interlinearly with the variant *aliquid*, but the way the corrector expressed it was as follows:

    vel quid
aliud

This produced the nonsense *aliudve quid*. As for *leniantur*, the manuscripts must simply be in error. The thing which is alleviated by the counsels of rulers is the *aliquid incognitum*. Hence, the singular *leniatur* – the plural can easily be explained as a misunderstanding of the preceding *medicinae*.

LIST OF WORKS CITED

In this list of works cited, we use the following bibliographical abbreviations:

ANRW	*Aufstieg und Niedergang der Römischen Welt*
Ant. Class.	*L'Antiquité Classique*
BHAC	*Bonner Historia-Augusta-Colloquium*
	(Antiquitas Reihe 4. Beiträge zur Historia-Augusta-Forschung), Bonn
BICS	*Bulletin of the Institute of Classical Studies*
CCCM	*Corpus Christianorum Continuatio Mediaevalis*
CCSA	*Corpus Christianorum Series Apocryphorum*
CCSL	*Corpus Christianorum Series Latina*
CCTC	*Cambridge Classical Texts and Commentaries*
CGL	*Corpus Glossariorum Latinorum*
CP	*Classical Philology*
CQ	*Classical Quarterly*
CR	*Classical Review*
CSEL	*Corpus Scriptorum Ecclesiasticorum Latinorum*
GRBS	*Greek, Roman, and Byzantine Studies*
HAC	*Historiae Augustae Colloquia*
Historia	*Historia: Zeitschrift für Alte Geschichte*
HLL	*Handbuch der Lateinischen Literatur der Antike*
HSCP	*Harvard Studies in Classical Philology*
IMU	*Italia Medioevale e Umanistica*
ISTC	*Incunabula Short Title Catalogue*
JHS	*Journal of Hellenic Studies*
JRS	*Journal of Roman Studies*
MGH	*Monumenta Germaniae Historica (AA = Auctores Antiquissimi)*
REA	*Révue des Études Anciennes*
REL	*Revue des Études Latines*
RhM	*Rheinisches Museum für Philologie*
RHT	*Revue d'Histoire des Textes*
Settimane di studio	*Settimane di studio del Centro italiano di studi sull'alto Medioevo*
USTC	*Universal Short Title Catalogue*
ZPE	*Zeitschrift für Papyrologie und Epigraphik*
ZSS	*Zeitschrift der Savigny-Stiftung für Rechtsgeschichte, romanistische Abteilung*

★ ★ ★

Adams, J.N. 1976: *The Text and Language of a Vulgar Latin Chronicle (Anonymus Valesianus II)* (*BICS* Supplement 36), London.

— 1978: 'Conventions of Naming in Cicero', *CQ* 28.1, 145–166.

— 1982: *The Latin Sexual Vocabulary*, London.

— 2013: *Social Variation and the Latin Language*, Oxford.

Adler, A. 1928–1938: *Suidae Lexicon*, 5 vols, Leipzig.

Adunka, E. 1952: 'Frankfurter, Salomon (1856–1941), Altphilologe und Bibliothekar', *Österreichisches Biographisches Lexikon ab 1815* 1.4, 346.

Aja Sanchez, J.R. 1993: 'Imprecaciones senatoriales contra Commodo en la "Historia Augusta"', *Polis: Revista de ideas y formas políticas de la Antigüedad Clásica* 5, 5–21.

Albertson, D. 2014: *Mathematical Theologies: Nicholas of Cusa and the Legacy of Thierry of Chartres*, Oxford.

Aldrete, G.S. 1999: *Gestures and Acclamations in Ancient Rome*, Baltimore, MD, and London.

Alföldi, A. 1952: *A Conflict of Ideas in the Late Roman Empire: The Clash Between the Senate and Valentinian I* (tr. H. Mattingly), Oxford.

— 1968: 'Die verlorene Enmannsche Kaisergeschichte und die "Caesares" des Julianus Apostata', *BHAC 1966/1967*, 1–8.

Alföldy, G. 1972: 'Der Sturz des Kaisers Geta und die antike Geschichtsschreibung', *BHAC 1970*, 19–51.

— 1976: 'Zwei Schimpfnamen des Kaisers Elagabal. Tiberinus und Tractatitius', *BHAC 1972–1974*, 11–21.

Allen, M.I. 2002: *Frechulfi Lexoviensis episcopi opera omnia* (*CCCM* 169–169A), 2 vols, Turnhout.

Altmayer, K. 2014: *Die Herrschaft des Carus, Carinus und Numerianus als Vorläufer der Tetrarchie* (*Historia Einzelschriften* 230), Stuttgart.

Anderson, W.S. 1965: 'Valla, Juvenal, and Probus', *Traditio* 21, 383–424.

Ando, C. 1995: [Review of Bird 1994], *Bryn Mawr Classical Review* 95.03.21 (https://bmcr.brynmawr.edu/1995/1995.03.21/) and *The Medieval Review* 95.03.11 (https://scholarworks.iu.edu/journals/index.php/tmr/article/view/14310).

Anspach, A.E. 1913: [Review of Lindsay 1913], *Deutsche Literaturzeitung* 34.48 [29 November 1913], 3040–3043.

— 1930: *Taionis et Isidori nova fragmenta et opera*, Madrid.

Appelt, H. 1990: *Die Urkunden Friederichs I. 1181–1190* (*MGH Diplomata: Die Urkunden der deutschen Könige und Kaiser* 10.4), Hannover.

Armstrong, D. 1984: 'Gallienus in Athens, 264', *ZPE* 70, 235–258.

Arnaudt-Lindet, M.-P. 1993: *L. Ampelius: Aide-Mémoire (Liber Memorialis)*, Paris.

— 1997: 'Le «Liber memorialis» de L. Ampelius', *ANRW* 2.34.3, 2301–2312.

Arnold, T. 1879: *Henrici Archidiaconi Huntendunensis Historia Anglorum. The History of the English by Henry, Archdeacon of Huntingdon*, London.

Arntzen, J. 1733: *Sexti Aurelii Victoris Historia Romana, cum notis integris Dominici Machanei, Eliae Vineti, Andreae Schotti, Jani Gruteri, nec non excerptis Frid. Sylburgii & Annae Fabri filiae*, Amsterdam (Jansson-Waesberg) and Utretch (Jakob Van Poolsum).

Ash, R. 2018: *Tacitus: Annals Book XV*, Cambridge.

Aßmann, E. 1940: 'Der Liber memorial des Lucius Ampelius', *Philologus* 94, 197–221.

Aussenac, E. 2001: 'L'*Origo Constantini*: rétroaction et approche d'une datation', *Latomus* 60.3, 671–676.

Avitabile, L. 1970: '[Roma, Biblioteca Vallicelliana] A 18', in A. Petrucci (ed.), 'Censimento dei codici dei secoli X–XII', *Studi Medievali* 3rd series 11.2, 1013–1133.

Badian, E. 1993: 'Livy and Augustus', in W. Schuller (ed.), *Livius. Aspekte seines Werkes*, Konstanz, 9–38.

Baker, A. 1988: 'Eunapius' Νέα Ἔκδοσις and Photius', *GRBS* 29.4, 389–402.

Baker, R. 2014: 'A Study of a Late Antique Corpus of Biographies [Historia Augusta]', D.Phil. Thesis, Oxford.

Baldini, A. 1984: *Ricerche sulla storia di Eunapio di Sardi. Problemi di storiografia tardo-pagana*, Bologna.

— 2000: *Storie perdute (III secolo d.C.)*, Bologna.

— 2002: 'Ancora sulla *Devotio* di Claudio Gotico: Aurelio Vittore fonte diretta della *Historia Augusta* e di Nicomaco Flaviano', in Bonamente and Paschoud 2002, 11–31.

— and Paschoud, F. 2015: 'ΕΥΝΑΠΙΟΥ ΙΣΤΟΡΙΑ', in B. Bleckmann and T. Stickler (eds), *Griechische Profanhistoriker des fünften nachchristlichen Jahrhunderts* (*Historia Einzelschriften* 228), Stuttgart, 19–50.

Baldwin, B. 1977: 'The Minor Characters in Athenaeus', *Acta Classica* 20, 37–48.

— 1978: 'Verses in the *Historia Augusta*', *BICS* 25, 50–58.

— 1981: 'Acclamations in the *Historia Augusta*', *Athenaeum* NS 59, 138–149.

— 1990: 'A Sallustian Echo in Tacitus', *Illinois Classical Studies* 15.2, 293–294.

— 1993: 'The *Epitome de Caesaribus*, from Augustus to Domitian', *Quaderni Urbinati di Cultura Classica* 43.1, 81–101.

— 1996: 'Photius, Phlegon, and Virgil', *Byzantine and Modern Greek Studies* 20.1, 201–208.

Balmaceda, C. 2017: Virtus Romana: *Politics and Morality in the Roman Historians*, Chapel Hill, NC.

Banchich, T.M. 2015: *The Lost History of Peter the Patrician: An Account of Rome's Imperial Past from the Age of Justinian*, London and New York.

— and Lane, E.N. 2009: The History *of Zonaras, from Alexander Severus to the Death of Theodosius the Great*, London and New York.

Bandy, A.C. 1983: *Ioannes Lydus: On the Powers or The Magistracies of the Roman State. Introduction, Critical Text, Translation, Commentary, and Indices*, Philadelphia, PA.

Barbieri, G. 1934: 'Il problema del cosidetto ultimo grande storico di Roma', *Annali della R. Scuola Normale Superiore di Pisa. Lettere, Storia e Filosofia* S. II, 3.4, 525–538.

— 1954: 'Mario Massimo', *Rivista di filologia e di istruzione classica* 32, 36–66 and 262–275.

Barchiesi, A. and Hardie, P. 2010: 'The Ovidian career model: Ovid, Gallus, Apuleius, Boccaccio', in P. Hardie and H. Moore (eds), *Classical Literary Careers and their Reception*, Cambridge.

Bardon, H. 1952–1956: *La literature latine inconnue*, 2 vols, Paris.

Barnes, T.D. 1967: 'Hadrian and Lucius Verus', *JRS* 57, 65–79.

— 1970a: 'The Lost Kaisergeschichte and the Latin Historical Tradition', *BHAC 1968/1969*, 13–43.

— 1970b: 'Three Notes on the *Vita Probi*', *CQ* 20.1, 198–203.

— 1971: *Tertullian: A Historical and Literary Study*, Oxford.

— 1972a: 'Ultimus Antoninorum', *BHAC 1970*, 53–74.

— 1972b: 'Some Persons in the Historia Augusta', *Phoenix* 26.2, 140–182.

— 1975: [Review of Kolb 1972], *Gnomon* 47.4, 368–373.

— 1976a: 'The *Epitome de Caesaribus* and Its Sources', *CP* 71.3, 258–268.

— 1976b: 'Imperial Campaigns, A.D. 285–311', *Phoenix* 30.2, 174–193.

— 1977: 'The Fragments of Tacitus' *Histories*', *CP* 72.3, 224–231.

— 1978: *The Sources of the Historia Augusta* (Collection Latomus 155), Brussels.

— 1981: *Constantine and Eusebius*, Cambridge, Mass.

— 1982: *The New Empire of Diocletian and Constantine*, Cambridge, Mass.

— 1984: 'The Composition of Cassius Dio's *Roman History*', *Phoenix* 38.3, 240–255.

— 1989: 'Jerome and the *Origo Constantini Imperatoris*', *Phoenix* 43.2, 158–161.

— 1991: 'Latin Literature between Diocletian and Ambrose' [Review of Herzog 1989], *Phoenix* 45.4, 341–355.

— 1993: *Athanasius and Constantius: Theology and Politics in the Constantinian Empire*, Cambridge, Mass.

— 1995: 'The Sources of the Historia Augusta (1967–1992)', in Bonamente and Paci (eds), 1–28.

— 1998: *Ammianus Marcellinus and the Representation of Historical Reality*, Ithaca, NY.

— 2002: [Review of Festy 1999a], *CR* 52.1, 25–27.

— 2008: 'Aspects of the Severan Empire I: Severus as New Augustus', *New England Classical Journal* 35.4, 251–267.

— 2011: *Constantine: Dynasty, Religion and Power in the Later Roman Empire*, Chichester.

Barrett, G. 2019: 'God's Librarian: Isidore of Seville and His Literary Agenda', in A. Fear and J. Wood (eds), *A Companion to Isidore of Seville*, Leiden and Boston, 42–100.

Bastomsky, S.J. 1967: 'The Death of the Emperor Titus – A Tentative Suggestion', *Apeiron* 1.2, 22–23.

Bauman, R. 1977: 'The Resumé of Legislation in the Early Vitae of the Historia Augusta', *ZSS* 94, 43–75.

— 1995: 'The Death of Ulpian, the Irresistible Force and the Immovable Object', *ZSS* 112, 385–399.

Baynes, N.H. 1926: *The Historia Augusta, Its Date and Purpose*, Oxford.

Bechmann, W. 1726: *Disputatio circularis de S. Aurel. Vict.*, Altdorf (the heirs of Johann Daniel Tauber).

Begbie, C.M. 1967: 'The Epitome of Livy', *CQ* 17.2, 332–338.

Behrens, H. 1917: *Quaestiones de libello, qui Origo gentis Romanae inscribitur*, Berlin.

Bell, Jr, A.A. 1987: 'Josephus and Pseudo-Hegesippus', in L.H. Feldman and G. Hata (eds), *Josephus, Judaism, and Christianity*, Detroit, MI, 349–361.

Benario, H.W. 1997: '"Ignotus", the "Good Biographer"(?)', *ANRW* 2.34.3, 2759–2772.

Benferhat, Y. 2015: '*Quousque tandem, quousque tandem* . . . Recherches sur la notion de *patientia* dans la vie politique à Rome (de César a Hadrien)', *Fundamina* 21.1, 1–13.

Bentley, R. [Phileleutherus Lipsiensis, *pseud.*] 1713: *Remarks upon a Late Discourse of Free-Thinking: In a Letter to F.H.D.D. . . . Part the Second*, London (John Morphew and E. Curl).

Béranger, J. 1974: 'L'hérédité dynastique dans l'Histoire Auguste: Procédé et tradition', *BHAC 1971*, 1–20.

Bertrand, C., Desbordes, B., and Callu, J.-P. 1986: 'L'*Histoire Auguste* et l'historiographie médiévale', *RHT* 14–15 (1984–1985), 97–130.

Bertrand-Dagenbach, C. 1990: *Alexandre Sévère et l'*Histoire Auguste (*Collection Latomus* 208), Brussels.

—— 2004: 'Aux sources de l'*Histoire Auguste* à travers les fragments de Marius Maximus et de Dexippe', *Ktèma: civilisations de l'Orient, de la Grèce et de Rome antiques* 29, 223–230.

—— 2014: *Histoire Auguste. Tome III, 2ᵉ partie: Vie d'Alexandre Sévère*, Paris.

Bessone, L. 1980: 'Echi di Aurelius Vittore (*Caes.* 5) nel *Chronicon* di Sulpicio Severo', *Rivista di filologia e di istruzione classica* 108, 431–441.

—— 1982: 'La tradizione epitomatoria liviana in età imperiale', *ANRW* 2.30.2, 1230–1263.

Bidez, J. and Cumont, F. 1922: *Imp. Caesaris Flavii Claudii Iuliani epistulae leges poematia fragmenta varia*, Paris.

Billanovich, G. 1956: 'Dall'antica Ravenna alle biblioteche umanistiche', *Aevum* 30.4, 319–353.

—— 1993: 'Ancora dalla antica Ravenna alle biblioteche umanistiche', *IMU* 36, 107–174.

Bird, H.W. 1971: 'Aurelius Victor and the Accession of Claudius II', *Classical Journal* 66.3, 252–254.

—— 1973: 'Further Observations on the Dating of Enmann's *Kaisergeschichte*', *CQ* 23.2, 375–377.

—— 1981: 'The Sources of the *De Caesaribus*', *CQ* 31.2, 457–463.

—— 1984: *Sextus Aurelius Victor: A Historiographical Study*, Liverpool.

—— 1985: 'Two Textual Notes on Aurelius Victor's Liber de Caesaribus', *Echos du monde classique / Classical Views* NS 39.4, 107–110.

—— 1989: 'A Strange Aggregate of Errors for A.D. 193', *Classical Bulletin* 65, 95–98.

—— 1994: *Aurelius Victor: De Caesaribus* (*Translated Texts for Historians* 17), Liverpool.

—— 1997: 'The *Historia Augusta* on Constantine's Lineage', *Arctos: Acta Philologica Fennica* 31, 9–17.

—— 1999: 'Mocking Marius Maximus', *Latomus* 58.4, 850–860.

Birley, A.R. 1966a: *Marcus Aurelius*, London.

—— 1966b: 'Two Names in the Historia Augusta', *Historia* 15.2, 249–253.

—— 1971: *Septimius Severus: The African Emperor*, London.

—— 1987: *Marcus Aurelius: A Biography*, London.

—— 1994: 'Further Notes on the HA Severus', in Bonamente and Paschoud (eds), 19–42.

—— 1995: 'Indirect Means of Tracing Marius Maximus', in Bonamente and Paci (eds), 57–74.

—— 1996: 'Fiction in the Epitome?', in Bonamente and Mayer (eds), 67–82.

—— 1997a: *Hadrian: The Restless Emperor*, Oxford.

—— 1997b: 'Marius Maximus: The Consular Biographer', *ANRW* 2.34.3, 2678–2757.

—— 2000: 'Senators as Generals', in E. Birley, G. Alföldi, B. Dobson, and W. Eck (eds), *Kaiser, Heer und Gesellschaft in der Römischen Kaiserzeit: Gedenkschrift für Eric Birley*, Stuttgart, 97–119.

—— 2003: 'The Historia Augusta and Pagan Historiography', in Marasco (ed.), 127–149.

—— 2004: [Review of Paschoud 2000], *Gnomon* 76.1, 45–50.

—— 2005: 'Attitudes to the State in the Latin Apologists', in A. Wlosok and F. Paschoud (eds), *L'apologétique chrétienne gréco-latine à l'époque prénicéenne*, Geneva, 249–277.

—— 2006: 'Rewriting Second- and Third-Century History in Late-Antique Rome: The *Historia Augusta*', *Classica* 19.1, 19–29.

Birt, Th. 1888: *Zwei politische Satiren des alten Rom. Ein Beitrag zur Geschichte der Satire*, Marburg.

—— 1920: 'Zu Marius Maximus', *Philologus* 76, 362–366.

Bischoff, B. 1994: *Manuscripts and Libraries in the Age of Charlemagne* (tr. ed. M. Gorman), Cambridge.

Blaudeau, P. 2015: 'Adapter le genre du bréviaire plutôt qu'écrire une histoire ecclésiastique? Autour du choix retenu par Liberatus de Carthage pour rapporter le déroulement des controverses christologiques des Ve-VIe s', in G. Greatrex and H. Elton (eds), *Shifting Genres in Late Antiquity*, 69–80, Farnham and Burlington, VT.

Bleckmann, B. 1992: *Die Reichskrise des III. Jahrhunderts in der spätantiken und byzantinischen Geschichtsschreibung: Untersuchungen zu den nachdionischen Quellen der Chronik des Johannes Zonaras*, Munich.

—— 1995a: 'Bemerkungen zu den *Annales* des Nicomachus Flavianus', *Historia* 44.1, 83–99.

—— 1995b: 'Zu den Quellen der Vita Gallieni duo', in Bonamente and Paci (eds), 75–103.

—— 1997: 'Überlegungen zur Enmannschen Kaisergeschichte und zur Formung historischer Traditionen in tetrarchischer und konstantinischer Zeit', in Bonamente and Rosen (eds), 11–37.

—— 1999: 'Epitome de Caesaribus, Landolfus Sagax und 300 000 Alamannen. Zwei Bemerkungen anläßlich der neuen Epitome-Ausgabe von M. Festy', *Göttinger Forum für Altertumswissenschaft* 2, 139–149.

— 2015: '*Last Pagans*, Source Criticism and Historiography of the Late Antiquity', *Millenium* 12.1, 103–115.

— and Brandt, H. (eds) 2017: *Historiae Augustae Colloquium Dusseldorpiense* (*HAC* NS 13), Bari.

— and Groß, J. 2016: *Historiker der Reichskrise des 3. Jahrhunderts, I*, Paderborn.

— and — 2018: *Eutropius. Breviarium ab urbe condita*, Paderborn.

Bloch, H. 1972: 'Monte Cassino's Teachers and Library in the High Middle Ages', *La scuola nell'Occidente latino dell'alto Medioevo: 15–21 aprile 1971* (*Settimane di studio* 19), 2 vols, Spoleto, 2.563–605.

Blockley, R.C. 1973: 'Tacitean Influence upon Ammianus Marcellinus', *Latomus* 32.1, 63–78.

— 1980: 'Was the First Book of Zosimus' New History Based on more than Two Sources?', *Byzantion* 50.2, 393–402.

— 1981–1983: *The Fragmentary Classicising Historians of the Later Roman Empire: Eunapius, Olympiodorus, Priscus and Malchus*, 2 vols, Leeds.

— 1996: 'Ammianus Marcellinus and His Classical Background – Changing Perspectives', *International Journal of the Classical Tradition* 2.4, 455–466.

den Boeft, J., den Hengst, D., and Teitler, H.C. 1991: *Philological and Historical Commentary on Ammianus Marcellinus XXI*, Groningen.

—, —, and — 2008: *Philological and Historical Commentary on Ammianus Marcellinus XXVI*, Leiden and Boston.

—, Drijvers, J.W., den Hengst, D., and Teitler, H.C. 2009: *Philological and Historical Commentary on Ammianus Marcellinus XXVII*, Leiden.

—, —, —, and — 2011: *Philological and Historical Commentary on Ammianus Marcellinus XXVIII*, Leiden.

—, —, —, and — 2018: *Philological and Historical Commentary on Ammianus Marcellinus XXXI*, Leiden.

Boehm, I. and Vallat, D. (eds) 2020: Epitome. *Abréger les textes antiques*, Lyon.

den Boer, W. 1972: *Some Minor Roman Historians*, Leiden.

Böhme-Schönberger, A. 2004: 'Wurde Alexander Severus in Bretzenheim ermordet?', *Mainzer Zeitschrift* 99, 11–16.

Böhringer, L. 1992: *Hinkmar von Reims. De divortio Lotharii regis et Theutbergae reginae* (*MGH Concilia* 4, *supp.* 1), Hannover.

Boissevain, U.P. 1906: *Excerpta historica iussu imp. Constantini Porphyrogeniti confecta IV: Excerpta de Sententiis*, Berlin.

Bonamente, G., Heim, F., and Callu, J.-P. (eds) 1998: *Historiae Augustae Colloquium Argentoratense* (*HAC* NS 6), Bari.

— and Mayer, M. (eds) 1996: *Historiae Augustae Colloquium Barcinonense* (*HAC* NS 4), Bari.

— and Paci, G. (eds) 1995: *Historiae Augustae Colloquium Maceratense* (*HAC* NS 3), Bari.

— and Paschoud, F. (eds) 1994: *Historiae Augustae Colloquium Genevense* (*HAC* NS 2), Bari.

— and — (eds) 2002: *Historiae Augustae Colloquium Perusinum* (*HAC* NS 8), Bari.

— and Rosen, K. (eds) 1997: *Historiae Augustae Colloquium Bonnense* (*HAC* NS 5), Bari.

Bonazzi, M: 2013. 'Eudorus of Alexandria and the "Pythagorean" Pseudepigrapha', in G. Cornelli, R. McKirahan, and C. Macris (eds), *On Pythagoreanism*, Berlin and New York, 385–404.

Borszák, I. 1976: 'Von Tacitus zu Ammian', *Acta Antiqua Academia Scientiarum Hungaricae* 24, 357–368.

Bostock, J. and Riley, H.T. 1855–1857: *The Natural History of Pliny*, 6 vols, London.

Bott, H. 1920: *De epitomis antiquis*, Marburg.

Botteon, Don V. 1907: *Un documento prezioso riguardo alle origini del Vescovado di Ceneda – e la serie dei vescovi cenedesi corretta e documentata. Illustrazione critico-storica*, Conegliano.

Bouffartigue, J. 1992: *L'Empereur Julien et la culture de son temps*, Paris.

Bowersock, G.W. 1975: 'The Greek-Nabatean Bilingual Inscription at Ruwwāfa, Saudi Arabia', in J. Bingen, G. Cambier, and G. Nachtergael (eds), *Le monde grec: pensée, littérature, histoire, documents. Hommages à Claire Préaux*, Brussels, 513–522.

— 1980: 'The Emperor of Roman History', *New York Review of Books* 6 March.

— 1982: 'The Emperor Julian on His Predecessors', *Yale Classical Studies* 27, 159–172.

— 1990: [Review of Matthews 1989], *JRS* 80, 244–250.

— 1994: 'Ronald Syme 1903–1989', *Proceedings of the British Academy* 84, 539–563.

Braccesi, L. 1973: *Introduzione al De viris illustribus*, Bologna.

Bradbury, S. 2000: 'A Sophistic Prefect: Anatolius of Berytus in the Letters of Libanius', *CP* 95.2, 172–186.

Brandt, H. 1996: *Kommentar zur Vita Maximi et Balbini der Historia Augusta*, Bonn.

Bray, J. 1997: *Gallienus: A Study in Reformist and Sexual Politics*, Kent Town.

Briquel, D. 1990: *L'Origine Lydienne des Étrusques: Histoire de la doctrine dans l'antiquité*, Rome.

Briscoe, J. 1998: *Valeri Maximi Facta et dicta memorabilia*, 2 vols, Stuttgart and Leipzig.

— 2018: *Valerius Maximus*, Facta et dicta memorabilia, *Book 8: Text, Translation, and Commentary*, Berlin and Boston.

Brodersen, K. 1993: 'Appian und sein Werk', *ANRW* 2.34.1, 341–363.

— 2011: 'Mapping Pliny's World: The Achievement of Solinus', *BICS* 54.1, 63–88.

— (ed.) 2014: *Solinus: New Studies*, Heidelberg.

— 2020: '*In modum fulminis*: Cniva und Ostrogotha bei Jordanes und in den Scythica Vindobonensia', in Mitthoff *et al.* (eds), 147–157.

Broekaert, W. 2011: 'Oil for Rome During the Second and Third Century AD: A Confrontation of Archaeological Records and the *Historia Augusta*', *Mnemosyne* 64, 591–623.

Broughton, T.R.S. 1951–1960: *The Magistrates of the Roman Republic*, 3 vols, New York.

Brown, P.R.L. 1967: 'The Later Roman Empire' [Review of Jones 1964], *Economic History Review* NS 20.2, 327–343.

— 1971: *The World of Late Antiquity*, London.

— 2000: *Augustine of Hippo. A Biography*, Berkeley and Los Angeles.

Browning, R. 1982: 'Biography', in E.J. Kenney and W.V. Clausen (eds), *The Cambridge History of Classical Literature II: Latin Literature*, Cambridge, 723–731.

Brugisser, P. 1989: 'Gratien, nouveau Romulus', in M. Piérart and O. Curty (eds), *Historia Testis: Mélanges d'epigraphie, d'histoire ancienne et de philologie offerts à Tadeusz Zawadzki*, Fribourg, 189–205.

Brugnoli, G. 1958: 'La latinità di Paolo Diacono: l'archeologia italicà', *Rivista Benedictina* 12, 185–203.

— 1960: 'Paolo Diacono e l'Origo gentis Romanae', *Rivista di cultura classica e medioevale* 2, 371–387.

Brunt, P.A. 1980: 'On Historical Fragments and Epitomes', *CQ* 30.2, 477–494.

Bruun, C. 1995: 'The Thick Neck of the Emperor Constantine: Slimy Snails and "Quellenforschung"', *Historia* 44.4, 459–80.

— 2003: 'Roman Emperors in Popular Jargon. Searching for Contemporary Nicknames I', in L. de Blois et al. (eds), *The Representation and Perception of Roman Imperial Power*, Amsterdam, 69–98.

von Büren, V. 2012: 'Les *Étymologies* de Paul Diacre? Le Manuscrit Cava de'Tirreni, 2 (XXIII) et le *Liber Glossarum*', *IMU* 53, 1–36.

Burgersdijk, D.W.P. 2010: 'Style and Structure of the Historia Augusta', Ph.D. Thesis, Amsterdam.

— 2013: 'Pliny's *Panegyricus* and the *Historia Augusta*', *Arethusa* 46.2, 289–312.

— 2016: '*Qui vitas aliorum scribere orditur*: Narratological Implications of Fictional Authors in the *Historia Augusta*', in K. de Temmerman, K. Demoen (eds), *Writing Biography in Greece and Rome: Narrative Technique and Fictionalization*, Cambridge, 240–256.

— 2017: 'Aurelius Victor, Festus and the Others: Minor Historians and Anonymous Sources in the *Historia Augusta*', in Bleckmann and Brandt (eds), 33–46.

Burgess, R.W. 1993a: '*Principes cum Tyrannis*: Two Studies on the Kaisergeschichte and Its Tradition', *CQ* 43.2, 491–500.

— 1993b: *The* Chronicle *of Hydatius and the* Consularia Constantinopolitana: *Two Contemporary Accounts of the Final Years of the Roman Empire*, Oxford.

— 1995a: 'Jerome and the *Kaisergeschichte*', *Historia* 44.3, 349–369.

— 1995b: 'On the Date of the *Kaisergeschichte*', *CP* 90.2, 111–128.

— 1997: 'The Dates and Editions of Eusebius' *Chronici Canones* and *Historia Ecclesiastica*', *Journal of Theological Studies* NS 48.2, 471–504.

— 1998: 'Jerome's *Chronici Canones*, Quellenforschung, and Fourth-Century Historiography', in Bonamente *et al.* (eds), 83–104.

— 1999: *Studies in Eusebian and Post-Eusebian Chronography* (*Historia Einzelschriften* 135) (with the assistance of Witold Witakowski), Stuttgart.

— 2000: '"Non duo Antonini sed duo Augusti': The Consuls of 161 and the Origins and Traditions of the Latin Consular *Fasti* of the Roman Empire', *ZPE* 132, 259–290.

— 2001: 'Eutropius *V.C. Magister Memoriae*?', *CP* 96.1, 76–81.

— 2005: 'A Common Source for Jerome, Eutropius, Festus, Ammianus, and the *Epitome de Caesaribus* between 358 and 378, along with Further Thoughts on the Date and Nature of the *Kaisergeschichte*', *CP* 100, 166–192.

— 2011: *Chronicles, Consuls, and Coins: Historiography and History in the Later Roman Empire*, Farnham.

— 2012: 'The Chronograph of 354: Its Manuscripts, Contents, and History', *Journal of Late Antiquity* 5.2, 345–396.

— 2014: *Roman Imperial Chronology and Early-Fourth-Century Historiography: The Regnal Durations of the So-Called Chronica urbis Romae of the Chronograph of 354* (*Historia Einzelschriften* 234), Stuttgart.

— and Kulikowski, M. 2013: *Mosaics of Time: The Latin Chronicle Traditions from the First Century* BC *to the Sixth Century* AD. *Volume I: A Historical Introduction to the Chronicle Genre from Its Origins to the High Middle Ages*, Turnhout.

Burrow, C., Harrison, S.J., McLaughlin, M., and Tarantino, E. 2020: *Imitative Series and Clusters from Classical to Early Modern Literature*, Berlin.

Butrica, J.L. 2005: 'Some Myths and Anomalies in the Study of Roman Sexuality', *Journal of Homosexuality* 49, 209–269.

— 2006: 'The Fabella of Sulpicia (*Epigrammata Bobiensia* 37)', *Phoenix* 60, 70–121.

Caldelli, E. 2006: *Copisti a Roma nel Quattrocento*, Rome.

Callens, P. 1972: *Prosperi Aquitani opera. Pars 2: Expositio Psalmorum, Liber sententiarum* (*CCSL 68A*), Turnhout.

Callu, J.-P. 1985: 'La premiere diffusion de "l'Histoire Auguste" (VIe-IXe S.)', in J. Straub, ed., *BHAC 1982/1983*, 89–129.

— 1996: 'Aurélius Victor et le interrègne de 275', in Bonamente and Mayer (eds), 133–145.

— 1999: 'En amont de l'Histoire Auguste 357–387', in Paschoud (ed.), 87–107.

—, Desbordes, O., and Gaden, A. 1992: *Histoire Auguste. Tome I, 1ʳᵉ Partie: Introduction génerale, Vies d'Hadrien, Aelius, Antonin*, Paris.

Cameron, A.D.E. 1964a: 'The Roman Friends of Ammianus', *JRS* 54, 15–28.

— 1964b: 'Literary Allusions in the Historia Augusta', *Hermes* 92.3, 363–377.

— 1965a: [Review of Works on the *HA*: Straub, *Heidnische Geschichtsapologetik* (Bonn, 1963); *Historia-Augusta-Colloquium Bonn 1963* (Bonn, 1964); *Atti del colloquio patavino sulla Historia Augusta* (Rome, 1964)], *JRS* 55, 240–250.

— 1965b: 'Two Glosses in Aurelius Victor', *CR* 15.1, 20–21.

— 1966: 'The Date and Identity of Macrobius', *JRS* 56, 25–38.

— 1967: 'Rutilius Namatianus, St. Augustine, and the Date of the *De Reditu*', *JRS* 57, 31–39.

— 1968: 'The First Edition of Ovid's *Amores*', *CQ* 18.2, 320–333.

— 1969a: [Review of Eadie 1967], *CR* 19.3, 305–307.

— 1969b: 'The Date of Zosimus', *Philologus* 113, 106–110.

— 1970: *Claudian: Poetry and Propaganda at the Court of Honorius*, Oxford.

— 1971: [Review of Syme 1968a], *JRS* 61, 255–267.

— 1980: '*Poetae Novelli*', *HSCP* 84, 127–175.

— 1985: 'Polyonomy in the Late Roman Aristocracy: The Case of Petronius Probus', *JRS* 75, 164–182.

— 1995: *Callimachus and His Critics*, Princeton, NJ.

— 1999: 'The Antiquity of the Symmachi', *Historia* 48.4, 477–505.

— 2004a: *Greek Mythography in the Roman World*, Oxford.

— 2004b: 'Vergil Illustrated between Pagans and Christians. Reconsidering the "Late-4th C. Classical Revival", The Dates of the Manuscripts, and the Places of Production of the Latin Classics', *Journal of Roman Archaeology* 17.2, 502–525.

— 2010: 'The Date of the Scholia Vetustiora on Juvenal', *CQ* 60.2, 569–576.

— 2011: *The Last Pagans of Rome*, Oxford.

— 2012: 'Nicomachus Flavianus and the Date of Ammianus's Lost Books', *Athenaeum* 100, 337–358.

— 2014: 'Momigliano and the *Historia Augusta*', in T.J. Cornell and O. Murray (eds), *The Legacy of Arnaldo Momigliano*, London and Turin, 147–164.

Cancelli, F. 2010: *La codificazione dell'edictum praetoris: dogma romanistico*, Milan.

Cardascia, G. 1950: 'L'Apparition dans le droit des classes d'«honestiores» et d'«humiliores»', *Revue historique de droit français et étranger* 4th series 27, 305–337 and 461–485.

Carlos Martín, J. 2005: 'El corpus hagiográfico latino en torno a la figura de Isidoro de Sevilla en la Hispania tardoantica y medieval (ss. VII–XIII)', *Veleia* 22, 187–228.

Castaldi, L and Martello, F. 2011: '"Tempera quasi aurum": origine, redazione e diffusione del "Liber testimoniorum" di Paterio', *Filologia mediolatina* 18, 23–107.

Cataudella, M.R. 2003: 'Historiography in the East', in Marasco (ed.), 391–447.

Cavallera, F. 1922: *Saint Jerôme: Sa vie et son œuvre*, 2 vols, Louvain.

Cavallo, G. 1975: 'La trasmissione dei testi nell'area Beneventano-Cassinese', in *La cultura antica nell'Occidente Latino dal VII all'XI secolo: 18–24 aprile 1974 (Settimane di studio 22)*, 2 vols, Spoleto, 1.357–424.

Cecconi, G.A. 2013: 'Alan Cameron's Virius Nicomachus Flavianus', in R. Lizzi Testa (ed.), *The Strange Death of Pagan Rome: Reflections on a Historiographical Controversy*, Turnhout, 151–164.

Cervani, R. 1978: *L'epitome di Paolo del* De verborum significatu *di Pompeo Festo. Struttura e metodo*, Rome.

Cessi, R. 1913a: *Fragmenta Historica ab Henrico et Hadriano Valesio primum edita [Anonymus Valesianus]*, Citta di Castello.

— 1913b: 'Di due miscellanee storiche medioevali', *Archivio muratoriano* 13, 71–96.

— 1942: *Documenti relativi alla storia di Venezia anteriori al mille*, 2 vols, Padua.

Chalmers, W.R. 1953: 'The Νεα Ἐκδοσις of Eunapius' *Histories*', *CQ* 3.3/4, 165–170.

Champlin, E. 1980: *Fronto and Antonine Rome*, Cambridge, Mass.

— 1982: 'The Epitaph of Naucellius', *ZPE* 49, 184.

Charlesworth, M.P. 1947: 'Imperial Deportment: Two Texts and Some Questions', *JRS* 37, 34–38.

Charlet, J.-L., Furno, M., Pade, M., Ramminger, J., and Abbamonte, G. 1998: *Nicolai Perotti Cornu Copiae seu linguae Latinae commentarii* VII, Sassoferrato.

Chastagnol, A. 1955: 'Notes chronologiques sur l'Histoire Auguste et le Laterculus de Polemius Silvius', *Historia* 4.2/3, 173–188.

— 1960: *La préfecture urbaine a Rome sous le Bas-Empire*, Paris.

— 1962: *Les fastes de la préfecture de Rome au Bas-Empire*, Paris.

— 1963: 'L'Administration du Diocèse Italien au Bas-Empire', *Historia* 12.3, 348–379.

— 1964: 'Le problème de l'Histoire Auguste: état de la question', *Historia-Augusta-Colloquium Bonn 1963*, 43–71.

— 1966: 'Zosime II, 38 et l'Histoire Auguste', *BHAC 1964/1965*, 43–78.

— 1967: 'Emprunts de l'*Histoire Auguste* aux *Caesares* d'Aurélius Victor', *Revue de Philologie, de Littérature et d'Histoire Anciennes* 41, 85–97.

— 1970: *Recherches sur l'Histoire Auguste, avec un rapport sur les progrès de las Historia Augusta-Forschung depuis 1963*, Bonn.

— 1974: 'L'empereur gaulois Marius dans l'Histoire Auguste', *BHAC 1971*, 51–58.

— 1976: 'Autour de la "sobre ivresse" de Bonosus', *BHAC 1972/1974*, 91–112.

— 1994: *Histoire Auguste: les empereurs romains de IIᵉ et IIIᵉ siècles*, Paris.

Chausson, F. 1997: '*Severus* XVII,5–XIX,4: une identification?', in Bonamente and Rosen (eds), 97–113.

— 2002: 'Variétés généalogiques I. Numa Pompilius ancêtre de Marc Aurèle', in Bonamente and Paschoud (eds), 109–147.

— 2007: *Stemmata Aurea: Constantin, Justine, Théodose. Revendications généalogiques et idéologie impériale au IVᵉ siècle ap. J.-C.*, Rome.

Chiesa, P. (ed.) 2000: *Paolo Diacono: Uno scrittore fra tradizione longobarda e rinnovamento carolingio. Atti del convegno internazionale di studi, Cividale del Friuli, 6–9 maggio 1999*, Udine.

Chisholm, J.E. 1967: *The Pseudo-Augustinian Hypomnesticon against the Pelagians and Celestians, vol. 1*, Fribourg.

Christ, K. 2005: 'Kaiserideal und Geschichtsbild bei Sextus Aurelius Victor', *Klio* 87, 177–200.

Christol, M. 1986: *Essai sur l'évolution des carrières sénatoriales dans la second moitié du IIIe siècle ap. J.C.*, Paris.

— 2014: 'Gallien, Claude et Aurélien', in C. Bertrand-Dagenbach and F. Chausson (eds), *Historiae Augustae Colloquium Nanceiense (HAC NS 12)*, 159–183.

— and Loriot, X. 2001: 'P. Alfius Avitus et P. Plotius Romanus, gouverneurs de Galatie', *Ant. Class.* 70, 97–121.

Clark, F. 2020: *The First Pagan Historian: The Fortunes of a Fraud from Antiquity to the Enlightenment*, New York.

Clarke, G.W. 1986: *The Letters of St. Cyprian of Carthage: Volume III, Letters 55–66*, New York, and Mahwah, NJ.

Clement, R.-W. 1985: 'Two Contemporary Gregorian Editions of Pope Gregory the Great's *Regula Pastoralis* in Troyes MS 504', *Scriptorium* 39.1, 89–97.

Cleve, R. 1998: 'Cassius Dio and Ulpian', *Ancient History Bulletin* 2, 118–124.

Cohn, A. 1884: *Quibus ex fontibus S. Aurelii Victoris et Libri de Caesaribus et Epitomes undecim capita priora fluexerint*, Berlin.

Colledge, M.A.R, 1977: [Review of Dufraigne 1975], *CR* 27.2, 287–288.

Colombo, M. 2017: 'Nota di critica testuale su Ammiano Marcellino', *Wiener Studien* 130, 201–243.

Conte, G.B. 1994: *Latin Literature a History* (tr. J.B. Solodow, rev. D. Fowler and G.W. Most), Baltimore, MD, and London.

Conti, S. 2004: *Die Inschriften Kaiser Julians*, Stuttgart.

Cooper, S.A. and Hunter, D.G. 2010: 'Ambrosiaster *redactor sui*: The Commentaries on the Pauline Epistles (Excluding Romans)', *Revue d'études augustiniennes et patristiques* 56, 69–91.

Corbett, P. B. 1949: 'The "De Caesaribus" Attributed to Aurelius Victor: Points Arising from an Examination of the MSS and of the Teubner Edition of F. Pichlmayr', *Scriptorium* 3, 254–257.

Corcoran, S. 1996: *The Empire of the Tetrarchs. Imperial Pronouncements and Government A.D. 284–324*, Oxford.

Cornelius, E. 1888: *Quomodo Tacitus, historiarum scriptor in hominum memoria versatus sit usque ad renascentes literas saeculis XIV. et XV.*, Marburg.

Cornell, T.J.H. (ed.) 2013: *Fragments of the Roman Historians*, 3 vols, Oxford.

Cornwell, H. 2015: 'The King Who Would Be Prefect: Authority and Identity in the Cottian Alps', *JRS* 105, 41–72.

della Corte, F. 1975: 'I "Caesares" di Ausonio e Mario Massimo', in S. Boldrini, S. Lanciotti, C. Questa, and R. Raffaelli (eds), *Gli storiografi Latini tramandati in frammenti (Urbino, 9–11 maggio 1974)*, Urbino, 483–491.

Costambeys, M. 2000: 'The Monastic Environment of Paul the Deacon', in Chiesa (ed.), 127–138.

Costantini, L. 2019: *Magic in Apuleius' Apologia: Understanding the Charges and the Forensic Strategies in Apuleius' Speech*, Berlin.

Courteault, P. 1921: 'An Inscription Recently Found at Bordeaux', *JRS* 11, 101–107.

Courtney, E. 1980: *A Commentary on the Satires of Juvenal*, London.

— 1993: *The Fragmentary Latin Poets*, Oxford.

Crawford, M.H. 2019: 'Paul the Deacon between Justinian and Bologna', *Revue de Philologie, de Littérature et d'Histoire Anciennes* 93.2, 29–82 and 227–228.

Crawford, M.R. 2020: 'The Influence of Eusebius' Chronicle on the Apologetic Treatises of Cyril of Alexandria and Augustine of Hippo', *Journal of Ecclesiastical History* 71.4, 693–711.

Crecelius, W. 1857: 'S. Aurelii Augustini de dialectica liber', *Jahresbericht über das Gymnasium zu Elberfeld . . . Schuljahr 1856–57*, Elberfeld, 1–20.

Criniti, N. 1993: 'Granio Liciniano', *ANRW* 2.34.1, 119–205.

Crivellucci, A. 1906: 'Un'opera *De terminatione Provinciarum Italiae* del secolo VII d.C.', *Studi Storici* 15, 115–122.

— 1908: 'Ancora di una pretesa opera *De terminatione provinciarum Italiae* del secolo VII', *Studi Storici* 17, 283–288.

— 1912: *Landolfi Sagacis Historia Romana*, 2 vols, Rome.

— 1914: *Pauli Diaconi Historia Romana*, Rome.

Crook, J. 1959: [Review of Syme 1958 and C.W. Mendell 1957: *Tacitus. The Man and His Work*, New Haven, CT], *Phoenix* 13.1, 38–41.

Dąbrowa, E. 2019: 'The Title of "Colonia" and Colonisation as Factors in the Development of Cities in Roman Syria', in N.J. Andrade, C. Marcaccini, G. Marconi, and D. Violante (eds), *Roman Imperial Cities in the East and in Central-Southern Italy*, Rome, 263–280.

Dacier, A. 1681: *Sex. Aurelii Victoris Historiae Romanae Compendium*, Paris (Denys Thierry).

Dahn, F. 1876: *Paulus Diaconus. I. Abtheilung: Des Paulus Diaconus Leben und Schriften*, Leipzig.

Daintree, D. 1990: 'The Virgil Commentary of Aelius Donatus – Black Hole or "Éminence Grise?"', *Greece and Rome* 37, 65–79.

Damsholt, T. 1977: 'Das Zeitalter des Zosimos. Euagrios, Eustathios und die Aufhebung des chrysargyron', *Analecta Romana Instituti Danici* 8, 89–102.

D'Anna, G. 1992: *Anonimo: Origine del Popolo Romano*, Milan.

Darrigol, O. 2005: 'The Genesis of the Theory of Relativity', in Th. Damour, O. Darrigol, and V. Rivasseau (eds), *Einstein, 1905–2005: Poincaré Seminar 2005*, Berlin, 1–22.

Davenport, C. 2019: *A History of the Roman Equestrian Order*, Cambridge.

De Bruyne, D. and Sodar, B. 1932: *Les anciennes traductions latines des Machabées*, Abbaye de Maredsous.

D'Elia, S. 1965: *Studi sulla tradizione manoscritta di Aurelio Vittore: Parte I: La tradizione diretta*, Naples.

— 1968: 'Per una nuova edizione critica di Aurelio Vittore', *Rendiconti della Accademia di Archeologia Lettere e Belle Arti* (Naples) NS 43, 103–194.

— 1973: 'Per una nuova edizione critica di Aurelio Vittore: Conclusioni', *Bollettino di Studi Latini* 3, 52–75.

De Nolhac, P. 1907: *Pétrarque et l'humanisme. Nouvelle édition*, 2 vols, Paris.

D'Ooge, M.L., Robbins, F.E., and Karpinski, L.C. 1926: *Nicomachus of Gerasa: Introduction to Arithmetic*, New York and London.

De Vregille, B. and Neyrand, L. 1986: *Apponii in Canticum Canticorum expositionem* (*CCSL* 19), Turnhout.

DeLaine, J. 1997: *The Baths of Caracalla: A Study in the Design, Construction, and Economics of Large-Scale Building Projects in Imperial Rome*, Portsmouth, RI.

Derolez, A. 2003: *The Palaeography of Gothic Manuscript Books: From the Twelfth to the Early Sixteenth Century*, Cambridge.

Dessau, H. 1889: 'Über Zeit und Persönlichkeit der Scriptores Historiae Augustae', *Hermes* 24.3, 337–392.

— 1892: 'Über die Scriptores Historiae Augustae', *Hermes* 27.3, 561–605.

Dey, H.W. 2011: *The Aurelian Wall and the Refashioning of Imperial Rome, A.D. 271–855*, Cambridge.

Dietz, K. 1980: *Senatus contra principem: Untersuchungen zur senatorischen Opposition gegen Kaiser Maximinus Thrax*, Munich.

Dill, U. 2013: 'Wölfflin, Eduard', in *Historisches Lexikon der Schweiz* (https://hls-dhs-dss.ch/de/articles/043464/2013–11–20).

Doignon, J. 1966: 'Le titre de *Nobilissimus Puer* porté par Gratien et la mystique littéraire des origins de Rome à l'avènement des Valentiniens', in R. Chevallier (ed.), *Mélanges d'archéologie et d'histoire offerts à André Piganiol*, 3 vols, Paris, 3.1693–1709.

von Domaszewski, A. 1900: 'Der Truppensold der Kaiserzeit', *Neue Heiderlberger Jahrbücher* 10, 218–241.

— 1918: *Die Personennamen bei den Scriptores historiae Augustae*, Heidelberg.

Doody, A. 2009: 'Authority and Authorship in the *Medicina Plinii*', in A. Doody and L.C. Taub (eds), *Authorial Voices in Greco-Roman Technical Writing*, Trier, 93–105.

Dorfbauer, L.J. 2017: *Fortunatianus Aquileiensis: Commentarii in Evangelia* (*CSEL* 103), Berlin.

Dreyer, B. 2011: *Polybios: Leben und Werk im Banne Roms*, Hildesheim.

Drijvers, J.W. and Hunt, D. (eds) 1999: *The Late Roman World and Its Historian: Interpreting Ammianus Marcellinus*, London.

Drinkwater, J.F. 1987: *The Gallic Empire: Separatism and Continuity in the North-Western Provinces of the Roman Empire, A.D. 260–274* (*Historia Einzelschriften* 52), Stuttgart.

— 1994: 'Silvanus, Ursicinus and Ammianus: Fact or Fiction', *Studies in Latin Literature and Roman History* 7, 568–576.

— 2007: *The Alamanni and Rome 213–496: Caracalla to Clovis*, Oxford.

— 2019: *Nero: Emperor and Court*, Oxford.

Drost-Abgarjan, A. 2006: 'Ein neuer Fund zur armenischen Version der Eusebios-Chronik', in M. Wallraff (ed.), *Julius Africanus und di christliche Weltchronistik*, Berlin and Boston, 255–262.

Droysen, H. 1878: 'Nachträge zu der Epitome des Nepotianus', *Hermes* 13.1, 122–132.

— 1879: *Eutropi Breviarium ab urbe condita cum versionibus Graecis et Pauli Landolfique additamentis* (*MGH AA* 2), Berlin.

Dubischar, M. 2010: 'Survival of the Most Condensed? Auxiliary Texts, Communications Theory, and Condensation of Knowledge', in Horster and Reitz (eds), 39–67.

Duff, T.E. 2011: 'The Structure of the Plutarchan Book', *Classical Antiquity* 30.2, 213–278.

Dufraigne, P. 1975: *Aurelius Victor: Livre des Césars*, Paris.

Dulaey, M. 1993: *Victorin de Poetovio, premier exégète latin*, 2 vols, Paris.

Durliat, J. 1990: *De la ville antique à la ville byzantine: le problème des subsistances*, Rome.

Dzino, D. 2005: '*Sabaiarius*: Beer, Wine and Ammianus Marcellinus', in W. Mayer and S. Trzcionka (eds), *Feast, Fast or Famine*, Brisbane, 57–68.

Eadie, J.W. 1967: *The* Breviarium *of Festus. A Critical Edition with Historical Commentary*, London.

Ebeling, P. 1881: *Quaestiones Eutropianae*, Halle.

Echols, E.C. 1962: *Sextus Aurelius Victor's Brief Imperial Lives*. Exeter, NH.

Eck, W. and Heil, M. 2021: 'Eine angebliche zweite Frau Kaiser Valerians – die nie gelebt hat', *ZPE* 217, 212–226.

Edgeworth, R.J. 1992: 'More Fiction in the *Epitome*', *Historia* 41.4, 507–509.

Egidi, R. 2010: 'L'area di Piazza Venezia. Nuovi dati topografici', in R. Egidi, F. Filippi, and S. Martone (eds), *Archeologia e infrastrutture. Il tracciato fondamentale della linea C della metropolitana di Rome: prime indagini archeologiche* (*Bollettino d'Arte*, volume speciale), Rome, 93–123.

Eigler, U. 2003: Lectiones vetustatis: *Römische Literatur und Geschichte in der lateinischen Literatur der Spätantike*, Munich.

Elm, S. 2012: *Sons of Hellenism, Fathers of the Church: Emperor Julian, Gregory of Nazianzus, and the Vision of Rome*, Berkeley.

Emonds, H. 1941: *Zweite Auflage im Altertum: Kulturgeschichtliche Studien zur Überlieferung der antiken Literatur*, Leipzig.

Enmann, A. 1880: *Untersuchungen uber die Quellen des Pompeius Trogus für die griechische und sicilicsche Geschichte*, Dorpat.

— 1884: 'Eine verlorene Geschichte der Römischen Kaiser und das Buch *De Viris Illustribus Urbis Romae*', *Philologus Supplementband* 4.3, 337–501.

— 1886: *Kritische versuche zur ältesten griechischen Geschichte. I. Kypros under ursprung des Aphroditeskultus*, St Petersburg.

Estiot, S. 2010: 'À propos d'un médaillon inédit de l'usurpateur Julien (284–285 AD): son règne et son monnoyage', *Revue Numismatique* 166, 397–418.

Eubank, W. 1933: *The Poems of Cicero*, London.

Fabia, P. 1900: *Onomasticon Taciteum*, Paris and Lyon.

Falque, E. 2008: *Eutropio: Breviario. Aurelio Víctor: Libro de los Césares*, Madrid.

Farnham, F. 1976: *Madame Dacier: Scholar and Humanist*, Monterey, CA.

Farrer, A.M. 1955: 'On Dispensing with Q', in D.E. Nineham (ed.), *Studies in the Gospels: Essays in Memory of R.H. Lightfoot*, Oxford, 55–88.

Feissel, D. 2000: 'Une constitution de l'empereur Julien entre texte épigraphique et codification (CIL III, 459 et CTh I, 16, 8)', in E. Lévy, *La codification des lois dans l'Antiquité: Actes du Colloque de Strasbourg, 27–29 novembre 1997*, Paris, 315–337.

Festy, M. 1994: 'À propos du *Corpus Aurelianum*: à la recherche des leçons du *Codex Metelli* perdu', *Pallas* 41, 91–136.

— 1998: 'En éditant l'*Epitome de Caesaribus*', in Bonamente *et al.* (eds), 153–166.

— 1999a: *Pseudo-Aurélius Victor: Abrégé des Césars*, Paris.

— 1999b: 'Aurélius Victor, source de l'*Histoire Auguste* et de Nicomaque Flavien', in Paschoud (ed.), 121–133.

— 2003: 'De *L'Epitome de Caesaribus* à la *Chronique* de Marcellin: L'*Historia Romana* de Symmaque le Jeune', *Historia* 52.2, 251–255.

Fisher, E. 1982: 'Greek Translations of Latin Literature in the Fourth Century A.D.', in J.J. Winkler and G. Williams (eds), *Later Greek Literature* (*Yale Classical Studies* 27), Cambridge, 173–215.

Fisher, W.H. 1929: 'The Augustan *Vita Aureliani*', *JRS* 19, 125–149.

Flach, D. 1972: 'Von Tacitus zu Ammian', *Historia* 21.1, 333–350.

Fleckeisen, A. 1898: *P. Terenti Afri comoediae*, Leipzig.

Fornara, C.W. 1992a: 'Studies in Ammianus Marcellinus I: The Letter of Libanius and Ammianus' Connection with Antioch', *Historia* 41.3, 328–344.

— 1992b: 'Studies in Ammianus Marcellinus II: Ammianus' Knowledge and Use of Greek and Latin Literature', *Historia* 41.4, 420–438.

Forni, G. and Angeli Bertinelli, M.G. 1982: 'Pompeo Trogo come fonte di storia', *ANRW* 1.30.2, 1298–1361.

Foucher, A. 2000: Historia proxima poetis. *L'influence de la poésie épique sur le style des historiens latins, de Salluste à Ammien Marcellin* (*Collection Latomus* 255), Brussels.

Frakes, R.M. 1995: 'Cross-References to the Lost Books of Ammianus Marcellinus', *Phoenix* 49.3, 232–246.

Frank, R.I. 1969: *Scholae Palatinae: The Palace Guards of the Later Roman Empire*, Rome.

Frankfurter, S. 1933: 'Hermann Dessau', *Jahresbericht über die Fortschritte der klassischen Altertumswissenschaft* 241 (4th Abt.), 80–107.

Fravventura, V. 2020: 'Varianti redazionali nella tradizione manoscritta del "De rerum naturis" di Rabano Mauro: il Gruppo γ', in L. Castaldi, A. Degl'Innocenti, E. Menestò, and F. Santi (eds), *Critica del testo e critica letteraria* (*mediEVI* 28), Florence, 25–58.

Freund, S. 2015: 'Die Hetäre Leaina in Ciceros "De Gloria"', *Rheinisches Museum* 158, 247–259.

Friedrich, A. 2002: *Das Symposium der XII Sapientes. Kommentar und Vergasserfrage*, Berlin and New York.

Frier, B.W. 1979: *Libri Annales Pontificum Maximorum: The Origins of the Annalistic Tradition* (*Papers and Monographs of the American Academy in Rome* 27), Rome.

Fukuyama, Y. 2013: 'The Intervention of Gods in the Punishment of "Bad" Emperors in the *Historia Augusta*', *Journal of Greco-Roman Studies* 52, 141–151.

Funck, J. 1744: *De vegeta Latinae linguae senectute commentarius*, Marburg (Philip Casimir Müller).

Gaertner, J.F. 2018: 'The *Corpus Caesarianum*', in L. Grillo and C.B. Krebs (eds), *The Cambridge Companion to the Writings of Julius Caesar*, Cambridge, 263–276.

Gainsford, P. 2012: 'Diktys of Crete', *Cambridge Classical Journal* 58, 58–87.

Galdi, M. 1922: *L'Epitome nella letteratura latina*, Naples.

Galimberti, A. 2017: 'P. Oxy. 471: Hadrian, Alexandria, and the Antinous Cult', in E. Grijalvo *et al.* (eds), *Empire and Religion: Religious Change in Greek Cities under Roman Rule*, Leiden, 98–111.

Galli Milić, L. and Hecquet-Noti, N. (eds) 2010: *Historiae Augustae Colloquium Genevense in honorem F. Paschoud septuagenarii. Les traditions historiographiques de l'antiquité tardive: idéologie, propagande, fiction, réalité* (*HAC* NS 11), Bari.

Gameson, R. 2019: 'Introduction: Conceiving the Life of Texts', in C. Caruso (ed.), *The Life of Texts: Evidence in Textual Production, Transmission and Reception*, London, 1–27.

Garnsey, P. 1970: *Social Status and Legal Privilege in the Roman Empire*, Oxford.

Gauville, J.-L. 2005: 'Abbreviated Histories: The Case of the *Epitome de Caesaribus* (AD c. 395)', Ph.D. Thesis, McGill.

Giacchero, M. 1974: *Edictum Diocletiani et Collegarum de pretiis rerum venalium*, 2 vols, Genoa.

Giardina, A. 1986: 'Le due Italie nella forma tarda dell'Impero', in A. Giardina (ed.), *Società romana e impero tardoantico I: Istituzioni, ceti economie*, Rome and Bari, 1–36.

Gilliam, J.F. 1980: 'Rostovtzeff's Obituary of Enmann', *BHAC 1977–1978*, 103–113.

Giomini, R. and Celentano, M.S. 1980: *C. Iulii Victoris Ars rhetorica*, Leipzig.

Girotti, B. 2004: '*Cornelia Gallonia Augusta*, seconda mogilie di Valeriano: un contributo epigrafico ad un problema storiografico?', *Epigraphica: Periodico internazionale di epigrafia* 66, 365–367.

— 2015: 'Nicomaco Flaviano, *Historicus disertissimus?*', *Hermes* 143.1, 124–128.

Gitner, A. forthcoming: '*Oribasius Latinus*', in Stover (ed.) forthcoming a.

von Gladiss, D. and Gawlik, A. 1941–1978: *Die Urkunden Heinrichs IV.* (*MGH Diplomata: Die Urkunden der deutschen Könige und Kaiser* 6.1–3), 3 vols, Hannover.

Glinister, F., North, J.A., and Woods, C. 2007: 'Introduction', in F. Glinister and C. Woods (eds), *Verrius, Festus, & Paul: Lexicography, Scholarship, & Society* (*BICS Supplement* 93), London.

Glorie, F. 1965: *Itineraria et Alia Geographica* (*CCSL* 175), Turnhout.

— 1972: *Scriptores 'Illyrici' Minores* (*CCSL* 185), Turnhout.

Goetz, G. 1892: *Hermeneumata Pseudodositheana* (*CGL* 3), Leipzig.

— and Gundermann, G. 1888: *Glossae Latinograecae et Graecolatinae* (*CGL* 2), Leipzig.

Goffart, W. 1988: *The Narrators of Barbarian History (A.D. 550–800): Jordanes, Gregory of Tours, Bede, and Paul the Deacon*, Princeton, NJ.

Goodacre, M.S. and Perrin, N. (eds) 2004: *Questioning Q: A Multidimensional Critique*, Downers Grove, IL.

Goodyear, F.R.D. 1981: *The Annals of Tacitus, Books 1–6. Volume II: Annals 1.55–81 and Annals 2* (*CCTC* 23), Cambridge.

Goold, G.P. 1970: 'Servius and the Helen Episode', *HSCP* 74, 101–168.

Gorman, M. 1997: 'The Oldest Epitome of Augustine's *Tractatus in Euangelium Ioannis* and Commentaries on the Gospel of John in the Early Middle Ages', *Revue des Études Augustiniennes* 43, 63–103.

Görres, F. 1868: *De primis Aureliani principatus temporibus dissertatio historica*, Bonn.

Goud, T.E. 1996: 'The Sources of Josephus *Antiquities* 19', *Historia* 45.4, 472–482.

Goulder, M. 1996: 'Is Q a Juggernaut?', *Journal of Biblical Literature* 115, 667–681.

Goulet, R. 1980: 'Sur la chronologie de la vie et des oeuvres d'Eunape de Sardes', *JHS* 100, 60–72.

— 2014: *Eunape de Sardes. Vies de philosophes et de sophistes*, 2 vols, Paris.

Gowers, E. 1993: *The Loaded Table: Representations of Food in Roman Literature*, Oxford.

Graebner, F. 1905: 'Eine Zosimosquelle', *Byzantinische Zeitschrift* 14.1, 87–159.

Grafton, A. and Williams, M. 2006: *Christianity and the Transformation of the Book: Origen, Eusebius, and the Library of Caesarea*, Cambridge, Mass., and London.

Greatrex, G. 2014: 'Perceptions of Procopius in Recent Scholarship', *Histos* 8, 76–121.

Green, R.P.H. 1981: 'Marius Maximus and Ausonius' *Caesares*', *CQ* 31.1, 226–236.

— 1991: *The Works of Ausonius*, Oxford.

— 1996: *Augustine: De Doctrina Christiana*, Oxford.

— 1999: 'Ausonius' *Fasti* and *Caesares* Revisited', *CQ* 49.2, 573–578.

Green, W.M. 1959: 'A Fourth Century Manuscript of Saint Augustine?', *Revue Bénédictine* 69, 191–197.

Greenwood, D.N. 2014: 'Five Latin Inscriptions from Julian's Pagan Restoration', *BICS* 57.2, 101–119.

— 2021: *Julian and Christianity: Revisiting the Constantinian Revolution*, Ithaca, NY, and London.

Gries, K. 1963: [Review of Echols 1962] *Classical Outlook* 40.5, 55–56.

Groß-Albenhausen, K. and Fuhrmann, M. 2009: *Die römischen Kaiser*, Düsseldorf.

Grundmann, C.H. 2015: 'Theodosius Andreas Harnack (1817–1889)', in M.L. Becker (ed.), *Nineteenth-Century Lutheran Theologians*, Göttingen, 255–274.

Grusková, J. 2013: 'Zur Textgeschichte der Chronik des Eusebios zwischen Okzident und Orient ("*Eusebii Chronici fragmentum Vindobonense*" – ein neues grichisches Handschriftenfragment)', in E. Juhász (ed.), *Byzanz und Abendland: Begegnungen zwischen Ost und West*, Budapest, 43–51.

Gruter, J. 1602: *Inscriptiones antiquae totius orbis Romani, in corpus absolutissimum redacta*, Heidelberg (Ex Officina Commeliniana) (*USTC*: 2039501).

Gryson, R. 1982: *Scripta Arriana Latina. Pars I* (*CCSL* 187), Turnhout.

Gurd, S.A. 2007: 'Cicero and Editorial Revision', *Classical Antiquity* 26.1, 49–80.

— 2014: 'Revision in Greek Literary Papyri', in V. Wohl (ed.), *Probabilities, Hypotheticals, and Counterfactuals in Ancient Greek Thought*, Cambridge, 160–184.

Haake, M. 2016: '"Durch Leiden lernen"? Aurelius Victor, Marc Aurel, Hipparchos und Nikaia – oder: Warum straft ein Kaiser eine Stadt? Überlegungen zu Aur. Vict. 41, 19–20', in H. Schwarzer and H.-Helge Nieswandt (eds), *'Man kann es sich nicht prächtig genug vorstellen!' Festschrift für Dieter Salzmann zum 65. Geburtstag*, 2 vols, Marsberg, 2.719–729.

Håkanson, L. 1978: *Calpurnii Flacci Declamationum excerpta*, Stuttgart.

— 1989: *L. Annaeus Seneca Maior. Oratorum et rhetorum sententiae, divisiones, colores*, Leipzig.

Haklai-Rotenberg, M. 2011: 'Aurelian's Monetary Reform: Between Debasement and Public Trust', *Chiron* 41, 1–39.

Hall, L.J. 2004: *Roman Berytus: Beirut in Late Antiquity*, London and New York.

Halporn, J. 2004: *Cassiodorus: Institutions of Divine and Secular Learning and On the Soul* (*Translated Texts for Historians* 42) (introduction by M. Vessey), Liverpool.

Hankius, M. 1669: *De Romanarum rerum scriptoribus liber*, Leipzig (Christian Michael).

Hanna, R. 1996: *Pursuing History: Middle English Manuscripts and Their Texts*, Stanford, CA.

Hansen, W. 1996: *Phlegon of Tralles' Book of Marvels*, Exeter.

Hanson, R.P.C. 1974: 'The Circumstances Attending the Death of the Emperor Flavius Valerius Severus in 306 or 307', *Hermathena* 119, 59–68.

von Harnack, A. 1873: *Zur Quellenkritik der Geschichte des Gnosticismus*, Leipzig.

— 1907: *Sprüche und Reden Jesu: Die zweite Quelle des Matthäus und Lukas*, Leipzig.

— 1908: *The Sayings of Jesus: The Second Source of St. Matthew and St. Luke* (tr. J.R. Wilkinson), New York and London.

Harries, J. 1978: 'Church and State in the *Notitia Galliarum*', *JRS* 68, 26–43.

Harrison, S.J. 2000: *Apuleius: A Latin Sophist*, Oxford.

Hartke, W. 1932: *De saeculi quarti exeuntis historiarum scriptoribus quaestiones dissertatio inauguralis quam consensu et auctoritate amplissimi philosophorum ordinis in litterarum universitate Friderica Guilelma Berolinensi ad summos in philosophia honores rite impretandos*, Leipzig.

Hartmann, U. 2006: 'Der Mord an Kaiser Gallienus', in K.-P. Johne, T. Gerhardt, and U. Hartmann (eds), *Deleto paene imperio Romano: Transformationsprozesse des Römischen Reiches im 3. Jahrhundert und ihre Rezeption in der Neuzeit*, Stuttgart, 81–124.

Hasebroek, J. 1921: *Untersuchungen zur Geschichte des Kaisers Septimius Severus*, Heidelberg.

Haverfield, F. 1916: 'Tacitus During the Late Roman Period and the Middle Ages', *JRS* 6, 196–201.

Hayashi, T. 2017: 'Sources et signification du *Liber de Caesaribus* d'Aurélius Victor', Ph.D. Thesis, Bourgogne.

Haynes, J. 2015: 'Citations of Ovid in Virgil's Ancient Commentators', in C. Kraus and C. Stray (eds), *Classical Commentaries: Explorations in a Scholarly Genre*, Oxford, 216–232.

Heath, C. 2016: 'Hispania et Italia: Paul the Deacon, Isidore, and the Lombards', in A.T. Fear and J. Wood (eds), *Isidore of Seville and His Reception in the Early Middle Ages: Transmitting and Transforming Knowledge*, Amsterdam, 159–176.

Heather, P. 1993: 'The Historical Culture of Ostrogothic Italy', in *Teoderico il Grande e i Goti d'Italia. Atti del XIII Congresso internazionale di studi sull'Alto Medioevo, Milano, 2–6 novembre 1992*, 2 vols, Spoleto, 1.317–353.

Hebblewhite, M. 2020: *Theodosius and the Limits of Empire*, London and New York.

Heck, E. 1972: *Die dualistischen Zusätze und die Kaiseranreden bei Lactantius*, Heidelberg.

— and Wlosok, A. 1994: *Lactantius: Epitome Divinarum Institutionum*, Stuttgart and Leipzig.

— and — 2005: *Lactantius: Divinarum Institutionum libri septem I: Libri I et II*, Munich and Leipzig.

Hedrick, C.W. 2000: *History and Silence: Purge and Rehabilitation of Memory in Late Antiquity*, Austin, TX.

Heer, J.M. 1904: 'Der historische Wert der Vita Commodi in der Sammlung der scriptores historiae Augustae', *Philologus Supplementband* 9, 1–208.

Helm, R. 1927a: 'Hieronymus und Eutrop', *RhM* NF 76.2, 138–170.

— 1927b: 'Hieronymus und Eutrop', *RhM* NF 76.3, 254–306.

— 1956: *Die Chronik des Hieronymus*² (*Eusebius Werke* 7), Berlin.

den Hengst, D. 1987: '*Verba non res*: Über die inventio in den Reden und Schriftstucken in der Historia Augusta', *BHAC 1984/1985*, 157–174.

— 1994: 'Some Notes on the *Vita Taciti*', in Bonamente and Paschoud (eds), 101–107.

— 2004: '"The Plato of Poets": Vergil in the *Historia Augusta*', in R. Rees (ed.), *Romane memento: Vergil in the Fourth Century*, London, 172–188.

Henriet, P. 1997: 'Hagiographie et politique a León au debut du XIIIe siècle: les chanoines réguliers de Saint-Isidore et la prise de Baeza', *Revue Mabillon* NS 8 (= 69), 53–82.

Henry, M. 1982: 'L'apparition d'une île: Sénèque et Philostrate, un même témoignage', *Ant. Class.* 51, 174–192.

Henry, P. 1935: *Recherches sur la Préparation évangélique d'Eusebe et l'édition perdue des oeuvres de Plotin publiée par Eustochius*, Paris.

— and Schwyzer, H.-R. 1959: *Plotini Opera. Tomus II: Enneades IV–V*, Paris and Brussels.

Heraeus, W. 1899: 'Varia', *RhM* NF 54, 305–311.

Herzog, R. (ed.) 1989: *Restauration und Erneureung: Die lateinische Literatur von 284 bis 374 n. Chr.* (*HLL* 5), Munich.

Heuser, P.H. 2003: *Jean Matal. Humanistischer Jurist und europäischer Friedensdenker (um 1517–1597)*, Cologne.

Hinard, F. 1987: 'Sur une autre forme de l'opposition entre *virtus* et *fortuna*', *Kentron* 3, 17–21.

Hock, R.P. 1982: 'Puns, Aelius Maurus, and the Composition of the *Historia Augusta*', *Transactions of the American Philological Association* 112, 107–113.

Hohl, E. 1911: 'Vopiscus und die Biographie des Kaisers Tacitus', *Klio* 11, 178–229.

— 1934: 'Zur Historia-Augusta-Forschung', *Klio* 27, 149–164.

— 1937: 'Bericht über die Literatur zu den Scriptores Historiae Augustae für die Jahre 1924–1935', *Jahresbericht über die Fortschritte der klassischen Altertumswissenschaft begründet von Conrad Bursian. Zweite Abteilung: Altertumswissenscht und Lateinische Autoren* 63.265, 127–156.

— 1950: 'Das Ende Caracallas, eine quellenkritische Studie', *Miscellanea Academica Berolinensia. Gessamelte Abhandlungen zur Feier des 250jährigen Bestehens der Deutschen Akademie der Wissenschaften zu Berlin*, Berlin, 276–293.

—1955: 'Die Historia Augusta und die Caesares des Aurelius Victor', *Historia* 4.2/3, 220–228.

Holford-Strevens, L. 1995: [Review of Arnaud-Lindet 1993], *Gnomon* 67.7, 600–604.

— 2019: *The* Disputatio Chori et Praetextati. *The Roman Calendar for Beginners*, Turnhout.

Hollerich, M.J. 2021: *Making Christian History: Eusebius of Caesarea and His Readers*, Oakland, CA.

Holtz, L. 1986: 'Quelques aspects de la tradition et de la diffusion des *Institutions*', in S. Leanza (ed.), *Atti della Settimana di studi su Flavio Magno Aurelio Cassiodoro, Cosenza-Squillace 19–24 settembre 1983*, Soveria Manelli, 281–312.

— 2005: 'Prolégomènes à une édition critique du commentaire de Pompée, grammarien africain', in I. Taifacos (ed.), *The Origins of European Scholarship: The Cyprus Millennium International Conference*, Stuttgart, 109–119.

Holtzmann, H.J. 1863: *Die synoptischen Evangelien: ihr Ursprung und geschichtlicher Charakter*, Leipzig.

Homo, L. 1919: 'La grande crise de l'an 238 ap. J. C. et le problème de l'Histoire Auguste', *Revue Historique* 131.2, 209–264 and 132.1, 1–38.

—1926: 'Les documents de l'Histoire Auguste et leur valeur historique', *Revue Historique* 151.2, 161–198 and 152.1, 1–31.

Hönn, K. 1911: *Quellenuntersuchungen zu den Viten des Heliogabalus und des Severus Alexander im Corpus der Scriptores Historiae Augustae*, Leipzig and Berlin.

Hopkins, K. 1983: *Death and Renewal*, Cambridge.

Hornung, S. 2011: *Luxus auf dem Lande: Die Romische Palastvilla von Bad Kreuznach*, Bad Kreuznach.

Horsfall, N. 1993: 'Trasmissione del Latino a Constantinopoli: ritorni dei testi in patria', *Messana. Rassegna di studi filologici linguistici e storici* NS 16, 75–94.

— 2008–2009: 'Dictys's *Ephemeris* and the Parody of Scholarship', *Illinois Classical Studies* 33–34, 41–63.

Horster, M. and Reitz, C. (eds) 2010a: *Condensing texts – Condensed Texts*, Stuttgart.

— and — 2010b: '"Condensation" of Literature and the Pragmatics of Literary Production', in Horster and Reitz (eds), 3–14.

Horsting, A.G.A. 2016: *Prosper Aquitanus: Liber epigrammatum* (*CSEL* 100), Berlin.

Housman, A.E. 1902: 'Remarks on the Culex', *CR* 16.7, 339–346.

Huemer, I. 1885: *Sedulii Opera Omnia* (*CSEL* 10), Vienna.

Hunt, D. 1999: 'The Outsider Inside: Ammianus on the Rebellion of Silvanus', in Drijvers and Hunt (eds), 46–56.

Hunt, R.W. 1975: *The Survival of Ancient Literature*, Oxford.

Hunt, T.J. 1998: *A Textual History of Cicero's* Academici Libri, Leiden, Boston, Cologne.

Huysmans, J.-K. 1884: *À rebours*, Paris.

Hwang, A.Y. 2009: *Intrepid Lover of Perfect Grace: The Life and Thought of Prosper of Aquitaine*, Washington, DC.

Iasiello, I.M. 2007: *Samnium: assetti e trasformazioni di una provincia tardoantica*, Bari.

Ihm, M. 1894: 'Zu Valerius Maximus und Ianuarius Nepotianus', *RhM* NF 49, 247–255.

Innes, M. 1997: 'The Classical Tradition in the Carolingian Renaissance: Ninth-Century Encounters with Suetonius', *International Journal of the Classical Tradition* 3.3, 265–282.

Jakobi, Richard, 1874: *De Rufi Festi breviarii fontibus*, Bonn.

Jakobi, Rainer, forthcoming: *Die Valerius Maximus-Epitome des Ianuarius Nepotianus*, Berlin and New York.

Janiszewski, P. 2006: *The Missing Link: Greek Pagan Historiography in the Second Half of the Third Century and in the Fourth Century AD*, Warsaw.

Jardé, A. 1925: *Études critiques sur la vie et le règne de Sévère Alexandre*, Paris.

Jędrzejczak, D. 2009: 'Sulpicia as a Woman-Singer', *Latomus* 68, 693–695.

Jeep, L. 1873: 'Aurelii Victoris de Caesaribus historiae e l'epitome de Caesaribus', *Rivista di filologia e di istruzione classica* 1, 505–518.

Johnson, M.J. 2009: *The Roman Imperial Mausoleum in Late Antiquity*, Cambridge.

Jones, A.H.M. 1964: *The Later Roman Empire, 284–602: A Social, Economic, and Administrative Survey*, 3 vols, Oxford.

— 1969: [Review of Syme 1968a], *Journal of Theological Studies* NS 20.1, 320–321.

de Jonge, P. 1972: *Philological and Historical Commentary on Ammianus Marcellinus XVI*, Groningen.

Joseph, T.A. 2012: *Tacitus and the Epic Successor. Virgil, Lucan, and the Narrative of Civil War in the Histories* (*Mnemosyne Supplements* 345), Leiden and Boston.

Kagan, K. 2006: *The Eye of Command*, Ann Arbor, MI.

Kajanto, I. 1965: *The Latin Cognomina* (*Commentationes Humanarum Litterarum* 36.2), Helsinki.

Kaldellis, A. 2017: 'How Perilous Was it to Write Political History in Late Antiquity?', *Studies in Late Antiquity* 1.1, 38–64.

Kaminsky, H.H. 1974: 'Zum Sinngehalt des Princeps-Titles Arichis' II. Von Benevent', *Frühmittelalterliche Studien* 8, 81–92.

Karst, J. 1911: *Die Chronik aus dem armenischen Übersetz mit textkritischem Commentar* (*Eusebius Werke* 5), Leipzig.

Kaster, R.A. 1988: *Guardians of the Language: The Grammarian and Society in Late Antiquity*, Berkeley.

— 2002: 'The Taxonomy of Patience, or When Is *Patientia* Not a Virtue?', *CP* 97.2, 133–144.

— 2011: *Macrobii Ambrosii Theodosii Saturnalia*, Oxford.

Keegan, J. 1976: *The Face of Battle*, London.

Keeline, T. 2013: 'Did (Servius') Virgil Nod?', *Vergilius* 59, 61–80.

— 2022: 'The Literary Artistry of Terentianus Maurus', *JRS* 112, 143–172.

Keenan, J.G. 1973: 'The Names Flavius and Aurelius as Status Designations in Later Roman Egypt', *ZPE* 11, 33–63.

— 1974: 'The Names Flavius and Aurelius as Status Designations in Later Roman Egypt (II)', *ZPE* 13, 283–304.

Keil, H. 1857–1880: *Grammatici Latini*, 8 vols, Leipzig.

Kelly, G. 2004: 'Ammianus and the Great Tsunami', *JRS* 94, 141–167.

— 2007: 'The sphragis and closure of the *Res gestae*', in J. den Boeft, D. den Hengst, H.C. Teitler, and J.W. Drijvers (eds), *Ammianus after Julian: The Reign of Valentinian and Valens in Books 26–31 of the Res Gestae*, Leiden, 219–241.

— 2008: *Ammianus Marcellinus: The Allusive Historian*, Cambridge.

— 2009: 'Ammianus Marcellinus: Tacitus' Heir and Gibbon's Guide', in A. Feldherr (ed.), *The Cambridge Companion to the Roman Historians*, Cambridge, 348–361.

— 2010: 'The Roman World of Festus' *Breviarium*', in C. Kelly, R. Flower, and M.S. Williams (eds), *Unclassical Traditions. Volume I: Alternatives to the Classical Past in Late Antiquity*, Cambridge, 72–91.

— 2011: [Review of Cameron 2011], *CR* 65.1, 230–233.

— 2013: 'Ammianus' Greek Accent', *Talanta* 45, 67–79.

— 2015: 'Ammianus Marcellinus and Funny Names' (http://ausonius.blogspot.com/2015/03/ammianus-marcellinus-and-funny-names.html).

— 2022: 'Why We Need a New Edition of Ammianus Marcellinus', in M. Hanaghan and D. Woods (eds), *Ammianus Marcellinus: From Soldier to Author*, Leiden, 19–58.

— and Stover, J.A. 2016: 'The Hersfeldensis and the Fuldensis of Ammianus Marcellinus: A Reconsideration', *Cambridge Classical Journal* 62, 108–129.

Kelly, J.N.D. 1975: *Jerome: His Life, Writings, and Controversies*, London.

Kemezis, A. 2012: 'Commemoration of the Antonine Aristocracy in Cassius Dio and the *Historia Augusta*', *CQ* 62.1, 387–414.

Kestemont, M., Stover, J.A.S., Koppel, M., Karsdorp, F., and Daelemans, W. 2016: 'Authenticating the Writings of Julius Caesar', *Expert Systems with Applications* 63, 86–96.

Kienast, D. 2004: *Römische Kaisertabelle: Grundzüge einer römischen Kaiserchronologie*, Darmstadt.

Kim, L.Y. 2010: *Homer between History and Fiction in Imperial Greek Literature*, Cambridge.

Klebs, E. 1889: 'Das Valesische Bruchstück zur Geschichte Constantins', *Philologus* 47, 53–80.

— 1890: 'Entlehnungen aus Velleius', *Philologus* 49 (NS 3), 285–312.

Knoell, P. 1885: *Eugipii Excerpta ex operibus S. Augustini* (*CSEL* 9), Vienna.

Koch, H. 1895: 'Proklus als Quelle des Pseudo-Dionysius Areopagita in der Lehre vom Bösen', *Philologus* 54, 438–454.

Koeheler, F. and Milchsack, G. 1913: *Die Handschriften der Herzoglichen Bibliothek zu Wolfenbüttel. Abth. 4: Die Gudischen Handschriften*, Wolfenbüttel.

Kolb, F. 1972: *Literarische Beziehungen zwischen Cassius Dio, Herodian und der Historia Augusta*, Bonn.

König, I. 1987: *Origo Constantini. Anonymus Valesianus. Teil 1: Text un Kommentar*, Trier.

Kornemann, E. 1905: *Kaiser Hadrian und der letzte grosse Historiker von Rom*, Leipzig.

Kulikowski, M. 2007: 'Marius Maximus in Ammianus and the *Historia Augusta*', *CQ* 57.1, 244–256.

— 2018: 'Classicizing History and Historical Epitomes', in S. McGill and E.J. Watts (eds), *A Companion to Late Antique Literature*, Hoboken, NJ, 143–159.

Kunkel, W. 1967: *Herkunft und soziale Stellung der römischen Juristen*, Graz, Vienna, and Cologne.

Kwakkel, E. 2012: 'Biting, Kissing and the Treatment of Feet: The Transitional Script of the Long Twelfth Century', in E. Kwakkel, R. McKitterick, and R. Thomson (eds), *Turning Over a New Leaf: Change and Development in the Medieval Manuscript*, Leiden, 79–125.

La Penna, A. 2004–2005: 'I *flosculi* sallustiani di Aurelio Vittore', *Acta Classica Universitas Scientiarum Debrecensis* 40–41, 377–384.

— and Funari, R. 2015: *C. Sallusti Crispi Historiae I: Fragmenta 1.1–146*, Berlin and Boston.

La Rocca, C. 2004: 'A Man For All Seasons: Pacificus of Verona and the Creation of a Local Carolingian Past', in Y. Hen and M. Innes (eds), *Using the Past in the Early Middle Ages*, Cambridge, 250–279.

Laistner, M.L.W. 1927: 'A Ninth-Century Commentator on the Gospel According to Matthew', *Harvard Theological Review* 20.2, 129–149.

Lambrechts, P. 1934: 'L'empereur Lucius Verus. Essai de réhabilitation', *Ant. Class.* 3.1, 173–201.

Lanciani, R. 1892: 'Le mura di Aureliano e Probo', *Bulletino della Commissione Archeologia Comunale di Roma* 4th S. 20.2, 87–111.

Lanciotti, S. 2000: 'Tra Festo e Paolo', in Chiesa (ed.), 237–250.

Langenfeld, K. 2017: 'Forging a History: The Inventions and Intellectual Community of the *Historia Augusta*', Ph.D. Thesis, Duke University.

Lankila, T. 2011: 'The Corpus Areopagiticum as a Crypto-Pagan Project', *Journal for Late Antique Religion and Culture* 5, 1–40.

Lapidge, M. 2013: 'Hilduin of Saint-Denis and the *Conscriptio Visbii*', in J. Elfassi, C. Lanéry, and A.-M. Turcan-Verkerk (eds), *Amicorum societas. Mélanges offerts à François Dolbeau pour son 65e anniversaire*, Florence, 409–416.

—— 2018: *The Roman Martyrs: Introduction, Translation, and Commentary*, Oxford.

Leaning, J.B. 1989: 'Didius Julianus and His Biographer', *Latomus* 48.3, 548–565.

Lécrivain, C.A. 1904: *Études sur l'Histoire Auguste*, Paris.

Lendinara, P. 2000: 'Gli *Scholia Vallicelliana* e i primi glossary anglosassoni', in Chiesa (ed.), 251–278.

Levillain, L. 1964: *Loup de Ferrières: Correspondance*, 2 vols, Paris.

Liebeschuetz, J.H.W.G. 2003: 'Pagan Historiography and the Decline of the Empire', in Marasco (ed.), 177–218.

Lindsay, W.M. 1903: *The Ancient Editions of Martial, with Collations of the Berlin and Edinburgh MSS*, Oxford.

—— 1904: *The Ancient Editions of Plautus*, Oxford.

—— 1913: *Sexti Pompei Festi de verborum significatu quae supersunt cum Pauli epitome, Thewrewkianis copiis usus*, Leipzig.

—— 1916: 'New Evidence for the Text of Festus', *CQ* 10.2, 106–115.

Lippold, A. 1991: *Kommentar zur Vita Maximini Duo der Historia Augusta*, Bonn.

Lloyd, R.B. 1961: 'Republican Authors in Servius and the Scholia Danielis', *HSCP* 65, 291–341.

Loew, E.A. 1980: *The Beneventan Script: A History of the South Italian Minuscule. Second Edition prepared and enlarged by Virginia Brown*, 2 vols, Rome.

Long, J. 1996: *Claudian's In Eutropium, Or, How, When, and Why to Slander a Eunuch*, Chapel Hill, NC.

Lőrincz, B. 2000: *Onomasticon provinciarum Europae Latinarum (OPEL), Vol. 3: Labareus-Pythea*, Vienna.

—— 2002: *Onomasticon provinciarum Europae Latinarum (OPEL), Vol. 4: Quadratia-Zures*, Vienna.

—— 2005: *Onomasticon provinciarum Europae Latinarum (OPEL), Vol. 1: Aba-Bysanus. Editio nova aucta et emendata*, Vienna.

Loriot, X. 1974: 'Les *Fasti Ostienses* et le *dies imperii* de Gordien III', *Mélanges d'histoire ancienne offerts à William Seston*, Paris, 297–312.

Loriot, X. 1975: 'Les premières années de la grande crise du IIIe siècle. De l'avènement de Maximin le Thrace (235) à la mort de Gordien III (244)', *ANRW* 2.2, 657–787.

Luce, T.J. 1977: *Livy: The Composition of His History*, Princeton, NJ.

Maas, M. 1992: *John Lydus and the Roman Past: Antiquarianism and Politics in the Age of Justinian*, London and New York.

MacCormack, S. 1976: 'Latin Prose Panegyrics: Tradition and Discontinuity in the Later Roman Empire', *Revue d'études augustiniennes et patristiques* 22, 29–77.

MacCoull, L.S.B. 1999: 'Who Was Eusebius of Alexandria?', *Byzantinoslavica: Revue Internationale des Études Byzantines* 60.1, 9–18.

McDermott, W.C. 1977: 'Plotina Augusta and Nicomachus of Gerasa', *Historia* 26.2, 192–203.

Macedo, G.N. 2016: 'Il *fragmentum Antinoense* e la fortuna di Giovenale nel mondo grecofono', in A. Stramaglia, S. Grazzini, and G. Dimatteo (eds), *Giovenale tra storia, poesia e ideologia*, Berlin, Munich, and Boston, 213–230.

McKitterick, R. 1999: 'Paul the Deacon and the Franks', *Early Medieval Europe* 8.3, 319–339.

MacLachlan, R. 2004: 'Epitomes in Ancient Literary Culture', Ph.D. Thesis, University of Cambridge.

MacMullen, R. 1962: 'Roman Bureaucratese', *Traditio* 18, 364–378.

—— 1982: 'The Epigraphic Habit in the Roman Empire', *American Journal of Philology* 103.3, 233–246.

Maehly, J. 1855: 'Zur Kritik der Caesares des Aurelius Victor', *Jahrbücher für classische Philologie* 1, 264–268.

Maenchen-Helfen, O.J. 1955: 'The Date of Ammianus Marcellinus' Last Books', *American Journal of Philology* 76.4, 384–399.

Magie, D. 1921–1932: *Historia Augusta* (*Loeb Classical Library* 139, 140, 263), 3 vols, London and Cambridge, Mass.

Makhlaiuk, A. 2020: 'Emperors' Nicknames and Roman Political Humour', *Klio* 102, 202–235.

Malcovati, E. 1943–1944: 'Le traduzioni greche di Eutropio', *Rendiconti dell'Istituto Lombardo di Scienze e Lettere. Classe di lettere* 77.8 (series 3), 273–297.

Malherbe, A.J. 1977: *The Cynic Epistles: A Study Edition*, Missoula, MT.

Mallan, C. 2013: 'The Style, Method, and Programme of Xiphilinus' *Epitome* of Cassius Dio's *Roman History*', *GRBS* 53, 610–644.

—— 2017: 'The Book Indices in the Manuscripts of Cassius Dio', *CQ* 66.2, 705–723.

Malloch, S.J.V. 2013: *The Annales of Tacitus, Book 11* (*CCTC* 51), Cambridge.

—— 2022: 'The Return of the King? Tacitus on the Principate of Augustus', *Hermes* 150.1, 82–100.

Manitius, M. 1892: *Philologisches aus alten Bibliothekskatalogen (bis 1300)* (*RhM* NF 47, *Ergänzungsheft*), Frankfurt.

—— 1935: *Handschriften antiker Autoren in mittelalterlichen Bibliothekskatalogen* (*Zentralblatt für Bibliothekswesen* 67), Leipzig.

Marasco, G. 1996: 'Giulia Domna, Caracalla e Geta. Frammenti di tragedia alla corte dei Severi', *Ant. Class.* 65, 119–134.

— (ed.) 2003: *Greek and Roman Historiography in Late Antiquity, Fourth to Sixth Century A.D.*, Leiden.

Marenbon, J. 2003: *Boethius*, Oxford.

Marié, M.-A. 1989: 'Virtus et Fortuna chez Ammien Marcellin', *REL* 67, 179–90.

Marincola, J. 1997: *Authority and Tradition in Ancient Historiography*, Cambridge.

Mariotti, S. 1961: 'Il *Codex Metelli* nella tradizione dell'*Origo gentis Romanae*', *Studi Classici e Orientali* 10, 102–111.

Marolla, G. 2021: 'Sidonio Apollinare e il concetto di satira nella tarda antichità', *Invigilata Lucernis* 43, 129–144.

Marshall, P.K. 1977: *The Manuscript Tradition of Cornelius Nepos* (*BICS* Supplement 37), London.

Martin, F. 1866: *De Fontibus Zosimi*, Berlin.

Martin, G. 2006: *Dexipp von Athen. Edition, Übersetzung und begleitende Studien*, Tübingen.

Martin, P.M. 2016: *Les Hommes Illustres de la Ville de Rome*, Paris.

Martín-Iglesias, J.C. 2016: *Scripta Medii Aevi de vita Isidori Hispalensis episcopi* (*CCCM* 281), Turnhout.

Martini, P.S. 1983: 'La produzione libraria negli *scriptoria* delle abbazie di Farfa e di S. Eutizio', *Atti del 9° congresso internazionale di studi sull'alto medioevo. Spoleto, 27 settembre-2 ottobre 1982*, 2 vols, Spoleto, 2.581–607.

Mason, D.J.P. 1988: '*Prata Legionis* in Britain', *JRS* 19, 163–189.

Mason, H.J. 1974: *Greek Terms for Roman Institutions: A Lexicon and Analysis*, Toronto.

Matthews, J.F. 1970: 'Olympiodorus of Thebes and the History of the West (A.D. 407–425), *JRS* 60, 79–97.

— 1975: *Western Aristocracies and Imperial Court A.D. 364–425*, Oxford.

— 1989: *The Roman Empire of Ammianus*, London.

— 2000: *Laying Down the Law: A Study of the Theodosian Code*, New Haven, CT.

Maurenbrecher, B. 1891–1893: *C. Sallusti Crispi Historiarum reliquiae*, 2 fascicles, Leipzig.

Meckler, M. 1996: 'The Beginning of the *Historia Augusta*', *Historia* 45.3, 364–375.

Mendelssohn, L. 1879–1881: *Appiani Historia Romana*, Leipzig.

— 1883: *Herodiani ab excessu divi Marci libri octo*, Leipzig.

— 1887: *Zosimi comitis et exadvocati fisci Historia nova*, Leipzig.

— and Wendland, P. 1900: *Aristea ad Philocratem epistula cum ceteris de origine versionis LXX interpretum testimoniis*, Leipzig.

Menghini, E. 1904: 'Dello stato presente degli studi intorno all vita di Paolo Diacono', *Bolletino della societa pavese di storia patria* 4, 15–100, 231–285, 314–366.

Mercogliano, F. 1997: *«Tituli ex corpore Ulpiani»: storia di un testo*, Naples.

Merkle, S. 1989: *Die Ephemeris belli Troiani des Diktys von Kreta*, Frankfurt.

— 1999: 'News from the Past: Dictys and Dares on the Trojan War', in H. Hofmann (ed.), *Latin Fiction: The Latin Novel in Context*, London and New York, 131–140.

Metzger, E. 2000: 'The Current View of the Extra-Judicial *vadimonium*', *ZSS* 117, 133–178.

Mewaldt, J. 1907: 'Selbstcitate in den Biographieen Plutarchs', *Hermes* 42.4, 564–578.

Meyer, P.M. 1932: 'In Memoriam [H. Dessau]', *ZSS* 52, 560.

Michael, B. 1990: *Die mittelalterlichen Handschriften der Wissenschaftlichen Stadtbibliothek Soest*, Wiesbaden.

Miglio, M. 1972: 'Bussi, Giovanni Andrea', *Dizionari Biografico degli Italiani*, Rome, 15, 565–572.

Migliorati, G. 2016: 'La morte di Gallieno e il suo contest politico (268 D.C.)', *Aevum* 90.1, 239–255.

Milani, C. 2009: 'Sardinia in testi latini medievali', *Il Nome nel testo. Rivista internazionale di onomastica letteraria* 11, 67–72.

Millar, F. 1964: *A Study of Cassius Dio*, Oxford.

— 1969: 'P. Herennius Dexippus: The Greek World and the Third-Century Invasions', *JRS* 59, 12–29.

Mitthoff, F., Martin, G., and Grusková, J. (eds) 2020: *Empire in Crisis: Gothic Invasions and Roman Historiography. Beiträge einer internationalen Tagung zu den Wiener Dexipp-Fragmenten (Dexippus Vindobonensis), Wien, 3–6 Mai 2017* (*Tyche* Supplementband 12), Vienna.

Mohler, L. 1923: *Kardinal Bessarion als Theologe, Humanist und Staatsmann. Funde und Forschungen. I. Band: Darstellung*, Paderborn.

Molinier, A. 1998: 'Marius Maximus Source Latine de la Vie de Commode?', in Bonamente, Heim, and Callu (eds), 223–248.

Molinier Arbo, A. 2009: 'Dion Cassius *versus* Marius Maximus? Éléments de Polémique entre les *Romaika* et l'*Histoire Auguste*', *Phoenix* 63.3/4, 278–295.

— 2010: 'Les documents d'archives dans la *Vita Commodi*: degré zéro de l'histoire ou fiction', in M.-R. Guelfucci (ed.), *Jeux et enjeux de la mise en forme de l'histoire. Recherches sur le genre historique en Grèce et à Rome* (*Dialogues d'histoire ancienne, Supplement* 4.1), Besançon, 87–112.

— 2021: 'L'histoire peut-elle se répéter? Le devenir de Rome selon l'auteur de l'*Histoire Auguste*', in S.C. Zinsli and G. Martin (eds), *Historiae Augustae Colloquium Turicense* (*HAC* NS 14), 117–134.

Mollea, S. 2018: 'In Maehly's Footsteps: *iterum* better than *etiam* in Aurelius Victor, *Liber de Caesaribus* 1.1?', *Mnemosyne* 71, 709–713.

Mombritius, B. 1477/1478: [*Sanctuarium*], 2 vols, Milan (*ISTC*: im00810000).

Momigliano, A. 1946: 'Friedrich Creuzer and Greek Historiography', *Journal of the Warburg and Courtauld Institutes* 9, 152–163.

— 1954: 'An Unsolved Problem of Historical Forgery: The *Scriptores Historiae Augustae*', *Journal of the Warburg and Courtald Institutes* 17, 22–46.

— 1958a: 'Some Observations on the "Origo Gentis Romanae"', *JRS* 48, 56–73.

— 1958b: 'Per una nuova edizione della «Origo gentis Romanae»', *Athenaeum* 36, 248–259.

— 1969: [Review of Syme 1968a], *English Historical Review* 84.332, 566–569.

— 1973: [Review of Syme 1971a], *English Historical Review* 88.346, 114–115.

— 1974: 'The Lonely Historian Ammianus Marcellinus', *Annali della Scuola Normale Superiore di Pisa* 3.4, 1393–1407.

— 1984: [Review of Syme 1983 and 1979–1991 vol. iii], *Times Literary Supplement* 12 October 1984, 1147–1148, repr. in Momigliano 1987, 392–398.

— 1987: *Ottavo contributo alla storia degli studi classici e del mondo antico*, Rome.

Mommsen, Th. 1850: *Über den Chronographien vom Jahre 354 mit einem Anhange über die Quellen der Chronik des Hieronymus*, Leipzig.

— 1866: 'Eutropius Breviarium ab urbe condita', *Hermes* 1, 468.

— 1877: 'Zu der Origo Gentis Romanae', *Hermes* 12.4, 401–408.

— 1881: 'Ammians Geographica', *Hermes* 16.4, 602–636.

— 1882: *Iordanis Romana et Getica* (*MGH AA* 5.1), Berlin.

— 1890: 'Die Scriptores Historiae Augustae', *Hermes* 25.2, 228–292.

— 1892: *Chronica Minora saec. IV, V, VI, VII volumen I* (*MGH AA* 9), Berlin.

— 1894: *Chronica Minora saec. IV, V, VI, VII volumen II* (*MGH AA* 11), Berlin).

Monfasani, J. 2011: 'Niccolò Perotti and Bessarion's *In Calumniatorem Platonis*', in M. Pade and C. Plesner Horster (eds), *Niccolò Perotti: The Languages of Humanism and Politics* (*Renæssanceforum* 7), 181–216.

Moore, J.M. 1965: *The Manuscript Tradition of Polybius*, Cambridge.

Moreau, J. 1968: *Excerpta Valesiana*, Leipzig.

Morgan, J.R. 1999: [Review of Hansen 1996], *Histos* 2, 302–307.

Morin, G. 1906: 'Notes sur Victorin de Pettau', *Journal of Theological Studies* 7.27, 456–459.

Mortensen, L.B. 2000: 'Impero Romano, *Historia Romana* e *Historia Langobardorum*', in Chiesa (ed.), 355–366.

Moscadi, A. 2001: *Il Festo Farnesiano (Cod. Neapol. IV. A. 3)*, Florence.

Mosig-Walburg, K. 2005: 'Hanniballianus rex', *Millennium: Jahrbuch zu Kultur und Geschichte des ersten Jahrtausends n. Chr.* 2, 229–254.

Mosshammer, A. 1979: *The Chronicle of Eusebius and the Greek Chronographic Tradition*, Lewisburg, PA.

Muhlberger, S. 1986: 'Prosper's *Epitoma Chronicon*: Was there an Edition of 443?', *CP* 81.2, 240–244.

— 1990: *The Fifth-Century Chroniclers: Prosper, Hydatius, and the Gallic Chronicler of 452*, Leeds.

— 1996: [Review of Bird 1994], *Medieval Review* 96.11.17 (https://scholarworks.iu.edu/journals/index.php/tmr/article/view/14437).

Mülke, M. 2010: 'Die Epitome – das bessere Original?', in Horster and Reitz (eds), 69–90.

Müller, F.L. 1998–1999: 'Ein unbemerktes Herodot-Zitat, Bildung und Karriere bei S. Aurelius Victor', *Acta Classica Universitas Scientiarum Debreceniensis* 34–35, 407–428.

Murgia, C.E. 2003: 'The Dating of Servius Revisited', *CP* 98, 45–69.

Murphy, F.X. 1945: *Rufinus of Aquileia (345–411): His Life and Works*, Washington, DC.

Mynors, R.A.B. 1937: *Cassiodori Senatoris Institutiones*, Oxford.

— 1964: *XII Panegyrici Latini*, Oxford.

Neff, K. 1908: *Die Gedichte des Paulus Diaconus: kritische und erklärende Ausgabe*, Munich.

Nelson, J. 1998: 'Making a Difference in Eighth-Century Politics: The Daughters of Desiderius', in A.C. Murray (ed.), *After Rome's Fall: Narrators and Sources of Early Medieval History. Essays Presented to Walter Goffart*, Toronto, 171–190.

Németh, A. 2018: *The Excerpta Constantiniana and the Byzantine Appropriation of the Past*, Cambridge.

Neri, V. 1992: *Medius princeps. Storia e immagine di Costantino nella storiografia latina pagana*, Bologna.

Nesselhauf, H. 1964: 'Patrimonium und Res Privata des Römischen Kaisers', *Historia-Augusta-Colloquium Bonn 1963*, 73–93.

— 1966: 'Die Vita Commodi und die Acta Urbis', *BHAC 1964/1965*, 127–138.

Netz, R. 2020: *Scale, Space and Canon in Ancient Literary Culture*, Cambridge.

Neumann, K.-G. 1987: 'Taciteisches im Werk des Ammianus Marcellinus', Ph.D. Thesis, Ludwig-Maximilians-Universität.

Nicholson, O. (ed.) 2018: *The Oxford Dictionary of Late Antiquity*, 2 vols, Oxford.

Nickbahkt, M.A. and Scardino, C. 2021: *Aurelius Victor: Historiae Abbreviatae*, Paderborn.

Nixon, C.E.V. 1971: 'An Historiographical Study of the Caesares of Sextus Aurelius Victor', Ph.D. Thesis, University of Michigan.

— 1985: [Review of Bird 1984], *Phoenix* 39.4, 410–413.

— 1991: 'Aurelius Victor and Julian', *CP* 86.2, 113–125.

Nowak, K. 1996: *Adolf von Harnack als Zeitgenosse. Reden und Schriften aus den Jahren des Kaiserreichs und der Weimarer Republik*, 2 vols, Berlin.

— and Oexle, O.G. (eds) 2001: *Adolf von Harnack: Theologe, Historiker, Wissenschaftspolitiker*, Göttingen.

O'Brien, P. 2006: 'Ammianus Epicus: Virgilian Allusion in the *Res gestae*', *Phoenix* 60.3/4, 274–303.

O'Donnell, J.J. 1979: *Cassiodorus*, Berkeley.

Oakley, S.P. 2020: 'Point and Periodicity: The Style of Velleius Paterculus and Other Latin Historians Writing in the Early Principate', in M.C. Scappaticcio (ed.), *Seneca the Elder and His Rediscovered* Historiae ab initio bellorum civilium*: New Perspectives on Early-Imperial Roman Historiography*, Berlin and Boston, 199–234.

Omissi, A. 2018: *Emperors and Usurpers in the Later Roman Empire: Civil War, Panegyric, and the Construction of Legitimacy*, Oxford.

Omont, H. 1894: *Inventaire des Manuscrit Grecs & Latins donnés a Saint-Marc de Venise par le Cardinal Bessarion en 1468*, Paris.

Opelt, I. 1962: 'Epitome', *Reallexikon für Antike und Christentum: Sachwörterbuch zur Auseinandersetzung des Christentums mit der antiken Welt* 5, 944–973.

Opitz, Th. 1872: *Quaestiones de Aurelio Victore*, Leipzig.

— 1874: 'Quaestiones de Aurelio Victore', *Acta Societatis Philologae Lipsiensis* 2, 198–279.

Ottaviano, S. 2013: '*Scholia non Serviana* nei manoscritti carolingi di Virgilio: prime notizie degli scavi', *Exemplaria Classica* 17, 221–244.

Pade, M. and Ramminger, J. 1994: *Nicolai Perotti Cornu Copiae seu linguae Latinae commentarii* IV, Sassoferrato.

Paniagua, D. 2018: *Polemii Silvii Laterculus*, Rome.

Panofsky, E. 1967: 'Hercules Agricola: A Further Complication in the Problem of the Illustrated Hrabanus Manuscripts', in D. Fraser and H. Hibbard (eds), *Essays Presented to Rudolf Wittkower on His Sixty-Fifth Birthday*, 2 vols London, 2.20–28.

Paraschiv, M. and Zugravu, N. 2012: *Pseudo-Aurelius Victor: Epitome de Caesaribus. Epitomă despre împăraţi*, Iaşi.

Pascal, C. 1906: 'Un'opera "De terminatione provinciarum Italiae" del secolo VII d.C.', *Archivio Storico Italiano*, serie V, 37, 301–321.

— 1907: 'Sull'opera *De terminatione Provinciarum Italiae*', *Archivio Storico Italiano*, serie V, 39, 101–105.

Paschoud, F. 1975: *Cinq études sur Zosime*, Paris.

— 1983: '*Frumentarii, Agentes in Rebus, Magistriani, Curiosi, Veredarii*: Problèmes de Terminologie', *BHAC 1979/1981*, 215–243.

— 1991: 'L'*Histoire Auguste* et Dexippe', in G. Bonamente and N. Duval (eds), *Historiae Augustae Colloquium Parisinum* (*HAC* NS 1), Macerata, 217–269.

— 1994: 'Nicomaque Flavien et la connexion Byzantine (Pierre le Patrice et Zonaras): A propos du livre récent de Bruno Bleckmann', *Antiquité Tardive* 2, 71–82.

— 1996: *Histoire Auguste. Tome V, 1re partie: Vies d'Aurélien et de Tacite*, Paris.

— 1998a: 'Quelques problèmes actuels relatifs à l'historiographie de l'antiquité tardive', *Symbolae Osloenses* 73, 74–87.

— 1998b: 'Aurélius Victor, Eutrope ou "Kaisergeschichte" d'Enmann?', in Bonamente, Heim, and Callu (eds), 269–270.

— (ed.) 1999a: *Historiae Augustae Colloquium Genevense* (*HAC* NS 7), Bari.

— 1999b: 'Propos sceptiques et iconoclastes sur Marius Maximus', in *idem* (ed.), 241–254.

— 2000: *Zosime. Histoire Nouvelle. Tome I: Livres I et II*, Paris.

— 2001: *Histoire Auguste. Tome V, 2ᵉ partie: Vies de Probus, Firmus, Saturnin, Proculus et Bonose, Carus, Numérien et Carin*, Paris.

— 2002: [Review of Baldini 2000], *Antiquité Tardive* 10, 487–489.

— 2006a: *Eunape, Olympiodore, Zosime: Scripta minora*, Bari.

— 2006b: 'Chronique d'Historiographie Tardive', *Antiquité Tardive* 14, 325–344.

— 2007: 'Chronique d'Historiographie Tardive', *Antiquité Tardive* 15, 349–364.

— 2009: 'Les enfants de Suétone', in R. Poignault (ed.), *Présence de Suétone: actes du colloque tenu à Clermont-Ferrand, 25–27 novembre 2003: à Michel Dubuisson in memoriam*, Tours, 175–185.

— 2010: 'Chronique d'Historiographie Tardive', *Antiquité Tardive* 18, 309–320.

— 2018: *Histoire Auguste. Tome IV, 1ʳᵉ partie: Vies des deux Maximins, des trois Gordiens, de Maxime et Balbin*, Paris.

Pasquali, G. 1952: *Storia della tradizione e critica del testo*, Florence.

Peachin, M. 1988: 'Gallienus Caesar (?)', *ZPE* 74, 219–224.

— 1989: 'Once More A.D. 238', *Athenaeum* 67, 594–604.

— 1990: *Roman Imperial Titulature and Chronology, A.D. 235–284*, Amsterdam.

— 1996: *Iudex Vice Caesaris: Deputy Emperors and the Administration of Justice during the Principate*, Stuttgart.

Pékary, T. 1993: 'Kaiser Mark Aurel, die Stadt Nikaia und der Astronom Hipparchos', *Epigraphica Anatolica. Zeitschrift für Epigraphik und historische Geographie Anatoliens* 21, 121–123.

Pelling, C. 2010: 'The Spur of Fame: *Annals* 4.37–8', in C.S. Kraus, J. Marincola, and C. Pelling (eds), *Ancient Historiography and Its Contexts: Studies in Honour of A.J. Woodman*, Oxford.

Penella, R.J. 1980a: 'Caracalla and His Mother in the *Historia Augusta*', *Historia* 29.3, 382–384.

— 1980b: 'A Lowly Born Historian of the Late Roman Empire: Some Observations on Aurelius Victor and His *De Caesaribus*', *Thought: A Review of Culture and Idea* 55.216, 122–131.

— 1981: 'Alexander Severus and the *Exsoleti*: An Unfulfilled Intention', *RhM* NF 124.2, 184–187.

— 1983a: 'A Sallustian Reminiscence in Aurelius Victor', *CP* 78, 234.

— 1983b: 'The Eloquence of the Emperor Numerian', *Ant. Class.* 52, 274–276.

— 1990: *Greek Philosophers and Sophists in the Fourth Century A.D.: Studies in Eunapius of Sardis*, Leeds

— 2007: *Man and the Word: The Orations of Himerius*, Berkeley and Los Angeles.

Perczel, I. 2009: 'The Earliest Syriac Reception of Dionysius', in S. Coakley and C. Stang (eds), *Re-thinking Dionysius the Areopagite*, Chichester, 27–42.

Perrin, M. 1987: *Lactance: Épitomé des Institutions Divines*, Paris.

Pertz, G.H. 1829: *Monumenta Germaniae Historica . . . Scriptorum Tomus II*, Hannover.

Pesditschek, M. 2008: 'Stein, Arthur (1871–1950), Historiker und Epigraphiker', *Österreichisches Biographisches Lexikon* 60, 146–147.

Peter, H. 1883: [Review of Enmann 1884], *Philologischer Anzeiger als Ergänzung des Philologus* 13, 548–552.

— 1897: *Die Geschichtliche Litteratur über die römische Kaiserzeit bis Theodosius I und ihre Quellen*, 2 vols, Berlin.

— 1906: *Historicorum Romanorum Reliquiae, Volumen Alterum*, Leipzig.

Petit, P. 1994: *Les Fonctionnaires dans l'Œuvre de Libanius*, Besançon.

Petoletti, M. 2019: 'Le migrazione dei testi classici nell'alto medioevo. Il ruolo dell'Italia settentrionale', in *Le migrazioni nell'Alto Medioevo, Spoleto, 5–11 aprile 2018* (Settimane di studio 66), 2 vols, Spoleto, 551–580.

Petre, Z. 1965: 'La pensée historique de Zosime', *Studii Clasice* 7, 263–272.

Petschenig, M. 1886: *Iohannis Cassiani Conlationes XXIIII* (*CSEL* 13), Vienna.

Pettorelli, J.-P. and Kaestli, J.-D. 2012: *Vita latina Adae et Evae* (*CCSA* 18–19), 2 vols, Turnhout.

Pflaum, H.-G. 1966: 'La valeur de la source inspiratrice de la Vita Pii à la lumière des personnalites nommement citées', *BHAC 1964/1965*, 143–152.

Piano, V. 2017: 'Il P.Herc. 1067 latino: il rotolo, il testo, l'autore', *Cronache Ercolanesi* 47, 163–250.

Pichlmayr, F. 1970 (1911): *Sexti Aurelii Victoris Liber de Caesaribus*, rev. R. Gründel, Zwickau.

Pichon, R. 1906: 'L'origine du recueil des "Panegyrici latini"', *REA* 8.3, 229–249.

Pirie, J.W. 1926: 'New Evidence for the Text of Placidus', *Archivum Latiniatis Medii Aevi* 2, 185–190.

Pirri, P. 1960: *L'abbazia di Sant'Eutizio in Val Castoriana presso Norcia e le chiese dipendenti* (*Studia Anselmiana* 45), Rome.

Pizzani, U. 1985: 'Gli scritti grammaticali attribuiti a S. Agostino', *Augustinianum* 25, 361–383.

Plater, W.E. and White, H.J. 1926: *The Grammar of the Vulgate, being an Introduction to the Study of the Latinity of the Vulgate Bible*, Oxford.

Plew, J. 1884: [Review of Enmann 1884], *Göttingische gelehrte Anzeigen* 1.5, 200–208.

Plommer, H. 1973: *Vitruvius and Later Roman Building Manuals*, Cambridge.

Polloni, S. 2007: 'Manoscritti liturgici della Biblioteca Capitolare di Verona (secolo IX). Contributo per uno studio codicologico e paelografico', *Medioevo. Studi e documenti* 2, 153–228.

Pontani, F. 2012: [Review of Horster and Reitz 2010], *Mnemosyne* 65.4/5, 853–857.

Popovíc, I. (ed.) 2011: *Felix Romuliana – Gamzigrad*, Belgrade.

Porena, P. 2003: *Le origini della prefettura del pretorio tardoantico*, Rome.

— 2021: 'Verso la provincializzazione dell'Italia romana: la carriera di A. Vitellius Felix Honoratus durante il principato di Valeriano e Gallieno', ὅρμος: *Ricerche di storia antica* NS 13, 251–286.

Potter, D.S. 1990: *Prophecy and History in the Crisis of the Roman Empire: A Historical Commentary on the* Thirteenth Sibylline Oracle, Oxford.

— 1991: 'The Inscription on the Bronze Herakles from Mesene: Vologeses IV's War with Rome and the Date of Tacitus' *Annales*', *ZPE* 88, 277–290.

Prag, J.R.W. 2006: 'Poenus plane est – But Who Were the 'Punickes'?', *Papers of the British School at Rome* 74, 1–37.

Prchlík, I. 2015: 'The Fiery Eyes of Augustus and the *Annales* of Nicomachus Flavianus', *Acta Universitatis Carolinae Philologica* 2/*Graecolatina Pragensia* 25, 9–20.

Prince, S. 2015: *Antisthenes of Athens. Texts, Translations, and Commentary*, Ann Arbor, MI.

Puccioni, G. 1958a: *La fortuna medievale della Origo gentis Romanae*, Messina.

— 1958b: *[Aureli Victoris] Origo Gentis Romanae*, Florence.

— 1958c: 'La composizione dell'Origo gentis romanae', *Annali della Sculoa Normale Superiore di Pisa. Lettere, Storia e Filosofia*, serie II, 27.3/4, 211–223.

— 1960: 'L'arceologia italica di Paolo Diacono', *Maia* 12, 63–73.

Quiroga Puertas, A.J. 2017: 'In Heaven unlike on Earth. Rhetorical Strategies in Julian's *Caesars*', in idem (ed.), *Rhetorical Strategies in Late Antique Literature. Images, Metatexts and Interpretation*, Leiden and Boston.

Ramorino, F. 1898: *Cornelio Tacito nella storia della coltura*[2], Milan.

Ramsey, J.T. 2003: *Cicero: Philippics I–II*, Cambridge.

— 2015: *Sallust: Fragments of the Histories, Letters to Caesar* (*Loeb Classical Library* 522), Cambridge, Mass.

Ranstrand, G. 1952: *Querolus siue Aulularia: Incerti auctoris comoedia una cum indice uerborum*, Göteborg.

Raschieri, A.A. 2020: 'Epitomare nella scuola di retorica: Giulio Paride e Ianuario Nepoziano', in Boehm and Vallat (eds), 153–167.

Ratti, S. 1999: 'Sur la source du récit de la mort de Gallien dans l'*Histoire Auguste* (*Gall.* 14, 1–11)', in Paschoud (ed.), 259–276.

Rebenich, S. 1992: *Hieronymus und sein Kreis: Prosopographische und sozialgeschichtliche Untersuchungen* (*Historia Einzelschriften* 72), Stuttgart.

— 1997: *Theodor Mommsen und Adolf Harnack. Wissenschaft und Politik im Berlin des ausgehenden 19. Jahrhunderts*, Berlin.

Reekmans, T. 1997: 'Notes on Verbal Humour in the *Historia Augusta*', *Ancient Society* 28, 175–207.

Rees, R. 1999: 'Ammianus Satiricus', in Drijvers and Hunt (eds), 125–137.

— 2012: 'Bright Lights, Big City: Pacatus and the *Panegyrici Latini*', in L. Grig and G. Kelly (eds), *Two Romes. Rome and Constantinople in Late Antiquity*, Oxford, 203–222.

Reeve, M.D. 1969: 'Author's Variants in Longus?', *Proceedings of the Cambridge Philological Society* NS 15 (195), 75–85.

— 1984: 'The Addressee of *Laus Pisonis*', *Illinois Classical Studies* 9.1, 42–48.

— 1988: 'The Transmission of Florus' *Epitoma de Tito Livio* and the *Periochae*', *CQ* 38, 477–491.

— 1997: [Review of Arnaud-Lindet, M.P. 1994: *Festus, Abrégé des haut faits du peuple romain*, Paris], *Gnomon* 69.6, 508–513.

— (ed.) 2004: *Vegetius: Epitoma rei militaris*, Oxford.

— 2007: 'The Editing of Pliny's *Natural History*', *RHT* NS 2, 107–179.

— 2014: 'Pliny's "Natural History" in the "Scholia Vallicelliana" on Isidore', in F. Lo Monaco and L.C. Rossi (eds), *Il mondo e la storia. Studi in onore di Claudia Villa*, Florence, 247–254.

— 2021: *The Transmission of Pliny's* Natural History, Rome.

Reimitz, H. 2016: 'The Early Medieval Editions of Gregory of Tours' *Histories*', in A.C. Murray (ed.), *A Companion to Gregory of Tours*, Leiden and Boston, 519–565.

Reitemeier, J.F. 1784: *Zosimi Historiae Graece et Latine*, Leipzig (apud Weidmanni Heredes et Reichium).

Reynolds, L.D. (ed.) 1983: *Texts and Transmission: A Survey of the Latin Classics*, Oxford.

— and Wilson, N.G. 1991: *Scribes and Scholars: A Guide to the Transmission of Greek & Latin Literature*, Oxford.

Rich, J. 2016: 'Annalistic Organization and Book Division in Dio's Books 1–35', in V. Fromentin, E. Bertrand, M. Coltelloni-Trannoy, M. Molin, and G. Urso (eds), *Cassius Dion: nouvelles lectures*, 2 vols, Bordeaux, 1.271–286.

Richard, J.-C. 1983: *Pseudo-Aurélius Victor: Les Origines du Peuple Romain*, Paris.

— 1993: [Review of D'Anna 1992], *REL* 71, 316–320.

Richlin, A. 2014: *Arguments with Silence: Writing the History of Roman Women*, Ann Arbor, MI.

Ridley, R.T. 1969–1970: 'Eunapius and Zosimus', *Helikon: Rivista di tradizione e cultura classica dell'università di Messina* 9–10, 574–592.

— 1972: 'Zosimus the Historian', *Byzantinische Zeitschrift* 65, 277–302.

Roberto, U. 2005: *Ioannis Antiocheni Fragmenta ex Historia chronica*, Berlin and New York.

Robinson, D.M. 1946: 'The Wheel of Fortune', *CP* 41.4, 207–216.

Roda, S. 1981: *Commento storico al libro IX dell'epistolario di Q. Aurelio Simmaco*, Pisa.

Rodgers, B.S. 1980: 'Constantine's Pagan Vision', *Byzantion* 50.1, 259–278.

— 1989: 'The Metamorphosis of Constantine', *CQ* 39.1, 233–246.

Rohrbacher, D. 2005: 'Why Didn't Constantius II Eat Fruit?', *CQ* 55.1, 323–326.

— 2006: 'The Sources for the Lost Books of Ammianus Marcellinus', *Historia* 55.1, 106–124.

— 2009: 'Enmanns' *Kaisergeschichte* from Augustus to Domitian', *Latomus* 68.3, 709–719.

— 2013: 'The Sources of the *Historia Augusta* Re-Examined', *Histos* 7, 146–180.

— 2016: *The Play of Allusion in the* Historia Augusta, Madison, WI.

— 2020: 'Martial and the *Historia Augusta*', *CQ* 70.2, 911–916.

Rolfe, J.C. 1935–1940: *Ammianus Marcellinus. History* (*Loeb Classical Library* 300, 315, 331), 3 vols, London and Cambridge, Mass.

Roman, Y., Rémy, B., and Riccardi, L. 2009: 'Les intrigues de Plotine et la succession de Trajan. À propos d'un aureus au nom d'Hadrien César', *REA* 111, 508–517.

Roncaglia, C. 2013: 'Client Prefects? Rome and the Cottians in the Western Alps', *Phoenix* 67.3/4, 353–372.

Rose, C.B. 2021: 'Reconsidering the Frieze on the Arch of Constantine', *Journal of Roman Archaeology* 34, 175–210.

Rose, E. 2013: '*Abdias scriptor vitarum sanctorum apostolorum*? The "Collection of Pseudo-Abdias" Reconsidered', *RHT* 8, 227–268.

Rose, H.J. 1996: *A Handbook of Latin Literature: From the Earliest Times to the Death of St. Augustine*, Wauconda, IL.

Rosellini, M. forthcoming: 'Julius Valerius' in Stover (ed.) forthcoming a.

Ross, A.J. 2015: 'Ammianus, Traditions of Satire and the Eternity of Rome', *Classical Journal* 110.3, 356–373.

— 2016a: *Ammianus' Julian: Narrative and Genre in the* Res Gestae, Oxford.

— 2016b: 'Libanius the Historian? Praise and the Presentation of the Past in *Or.* 59', *GRBS* 56, 293–320.

— 2018: 'Ammianus and the Written Past', in O. Devillers and B. Sebastiani (eds), *Les historiens grecs et romains: entre sources et modèles*, Bordeaux, 319–334.

Rossbach, O. 1897: 'Der prodigiorum liber des Iulius Obsequens', *RhM* NF 52, 1–12.

Rouse, R. and McNelis, C. 2001: 'North African Literary Activity: A Cyprian Fragment, the Stichometric Lists and a Donatist Compendium', *RHT* 30, 189–238.

Rubin, Z. 1974: [Review of Birley 1971], *JRS* 64, 231–233.

— 1980: *Civil-War Propaganda and Historiography* (*Collection Latomus* 173), Brussels.

Rudoni, E. 2010: 'Sei note testuali ad Aurelio Vittore', *Studi Classici e Orientali* 56, 309–314.

Rühl, F. 1867: *Die quellen Plutarchs im Leben des Kimon*, Marburg.

— 1871: *Die Verbreitung des Justinus im Mittelalter: Eine Literarhistorische Untersuchung*, Leipzig.

— 1872: *Die Textesquellen des Justinus*, Leipzig.

— 1887: *Eutropi Breviarium ab urbe condita*, Leipzig.

Rummel, E. 2015: *The Collected Works of Erasmus. Controversies*, Toronto.

Ruysschaert, J. 1968: *Miniaturistes «Romains» sous Pie II*, Siena.

Sacchi, P.F. and Formisano, M. 2022: *Epitomic Writing in Late Antiquity and Beyond: Forms of Unabridged Writing*, London.

Saffrey, H.D. 1990: *Recherches sur le néoplatonisme après Plotin*, Paris.

— 2000: *Le néoplatonisme après Plotin*, Paris.

Sage, E.T. 1936: *Livy. Books XXXVIII–XXXIX (Loeb Classical Library* 313), London and Cambridge, Mass.

Sallmann, K. (ed.) 1997: *Die Literatur des Umbruchs. Von der römischen zur christlichen Literatur, 117 bis 284 n. Chr. (HLL* 4), Munich.

Salomies, O. 1987: *Die Römischen Vornamen. Studien zur römischen Namengebung (Commentationes Humanarum Litterarum* 82), Helsinki.

— 1992: *Adoptive and Polyonymous Nomenclature in the Roman Empire (Commentationes Humanarum Litterarum* 97), Helsinki.

Salway, B.W. 1994: 'What's in a Name? A Survey of Roman Onomastic Practice from *c.* 700 B.C. to A.D. 700', *JRS* 84, 124–145.

— 2013: 'The Publication and Application of the Theodosian Code', *Mélanges de l'École Française de Rome – Antiquité* 125.2.

Sancho Gómez, M.P. 2019: 'Duces praeclarissimos instituit. La "escuela de generales" del emperador Probo en la Historia Augusta: ¿invención literaria o realidad?', *Classica et Christiana* 14, 243–368.

Sandys, J.E 1903–1908: *A History of Classical Scholarship*, 3 vols, Cambridge.

Santini, C. 1979: *Eutropii Breviarium ab urbe condita*, Leipzig.

Sartre, M. 1984: 'Le *dies imperii* de Gordien III: une inscription inédite de Syria', *Syria* 61, 49–61.

Saunders, R.T. 1992: 'Who Murdered Gallienus?', *Antichthon* 26, 80–94.

Savelli, R. 2018: 'Sulla stampa del *Corpus iuris civilis* nel Cinquecento. Standardizzazione, innovazioni, contaminazioni', in S. Levati and S. Mori (eds), *Una storia di rigore e di passione. Saggi per Livio Antonielli*, Milan, 103–125.

Savino, E. 2017: *Ricerche sull'Historia Augusta*, Naples.

Scavone, D.C. 1970: 'Zosimus and His Historical Models', *GRBS* 11.1, 57–67.

Schamp, J. 2009: 'Pour une étude des milieux Latins de Constantinople', in F. Biville and I. Boehm (eds), *Autour de Michel Lejeune. Actes des Journées d'études organisées à l'Université Lumière-Lyon 2 – Maison de l'Orient et de la Méditerranée 2–3 février 2006*, Lyon, 255–272.

Schiller, H. 1883: *Geschichte der römischen Kaiserzeit I.2: Von der Regierung Vespasians bis zur Erhebung Diokletians*, Gotha.

Schlumberger, J.A. 1974: *Die "Epitome de Caesaribus": Untersuchungen zur heidnischen Geschichtschreibun des 4. Jahrhunderst n. Chr.*, Munich.

— 1976: 'Die Epitome de Caesaribus und die Historia Augusta', *BHAC 1972/1974*, 201–219.

— 1985: 'Die verlorenen Annalen des Nicomachus Flavianus: Ein Werk über Geschichte der Römischen Republik oder Kaiserzeit?', *BHAC 1982/1983*, 305–329.

— 2010: 'Epitome, Historia Augusta und Marius Maximus?', in Galli Milić and Hecquet-Noti (eds), 195–209.

Schmidt, M.G. (ed.) 2009: *Hermann Dessau (1856–1931): zum 150. Geburtstage des Berliner Althistorikers und Epigraphikers. Beiträge eines Kolloquiums und wissenschaftliche Korrespondenz des Jubilars*, Berlin.

Schmidt, P.L. 1968: *Iulius Obsequens und das Problem der Livius-Epitome: Ein Beitrag zur Geschichte der lateinischen Prodigienliteratur*, Wiesbaden.

— 1978: 'Das Corpus Aurelianum und S. Aurelius Victor', *Paulys Realencyclopädie der classischen Altertumswissenschaft, neue Bearbeitung. Supplementband XV: Acilius bis Zoilos*, Munich.

Schmidt-Hofner, S. 2020: 'An Empire of the Best: Zosimus, the Monarchy, and the Eastern Administrative Elite in the Fifth Century CE', *Chiron* 50, 217–251.

Scholtemeijer, J. 1976: 'Historia Augusta: Nomen Antoninorum', *Acta Classica* 19, 105–113.

Schöne, A. 1900: *Die Weltchronik des Eusebius in ihrer Bearbeitung durch Hieronymus*, Berlin.

van de Schoor, R. 2016: *Georgius Cassander's* De officio pii viri *(1561)*, Berlin and Boston.

Schott, A. 1579: *Sex: Aurelii Victoris Historiae Romanae Breviarium*, Antwerp (Christopher Plantin) (*USTC*: 402815).

— 1609: *Cornelii Nepotis opera quae quidem extant historica virorum domi militiaeque illustrium Graecorum Romanorumque*, Frankfurt (Claude de Marne and the heirs of Jean Aubry) (*USTC*: 2134640).

Schreckenberg, H. 1972: *Die Flavius-Josephus-Tradition in Antike und Mittelalter*, Leiden.

Schullian, D.M. 1981: 'A Revised List of Manuscripts of Valerius Maximus', *Miscellanea Augusto Campana*, Padua, 2 vols, 2.695–728.

Schulz, E. 1926: 'Zur Entstehungsgeschichte der Werke Gotfrids von Viterbo', *Neues Archiv der Gesellschaft für ältere deutsche Geschichtskunde* 46, 87–131.

Schulz, O.Th. 1907: *Das Kaiserhaus der Antonine und der letzte Historiker Roms, nebts einer Beigabe das Geschichtswerk des Anonymus*, Leipzig.

Schulz, V. 2019: *Deconstructing Imperial Representation: Tacitus, Cassius Dio, and Suetonius on Nero and Domitian*, Leiden.

Schumacher, L. 1982: *Römische Kaiser in Mainz im Zeitalter des Principats (27 v. Chr. – 284 n. Chr.)*, Bochum.

— 2004: 'Die *Sicilia* in Mainz-Bretzenheim. Zur Lokalisierung der Ermordung des Kaisers Severus Alexander', *Mainzer Zeitschrift* 99, 1–10.

Schwartz, J. 1964: 'Avidius Cassius et les sources de l'Histoire Auguste (à propos d'une légende rabbinique)', *Historia-Augusta-Colloquium Bonn 1963*, 135–164.

— 1980: 'À propos d'une notice de la chronologie de Jérôme', in *BHAC 1977/1978*, 225–232.

Schweitzer, A. 1906: *Von Reimarus zu Wrede, eine Geschichte der Leben-Jesu-Forschung*, Tübingen.

— 1910: *The Quest of the Historical Jesus: A Critical Study of Its Progress from Reimarus to Wrede* (tr. W. Montgomery), London.

Schwendemann, J. 1923: *Der historische Wert der Vita Marci bei den Scriptores Historiae Augustae*, Heidelberg.

Seeck, O. 1883: *Q. Aurelii Symmachi quae supersunt* (*MGH AA* 6.1), Berlin.

— 1890: 'Studien zur Geschichte Diocletians und Constantins', *Jahrbücher für classische Philologie* 36, 609–639.

— 1911: *Geschichte des Untergangs der antiken Welt IV*, Stuttgart.

— 1919: *Regesten der Kaiser und Päpste für di Jahre 311 bis 476 n. Chr. Vorarbeit zu einer Prosopographie der Christlichen Kaiserzeit*, Stuttgart.

Sehlmeyer, M. 2009: *Geschichtsbilder für Pagane und Christen. Res Romanae in den spätantiken Breviarien*, Berlin.

— 2020: 'More Publicity through Very Short Books. Epitomes in Late Antiquity and the Renaissance', in J. Muñoz Morcillo and C.Y. Robertson-von Trotha (eds), *Genealogy of Popular Science: From Ancient Ecphrasis to Virtual Reality*, Bielefeld, 315–344.

de Senneville-Grave, G. 1999: *Sulpice Sévère. Chroniques*, Paris.

Sepp, B. 1885: *Incerti auctoris liber de Origine gentis Romanae*, Eichstadt.

Seston, W. 1966a: 'Marius Maximus et la date de la «Constitutio Antoniniana»', in *Mélanges d'Archéologie, d'Épigraphie et d'Histoire offerts à Jérôme Carcopino*, Paris, 877–888.

— 1966b: 'Sur les traces de Marius Maximus: I. Marius Maximus et les Consuls de 209', *BHAC 1964/1965*, 211–219.

Shackleton Bailey, D.R. 1981: 'Textual Notes on Lesser Latin Historians', *HSCP* 85, 155–184.

— 2000: *Valerius Maximus. Memorable Doings and Sayings* (*Loeb Classical Library* 492, 492), 2 vols, Cambridge, Mass.

Shanzer, D. 2006: 'Latin Literature, Christianity and Obscenity in the Later Roman West', in N. McDonald (ed.), *Medieval Obscenities*, Woodbridge, 179–202.

Sharpe, R. 2003: Titulus: *Identifying Medieval Latin Texts: An Evidence-Based Approach*, Turnhout.

Shaw, B.D. 2013: *Bringing in the Sheeves: Economy and Metaphor in the Roman World*, Toronto.

Sherwin, W.K. 1972: '*De viris illustribus*: Two Unexamined MSS in the Walters Art Gallery', *Classical World* 65.5, 145–146.

— 1973: *Deeds of Famous Men (De viris illustribus): A Bilingual Edition*, Norman, OK.

Sinnigen, W.G. 1957: *The Officium of the Urban Prefecture during the Later Roman Empire* (*Papers and Monographs of the American Academy in Rome* 17), Rome.

Sivan, H. 1992: 'The Historian Eusebius (of Nantes)', *JHS* 112, 158–163.

Smith, C.J. 2005: 'The *Origo gentis Romanae*: Facts and Fictions', *BICS* 48, 97–136.

Smith, G.S. 2014: *Guilt by Association: Heresy Catalogues in Early Christianity*, Oxford.

Smith, K.F. 1913: *The Elegies of Albius Tibullus. The Corpus Tibullianum Edited with Introduction and Notes on Books I, II, and IV, 2–14*, New York.

Smith, W. (ed.) 1854–1857: *Dictionary of Greek and Roman Geography*, 2 vols, London.

Søby Christensen, A. 1980: *Lactantius the Historian. An Analysis of the* De Mortibus Persecutorum, Copenhagen.

Sogno, C. 2012: 'Persius, Juvenal, and the Transformation of Satire in Late Antiquity', in S. Braund and J. Osgood (eds), *A Companion to Persius and Juvenal*, Chichester, 363–385.

Solaro, G. 2022: 'André Schott e la paternità dei *Viri illustres*', *Bolletino di studi latini* 52, 151–163.

Solin, H. 2003: *Die griechischen Personennamen in Rom: Ein Namenbuch*, 3 vols, Berlin and New York.

— and Salomies, O. 1994: *Repertorium nominum gentilium et cognominum Latinorum*, Hildesheim.

Sólyom, M. 2018: 'Epitome de Caesaribus. Az utolsó latin nyelven írt pogány történeti munka', Ph.D. Thesis, Eötvös Loránd University.

Southern, P. 1989: 'The Numeri of the Roman Imperial Army', *Britannia* 20, 81–140.

Soverini, P. 1984–1985, 'Note ad Aurelio Vittore', *Museum Criticum* 19–20, 235–240.

Speck, P. 1991: 'Wie dumm darf Zosimus sein? Vorschläge zu seiner Neubewertung', *Byzantinoslavica* 52, 1–14.

Speidel, M.P. 1993: 'Commodus the God-Emperor and the Army', *JRS* 83, 109–114.

Speyer, W. 1963: *Epigrammata Bobiensia*, Leipzig.

— 1971: *Die literarische Fälschung im heidnischen und Christlichen Altertum: Ein Versuch ihrer Deutung*, Munich.

Stadter, P.A. 1980: *Arrian of Nicomedia*, Chapel Hill, NC, and London.

Staffa, A.R. 2010: 'I longobardi nell'Abruzzo adriatico fra VI e VIII secolo', in G. Roma (ed.), *I longobardi del sud*, Rome, 175–239.

Stancliffe, C. 1983: *St Martin and his Hagiographer: History and Miracle in Sulpicius Severus*, Oxford.

Starr, C.G. 1956: 'Aurelius Victor: Historian of Empire', *American Historical Review* 61.3, 574–586.

Steele, R.B. 1918: 'Roman Personal Names', *Classical Weekly* 11.15, 113–118.

Stefan, A. 2016: 'La date de la Victoire de Dioclétien sur Carin au *Margus*. À propos de *P. Oxy.* L 3569 et de *CJ* 2.53.3', *ZPE* 198, 271–282.

Stein, A. 1932: 'Hermann Dessau', *Klio* 25, 226–244.

Stern, H. 1953: *Date et Destinataire de l'*Histoire Auguste, Paris.

Stewart, C. 1998: *Cassian the Monk*, Oxford and New York.

Stiglmayr, J. 1895: 'Der neuplatoniker Proclus als Vorlage des sogennanten Dionysius Areopagita in der Lehre vom Übel', *Historisches Jahrbuch* 16, 253–273 and 721–748.

Stover, J.A. 2015: 'Olybrius and the *Einsiedeln Eclogues*', *JRS* 105, 288–321.

— 2016: *A New Work by Apuleius: The Lost Third Book of the* De Platone, Oxford.

— 2017: '*Epitome de Caesaribus* 1.24 and Ovid's Exile', *CP* 112.2, 267–275.

— 2019: [Review of Velaza 2016a], *Exemplaria Classica* 23, 459–464.

— 2020: 'New Light on the *Historia Augusta*', *JRS* 110, 167–198.

— 2021a: 'The Ciceronian Book and Its Influence: A Statistical Approach' *Ciceroniana Online* 5.2, 263–283.

— 2021b: [Review of Nickbahkt and Scardino 2021], *Bryn Mawr Classical Review* 21.10.41 (https://bmcr.brynmawr.edu/2021/2021.10.41/).

— 2022: [Review of Paschoud 2018], *Gnomon* 94.5, 410–414.

— (ed.) forthcoming a: *The Oxford Guide to the Transmission of the Latin Classics*.

— forthcoming b: 'Victorinus and Isidore in a Bamberg Miscellany'.

— forthcoming c: 'Sex. Aurelius Victor. Epitome de Caesaribus', in Stover (ed.) forthcoming a.

— forthcoming d: '*De viris illustribus*', in Stover (ed.) forthcoming a.

— forthcoming e: 'The Book in the Roman and Post Roman World', in G. Kelly and A. Pelttari (eds), *Cambridge History of Later Latin Literature*, Cambridge.

— and Kestemont, M. 2016: 'The Authorship of the *Historia Augusta*: Two New Computational Studies', *BICS* 59.2, 140–157.

— and Woudhuysen, G. 2017: 'Giovanni de Matociis and the *Codex Oratorianus* of the *De viris illustribus urbis Romae*', *Exemplaria Classica* 21, 125–148.

— and — 2020: 'Aurelius Victory and the Ending of Sallust's *Jugurtha*', *Hermathena* 199 [2015 issue], 93–134.

— and — 2021: 'Jordanes and the Date of the *Epitome de Caesaribus*', *Histos* 15, 150–188.

— and — 2022a: 'The Poet Nemesianus and the *Historia Augusta*', *JRS* 112, 173–197.

— and — 2022b: '*Historiarum libri quinque*: Hegesippus and the *Histories* of Sallust', *Histos* 16, 1–27.

— and — 2023: 'The Circulation of the *Scholia Vallicelliana* to Isidore', *RHT* NS 18.

— and — forthcoming a: 'Eutropius', in Stover (ed.) forthcoming a.

— and — forthcoming b: 'Aurelius Victor, *Caes.* 27.1 and the Name of the Father of Gordian III'.

Straub, J. 1970: 'Severus Alexander und die mathematici', *BHAC 1968/1969*, 247–272.

Stroheker, K.F. 1966: 'Die Aussenpolitik des Antoninus Pius nach der Historia Augusta', *BHAC 1964/1965*, 241–256.

Stuart, D.R. 1908: 'The Point of an Emperor's Jest', *CP* 3, 59–64.

Sturm, J.J. 1687: *Disputationem circularem de Sex. Rufo*, Altdorf (Heinrich Meyer).

Suski, R. 2005: 'Why Eusebius of Nantes Was Not the Author of Kaisergeschichte', in J. Styka (ed.), *Studies of Roman Literature. Classica Cracoviensia, IX*, Kraków, 43–71.

Swan, P.M. 2004: *The Augustan Succession: An Historical Commentary on Cassius Dio's Roman History, Books 55–56 (9 B.C.–A.D. 14)*, Oxford.

Syme, R. 1928: 'Rhine and Danube Legions under Domitian', *JRS* 18, 41–55.

— 1930: 'The Imperial Finances under Domitian, Nerva and Trajan', *JRS* 20, 55–70.

— 1938: 'The First Garrison of Trajan's Dacia', *Laureae Aquincenses memoriae Valentini Kuzsinszky dicatae I*, Budapest, 267–286.

— 1939: *The Roman Revolution*, Oxford.

— 1958: *Tacitus*, 2 vols, Oxford.

— 1960: 'Pliny's Less Successful Friends', *Historia* 9.3, 362–379.

— 1962: 'The Wrong Marcius Turbo', *JRS* 52, 87–96.

— 1964a: *Sallust*, Berkeley and Los Angeles.

— 1964b: 'Hadrian and Italica', *JRS* 54, 142–149.

— 1964c: 'Pliny and the Dacian Wars', *Latomus* 23.4, 750–759.

— 1965a: 'Hadrian the Intellectual', in *Les Empereurs Romains d'Espagne*, Paris, 243–253.

— 1965b: 'Governors of Pannonia Inferior', *Historia* 14.3, 342–361.

— 1966: 'The Bogus Names in the Historia Augusta', *BHAC 1964/1965*, 257–272.

— 1967: 'Les proconsuls d'Afrique sous Hadrien', *REA* 67.3–4, 342–352.

— 1968a: *Ammianus and the* Historia Augusta, Oxford.

— 1968b: 'Not Marius Maximus', *Hermes* 96.3, 494–502.

— 1968c: 'The Ummidii', *Historia* 17.1, 72–105.

— 1968d: 'Fiction and Archaeology in the Fourth Century', *Atti del convegno internazionale sul tema: tardo antico e alto medioevo. La forma artistica nel passaggio dall'antichità al medioevo (Roma 4–7 aprile 1967)*, Rome, 23–30.

— 1968e: 'Ignotus the Good Biographer', *BHAC 1966/1967*, 131–153.

— 1970a: 'The Secondary Vitae', *BHAC 1968/1969*, 285–307.

— 1970b: 'Three Jurists', *BHAC 1968/1969*, 309–323.

— 1971a: *Emperors and Biography: Studies in the Historia Augusta*, Oxford.

— 1971b: *The* Historia Augusta: *A Call of Clarity*, Bonn.

— 1971c: 'The *Historia Augusta*: Three Rectifications', *Journal of Theological Studies* NS 21.1, 101–104.

— 1972a: 'The Composition of the Historia Augusta: Recent Theories', *JRS* 62, 123–133.

— 1972b: 'Marius Maximus Once Again', *BHAC 1970*, 287–302.

— 1972c: 'The Son of the Emperor Macrinus', *Phoenix* 26.3, 275–291.

— 1974: 'The Ancestry of Constantine', *BHAC 1971*, 237–253.

— 1976a: 'Bogus Authors', *BHAC 1972–1974*, 311–321.

— 1976b: 'Astrology in the Historia Augusta', *BHAC 1972–1974*, 291–309.

— 1978a: 'The *Pomerium* in the Historia Augusta', *BHAC 1975/1976*, 217–231.

— 1978b: 'Propaganda in the Historia Augusta', *Latomus* 37.1, 173–192.

— 1979–1991: *Roman Papers*, 7 vols (E. Badian (ed.) I–II, A.R. Birley (ed.) III–VII), Oxford.

— 1980a: 'The End of the Marcomanni', *BHAC 1977/1978*, 265.

— 1980b: 'Fiction in the Epitomators', *BHAC 1977/1978*, 267–278.

— 1981: 'Hadrian and the Vassal Princes', *Athenaeum* NS 59.3–4, 273–283.

— 1982–1983: 'Spaniards at Tivoli', *Ancient Society* 13/14, 241–263.

— 1983: *Historia Augusta Papers*, Oxford.

— 1992: 'Trogus in the H.A., Some Consequences', in M. Christol, S. Demougin, Y. Duval, C. Lepelley, and L. Pietri (eds), *Institutions, Société et Vie Politique dans l'Empire Romain au IV*ᵉ *siècle ap. J.-C.*, Rome, 11–20.

Tabacco, R. 2000: *Itinerarium Alexandri*, Florence.

Tacoma, L.E. 2020: *Roman Political Culture: Seven Studies of the Senate and City Councils of Italy from the First to the Sixth Century AD*, Oxford.

Tarrant, R.J. 1978: [Review of Dufraigne 1975], *Gnomon* 50.4, 355–362.

— 2016: *Texts, Editors, and Readers: Methods and Problems in Latin Textual Criticism*, Cambridge.

Tenney, M.F. 1935: 'Tacitus Through the Centuries to the Age of Printing', *University of Colorado Studies* 22.4, 341–363.

Thomas, P. 1896: *Catalogue des Manuscrits de Classiques Latins de la Bibliotheque Royale de Bruxelles*, Ghent.

Thomissen, J.-J. 1886–1887: 'Huybrechts (Jean)', *Biographie Nationale de Belgique* IX, Brussels, col. 726.

Thompson, E.A. 1943: 'Ammianus' Account of Gallus Caesar', *American Journal of Philology* 64.3, 302–315.

— 1947: *The Historical Work of Ammianus Marcellinus*, Cambridge.

Thomson, M. 2012: *Studies in the* Historia Augusta (*Collection Latomus* 337), Brussels.

de Tillemont, L. 1701: *Histoire des Empereurs . . . Tome cinquieme, qui comprend depuis Valentinien I. Jusqu'à Honoré*, Paris (Charles Robustel).

Toher, M. 2009: 'Augustan and Tiberian Literature', in M. Griffin (ed.), *A Companion to Julius Caesar*, Malden, MA, 224–238.

Tolkhien, J. 1913: 'Ludwig Jeep', *Biographisches Jahrbuch für die Altertumswissenschaft* 35, 121–133.

Tondini, G. 2011: 'Un modello per il regno dei Carolingi in Italia. L'*Epitome Phillipsiana* e l'identità urbana di Verona dopo il 774', Ph.D. Thesis, Padova.

Townend, G.B. 1972: 'The Earliest Scholiast on Juvenal', *CQ* 22.2, 376–387.

Townsend, P.W. 1955: 'The Revolution of A.D. 238: The Leaders and Their Aims', *Yale Classical Studies* 14, 49–105.

Treadgold, W. 2007: *The Early Byzantine Historians*, Basingstoke.

Troncarelli, F. 2014: '*Inaudita in excerpta*: la «Vita di Boezio» di Jordanes e i suoi lettori (Giovanni de' Matociis, Jacques Sirmond, Nicolas Caussin)', *RHT* NS 9, 157–199.

Tropea, G. 1899: *Studi sugli Scriptores Historiae Augustae III. Mario Massimo: Vita e frammenti*, Messina.

Trout, D.E. 1999: *Paulinus of Nola: Life, Letters, and Poems*, Berkeley and Los Angeles.

Turcan, R. 1993: *Histoire Auguste. Tome III, 1ère partie: Vies de Macrin, Diaduménien, Héliogabale*, Paris.

Turcan-Verkerk, A.-M. 1999: 'Mannon de Saint-Oyen dans l'histoire de la transmission des textes', *RHT* 29, 169–243.

Ughelli, F. 1720: *Italia sacra sive de episcopi Italiae et Insularum Adjacentium. Tomus Quintus*, Venice (Sebastian Coleti).

Ullman, B.L. 1960: *The Origin and Development of Humanistic Script*, Rome.

Ulrici, H. 1833: *Charakteristik der antiken Historiographie*, Berlin.

Van Hoof, L. and Van Nuffelen, P. 2013: '"No Stories for Old Men": Damophilus of Bithynia and Plutarch in Julian's *Misopogon*', in A. Quiroga Puertas (ed.), *The Purpose of Rhetoric in Late Antiquity: From Performance to Exegesis*, Tübingen, 209–222.

— and — 2017: 'The Historiography of Crisis: Jordanes, Cassiodorus and Justinian in Mid-Sixth-Century Constantinople', *JRS* 107: 275–300.

— and — 2020a: *The Fragmentary Latin Histories of Late Antiquity (AD 300–620). Edition, Translation and Commentary*, Cambridge.

— and — 2020b: *Clavis Historicorum Antiquitatis Posterioris: An Inventory of Late Antique Historiography (A.D. 300–800)*, Turnhout.

Van Nuffelen, P. 2012: *Orosius and the Rhetoric of History*, Oxford.

— 2015: 'Greek Secular Historians in Late Antiquity', *Histos* 9, ix–xv.

Vanderspoel, J. 1995: *Themistius and the Imperial Court. Oratory, Civic Duty, and* Paideia *from Constantius to Theodosius*, Ann Arbor, MI.

Vansteenberghe, E. 1920: *Le cardinal Nicolas de Cues*, Paris.

Vecchi, G. 1950: 'Praecepta artis musicae collecta ex libri Aurelii Augustini De Musica post Angelum Maium novis collatis codicibus', *Memorie dell'Accademia delle scienze dell'Istituto di Bologna. Classe di scienze morali* 5th series 1, 91–153.

— 1986: *Aurelii Augustini Praecepta artis musicae*, Bologna.

Velaza, J. (ed.) 2016a: *From the Protohistory to the History of the Text*, Frankfurt.

— 2016b: 'The Protohistory of the Text of Martial', in *idem* (ed.), 279–294.

Venturini, T. 1929: *Ricerche paleografiche intorno all'archdiacono Pacifico di Verona*, Verona.

Versnel, H.S. 1976: 'Two Types of Roman *Devotio*', *Mnemosyne* 29.4, 365–410.

Villa, C. 1984: 'Uno schedario di Paolo Diacono: Festo e Grauso di Ceneda', *IMU* 27, 56–80.

— 1987: 'II. I programmi scolastici', *Dall'eremo al cenobio. La civiltà monastica in Italia dalle origini all'età di Dante*, Milan, 292–320.

Vossius, G.I. 1627: *De historicis latinis libri tres*, Leiden (Joannes Maire) (*USTC*: 1011719).

Vout, C. 2005: 'Antinous, Archaeology and History', *JRS* 95, 80–96.

— 2007: *Power and Eroticism in Imperial Rome*, Cambridge.

Waitz, G. 1872: 'Gotifredi Viterbiensis Opera', in G.H. Pertz (ed.), *Monumenta Germaniae Historica, Scriptorum Tomus XXII*, Hannover, 1–338.

— 1878: *Scriptores Rerum Langobardicarum et Italicarum Saec. VI–IX* (*MGH*), Hannover.

Wallenwein, K. 2017: *Corpus Subscriptionum: Verzeichnis der Beglaubigungen von spätantiken und frühmittelalterlichen Textabschriften (saec. IV–VIII)*, Stuttgart.

Wankenne, J. 1986: [Review of Bird 1984], *Ant. Class.* 55, 468–469.

Wardle, D. 1995: 'Aurelius Victor' [Review of Bird 1994], *CR* 45.2, 266–267.

Warner, L. 2011: *The Lost History of* Piers Plowman*: The Earliest Transmission of Langland's Work*, Philadelphia, PA, and Oxford.

Wasselynck, R. 1962: 'Les compilations des «Moralia in Job» du VIIᵉ au XIIᵉ siècle', *Recherches de théologie ancienne et médiévale* 29, 5–32.

Watts, E.J. 2006: *City and School in Late Antique Athens and Alexandria*, Berkeley.

Wear, S.K. and Dillon, J.M. 2007: *Dionysius the Areopagite and the Neoplatonist Tradition: Despoiling the Hellenes*, Aldershot.

Weber, L.J. 1994: 'The Historical Importance of Godfrey of Viterbo', *Viator* 25, 153–195.

Wessner, P. 1931: *Scholia in Iuvenalem Vetustiora*, Leipzig.

Westerbergh, U. 1956: Chronicon Salernitanum*: A critical Edition with Studies on Literary and Historical Sources and on Language*, Stockholm.

Weyman, C. 1904: 'Zu den Sprichwörtern und sprichwörtlichen Redensarten der Römer', *Archiv für lateinische Lexikographie und Grammatik* 13, 253–270 and 379–406.

Whatmough, J. 1925: 'Scholia in Isidori Etymologias Vallicelliana', *Archivum Latiniatis Medii Aevi* 2, 57–75 and 134–169.

Wijga, I.R. 1890: *Liber de viris illustribus urbis Romae*, Groningen.

von Wilamowitz-Moellendorff, U. 1921: *Griechische Verskunst*, Berlin.

Williams, M.H. 2006: *The Monk and the Book: Jerome and the Making of Christian Scholarship*, Chicago, IL, and London.

Wilshire, L.E. 1973: 'Did Ammianus Marcellinus Write a Continuation of Tacitus?', *Classical Journal* 68.3, 221–227.

Winterbottom, M. 1967: 'Fifteenth-Century Manuscripts of Quintilian', *CQ* 17.2, 339–369.

— 1993: 'The Transmission of Cicero's *De Officiis*', *CQ* 43.1, 215–242.

Wiseman, T.P. 2013: *The Death of Caligula: Josephus Ant. Iud. XIX 1–273, Translation and Commentary*, Liverpool.

Witakowski, W. 1987: *The Syriac Chronicle of Pseudo-Dionysius of Tel-Mahre. A Study in the History of Historiography* (*Studia Semitica Upsaliensi* 9), Uppsala.

Witke, C. 1971: *Numen litterarum: The Old and the New in Latin Poetry from Constantine to Gregory the Great*, Leiden.

Wolff, E. 2007: *Rutilius Namatianus: Sur son retour* (with the collaboration of S. Lancel and J. Soler), Paris.

Wölfflin, E. 1874: 'Aurelius Victor', *RhM* NF 29, 282–308.

— 1902: 'Zur Latinität der Epitome Caesarum', *Archiv für Lateinische Lexikographie und Grammatik mit Einschluss des älteren Mittellateins* 12, 445–453.

Womersley, D. 1994: *The History of the Decline and Fall of the Roman Empire: Edward Gibbon*, 3 vols, London.

Woodman, A.J. 1975: 'Questions of Date, Genre, and Style in Velleius: Some Literary Answers', *CQ* 25.2, 272–306.

— 1977: *Velleius Paterculus: The Tiberian Narrative, 2.94–131* (*CCTC* 17), Cambridge.

— 2018: *The Annals of Tacitus: Book 4* (*CCTC* 58), Cambridge.

Woods, D. 1993: 'A Historical Source of the Passio Typasii', *Vigiliae Christianae* 47, 78–84.

— 1994: 'An Unnoticed Official: The *Praepositus Saltus*', *CQ* 44.1, 245–251.

Woudhuysen, G. 2018a: 'Uncovering Constans' Image', in D.W.P. Burgersdijk and A.J. Ross (eds), *Imagining Emperors in the Later Roman Empire*, Leiden, 158–182.

— 2018b: 'Gibbon among the Barbarians', in K. O'Brien and B. Young (eds), *The Cambridge Companion to Edward Gibbon*, Cambridge, 93–109.

— 2019: 'Myrmeicus or Myrmecius?', *Mnemosyne* 72.5, 840–860.

— 2021a: '*Codex Nicholsonianus*', *JRS* 111, 225–238.

— 2021b: '"A Faraway Land of Which We Know Little"? Britain in the Politics of the Fourth-Century Empire', in B. Ward-Perkins, R. Miles, and M. Hessérus (eds), *Roman Britain in the Roman Empire*, Stockholm, 63–73.

Xeravits, G.G. and Zsengellér, J. (eds) 2007: *The Books of the Maccabees: History, Theology Ideology. Papers of the Second International Conference on the Deuterocanonical Books, Pápa, Hungary, 9–11 June, 2005*, Leiden and Boston.

Yardley, J.C. 2010: 'What is Justin doing with Trogus?', in Horster and Reitz (eds), 469–490.

Zahn, T. 1916: 'Ein Kompendium der biblischen Prophetie aus der afrikanischen Kirche um 305–325', in *Geschichtliche Studien Albert Hauck zum 70. Geburtstag dargebracht*, Leipzig, 52–63.

Zainaldin, J.L. 2020: *Gargilius Martialis: The Agricultural Fragments (CCTC* 60), Cambridge.

Zecchini, G. 1993: *Ricerche di storiografia latina tardoantica*, Rome.

— 2010: 'L'*Historia Augusta* da Memmio Simmaco a Paolo Diacono', in Galli Milić and Hecquet-Noti (eds), 229–235.

— 2017: 'Il Nuovo Dexippo e l'Historia Augusta', in Bleckmann and Brandt (eds), 189–196.

Zetzel, J.E.G. 2005: *Marginal Scholarship and Textual Deviance: The Commentum Cornuti and the Early Scholia on Persius*, London.

— 2018: *Critics, Compilers, and Commentators. An Introduction to Roman Philology, 200 BCE–800 CE*, Oxford.

Zinsli, S.C. 2014: *Kommentar zur Vita Heliogabali der Historia Augusta*, Bonn.

Zorzetti, N. 1982: *Iulii Exuperantii Opusculum*, Leipzig.

Zurli, L. 2017: *The Manuscript Transmission of the* Anthologia Latina, Hildesheim.

Maps of Victor's World

The maps on the following five pages respectively show:

These maps were created using QGIS 3.16.13. The data for the Roman roads came from M. McCormick *et al.* (2013) 'Roman Road Network (version 2008)', DARMC Scholarly Data Series, Data Contribution Series #2013-5. DARMC, Center for Geographic Analysis, Harvard University, Cambridge MA 02138.

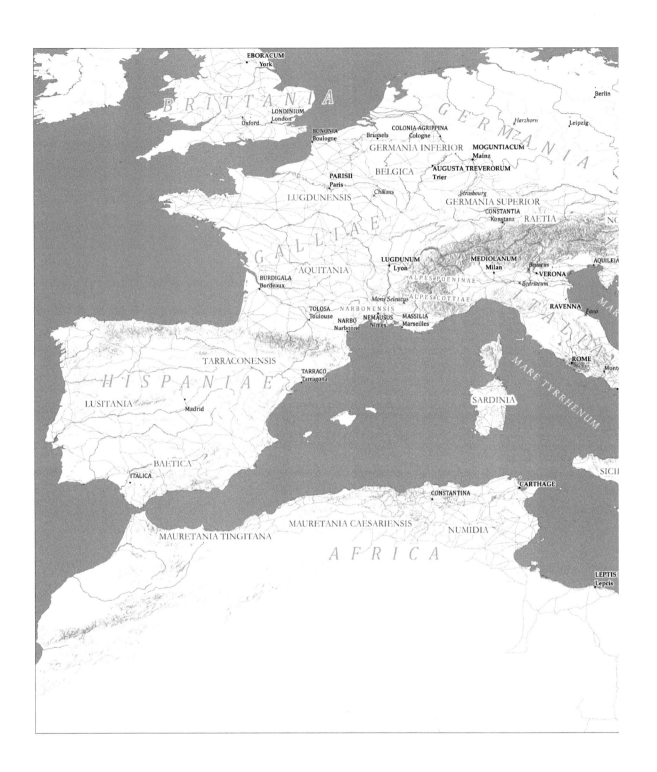

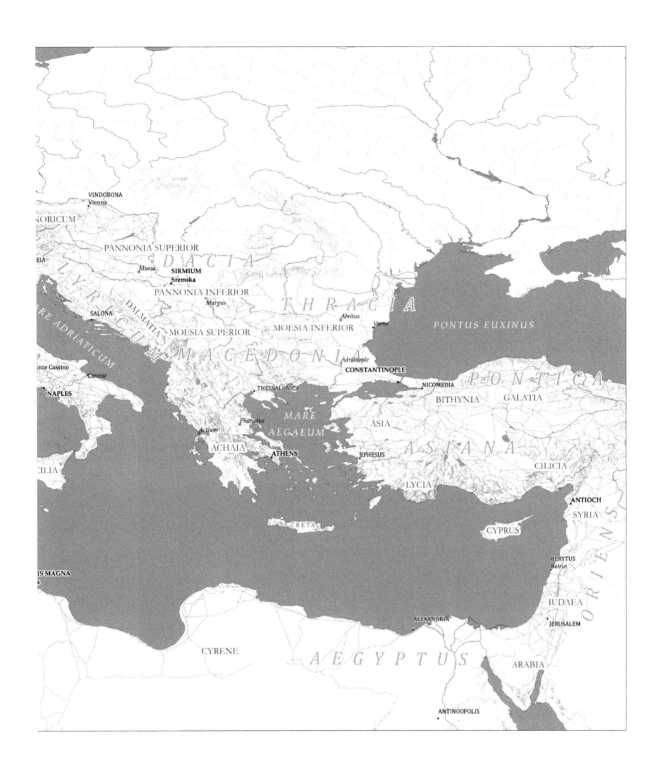

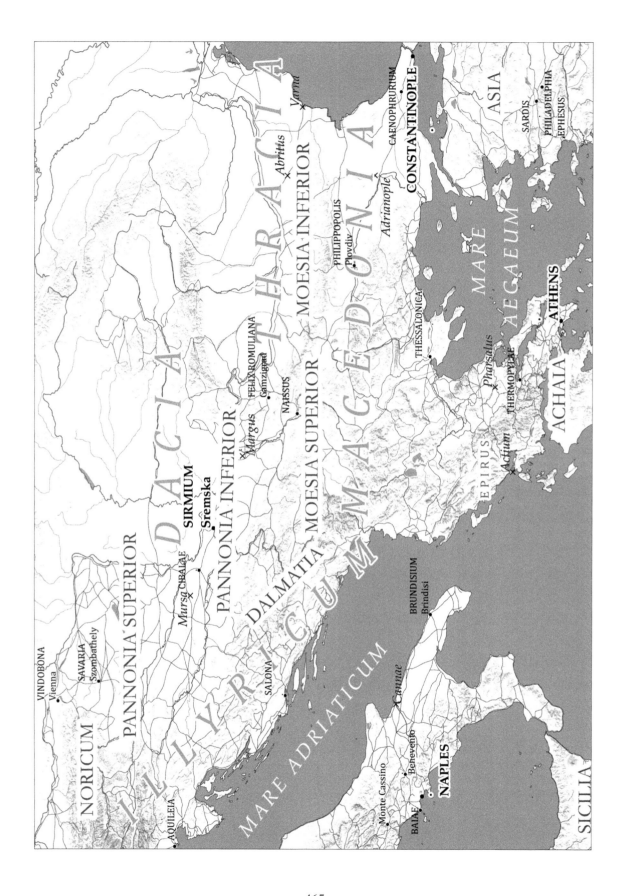

465

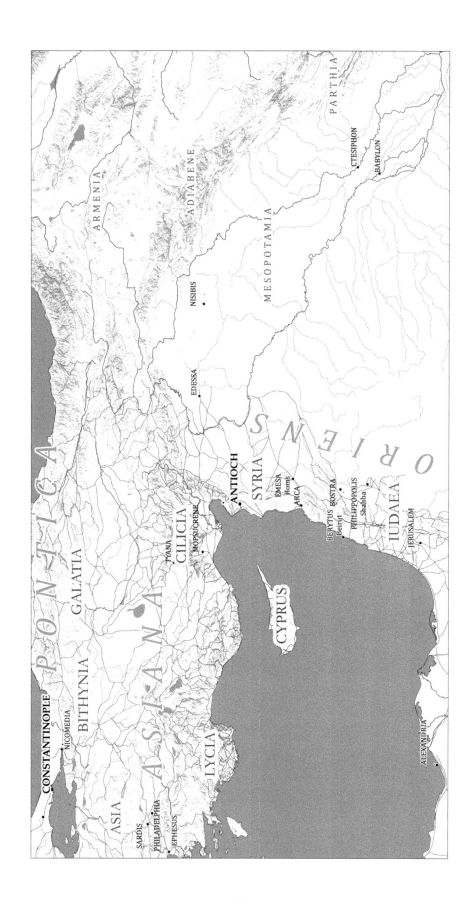

Index of Manuscripts Cited

Index of Sources

Historiae abbreviatae (*Liber de Caesaribus*)

VICTOR OF VITA

Historia persecutionis Africanae Provinciae

VICTORINUS OF PETTAU

Commentarii in Apocalypsin

VINDICIANUS

DE VIRIS ILLUSTRIBUS URBIS ROMAE

Epigraphica

General Index

This is an analytical general index. It is designed to lead the inquiring reader not to every single instance of a word or a concept, but rather to those that matter and especially to those that could not be easily found by perusing the table of contents. It is primarily an index of names – individuals, the titles of texts and places – and much about ideas or events can best be recovered by (for example) looking at the sub-entries for emperors or important places. For texts and their authors, it ought to be used in combination with the 'Index of Sources', which is (or is meant to be) comprehensive. Where a headword appears throughout the book, it will tend to have a number of sub-entries. Where it is featured only once or a few times, it is less likely to be so subdivided and it would be wise to consult all the pages listed.

Within entries, general references to the headword are grouped first, followed by sub-entries (separated by a semi-colon) – some sub-entries are themselves further divided (by commas). In both headwords and sub-entries, the most important discussion is sometimes indicated by 'esp.', (generally) placed first. For headwords, contextual information is given in parentheses. Modern individuals are listed by surname. Ancient figures appear usually by their last name (the *cognomen* or diacritic), with other names placed after a comma (in the order that they were used in antiquity). Where they are so famous under another name as to make that rule unhelpful, they can be found under the name of common reference. We have taken an appropriately unstandardised approach to medieval figures, who can be found under the name by which they are usually known. Readers who in perplexity discover that some important figure appears to be absent should first check that he or she is not to be found under another appellation. As Gibbon said, it is sometimes easier to feel than to explain the motives behind any such distinction.

A page number followed by a note means that the headword is discussed in the note – where the page number is followed by 'and n.', both main text and note(s) should be consulted.